A TREASURY *of*

AMERICAN HERITAGE

A TREASURY

of AMERICAN HERITAGE

A selection from the first five years
of The Magazine of History

SIMON & SCHUSTER
NEW YORK

PUBLISHER
James Parton
EDITORIAL DIRECTOR
Joseph J. Thorndike, Jr.
SENIOR EDITOR
Bruce Catton

EDITOR
Oliver Jensen
MANAGING EDITOR
Eric Larrabee
ASSOCIATE EDITORS
Richard M. Ketchum
Joan Paterson Mills
Robert L. Reynolds
ASSISTANT EDITORS
Helen M. Brown, Robert Cowley
Stephen W. Sears
LIBRARIAN
Caroline Backlund
COPY EDITOR
Beverly Hill
ASSISTANT: Naomi S. Weber

ART DIRECTOR
Irwin Glusker
ASSOCIATE ART DIRECTOR: Murray Belsky
STAFF PHOTOGRAPHER: Herbert Loebel

ADVISORY BOARD
Allan Nevins, *Chairman*

Ray A. Billington	Alvin M. Josephy, Jr.
Carl Carmer	Richard P. McCormick
Albert B. Corey	Harry Shaw Newman
Christopher Crittenden	Howard H. Peckham
Marshall B. Davidson	S. K. Stevens
Louis C. Jones	Arthur M. Schlesinger, Sr.

SPONSORED BY
American Association for State & Local History
Society of American Historians

CIRCULATION DIRECTOR
Richard V. Benson

AMERICAN HERITAGE is published every two months by American Heritage Publishing Co., Inc., 551 Fifth Avenue, New York 17, N.Y. Single Copies: $3.95; Annual Subscriptions: $15.00 in U.S. & Canada; $16.00 elsewhere.

FOREWORD

This book is, in a general sense, the pick of the first five years of the new AMERICAN HERITAGE Magazine. It includes more than forty articles and picture portfolios chosen by the editors from more than four hundred published between December, 1954, and the end of 1959. The arrangement roughly follows the order of American history itself, as the wilderness blooms into the great republic and as the story turns anxiously to the convulsions and crises of the twentieth century.

A few qualifications should be stated at once about the selections. We have tried to include both thoughtful and lighter articles. We have arbitrarily limited each author, with slight exceptions, to one contribution. Even a book ten times this size would have had to exclude many themes and many fine writers, and we must warn readers with regret that some matters perforce are missing; there is nothing here for the Whiskey Rebellion Round Table, the Scrimshaw Collectors Society, or the War of Jenkins' Ear Book Club. But there is a good deal else which we hope will help interpret the drama and significance of the American experiment, so greatly challenged today yet so surely the best hope of mankind.

History, of course, is an enormous subject, for it is all the big and little business of the past. "The witness of the ages," Cicero called it, "the light of truth, the life of memory, the mistress of life, the messenger of antiquity." During the last decade, in addition—as Allan Nevins, the Chairman of our Advisory Board, points out—history has been enjoying an unprecedented boom. Swarming universities, proliferating institutes, bulging museums, specialty-pursuing societies of all sorts and sizes, libraries sagging under the load of great collections—all testify to a rediscovery, in mass terms, of the truth of Cicero's assertion. Why? Perhaps, Dr. Nevins suggests, "the unprecedented events in the last generation have stimulated an appetite for parallels, contrasts and interpretation."

Beyond this, however, history has an intrinsic value, like literature or art; indeed, it can scarcely be separated from them. Conceivably, the editors hope, the art is returning to Parnassus, and to a time in which the historian can resume the place once occupied by the Macaulays, Prescotts, and Parkmans of the last century in the very forefront of literature. Such a restoration must be the aim of anyone who feels the past has lessons for the future.

During the last hundred years many scholars have tended to lock serious history away in a kind of Fort Knox, hidden away from the public, where members of the orthodoxy might paw over the materials and reshuffle their conclusions in sterile privacy. For the outsider there seemed to remain only on one hand the schoolboy's stultifying parade of dates and "trends," and, on another, a mixture of Flag Day oratory and stereotype. Nonspecialist history trembled between boredom and Hollywood, dull when not vulgar, well calculated to bear out the otherwise indefensible remark of Henry Ford's that "history is bunk."

It does not have to be that way. The historian has more weapons at his command than he is always ready to use; when he does use them, history comes alive, speaking to the general reader in terms that he will understand and that will hold his interest, but retaining its solid foundation of fact. A historical magazine can recapture the look and feel of a vanished era by reprinting that era's own art—its paintings, prints, and drawings, its music, its posters, even its fragile manuscripts. It can present these with good layout and typography, uninterrupted by mood-shattering modern advertising. It can, in short, recreate the past so that the present age can see how things were with its ancestors; and to this concept AMERICAN HERITAGE has dedicated itself.

No one has done more than AMERICAN HERITAGE's senior editor, Bruce Catton, to lead modern historians away from both the stereotypes and the dry rot of the Fort Knox school of history. His words in the introduction to the first issue of AMERICAN HERITAGE express clearly the spirit of this volume:

History after all is the story of people: a statement that might seem too obvious to be worth making if it were not for the fact that history so often is presented in terms of vast incomprehensible forces moving far under the surface, carrying human beings along, helpless, and making them conform to a pattern whose true shape they never see. The pattern does exist, often enough, and it is important to trace it. Yet it is good to remember that it is the people who make the pattern, and not the other way around.

The difficult task of organizing, rearranging, and making a few necessary revisions in the materials used in this volume has been ably performed by Miss Beverly Hill; the art direction has been furnished by Murray Belsky. They have been assisted by others on the AMERICAN HERITAGE staff, which is listed on the page at left as it stood at the beginning of 1960. The staff in turn is indebted beyond measure not only to the authors, but to the libraries, museums, publishers, historical societies, and private collectors (specified where they occur in the book) who have given so freely of their resources and enthusiasm. We must also thank our advisory and sponsoring societies, the Association for State and Local History and the Society of American Historians, and all those who, by subscribing and contributing, make AMERICAN HERITAGE possible.

—Oliver Jensen

5

Table of Contents

Trading at Fort Laramie in 1837, by Alfred Jacob Miller

IRVING S. OLDS COLLECTION

Her crew rows the Constitution *to safety in the War of 1812.*

MYTHS THAT HIDE THE
American Indian

Forget the stereotypes. The red man

By OLIVER LA FARGE

was of many tribes, with variations

much broader than tradition supposes.

E ver since the white men first fell upon them, the Indians of what is now the United States have been hidden from white men's view by a number of conflicting myths. The oldest of these is the myth of the Noble Red Man or the Child of Nature, who is credited either with a habit of flowery oratory of implacable dullness or else with an imbecilic inability to converse in anything more than grunts and monosyllables.

That first myth was inconvenient. White men soon found their purposes better served by the myth of ruthless, faithless savages, and later, when the "savages" had been broken, of drunken, lazy good-for-nothings. All three myths coexist today, sometimes curiously blended in a schizophrenic confusion such as one often sees in the moving pictures. Through the centuries the mythical figure has been variously equipped; today he wears a feather headdress, is clothed in beaded buckskin, dwells in a tepee, and all but lives on horseback.

It was in the earliest period of the Noble Red Man concept that the Indians probably exerted their most

In the Indian Chief, *a primitive c. 1820, the unknown artist was apparently inspired by the myth of the Noble Red Man.*

important influence upon Western civilization. The theory has been best formulated by the late Felix S. Cohen, who, as a profound student of law concerning Indians, delved into early white-Indian relations, Indian political economy, and the white men's view of it. According to this theory, with which the present writer agrees, the French and English of the early Seventeenth Century encountered, along the East Coast of North America from Virginia southward, fairly advanced tribes whose semi-hereditary rulers depended upon the acquiescence of their people for the continuance of their rule. The explorers and first settlers interpreted these rulers as kings, their people as subjects. They found that even the commonest subjects were endowed with many rights and freedoms, that the nobility was fluid, and that commoners existed in a state of remarkable equality.

Constitutional monarchy was coming into being in England, but the divine right of kings remained firm doctrine. All European society was stratified in many classes. A somewhat romanticized observation of Indian society and government, coupled with the idea of the Child of Nature, led to the formulation, especially by French philosophers, of the theories of inherent rights in all men, and of the people as the source of

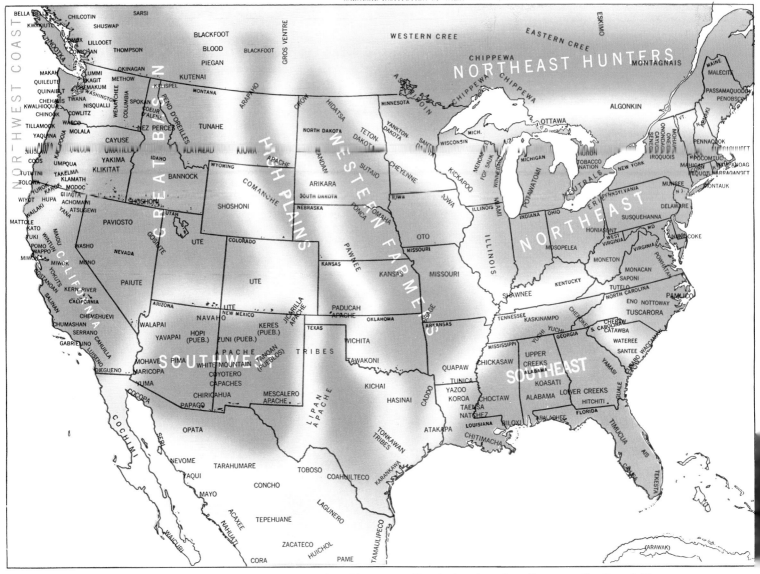

In 1650, shortly after the coming of the white man to North America, the tribes were distributed like this. Shadings mark the general cultural areas; the author's discussion centers around the three—Southeast, Southwest, and Northwest Coast—which had achieved the highest cultural level in this period.

the sovereign's authority. The latter was stated in the phrase, "consent of the governed." Both were carried over by Jefferson into our Declaration of Independence in the statement that "all men are created equal, that they are endowed by their Creator with certain unalienable Rights" and that governments derive "their just powers from the consent of the governed. . . ."

Thus, early observations of the rather simple, democratic organization of the more advanced coastal tribes, filtered through and enlarged by the minds of European philosophers whose thinking was ripe for just such material, at least influenced the formulation of a doctrine, or pair of doctrines, that furnished the intellectual base for two great revolutions and profoundly affected the history of mankind.

In the last paragraph I speak of "the more advanced" tribes. Part of the myth about the first Americans is that all of them, or most of them, had one culture and were at the same stage of advancement. The tribes and nations that occupied North America varied enormously, and their condition was anything but static. The advent of the white men put a sudden end to a phase of increasingly rapid cultural evolution, much as if a race of people, vastly superior in numbers, in civilization, and above all in weapons, had overrun and conquered all of Europe in Minoan times. Had that happened, also, the conquerors would undoubtedly have concluded, as so many white men like to conclude about Indians, that that peculiar race of light-skinned people was obviously inferior to their own.

Human beings had been in the New World for at least 15,000 years. During much of that time, as was the case in the beginning everywhere, they advanced but little from a Palaeolithic hunting culture. Somewhere around 2,500 B.C. farming began with the domestication of corn either in Peru or in Meso-America * in the vicinity of western Guatemala. Farming brought about the sedentary life and the increased food supply necessary for cultural progress. By the time of the birth of Christ, the influence of the high cultures, soon to become true civilizations, in Meso-America was beginning to reach into the present United States. Within the next 1,500 years the Indians of parts of North America progressed dramatically. When the white men first landed, there were three major centers of high culture: the Southeast-Mississippi Valley, the Southwest, and the Northwest Coast. None of the peoples of these regions, incidentally, knew about war bonnets or lived in tepees.

The Southeast-Mississippi Valley peoples (for brevity, I shall refer to the area hereafter simply as "Southeast") seem to have had the strongest influences from Meso-America, probably in part by land along the coast of Texas, in part by sea across the Gulf of Mexico, whether direct from Mexico or secondhand through the peoples of the West Indies. There is a striking resemblance between some of their great earthen mounds, shaped like flat-topped pyramids, with their wood-and-thatch temples on top, and the stone-and-mortar, temple-topped pyramids of Meso-America. Some of their carvings and engravings strongly suggest that the artists had actually seen Meso-American sculptures. The full list of similarities is convincingly long.

There grew up along the Mississippi Valley, reaching far to the north, and reaching also eastwards in the far south, the high culture generally called "Mound Builder." It produced a really impressive art, especially in carving and modeling, by far the finest that ever existed in North America. The history of advancing civilization in the New World is like that of the Old—a people develops a high culture, then barbarians come smashing in, set the clock part way back, absorb much of the older culture, and carry it on to new heights. A series of invasions of this sort seems to have struck the Mound Builders in late prehistoric times, when they were overrun by tribes mainly of Muskhogean and Iroquoian linguistic stock. Chief among these were the ancestors of the well-known Five Civilized Tribes—the Seminoles, Creeks, Choctaws, Chick-

* Meso-America denotes the area in which the highest civilizations north of Peru developed, extending from a little north of Mexico City into Honduras.

asaws, and Cherokees. When white men first met them, their culture was somewhat lower than that of the earlier period in the land they occupied. None the less, they maintained, in Florida, Alabama, Mississippi, Louisiana, and Georgia, the highest level east of the Rockies. A late movement of Iroquoian tribes, close relatives of the Cherokees, among them the Iroquois themselves, carried a simpler form of the same culture into Pennsylvania, New York, Ohio, and into the edge of Canada.

All of these people farmed heavily, their fields stretching for miles. They were few in a vast land—the whole population of the present United States was probably not over a million. Hunting and fishing, therefore, were excellent, and no reasonable people would drop an easy source of abundant meat. The development of their farming was held in check quantitatively by the supply of fish and game. They farmed the choice land, and if the fields began to be exhausted, they could move. They moved their habitations somewhat more freely than do we, but they were anything but nomadic. The southern tribesmen lived neither in wigwams nor tepees, but in houses with thatched roofs, which in the extreme south often had no walls. They had an elaborate social structure with class distinctions. Because of their size, the white men called their settlements "towns." The state of their high chiefs was kingly. They were a people well on the road towards civilization.

The Natchez of Mississippi had a true king, and a curious, elaborate social system. The king had absolute power and was known as the Sun. No ordinary man could speak to him except from a distance, shouting and making obeisances. When he went out, he was carried on a litter, as the royal and sacred foot could not be allowed to touch the ground. The Natchez nation was divided into two groups, or moieties: the aristocracy and the common people. The higher group was subdivided into Suns (the royal family), Nobles, and Honored Ones. The common people were known simply as Stinkers. A Stinker could marry anyone he pleased, but all the aristocrats had to marry out of their moiety, that is, marry Stinkers. When a female aristocrat married a Stinker man, her children belonged to her class; thus, when a Sun woman married a Stinker, her children were Suns. The children of the men, however, were lowered one class, so that the children of a Sun man, even of the Sun himself, became Nobles, while the children of an Honored One became lowly Stinkers.

This system in time, if nothing intervened, would lead to an overwhelming preponderance of aristocrats. The Natchez, however, for all their near-civilization, their temples, their fine crafts and arts, were chronically warlike. Those captives they did not torture to death they adopted, thus constantly replenishing the supply of Stinkers (a foreigner could become nothing else, but his grandchildren, if his son struck a royal fancy, might be Suns).

The Natchez were warlike. All of the southeasterners were warlike. War was a man's proper occupation. Their fighting was deadly, ferocious, stealthy if possible, for the purpose of killing—men, women, or children, so long as one killed—and taking captives, especially strong males whom one could enjoy torturing to death. It is among these tribes and their simpler relatives, the Iroquois, that we find the bloodthirsty savage of fiction, but the trouble is that he is not a savage. He is well on the road toward civilization.

With the Iroquois, they shared a curious pattern of cruelty. A warrior expected to be tortured if captured, although he could, instead, be adopted, before torture or at any time before he had been crippled. He entered into it as if it were a contest, which he would win if his captors failed to wring a sign of pain from him and if he kept taunting them so long as he was conscious. Some of the accounts of such torture among the Iroquois, when the victim was a member of a tribe speaking the same language and holding to the same customs, are filled with a quality of mutual affection. In at least one case, when a noted enemy proved to have been too badly wounded before his capture to be eligible for adoption, the chief, who had hoped that the man would replace his own son, killed in battle, wept as he assigned him to his fate. At intervals between torments so sickening that one can hardly make one's self read through the tale of them, prisoner and captors exchanged news of friends and expressions of mutual esteem. Naturally, when tribes who did not hold to these customs, including white men, were subjected to this treatment, it was not well received.

This pattern may have come into North America from a yet more advanced, truly civilized source. The Mexicans—the Aztecs and their neighbors—expected to be sacrificed if they were captured, and on occasion might insist upon it if their captors were inclined to spare them. They were not tortured, properly speaking, as a general rule, but some of the methods of putting them to death were not quick. What we find in North America may have been a debasement of the Mexican practices developed into an almost psychopathic pleasure among people otherwise just as capable of love, of kindness, of nobility, and of lofty thought as any anywhere—or what the conquistadores found in Mexico may have been a civilized softening of earlier, yet more fearful ways. The Aztecs tore fantastic numbers of hearts from living victims and, like the people of the Southeast, when not at war said "We are idle." They were artists, singers, dancers, poets, and great lovers of flowers and birds.

The Iroquois and Muskhogeans had a real mental sophistication. We observe it chiefly in their social order and what we know of their religions. The Iroquois did not have the royalty and marked divisions of classes that we find farther south, but their well organized, firmly knit tribes were what enabled them, although few in numbers, to dominate the Algonkians who surrounded them. The Iroquois came nearer to having the matriarchy that popular fable looks for among primitive people than any other American tribe. Actual office was held by the men, but the women's power was great, and strongly influenced the selection of the officers.

Five of the Iroquois tribes achieved something unique in North America, rare anywhere, when in the Sixteenth Century they formed the League of the Five Nations—Senecas, Onondagas, Mohawks, Cayugas, and Oneidas—to which, later, the Tuscaroras were added. The league remained united and powerful until after the American Revolution, and exists in shadowy form to this day. It struck a neat balance between sovereignty retained by each tribe and sovereignty sacrificed to the league, and as so durable and effective a union was studied by the authors of our Constitution.

The league was founded by the great leader Hiawatha. Any resemblance between the fictional hero of Longfellow's poem and this real, dead person is purely coincidental. Longfellow got hold of the name and applied it to some Chippewa legends, which he rewrote thoroughly to produce some of the purest rot and the most heavy-footed verse ever to be inflicted upon a school child.

The Iroquois lived in "long houses," which looked like extended Quonset huts sheathed in bark. Smaller versions of these, and similarly covered, domed or conical structures, are "wigwams," the typical housing of the Northeast. Many people use the word "wigwam" as synonymous with "tepee," which is incorrect. A tepee, the typical dwelling of the Plains Indians of a later period, is a functional tent, usually covered with hides or, in recent years, canvas, and one of its essential features is that it is the shelter of constantly mobile people. A tepee, incidentally, is about the most comfortable tent ever invented, winter or summer—provided you have two or three strong, competent women to attend to setting it up and striking it.

The great tribes we have been discussing showed their sophistication in a new way in their response to contact with Europeans. Their tribal organizations became tighter and firmer. From south to north they held the balance of power. The British success in establishing good relations with many of them was the key to driving the French out of the Mississippi area; to win the Revolution, the Americans had to defeat the Iroquois, whose favor up to then had determined who should dominate the Northeast. The southern tribes radically changed their costume, and quickly took over cattle, slaves, and many arts. By the time Andrew Jackson was ready to force their removal, the Cherokees had a stable government under a written constitution, with a bicameral parliament, an alphabet for writing their language, printing presses, a newspaper, schools, and churches.

Had it not been for the white men's insatiable greed and utter lawlessness, this remarkable nation would have ended with a unique demonstration of how, without being conquered, a "primitive" people could adapt itself to a new civilization on its own initiative. They would have become a very rare example of how aborigines could receive solid profit from the coming of the white men.

After the five Civilized Tribes were driven to Oklahoma, they formed a union and once again set up their governments and their public schools. Of course we could not let them have what we had promised them; it turned out that we ourselves wanted that part of Oklahoma after all, so once again we tore up the treaties and destroyed their system. None the less, to this day they are a political power in the state, and when one of their principal chiefs speaks up, the congressmen do well to listen.

The tribes discussed until now and their predecessors in the same general area formed a means of transmission of higher culture to others, east and west. Their influence reached hardly at all to the northward, since north of the Iroquois farming with native plants was difficult or impossible. On the Atlantic Coast of the United States the tribes were all more or less affected. Farming was of great importance. Even in New England, the status of chiefs was definite and fairly high. Confederacies and hegemonies, such as that of the Narragansetts over many of the Massachusetts

This sturdy warrior was painted in the 1580's by John White. He is typical of the southeastern Indians whom the white men encountered.

tribes, occurred, of which more primitive people are incapable.

To the westward, the pattern of farming and sedentary villages extended roughly to the line that runs irregularly through Nebraska and Kansas, west of which the mean annual rainfall is below twenty inches. In wet cycles, there were prehistoric attempts to farm farther west, and in historic times the Apaches raised fair crops in the eastern foothills of the southern tip of the Rockies, but only the white men combined the mechanical equipment and the stupidity to break the turf and exhaust the soil of the dry, high plains.

An essay as short as this on so large a subject is inevitably filled with almost indefensible generalizations. I am stressing similarities, as in the case of the Iroquois-Southeast tribes, ignoring great unlikenesses. Generalizing again, we may say that the western farmers, whose cultures in fact differed enormously, also lived in fairly fixed villages. In the southern part, they built large houses covered with grass thatch. At the northwestern tip of the farming zone we find the Mandans, Hidatsa, and Crows, who lived in semi-subterranean lodges of heavy poles covered with earth, so big that later, when horses came to them, they kept their choice mounts inside. These three related, Siouan-speaking tribes living on the edge of the Plains are the first we have come to whose native costume, when white men first observed them, included the war bonnet. That was in the early Nineteenth Century; what they wore in 1600, no one knows.

The western farmers had their permanent lodges; they also had tepees. Immediately at hand was the country of the bison, awkward game for men on foot to hunt with lance and bow, but too fine a source of meat to ignore. On their hunting expeditions they took the conical tents. The size of the tepees was limited, for the heavy covers and the long poles had to be dragged either by the women or by dogs. Tepee life at that time was desirable only for a short time, when one roughed it.

The second area of Meso-American influence was

13

the Southwest, as anthropologists define it—the present states of New Mexico and Arizona, a little of the adjacent part of Mexico, and various extensions at different times to the north, west, and east. We do not find here the striking resemblances to Meso-America in numbers of culture traits we find in the Southeast: the influence must have been much more indirect, ideas and objects passing in the course of trade from tribe to tribe over the thousand miles or so of desert northern Mexico.

In the last few thousand years the Southwest has been pretty dry, although not as dry as it is today. A dry climate and a sandy soil make an archaeologist's paradise. We can trace to some extent the actual transition from hunting and gathering to hunting plus farming, the appearance of the first permanent dwellings, the beginning of pottery-making, at least the latter part of the transition from twining and basketry to true weaving. Anthropologists argue over the very use of the term "Southwest" to denote a single area, because of the enormous variety of the cultures found within it. There is a certain unity, none the less, centering around beans, corn, squashes, tobacco, cotton, democracy, and a preference for peace. Admitting the diversity, the vast differences between, say, the Hopi and Pima farmers, we can still think of it as a single area, and for purposes of this essay concentrate on the best-studied of its cultures, the Pueblos.

The name "Pueblo" is the Spanish for "village," and was given to that people because they lived—and live—in compact, defensible settlements of houses with walls of stone laid up with adobe mortar or entirely of adobe. Since the Spanish taught them how to make rectangular bricks, pure adobe construction has become the commoner type. They already had worked out the same roofing as was usual in Asia Minor and around the Mediterranean in ancient times. A modern Pueblo house corresponds almost exactly to the construction of buildings dating back at least as far as 600 B.C. in Asia Minor.

The Pueblos, and their neighbors, the Navahos, have become well enough known in recent years to create some exception to the popular stereotype of Indians. It is generally recognized that they do not wear feathers and that they possess many arts, and that the Pueblos are sedentary farmers.

Farming has long been large in their pattern of living, and hunting perhaps less important than with any people outside the Southwest. Their society is genuinely classless, in contrast to that of the Southeast. Before the Spanish conquest, they were governed by a theocracy. Each tribe was tightly organized, every individual placed in his niche. The power of the theocracy was, and in some Pueblos still is, tyrannical in appearance. Physical punishment was used to suppress the rebellious; now more often a dissident member is subjected to a form of being sent to Coventry. If he be a member of the tribal council, anything he says at meetings is pointedly ignored. If he has some ceremonial function, he performs it, but otherwise he is left in isolation. I have seen a once self-assertive man, who for a time had been a strong leader in his tribe, subjected to this treatment for several years. By my estimation he lost some thirty pounds, and he became a quiet conformist. The power of the theocracy was great, but it rested on the consent of the governed.

The Pueblos had many arts, most of which still continue. They wove cotton, made handsome pottery, did fine work in shell. Their ceremonies were spectacular and beautiful. They had no system of torture and no cult of warfare. A good warrior was respected, but what they wanted was peace.

The tight organization of the Pueblo tribes and the absolute authority over individuals continues now among only a few of them. The loosening is in part the result of contact with whites, in part for the reason that more and more they are building their houses outside of the old, solid blocks of the villages, simply because they are no longer under constant, urgent need for defense.

It is irony that the peace-loving southwestern farmers were surrounded by the worst raiders of all the wild tribes of North America. Around A.D. 1100 or 1200 there began filtering in among them bands of primitives, possessors of a very simple culture, who spoke languages of the Athabascan stock. These people had drifted down from western Canada. In the course of time they became the Navahos and the Apaches. For all their poverty, they possessed a sinew-backed bow of Asiatic type that was superior to any missile weapon known to the Southwest. They traded with the Pueblos, learned from them, stole from them, raided them. As they grew stronger, they became pests. The Navahos and the northeastern branch of the Apaches, called Jicarilla Apaches, learned farming. The Navahos became artists, above all the finest of weavers, but did not give up their raiding habits.

These Athabascans did not glorify war. They made a business of it. Killing enemies was incidental; in fact, a man who killed an enemy had to be purified afterwards. They fought for profit, and they were about the only North Americans whose attitude toward war resembled that of the professional soldier. This did not make them any the less troublesome.

The last high culture area occupied a narrow strip along the Pacific Coast, from northern California across British Columbia to southern Alaska—the North-

George Catlin in 1832 first painted the Bull Dance of the Mandans (above), a celebration of the buffalo's coming which took place in a clearing between the earth-covered lodges. The disrupting figure at left is the evil spirit, soon to be neutralized by a magic medicine pipe and driven from the village by squaws.

Another form of buffalo worship practiced by the Plains Indians was the so-called "medicine circles," shown at left by Miller as they appeared near the Platte River. Composed of buffalo (and, reportedly, sometimes human) skulls, it is thought that they were meant in some mystic way to attract the herds.

west Coast culture. There was no Meso-American influence here, nor was there any farming. The hunting and fishing were so rich, the supply of edible wild plants so adequate, that there was no need for farming—for which in any case the climate was unfavorable. The prerequisite for cultural progress is a food supply so lavish that either all men have spare time, or some men can specialize in non-food-producing activities while others feed them. This condition obtained on the Northwest Coast, where men caught the water creatures from whales to salmon, and hunted deer, mountain sheep, and other game animals.

The area was heavily forested with the most desirable kinds of lumber. Hence wood and bark entered largely into the culture. Bark was shredded and woven into clothing, twined into nets, used for padding. Houses, chests, dishes, spoons, canoes, and boats were made of wood. The people became carvers and woodworkers, then carried their carving over onto bone and horn. They painted their houses, boats, chests, and their elaborate wooden masks. They made wooden armor, including visored helmets, and deadly wooden clubs. The chiefs placed carvings in front of their houses that related their lineage, tracing back ultimately to some sacred being such as Raven or Bear—the famous, so-called totem poles.

I have said that the finest prehistoric art of North America was that of the Mound Builders; in fact, no Indian work since has quite equaled it—but that is, of course, a matter of taste. The greatest historic Indian art was that of the Northwest Coast. Their carvings, like the Mound Builder sculptures, demand comparison with our own work. Their art was highly stylized, but vigorous and fresh. As for all Indians, the coming of the white men meant ruin in the end, but at first it meant metal tools, the possession of which resulted in a great artistic outburst.

Socially they were divided into chiefs, commoners, and slaves. Slaves were obtained by capture, and slave-raiding was one of the principal causes of war. Generosity was the pattern with most Indians, although in the dry Southwest we find some who made a virtue of thrift. In the main, a man was respected because he gave, not because he possessed. The Northwest Coast chiefs patterned generosity into an ugliness. A chief would invite a rival to a great feast, the famous potlatch. At the feast he would shower his rival and other guests with gifts, especially copper disks and blankets woven of mountain sheep wool, which were the highest units of value. He might further show his lavishness by burning some possessions, even partially destroy a copper disk, and, as like as not, kill a few slaves.

If within a reasonable time the other chief did not

reply with an even larger feast, at which he gave away or destroyed double what his rival had got rid of, he was finished as a chief—but if he did respond in proper form, he might be beggared, and also finished. That was the purpose of the show. Potlatches were given for other purposes, such as to authenticate the accession of the heir to a former chief, or to buy a higher status

This impression of An Indian Chief before and after his Visit to Washington *was painted by George Catlin in 1841.*

but ruinous rivalry was constant. They seem to have been a rather disagreeable, invidious, touchy people. The cruelty of the southeasterners is revolting, but there is something especially unpleasant about proving one's generosity and carelessness of possessions by killing a slave—with a club made for that special purpose and known as a "slave-killer."

The Meso-American culture could spread, chang-

16

ing beyond recognition as it did so, because it carried its food supply with it. The Northwest Coast culture could not, because its food supply was restricted to its place of origin.

North and east of the Northwest Coast area stretched the sub-Arctic and the plains of Canada, areas unsuitable for primitive farming. To the south and east were mountains and the region between the Rockies and the Coastal ranges called the Great Basin. Within it are large stretches of true desert; most of it is arid. Early on, Pueblo influences reached into the southern part, in Utah and Nevada, but as the climate grew drier, they died away. It was a land to be occupied by little bands of simple hunters and gatherers of seeds and roots, not strong enough to force their way into any place richer.

In only one other area was there a natural food supply to compare with the Northwest Coast's, and that was in the bison range of the Great Plains. But, as already noted, for men without horses or rifles, hunting bison was a tricky and hazarous business. Take the year 1600, when the Spanish were already established in New Mexico and the English and French almost ready to make settlements on the East Coast, and look for the famous Plains tribes. They are not there. Some are in the mountains, some in the woodlands to the northeast, some farming to the eastward, within the zone of ample rainfall. Instead we find scattered bands of Athabascans occupying an area no one else wanted.

Then the white men turned everything upside down. Three elements were most important in the early influence: the dislodgment of eastern tribes, the introduction of the horse, and metal tools and firearms. Let us look first at the impact on the centers of high culture.

White men came late to the Northwest Coast, and at first they came only as traders. As already noted, early contact with them enriched the life of the Indians and brought about a cultural spurt. Then came settlers. The most advanced, best organized tribes stood up fairly well against them for a time, and they are by no means extinct, but of their old culture there are now only remnants, with the strongest survivals being in the arts. Today, those Indians who are in the "Indian business," making money from tourists, dress in fringed buckskin and war bonnets, because otherwise the tourists will not accept them as genuine.

The tribes of the Atlantic Coast were quickly dislodged or wiped out. The more advanced groups farther inland held out all through colonial times and on into the 1830's, making fairly successful adjustments to the changed situation, retaining their sovereignty, and enriching their culture with wholesale taking over of European elements, including, in the South, the ownership of Negro slaves. Finally, as already noted, they were forcibly removed to Oklahoma, and in the end their sovereignty was destroyed. They remain numerous, and although some are extremely poor and backward, others, still holding to their tribal affiliations, have merged successfully into the general life of the state, holding positions as high as chief justice of the state supreme court. The Iroquois still hold out in New York and in Canada on remnants of their original reservations. Many of them have had remarkable success in adapting themselves to white American life while retaining considerable elements of their old culture. Adherents to the old religion are many, and the rituals continue vigorously.

The British invaders of the New World, and to a lesser degree the French, came to colonize. They came in thousands, to occupy the land. They were, therefore, in direct competition with the Indians and acted accordingly, despite their verbal adherence to fine principles of justice and fair dealing. The Spanish came quite frankly to conquer, to Christianize, and to exploit, all by force of arms. They did not shilly-shally about Indian title to the land or Indian sovereignty; they simply took over, then granted the Indians titles deriving from the Spanish crown. They came in small numbers—only around 3,000 settled in the Southwest—and the Indian labor force was essential to their aims. Therefore they did not dislodge or exterminate the Indians, and they had notable success in modifying Indian culture for survival.

In the Southwest the few Spaniards, cut off from the main body in Mexico by many miles of difficult, wild country, could not have survived alone against the wild tribes that shortly began to harry them. They needed the Pueblo Indians and the Pueblos needed them. The Christian Pueblos were made secure in their lands and in their local self-government. They approached social and political equality. During the period when New Mexico was under the Mexican Republic, for two years a Taos Indian, braids, blanket, and all, was governor of the territory. Eighteen pueblos survive to this day, with a population now approaching 19,000, in addition to nearly 4,000 Hopis, whose culture is Pueblo, in Arizona. They are conservative progressives, prosperous on the whole, with an excellent chance of surviving as a distinctive group for many generations to come. It was in the house of a Pueblo priest, a man deeply versed in the old religion as well as a devout Catholic, that I first saw color television.

The Spanish, then, did not set populations in motion. That was done chiefly from the east. The great

Spanish contribution was loosing the horses. They did not intend to; in fact, they made every possible effort to prevent Indians from acquiring horses or learning to ride. But the animals multiplied and ran wild; they spread north from California into Oregon; they spread into the wonderful grazing land of the high Plains, a country beautifully suited to horses.

From the east, the tribes were pressing against the tribes farther west. Everything was in unhappy motion, and the tribes nearest to the white men had firearms. So the Chippewas, carrying muskets, pushed westward into Minnesota, driving the reluctant Dakotas, the Sioux tribes, out of the wooded country into the Plains as the horses spread north. At first the Dakotas hunted and ate the strange animals, then they learned to ride them, and they were off.

The Sioux were mounted. So were the Blackfeet. The semi-civilized Cheyennes swung into the saddle and moved out of the farming country onto the bison range. The Kiowas moved from near the Yellowstone to the Panhandle; the Comanches came down out of the Rocky Mountains; the Arapahos, the Crows, abandoning their cornfields, and the Piegans, the great fighting names, all followed the bison. They built their life around the great animals. They ate meat lavishly all year round; their tepees, carried or dragged now by horses, became commodious. A new culture, a horse-and-bison culture, sprang up overnight. The participants in it had a wonderful time. They feasted, they roved, they hunted, they played. Over a serious issue, such as the invasion of one tribe's territory by another, they could fight deadly battles, but otherwise even war was a game in which shooting an enemy was an act earning but little esteem, but touching one with one's bare hand or with a stick was the height of military achievement.

This influx of powerful tribes drove the last of the Athabascans into the Southwest. There the Apaches and the Navahos were also mounted and on the go, developing their special, deadly pattern of war as a business. In the Panhandle country, the Kiowas and Comanches looked westward to the Spanish and Pueblo settlements, where totally alien peoples offered rich plunder. The Pueblos, as we have seen, desired to live at peace. The original Spanish came to conquer; their descendants, becoming Spanish-Americans, were content to hold what they had, farm their fields, and graze their flocks. To the north of the two groups were Apaches and Utes; to the east, Kiowas and Comanches; to the south, what seemed like unlimited Apaches; and to the west the Navahos, of whom there were several thousands by the middle of the Seventeenth Century.

The tribes named above, other than the Kiowas and

Comanches, did not share in the Plains efflorescence. The Navahos staged a different cultural spurt of their own, combining extensive farming with constant horseback plundering, which in turn enabled them to become herdsmen, and from the captured wool develop their remarkable weaving industry. Their prosperity and their arts were superimposed on a simple camp life. With this prosperity, they also developed elaborate rituals and an astoundingly rich mythology.

The Dakotas first saw horses in 1722, which makes a convenient peg date for the beginning of the great Plains culture. A little over a hundred years later, when Catlin visited the Mandans, it was going full blast. The memory of a time before horses had grown dim. By 1860 the Plains tribes were hard-pressed to stand the white men off; by 1880 the whole pattern was broken and the bison were gone. At its height, Plains Indian culture was brittle. Materially, it depended absolutely on a single source of food and skins; in other aspects, it required the absolute independence of the various tribes. When these two factors were eliminated, the content was destroyed. Some Indians may still live in tepees, wear at times their traditional clothing, maintain here and there their arts and some of their rituals, but these are little more than fringe survivals.

While the Plains culture died, the myth of it spread and grew to become embedded in our folklore. Not only the Northwest Coast Indians but many others as unlikely wear imitations of Plains Indian costume and put on "war dances," to satisfy the believers in the myth. As it exists today in the public mind, it still contains the mutually incongruous elements of the Noble Red Man and the Bloodthirsty Savage that first came into being three centuries and a half ago, before any white man had ever seen a war bonnet or a tepee, or any Indian had ridden a horse.

Oliver La Farge was a professional anthropologist before he turned to writing as his career. Since then he has pursued anthropology, especially American Indian ethnology, as an avocation. He is the author of a number of popular books, among them Laughing Boy *(Pulitzer Prize novel for 1929), as well as scientific works, and many short stories. He is active in the Association on American Indian Affairs, the American Anthropological Association, and the American Academy of Arts and Sciences.*

Of Raleigh and the First Plantation

The fate of the Virginia Colony rested on the endurance of adventurers, the financing

of London merchants, and the favor of a courtier with his demanding spinster Queen

By A. L. ROWSE

In the marvelous 1580's everything was beginning to ripen together in the heat of the tension between England and Spain. Poetry and the drama that had been so sparse and backward were coming to a head with Sidney and Spenser and Marlowe; the first Elizabethan madrigals appear in the very year the war against Spain begins. And this is the moment when the idea of American colonization takes shape and wing—or, perhaps I should say, takes sail.

The person who had first undertaken to carry out the idea, as to which there had been so much discussion and so many abortive gestures in the direction of it, was Humphrey Gilbert. And from the Crown's patent he was granted in 1578 sprang the ultimate achieve-

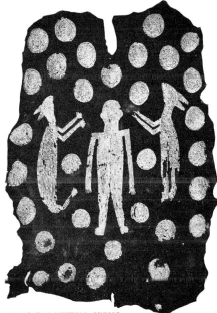

For all the ruffles and earrings of his court costume, Sir Walter Raleigh (left) embodied qualities the Elizabethan Age admired: style, poetry, good looks, and pride. Men such as he revealed the wonders of the New World to the Old, bringing back tobacco and trophies like the ceremonial cloak of Chief Powhatan (right), made of deerskin decorated with tiny shells, in the figure of a man with an animal on each side.

ASHMOLEAN MUSEUM, OXFORD

ment. That patent gave him license for six years "to search, find out and view such remote, heathen and barbarous lands, countries and territories not actually possessed of any Christian prince or people." That was the regular formula, in pursuance of the government's consistent stand on American settlement.

Humphrey Gilbert had been from the days of his youth a personal servant of Queen Elizabeth, from the time when, as Princess, she was in disgrace with her sister Mary. We know little of Gilbert's expedition of 1578, which was secret, very mixed in its make-up—to which some genuinely piratical elements were attached and which turned out a complete failure. It is thought that he was aiming at settlement in Florida. The Queen contributed a ship of her own, the *Falcon:* captain, Walter Raleigh. I cannot help thinking she must have known him, certainly have known of him, long before the traditionally romantic account of her sudden falling for him—to which we have all subscribed.

Walter Raleigh was no new man: he came from a very old family which had already made its place by the time of Henry II.

This delicately drawn map of the south coast of England in the time of Henry VIII, marked with notices to mariners and as accurate as it is decorative, is in the British Museum and has never been reproduced in its entirety. Above are three sections of it covering the coast of Cornwall and Devon, from Land's End (far left) to Exmouth, showing the harbors from which nearly all the West Country voyages to America set sail. The pivot is Plymouth Sound, shown with St. Nicholas' Island lying off the Hoe—after the Armada it became known as

COURTIER-BACKER: *The third Earl of Southampton was a supporter of the Virginia Company and for a time its treasurer. History knows him best as the generous patron of Shakespeare. As a young man he played a part in the Earl of Essex's conspiracy and narrowly escaped with his life.*

POET-BACKER: *England had Sir Philip Sidney's heart, and he hers, to paraphrase him. The soldier who died so young, the author of famous poems to "Stella," took an eager interest in the enterprises of Frobisher, Drake, and Raleigh. Only Elizabeth's own order kept him from joining Drake against the Spaniards in 1585. Next year, at only 32, he fell fighting in Holland.*

But by Raleigh's time the family had lost most of its property and become rather impoverished—a most humiliating and irritating situation, especially for an ambitious young man, to feel that you are somebody and haven't a bean. Something of this irritation may be seen all through Raleigh's career: he was always a man in a hurry, conscious of his gifts and abilities, yet always made to wait on circumstances—and maddened by frustration. And there *was* a yellow streak in Raleigh too—he was a great liar—a rift in him by which perhaps came the genius, for men have the qualities of their defects. There is no doubt of the genius; he bore all the stigmata of it.

Raleigh's mother was by birth a Champernowne, and widow of a Gilbert, so that these Gilberts—John, Humphrey, Adrian—were half brothers of Walter and Carew Raleigh. The Gilberts were brought up at Greenway on the Dart, the family seat being Compton Castle, that delightful rose-red H-shaped house of

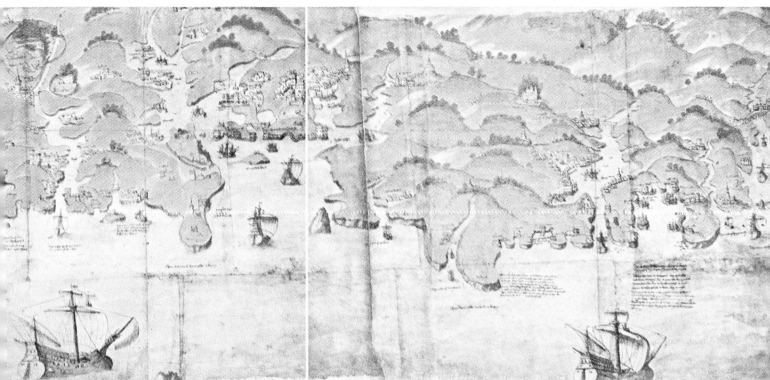

Drake's Island. At Cattewater began the voyages of Hawkins and Drake, and here Drake returned from his voyage round the world. From here too departed the New England ventures of Sir Ferdinando Gorges; and hence set out the Mayflower. Near the estuary of the Dart, with its port of Dartmouth, lived the Gilberts. From this haven Sir Humphrey Gilbert made sail on his Newfoundland voyage, and John Davis, in his search for the Northwest Passage. Near Exmouth, Sir Walter Raleigh was born.

SPENCER COLLECTION, THE
NEW YORK PUBLIC LIBRARY

NATIONAL PORTRAIT GALLERY, LONDON

the fourteenth century, near Torquay, of which the roofless hall has been restored by Commander Walter Raleigh Gilbert in recent years. Humphrey Gilbert was some fifteen years older than Raleigh, and to him the young Walter owed his lead in sea enterprises and ideas of American colonization. Where Gilbert led—at Oxford, in France and Ireland, at sea, over America—Raleigh followed. They had strong family characteristics in common: they were impulsive and intemperate, impatient of any opposition (they had all the more to put up with). They were not very nice men, but they had fascination and they were well educated. They were men of ideas—indeed with them ideas went to their head—and they had great imagination: they were projectors.

Gilbert's failure and, no doubt, the Queen's intimate knowledge of his defects of temperament made her reluctant to support his last and most elaborate project, which has been described as branching out

SAILOR-BACKER: Sir Humphrey Gilbert, well-born, well-educated (Eton and Oxford) half brother of Raleigh, was a long-time advocate of the Northwest Passage, sailed from Plymouth in 1583 to make a "Western Planting" in America. The Queen had complained that Gilbert was "of not good hap by sea," and sure enough he was lost during the voyage back to England.

BISHOP-BACKER: Even the cloth ventured money in the new lands. Among the investors was the Archbishop of Canterbury, George Abbot, the first Oxford man to become Archbishop since the Reformation. A Surrey clothworker's son, he founded a hospital in his native town of Guildford.

23

into "a maze of individual and corporate enterprises for the conquest and settlement of North America. . . ." She held Gilbert to be "a man noted of not good hap by sea"; however, against her better judgment, she relented and gave him permission to go. Before he left, with characteristic graciousness, she sent him by Walter Raleigh, now in the first flush of favor—her good wishes, with a jewel for token, "an anchor guided by a Lady." She asked him to leave his portrait with Raleigh for her; she did not invest in the voyage. Gilbert went, took possession of Newfoundland, lost his flagship with all his stores, and was drowned in the barque *Squirrel* on the way home.

Walter Raleigh was the heir to Gilbert's colonizing projects, the man who carried them into execution. But it was entirely his favor with the Queen that gave him the resources to put his plans into operation: the prestige and opportunities of his position, the support and service he could now command, the gifts of lands and licenses, the cash. Notice that the Queen's favor was not given for noth-

ing: there was an implied contract of service. It was her way of attaching men of ability to the service of the state, and from the men she delighted to favor, the state got good service. In all Raleigh's efforts for Virginia she was behind him: she backed him, she provided his resources. In addition, she made her own direct contribution.

In preparation for Raleigh's first Virginia colony, the geographer Richard Hakluyt wrote his *Discourse of Western Planting:* "Certain Reasons to induce her Majesty and the state to take in hand the western voyage and the planting therein." It was an extremely able state paper, unique in that age in putting forth a complete argument for colonial expansion, on every ground—economic, political, strategic, religious—with a plan for its execution and a program of settlement. Raleigh got Hakluyt an audience with the Queen, to whom he presented it on his knees. No doubt she read it: it was meant for her eyes, and was never printed until our own time. But she was not persuaded.

The argument was that only the resources of the state could accomplish the colonization of America.

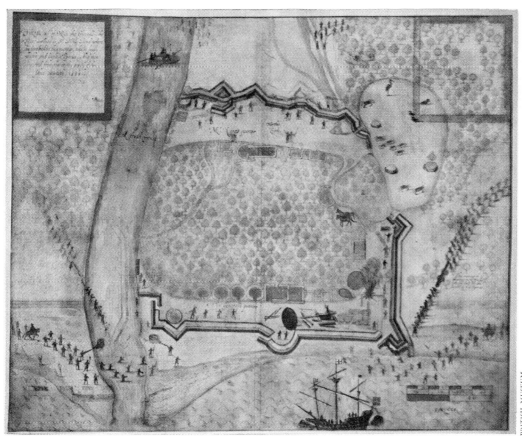

Since the Queen could not spare Raleigh, command of the first Virginia colony went to his cousin, Sir Richard Grenville, who built the fort on St. John's Island in the West Indies (shown in John White's map, above) before he landed in Virginia in 1585. The Tyger is at anchor, Grenville's quarters are at center, while Grenville himself, on horseback, is across the river (left).

An·DÑI·1571·
ÆTATIS·SVÆ·
·29·

Sir Richard Grenville, sea captain, commander of the first English colony to get a secure foothold on American shores.

There was something in that: so many were to fail, fall by the wayside, having ventured everything and lost; the sacrifices in wealth and manpower, in suffering, privation, and human life, were immense and terrible. But—a state enterprise? In that age everyone plundered the government and every governmental undertaking. The Queen knew that better than anyone. Had she not often had occasion to utter a *cri de coeur* against the "insatiable cupidity of men"? Then, too, a state enterprise meant a head-on collision with Spain, a frontal challenge from which no retreat was possible. Failure would mean a total loss of prestige to the state. There can be no doubt that the Queen was right to put it aside, and there it remained unknown till our day.

But this did not mean that she was not as anxious as anyone that colonization should succeed. Ultimately it did, under a characteristically mixed English form of enterprise, with private and public elements, and the Crown making a quasi-official contribution. The colonizing Queen made a good profit on her investments, and not least important, she contributed the symbolic name to Virginia.

Everything with this politic woman meant something. The permission to use the name was not mere coquettishness, not only the suggestion of romance which, genuine enough in that day, it has come chiefly to signify for us. It was, like everything with her, an intensely personal act, calling attention to an aspect of her personality which, if not unique in a ruler, was an unforgettable element in her fame. But it was also politics, a characteristically ambivalent notice to the world that she personally was involved as well as the Crown of England; her good name pledged. It was therefore an unmistakable underlining of her claim, which could not chivalrously be disregarded, a warning to others to keep off.

The name caught on at once—it evidently had life in it—with the poets no less than the seamen, the politicians, and merchants. In these same eighties, while Ralph Lane was writing from Virginia to her Secretary Walsingham of the "assurance of her Majesty's greatness hereby to grow by the addition of such a kingdom as this is to the rest of her dominions," Raleigh's friend Edmund Spenser was writing:
Or fruitfullest Virginia who did ever view?

In April, 1584, Raleigh dispatched two barques, under Captains Philip Amadas and Arthur Barlow, to reconnoiter a site for a colony in the southern section of the North American coast. They went out by the southern route via the Canaries and West Indies and then up to Cape Hatteras to the low-lying coast of what is now North Carolina, where among the shoals and lagoons they pitched on an island which they considered a promising site. The advantages of an island for purposes of defense are obvious, and the fact that it was situated among those sounds, with about the most difficult navigation in the world, afforded it some protection from Spanish attentions. Amadas and Barlow brought back a lyrical account of the country and its commodities, and also two lusty young Indians of standing, Wanchese and

The largest venture yet, eight sail commanded by Sir George Somers (right), set out in 1609. But the flagship was wrecked in Bermuda (above), suggesting Shakespeare's The Tempest.

Behind the scenes in London two rival figures were Sir Edwin Sandys (left), professional politician and for a time treasurer of the Virginia Company;

and capable Sir Thomas Smythe, the first governor of the East India Company and one of the most influential merchants engaged in colonial affairs.

Manteo, the first of whom was to belie these sanguine hopes, the second to remain ever faithful to the English. In that, the pattern of so much in the subsequent story of relations between the races was foreshadowed early.

That same year, while they were away, Raleigh's first big colonial effort was taking shape. In December the bill confirming his letters patent was before Parliament, and on second reading was handed over to a committee with an interesting membership. There were the Queen's Vice-Chamberlain, Sir Christopher Hatton; her principal Secretary, Sir Francis Walsingham; Sir Philip Sidney, Sir Francis Drake, Sir Richard Grenville, Sir William Courtenay, Sir William Mohun, and other West Country members specially interested in these matters. Upon third reading, the bill, "after many arguments and a proviso added unto it, passed." No one has observed that this long proviso was directed against the expedition undertaking hostilities by sea or land; no doubt that was due to Lord Burghley's influence, and represented a concession to his point of view. By the time the little fleet set sail, open war with Spain made the proviso out of date—and privateering on the way home more than paid the expenses.

The Queen at this time not being able to part with Raleigh, the command was handed over to his cousin, Sir Richard Grenville. There are things to be said against Grenville, all (and rather more than all) said by his second-in-command, Ralph Lane, a cousin of

Sir Edward Dyer and an equerry to the Queen—but he did the job. He made a successful cruise to the West Indies, where he took on board horses and kine to stock the colony, and plants, including sugar, to plant. At the end of June he landed the colony on Roanoke Island. He remained there for a month exploring and prospecting, and then hovered off Cape Hatteras for another month—watching out for what he could find, I suppose—at the end of which he set sail for England. On September 18 "the general came with the prize to Plymouth and was courteously received by divers of his worshipful friends."

That expedition to plant the first colony in America had an interesting membership. In addition to Grenville and Ralph Lane, there was the brilliant young navigator Thomas Cavendish from Suffolk, the second Englishman to make a successful voyage round the world. Also upon it were Thomas Hariot—the first scientist in the country—and John White, one of its best draftsmen, cartographer and illustrator of the expedition. Most of the leading spirits were West Country relations or neighbors of Grenville and Raleigh: one observes among the names an Arundell, a Stukeley, a Prideaux, a Bonython, a Kendall and, I am glad to say, Anthony Rouse, a friend of Drake.

Left to himself in command, Lane responded with a violent outburst against Grenville, full of the usual Elizabethan persecution mania and complaining of the unruliness of "the wild men of mine own nation," let alone living among savages. It is clear that what they needed was a Grenville to keep them in order; it is also clear that the Queen's equerry was not the type, and indeed he does not appear again in colonial enterprises.

It is not my purpose to tell once more the story of this first English colony in America, what happened to the hundred or so men—that became the usual number dispatched in these early efforts at settlement—upon Roanoke Island during the year almost that they remained there. But in fact, everything goes back to that first colony, to the colonial experience they gathered there, the knowledge as to the physical conditions, the flora and fauna, the products of the soil—above all, what they learned about Indian life, native ways and food, the difficulties of relations with the Indians.

The fundamental lesson that early colonists failed to learn was the absolute necessity of getting down to cultivate the soil. But we must remember to what an extent they consisted of rag, tag, and bobtail who would not learn anything, idle and listless, recalcitrant to all discipline. (Here is where the grand advantage of the Puritans came in, when it came to their turn, in moral fiber and self-discipline.) The dependence of the early colonists on the Indians for food supplies naturally created acute troubles between them, for there was not enough to go round. Their relations, the characters of the Indian chiefs, the troubles between the natives and the newcomers, provide the chief interest of the story.

Raleigh's promised supply ship was late in getting to sea; meanwhile, Grenville was fitting out a larger expedition upon the North Devon coast. The Roanoke colonists were ready to remain and wait, when their nerve was suddenly broken by one of those tornadoes that that coast enjoys—and the prime defect of Roanoke was that it had no satisfactory harbor. When in June, 1586, Drake arrived off the coast with a powerful fleet from his West Indian expedition, on which he had wrought so much destruction, he offered to take the colonists back with him, and on a sudden impulse they decided to accept. If Lane had been a stronger man, he would have stuck it out. . . . And

At right, a map of the American coast from Florida to the Chesapeake by John White, who came over with Raleigh's first colony, shows with red dots the points in "La Virgenia Pars" where English settlers landed. Raleigh's coat of arms in bright scarlet, ships, flying fish, and disporting dolphin, decorate the map, remarkably accurate for the time

THE *Fall* OF *R*ALEIGH

Elizabethan court life centered on the Queen, as when one of her maids of honor was being married (above). The scene, painted by Marcus Gheeraerts the Younger, shows Elizabeth on the way to Blackfriars on June 16, 1600. The bride, Anne Russell, is at right; the bridegroom's father, the Earl of Worcester, a Knight of the Garter, is at center in his pink doublet; but the figure of the Queen in her palanquin, borne by six knights, dominates the occasion. For those who sought her support, she was a jealous mistress. Hot-blooded men like Raleigh had to pay constant suit to their unmarried sovereign, a woman as willful as they were, and walk a narrow path, never too close, never too far. Sometimes they slipped.

Raleigh fell decisively from favor in 1592, a result of his affair with Elizabeth Throckmorton (right), another of the royal maids of honor, whom he was compelled to marry. Raleigh was devoted to her until the end. When "the wisest fool in Christendom," James I (above), became king, Raleigh's warlike anti-Spanish policies were doomed, and in 1618 he was beheaded (below). His last poem (below right) was written the evening before he died.

Even such is time, that takes in trust
Our youth, our joys, our all we have,
And pays us but with age and dust;
Who in the dark and silent grave,
When we have wandered all our ways,
Shuts up the story of our days.
But from this earth, this grave, this dust,
My God shall raise me up, I trust!

this provides one of the tantalizing "ifs" of history; for immediately after they had gone, Raleigh's supply ship turned up, looked for the colonists and, not finding them, returned with her provisions to England. A fortnight after that, Grenville arrived with three ships well-provided. He himself traveled "up into divers places of the country" seeking for news of the colony in vain.

Then, "unwilling to lose the possession of the country which Englishmen had so long held, after good deliberation," he left a post of fifteen men on Roanoke provisioned for two years, to hold the fort. He has been criticized for a wrong decision; but we do not know his circumstances or his instructions. It looks clear to me that he was expected to reinforce the existing colony, not plant a new one, nor is it likely that his people would volunteer to make a new settlement unprepared. The real point is that Drake's unintended taking off of the colonists completely upset the planned synchronization of Raleigh's efforts and spoiled the best chance of settlement. After that everything went wrong.

In 1587 Raleigh sent out his second colony—actually it was the fourth voyage he had set forth—under John White. This had a somewhat different plan: it was not intended to supersede Roanoke but to supplement it with a settlement on the Chesapeake, and Raleigh gave White, as governor with twelve assistants, a charter to found the city of Raleigh in Virginia—a measure of self-government. Raleigh's directions were never carried out, for the sailors refused to carry the colonists to the Chesapeake and insisted on landing them on Roanoke. The colonists insisted on John White returning for further supplies, and that was the last that was ever heard of them. Some think that they perished on their way through the forest to the Chesapeake, and that is likely enough: in their fate forerunners to how many countless pioneers who perished in the American wilderness.

In the spring of 1588, Raleigh sent out a couple of small pinnaces, which never got across the Atlantic in the disturbed conditions of that memorable summer. At Bideford, Grenville was fitting out his strongest expedition yet, three tall ships and four barques. But with the Armada on the way he was not allowed to go. His Virginia voyage countermanded, he was ordered to take his ships around to Plymouth and serve under Drake. In 1589, everything in the West Country went into the big Lisbon expedition under Drake and Norris, which was England's riposte to the Armada.

These years were full of work and activity for Raleigh and Grenville. As Lord Lieutenant of Cornwall, Raleigh was responsible for the land defenses of the county most exposed to invasion. He was kept busy in the west, at court, and in Ireland. In 1591 Grenville was killed in the last fight of the *Revenge,* celebrated by Raleigh in unforgettable prose. The next year, with tension relaxed, Raleigh fell into utter disgrace with the Queen. Everything that he had so far been able to do was due to his favor with her: he had no independent position or footing, he was not a peer of the realm with estates and a feudal dependence, he had no fortune of his own. It all depended on his position with the Queen.

A man like Raleigh had a difficult razor-edge to walk. The Queen liked very masculine types—though they also had to be intelligent. The language in which this maiden lady delighted was the language of love: a difficult situation for these high-spirited, highly sexed men, supposed to be in love with her, though of course it was a platonic relationship, always at a certain distance. Nothing more exacting than to be admitted to so privileged an intimacy and at the same time to keep your distance and your head. For their vestal virgin who presided over it all was a jealous deity: they could have neither the Queen nor anybody else. It was more than flesh and blood could stand, particularly the hot flesh and blood of these Elizabethan courtiers. One after the other lost his balance, toppled over, and fetched up for a spell in the Tower of London.

Raleigh was pretty free with women; at last he fell seriously in love with one and was caught; another Elizabeth, a Throckmorton and—what made it worse—a maid of honor to the Queen. It became evident, I think, that Raleigh had, in the technical sense, behaved badly: he compromised her, or they compromised each other. To the Queen, for psychological reasons that one can understand though perhaps not wholly sympathize with, the offense was unpardonable—after such protestations of love, a passion on an altogether higher plane, for her. Raleigh made it worse by denying that he had any intention of marrying the lady. The Queen clapped them both in the Tower and had them ignominiously married, no one knows when or how.

She never admitted Lady Raleigh to her presence again; for her, poor lady, the marriage was a prelude to a lifetime of trouble. I hope that Raleigh's fine phrase when condemned to death by James—"I chose you, and I loved you, in my happiest times"—made up a little for it with her. They seem to have remained always in love; perhaps it was just as well, though

Raleigh may have had some doubts when, for the next five years, the Queen kept him away from court and all influence, in the prime of his powers.

In the last years of the Queen's reign Raleigh came back to his place at court, though things were never quite the same between them again. In 1600 he was made governor of Jersey, and local tradition there credits him with beginning the trade between the Channel Islands and Newfoundland. Raleigh was preparing to renew his contacts when James came to the throne, and Raleigh not long after was condemned for treason. He spent practically the rest of his life in the Tower; not a very good base from which to conduct colonial enterprises. However, he maintained his interest and his belief in the future of Virginia. "I shall yet live to see it an English nation," he wrote grandly from imprisonment.

How to strike a balance in estimating Raleigh's colonial achievements, his services to America? He was criticized in his own day, as he has been in ours, for not doing more. That splendid intellect but not very nice man, Francis Bacon, who was not above kicking a man when he was down, wrote in his essay "Of Plantations," "it is the sinfullest thing in the world to forsake or destitute a plantation once in forwardness, for besides the dishonour, it is the guiltiness of blood of many commiserable persons." Everyone would know whom he had in mind. But Hakluyt, who knew all the facts and was in a better position to judge, says simply that Raleigh was disheartened by the great expense and by the unfaithfulness of those he employed, "after he had sent (as you may see by these five several times) colonies and supplies at his own charges and now at length both himself and his successors [are] thus betrayed."

We have seen something, not only of his difficulties and disappointments, the obstacles in the way, but of the sheer impossibility of getting his orders executed on the other side of the Atlantic in his own enforced absence. Armchair critics of today often do not have the imagination to appreciate the physical and other conditions upon which achieving anything in the Elizabethan Age depended, how much men were at the mercy of circumstances, of wind and weather, of personal caprice or royal favor, the undependability of agents, the perversity of things.

Yet Raleigh's efforts did bear fruit: a people's mem-

Fortifications in Bermuda, here and on the following pages, as illustrated in John Smith's Generall Historie *(1624).*

ory is more generous, and perhaps speaks more truly, than the professors'. Raleigh put Virginia on the map. The first Roanoke colony was of prime formative significance; subsequent colonial enterprise in America built on that foundation. By his position at Elizabeth's court he gave the most powerful impetus in practice to the idea of English settlement in America. Even his patronage of smoking tobacco, giving it social cachet, was not without its effect in helping Virginia's staple product, the crop by which she ultimately achieved economic viability.

The approaching end of the war with Spain, at the turn of the century, made it certain that the English would now resume their efforts to settle in North America. After all, that was what they had fought Spain for—with success. The Queen would not make peace without guarantees for the Netherlands and the principle of the open door in America. On that, negotiations had broken down in 1598 and 1599. When they were renewed, after her death, Spain was in a still weaker position to insist, and peace was made in London, the negotiations dominated by Cecil, who represented the continuity of Elizabethan policy. The government obtained all that it wished in regard to the Netherlands. With regard to America, there was no agreement. The Spaniards refused to accept the English position of freedom of trade with all parts not in effective occupation: hence the continuance of "war beyond the line," *i.e.*, the Pope's line, and the subsequent romantic and bloody history of the buccaneers. On the subject of English colonization, most important of all, nothing was said. The English were not going to admit that it was a subject for discussion. The only implication to be drawn was that they would now go ahead.

Already, exploratory voyages to the coast had been resumed, and with a clear sense, expressed in the narratives, of the continuity with those of the 1580's. The French, also, now released from civil war and from war with Spain by the Treaty of Vervins (1598), took up once more their long-suspended colonial ambitions, and there followed the first settlement in Acadia, at Port Royal. In these years the great Champlain was exploring these coasts and in 1608 clinched French power in the St. Lawrence with the founding of Quebec. Already the intrepid navigator Henry Hudson was scouring the Arctic ice from Greenland to Spitsbergen to find a way through to the East, and the next year (1609) was exploring the Hudson and the Delaware river valleys on behalf of the Dutch. A new phase of international rivalry for North America was beginning.

In 1606 a body chiefly of West Countrymen came together to petition James I for license to plant a colony—Raleigh's rights having lapsed by his condemnation for treason. From this patent the subsequent colonization sprang, in the northern part of Virginia (*i.e.,* New England) as well as the south. For it constituted two companies to carry out the twin projects envisaged in north and south. The southern company was to plant between 34 and 41 degrees north, and was backed mainly from London. The northern colony was to plant between 38 and 45 degrees north; it was backed mainly from Bristol, Exeter, and Plymouth, but came to be known as the Plymouth Company. The strength of the Plymouth Company, it was hoped, would lie in its fishing interests; the London Company's in finance. Finance and fishing—there could be no doubt which would emerge the stronger. Though there was some interaction between the two, and more friction, I leave the Plymouth Company to a later article: from it sprang, if in various ways and in varying degrees, the colonization of New England.

M oney and management were to be supplied by the city of London; and here the merchants weighed in, above all the East India magnate Sir Thomas Smythe, to whom the establishment and survival of the colony at Jamestown is chiefly due. It is significant that where the independent and ill co-ordinated resources of courtiers, gentlemen, and merchants had not answered earlier, the resources of the City merchants, made more maneuverable by the mechanism of the joint-stock company, succeeded. One must pay tribute to the unfaltering leadership of these merchant magnates—both Smythe and his opponent, Sir Edwin Sandys, with their supporters in the City—in all the discouragements and disasters that befell Virginia, for its ill luck continued, on the Chesapeake as at Roanoke. Lesser men would have given up in despair, would have had to for want of resources. But these men had, no less important, resource, resilience, flexibility; they turned their hands to anything rather than see it fail. And this time they saw it through.

The little fleet of three ships, the *Susan Constant, Godspeed,* and *Discovery,* with the usual complement of 100 men, sailed in December, 1606, under the command of

Pembroks forte
K

Captain Christopher Newport. Now a man of forty, who had been concerned in the capture of the *Madre de Dios,* richest of the prizes in the war, he was one of the best-esteemed sea captains of the day.

Newport brought his ships safe into the Chesapeake without let or hindrance. George Percy, brother of Raleigh's companion in the Tower—the "Wizard Earl" of Northumberland, tells us of "fair meadows and goodly tall trees, with such fresh-waters running through the woods, as I was almost ravished at the first sight thereof." They picked on the site of Jamestown, low and marshy as it was, unhealthy as it proved to be, because, being almost an island, it was defensible. There they constructed their fort. In obedience to their instructions they explored up the James River, till they were checked at the falls where now Richmond is.

We note the continuing stress upon finding a passage through to the Pacific; they were continually led to hope by stories of the Indians about a sea just beyond the mountains, and hope was not entirely extinguished until the end of the century. It is tribute to Captain John Smith's sense that he describes the bounds of Virginia as on the east "the great ocean; on the south lieth Florida; on the north Nova Francia; as for the west thereof, the limits are unknown." To discover them constituted the saga of the American people, and not until a couple of generations ago was the process, set in being by the Elizabethans, complete. In that sense, looking over the last prairie country to be settled, going through Rockies or Cascades, we may feel ourselves for a moment linked, in touch, with those first Elizabethans who started it all.

Theirs were the sacrifices; and the cost in human life in the first two decades of Virginia was terrible. No doubt this first venture was experimental and exploratory. Captain John Smith says that they had eaten up their provisions on too long a sea voyage, had arrived too late to plant, and in any case were insufficiently provided. He adds philosophically, "such actions have ever since the world's beginning been subject to such accidents, and everything of worth is found full of difficulties, but nothing so difficult as to establish a commonwealth so far remote from men and means, and where men's minds are so untoward as neither do well themselves nor suffer others." In other words, there was what is called the human factor—and it proved very human.

There is no point in entertaining illusions about it —these voyages transported the flotsam and jetsam of humanity, even the better-than-average proved selfish and listless and would not work to save themselves, let alone others. Famine and the marshes bred disease, and men began to die. Without any concentration of authority, bickerings and quarrels increased. By the end of the first winter, they were down to 38 men left alive.

Then the first supply arrived just in time, for they might have given up. (The colony planted contemporaneously by the Plymouth Company in the north at Sagadahoc did give up and went home.) With two supplies sent out in 1608 things began to look up; buildings that had been burned down were repaired, and the colonists began to plant a little. Faced with a second winter of privation, Captain John Smith, "whom no persuasions could persuade to starve," came to the fore and as president took matters forcefully in hand. "If any would not work, neither should he eat"; he threatened to drive those who would not work into the wilderness.

By these means, and by his own energy and force of character, Smith carried the colony successfully through the second winter with few losses.

That winter the colonists had enough novelties, excitements, dangers, consolations, to last them a lifetime. They kept Christmas in bad weather, "among the savages, where we were never more merry, nor fed on more plenty of good oysters, fish, flesh, wild fowl and good bread, nor never had better fires in England than in the dry smoky houses of Kecoughtan." Relations with the Indians had all the complexity of contacts between races at very different levels of civilization, by turns friendly and hostile—or rather, the same emotions in the same breast, so that a sharp lookout had to be kept all the time. The company at home insisted on the coronation of Powhatan, the leading chief of the area, against Smith's better judgment: of "subtle understanding and politic carriage," he was rendered all the more difficult to deal with.

The most dangerous moment came when the small group of Germans in the colony conspired, characteristically, to betray it. They surreptitiously smuggled weapons to the natives and hoped to betray the colony to Spain. Equally characteristically, they got what was coming to them; a brace who got away to Powhatan had their brains beaten out for their treachery to the English. Then the Indians gave a masque, or entertainment, in the woods, after which their women pursued the embarrassed Smith with their pressing endearments. Or Powhatan's pretty daughter Pocahontas, not yet however nubile, would turn cart wheels naked in the streets of Jamestown to delight the hearts of the planters.

At home in England a wave of interest in Virginia was rising to the height of a national enterprise. The undertaking was gathering way and was launched in 1609 with the second charter, the effective instrument in the creation of Virginia. For this incorporated the Virginia Company that governed the colony and saw it through its infancy to a permanent existence, and separated it from the Plymouth Company, concerned now only with the north. The Virginia Company drew upon a most impressive array of support that can truly be said to represent the nation. It came to include 56 city companies and some 659 individuals—21 peers, 96 knights, 28 esquires, 58 gentlemen, 110 merchants, 282 citizens, and so on. To read the names of the adventurers is like hearing a roll call of the most active elements in the society of the last years of Shakespeare. There they all are, from the Archbishop of Canterbury and Shakespeare's own patrons, the Earls of Southampton, Pembroke, and Montgomery, through many names with more distant echoes, for there are Cecils and Cromwells and Chamberlains, Lord North along with the Spencer ancestor of the Churchills, while the Winston ancestor took shares later; Anglican bishops alongside of Puritans and Catholics; famous figures in the life of London down to an obscure Cornish squire like William Roscarrock, living there on the Atlantic coast near Padstow; or Gabriel and John Beadle, two poor gentlemen who went out to Virginia in the first supply (1608). Everybody who was anybody seems to have been in it, except the poets—and they as usual were short of cash.

The jealous attentions of the Spanish ambassador Zuñiga were aroused. Amazed at the response to Virginia in English society, he wrote home to Philip III that "fourteen earls and barons have given 40,000 ducats, the merchants give much more, and there is no poor little man nor woman who is not willing to subscribe something . . . Much as I have written to your Majesty of the determination they have formed here to go to Virginia, it seems to me that I still fall short of the reality."

For Virginia itself the effective change made by the second charter was the appointment of a governor with real power and authority, advised but not displaceable by the council there. The governor appointed, Lord De la Warr, was to follow Sir Thomas Gates, who meanwhile went as his deputy, with Sir George Somers as admiral of the fleet of eight ships that left Plymouth in May. This had some six hundred colonists on board, including one hundred women: the largest expedition for America until the mass emigration to Massachusetts started in 1630.

The sailing of Somers' little fleet has been described as "the true beginning of one of the great folk movements of history," but Virginia's ill luck held good. To avoid Spanish attentions and a long sea voyage, Somers' fleet took a direct course across the Atlantic from the Canaries. They ran into a hurricane, and Somers' flagship was cast away upon the coast of Bermuda, though all the folk were saved. The "still-vexed Bermoothes" were thought by the Elizabethans to be haunted by evil spirits. Out of the fusion of those two inspirations—for several accounts of it circulated at home—came *The Tempest*.

The castaways found it pleasant and healthful, with plenty to eat; and there they passed an agreeable winter, while building a couple of pinnaces to take them to Virginia. The rest of the fleet, with four hundred of the people, had arrived there in a battered condition and went through a terrible winter. This was the real "starving time" in Virginia history. By the time their leaders arrived from Bermuda in the spring, of all the four hundred and those there before, only some sixty remained alive. No doubt they brought disease with them, after so exhausting a journey, but the main reason for the disaster—it was no less—was the absence of leadership, of all authority and discipline. Elizabethans simply could not operate without it. With their leaders wrecked in Bermuda—for all they knew, drowned—the colony went to pieces.

Provisions and livestock were all consumed; the Indians refused trade except for the colonists' arms, implements, and utensils, and then turned on them, till "there remained not past sixty men, women and children, most miserable and poor creatures; and those were preserved for the most part, by roots, herbs, acorns, walnuts, berries, now and then a little fish . . ." There was, in fact, an instance or two of cannibalism.

When Gates arrived he set himself to restore order sternly; but there was little he could do; men went on dying, and there were only four days' provisions left when the colony gave up and set sail down the river. On their way they met the incoming governor, Lord De la Warr, so long delayed, and they were turned back to Jamestown. Here, under proper authority, they were set to work once more: "every man endeavoureth to outstrip other in diligence: the French preparing to plant the vines, the English labouring in the woods and grounds; every man knoweth his charge, and dischargeth the same with alacrity."

At home Sir Thomas Smythe needed every ounce of confidence to keep the adventurers to the task. In the absence of any return on their money, with repeated calls for further supplies, the discouragements of all these disasters, the persistent run of ill luck, and the rumors circulating against the colony in consequence, Smythe needed courage and statesmanship of the highest order to pull things round. These he possessed. He was a man of immense capacity and experience, of unhurried judgment and weighty decision, a somewhat impersonal man, who had the confidence of both the city and the court.

Faced with a crisis in those affairs and finding that Bermuda now looked more promising, he called in Bermuda to redress the balance of Virginia. He obtained from the Crown a third charter for Virginia, extending her bounds 300 leagues from the continent to include Bermuda. A Bermuda, or Somers Islands, company was floated on a joint-stock, began to make profits from an immense piece of ambergris found on the coast, and started to colonize.

The new charter permitted a lottery to be started, with prizes, to raise cash. And later the company became chiefly a land company, "its one asset the land that had been bought with the sacrifices of the first ten years." The company appealed to intending planters with an offer of fifty acres for every person to be sent to the colony; on this basis plantation continued and was extended—whatever the setbacks now, settlement went on.

Within the colony, too, the corner may be said to have been turned with the change from communal arrangements to private ownership. No doubt the first tasks in a new settlement were communal in their nature. But when the soldier-governors allotted every man in the settlement three acres of clear ground to his own, they turned from bowling in the street to cultivating their gardens. Progress was at once to be seen. At the same time, what was to become Virginia's staple export, tobacco, makes its first appearance. The credit for the first experiments is thought to be John Rolfe's. He made another experiment, too, which has brought him greater fame; he fell in love with Pocahontas, and she with him. After much deliberation with his friends, and some prayer, he married her properly. This favorably impressed the Indians, and for some years there was a blissful interval of peace and good relations.

Rolfe later brought Pocahontas to England, where she "unexpectedly" died—of the climate, perhaps.

Now that the colony had been brought round, the man by whose efforts it had been accomplished, Sir Thomas Smythe, lost control of the Virginia Company and received his dismissal, in the usual way of such things. There always had been a division in the company between the big City merchants and the more numerous small adventurers, between the platform and the floor of the house. (As usual, the platform was generally right, the floor generally wrong.) Again, as usual, the discontented majority found leadership among the magnates: in the Earl of Warwick, in Shakespeare's Southampton, and above all in Sir Edwin Sandys.

Sandys, who became treasurer of the company in 1619, was a remarkable man. Educated under Richard Hooker at Oxford, where he became a Fellow of Corpus Christi College, he was much more of an intellectual than Sir Thomas Smythe. He toured Europe with Archbishop Cranmer's great nephew and dedicated the book he wrote, *Europae speculum,* to Archbishop Whitgift. We see that his early associations were archiepiscopal. This did not prevent him from being rather a demagogue in the House of Commons, where he was very forward in opposition.

In the Virginia Company Sandys captured the leadership of the lesser shareholders, many of whom, including fifty Members of Parliament, had not paid up their subscriptions. Sandys thereupon resorted to lotteries; he was very ingenious and resourceful, full of energy and ideas, up to anything and everything to raise money. And we must do him this justice: he did infuse new energy into, gave a fresh impetus to, the colony. After his first year of office, James refused to have him renominated: "Choose the Devil, if you will, but not Sir Edwin Sandys." So Southampton was elected treasurer, though Sandys remained the moving spirit.

Sir Edwin, I fear, was a sharp customer. When it came to depressing reports from Virginia, he and John and Nicholas Ferrars doctored the minutes. An adept at maneuvering votes in council, by 1622 he had got into control of both companies. He now proposed a scheme of salaries for himself and offices for his supporters that was unprecedented. He as director was to receive £500 a year. Smythe, after five years as governor of the East India Company, had refused to accept more than £400 gratuity. For twelve years' service as treasurer of the Virginia Company he was rewarded with twenty shares; Sandys got as much for one year, and John Ferrars as his deputy, the same amount for three years. It is not the first time that a reformer has been revealed as self-interested.

Meanwhile, so engrossed were they in these characteristic amenities of committees, idiotic dissensions, and personal maneuvers that the terrible Indian massacre of that year—in which 350 were killed and 500 more died within the twelvemonth—went unnoticed, so far as remedies went. Sandys and the Ferrarses suppressed information as to the worst miseries the colony endured, and put about misleading reports. But disquiet about Virginia grew, and Smythe's governor, back from Bermuda, revealed the facts of Sandys' feverish overshipping of colonists and the fearful mortality in consequence. He had certainly been energetic. In the four years of Sandys' administration 4,000 had been transported; the net increase to the population was 275. In all, by 1622 some 10,000 souls had gone out to Virginia; of these only 2,000 were alive. As to money, under Smythe £80,000 had been expended; in the far shorter period of Sandys, between £80,000 and £90,000.

No: the effective founder of Jamestown colony was Sir Thomas Smythe.

These facts were revealed by a committee appointed by the Crown, which exonerated Smythe's administration, going through all the books and figures, and condemned Sandys. There was furious dissension, for of course Sandys retained the support of the Commons. But the government had had enough of it; when Sandys and his allies appealed to the Commons, the Crown recalled the Virginia charters and resumed the government of the colony into its own hands: henceforth this took the classic shape of royal governors with assistants nominated by the Crown, with a representative assembly.

We may take this to end the founding phase in the colony's history. Up to 1624 the whole cost of the plantation of Virginia was about £200,000, with what little return we have seen. We may profitably contrast the money poured out by England to settle her stock in Virginia with Spain's ruthless exploitation of the West Indies—the regular drain of treasure from Mexico and Peru.

Within the colony, after such tribulations, all was at last set fair. Even before the last of them, the Indian Massacre of 1622, a most important development in government took place, from which the ultimate form of American government was shaped: the first representative assembly, based on popular election, met there in the tiny church beside the river at Jamestown. A touching scene in its simplicity and yet in all that it signifies—the heart of the political experience of the English-speaking peoples and the peculiar contribution they have to make to the world.

At home the interest displayed in very different quarters tells its own story. In matters of policy James I did not depart from the stand Queen Elizabeth had taken on America, though there were people, Sir Edwin Sandys among them, who were afraid that he might give way to the Spaniards. Anyway, in the first

THE PORTRAICTUER OF CAPTAYNE JOHN SMITH ADMIRALL OF NEW ENGLAND.

Æta 37
A° 1616

This portrait of John Smith was made by Simon de Passe, one of the foremost engravers of his day, for Smith's map of New England. The map, with the places named by Prince Charles himself, appeared in A Description of New England, *written while Smith was a prisoner of pirates who had captured him on his second trip to New England.*

years that mattered most, he had Cecil beside him to guide policy on the Elizabethan lines. James's own interest did not amount to much. We have an exchange between Southampton and Salisbury in 1609 which shows what they thought. James had heard of the Virginia squirrels that were said to fly, and asked Southampton whether there were none for him, and whether Salisbury had not provided some for him. Southampton would not have told Salisbury, "but that you know so well how he is affected to these toys." One notices the contrast between the lightheaded James in these matters and the profound and tenacious concern of the great Queen. And indeed nothing could have advertised that contrast more signally to the world than James's execution of Raleigh at the behest of Spain.

More worthy of respect is the interest of ordinary Englishmen in all walks of life in the new England rising on the other side of the Atlantic. The bishops raised a fund of some £2,000 for an Indian college and for the support of an Indian school, though the company was too short of funds to use them for the purpose. One day in November, 1620, a stranger stepped into a meeting of the court and presented Raleigh's history of Guiana, with a map and four great books, for the college; twelve months later a stranger again came forward with more books for the college. Most touching of all are the collections made on board the East Indiamen for Virginia. In 1621 at the Cape of Good Hope, the *Royal James* collected £70 6s. 8d. toward building a free school, the highest amount ten marks from Captain Pring, and so down to 1 shilling from the mariners. Two other ships collected 100 marks—in all £192 1s. 10d.—that Virginia might have a school. When we think of the hard conditions of those sailors' lives, and out of their little pay contributing their shillings, we glimpse something of what America meant for those simple English folk.

On the other hand, there is all that the old country meant for the new. Professor Wesley Frank Craven rightly emphasizes that the beginnings of American history can properly be read only forward from the Elizabethan England of which it was an extrapolation, not backwards from modern America. He is writing in particular about the South, though what he says also applies with little change to the North:

The historian who would trace the main threads woven into the pattern of Southern life must, therefore, turn first to England. . . . For it was the Elizabethan Englishman who planned and undertook the settlements to which most of us look back as on our beginnings. The Elizabethan tongue that once rang out across the James and the York may still be heard in certain out-of-the-way spots of the South. The Elizabethan devotion to Protestantism, born of a long defense of Elizabeth's church settlement and fed on the fiery materials of John Foxe's *Book of Martyrs,* still survives to shape the fundamental tenets of the great majority of Southerners. Even the institutional pattern our forefathers adapted to the peculiar requirements of a new-world environment was more Elizabethan than anything else. Though sheriffs, coroners, constables, justices of the peace, juries, and representative assemblies were ancient parts of the English scene, it was as their place and function had been defined under Elizabeth that the early colonists understood them. Here, too, has the South, ever prompt to recognize individual achievement, discovered the first heroic figures of her history—Elizabeth herself and Raleigh.

This article formed part of a series especially prepared for AMERICAN HERITAGE *by Dr. A. L. Rowse, Fellow of All Souls College, Oxford, and a noted authority on the Elizabethan era. The entire series may be read in his book,* The Elizabethans and America, *recently published by Harper & Brothers.*

☆ ☆ ☆ ☆ ☆ ☆ ☆ ☆ ☆ ☆ ☆

One of the most striking characteristics of an American is his self dependence. Born to no fortune, he knows from his earliest years that he has nothing but his own mental and bodily exertions to rely on in the great struggle of existence. This self dependence produces a remarkable quickness and versatility of talent. He turns his mother wit, as the Indian does his knife, to all purposes, and is seldom at a loss. At his first outset in life the world lies before him, like the wilderness of his own country, a trackless waste through which he must cut his own path; but what would be a region of doubt and despondency to another mind appears to him a land of promise, a region of glorious enterprize tinted with golden hope.

—From an unpublished essay by Washington Irving, 1831; courtesy of Mary A. Benjamin, Director, Walter R. Benjamin Autographs.

Philip was crowned on the ceremonial rock called King Philip's Throne; close to it, he was killed.

The
TRAGEDY of KING PHILIP
and the DESTRUCTION of the
NEW ENGLAND INDIANS

By GEORGE HOWE

The most serious threat to white colonization of New England was the Indian uprising of 1675-76, known as King Philip's War. What follows is the story of the tragic man who led that futile struggle, Philip, chief of the Wampanoags. But perhaps it is just as much the story of Philip's erstwhile friend and resourceful pursuer, Benjamin Church. This account is taken from George Howe's book, Mount Hope, *a superb history of Bristol, Rhode Island, published by the Viking Press in 1959.*

AN AMERICAN HERITAGE BOOK SELECTION

"Where there is love there is no fear"

Behind the present town of Bristol, Rhode Island, on Narragansett Bay, rises the 200-foot hill called Mount Hope. East of it is an estuary dividing Rhode Island from Massachusetts; west of it is Bristol harbor, and west again, the peninsula of Poppasquash.

In 1620, when the Pilgrims landed forty miles to the east at Plymouth, Mount Hope was the seat of Massasoit, King of the Wampanoags. They were a branch of the Algonquin nation; the name of the tribe means "Eastern People," and his own name means "Great Chief." He was chief of all the lesser sachems from Cape Cod to Narragansett Bay. He lived comfortably in a tent village that he called Pokanoket, north of the hill. His lodges, framed on poles, were covered with reed mattings sewn together with hemp and bound tight at the smoke hole with walnut bark. Having a flap at each end, they caught the breeze whichever way it blew. The biggest of them, the long house, stretched a hundred feet. The village was built at the foot of Mount Hope, not on top of it, in order that the smoke of the campfire might not be mistaken for signals.

When the fish hawks arrived in March, Massasoit knew that scup had moved up from the sea. When the bud of the white oak had reached the size of a mouse's ear, his squaws planted corn, laying a ripe herring at each hill for fertilizer. They hoed with quahog shells. His braves, who scorned labor, stalked deer on Poppasquash with bow and arrow, and netted tautog in the channel. There were soft-shelled clams in the mud at low tide for the digging, and eels, quahogs, and scallops offshore for the treading, all of which were brewed into a chowder called nasaump. Groundnuts, which are the roots of the wild bean, needed no labor at all; and huckleberries grew wild in the clearings. Over open fires, the squaws broiled roe, boiled succotash, baked corn bread, and refined the sugar of the maples. Winter was a season of semistarvation, but meat and fish, tanned in the sun the previous summer, saw the tribe through all but the hardest seasons. (The Indians never learned the use of salt to preserve their meat, though they were surrounded by sea water). Fifteen miles inland, at what is still called Fowling Pond, Massasoit had a winter game preserve. He might shift camp a little when his firewood gave out; even now, heaps of clamshells, marking a camp site, are sometimes dug up behind Mount Hope. But with fair weather he always returned to his hill. Mount Hope was his home and his throne.

On March 22, 1621, with his brother, Quadequina,

and sixty of his braves, he visited the Pilgrims at Plymouth. The royal party walked all the way from Mount Hope; horses were unknown to them. The *Mayflower*, which had brought the Englishmen from England the previous autumn, still lay in the harbor; she was not to return till April 5. The King's hair, high in front and long behind, was greased, and his face was painted with the royal mulberry. He looked like the gypsies the English had seen at home. He wore mooseskin moccasins, deerskin leggings, and a squirrel coat with the fur inside. A string of bone beads hung at his neck. He carried a knife in his coat-strap and a wooden tomahawk in his hand. As interpreter, he brought one of his subjects named Squanto. Seven years earlier, an English raider named Hunt had kidnapped Squanto from the coast and sold him to slavery in Spain. He had escaped to London, where he had learned English, and from London, as recently as 1619, he had escaped back to his own country.

Squanto stood beside the King on a rise above the Pilgrims' stockade at Plymouth.

"Welcome, Englishmen," he called down to them.

Governor Carver must have been astounded to hear his own language from a red man. He sent his young secretary, Edward Winslow, up to the hill with presents in his hand: a knife, a jewel for the ear, a pot of "strong water," a good quantity of biscuit, and some butter. They were gratefully accepted.

"Do you dare to walk among us alone?" Squanto asked Winslow. "Where there is love there is no fear," the secretary answered.

Winslow was detained on the hill as a hostage, while Massasoit followed Squanto down to the stockade. The newest cabin in the colony was made ready to receive him. It was not much better than the royal long house at Mount Hope. A green rug had been laid on the earth floor, with three or four cushions on it. Drift-

The English arrive, an engraving from An Illuminating History of North America, *by John Frost.*

wood blazed in the clay fireplace. The room was lighted by paper windows, and, when darkness fell, by bayberry dips. Little Miles Standish, with a file of six men, presented arms. To the sound of a trumpet and drum, Governor Carver himself entered. He bent his chin over Massasoit's hand and kissed it. He gave him a great draught of strong water, whereat the King's whole body broke into a sweat. He had never tasted liquor before. Massasoit sat all afternoon beside the Governor, trembling with fear. Before he started home he had put his mark to a treaty of alliance with King James I of England. The white men who had landed on his shore, with cuirasses instead of leather for armor, with muskets and cutlasses for weapons instead of arrows, with sailboats and rum and tobacco, were lucky allies for him. He called them *Wautoconoag*, which means "men who wear clothes."

Massasoit was a portly and dignified sachem of 41, grave of countenance and spare of speech. Once he had been subject to the Narragansetts, westward across the bay. A four-year plague, beginning in 1617, had so reduced his tribe that they were making ready to subdue him again. Once there had been three thousand Wampanoags; now there were hardly more fighting men than the sixty who attended the King to Plymouth. As a later governor put it, "Providence was visible in thinning the Indians to make room for the English."

The dour John Winthrop in 1634 gloated that "The natives are neere all dead of the small poxe, so as the Lord hathe cleared our title to what we possess." (There is reason to believe, however, that the plague was not smallpox, but jaundice.)

But the Pilgrims, so far, were the only Englishmen north of Virginia. They had hardly survived their first winter in the New World, and had nothing to lose by making friends with the Indians.

Four months later they sent an embassy to Mount Hope to return Massasoit's visit. They brought him a horseman's laced coat of red cotton, though he still had no horse, and a necklace of copper beads to serve as a passport for future visits. Since warm weather had come, the King had reversed his squirrel coat so the fur was on the outside. Not being forewarned of the visit, he had to do his hasty best. For the reception he donned his turkey-feather mantle, tied at the throat with twine. The English, squatting on skins outside his wigwam, shared the dried beef which the squaws brought from the storepit, and two tautog shot by the braves with bow and arrow. The King had forty guests that afternoon: two Englishmen and thirty-eight Indians. They smoked his pipe of hemlock and ground-up ivy. They played the dice game which their host called Hubbub.

Edward Winslow succors Massasoit.

The English ambassadors slept that night on the same plank bed with the King, his wife, and two of his chiefs.

"We were worse weary of our lodging," they reported to Plymouth, "than with our journey. What with the savages' barbarous singing (for they are wont to sing themselves asleep), with lice and fleas within door and mosquitos without, we could hardly sleep all the time of our being there."

Claiming they must keep Sabbath at home, but actually "much fearing if we should stay any longer we should not be able to recover home for want of strength," they started back on Saturday morning and rode into Plymouth on the same night.

In December, when the Pilgrims gave thanks for their first year of survival, Massasoit returned the visit. His braves killed four deer, and the King contributed them to the first Thanksgiving dinner.

Two years later, Winslow heard that Massasoit was on his deathbed. He visited him again. He found the royal wigwam so crowded with mourners that he could hardly elbow his way inside. Beside the pallet stood the King's wife; his brothers, Quadequina and Akkompoin; and his medicine men.

Massasoit, who suffered from constipation, had not eaten for two days. He lay among the howling sorcerers with his eyes closed. His sight had gone.

"*Kéen Winsnow?*" he asked faintly, meaning "Art thou Winslow?"

Indians could not pronounce the letter *l*.

"*Ahhé,*" Winslow answered for yes.

"*Matta néen wonckanet nanen, Winsnow.*" ("Ah, Winslow, I shall never see thee again.")

But Winslow had brought with him from Plymouth

Paul Revere's fanciful portrait of King Philip.

"a confection of many comfortable conserves." He forced it between Massasoit's stiffening jaws with his knife blade. When the King had swallowed a little of it, the ambassador washed out his mouth and scraped his furry tongue. Next day he sent couriers to Plymouth for some chickens, for poultry was unknown to the Indians. While they were gone, he brewed a vegetarian pottage out of strawberry leaves and sassafras—all he could find in March—which a squaw ground up with a little corn and boiled in a pipkin. He strained the broth through his own handkerchief and fed it to the King. The next meal was goose soup, thanks to a pretty bull's-eye of his blunderbuss at 120 yards. (The Indian word for goose was *honck*.) The soup restored the King's eyesight but was too rich for his stomach. He vomited, and bled for four hours from the nose. But after the nosebleed, he slept for six. When he waked, Winslow washed his face and suppled his beard. By the time the chickens arrived, the King was well enough to order them saved for breeding instead of being slaughtered for broth. His friends came from

as far as a hundred miles to see the miracle of his recovery and listen to his praises of his English friends.

Massasoit begat three sons—Wamsutta, Metacom, and Suconewhew—and two daughters, one named Amie and one whose name is lost. He lived to see his two older sons marry two sisters from across Mount Hope Bay. Weetamoe, the wife of Wamsutta, was in her own right Queen of Pocasset—the hillside which is now Tiverton, Rhode Island.

Over the rest of his long reign, Massasoit recklessly ceded tracts of his depopulated kingdom to the Pilgrims in exchange for their weapons, horses, rum, and currency.

The English converted some of the Wampanoags to Christianity, and a good many more of the inland Nipmucks. Massasoit clung to his traditional gods: Kichtan, for good, and Abemecho, for evil. He believed vaguely that Heaven lay in the southwest, the direction of fair-weather winds. Kichtan had made the first man and woman out of stone; when they proved unsatisfactory, he destroyed them and made another couple out of a tree. The Pilgrims' story of Noah and the flood was not much different. He was willing to let the Nipmucks, and even his own Wampanoags, accept the English God, provided he did not have to give up his own. He did not object when John Eliot, the Apostle to the Indians, carried away Sassamon, his secretary, to study the new religion at Harvard, nor even when his youngest boy, Suconewhew, went there, too. But for himself, he was too old to change.

Other sachems were more receptive. When the Pilgrims asked them "to worship ye only true God, which made Heaven and earth, and not to blaspheme Him," one of them answered wistfully:

"We do desire to reverence ye God of ye English, and to speak well of Him, because we see He doth better to ye English than other gods do to others."

The English always paid for their land, but they seemed always to buy the best. The deeds, written in English, were witnessed and recorded in the General Court at Plymouth. They took over the choicest fishing grounds and cleared the woods of game. When their trade goods had long been spent or drunk up, the land was still theirs. Even so, Massasoit was so grateful to his allies that he petitioned the General Court at Plymouth to assign English names to his two older sons. The Pilgrims would not grant them Christian names, and the only two close relatives from pagan history who came to mind were the warrior kings of Macedon. In 1656 Wamsutta became Alexander; Metacom became Philip. The brothers were flattered by the comparison. Aware that the Greek name Philip means "a lover of horses," the governor gave the young prince a black stallion.

The English called their converts Praying Indians. They made them bailiffs and marshals in the villages around Boston, let them attend court and serve on juries, and even placed some of them over the white constables. The copper-skinned magistrate of the Praying Village at Natick issued this mandamus to his white assistant:

"You, you big constable! Quick you catch um Jeremiah Offscow, strong you hold um, safe you bring um before me—Waban, Justice of Peace."

When a new magistrate asked Waban what he did when the non-praying Indians got drunk and quarreled with each other, he told him, "Tie um all up and whip um plaintiff, whip um fendant, whip um witness."

The converted Indians hung around the fringes of the settlements, helping the English cultivate their corn, butchering their hogs in the fall, and digging clams or treading eels for them in exchange for food and rum. The English settlers at Weymouth, a village between Plymouth and Boston, complained that the Indians plucked their food from the kettles before they could get at it themselves.

Most of the sachems resented the conversions, and the tolerant Roger Williams at Providence agreed with them. In 1654 he wrote the Puritan governor of Massachusetts Bay:

At my last departure for England, I was importuned by the Narragansett Indians to present to the high sachems of England that they might not be forced from their religions, and, for not changing them, be invaded by war. For they say they are daily visited with threatenings by [Praying] Indians that come from about the Massachusetts, that if they would not pray, they should be destroyed by war. Are not all the English of this land generally a persecuted people from their native land? And hath not the God of peace and Father of mercies made the natives more friendly to us in this land than our countrymen in our own? Are not our families grown up in peace amongst them? Upon which I humbly ask how it can suit with Christian ingenuity to take hold of some seeming occasions for their destruction.

"*In the posture of war*"

Massasoit died in 1661 at the venerable age of 81. The haughty Alexander, his oldest son, succeeded him. After he had been dismissed by the Pilgrims, Alexander was suddenly taken ill. One story has it that their suspicions (which seem to have been well-founded) so outraged him that he broke into a burning fever before his trial even began; another that he was poisoned by Josiah Winslow, at whose house in Marshfield he stayed on the return. In light of the existing record there is no reason to believe either story.

Benjamin Church, also as imagined by Revere.

Alexander seems to have been well treated both at Duxbury and at Marshfield. He died on the way home to Mount Hope, having reigned only a year.

Philip succeeded his brother. He was 24 years old. On the rock now called King Philip's Throne, on the east side of Mount Hope, he donned the nine-foot stole of wampum, fringed with red deerskin and embroidered with beasts and birds, the headband with two flags behind, the breastplate engraved with a star, and the scarlet cloak that were his "royalties." Paul Revere's crude portrait of him, engraved a century later from imagination, and a hostile one at that, shows him as a square-set man of medium height, with a trace of a beard below his chin, standing before Mount Hope in his regalia, with bare legs above his moccasins, a musket in his hand, and a tomahawk and powder horn at his feet. But it is likely that he was taller than most of the English.

One of Philip's hands was scarred from the explosion of a pistol. He had undergone the tests of manhood. He had spent the winter alone in the forest with only a bow and arrow, a hatchet, and a knife to defend himself against the wolves and wildcats. He had drunk the juice of poisonous herbs, with the medicine man standing by with emetics in case of danger, until he had proved himself immune. Legend says that, with the Devil to help him, Philip could throw a stone

45

across the harbor from the crest of Mount Hope to Poppasquash, two miles away.

Like the widowed Weetamoe, he believed that English poison, and not a broken heart, had killed Alexander. He was determined to avenge his brother. So fierce were his loyalties that he had once pursued the  Indian called John Gibbs all the way to Nantucket Island, across forty miles of open water, because he had spoken ill of the dead Massasoit. Somehow the traducer escaped him in the dunes, but Philip would not leave the island until the English gave him all the money they could scrape together. It came to nineteen shillings.

By Massasoit's treaty, the English had agreed to respect the Indians' land. There was certainly enough for both. The treaty made it illegal for an Englishman to buy land from an Indian without the consent of the General Court at Plymouth. This rule was designed to protect the Indians from fraud, for it had never occurred to them that they owned the land anyway; they simply occupied it. Massasoit's generosity, and the greed of the colonists, made the law impossible to enforce. When Philip belatedly saw that he was not sharing his territory with the white settlers, but losing it to them, he determined to retain what little was left. His English friend John Borden reports that he told him:

"But little remains of my ancestor's domain, I am resolved not to see the day when I have no country."

One of his surviving letters to the Governor of Plymouth Colony, probably in the hand of John Sassamon, shows his state of mind:

KING PHILIP desire to let you understand that he could not come to the Court, for Tom his interpreter has a pain in his back, that he could not travil so far, and Philip sister is very sick. Philip would entreat that favor of you and aney of the majestrates, if aney English or Enjians speak about aney land, he pray you to give them no answer at all. This last somer he made that promis with you, that he would sell no land in 7 yers time, for he would have no English trouble him before that time. He has not forgot that you promis him. He will come as sune as possible he can speak with you, and so I rest

          Your verey loveing friend
          Philip, dwelling at mount hope nek.

In 1671 he confirmed his father's treaty at a conference in the Taunton meetinghouse, where the English sat on one side of the aisle and the Indians on the other. Later in the same year he even agreed to pay tribute to the Pilgrims, but did all he could to evade it by pleading poverty:

"I am willing and do promise to pay unto the government of Plymouth one hundred pounds in such things as I have, but would entreat the favour that I might have three years to pay it in, forasmuch as I do not have it at present. I do promise to send unto the Governor, or whom he shall appoint, five wolves' heads, if I can get them; or as many as I can procure until they come to five wolves yearly."

The settlers no longer needed the friendship of Indians. Three times they summoned Philip, as they had summoned Alexander, to answer charges of conspiracy. The first time, he meekly gave up the seventy guns his braves had brought with them. The braves were disgusted, for they had almost forgotten how to hunt with bow and arrow, and even though they did not know how to repair their guns themselves, there was a friendly English blacksmith named Uriah Leonard, near Fowling Pond, who was always ready to forge their spare parts from the bog iron nearby, though he broke the law when he did so.

In return for the seventy muskets, the settlers promised that all future charges should be arbitrated by the Puritans of the Province of Massachusetts Bay. The Puritans were richer, more numerous and sharper than their Pilgrim brethren at Plymouth, but Plymouth had the advantage of seniority, and was respectfully referred to as the Old Colony. The Puritans deferred to the sanctity of the Pilgrims, who in return were forever asking their help and advice. A saying grew up that the Plymouth saddle was always on the Bay horse.

The second time the settlers complained, Philip went to Boston direct, and convinced the Puritans that the charges against him were unfounded. The third time, he wrote angrily back to Plymouth:

"Your governor is but a subject. I shall treat only with my brother, King Charles of England. When he comes, I am ready."

By 1671 there were perhaps 40,000 Englishmen in all New England, and only half as many Indians. Before long there would be none at all, unless the English were driven out. They were beginning to surround Mount Hope itself. They had built a garrison house at Swansea to the north, and settled in numbers on Aquidneck Island, to the south, across the channel. Queen Awashonks of Sakonnet, whose kingdom adjoined Queen Weetamoe's, had sold land on the east side of Mount Hope Bay, within sight of King Philip's lodges, to an English carpenter named Benjamin Church. Philip himself, in spite of his resolution, sold off the present New Bedford in 1665, and in 1670 granted 100 acres, only a mile west of Pokanoket, to a certain John Gorham. In all, he sold some thirty-five square miles in the nine years after his brother's death, at an average price of elevenpence an acre. But legally, Mount Hope was still sovereign Indian territory, hemmed in on the north by the Baptist colony of

Providence Plantations, on the south by the Quakers of Aquidneck (now called Rhode) Island, on the east by the Pilgrims themselves, and on the west by Narragansett Bay.

Philip had many grievances. The English let their cattle destroy the Indian cornfields, which were never fenced. In any lawsuit, they took the word of a single Praying Indian against that of twenty unconverted ones. As Philip told John Easton, a Quaker who ferried over from Aquidneck to pacify him:

"The English are so eager to sell the Indians liquor that most of the Indians spend all in drunkenness, and then raven upon the sober Indians."

The Pilgrim clergy kept one eye on Heaven and the other on earth. This land, they sincerely believed, belonged to God. He had chosen them to bring it back to Him, and the Indians with it, if they would come. The Indians did not share this view—not even the Praying Indians.

The Wampanoags alone were too weak to attack the English, but Philip dreamed of an alliance with other tribes, from the Kennebec to the Hudson. They had never united before; it was their jealousies which gave the English their power, as the English themselves well knew.

But before his conspiracy could ripen it was betrayed to Governor Winslow by Philip's own secretary, the Harvard-educated convert John Sassamon, in revenge. On January 29, 1675, Philip had Sassamon murdered. Three of his braves broke the traitor's neck on the shores of Middleboro Pond. To pretend that he had drowned, they pushed his corpse under the ice, but left his gun and hat on the ice nearby. The English caught the assassins anyway, and tried them before a mixed jury of white men and red. The Rever-

end Increase Mather of Boston, who attended the trial, reported to his young son Cotton that one of the three, called Tobias, was proved guilty by the fact that Sassamon's body bled afresh when he approached it. Two were hanged, including Tobias; the third was reprieved for a month and then shot. To the Plymouth Colony, the Mathers were the very voice of God.

The execution enraged Philip. He claimed that foreigners had no right to punish Indians who murdered each other. Worst of all, the trial exposed his conspiracy. Now he dared wait no longer to attack, though he was not quite ready for war. In June he sent six warriors across Mount Hope Bay to Sakonnet, by canoe, to draw the Squaw Sachem Awashonks into an alliance. She had an army of 300. She honored his envoys with a ceremonial dance; but as it began, two of her own tribe slipped down to Benjamin Church's farm to invite him up to join it. Church, unarmed, followed them back to the longhouse. He found Awashonks herself in a foaming sweat—the phrase is his—leading the dance. When he entered, she broke off the festivities and called him before her.

Church was a married man of 35. If his Bristol descendants favor him, he was not bad-looking. Awashonks was the widow of a chief called Tolony. Her age is unknown now and was perhaps a secret even then. She had a grown son named Peter, so can hardly have been younger than her unexpected guest. Church does not boast, but Awashonks' behavior made it clear that he pleased her.

Inside the lodge, King Philip's men crowded around him, "in the posture of war." Their faces and chests were painted with totems of yellow and red. Their hair was trimmed to a coxcomb. Some wore rattlesnake skins down their backs. Their shot bags and powder

This 1810 engraving gives a tidy, if highly imaginative picture of King Philip's War.

47

horns hung from their shoulders. Church felt the shot bags and asked what they were for.

"To shoot pigeons with," was the mocking answer.

Church turned to the Queen and told her:

"If Philip is resolved to make war, the best thing for Your Majesty will be to knock all these Mount-hopes on the head and shelter yourself with me for protection. For my part, I desire nothing more than peace, yet if nothing but war will satisfy them, I believe I shall prove a sharp thorn in their sides."

His boldness drew him a promise that Awashonks and her army would at least be neutral if war should come.

Philip, ignoring her, held a two-week war dance atop Mount Hope. The visiting chieftains, the medicine men, and the oldest squaws squatted in a ring around the bonfire. The braves stood behind them and the rabble milled on the outskirts. Each brave, as the name of an English settlement was called out, picked up a firebrand, danced around the circle in a mock battle with the flame, and finally conquered the town by quenching the torch in the earth.*

Philip was ruthless and sentimental, wily and indecisive, noble and niggardly, all at the same time. His sorcerers, in snakeskin cloaks and wooden masks, consulted their oracles—the notes of the whippoorwill? the entrails of the owl?—and reported that no Englishman would ever kill him. That was enough for him. He sent a canoe up Mount Hope Bay to warn his English friend Hugh Cole to fly before it was too late. It was a favor that might have cost him the war, if Cole had warned his fellow Englishmen. Then he let the war begin, though it is said he threw himself weeping to the ground as he gave the command.

It was a superstition that the side which drew first blood would lose. On Sunday, June 20, 1675, while the settlers of nearby Swansea were at meeting, the Indians shot some of their cattle. This did not count as bloodshed, perhaps, but was enough to drive the white men from their scattered thatch-roofs to the shelter of their garrison house. Philip ransacked their farmsteads without hindrance. On Wednesday a lad named John Salisbury, emerging from the garrison to salvage his geese, found their necks wrung and a band of Indians searching his father's keeping room for rum. He fired into the band and wounded an Indian. First blood was thus drawn by the English. Next day the Indians returned. They murdered the boy and his father.

The frightened settlers sent a messenger to Plymouth for help. A troop of 36 under Captain Matthew Fuller reached Swansea on the twenty-eighth. Benja-

* This description of Philip's war dance is based on Church's account of a similar dance held a year later, but undoubtedly the two were much the same.

An Indian ambush.

min Church was second in command. Weighted down by their heavy buffcoats, their breastplates, swords, carbines, and pistols, they had taken four days to march from the Old Colony. Behind the infantry lumbered the pack train. The troops' ration was biscuit, dried fish, pork, oil, raisins, sugar, peas, wine, and rum. Another "army" arrived from Boston equipped with hunting dogs. One-third of each troop was armed with fourteen-foot pikes; and two-thirds with matchlock muskets so long that they required a forked rest for the barrel. It took 56 separate motions to fire a matchlock.

By the time the two details converged at Swansea, six more Englishmen had been tomahawked in the village. The troops killed six Indians in revenge. Two weeks afterward, marching down the Kickemuit River, one hundred and seventy-six strong, to besiege Mount Hope, they found eight flayed heads on poles, and later the torn leaves of a Bible scattered blasphemously on the ground. Lieutenant Church went ahead with half of the army to attack Mount Hope, and the other half set to building a fort in case Philip should attack *them*. Church did not believe in static warfare. He fought as the Indians did themselves. He had heard one of them say, "The English always keep in a heap together, so it is as easy to hit them as to hit a house."

Church's troop of Englishmen crept down to Mount Hope, sometimes waist-deep in the swamp and sometimes on their bellies in the grass, but always deployed at a distance from one another.

They found the hill deserted. Philip was too wily to let himself be trapped on a peninsula. He had shipped the squaws and papooses across Narragansett Bay to shelter with his allies on that side of the water.

Church decided that there was only one direction Philip himself could have taken: eastward across Mount Hope Bay to the kingdom of his sister-in-law, Weetamoe. He ferried across to Aquidneck Island and wheeled left to the straits which divide it from Pocasset. On the far side he caught sight of the enemy, lurking in the bushes at the top of the hill.

With 17 men he crossed the narrows by boat. On the far side he took cover under the fence in John Almy's peasefield. More Indians were on the hill than he had thought: 300 of them, it turned out afterward. The "Battle of the Peasefield" lasted six hours. The English advanced as far as a well on the far side of the field, but were driven back by a rain of bullets from the stumps and boulders above them. At last their ammunition gave out, and they retreated to the shore. By luck, a Quaker sloop from Aquidneck Island came sailing through the strait just in time to rescue them. Two by two she took them off in a canoe, but not before Church, under fire, made his way alone once more across the peasefield to retrieve his hat and cutlass, which he had left behind at the well.

A few days later, with some reluctant reinforcement from Captain Fuller, he made another assault on the hill. This time he had better luck. The Indians fled before him. At the Pocasset cedar swamp, in the kingdom of Queen Weetamoe, the first of the royal family fell: Philip's young brother, Suconewhew, who had studied at Harvard.

For a time the English were certain that they had trapped Philip in the swamp, and need only keep him surrounded until hunger forced him to surrender. Leaving a skeleton force behind for this purpose, the greater part of the armies returned to Boston after July 19. But one night late in July—probably the twenty-ninth—Philip and his warriors escaped the victors by crossing the Taunton River at low tide, far upstream, and fanned out to the open Nipmuck country in western Massachusetts.

Except for a guard over the prisoners taken in the Pocasset cedar swamp, the remainder of the armies of Plymouth and Massachusetts, which had taken the field on June 24, disbanded. The campaign had been short. Church got back to his farm in Awashonks' kingdom in time for the fall harvest.

"So let all thine enemies perish, O Lord!"

The strategists of the two colonies saw that Philip's escape meant that the war might spread westward toward the Hudson, and that he might return with reinforcements to attack them again. On July 15 they forced a treaty on the Narragansetts, who were still sheltering the Wampanoag women and children. It promised them immunity and set a bounty of two yards of cloth, worth five shillings the yard, for each Wampanoag scalp they brought in, four yards for each live Wampanoag, forty for Philip's scalp, and eighty for Philip alive. Trusting to the treaty, 150 Indians trudged into Plymouth to put themselves under the colony's protection. No Wampanoag scalps were ever delivered, but for three months the Narragansetts were at least neutralized.

Little is known of Philip's own activities during the remainder of the summer campaign. Though there is no record that he appeared in battle himself, all the western reaches of the English colonies were terrorized by the lightning raids of his warriors. On August 4 they besieged Brookfield. In September they burned Deerfield and attacked Hadley and Northfield. On the eighteenth they killed ninety Englishmen guarding a provision train from Deerfield to Hadley. On the twenty-eighth, at Northampton, they scalped Praisever Turner and Unzakaby Shakespeare when they ventured too far from the garrison house in search of firewood. On October 5 they burned 32 houses in Springfield, and on the nineteenth, with a troop of 800, they attacked Hatfield, but were repulsed.

Clad in the *wamus*, a slipover buckskin hunting jacket, and shod with noiseless moccasins, they shot flaming arrows into the settlers' thatched roofs. They pushed fire wagons against the log walls, edging them forward at the end of lashed poles from as far away as seventy yards. That distance was about the effective range of the colonists' muskets. When they broke through, they had no mercy.

Luck was not always on Philip's side. Sometimes a providential rain extinguished the firebrands. The settlers' own muskets, if the range was close enough, accounted for many of the enemy. At the attack on Hadley, says legend, a bearded stranger emerged from Parson Russell's attic, rallied the defenders, and vanished as mysteriously as he had appeared. They thought he was an angel. Long afterward they learned that he was William Goffe, one of the Roundhead judges who had condemned Charles I to the axe in 1649. He was hiding now in the New World from the long-armed vengeance of Charles II.

The Indians were merciless to the men they captured, but rarely mistreated the women. At Northfield they hung up two Englishmen on chains, with hooks under their jaws. The colonists, whose status as God's chosen exempted them from conscience, were no less cruel. At Springfield they ordered an old squaw "to be torn in pieces by dogs, and she was so dealt withal." On another occasion they massacred 126 Indians, including Quaiapen, the old queen of the Narragansetts, whom Major John Talcott described as "an old piece of venom."

Cruelest of all were the Indians who fought for the English. In Boston once, the Puritans were in the long process of executing an Indian prisoner by hoisting him to the gallows with a rope at his neck, and letting him down again three or four times to prolong his departure. Another Indian, a friend of his, stepped forward, drove a knife into him, and sucked out his heart-blood. He explained to the spectators, "Me stronger as I was before. Me be so strong as me and he too. He be very strong man fore he die."

The war was no longer local. It was known that the Narragansetts had a great fort in the swamp west of what is now Kingston, Rhode Island. Hospitality was sacred to them. Besides the women and children whom they already sheltered, and in spite of the bounty offered by the July treaty, they gave refuge to Philip's wounded and the aged who could not keep up with his fast-moving campaign. There was a chance that Philip might himself be in the camp, for he had not been seen since his escape at Pocasset. Spies reported that Weetamoe, his sister-in-law, was surely there, with her current husband. The fact that the Narragansetts had not surrendered her was excuse enough for the English to attack them. As one colonist put it, "If she be but taken, her lands will more than pay for all the charges we have been at in this unhappy war."

Canonchet, the Narragansett sachem, was summoned to Boston. On October 18 he signed a second treaty, agreeing to give her up within ten days. The governor of Plymouth, Josiah Winslow (he was the son of Massasoit's friend, Edward), gave him a silver-trimmed coat as a reward. The ten days passed, but Weetamoe was not delivered. The ultimatum having expired, Plymouth sold off the 150 Indians who had surrendered in July. They were shipped to Cadiz, Spain, as slaves—"sent off by the Treasurer," in the politer words of the official record. They averaged two shillings and twopence a head.

On November 12, the united colonies of Plymouth, Massachusetts Bay, and Connecticut had declared war on the Narragansetts. (The peaceful Quakers of Aquidneck Island and the Baptists of Providence, separated from each other by Mount Hope itself, took no part in the hostilities.) They mustered an army a thousand strong, under the command of Governor Winslow. There were 158 from Plymouth, 527 from Massachusetts Bay, and 315 from Connecticut, not counting teamsters, servants, and "volunteers." Winslow offered Benjamin Church the command of a company. Church, who had no taste for the classic warfare that was the only kind the Governor understood, declined. But he promised, as he puts it, to "wait upon him through the expedition as a Reformado," which means what is now called a guerrilla.

The three contingents were to make contact at Richard Smith's garrison house, which still stands, greatly altered, near Wickford on the west shore of Nar-

ragansett Bay. Church got there by sloop several days before they arrived overland. He had captured eighteen Indians by the time the regulars marched in.

The regulars were uniformed in leather jerkins and breeches, and wore Monmouth caps on their heads. Each man carried a six-foot flintlock musket and a bandolier which held a pound of powder, twenty bullets, and two fathom-length of match. They had no tents; each night of the march down from Providence they had slept under blankets on the frozen ground. But they had taken 47 prisoners themselves. Captain Nathaniel Davenport of the 5th Massachusetts Company bought them in for his own account as slaves at a bargain: eighty pounds for the lot.

The Narragansett fortress, which was under Canonchet's command, covered a four-acre rise in the middle of the trackless swamp, eighteen miles inland from the garrison house. The English might not have found it at all if Peter Freeman, one of Church's Indian prisoners, had not guided them. It was hidden from sight, even on a clear day, by a jungle of cedars. On December 19, 1675, the day of the assault, it was snowing hard, and there was a two-foot fall by afternoon. That was almost the shortest day of the year, with the sun setting by four o'clock. The fort had been designed by an Indian engineer called Stonewall John, with the help of Joshua Tefft, a renegade white man. Inside it, 3,000 Indians were crowded into 500 wigwams. Their winter provisions, in tubs hollowed out of sawn-off butternut trunks, were stacked against the walls to deaden the English bullets. The fort was even equipped with a forge for the repair of ordnance. Around its perimeter a sixteen-foot abatis of felled trees, with the branches forward, was backed by a stockade of logs. The only bridge between the fort and the tussocks of the swamp was a single log, with the inner end set between four-foot palisades with loopholes in them.

The attack began at two in the afternoon while the squaws were preparing dinner inside the fort. As fast as the English ventured onto the log, the Indians shot them from the loopholes, and they toppled into the icy stream. Six captains went down. Among them was Davenport, who had just paid eighty pounds for his slaves.

Away from the stream, the stagnant swamp was frozen over. Church, who had been stationed on solid ground with the governor's staff, saw his chance. With thirty men, he crossed the ice and broke into the fort from the flank, through the tangle of the abatis. It was a feat that, under heavy armor, would have been impossible in a thaw, and was almost a miracle now in the twilight and the snow. In his own modest words,

He encouraged his company and ran right on, till he was struck with three bullets; one in his thigh, which was near cut off as it glanced on the joint of his hip-bone; another through the gatherings of his breeches and drawers with a small flesh wound; a third pierced his pocket and wounded a pair of mittens he had borrowed of Capt. Prentice, which, bring wrapped together, had the misfortune of having many holes cut through them with a single bullet.

His troop poured through the breach. After a hopeless hand-to-hand fight, the Indians fled through the dark across the ice into the fastness of the swamp. "They run, they run!" someone shouted over the tumult. A few of the squaws strapped their papooses to their backs and plodded away through the drifts. They had no time nor strength to carry anything else with them into the blizzard. Most were left behind, cowering in the wigwams.

The regulars prepared to fire the camp. Church tried to dissuade them, if only because the English would need the shelter and provision for themselves. Since he was only a "reformado," no one listened. In the darkness and terror, it was easier to burn the wigwams than to spare them. He dragged himself back to Governor Winslow, who also bore the title of general, to plead against the burning.

The general [his story goes on] moved toward the fort, designing to ride in himself and bring in the whole army; but just as he was entering it one of his captains met him, and asked whither he was going. He told him, "Into the fort." The captain laid hold of his horse and told him his life was worth a hundred of theirs, and that he should not expose himself. The general answered that he supposed the brunt was over, and that Mr. Church had informed him the fort was taken, and he was of the mind that it was most practicable for him and his army to shelter themselves therein. The captain replied in a great heat that Church lied, and told the general that if he moved another step toward the fort he would shoot his horse under him.

Then bristled up another gentleman, a certain doctor, and opposed Mr. Church's advice, and said that if it were complied with, it would kill more men than the enemy had killed. And looking upon Mr. Church, and seeing the blood flow apace from his wounds, told him that if he gave such advice as that was, he should bleed to death like a dog before he would endeavor to stanch his blood.

They prevailed against Mr. Church's advice. Burning up all the houses and provisions in the fort, the army returned that night [to Smith's garrison house] in the storm and cold. And I suppose that everyone who is acquainted with that night's march deeply laments the miseries that attended them, especially the wounded and dying men. Some of the enemy that were then in the fort have since informed us that near a third of all the Indians belonging to the Narragansett country were killed by the English or by the cold of that night; that they fled out of their fort so hastily that they carried nothing with them; and that if the English had kept in the fort, the Indians would certainly have been necessitated either to surrender themselves or to have perished by hunger and the severity of the season.

As it was, more than eighty of the militia were killed that day, or died that night jolting through the blizzard to the garrison house on stretchers slung from their comrades' muskets. One account says the Indians lost 500 warriors, and that 500 women, children, and invalids, despite Church's effort to spare them, were burned to death. The true figure is unknown, but only a few survived. Cotton Mather, in his *Magnalia*, exulted:

We have heard of two and twenty Indian captains slain, all of them brought down to Hell in one day. When they came to see the ashes of their friends, mingled with the ashes of their fort, and the Bodies of so many of their Country terribly *Barbikew'd*, where the English had been doing a good day's work, they Howl'd, they Roar'd, they Stamp'd, they Tore their hair; and though they did not swear (for they know not how) yet they Curs'd, and were the pictures of so many *Devils* in Desperation.

And his father, Increase, exclaimed, "So let all thine enemies perish, O Lord!"

This engraving from an 1875 schoolbook depicts the struggle at the single entrance of the Narragansett swamp fortress.

"God sent 'em in the head of a Leviathan"

After the victory, the colonies again foolishly disbanded their army. Queen Weetamoe escaped from the swamp. King Philip, after all, had not been in it, but in his camp at what is now Schaghticoke on the Hudson. Canonchet led the surviving Narragansetts westward to join him. There was no doubt now which side he was on. On the way across the Nipmuck country, he joined forces with Philip's field commander, Anawon, whom Church describes as "a great surly old fellow." For four months, while Church remained at home recovering from his wounds, the two tribes harried the English settlements almost without hindrance.

The Mohawks of the Hudson had given Philip no help. When he attacked three of their men in the woods near the Schaghticoke camp, hoping the English would be blamed, one of them recovered and accused him instead. The angry Mohawks set upon him, and he barely escaped with his life. He fled eastward, desperately short of provisions. At what is now South Vernon, Vermont, Weetamoe and the few survivors of the Narragansett swamp fight met him on March 8, 1676.

In the Nipmuck country in the valley of the Connecticut, Philip's spring campaign promised well. At a war council in Northfield, Canonchet and he decided to strike still farther east, into the heart of the colonies. Medfield, just outside Boston, was burned. After the attack, a Praying Indian still loyal to his race, James the Printer (he had helped Apostle Eliot with the Bay Psalm Book), posted this defiance on the bridge across the Charles:

"Know by this paper that the Indians whom thou hast provoked to wrath and anger will war these 21 years, if you will. There are many Indians yett. We come three hundred at this time. You must consider that the Indians lose nothing but their lives, while you must lose your fair houses and cattle."

Philip's men raided Bridgewater, Scituate, and Rehoboth once, and Marlborough and Sudbury twice. At Marlborough the squaws scalped and mutilated two Englishmen. At Sudbury they annihilated a whole company under Captain Wadsworth and prevented reinforcements from reaching them by setting fire to the windward meadows. But legend has it that the only person killed in the attack on the village of Providence was a man named Wright, described as being "of a singular and sordid humour." The braves disemboweled him and stuffed his Bible in his belly. Philip even struck at Plymouth itself and burned Clark's garrison house only two miles outside of the town. Yet he gave orders to spare the village of Taunton, for it was there that Leonard, the friendly blacksmith, had his forge.

In April, Canonchet was captured by the English. They taunted him with his broken promise to deliver the Wampanoag scalps.

"I shall not give up a Wampanoag or the paring of a Wampanoag's nail," he told them.

When they sentenced him to be shot, he said, "I like it well. I shall die before my heart is soft, or I have said anything unworthy of myself."

The English divided the privilege of his execution among three tribes in their service. A Pequot shot him, a Mohegan quartered him, and a Niantic burned his corpse. His head was sent to Connecticut "as a token of love and affection."

Worst of all for Philip, Church's wounds were healing. Governor Winslow offered to put him in command of sixty men as soon as he should be well enough to take the field. Church answered that he would need 300, half of whom must be friendly Indians. He knew that he could never win without them, and added that if the English intended to defeat Philip, they must make a business out of war as he did. The governor answered that the colony could not afford so large a force and that it would not recruit Indians in any case.

While they argued, Philip and his warriors struck again. On the eleventh of May, he burned sixteen more houses in Plymouth. Governor Winslow, outraged and frightened by this second raid on the capital, yielded to Church. He offered him a captain's commission, the command of 60 Englishmen and 140 Indians (if they could be found), and the right, which Church demanded, to grant clemency to any of the enemy except Philip himself and "such as have been principal Actors in those Villainies." It was Church's very softheartedness that had so far slowed up his promotion.

His first task was to recruit his 140 Indians. As he was returning to Rhode Island by canoe, he accidentally met Honest George, the courtier who had invited him to Awashonks' dance before the war began. The two arranged a parley for the next day on the beach at Sakonnet Point in her kingdom. When Church arrived to meet the Queen, her troops, fully armed, stood sullenly behind her on the dunes. Church carried nothing with him except a twist of tobacco and a calabash full of strong water. The result of this parley was that Awashonks' chief captain stood up and said to Church with a bow:

The escape of King Philip.

"Sir, if you will please to accept of me and my men, and will head us, we will fight for you, and will help you to Philip's head before the Indian corn be ripe."

Church understood swamp warfare as well as Philip himself, and the Indian character a little better. Awashonks' men were as good as bloodhounds at following a trail. They led the force, skimming the tussocks as lightly as the enemy ahead of them. The English came ponderously behind for fear of being mired. A whistle from Church was the signal of danger; every man dropped to the ground when he heard it.

He tracked Philip to the Bridgewater swamp, between Plymouth and Mount Hope. They made contact on Tuesday, August 1, 1676. In the action he captured or killed 173 Indians. Among the captives were Philip's wife and son: the lusterless Nanuskooke, so dim beside the lusty Weetamoe and the coquettish Awashonks; and the princeling whose very name is unknown. Philip's uncle, Akkompoin, was killed. Philip just missed death himself. Church saw him sitting on a tree stump, but recognized him an instant too late to bring the musket to his shoulder. The King escaped again.

"It must be as bitter as death to him," Mather gloated, "to lose his wife and only son, for the Indians are marvelously fond and affectionate toward their children."

Church sent 153 prisoners into Bridgewater pound the night of August 3. Being well treated with victuals and drink, he says, they had a merry night, and the prisoners laughed as loud as the soldiers, not having been so well treated for a long time before.

It was not his long retreat that broke Philip's spirit "so that he never joyed after," nor Canonchet's death, nor even the capture of his wife and son, but the knowledge that many of his own tribe had deserted to the English. Even before Bridgewater, 300 of them

had begged Governor Leverett of Massachusetts Bay to intercede with Plymouth for pardon. They seem to have thought that the Puritans would be more lenient than the Pilgrims.

If Leverett did plead for them, he was unsuccessful. Plymouth spared their lives, but sold them into slavery at the new low price of one pound apiece or seven bushels of corn in trade.

Church's own magnanimity was repaid. At Bridgewater he captured Lightfoot and Littleyes, two of Philip's men who had threatened to kill him the night of Awashonks' dance. Instead of hanging them, as his own Indians urged, he spared them. He even made Lightfoot a sergeant. It was not Englishmen's fashion, he said, to seek revenge; they should have the same quarter as other prisoners. He would go up to a likely-looking prisoner, clap him on the back, and say: "Come, come; you look wild and surly, but that means nothing. My best soldiers, a little while ago, were as wild and surly as you are now. By the time you've been with me a day or two you'll love me, too, and be as brisk as any of them."

It was true. He sent a file of them on Philip's track, with Lightfoot in command, and bade them quit themselves like men. Away they scampered on the trail, like so many horses. Three days later they caught Philip at breakfast in Swansea, where the war had started. But he escaped again, leaving the kettles boiling on the campfire and the meat roasting on the wooden spits. On August 6, Weetamoe was drowned trying to float a raft to her kingdom of Pocasset. The tide washed her naked old body ashore, and the English added her head to the row of poles at Plymouth. Philip fled through the salt meadows toward Mount Hope as if he must, like her, go home to die.

Even then he would not surrender. With his own tomahawk he killed one of his braves for suggesting peace. Church could afford to wait, for Philip could not escape. A Connecticut troop blocked him on the west, the armies of Massachusetts Bay and Plymouth on the north and east, and the sea itself on the south.

Church had sent his wife, Alice, to stay with Quakers on Aquidneck for safety during the campaign. He deserved a visit with her. After breaking contact with Philip, he made his leisurely way overland toward the Island, across the kingdom of the dead Weetamoe. En route he beat up the cedar swamp where he had fought the year before. Discovering no Indians, he crossed by ferry to Aquidneck and there took a horse to the house where his wife waited. She fainted with surprise when he walked into her lodging.

The Indian whom Philip had slain for talking peace left a brother named Alderman. On the morning of

August 11, Alderman stole down the two miles from Philip's camp at Mount Hope to the ferry. He signaled over to the Island that he had news. (The abutment of the Mount Hope Bridge now rests on the sandspit where he stood.) Church, summoned by messenger over the eight miles from his wife's lodging on Aquidneck Island, left her at once. The vindictive Alderman paddled across the ferry to tell him that Philip and Anawon were encamped on an upland rise above the miry swamp at the foot of Mount Hope. It was a spot which Church knew well; he could see it from where he stood. His wife must be content with a short visit, said he, when such game was ahead. Having collected what men he could in one afternoon—eighteen Englishmen and twenty-two Indians—he paddled across to the mainland in the darkness.

It was a summer of drought. On Mount Hope a little corn had sprouted from the ears that he had trampled down the summer before, but its leaves were curling on the prostrate stalks. Philip slept that night in a lean-to below the flat top of the forty-foot rock called his throne. Anawon lay beside him.

Philip slept badly that night. He waked out of a nightmare to tell Anawon that he had dreamed Church had caught him. Then he resumed his uneasy sleep.

At dawn on August 12, Church deployed his men in pairs, an Englishman and an Indian in each, to close in below the camp. As the swollen sun was rising over Pocasset, a shot and then a volley rang out on the morning air. An Indian, wandering on the edge of the camp, had stumbled into one of Church's parties. Suddenly the camp came alive. Philip leaped from the bed with nothing on but his breechclout and stockings. He seized his gun, slung his shot bag and powder horn over his shoulder, and ran down hill, southwestward, into the swamp. Unwittingly, he raced directly into an ambush where two men, their gun muzzles marking his flight, waited.

The Englishman was Caleb Cook; the Indian was Alderman. On the crest of the hill, Anawon shouted the war cry *Iootash! Iootash!* to rally the braves. (The word meant "Stand fast!") He was too late. Cook's gun misfired because of the dampness; but Alderman's, which had two barrels, sent one bullet through Philip's heart and another two inches above it. The King fell on his face in the mud, with his gun under him. The oracles were proved right: it was not an Englishman who killed him. But as Increase Mather put it, the English had *prayed* that bullet through his heart.

Church did not relax his ambush at the news, but Anawon had seen the death from the hilltop. He guided the fifty survivors—all that were left of the Wampanoag tribe—through the trap over the very

path the English had made when they set it. Soon the sun dried the dew; it was now too late to track him.

Church called his company together on the ledge where Philip and Anawon had slept. When he told them Philip was dead, the whole army, he says, gave three loud huzzas. His Indians pulled the body from the mud by its heels and dragged it before him. He knew it was Philip's from the scarred hand.

"And a doleful, great, naked dirty beast he looked like," says the *Entertaining History.*

Because Philip had left so many Englishmen unburied and rotting above ground, Church ordered that "not one of his bones should be buried." The body was quartered, and a piece hung on each of four trees. The head was set on a pole and carried to Plymouth, where it remained for 25 years. As Cotton Mather rejoiced some years later, "God sent 'em in the head of a *leviathan* for a *thanksgiving feast.*" Church gave the scarred hand to Alderman as a reward. For months thereafter he exhibited it in a pail of rum "to such gentlemen as would bestow gratuities on him."

"*The last that war against the English*"

Anawon, who had escaped with the remnant of the tribe, had vowed never to be taken alive. It seemed hardly worth pursuing him now that Philip was dead. Captain Church had surely earned a rest. He went back to his wife on the Island. Two weeks later word reached him that Anawon had begun to raid the long-suffering settlements of Rehoboth and Swansea. He learned through a deserter that the old chief was kenneled at the base of a steep rock a few miles above Mount Hope. It was surrounded on all sides but one by the dismal Rehoboth swamp.

Church asked Caleb Cook, who had missed his chance of glory on the morning of Philip's death, whether he would follow him that very night to find the hiding place.

"Sir," Cook answered, "I am never afraid of going anywhere when you are with me."

Church, with Cook and the deserter beside him, waited on the edge of the swamp until dark, when Anawon would have stacked his guns for the night. By luck, he caught an old brave returning from the swamp with his daughter. He held the two of them for decoys. When the moon had risen, he forced the brave to sound the wolf call which was the password of the camp. An answering howl came back from the rock. He could hear someone pounding corn in a mortar at the foot of it. The noise covered the scraping of Church's clumsy boots. With his hatchet in one hand, he pushed the captives ahead of him as a screen, and then crashed down a fissure in the rock behind them, clutching at the bushes on the side with the other hand to steady himself. Cook and the deserter tumbled down behind him.

Anawon and his young son, who had been asleep by the campfire, started up. When they saw Church, the boy whipped his blanket over his head and shrank up into a heap. Anawon cried out *"Howoh!"* which meant "They've caught me!"

Church stationed Cook in front of the stack of guns. With the deserter translating for him, he ordered Anawon's fifty men to toss their tomahawks alongside, and they obeyed. He turned to Anawon.

"What have you got for supper, Captain?" he asked through the interpreter. "I've come to eat with you."

"Taubut," Anawon answered in his deep voice (the word meant "Welcome"). "I have cow-beef and horse-beef."

Church chose cow-beef. It was soon got ready by the squaws. Church seasoned his supper—and Anawon's, too—from the bag of salt that he always carried.

He had been on his feet for sixty hours. After supper he ordered Cook to stand watch while he rested. But he could not sleep. After lying some time beside Anawon, he opened his eyes. Cook was fast asleep, and so were all the Indians except Anawon himself.

For an hour the two soldiers stared at each other in silence. Church spoke only a few words of Algonquin, and supposed that Anawon spoke no English. At last Anawon stood up with a groan, throwing off his blanket. With nothing on but his breechclout, he walked out of sight around a corner of the rock. Church, supposing he went to ease himself in private, let him go, but took care just the same to lift a gun from the stack and shelter himself behind Anawon's son in case of a trap.

Then by the moonlight he saw the old warrior returning with a deerskin pack in his hands. Church stood up, grasping the gun. Anawon dropped to his knees before him.

"Great Captain," he said in his slow, but perfectly plain English, "you have killed Philip and conquered his country. I and my company are the last that war against the English. The war is ended by your means; therefore these things belong to you."

He opened the pack. It held Philip's regalia. He draped the wampum stole on Church's neck. Its fringe reached the ground at the Captain's boots. He laid the red cloak on Church's shoulder, the breastplate on his chest, the fillet on his head. He offered him two hornfuls of glazed powder and a red blanket.

The two men sat down to smoke while the others still snored. A curious sight they made to the moon: the naked old Indian and the young Englishman decked in his victim's regalia. They talked the night through. Church let Anawon boast of the victories he had won for Massasoit in the old days, against the Narragansetts. Old soldiers are seldom so patient with each other.

Church sent Anawon and his men to Plymouth under guard. He promised that the lives of the braves would be spared. He could not give the old chieftain the same pledge, but assured him that he would beg the Governor for mercy. But the Governor was not so lenient. When Church got there himself, he found Anawon's head on a pole. Beside it was that of Tispaquin, the Black Sachem, who had married Philip's sister, Amie. He was the last straggler of the royal family to be captured.

Only Nanuskooke and her son were left alive. They had lain in Plymouth jail for a month. John Eliot, the old apostle, asked the General Court to set them free now that the war was over. Church agreed with him. He reminded the Governor that he had given him the right of pardon. Most of the colony, however, were for executing the two prisoners before the boy could grow up to avenge his father.

However, the General Court tempered justice with mercy, and made a little money for the colony besides. It ordered them sold into slavery in Bermuda. On March 20, 1677, Parson Cotton wrote casually to his brother, "Philip's boy goes now to be sold."

Nanuskooke and he were never heard of again. A century and half later, the orator Edward Everett flung Cotton Mather's exultation back at him. "An Indian princess," he declaimed, "sold from the cool breezes of Mount Hope, from the wild freedom of a New England forest, to gasp under the lash, beneath the blazing sun of the tropics! Bitter as death? Aye, bitter as Hell! . . ."

The death of King Philip.

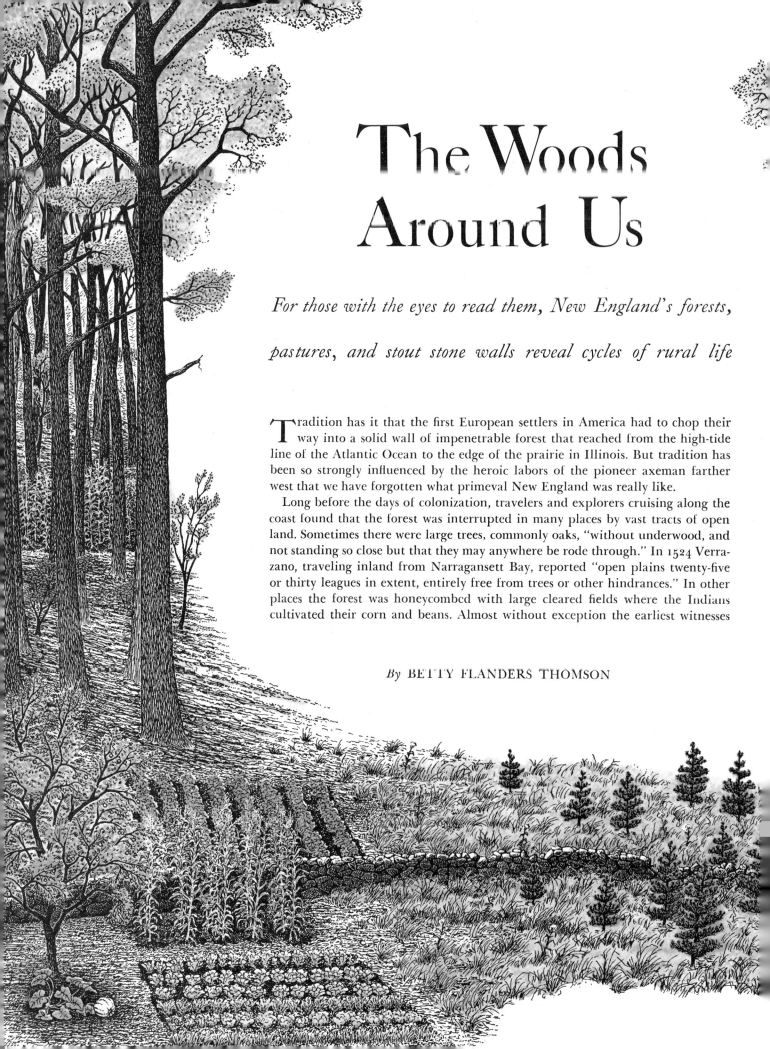

The Woods Around Us

For those with the eyes to read them, New England's forests,

pastures, and stout stone walls reveal cycles of rural life

Tradition has it that the first European settlers in America had to chop their way into a solid wall of impenetrable forest that reached from the high-tide line of the Atlantic Ocean to the edge of the prairie in Illinois. But tradition has been so strongly influenced by the heroic labors of the pioneer axeman farther west that we have forgotten what primeval New England was really like.

Long before the days of colonization, travelers and explorers cruising along the coast found that the forest was interrupted in many places by vast tracts of open land. Sometimes there were large trees, commonly oaks, "without underwood, and not standing so close but that they may anywhere be rode through." In 1524 Verrazano, traveling inland from Narragansett Bay, reported "open plains twenty-five or thirty leagues in extent, entirely free from trees or other hindrances." In other places the forest was honeycombed with large cleared fields where the Indians cultivated their corn and beans. Almost without exception the earliest witnesses

By BETTY FLANDERS THOMSON

The panoramic drawing on these two pages illustrates the growth cycles of the New England woods. At far left is the primeval oak forest. This (proceeding counterclockwise) was cleared and planted by early settlers, who marked off their property lines with stone walls. Farmland, gradually deserted after the Civil War, was slowly taken over by dry grass and goldenrod. Here, tiny white pines took root, and as they grew, formed a canopy which shut out the sun and smothered the pasture grass and weeds. Between 1890 and 1925 the pines were cut for lumber. They did not sprout again from the stumps, but fast-growing hardwoods—oak, maple, and beech—also lost in the lumbering, did; hence the new forest (above) consists largely of these hardwoods, plus birch, poplar, and cherry. Only the stone walls survived unchanged.

ILLUSTRATED FOR AMERICAN HERITAGE BY JOHN LANGLEY HOWARD

remarked upon the large treeless areas they saw everywhere from the Saco River in Maine southward beyond the Hudson and even far up the river valleys into what we know as central New York State.

All the Indians of the northeast were part of the great Algonkian relationship. Those near the coast were to some extent hunters and fishermen, but the staple of their living came from agriculture. These tribes lived in more or less permanent villages of dome-topped wigwams with a wooden framework covered with bark or skin. Around each village lay the cornfields, cleared by the men with fire and stone axe, cultivated by the women with hoes of bone or shell, and fertilized with the well-known fish that was laid in each hill at planting time. Primitive as the operation was, the fields produced large quantities of corn of many kinds, as well as beans, squash, and various other crops. Judging from the early accounts, the amount of land under cultivation must have been truly impressive. William Wood, for example, in an early piece of promotional literature published in 1634 and called *New England's Prospect*, described one Indian cornfield after another in specifically named places all along the coast.

Because the same field was cultivated for several years running, the fertility of the soil eventually declined and the crop yield began to fall off. When that happened, new land was cleared and the old abandoned, to grow up in time to brush and trees. Trees were also cut lavishly for fuel, and the woods were in constant retreat around each village as long as it remained in one place.

Beyond the cultivated lands the forests were repeatedly burned. Many early voyagers spoke of the number of fires they saw all along the eastern coast and at the same time commented on the open, brushless nature of the forest. Students of vegetation do not agree as to whether it was fire that kept out the underbrush or whether the forest burned readily because it was naturally dry and open for reasons of climate and soil. We do know that the Indians deliberately set fires in order to improve the growth of grass in early spring for the benefit of game animals and to clear out the underbrush and so make their hunting generally easier. Probably most of these were small ground fires that did relatively little harm to large, thick-barked trees. But even a fast-running grass fire will kill the small seedlings on which the perpetuation of a forest depends; and as the older trees succumbed to blight or tempest, the forest became more and more open until it resembled a park-like plantation. Early observers also recorded that wet, swampy land, where fires could not easily penetrate, was commonly covered with a dense, thickety growth. So it seems likely that the openness of the woods was at least in part the doing of the Indians.

When the Pilgrim Fathers at last dropped anchor in Plymouth Harbor, the prospect of the bare December woods must have made many a heart secretly sink. One may wonder if the Pilgrims could have survived even as well as they did if, in their weakened, half-starved condition, they had had to make a clearing in the forest before they could put in their first crop the next spring. Fortunately the kind Providence in which they so fervently believed had led them to the site of an abandoned Indian village. Only three or four years earlier the original inhabitants of the place had been virtually wiped out by a plague of smallpox. So it turned out that the Pilgrims found land already cleared for them, as well as a hidden store of unused grain that carried them through that first grim winter.

Then in the spring Squanto, the Indian who was to become their fast friend and helper, appeared from the woods to begin their initiation into the uses of Indian corn.

In the first years at Plymouth there was little occasion for any undertaking beyond securing the necessities of life. But soon more venturesome scouting parties penetrated farther inland. When the first explorers returned from the north, they told with awe of the dense, dark forests of the interior. There were no sunny fields there where women chattered at their work; only an occasional band of hunters, passing along narrow woodland trails, broke the deep stillness.

Once the first settlements were chipped out of the edge of the wilderness, immigrants arrived in increasing numbers. In many cases entire communities came directly from England to start a new life together in the New World. Then, as immigration and natural increase brought crowding in the first tight little communities, groups began to split off and settle in new places.

Naturally the most fertile and accessible regions filled up first. By 1700 there were 80,000 people living in the low-lying areas along the coast and up the great central valley of Connecticut and Massachusetts as far as Northfield. By 1776 Thomas Pownall could write that the land between New Haven and Hartford was "a rich, well cultivated Vale thickly settled & swarming with people. . . . It is as though you were still traveling along one continued town for 70 or 80 miles on end."

As time went on, the flood tide of settlement moved westward and northward, creeping up out of the broad valleys and into the more rigorous hills. Litchfield, in the upland of western Connecticut, was founded in 1719. Petersham in central Massachusetts was settled between 1733 and 1750; Grafton County, New Hampshire, between 1760 and 1772. By 1780 the farthest frontier stood in central Maine and Vermont.

The years between 1830 and 1860 were the heyday of New England agriculture. Probably every American's response to the idea of living in the country is colored by the image of the family-size New England farm of those days. The farm was as nearly as possible a self-contained economic unit, with useful work for everyone, however large the family might grow. The littlest ones could hold the skein of yarn to be wound for grandmother's knitting or set out milk for the cats, who in turn earned their keep as mousers. A boy was needed for man's work as soon as his muscles were strong enough. And a woman's life was filled with the routine but tangibly constructive work of sewing and cooking and the eternal details of keeping a family clean and comfortable.

Pleasures were simple and homemade. If the household needed outside distractions, there were plenty of neighbors within gathering distance for barn-raisings or quilting parties. Odell Shepard, writing about Connecticut, said, "In early days our people could see the lights in one another's windows and could communicate by shouting from farm to farm. An old man has told me that in his youth it was possible to arrange a barn dance among a dozen of his neighbors without any man's stirring from his front door. . . . Another old man has told me of the time, far back, when he, sitting under his elm tree on a Sunday afternoon, could see seven or eight friends of his sitting in front of their several houses and under their own elms." For the most sobersided there was always Sunday church meeting and the excitement of occasional camp-meeting revivals.

We have an outsider's picture of the times from

Harriet Martineau, an English "authoress" who traveled widely in America in 1834–36 and wrote a charming and lively account of what she saw and what she thought about it. One of the houses where she visited stood on a hilltop in Stockbridge, a handsome old town in the Berkshires of Massachusetts. From her host's doorway she could see everything that went on in the busy village, since, apart from the forest-covered mountains, the entire landscape consisted of lush green fields, broken only by the road and the Housatonic River.

She also visited in Gloucester and thought that "the place has the air of prosperity that gladdens the eye wherever it turns, in New England"; and she saw what Karl Marx never realized, that "as a mere matter of convenience, it is shorter and easier to obtain property by enterprise and labour in the United States, than by pulling down the wealthy."

Although the first aim of a farm in those days was to provide the family's material needs, a cash crop of some sort was needed on even the meagerest place to provide for a few necessities such as iron tools and salt; and many of life's amenities were available for the buying. Most of the scant plowable land was needed for subsistence crops, but there was plenty of steep and stony land that made satisfactory grazing for cattle as soon as it was cleared of trees. Over the years, consequently, more and more cattle were raised for a market crop, and an increasing proportion of farmland was devoted to hay and pasture, which would sustain the animals.

Even in the midst of this happy summer season, and before the frontier tide had reached the northern limits of the country, the ebb had begun almost unnoticed from the earlier settled regions. It was the little towns in the hills that slipped first. It took only a generation or two of life on a high, remote farm, where summers are short and winters long and bitter, and where the sheep need sharp noses to graze between the rocks, to make a farmer pack up his belongings and set off to look for a more promising place.

There is the case of the Connecticut hill town of Hartland, scarcely twenty miles from Hartford. The population of Hartland Township has shown a decrease in every federal census since the first one was taken in 1790. The condition soon spread; and by 1820 many towns in rural areas of southern Vermont and New Hampshire had begun to lose population.

For a long time the trend of the migration was northward into the still-empty parts of upper New England. Gradually,

however, an even stronger tide to the west set in as the front line of advancing settlement poured out onto the fertile, level lands beyond the Alleghenies. The floodgates to the Midwest really swung wide with the opening in 1825 of the Erie Canal, the great watery highway to the West, and the beginning of steam navigation on the Great Lakes in the 1830's.

Contrary to what many people believe, there is nothing inherently wrong with the fertility of New England's soil—what there is of it. Until recently, the highest yield of corn per acre in this country was produced in Connecticut. The difficulty lies in what the glaciers did to the topsoil, and the key to the matter is that phrase, "what there is of it." All the soil that once mantled the landscape was scraped away by the ice. Much of it was carried off and dumped into the ocean, and the rest was thoroughly mixed with rocks of all shapes and sizes and of great abundance before it was set down again. Fortunately there were rivers and lakes that washed some of the soil out from among the rocks and assembled it into usable masses here and there. But relatively few of these patches are large enough to do more than provide turning space for a small horse-drawn hayrake.

It is worth noting that when the ice sheets of the last glacial age pushed down into what is now the Middle West, they did not encounter mountains or hard rocks. Unlike New England, the limestones, sandstones, and shales of that region were soft; and as a result, the same glaciers that scraped New England bare of soil brought riches to the present states of Ohio, Indiana, and Illinois. The ice crushed and ground rocks to fine powder, and mixed the old surface with this and with fresh minerals brought up from deep in the subsoil, creating a new topsoil that has remained bountiful to this day.

It was the competition from cheap western land, level and clear enough to allow the use of large farm machinery, that put the pinch on New England agriculture. When canals and then railroads came along and provided low-cost transportation for bulk freight from the west, the bottom fell out of the old farm economy. As a result, hordes of Yankees gave up and went off to populate the new lands; and it is not always as easy as you think to tell an old-stock Ohioan or Iowan from an old-stock Vermonter.

Defection from the hills received a further push from the expansion of water-powered industries; and this in turn was enormously stimulated by the Civil War. People who did not go west moved down into the mushrooming factory towns nearer home. While the farmer's daughters went to work in the mills, his sons went off to fight in the war. Perhaps it was the general restlessness of soldiers going back to civilian life; perhaps it was just seeing other parts of the country and other ways of living that offered greater rewards for toil, but in any case, large numbers of young men never returned to the old hill farms.

By the 1870's farms were being abandoned wholesale, even in the recently opened parts of northern New Hampshire and Maine. Deserted farmhouses became increasingly conspicuous in the landscape, and soon it was apparent to even the least observant that a great change was taking place in rural New England. The general public grew highly excited and a loud cry of alarm went up over the decline of a way of life that had become centrally embedded in our national tradition. Files of popular magazines of the 1880's and 1890's show the state of public opinion. Every volume for those years has articles written from all points of view, impassioned, reasoned, or merely sentimental, setting forth proposals for keeping people on the farms in order to preserve our great heritage of plain living and high thinking, and of course in an idyllic rural setting.

The farmers who were trying to squeeze a decent living from the rocky hills took a different view of the matter. When a family decided to leave, there were few takers for the farm. Many simply moved out and, after a last lingering look at the old home, shut the door and went away, leaving the place to the forces of nature.

With no one on hand to repair a leaky roof or replace the first broken window, it took only a few years for an abandoned house to fall into decay. No one was there to grieve over the more complete havoc wrought by fire or violent windstorm. With the garden unweeded, the paths untrod, even the pastures ungrazed, the land that had been so laboriously cleared soon grew up to brush, its very existence as a homesite all but forgotten. In less than a generation there might be nothing left but a cellar hole far in the woods on a road no longer kept up by the town. A man from southwestern New Hampshire once said that when he was a child in 1865 he knew of nine old cellar holes within a mile of his country school. In the same area in 1887 he counted 23 of them.

To catch the flavor of the changing times, one can make a pilgrimage to the Berkshire plateau, the little highland that stands between the Connecticut River and the Housatonic in western Massachusetts. Pioneer settlers first pushed into these hills in the 1720's along the old trail that is followed by the present road from Westfield to Great Barrington. Once settlement was begun, the hill country developed rapidly. It reached its vigorous prime about the time of the Revolution and continued for several decades in this happy state. But with clearing for farms, logging for sawmills and tanneries, and making charcoal to feed the local iron foundries, the entire primeval forest was either removed or at least drastically altered. Then, around the time of the Civil War, the great rural decline struck hard at the farms and towns of the Berkshires.

Pay a visit first to the boyhood home of William Cullen Bryant. He was born at Cummington, Massachusetts, in 1794, the son of a frontier doctor. The house has been preserved, a substantial dwelling that still looks out over open, rolling hayfields. One can easily in imagination picture the countryside flourishing with many small farms and reconstruct the village as a busy little place with a surprisingly large number of small industries. Then go to Buckland and search out Mary Lyon's birthplace. When she set out on the path that finally led her to the founding of Mount Holyoke Seminary in 1837, she came down from a home in a well-populated rural country, with neighboring houses in sight here and there across the fields. Today you follow a back road up into the lonely hills and find at journey's end only a cellar hole in a small clearing in the woods, the spot marked by a bronze plaque on one of the ever-present boulders.

The course of farm abandonment in New England can be read in the changing proportions of cleared and wooded land. From 1815 to 1820 all but 27 per cent of the entire area of Connecticut had been cleared of forest. Those were the peak years. By 1910 the woods had expanded to cover 45 per cent, and by 1955, 63 per cent of the state. Farther north the cleared area never reached such an extent, and the maximum came later. Only 25 per cent of Maine has ever been open country and that was in 1880. At the present time about three-quarters of all New England is covered with woodland or forest; the remaining quarter includes all the cities and their sprawling suburbs.

When the trees begin to reclaim their old dominion, the course of events follows a well-defined pattern. In the south and southeastern parts of New England, encroachment by the woods begins with the appearance of tiny red cedars scattered among the dry, skimpy grass and goldenrod of a neglected pasture. In the extreme north and northeast and at higher elevations elsewhere, the edging-in of red spruce, with a spatter of balsam fir, betrays the deterioration of pasture land. Throughout the great central region, however, it is white pine that first takes over the old fields.

Even today, pines are so characteristic of the region that for a vignette symbolic of New England, one might use a rough, bouldery hillside covered with short grass and clumps of fern, a bit of stone wall, and a single ancient pine, gnarled of trunk, horizontal of bough, and soft and delicate of foliage.

At the height of agricultural development many old pines survived in wood lots or along roadside walls or in pastures. In a good seed year an old pine produces seeds by the million; being light, and each equipped with its little sail, these easily blow out across the fields. The open, sunny grassland of an old pasture suits an infant pine very well; and in a few years an unused field becomes thickly stocked with thrifty young trees. By the time these are head-high to a grown man, their branches may meet in a completely closed canopy that darkens the ground below and smothers the old pasture grass and weeds. In the deep shade and in the dense, springy mat of fallen needles that soon forms under a pinewood, few other plants can get a foothold; and the pine grows up in a virtually pure stand.

As the trees grow older and larger and the thick canopy of foliage rises, occasional breaks appear in the ceiling where a tree succumbs to windstorm or blight. Such islands of light are quickly floored over by a brushy thicket. Elsewhere the woods are dim and quiet. No sun-loving pine seedling can survive in the darkness; but certain shade-tolerant hardwoods begin to infiltrate, sparsely, at first, and slowly, but persistently. By the time the old-field pines are some forty years old, the leafy underbrush is becoming conspicuous, and it is clear to a thoughtful observer that the next generation in these woods is going to be different. At about this time, too, the growth of the pines begins to taper off, and in another twenty years or so they all but cease to grow.

When they are full grown and just before the younger hardwoods begin to crowd in on them, the pines are ripe for lumbering. Although most of their wood is knotty and by no means up to the quality of slowly grown virgin timber, still it is useful for boxes and crates and matchsticks; and when there is a market nearby, it can provide a tidy return to both landowner and lumberman.

It was between 1890 and 1925 that the great harvest of old-field pine was reaped in New England. In those years lumbering was done by clear-cutting. This is essentially a mowing operation in which everything is cut off close to the ground. Scattered among the raw stumps are ferns and a few little flowering plants. Small tree seedlings and saplings that are flex-

ible enough to bend rather than break under a skidding log will remain, if somewhat the worse for wear. But with the overhead trees gone, the climate in which the forest survivors live is abruptly and drastically changed. The new conditions are too much for some of the forest plants, and many of them languish and die.

For others, though, the going of the pines brings a new lease on life. Young broad-leaved trees go into a rapid spurt of growth and soon make a thick coppice that consists largely of oak, maple, and beech, and, in the old days, chestnut. Any of these that were large enough to be cut in the lumbering operation sprouted vigorously from the stump. Pines, on the other hand, like all conifers, do not sprout, and a tree cut down is a tree gone forever. Moreover, any pine seedling that starts among fast-growing stump sprouts is shaded to death in its infancy. So wherever hardwoods have a firm foothold they effectively shut out any new pines, and the next generation of forest bears little resemblance to the old.

Any parts of the old forest that were not yet infiltrated by hardwoods at the time of lumbering soon became restocked with seedlings of one kind or another. If a good pine seed year follows directly after the cutting operation, and if there are enough old seed trees left in the neighborhood, the new stock may consist at least partly of pine. Chances are that there will also be plenty of birch, poplar, and cherry, whose seeds are light and easily distributed by birds or the wind. Even when outnumbered by pines, the hardwood seedlings grow so much faster in their first few years of life that they offer strenuous competition to the new generation of pine. Here things are quite different from the dense sod of an old pasture, where the pine is much less inhibited than the hardwoods by the close company of grass and weeds. As a result, the new generation of woodland is promptly dominated by broad-leaved trees, and the old-field pine goes the way of all transients.

In the thirty to sixty years since the great pine harvest, landowners have taken from the new growth whatever they could find that was useful or salable. Most often this has meant repeated clear-cutting for cordwood. The little selective logging that has gone on has removed the better trees of kinds that could be sold for saw logs, leaving the trash to develop for the future. Though sprouts from a very small, cut-off tree of a desirable species may grow into quite respectable timber, those from a large old stump never form usable logs. Moreover, the most vigorous sprouters are not the best timber trees. As a result, the "forest" cover of much of central and southern New England is now a sorry mixture of the most persistent weed trees and low-grade stump sprouts.

To the informed eye, however, this scraggly woodland reveals many clues to its past history, especially in winter, when most of the trees are bare. Chief and most eloquent are the stone walls that outline roads and fields and woodlands everywhere in New England. Proper New England walls are dry-built, not rigid with mortar, their stones kept in place only by skillful arrangement and balance. Sometimes the stones have been cut and shaped so that only the smallest chinks interrupt the flat surfaces of top and sides. But true country walls are made of rough stones just as they were carted from the field in a horse-drawn stoneboat and piled into straightforwardly functional fences, full of sheltering crannies for mice and chipmunks.

The miles upon miles of wall that the winter traveler sees from the road are the accumulation of two, even three, centuries of labor. From earliest colonial days the building and upkeep of fences was one of man's most important private and civic duties; and considering the local situation, fence usually meant stone wall. Public records of the Colony of Connecticut show that the General Court strove mightily with the problem of proper fencing. Repeatedly it handed down regulations intended to enforce the maintenance of fences adequate to keep cattle on the property of their owner and more especially out of the neighbor's cornfield.

In 1634, after a number of individual judgments, the court ordered that each town should forthwith "chuse fro among theselves seaven able and discreet men" to ponder and make recommendations for improving the common lands. "And whereas also, much damage hath risen not only fro the unrulynes of some kynd of Cattell but also fro the weakness & insufficiency of many fences, whereby much variance and difference hath followed, which if not prevented for the future may be very prejudiciall to the publique peace; It is therefore likewise Ordered, that the said 7 men soe chosen, or at least 5 of the, shall sett downe what fences are to be made in any Comon grownds, and after they are made to cause the same to be vewed, and to sett such fynes as they judge meet upon any as shall neglect or not duly attend their Order therein. And when fences are made and judged sufficient by the, whatsoever damage is done by hoggs or any other cattle shall be paid by the owners of the said cattle, without any gaynesaying or reliefe . . ."

Even this firm dictum did not settle the matter, and later courts had to order the fence-viewers time after time to tend more conscientiously to their duties. More than a century and a half later the office of Fence Viewer was still important enough to be incorporated into the governmental machinery of new territories, such as Ohio, then being admitted to the Union.

For generations wall-building went on as fields were cleared of rocks and trees, until most of New England became laced over with a fine-meshed network of stone. Though the walls often run with no discernible meaning through the woods today, they mark off what once were open fields and lanes or show the course of the local road before it was leveled and straightened to suit the demands of traffic moving so much faster than the horse or the ox. Many a roadside picnic area makes use of a nook left by a rounded-off curve or a relocated bridge, and one of its charms may be the wall that still separates private field from public way.

In this land the trees, too, record details of local history. The ordered row of wide-spreading maples edging the woods by the roadside once graced the front of a house that may have fallen before that horror, fire in the country. That ancient oak with its low, heavy boughs forming a crown as wide as it is high clearly lived its formative years in the open, without the jostle of slim young things that now crowd around its knees. Long ago it was left in the open pasture to provide shade and shelter for the animals, and it had grown to stately size when the farmer gave up the struggle and the brush crept in. The tall red cedars now deep in the woods certainly started in an open, grassy place a long time ago when there were no fast-growing, broad-leaved trees nearby to overtop them and shade them to death.

Many patches of woods have no ancient giants among the smaller trees. But look at the way the trunks grow from the ground. Nearly all of them stand in bouquet-like clusters. Perhaps you can find the remains of the stump in the center from which the present trees sprouted when the wood lot was clear-cut between fifteen and forty years ago. The parent woods, too, may have originated as coppice or sproutwood that grew up after an earlier woodland was cut for charcoal and posts and cordwood; and the present trees may be as much as the fourth or fifth generation of sprouts from the original forest.

Fires and grazing, too, leave their marks on the land. Where a poor sort of pasture is being invaded by trees, there is an abundance of red cedar. Cattle eat the seedlings of broad-leaved trees as fast as they appear but leave the prickly cedars strictly alone. Fire, on the other hand, kills red cedar but encourages the increase of the fast-growing black cherry, which only sprouts more vigorously from every root and stump when its above-ground parts are destroyed. Aspen and the little, gray old-field birch will seed in on bare soil when an old cultivated field is abandoned or when a hot fire sweeps through a dry woodland, burning off the protective humus mat from the ground.

Of course not all the land once cleared for farming has been abandoned to grow up to forest. New England agriculture has not dried up but rather has taken other channels. Recent decades have brought a shift to the production of specialized, high-value crops such as tobacco, cranberries, and maple syrup; and the countless part-time farmers who keep a few dairy cows or a flock of laying hens contribute a substantial share of the total agricultural output of the region.

Under the term "rural non-farm population" the federal census lists other thousands of happy people who are enjoying country scenes with the comfort of city incomes and whose "farm," as they will call it, may consist of little more than a few decrepit but delectable apple trees and a few acres of grassy field that are mowed more to keep the brush down than for the sake of the few wisps of hay they may yield. The houses that time passed by and the villages where nothing much has happened for a hundred years may bespeak a functionally decadent landscape; but they please our eye and give us a sense of having roots. And today's non-farmers can look with joy on the wooded hills that so discouraged their great-grandfathers, the spiritual if not the literal ancestors of us all.

Betty Flanders Thomson is associate professor of botany at Connecticut College in New London and is the author of The Changing Face of New England, *which was recently published by the Macmillan Company.*

Forgotten First Foothold
in the New England Woods

Unlike the Spanish and the French, the English were late to explore and exploit the New World. Not until 1585, almost a century after Columbus' first momentous landfall, did they establish the ill-fated Roanoke colony on the Carolina coast; twenty-two more years were to pass before they attempted to penetrate the New England wilderness. Then, in the summer of 1607, two boatloads of would-be settlers landed on the coast of Maine. For a year their precarious outpost survived; but, like Roanoke, it was to prove in the end a forlorn hope.

The man responsible for this venture was Sir Ferdinando Gorges, a much-decorated veteran of the wars with Spain, who spent most of his adult life and a sizeable fortune promoting the colonization of New England. In the early years of the seventeenth century, Gorges commanded the fortress at Plymouth—then the main port of embarkation for the occasional explorers and fishermen who journeyed to the New World. Gorges kept closely in touch with these mariners, and was particularly excited by their reports of the coast of New England. With his influential friend, the Lord Chief Justice Sir John Popham, he helped to organize the Plymouth Company, with the intention of planting a colony there.

In 1607, the Plymouth Company sent out two ships carrying some one hundred colonists—the *Gift of God*, captained by Sir John's relative, George Popham, and the *Mary and John*, under Raleigh Gilbert. Late that summer the expedition arrived off the coast of Maine, and founded a small settlement on a lovely, rugged peninsula at the mouth of the Sagadahoc River—or Kennebec, as it was later called.

As long as the weather held good, the future augured well for the young colony. Under the leadership of George Popham, the settlers constructed a fort, and within it, a church, storehouse, and shelters. At the same time, they began work on a thirty-ton pinnace, the *Virginia*. The photograph at right shows Popham Beach, where they cradled this first English ship built in North America.

With the coming of an early and unusually severe winter, their bright hopes vanished. Cooped up in their tiny fort, the colonists quarreled and split into irreconcilable factions. All at once everything seemed to go wrong. Their storehouse burned down. George Popham died and was succeeded by Raleigh Gilbert, who, in turn, had to return to England to claim an inheritance. Without a capable leader, the colonists lost heart, and by the time another winter had set in, the Sagadahoc settlement was deserted, and all but forgotten. Fame waited for Plymouth, twelve years later.

Eliot at 55, in a formal portrait painted from life by an unknown artist in 1659.

Apostle TO THE Indians

John Eliot preached to the Massachusetts savages, printed the Bible in their "barbarous Linguo," and tried to reply to their disquieting questions

By FRANCIS RUSSELL

Whenever the Reverend John Eliot walked along the Indian trail from Roxbury to Dorchester Mill in the autumn weather, he tried to put the time to proper use by continuing the metrical version of the Psalms that he and Richard Mather and Thomas Weld were working on. His somber figure pinpointed the brightness of the afternoon as he strode along, heedless of the crickets' antiphonal shrilling. Late goldenrod and Michaelmas daisies encroached on the way, brushing against his cloak. Slowly, so very slowly, the Old Testament lines formed themselves in his mind:

> *Like Pelican in wilderness*
> *like Owle in desart so am I;*
> *I watch, and like a sparrow am*
> *on house top solitarily.*
> *Mine enemies daily mee reproach . . .*

But then, as had happened so many times before, he would find himself caught up in the immediacy of the sun-drenched moment, the shout of the crickets drowning out the psalm. And he would become aware again of sweet fern and the salt scent of the marsh and the harbor in the middle distance and the russet patches of oak and blueberry. Lemon-pale witch hazel fila-

ments, that New World shrub that flowered so strangely in the autumn, came just on a level with his eye. *Nova Anglia*—New England. This, he now knew with loving thankfulness, was his world.

According to the 1628 charter of Massachusetts Bay the "royall intention and the adventurer's free profession, the principall ende of this Plantation" was "to wynn the natives of the country to the knowledge and obedience of the onlie true God and Saviour of mankinde." It was not a profession which many of the earlier settlers shared. Fortunately for them, the Indians of the region had been almost exterminated by a plague a few years before, and there was little challenge in the broken remnants of the Massachusetts Bay tribes. For those transplanted Englishmen the Indians were a subhuman nuisance, when they were not devils. "The veriest Ruines of Mankind," Cotton Mather said of them. And even the gentle Roger Williams called them "wolves with the brains of men."

John Eliot was one of the very few to take the intentions of the charter to heart. Holding the Bible as the literal word of God, the ultimate source of all knowledge, he was drawn to the Indians at least in part by his belief that they were the descendants of

67

the lost tribes of Israel. But more fundamentally they were to him human beings created by God, souls to be saved. This conviction expanded in his inner self until it dominated his life. As he wrote in later years: "Pity to the poor Indians, and desire to make the name of Christ chief in these dark ends of the earth —and not the rewards of men—were the very first and chief moves, if I know what did first and chiefly move in my heart, when God was pleased to put upon me that work of preaching to them."

John Eliot, known to after generations as the Apostle to the Indians, was born at Widford, Hertfordshire, in 1604. At the customary age of fourteen he entered Jesus College, Cambridge, taking his B.A. degree in 1622. He then became an usher in the Reverend Thomas Hooker's school at Little Baddow, an employment that Cotton Mather in later years tried anxiously to show as not really menial. Hooker, a Puritan of the milder sort and much honored in the countryside, was finally forced by Laud's high church policies to flee to Holland as the first step on his way to America. Eliot followed him.

Though John Eliot never wavered from the ferocious creed of Calvin, he kept beneath all the doctrines of predestination a warm and loving heart. Children and Indians he cherished with much patience. There was no Barebones self-righteousness about him. When he left England, a "select number of his pious and Christian friends" followed him on the promise that he would be their New World pastor—an indication of this unordained young man's winning ways. On his arrival he was probably the first New England minister to take orders in the Congregational manner. A year later his bride-to-be, Anne Mumford, came to join him.

At first, he filled in as a substitute in Boston's First Church, and although the elders would have kept him, he was mindful of his friends. There, in the hilly country beyond Boston Neck with its outcroppings of conglomerate and the broken glimpses of the harbor islands, he and his congregation that had followed him so far made their settlement. So was the church in Roxbury established in 1632, and there Eliot remained through wars and changes of governments and dynasties for over fifty years.

In 1646 the General Court of Massachusetts passed an order to promote the diffusion of Christianity among the natives, and the elders of the churches were requested to consider how it might best be effected. Although John Eliot had spent a dozen years tending the rude and straggling Roxbury settlement, he had long been considering just this. He now took into his house Cockenöe, an Indian made prisoner in the Pequot War of 1637, who had been serviced to a

Dorchester planter, and who could speak and even read English. Later, an Indian youth named Job Nesutan replaced Cockenöe as Eliot's teacher and helper. With him Eliot began his study of the Indian language, tentatively translating the Commandments and the Lord's Prayer. After two years he was able to preach, if haltingly, in this acquired tongue.

The language of the Massachusetts Bay tribes was Algonquian, a Mahican dialect called by Eliot and others the "Massachusetts language." With the Indian method of compressing complex ideas into extended

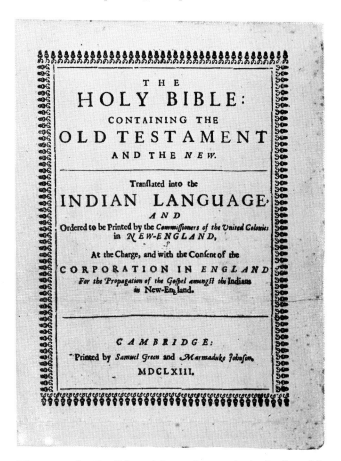

These are the English and (opposite page) the Indian title pages of Eliot's Algonquian Bible. Financed by a London missionary society, it was the first Bible printed in America.

single words, it was not a facile tool. Eliot did his best to develop grammatical usages. Cotton Mather held that it would have been more effective to teach the Indians English than to translate Scriptures into their "barbarous Linguo." Even the demons of Hell could not understand it, he said. Gravely Mather explained that he had tried out some languages on a captive audience of demons (whom he reached through conversing with a "possessed" young woman); during the séance, he went on, his infernal friends did well enough with Latin, Greek, and Hebrew, but failed miserably to understand his questions in Algonquian.

Eliot's first mission, when he felt he had mastered the language sufficiently, was at the small Indian settlement near the falls of the Charles River a few miles above Cambridge. Here, on a hill beyond the river's great S curve, Waban—in Algonquian, "the Wind"—a peaceful Indian, half trader, half sachem, had gathered together a settlement out of the fragmented tribes. Waban's group had been friendly to the English from the beginning, and Waban would gladly listen to the stocky man in black who spoke,

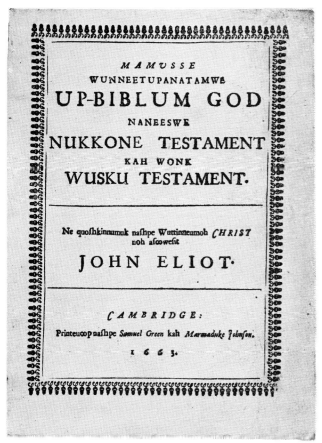

As the title page shows, Algonquian was, like German, agglutinative. The Bible's longest word (34 letters) is Wutappesittukqussunnookwehtunkquoh—"kneeling down to him."

or seemed to speak, the Indian tongue.

It was a fading October day with the hard-rimmed sky beginning to take on tones of winter, when Eliot and three clergymen companions first arrived before Waban's wigwam. There at the council fire Eliot preached the first Protestant sermon in the Indian tongue on the North American continent. He took as his text Ezekiel 27:9, "Prophesy unto the wind, prophesy, son of man, and say to the wind, Thus saith the Lord God." It was a shrewd and happy choice, appealing both to the pride of Waban the Wind and to the superstition of his listeners. Snake eyes reflected by the firelight, elders with bronze impassive faces, the restless children, the shrill-voiced crones silent for once, all watched the Englishman. He preached to them for an hour and a quarter, moderate by that day's standard, adapting as he could the Institutes of Calvin to their forest ways.

After prayers in English—for he did not as yet feel himself equal to praying in Algonquian—some of the Indians began to ask him questions, and he encouraged them then and for all future meetings.

Why, they would ask him around their smoldering fires and later in the lodges of the praying towns, why does not God who has full power kill the Devil that makes all men so bad? Was the Devil or man made first? Might there be something, if only a little, gained by praying to the Devil? If God made Hell in one of the six days, why did he make it before Adam had sinned? If all the world be burned up, where shall Hell be then? Are all the Indians who have died now in Hell, while only we are in the way of getting to Heaven? Why does not God give all men good hearts that they may be good? Whither do dying little children go, seeing they have not sinned? "This question," said Eliot, "gave occasion to teach them more fully original sin and the damned state of all men. I could give them no further comfort than that, when God elects the parents, he elects their seed also."

There were also the curious, the doubting, and the malicious. How is it that sea water is salt and land water fresh? they asked the white man facing them with the clasped book. Or—If a man should be enclosed in iron a foot thick, and thrown into a fire, how would his soul get out? Why do Englishmen kill all snakes?

Waban, however he understood predestination, became a convert to Eliot's teaching. Under his leadership and with Eliot's instructions, the Indians of his settlement formed themselves into the Christian village of Nonantum—meaning "Rejoicing"—after the white man's pattern. From Eliot they received clothing, blankets, spades, axes, and other tools. The squaws were given spinning wheels. For out of these nomad hunters he would make husbandmen, that they should eat bread in the sweat of their dark faces. The Indians laid out streets and fenced and planted their fields. Eliot was understanding, and they trusted him. He knew he could not push the mercurial savages too hard, and he was content at first if they observed the decent minimum of outer forms. One group of Indians, instructed not to do any unnecessary work on Sunday, replied that it would be easy for them since they had little to do on any day.

Nonantum developed into a small trading center

where the Indians made brooms, baskets, and eelpots for the colonists and sold fish and venison and berries in season. Yet the Praying Indians, as they were called, were looked on with contemptuous distrust by most whites, and finally Eliot resolved to move them up the Charles River to a remote place of hills called Natick, eighteen miles away. On this virgin ground he would set up a town according to the principles laid down in the Bible. Eliot would have his Indians "wholly governed by Scriptures in all things, both in church and state."

Natick was laid out for some 800 inhabitants. Except for the temporary assistance of an English carpenter, all the work was done by Indians. Two streets on one side of the river were joined to one on the far side by a bridge. After the lots were measured they were assigned one to a family. A circular fort was built and after that a rectangular meetinghouse fifty feet long, twenty-five feet wide, and twelve feet high. The latter was used as a schoolroom during the week, one section of it being partitioned off for Eliot's particular use and known as the Prophet's Chamber. There were several other houses of the English kind, but for the most part the Indians preferred their accustomed wigwams.

nce every fortnight, during the summer weather, Eliot visited his Praying Indians at Natick. Summoned by two drums, the congregation assembled in the meetinghouse. There, in the church he had helped build with his own hands, in the smoky, rush-lit room with the noise of running water outside and inside the high-pitched buzz of mosquitoes, Eliot would deliver one of those massive seventeenth-century sermons, expounding the Scriptures in the tongue he had learned with so much difficulty. The Indians had come to regard him as a father. Beyond the dogma which they scarcely understood they sensed the goodness of the man. So they served him, with only occasional backsliding, and when the times of trouble came most of them held loyally to him.

Natick became a show place, visited frequently by Boston clergymen who were pleased to catechize the congregation through an interpreter and delighted at the answers that were roared back. Men like Governor Endicott and President Dunster of Harvard, who came to Natick and saw the domesticated Indians hoeing, reaping, picking hops, cutting wood, making hay, and building stone fences, were happily convinced. The harder minds among the colonists were not. Most of the settlers looked sourly on Eliot's Indians, maintaining that their piety was a fable, a device for raising money to support a group of hypocritical and shiftless "foreigners."

Although Eliot's biographers do not emphasize the fact, there were tangible advantages in becoming a Praying Indian. The apostle wanted his converts to be prosperous as a mark of election, and he had the means to reward those who listened to the Gospel message. Clothing, food, and implements were on hand for them. Never did he enter a settlement without bringing gifts, for children as well as the others. No Indian was ever turned away empty-handed from the door of the Roxbury parsonage. It has been estimated that the cost of conversion ran to £10 per Indian, a large sum in those days.

Eliot, selfless and austere, had been known to give away his monthly stipend in a fit of absent-minded benevolence; but like many such unworldly men he could be singularly practical in raising money for a cause. The funds for his missionary work came from England, through the middle-aged piety of dowagers of wealthy Puritan families and occasional aristocrats like the daughter of the Earl of Shrewsbury. Eliot planned his touches with care. He was the earliest and one of the most successful writers of dunning letters in America, the first transatlantic promoter of a fund-raising campaign. In 1649 a London corporation, the Society for Promoting and Propagating the Gospel of Jesus Christ in New England, was established, and on this society Eliot came to depend for much of his later support, including the subsidizing of his Bible translation.

The question of the sincerity of the Indian converts is a complex one. How much they were swayed by religious conviction is impossible to say. Certainly the awe and admiration they felt for the dominant white men was easily transferable to the white men's peculiar God. Then, too, in their eroded tribal state they were driven to the shelter of the white settlements by fear of the Mohawks. By becoming converts they freed themselves of the oppressive exactions of sachem and medicine man. There were the things of this world—not to be neglected—that were to be had in Christ's name. Finally there was the influence of the Reverend John Eliot himself, the doughty, paternal figure whose kindliness even Calvin's creed could not conceal.

Eliot's translation of the Bible into Algonquian, *Mamusse Wunneetupanatamwe Up-Biblum God* ("The-whole Holy his-Bible God"), was his most cherished achievement, the goal of all his studies. From his first days in New England he had seen it as his sacred task to bring the word of God to the Indians. Only when they could read the Bible could he be assured of the permanence of their faith.

WUNAUNCHEMOOKAONK NASHPE

MATTHEVV.

CHAP. I.

a Luke
3.23.
b Gen.
21.3.
c Gen.
25.26.
d Gen.
29.35.
e Gen.
38.27.
f 1 Chr.
2.5.
Ruth
4.18.

Ppometuongane *a* book Jesus Christ, wunnaumonuh David, wunnaumonuh Abraham.

2 *b* Abraham wunnaumonieu Isaakoh, kah Isaak wunnaumonieu Jakobuh, kah *d* Jakob wunnaumonieu Judasoh, kah weematoh.

3 Kah *e* Judas wunnaumonieu Pharesoh kah Zarahoh wutch Tamarhut, kah *f* Phares wunnaumonieu Ezromoh, kah Ezrom wunnaumonieu Aramoh.

4 Kah Aram wunnaumonieu Aminadaboh, kah Aminadab wunnaumonieu Naassonoh, kah Naasson wunnaumonieu Salmonoh.

5 Kah Salmon wunnaumonieu Boazoh wutch Rachab, kah Boaz wunnaumonieu Obeduh wutch Ruth, kah Obed wunnaumonieu Jesseoh.

g 1 Sam.
16.1.
& 17.
12.

6 Kah *g* Jesse wunnaumonieu David ketassootoh, kah *h* David ketassoot wunnaumonieu Solomonoh wutch ummittamwussuh Uriah.

h 2 Sam.
12.24.
i 1 Chr.
3.10.

7 Kah *i* Solomon wunnaumonieu Rehoboamoh, kah Rehoboam wunnaumonieu Abiahoh, kah Abia wunnaumonieu Asahoh.

8 Kah Asa wunnaumonieu Josaphatoh, kah Josaphat wunnaumonieu Joramoh, kah Joram wunnaumonieu Oziasoh.

9 Kah Ozias wunnaumonieu Jothamoh, kah Jotham wunnaumonieu Achazoh, kah Achaz wunnaumonieu Ezekiasoh.

k 2 Kin.
20. 21.
1 Chro.
3.10.

10 Kah *k* Ezekias wunnaumonieu Manasses, kah Manasses wunnaumonieu Ammonoh, kah Ammon wunnaumonieu Josiasoh.

11 Kah Josias wunnaumonieu Jechoniasoh, kah wematoh, ut papaume na uttooche masinneohteamuk ut Babylon.

l 1 Chr.
3. 16,
17.

12 Kah mahche missinneohteabettit ut Babylon, *l* Jechonias wunnaumonieu Sa'athieloh, kah Salathiel wunnaumonieu Zorobabeloh.

13 Kah Zorobabel wunnaumonieu Abiudoh, kah Abiud wunnaumonieu Eliakimoh, kah Eliakim wunnaumonieu Azoroh.

14 Kah Azor wunnaumonieu Sadokoh, kah Sadok wunnaumonieu Achimoh, kah Achim wunnaumonieu Eliudoh.

15 Kah Eliud wunnaumonieu Eleazaroh, kah Eleazar wunnaumonieu Matthanoh, kah Matthan wunnaumonieu Jakoboh.

16 Kah Jakob wunnaumonieu Josephoh, weisukeh Mary noh mo wachegit Jesus uttiyeuoh ahennit Christ.

17 Nemehkuh wame pometeongash wutch Abrahamut onk yean Davidut, nabo yauwudt pometeongash; neit wutch Davidut onk yean unmissinohkonauh ut Babylon, nabo yauwudt pometeongash: neit wutch ummissinohkonaoh ut Babylon nô pajeh uppeyonat Jesus Christ, nabo yauwudt pometeongash.

18 Kah Jesus Christ *m* wunneetuonk yeu mo, nagum okasoh Maryhoh kah Joseph quoshodhettit (asquam naneesinhettekup) miskauau wutchéketeauónat nashpe Nathauanittooh.

m Luke
1.27.

19 Neit wessukeh Josephuh wunnomwaénuooh, matta mo wuttenantamooun wutáyimáuoh mussissewautut, unnantam kemeu nuppogken yeuoh.

20 Webe natwontog yeushog kusseh wutangelsumoh Lord wunnaeihtunkquoh ut unnukquomuonganit, noowau, Joseph ken wunnaumonuh David, ahque wabesish nemunon Mary kummittamwos, newutche uttiyeuoh wachegit, ne nashpe wunneetupanatamwe Nathauanittooout.

21 Kah woh neechau wusñaumon woh kuttissowen *n* Jesus, newutche woh wadchanau ummissinninnumoh wutch ummatchesseonganooout.

n Luke
1.31.

22 Wame yeush *n* nihyeupash ne woh nnih toh ancoowop Lord nashpeu manittoowompuh noowau.

23 *o* Kusseh peenomp pish wompequau, kah pish neechau wannaumonuh, kah pish wuttissowenuh Emanuel, yeu nauwuttamun, God koowetomukqun.

o Isaiah
7.14.

24 Neit Joseph omohket wutch koué nat, wutussen uttoh ánukqut wutangelsumoh Lord, kah neemunau ummittamwussuh.

25 Kah matta cowabeuh nô pajeh wunneechanat mohtommeginitcheh wunnaumonuh, kah wuttissowenuh Jesus.

CHAP. II.

JESUS *a* neekit ut Bethlem ut Judea ukkesukkodtumut Herod Sontim, kusseh waantamwáenhog wamohettit wutchepwoeiyeu Jerusalemwaut.

a Luke
2.6.

A 2   2 Noo-

Job Nesutan often did not know. And some Indians with childish malice would deliberately trick him, supplying a wrong or sometimes an obscene word.

With his other burdens it is a marvel that he found time to carry on his translating. For in all weathers and all seasons he made his visitations in the towns and friendly settlements, sometimes as far as sixty miles afield. An indomitable figure who could bend to a nor'easter and yet not draw back, who did not hesitate in a pinch to adopt Indian dress, who would stop on a rainy night at any wigwam and wring the water from his socks and be off the next morning, who when hostile Indians barred his path could say: "I fear neither you nor all the sachems in the country. I will go on, and do you touch me if you dare."

Then there was his Roxbury congregation, and the education of his own people. "Lord! For schools everywhere among us!" he prayed. He founded the Indian College at Cambridge. He established the Free School in Roxbury. (Founded in 1645, the Roxbury Latin School, as it was subsequently known, is the oldest endowed school in the United States. It is at present a country day school of 150 students in West Roxbury, Massachusetts.) He made teachers and ministers of his Indian converts. And he wrote reports over the years that were published regularly by the society and came to be known as the Indian Tracts.

For ten years he labored at his self-appointed task, in the long summer evenings, through the waning autumn days, with winter biting at his study door, testing each sentence, each verse. It was a tremendous effort to adapt the restricted Indian tongue to the subtle and majestic cadences of the King James Version. For so many things there were no equivalents.

When Eliot began his Bible translation there was no assurance it would ever be printed, yet he continued at it through the years, trusting in Providence and in the London society. He did not trust in vain, for—as that unpractical man shrewdly realized—such a project was attuned to the very premises on which the society was founded. Its governors agreed to underwrite the expenses of the Indian Bible.

The *Up-Biblum* was printed by Samuel Green at the Cambridge Press, housed in the Indian College inside the Harvard Yard. This small hand press, the only one in the colonies, had come into Harvard's possession through President Dunster's marriage. In the lingering aftermath of the 1640 depression, it existed in a moribund state until it was revivified by the society's remittances for printing Eliot's Bible. Directly and indirectly this undertaking was worth the then very large sum of £1,000 a year to the Boston commercial community.

Eliot completed his translation in 1659. That same year printing was begun, and almost at once the society shipped an additional press to Cambridge. Special type had to be sent as well, the Indian language requiring a double *o* logotype and more than the normal proportions of *o*'s, *k*'s, and *q*'s.

The final chapters of Revelation were printed in 1663. Fifteen hundred copies of the *Up-Biblum* were run off, 200 copies being bound in stout leather for the immediate use of the Indians. This was the first Bible printed in America, the earliest example in history of the translation and printing of the entire Bible as a means of evangelization. It was Eliot's most durable monument.

King Charles' acceptance of the sudden and politic dedication of the *Up-Biblum* was gracious, considering the fact that only three years before Eliot, in a slim volume called *The Christian Commonwealth*, had applauded Cromwell, denounced Charles I as anti-Christ, and anathematized the Lords and Commons.

The following dozen years were to climax Eliot's labors. Captain Daniel Gookin, a layman of some military and political prominence in the colony, was appointed superintendent of the Praying Indians and became Eliot's principal colleague. The original settlement at Natick throve, and additional towns were set up at Stoughton, Grafton, Marlboro, Littleton, and Tewksbury. Eliot composed an Indian Primer, an Indian Grammar, and an Indian Psalter and translated Baxter's *Call to the Unconverted*. In 1674 there were two established Indian churches, fourteen Indian towns, and 1,100 Praying Indians.

An unusual glimpse of Eliot comes to us from a novel source. In the mid-seventeenth century the Jesuit Father Druillette was sent by the governor of Canada to Boston to discuss commercial relations. Although Jesuits were nominally under sentence of death in Massachusetts, Father Druillette was received cordially both by Governor Endicott and by Governor Bradford of Plymouth. On one of his journeys he was an overnight guest of Eliot. That meeting of the priest and the Puritan conversing by the fireside as best they could in church and school Latin became the subject of a number of sentimental Victorian illustrations.

Eliot's vision of a Christianized Indian fellowship of thriving and expanding towns was shattered in 1675 by the outbreak of King Philip's War. Philip was the son of Massasoit, the sachem of the Rhode Island Wampanoags, whose early treaty with Plymouth banned any missionaries within his territory. More instinctively hostile to the whites than his politic father, Philip carried this anti-Christian bias even further. Once on a chance meeting with Eliot he had twisted a button of the latter's coat, telling him he cared no more for the Gospel than he did for that button.

To Philip's innate hostility was added his resentment at the encroaching whites. The old Pawtucket chieftain Passaconaway had warned him that though he might harm the colonists, they would in the end surely destroy him. That might be true, Philip thought, but only if he failed to strike in time. He planned with much cunning for a federation of tribes from Long Island Sound to the Penobscot that would rise at a given signal and exterminate the English settlements. For four years he made his preparations, formed secret alliances with the other tribes, collected guns and munitions and supplies, and planned his strategy.

The outbreak, in the middle of June, was sudden, bloody, and disastrous for the colonists. From Springfield east a hundred miles to within sight of Boston the towns went up in flames, and women and children were butchered with malignant savagery. Although Waban had warned the colonists some time before, they were unprepared. Before the militia could muster any effective counterattack the western garrisons were besieged and in some cases annihilated. No small town or isolated farm was safe. Terror of the savages reinforced all the colonists' earlier prejudices. Praying or not, an Indian was an Indian, better locked up, best dead.

Eliot's Indians lived in danger of their lives. Sometimes they were murdered out of hand, as at Chelmsford, or, as at Marlboro, seized and marched to the Boston jail. Yet in spite of ill will, suspicion, and harsh treatment which was to grow harsher, the great majority of the Praying Indians remained loyal. There were exceptions. James the Printer, who had helped print Eliot's *Up-Biblum*, abandoned his press and his hand-me-downs to put on war paint with King Philip, as did Old Jethro, an Indian preacher Eliot had trained, who was later taken prisoner and hanged.

Eliot and Gookin did all they could to protect the lives and substance of their wards; but they were increasingly isolated by the hysterical clamor against the Praying Indians. Gookin's life was threatened in the streets of Boston. When Eliot's boat tipped over in the harbor and was nearly run down by another boat, several people said it was a pity he had not drowned.

At the autumn period of Philip's greatest successes, the colonists packed off the Praying Indians from Natick and the other towns just before the harvest and shipped them down Boston Harbor to Deer Island. There they were left, women, children, and old men indifferently, to shift for themselves on that bleak drumlin lying open to the Atlantic. Eliot went to the water front to see the miserable converts embark, his most faithful among them—his ministers, his teachers, his interpreters. Whenever he could he visited them that winter, bringing small amounts of corn, provisions, and odds and ends of clothes. Those who survived did so mostly by grubbing for shellfish, threatened even there by some of the more hotheaded colonists, who as a reprisal for burnt villages were for going to Deer Island to kill the lot.

Yet through all their wretchedness the Indians still remained firm in their affection for John Eliot. And when some of the less fanatical and more practical-minded colonists decided to try to raise an Indian scouting company from among them, sixty volunteered. In the end, Indian aid to the English was substantial. The Praying Indians, resuming their forest ways, killed over 400 of the enemy, and Gookin maintained that they "turned yᵉ balance to yᵉ English side, so that yᵉ enemy went down yᵉ wind amain."

The war lasted until the middle of the following year. Philip was finally surrounded and brought to bay in Mount Hope Swamp in Rhode Island, a Praying Indian firing the shot that finished him. The militiamen found him lying in the mud, "a doleful, great, naked, dirty beast." They cut off his head and brought it to Plymouth, where it stood impaled for the next quarter of a century.

With the end of this threat the Praying Indians were allowed to leave Deer Island for their old homes, but only a poor minority survived. Whatever creative spark Eliot had managed to kindle in them had gone out. The end of Philip was the knell of the Massachusetts Indians. Over Eliot's distressed protests the war captives, including Philip's wife and young children, were sold into slavery in the West Indies. Where fourteen thriving Indian towns had existed, there were now only four listless and dwindling settlements.

The London society, however, continued its help. Most of the Indian Bibles had been burnt or destroyed during the war, and Eliot prepared a revised edition with the help of his friend John Cotton of Plymouth, who knew the language even better than he did. He still visited his remaining Indians when he could, although less frequently now that old age was on him.

John Eliot was to live another fifteen years, a patriarchal figure, revered now in the harmlessness of his broken dream, one of the last thin links with that first generation from across the ocean. His Praying Indians were no longer a problem in the expanding colony, and the bitterness was glossed over now. From Roxbury to Boston he had become such a time-accustomed figure over half a century that he seemed almost beyond time, and a saying grew up that Massachusetts could not come to an end as long as the Reverend John Eliot lived.

He himself knew that his time was almost out and how vain most of it had been. "There is a cloud," he wrote finally, "a dark cloud upon the work of the Gospel among the poor Indians."

He lived to see his wife Anne and four of his six children with Christ, his Cromwell with Christ, Charles with the Devil, God's Commonwealth pilloried, and every hand against his copper-colored children. And he remembered his *Up-Biblum*. Cotton Mather, pursuing a fancy of which he was fond, discovered that the anagram of his name was Toile.

John Eliot waited for the end with desire. For him the Great Perhaps was a certainty. When he was very old he liked to say that John Cotton and Richard Mather and the friends of his youth would suspect him of having gone the wrong way because he remained so long behind them. At the last, when he was dying, he dismissed the young clergymen who had come to pray superfluously over him. "Welcome Joy!" were his last words.

Francis Russell became interested in John Eliot while a student at Roxbury Latin School, America's oldest private school, which Eliot founded in 1645. Now a resident of Wellesley Hills, Massachusetts, Mr. Russell has been a frequent contributor to AMERICAN HERITAGE *on subjects as diverse as the Sacco-Vanzetti case (October, 1958); Sir William Johnson, the "Father to the Six Nations" (April, 1959); and James Michael Curley, the boss of Boston (June, 1959).*

"An unconquerable mind in a frame of iron"

LA SALLE ON

Beneath the walls of Fort Frontenac, the first boatload of La Salle's expedition set sail on Lake Ontario, heading west toward Niagara. La Salle, soon to follow with the rest of the explorers, stood in his scarlet cloak waving farewell. Beside him were Governor Frontenac and his lady. Three years ahead—three years of hardship, heartbreak, and death—lay the mouth of the Mississippi. **Never [says Parkman] under the impenetrable mail of paladin or crusader, beat a heart of more intrepid mettle than within the stoic panoply that armed the breast of La Salle. . . . America owes him an enduring memory; for, in this masculine figure, she sees the pioneer who guided her to the possession of her richest heritage.**

THE MISSISSIPPI

Forgotten paintings by George Catlin, who saw the West

unspoiled, turn up again to recall the marvels that un-

folded before the eyes of the heroic French explorer

The annals of American exploration, studded as they are with action and adventure, hold no story more heroic, in the exact, Homeric sense of this much abused word, than that of the Sieur de la Salle, fighting every obstacle which civilization, savage man, and nature could devise to penetrate to its end the valley of the Mississippi. No one has described it better, although his book is largely forgotten, than Francis Parkman. No artist, as one may see in the portfolio beginning here, has illustrated it with such faithful charm as George Catlin, the tireless traveler who recorded the Mississippi and the Plains before the white man had greatly altered them.

In the mid-1840's while traveling in Europe with his exhibition of Indian paintings, Catlin met and caught the fancy of King Louis Philippe, who had floated down the Ohio and Mississippi himself, in a small boat, while an exile from France between 1797 and 1800. The King commissioned a series showing La Salle's expedition in this former French dominion, against the backgrounds both men knew so well; together they sat down and planned the scenes. In time Catlin delivered them, as stipulated, to the Louvre—just before the outbreak of the Revolution of 1848. The monarch fled and Catlin was never paid. Recovered with difficulty five years later, the series formed part of a disappointing exhibition of Catlin's work in 1870; the often childlike simplicity of his style was not esteemed highly in his own lifetime. With a large collection of his paintings, the La Salle series was purchased in 1912 by Ogden Mills for the American Museum of Natural History in New York. But this special set—originally 28 in all—was never exhibited until recently, when it was displayed at the Kennedy Galleries in New York. AMERICAN HERITAGE is indebted to both the museum and the galleries for permission to reproduce this series; and it takes the opportunity to accompany it, beginning on the next page, with parallel quotations (in boldface) from Parkman's classic history.

In order to get above the Falls, to a place where they could build a ship to sail on Lake Erie, the explorers dragged their equipment around them. The expedition's friar, Father Hennepin, noted them in his journal: **Hennepin's account of the falls and river of Niagara —especially his second account, on his return from the West—is very minute, and on the whole very accurate. He indulges in gross exaggeration as to the height of the cataract, which in the edition of 1683, he states at five hundred feet, and raises to six hundred in that of 1697.** [The *Britannica* says 167 feet for the American Falls.] **He also says that there was room for four carriages to pass abreast under the American Fall without being wet. This is, of course, an exaggeration at the best; but it is extremely probable that a great change has taken place since his time. He speaks of a small lateral fall at the west side of the Horse Shoe Fall which does not now exist. Table Rock, now destroyed, is distinctly figured in his picture.**

Winter
1679

▲ When the carpenters were ready to lay the keel of the vessel, La Salle asked the friar to drive the first bolt; "but the modesty of my religious profession," he says, "compelled me to decline this honor." Seneca warriors . . . loitered sullenly about the place, expressing displeasure at the proceedings.

La Salle went back for supplies: The distance was some 250 miles, through the snow-encumbered forests . . . and over the ice of Lake Ontario. Two men attended him, and a dog dragged his baggage. . . . For food, they had only a bag of parched corn, which failed them two days before they reached the fort. ▼

The *Griffin,* first ship on Lake Erie, is launched: **The friar pronounced his blessing on her; the assembled company sang *Te Deum;* cannon were fired; and French and Indians, warmed alike by a generous gift of brandy, shouted and yelped in chorus as she glided into the Niagara. Her builders towed her out and anchored her in the stream. . . . The Indians gazed on her with amazement. Five small cannon looked out from her portholes; and on her prow was carved a portentous monster, the Griffin, whose name she bore, in honor of the armorial bearings of Frontenac. La Salle had often been heard to say that he would make the griffin fly above the crows, or, in other words, make Frontenac triumph over the Jesuits.** Catlin erred in showing La Salle at this great event; he was still back at Frontenac, battling his enemies and his creditors. Finally, in August, 1679, he returned. Soon the expedition set sail, passed through lakes Erie, Huron, and Michigan, and after many adventures, including the loss of the *Griffin* in a wreck, took to bark canoes to go down the Illinois River in January, 1680.

5
January
1680

Descending the Illinois River by canoe, the expedition came to an Indian village: La Salle leaped ashore, followed by his men. None knew better how to deal with Indians; and he made no sign of friendship, knowing that it might be construed as a token of fear. His little knot of Frenchmen stood, gun in hand, passive, yet prepared for battle. The Indians, on their part, rallying a little from their fright, made all haste to proffer peace. Two of their chiefs came forward, holding out the calumet. . . . La Salle, responding to these friendly overtures, displayed another.

▲ That afternoon: **Food was placed before them; and, as the Illinois code of courtesy enjoined, their entertainers conveyed the morsels with their own hands to the lips of these unenviable victims of their hospitality, while others rubbed their feet with bear's grease. La Salle, on his part, made them a gift of tobacco and hatchets; and, when he had escaped from their caresses, rose and harangued them. . . . He had come, he said, to protect them . . . and teach them to pray to the true God.**

◄ Near the Illinois village, La Salle built a stockade, Fort Crève-cœur, and commenced a new brigantine. The party split up, La Salle returning again to Canada for supplies, Tonty remaining in command, and Hennepin setting out with two men to descend the Illinois. It would be two years—full of mutiny, Indian fighting, struggles at home, endless journeyings—before La Salle, Tonty, his one truly faithful follower, and an otherwise almost new expedition could set forward again from the same site. Hennepin, who never rejoined, was captured and "adopted" by the fierce Sioux. Before his eventual return to Canada and France, he explored much of the upper Mississippi. On May 1, 1680, with the French soldier Du Gay and a number of his self-imposed "kinsmen," Hennepin came on a great falls (*left*), which he christened "St. Anthony," after his patron saint.

Hennepin's notice of the Falls of St. Anthony . . . is sufficiently accurate. . . . Great changes, however, have taken place here, and are still in progress. **The rock is a very soft, friable sandstone, overlaid by a stratum of limestone and [crumbling so rapidly] that the cataract will soon be little more than a rapid. . . . Beside the falls stands a city, which, by an ingenious combination of the Greek and Sioux languages, has received the name of Minneapolis, or City of the Waters.**

With Tonty, the friar Membré, and a new force, La Salle started south again. **It was the dead of winter, and the streams were frozen. They made sledges, placed on them the canoes, the baggage and a disabled Frenchman;** crossed from the Chicago to the northern branch of the Illinois, and filed in a long procession down its frozen course.

They embarked again, floating prosperously down between the leafless forests that flanked the tranquil river; till, on the sixth of February, they issued upon the majestic bosom of the Mississippi. To the explorers the river was the "Colbert," after the great minister of Louis XIV. La Salle lifted a banner and Membré his cross.

At the mouth of the Arkansas, they erected a cross: With every stage of their adventurous progress, the mystery of this vast New World was more and more unveiled. "I cannot tell you the civility and kindness we received from these barbarians . . . [writes Friar Membré to his superior] who are gay, civil, and free-hearted. The young men, the most alert and spirited we had seen . . . are so well formed that we were in admiration at their beauty. We did not lose the value of a pin while we were among them."

IO

March

1682

OVERLEAF: A great Taensas sachem receives La Salle: When he spoke, his wives howled to do him honor; and the assembled councillors listened with the reverence due to a potentate for whom, at his death, a hundred victims were to be sacrificed. . . . When all was ready, he was seen advancing, clothed in a white robe, and preceded by two men bearing white fans, while a third displayed a disk of burnished copper, doubtless to represent the Sun, his ancestor, or, as others will have it, his elder brother.

20

March ▶

1682

9
April
1682

Where the muddy waters discharged in the Gulf, success at last crowned the great enterprise. Up went the cross and the lily banner of the Bourbons, while to the [illegible] people assembled for this moment of history La Salle read a resounding proclamation: "In the name of the most high, mighty, invincible, and victorious Prince, Louis the Great, by the grace of God King of France and of Navarre, Fourteenth of that name, I . . . in virtue of the commission of His Majesty, which I hold in my hand, have taken, and do now take possession of this country of Louisiana . . . as also along the river Colbert, or Mississippi."

This was La Salle's greatest moment; nearly all that followed was tragedy. Well received by his king, he organized a new and bigger expedition which came by sea to the Gulf in 1685, but never found the river mouth again. One ship was wrecked on the coast of Texas (*below*), then another. The survivors wandered off, starved or died of disease. And while La Salle was resolutely searching his lost river, several of his men ambushed and killed him: **The friar at his side stood terror-stricken, unable to advance or to fly. . . . The murderers now came forward, and with wild looks gathered about their victim. "There thou liest, great Bashaw! There thou liest!" exclaimed Liotot in base exultation over the unconscious corpse. [They stripped it naked and] left it there, a prey to the buzzards and the wolves. Thus in the vigor of his manhood, at the age of forty-three, died Robert Cavelier de la Salle, "one of the greatest men,"** writes Tonty, **"of this age"**; without question one of the most remarkable explorers whose names live in history.

March
1685

*19
May
1686*

Benjamin Franklin's GRAND DESIGN

The Albany Plan of Union might have made the Revolution unnecessary

By RICHARD B. MORRIS

In one of the world's great success stories Ben Franklin adverts to a resounding failure with which his name is associated. Quoting from Dryden's rendition of a Juvenal *Satire*, he counsels us:

Look round the habitable world: how few
Know their own good, or, knowing it, pursue!

Franklin's brain child, the Albany Plan of Union, failed of adoption because neither the colonists nor the mother country knew their own good. "Such mistakes are not new," the scientist-statesman reflects in his *Autobiography*. "History is full of the errors of states and princes." The best measures of statesmanship, he shrewdly remarks, are seldom "adopted from previous wisdom, but forced by the occasion."

One of the richest opportunities the study of history affords statesmen is the chance to learn from past failures in shaping policy for present realities. From the failure to ratify the Albany Plan of Union, for which British and American statesmen must share the blame, a good deal was salvaged, perhaps more by the Americans than the British. When it came to applying the lessons learned at Albany to setting up their own federal system, the Americans showed that the experience was by no means wasted. On the other hand, the unwillingness of the British government to set up a truly federal system at a decisive period cost Britain

This view of Albany, New York, shows how it looked not too long before the delegates arrived. The painting of Franklin at left, probably by John Greenwood, shows him in his vigorous early forties. It was made about 1748, some six years before these events.

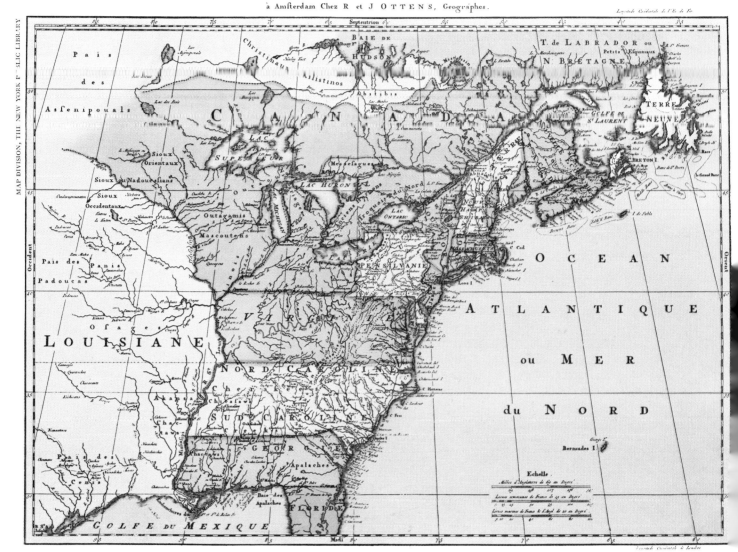

This map of the colonies and the Indian lands was published in French and Dutch about 1754, the year of the Albany Plan. All but the northernmost colony, Nova Scotia, and the southernmost, Georgia, were included in the Plan of Union.

a large slice of her old empire. Eventually Britain did apply the lessons of federalism learned at Albany, but by then America had been irretrievably lost to her.

The Albany Plan of Union was a grand design of statesmanship, the kind that is envisioned perhaps not more than once a century. It was devised to deal specifically with the first of a series of crises in the relations between Great Britain and her North American colonies.

In the summer of 1754 the shadow of France's aggressive intentions lay darkly over the British Empire in America. Already a young lieutenant colonel of the Virginia militia had met the enemy at the forks of the

Ohio, routed a French reconnaissance party, and, while the Albany Congress was still in session, had been obliged to surrender to a larger French force. The following year that young officer was to secure tragic proof of the inadequacy of Britain's military preparations and of the formidable capacity of her enemy to wage war. The experience George Washington gained on the Monongahela served his country well at a later day.

The French and Indian War, or the Seven Years' War as it was called when it spread from America to Europe, to Africa, to India and to the seven seas, was really a clash of two world empires. In the American

90

colonies England's military security rested in no small part upon her traditional alliance with the Iroquois, the Six Confederated Nations. But the bonds between England and her Indian allies had been stretched to the breaking point as the Iroquois observed with increasing alarm the rising military might of France.

The Iroquois saw the French using the interlude between Queen Anne's and King George's Wars to expand on the Mississippi and in the Illinois country. Their tension mounted when the French boldly established Fort Niagara on Lake Erie as a bastion against them. To the Six Nations the alliance with England seemed to have less and less military value. As the French became more aggressive the Six Nations moved toward neutrality.

The English erected Fort Oswego on Lake Ontario. They dispatched to the Six Nations their old friend William Johnson, Indian trader and honorary sachem of the Mohawks. But these measures fell short of guaranteeing continued Iroquois loyalty. Already some of the tribes had forged close French ties.

With a world war in the offing, glaring defects in the British colonial system were apparent equally to the Indians and the British government. No unified policy had been established. Each colony acted for itself. Regional and sectional differences made it virtually impossible to reach agreement with the Indians on a number of outstanding issues.

These imperial problems were uppermost in the mind of the Board of Trade when, in September, 1753, it instructed Sir Danvers Osborne, governor of New York, to summon an intercolonial conference to restore friendship with the Iroquois and to determine whether the colonies would "enter into articles of union and confederation with each other for the mutual defense of His Majesty's subjects and interests in North America, as well in time of peace as war." The order never reached Osborne. Suicide, brought on by private grief, ended his brief career in the province, and the letter was placed in the hands of Lieutenant Governor James De Lancey, who had assumed Osborne's duties.

At long last, on June 19, 1754, 24 delegates from seven of the fourteen continental colonies assembled in the old city hall of the compact Dutch fortress town of Albany. Under one roof were assembled a remarkable group of colonial statesmen, a group predisposed toward a liberal solution of political problems and not given to taking orders. While there was no official presiding officer, James De Lancey chaired the sessions he attended. De Lancey had long been feuding with the more liberal-minded Livingston faction, and had earned a reputation, not entirely deserved, of being the leader of the prerogative party in New York, the party which supported the Crown, the governor, and the other royal officials against the pretensions of the assembly.

Massachusetts sent a five-man delegation, including one of her most distinguished sons. He was Thomas Hutchinson, then a member of the provincial council, later chief justice and Tory lieutenant governor. Rhode Island dispatched Chief Justice Stephen Hopkins, whose election the very next year to the governorship marked a shift in power in that colony from the Newport to the Providence faction. Connecticut's Deputy Governor William Pitkin headed that delegation. He had already gained a reputation as a champion of colonial rights against the royal prerogative.

The strongest delegations came from New York and Pennsylvania. In addition to De Lancey, New York was represented by William Johnson, most deeply versed of all the delegates in Indian problems and most beloved by the Iroquois. Johnson advocated fraternization toward the red man and carried it out in his own private life. He was slated to become superintendent of Indian affairs and was to compile a formidable military record in the French and Indian War, a record which won him a knighthood. Two other prerogative men were in the New York delegation. They were the lawyers Joseph Murray and John Chambers. Another delegate was William Smith, a member of the governor's council and a leader of the liberal or anti-prerogative party.

Pennsylvania sent a formidable delegation, including John Penn, grandson of William Penn, a member of the proprietary family and later to become lieutenant governor. Accompanying him were Richard Peters, secretary of the province, Isaac Norris, speaker of the assembly, and Benjamin Franklin, then postmaster general of the colonies and a member of the legislature.

Franklin had already established his reputation. Then in his forty-ninth year, Franklin at Albany was to demonstrate his right to rank with the most constructive political thinkers of his century.

A crisis brought these minds together. A later crisis would divide them. Some, like Thomas Hutchinson and John Penn, became loyalists; others, like Hopkins and Franklin, led the rebellion against the Crown. But in the year 1754 they all considered it to be feasible for the colo-

JOIN, or DIE.

This first American cartoon was published by Franklin in his Pennsylvania Gazette, May 9, 1754.

nies to work in co-operation with the British government. Some even went so far as to regard the interests of the empire as paramount to those of their own sections and provinces. That time never came again.

The primary business of the Albany Congress was the making of a firm treaty with the Iroquois. In all, 150 Indian chiefs attended. They spared no pains to point out to the English their defenseless condition. Most eloquent perhaps was Chief Hendricks of the Mohawks. "Look at the French," he declared. "They are men. They are fortifying everywhere. But—we are ashamed to say it—you are like women." Taking a stick and throwing it behind him, he asserted: "You have thus thrown us behind your back and disregarded us."

Soothing words, vague promises and bribes headed off what had threatened to be an explosive situation. On behalf of all the delegates De Lancey gave a chain belt to the Indians, signifying that the colonies were acting jointly with the entire body of the Six Nations. Then New York, Pennsylvania and Connecticut each held separate sessions with the Indians. When the Iroquois chiefs left the conference they were in a far happier frame of mind than when they came. Thirty wagonloads of presents, including guns, may well have contributed to their cheerful mood on departure. The English had good reason to feel that the old Indian alliance had been re-established on a firm basis.

While these talks with the Indians were in progress, the delegates debated the question "whether a Union of all the Colonies is not at present absolutely necessary for their security and defence." They unanimously agreed that such a union was imperative, and a committee consisting of one member appointed by each delegation was set up at once to prepare and receive plans of union.

Now the idea of a union of the colonies was by no means novel. As far back as 1643 a notable step in that direction had been taken when the New England Confederation was formed. In that federation delegates from all the New England colonies except Rhode Island were empowered to decide on war and peace, to enact laws for the protection of the colonies, and to levy as well as collect taxes. The New England Confederation functioned down to the revocation of the Massachusetts charter in 1684. It had performed its greatest service in directing colonial military operations in King Philip's Indian war.

During the early intercolonial wars various plans for troop quotas were proposed. That original imperial thinker, the humanitarian William Penn, in 1697 had advocated an intercolonial assembly under a royal commissioner, but with an extremely limited jurisdiction.

Proposals for union kept cropping up. In 1751 Archibald Kennedy, a defense-conscious official who was receiver-general (tax collector) of New York and a member of the governor's council, proposed an intercolonial confederacy to hearten the Indians and curb the French. Meeting annually, the commissioners were to have power to supervise military affairs. Perhaps most significant, in the light of the later Albany Plan, was Kennedy's suggestion that the confederacy be established by act of Parliament.

Kennedy sent his ideas on to Benjamin Franklin, who seized upon them with enthusiasm. It would be a very strange thing, he wrote the New Yorker, if Six Nations of ignorant savages should be capable of forming a union that had subsisted for ages, and yet a like union should be impracticable for ten or a dozen English colonies to whom it was necessary. Going further than Kennedy, Franklin at this time proposed an intercolonial government, to be set up by voluntary action on the part of the colonies.

En route to Albany in 1754 Franklin stopped off in New York City to discuss with his friend Kennedy and with James Alexander, a noted colonial attorney and long a leader of the anti-prerogative forces, the refurbished plan of union which he had first evolved, at Kennedy's prompting, three years earlier. As Alexander wrote Cadwallader Colden, their talk had turned on the difficulty of forming a union without "affecting our liberties on the one hand, or being ineffectual on the other." Thus, in the late spring of 1754, these three colonial thinkers came to grips with the crucial problem raised by any design of government—that of liberty versus authority.

In addition to seeking the support of influential persons, Franklin recognized the necessity of rallying public opinion behind the plan. Before leaving Philadelphia he had prepared for his newspaper, the *Pennsylvania Gazette*, an article pointing out the need for union and stressing the fact that "our enemies have the great advantage of being under one direction, with one council, and one purse." Datelined Philadelphia, May 9, his article was illustrated by one of the very earliest cartoons in American journalistic history, a woodcut of a snake separated into parts, representing the colonies, with the motto beneath it: "JOIN OR

Richard B. Morris is professor of history at Columbia University and author of several books on the colonial and Revolutionary periods—not to mention the perennially useful Encyclopedia of American History. *This article was the first of a series in* AMERICAN HERITAGE *entitled* Times of Trial in American Statecraft, *since published in book form by Alfred A. Knopf, Inc., New York.*

DIE"—a device that was employed again at the start of the American Revolution.

Franklin's plan was so much bolder in conception than various other plans which were advanced, and so much better conceived for the purposes at hand, that it caught on at once. In fact, the "Plan of Union" as it was finally adopted at the Albany Congress was essentially based upon the "Short Hints Towards a Scheme for Uniting the Northern Colonies," which Franklin had prepared in advance of the congress and talked over with Kennedy and Alexander.

But there was one significant difference between Franklin's first proposal of 1751 and the later one embraced in the "Short Hints." The new plan was to be imposed by parliamentary authority. A thorough realist, Franklin by now saw no hope of achieving union through voluntary action on the part of the colonies. Perhaps no move better typifies the temper of the Albany Congress than the vote of that assembly on this particular proposal. Every delegate except three from Connecticut and two from Pennsylvania voted in favor of having Parliament legislate a federal union into existence. Twenty years later a number of these very same men, chief of them Franklin himself, were to deny Parliament's authority either to tax or to legislate for the colonies.

In conference Franklin's "Short Hints" underwent some minor revisions. His original plan provided for a governor-general, appointed and paid by the Crown, who was to have a veto over all acts of the grand council, in addition to executive powers. Except for changing the name from governor-general to president-general and adding to his authority the power to make Indian treaties and to declare war and peace with the advice and consent of the grand council, the executive in the final plan remained substantially as Franklin had proposed it. The legislature was to consist of a grand council to be chosen triennially by the assemblies of the colonies in numbers proportionate to the taxes paid into the general treasury.

Although the proportions of the first grand council were fixed in the final plan, provision was made that in later elections representation was to be based upon taxation rather than population. However, the fact that Franklin had conferred the power of election upon the assemblies rather than the more aristocratic and prerogative-minded governors' councils constituted a notable democratic innovation. Franklin's plan set up a general treasury for the united colonies. So did the final plan, which also provided for a union treasurer in each colony.

One of the most important areas reserved for the proposed continental government was the West. The

Thomas Hutchinson, member of the provincial council.

Albany Plan would have given the federal government the power to deal with the problems of defense, to raise arms, build forts, equip vessels of war, regulate the Indians, and administer territorial expansion. The final plan authorized the president-general and council to make laws for regulating the new settlements until they were formed into particular governments.

That these proposals were meant to curb the power of the original colonies over the western lands is perfectly clear from a representation to the King in Council, drawn up by Thomas Hutchinson and adopted at the congress. This imperialistic document urged that "the bounds of these Colonies which extend to the South Sea, be contracted and limited by the Alleghenny or Apalachian mountains." The Albany Plan, combined with the representation of that congress, would in effect have written off the trans-Appalachian claims of colonies like Virginia, and in fact was embodied in the Royal Proclamation of 1763.

Perhaps equally significant is the authority which the plan conferred upon the continental government to levy taxes. Finally, the continental government was empowered to make laws concerning matters within its jurisdiction, but such laws were to be submitted to the King in Council for approval or disallowance. If not disallowed within three years after submission, they were to remain in force.

At the Albany Congress the only real opposition to the Plan of Union seems to have been offered by the Connecticut delegates. They made various objections.

They felt that the territory was too large to administer and that it would be dangerous to unite under one head a population so rapidly growing. They objected to the president-general's veto and found that the power of levying taxes was "a very extraordinary thing" and ran counter to the rights of Englishmen. Some slight opposition was also made by De Lancey, who would have preferred to lodge with the colonial governors a veto on the election of representatives to the grand council.

But both Franklin and Pownall assert that the plan was unanimously adopted at the conference, and Thomas Hutchinson on his return to Massachusetts so informed the press. Hence, the Connecticut delegates must have abstained from casting a negative vote.

In America public opinion was never sufficiently aroused to put the plan across. The Connecticut assembly went on record opposing its adoption. New Jersey, which did not attend the congress, held that the plan adversely affected its constitution. The Pennsylvania assembly, despite Franklin's own prestige, voted it down without discussion. The Massachusetts assembly debated the plan at length and then defeated it. In short, with the exception of New York, whose legislature went on record favoring the proposal, every assembly which considered the plan turned it down.

In England the Albany Plan received as frigid a reception as in America. The Board of Trade submitted the plan to George II without comment, but the Privy Council took no action. Lord Halifax, head of the Board of Trade, urged instead a thoroughly undemocratic scheme of union, with a permanent revenue as its paramount objective. Other plans, like Cadwallader Colden's hereditary council of landholders in America in imitation of the House of Lords, contemplated sweeping revisions in the colonial charters, even the setting up of three regional unions. Such plans would not have enlarged colonial self-government, but delimited it.

Many years later Franklin pithily summed up the rejection of his plan on both sides of the water.

"The crown disapproved it," he pointed out, "as having too much weight in the democratic part of the constitution, and every assembly as having allowed too much to prerogative; so it was totally rejected." In short, the thinking of the men who met at Albany in 1754 was too bold for that day. In evolving the Plan of Union Franklin had shown himself to be an imperial-minded thinker who placed the empire above individual states' rights.

During the discussion over the ratification of the Albany Plan Franklin's own pen was not idle. Governor Shirley of Massachusetts proposed a drastic revision of the Albany Plan. He would have permitted Parliament to tax the colonies directly and have excluded the colonists from all share in the choice of the grand councilors.

In a stinging rebuttal Franklin pointed out that "compelling the colonies to pay money without their consent would be rather like raising contributions in an enemy's country than taxing of Englishmen for their own public benefit. It would be treating them as conquered people, and not as true British subjects."

These words of Franklin penned in 1754 forecast the constitutional arguments of the American colonists when, in 1765, Parliament for the first time instituted direct taxation of the colonies. The Stamp Act, which provoked the calling of another congress in New York —this one without permission of the Crown—touched off the great controversy which was fated to end in war. Had it been put in operation the Albany Plan would very likely have obviated the necessity for Parliament to levy taxes for the military defense and administration of the colonies.

Perhaps the British government recognized its mistake in failing to adopt the plan, but not until long after the Revolution had broken out and military currents were running adverse to the mother country. Following Burgoyne's defeat at Saratoga the British government instructed the Carlisle Peace Commission to concede to the colonies, if necessary, "Congress as a permanent institution so long as it did not infringe the sovereignty of Parliament." But America was by then irrevocably committed to independence and the offer was flatly rejected. In fact, the federal principle embodied in the Albany Plan would not be accepted by Great Britain for another half century, and then it was still another colonial revolt, this time in Canada, which converted the government to federalism.

For Americans the failure of statesmanship in 1754 was a lesson that was not soon forgotten. The Albany Plan constituted the basic core of that federal system that came into effect with the First Continental Congress. Even the notion that such a plan might keep the colonies in the empire was not lightly abandoned. At the First Congress the conservative Pennsylvanian and later loyalist, Joseph Galloway, proposed a watered-down version of the Albany Plan of Union, virtually identical with Franklin's plan except in one respect. He proposed that *both* Parliament and the intercolonial council should be empowered to legislate for the colonies, each to have a negative on the other. Again, it is significant of the temper of the year 1774 that this proposal was narrowly defeated by a vote of six states to five.

Despite the defeat of Galloway's proposal the old Albany Plan was not allowed to die. In June, 1775, as a delegate to the Second Continental Congress, Franklin proposed a plan of confederation substantially based on the Albany Plan. This plan substituted for the strong provision granting the powers of taxation to the grand council a proposal to allow Congress the right to make requisitions. But the new plan pointed toward national sovereignty in the large powers it conferred on Congress in other respects, powers extending to all matters "necessary to the general welfare." The proposal was shelved. After independence was declared the government was administered by congressional committees, and their meddlesome incompetence severely taxed the patience of the commander in chief.

As finally adopted, the Articles of Confederation incorporated a number of the ideas of the Albany Plan, including the control of the West by the federal government. Nevertheless, it continued the voting equality of the states which had been established by the First Congress. Again Franklin tried to introduce the idea of representation in proportion to population, but again he lost. The Articles set up a union of limited powers between equal sovereign states. By failing to go as far as the Albany Plan in limiting state sovereignty, the Articles of Confederation fell far short of what the delegates at Albany had proposed 24 years earlier.

But at least in one respect, the Congress of the Confederation did achieve one of the principal objectives of the Albany Plan—federal control of the western territories. The Northwest Territory Ordinance of 1787, in which Congress set up a government for the territories and laid down principles for the admission of new states, was a triumph for the federal dreamers at Albany.

Ultimate recognition of the practicality of the Albany Plan was attained at the Constitutional Convention. If you substitute a president for a president-general and add a second house you will find that in substance the Albany Plan was embodied in the federal Constitution.

Consider some of the basic concepts of the Albany Plan. The members of the council were to have been elected by the legislatures of the various colonies in the same manner in which United States senators were provided for in the Constitution. The colonies were represented as colonies, as in the Senate, yet a proportionate and varying representation was adopted, as we find in the House of Representatives. True, the system of proportionate representation which was finally adopted was based more appropriately on the democratic principle of population. Each of the powers granted the council were specifically given to Congress

William Shirley, governor of Massachusetts.

by the Constitution, except the power to purchase Indian lands and make new colonies of the land so acquired. Had these powers been spelled out in the Constitution, Jefferson might have been spared some anxious moments at the time of the Louisiana Purchase.

Writing in 1789, when the new federal government had become effective, Franklin indulged some speculations about the significance of the great failure of 1754. In a magazine article in which he analyzed his old Plan of Union, he made these observations:

On reflection, it now seems probable, that, if the foregoing plan, or something like it, had been adopted and carried into execution, the subsequent separation of the colonies from the mother country might not so soon have happened, nor the mischiefs suffered on both sides have occurred, perhaps, during another century. For the colonies, if so united, would have really been, as they then thought themselves, sufficient to their own defense; and, being trusted with it, as by the plan, an army from Britain, for that purpose, would have been unnecessary. The pretences for framing the Stamp Act would then not have existed, nor the other projects for drawing a revenue from America to Britain by acts of parliament, which were the cause of the breach, and attended with such terrible expense of blood and treasure; so that the different parts of the empire might still have remained in peace and union.

Of all the failures of British-American statesmanship, this first major failure may well have had the most momentous consequences for the world. ●

95

In the well-known Gilbert Stuart portrait of George Washington, many of the traces of age and illness have been carefully concealed by the painter's art.

A MEDICAL PROFILE OF
George Washington

Stalwart as he was, the general was often ill. A doctor studies his record and notes shortcomings in Eighteenth-Century medical care.

By RUDOLPH MARX, M.D.

If one looks closely at Gilbert Stuart's well-known portrait of George Washington, one observes an artificial bulging of the cheeks, as if they had been stuffed with cotton.

It has been reported that Stuart actually did use cotton to fill out the sunken cheeks of the illustrious sitter for this portrait, who at the time was wearing a set of ill-fitting dentures. In 1796, when the picture was painted, Washington was the proud possessor of two sets of these awkward and noisy contraptions, made of ivory. Up to the Nineteenth Century dentistry in the modern sense was unknown. When something was wrong with a tooth, it was pulled out. So, at the age of 22, Washington had a toothache which was relieved by having the tooth pulled. This same radical treatment was used for every aching tooth over the years, and by the age of 57 he had hardly any teeth left and had to wear false teeth. Six years later his last surviving tooth was pulled.

The face of the President is covered with a rosy glaze in the picture. His real complexion was described by his contemporaries as sallow, a color that was even visible through the tan which the sun and wind had burned on his face.

The painter also carefully retouched the pockmarks that deeply pitted Washington's features. These blemishes Washington had acquired at the age of nineteen during an ill-fated journey to Barbados Island. He was at that time accompanying his brother and guardian, Lawrence, who was suffering from active tuberculosis of the lungs and was vainly looking for salvation in the balmy climate of the West Indies.

In his diary, Washington notes that he was "strongly attacked" by smallpox and was confined to his bed for three weeks. When he finally arose from his sickbed, he bore the marks of the disease and carried them to his grave.

In most portraits, the Father of His Country is shown as having a chest bulging with well-deserved pride. The chest must have been tailor-made. Under the well-padded coat, Washington's chest was flat and somewhat hollow in the center, probably from early rickets. And the shoulders were not as broad as they appeared from the outside.

Colonel Tobias Lear, his devoted secretary and faithful friend, immediately after the death of the General, took his bodily measurements for posterity. He recorded Washington's shoulders as one foot nine inches across, which is average for a man of the unusual height of Washington. He measured six feet three and a half inches tall. If Washington was that tall at the age of 67, he must have been at least one inch taller at the prime of life.

Like Lincoln, with whom he had many physical characteristics in common, Washington was in his youth a champion wrestler and rail-splitter. It is a curious phenomenon that the two greatest Presidents of the United States were also physical giants. Even by present standards Washington and Lincoln would be considered unusually tall men. They were more outstanding for their size in their own time, when the average man was considerably smaller.

In spite of great physical strength and endurance, Washington was subjected to a host of diseases in his lifetime. He suffered from at least ten attacks of serious illness which on several occasions brought him to the brink of death. The question is whether Washington had more than his share of sickness in a period of history when a number of diseases were taken for granted, diseases which modern science has virtually conquered and which we have almost forgotten.

In Washington's world a great percentage of babies died from nutritional deficiencies and diarrhea. If they survived they were exposed to the prevalent epidemics of which the most contagious ones were most apt to be acquired in early childhood. A number of such diseases confer upon their victims, if they recover, a lasting, even lifelong immunity. Therefore they occur rarely in later life, and so were called children's diseases. Among them were measles, scarlet fever, whooping cough, and diphtheria. Before the introduction of vaccination, even smallpox was considered a children's disease in many countries.

If a person in the Eighteenth Century survived the trial period of infancy and childhood, he had to run the gantlet of a legion of other diseases waiting for him on his life's path. He was forever threatened by the White Plague, tuberculosis, which was the number one killer of the time. Then there was always malaria lurking in the swamps; ever present were the various strains of dysentery easily transmitted by uncooked food and drink, and the enteric fevers—typhoid and para-typhoid, harbored in human carriers and transmitted by food, drinking water, and the ubiquitous flies. Ever threatening were the pneumonias of different types.

Uncontrolled by antiseptics were the septic bacteria, the staphylococci and streptococci, which had a field day feasting in every wound. Like other disease germs, these shock troops of death can also enter the body through microscopic channels in the apparently unbroken skin and mucous lining.

Doctors of Washington's time were incapable of giving a scientific explanation of most disease phenomena. The medical concepts of the time were based upon a hodgepodge of ancient beliefs, time-honored traditions, and the doctrines formulated over the centuries by the accepted authorities of medicine.

Unknown was the science of bacteriology. The causes of most diseases were absolutely obscure, as were the pathways of their transmission. A contamination of the air by a miasma was blamed for the spread of the majority of diseases. The miasmas were thought to emanate from putrescent matter and from swamps, and to float in the air. Some diseases were believed to be transmitted by polluted water, a theory which came close to the truth in the case of typhoid.

No specific remedies against most infections were known, except for quinine which had been found effective against the rigors of malaria, as had mercury against the sores of syphilis.

In his last play, Le Malade Imaginaire, Molière wrote the lines, "Nearly all men die of their remedies and not of their illnesses." The medical therapy of Washington's time had changed very little in the hundred years since Molière. It still used the same murderous arsenal consisting mainly of bloodletting, purgatives, emetics, enemas, and blistering.

In order to understand some of the theories and methods of pre-scientific medicine as it was still practiced in Washington's time, we must realize that the first concepts and practices of the healing art originated in magic and religion in ancient times. Beneath the surface the doctors took over from the medicine men some of their rituals, and rationalized them as therapeutic measures. The most dramatic of these was the ceremony of bloodletting, which had been performed by savage tribes since prehistoric times. The object of this rite was either to let the bad demons escape with the flowing of blood, or to appease the spirits and gods by the sacrifice of blood.

Superstitions and traditions die hard, especially when they take the disguise of reason. Medicine justified the practice of bleeding by adopting the popular belief that blood was the carrier of the impurities and poisons of disease, and that by the removal of "bad" blood, the formation of new healthy blood would be engendered.

At the time of Washington the average amount removed in one bloodletting was one pint. The more serious the illness, the more blood was taken. It was then unknown that the mean blood volume of a person measures not more than eight and one-half per cent of the body weight, which meant about seventeen pints for a man of Washington's weight at the age of 67. It was believed that some glandular secretion in the body could replace the amount of drained blood within a few hours, instead of the weeks that are actually required.

Since the dawn of history people have used laxatives and emetics, in the majority of cases doing more harm than good by dehydrating and weakening the patient. Laxatives have killed thousands of victims suffering from appendicitis by distending an inflamed and brittle appendix. Enemas were somewhat less dangerous if used with discrimination, but repeated colonic flushings as practiced by the doctors of the Seventeenth and Eighteenth Centuries weakened and exhausted the patient and seriously strained his tired heart.

Another practice often used by colonial physicians was the raising of blisters on the skin. This was based on the belief that an inflammatory process could be "drawn" from the inside to the outside by counter-irritation. As it was usually done with caustic concoctions, it often produced severe chemical burns and inflicted unnecessary pain on the sufferer.

Altogether, if we consider the primitive state of preventive and therapeutic medicine in Washington's time, it is small wonder that few persons reached old age. In the case of Washington, we know that his grandfather died at 37, his father at 49, probably from infectious diseases; on his maternal side we only know that his mother reached the age of 82.

From his mother, her first-born son George inherited not only his physical features but also his unusually strong constitution and powers of endurance. However, if we consider his medical history, we marvel that he ever reached the age of 67, when he succumbed to a streptococcic throat infection and to the medical mistreatment he received.

We do not know anything about the childhood diseases of Washington. From the diaries and letters of Washington and from the reports of his doctors and friends, we have an exact knowledge of the illnesses which attacked him after his sixteenth year. In his seventeenth year Washington was licensed by William and Mary College in Virginia as a public surveyor, a profession which he practiced for several years in Fairfax County. At that time great stretches of Virginia were dotted with swamps infested with malaria-carrying mosquitoes. Camping outdoors as a surveyor, Washington was promptly bitten by these malaria-carrying mosquitoes and suffered his first attack of malaria, called "ague." During his later life Washington had repeated bouts of this intermittent fever.

We have already mentioned the severe case of smallpox which he contracted at nineteen during his sojourn at Barbados. This calamitous trip not only failed to cure the consumption of his brother, who died a few months later, but it brought George into close contact with the virulent tuberculosis bacilli as he nursed his brother, and they promptly invaded his body. Washington had barely returned to Mount Vernon, still weak from the smallpox, when the tubercular infection broke through the exhausted defenses of his system and manifested itself in the form of acute pleurisy. He recovered slowly and was in poor health many long months.

After two years the process must have been arrested, since Washington felt strong enough to enter military

How would Washington's "medical history" look on a modern Army form? Here is a glimpse of what it might show, as based on the findings brought forward in Dr. Marx's study.

service. In October, 1753, he received a commission as major in the Virginia militia and was immediately ordered on a fruitless mission to the French commander of the Ohio Territory. During the next year he led a military expedition against the French at Fort Duquesne and was badly defeated. He had hardly returned when he was stricken with a severe attack of malaria.

In 1755 the English general Edward Braddock ar-

99

rived in Virginia with several battalions of English troops. Braddock asked Washington to join his expedition against the French and Indians. The campaign had not progressed far when Washington fell ill with a febrile disease, apparently of the influenza type. He describes the experience in his diary in these words:

Immediately upon leaving the camp at George's Creek on the 14th, I was seized with violent fevers and pains in my head which continued without intermission until the 23rd following when I was relieved by General Braddock's absolutely ordering the physicians to give me Dr. James' Powders, one of the most excellent medicines in the world for it gave me immediate ease and removed my fevers and other complaints in four days time. [This remedy was a ferocious nostrum, which in full doses produced vomiting, sweating and diarrhea.] My illness was too violent to suffer me to ride, therefore I was indebted to a covered wagon for some part of my transportation.

On the day before the battle of Monongahela, Washington rose from his sickbed, still weak and barely able to sit on his horse. The battle itself, as every schoolboy knows, was a complete disaster. Braddock was killed, his troops were routed, and Washington managed to extricate the remainder of the detachment after two horses had been killed under him and his uniform pierced by four balls. He returned to Mount Vernon and wrote to one of his half brothers: "I am not able were I ever so willing, to meet you in town for I assure you that it is with some difficulty and much fatigue that I visit my plantations in the Neck; so much has a sickness of five weeks duration reduced me." Two years later Washington contracted a severe type of dysentery accompanied by high fever and a deep prostration which lasted for several months. Recovery was so slow and tedious that Washington became depressed and worried a good deal about his condition.

In the meantime the English government had sent a new general, John Forbes, with considerable reinforcements for a new campaign against the French and Indians in the Ohio Basin. The tonic of excitement invigorated Washington enough to accompany the English general as the commander of the advance guard. Washington had the great satisfaction that this, the third attempt to defeat the French in which he had participated, was successful. Fort Duquesne was taken and renamed Fort Pitt, later Pittsburgh.

After this campaign Washington resigned his commission, returned, and in January, 1759, married the widow Martha Custis. Apparently marriage had a beneficial influence on Washington's health. No sickness is reported in his diaries until 1761 when he had another attack which he believed to be malaria, though it may have been typhoid fever. He was bedfast for several weeks with pain and great prostration. Barely recovered, he had a relapse of fever which made him

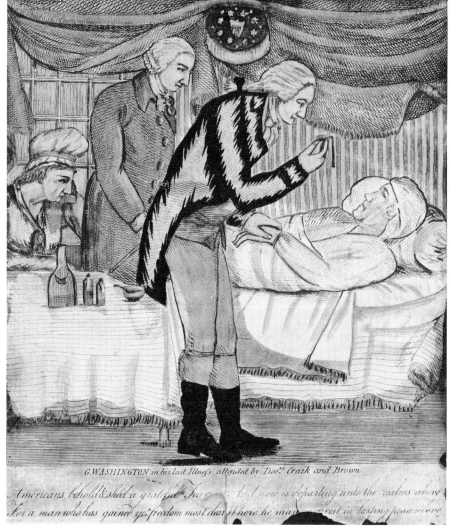

G.WASHINGTON in his last Illness attended by Doc^rs Craik and Brown

Americans behold & shed a grateful Tear   And now is departing unto the realms above
For a man who has gained ye freedom most dear   Where he may — rest in lasting peace & love

An unknown artist drew Washington dying, attended by Doctors Craik and Brown.

once more despondent and fearful that he was very near his "last gasp."

There is no mention of any disabling sickness for the next six years; then he suffered another attack of dysentery. This was followed by the longest period of freedom from illness that Washington ever enjoyed, and which included the long years of the Revolutionary War.

If one scans the diaries of Washington, one is astonished by his gloomy outlook each time he was stricken by serious illness, and his readiness to anticipate a fatal outcome. Washington's apprehensions were well founded. Of his nine brothers, half brothers, and sisters, two died in infancy and the other seven between the ages of thirteen and sixty-four. George survived them all, as well as his two adopted children. How could he have expected to outlive all his close relatives with the exception of his wife, Martha?

Sickness affects different people in different ways. Long periods of disease accompanied by disability, pain, and danger, such as Washington had to endure, exert a profound influence in molding a character. They are times of trial which soften the weak and temper the strong. Long periods of physical disability gave Washington the time to find himself and his ideal. Self-control and patience are masks which are acquired by long and painful practice in suppressing the natural outbursts of emotion and impatience. The sickbed is the best school in which to learn patience.

It can be assumed that other qualities which the mature Washington exhibited, his courage and unyielding determination, were also conditioned by his medical history. A man who has repeatedly faced death when attacked by unknown diseases, encounters with a feeling of relief enemies whom he can see and understand. And Washington's singleness of purpose may have derived its force from the store of energy dammed up by the frustrations of sickness.

We have only one record of Washington being incapacitated during the Revolutionary War, for a short time, probably by a bad cold. Even at Valley Forge there was not a day when Washington was not at his post. The continuous strain of his responsibility and the consciousness of his mission kept on stimulating his adrenal glands, raising his normal powers of endurance, resistance, and immunity. Destiny kept alive and well the only man of his time who could lead the American Revolution to victory.

Washington remained free of any disabling disease until 1786. Then, following the conclusion of the war and his election to the Presidency, came a letdown and he fell ill once more with "ague and fever." He was treated by Dr. James Craik, who had been his physi-

cian for the preceding 32 years and had become his close personal friend.

In 1786 Dr. Craik for the first time employed "the bark" on Washington for malaria with excellent results. "The bark" meant the bark of the Chinchona tree which had been used for 140 years against malaria in South America and southern Europe. It was given in the form of a powder, decoction, or extract, and was one of the first specific remedies employed for any disease.

In the first year of his Presidency there developed what the doctors called "a malignant carbuncle" on Washington's left hip, probably of staphylococcic origin. For several weeks he was desperately sick and septic. He was cared for by Dr. Samuel Bard, a well-known New York physician, who watched over the patient for many days and nights.

Finally Dr. Bard summoned all his courage, incised the carbuncle, and drained the pus, with immediate improvement. Washington was confined to the house for nearly six weeks. When he was able to go out, his coach had to be reconstructed to enable him to lie at full length.

In 1789 Washington went on an official visit to New England. In the outskirts of Boston he was delayed a considerable time in rain and stormy weather because the city and state authorities were unable to settle a dispute as to the etiquette of receiving the Chief of State, for which there was no precedent. As a result, Washington developed a bad cold with some inflammation of the eyes. Following this visit, an epidemic of respiratory infections spread through the city, and the die-hard Loyalists of Boston promptly named it "the Washington Influenza."

As the result of colds and the large doses of quinine taken for his malaria, Washington's hearing noticeably deteriorated during the last decade of his life. The deafness made it difficult for him to carry on conversations at public affairs, and increased his native diffidence. Therefore he acquired a reputation of being cold and aloof in society.

Like every person with normal vision, after reaching middle age Washington had to wear glasses for reading. In those days, the wearing of glasses was just as unfashionable as has been the wearing of hearing aids until quite recently. People were ashamed to wear glasses, considering them a humiliating disfigurement, like a clubfoot or hunchback. Washington used his reading glasses only in the privacy of his family and among intimate friends.

In 1790 the federal government was removed from New York to Philadelphia. In the spring of the same year Washington was taken with an attack of pneumonia followed by a relapse which almost proved fatal. He wrote: "I have already within less than a year had two severe attacks, the last worse than the first. A third probably will put me to sleep with my fathers."

There is no doubt that the responsibility and the nervous strain connected with the Presidency were a great drain on the physical strength and stamina of Washington, as on all other Presidents since. Sixty-five years old, sick, and tired of public service, he declined to be nominated for a third term and retired to the privacy of Mount Vernon in the spring of 1797. He was allowed only two and a half years of well-deserved rest at his beloved Mount Vernon. In 1798 his old nemesis, malaria, recurred, and responded only tardily to "the bark."

On the day of December 12, 1799, as was his custom, Washington was riding about his farm from 10 A.M. until 3 P.M. The weather that day was bad, rain, hail, and snow falling alternately, driven by an icy wind. Washington was a stickler for punctuality in all his activities, including his meal hours. On this December day in 1799, Washington was late for dinner. Served promptly at three o'clock, the meal was on the table when he entered the house. Colonel Lear, his faithful friend and secretary, observed that the neck of the general appeared wet and that snow was sticking to his hair, but Washington refused to change his clothes and sat down to the dinner.

The next day he complained of a cold and sore throat and did not go out as usual in the morning. In spite of his cold he went outside in the afternoon to mark some trees which he wanted cut down. In the evening a severe hoarseness developed, but he made light of it. Upon retiring, Colonel Lear suggested that the general take something for his cold, but Washington answered, "No, you know I never take anything for a cold; let it go as it came."

On the following day at three o'clock in the morning Washington told Martha that he was very unwell, that he had the ague. He could scarcely speak and breathed with difficulty. Martha begged him to let her awaken the servants and fetch him a home remedy. But Washington sternly refused to let her get up for fear she, too, would catch a cold.

At daybreak a servant came and lighted the fire. Soon Colonel Lear arrived and found the general voiceless, hardly able to utter an audible sound. A loathsome mixture of molasses, vinegar and butter was offered to Washington but he could not swallow a drop. As he tried harder to get it down, he started to cough convulsively, and almost suffocated. Rawlins, the overseer of the farm, was sent for with Washington's request to bleed him.

The overseer had acquired his surgical acumen in the practice of veterinary medicine. He took a pint of blood from Washington, but there was no relief. Colonel Lear next applied "sal volatile," the menthol-vapor rub of the time, to the throat of the sick man, rubbing it gently with his hand, upon which the patient complained that his throat was very sore. A piece of flannel saturated with the same evil-smelling salve was wound around his neck, and the feet bathed in warm water, all to no avail.

About eight o'clock Washington got up for two hours, but obtained no relief from the changed position. Dr. Craik arrived shortly after nine o'clock. He applied a blister of Spanish flies (derived from dried and powdered blister beetles) to the throat, took some more blood, and prescribed a gargle of vinegar and sage tea. He also ordered vinegar and hot water for steam inhalation. In attempting to use the gargle, the patient almost choked and regurgitated the liquid. At eleven o'clock the bleeding was repeated but the difficulty in swallowing and breathing did not improve. In the meantime Dr. Gustave Richard Brown, of Port Tobacco, and Dr. Elisha Cullen Dick, of Alexandria, had been summoned as consultants.

Both consultants arrived around three o'clock and sat down at the bedside of the patient. The clinical diagnostic methods of percussion and auscultation, tapping the chest and listening to the breath sounds, were not yet practiced at that time. Neither is there any record that the interior of the throat of Washington was ever inspected by the attending physicians. A diagnosis was arrived at by watching the patient, observing his external symptoms, and taking his pulse. The three doctors attending Washington saw their patient struggle for breath, each inspiration producing a shrill, harsh sound as the air was painfully sucked in through the obstructed air passage. His skin was blue and the nostrils dilated and contracted with the effort of breathing. In addition to this, the patient had great difficulty in swallowing.

The first diagnosis thought of was quinsy, which means "peritonsillar abscess." Later on the diagnosis was changed to "cynanche trachealis," an indefinite medical term of the time for a severe sore throat involving the voice box, in which the inflammatory swelling of the vocal chords encroaches upon the breathing space. Dr. Brown suggested using the standard treatment for this condition; namely, to resort to a more copious bleeding. The young American doctor, Dick, objected. He argued, "He needs all his strength—bleeding will diminish it." He was overruled by his two senior colleagues who were supported by the good soldier, Washington. A whole quart of blood was taken this time and it was observed that the blood came "slow and thick," which was undoubtedly the effect of dehydration.

To add insult to injury, the laxative, calomel, and the emetic, tartar, were administered, weakening the patient still further. About half past four Washington gave instructions about his will, and about five o'clock he tried to sit up, but was too weak to remain upright for more than half an hour. In the course of the afternoon he appeared in great distress and pain, and frequently changed his position in bed, struggling for breath.

As a last resort Dr. Dick suggested the use of a new, revolutionary method, the only one available which could have saved the patient from slow suffocation caused by the obstruction of the larynx, tracheotomy —the surgical cutting of an opening into the windpipe below the point of obstruction. In a communication several years later Dr. Dick reasoned, "I proposed to perforate the trachea as means of prolonging life and of affording time for the removal of the obstruction to respiration in the larynx which manifestly threatened immediate dissolution."

The older colleagues refused to take a chance on their illustrious patient by using such an unproved and daring procedure, which, in the annals of medicine, had been employed in only a few instances up to this time with success. The urgent entreaties of Dr. Dick were in vain. Instead of it, the polypragmatic senior physicians continued their futile measures by applying blisters and cataplasms of wheat bran to the legs and feet of the dying patient. The process of gradual suffocation progressed inexorably until about ten minutes before the general expired, when the breathing became easier. The exhausted heart stopped beating between ten and eleven o'clock on the evening of December 14, 1799.

From the first, Washington as usual had been exceedingly pessimistic about his illness. He had made up his mind that he was going to die and did what he could to dissuade his doctors from making special efforts for him, and begged them to let him die in peace.

"I find I am going," he whispered to Colonel Lear. "My breath cannot last long. I believed from the first that the disorder would prove fatal." And a little later he repeated the same conviction to Dr. Craik: "Doctor, I die hard, but I am not afraid to go." And later when Dr. Brown came into the room: "I feel myself going; I thank you for your attention but I pray you to take no trouble for me. Let me go quietly. I cannot last long."

The exact diagnosis of Washington's last sickness is still a matter of dispute among medical historians. The most convincing study was made by Dr. W. A. Wells of Washington, D. C., in 1927. Up to that time it was believed that Washington had died from diphtheria, corresponding to the diagnosis of "croup," which Dr. Dick had suggested in retrospect. A final diagnosis cannot be made with certainty, as no clinical description of the appearance of the inflammatory process has been given, and bacteriological confirmation of a diagnosis was unknown. In spite of this lack of evidence, Dr. Wells concluded from all the known data that Washington died from a streptococcic laryngitis, an inflammatory swelling of the larynx and the vocal chords caused by a strain of virulent streptococci. We are unable to estimate how much the treatment with depleting venesections and dehydrating cathartics and emetics contributed to the fatal outcome.

A graduate of Heidelberg University, Dr. Rudolph Marx has been practicing surgery in Los Angeles since 1923. He has written a number of articles on medical history. This article is an adaptation of a chapter in a book of medical profiles on the Presidents of the United States to be published in November, 1960, by G. P. Putnam.

Harold Murdock's "THE NINETEENTH OF APRIL 1775"

Forty years ago a Boston banker suggested

that the Battle of Lexington had become a

myth, and later evidence proves him right

With introduction and comment by Arthur Bernon Tourtellot

The most accurate depiction of th

Few episodes in American history lend themselves more easily to romanticizing than the stand of the embattled patriots on Lexington Common. It has all the necessary ingredients: good American farmers shot down, virtually on their doorsteps, by bloodthirsty British troops outnumbering them fourteen to one; farmhouses burned; a civilian population involved. For six generations our desire to think well of ourselves worked on the episode, softening the hard outlines of fact with the haze of romance.

But forty years ago a voice was raised against the chorus of national self-exaltation. It belonged to a Boston banker named Harold Murdock, a descendant of the original settlers, a man of wit, of insight, of scholarly persistence in tracking down details, and of a judicious temperament. Not an academic historian, Murdock had collected his own library of books and original manuscripts, which over the years had become particularly rich in early American history and eight-

eenth-century English history and Johnsoniana. In 1910, then vice-president of the National Shawmut Bank, he was elected to resident membership in the Massachusetts Historical Society—an honor that is conferred upon only 100 living people. Six years later he read his first paper, called "Historic Doubts on Lexington," before the society. Later it was published as the first essay in his book, The Nineteenth of April 1775.

Murdock was the first fully to explore and then explode the traditional version of what had happened on that memorable day, but in the three decades since he wrote, new evidence has come to light which reinforces his skeptical, though tentative, conclusions. The significance of Murdock's achievement as a triumph of American historiography has been confirmed. "Historic Doubts," somewhat shortened but with all its major assertions intact, was reprinted for the first time since 1925 in the August, 1959, AMERICAN HERITAGE. The text is interrupted with editorial comment.—A.B.T.

battle is this engraving made just afterward by Connecticut militiaman Amos Doolittle. Minutemen show no signs of resistance.

On the 2nd of September, 1824, Lafayette was a visitor in Concord, and the Honorable Samuel Hoar took occasion to remind him, in a public address, that he stood upon the spot where "the first forcible resistance" was made to the British arms. This simple assertion proved in a measure epoch-making. A half-century had passed since the great events to which Mr. Hoar referred, but his claim for Concord roused a storm of protest in Lexington. A bitter controversy ensued, and local pride and local historians were stirred to an extent that imperilled historic truth. The Town of Lexington took official cognizance of the Concord claim, and Elias Phinney, Esq., was charged with the task of demonstrating to all impartial minds that it was at Lexington, and not at Concord, that the embattled farmer fired that far-echoing shot that heralded American independence.

To assist Phinney in his work, depositions were extracted from ten aged citizens of Lexington, some of whom, fifty years before, had attended that early morning roll-call on the Common. Those venerable men, whose comrades in 1775 had been anxious to prove the peaceful intent and behavior of the minutemen, were now summoned to lend color to quite a contradictory theory. . . . Phinney's pamphlet on the battle appeared in 1825. Concord had old men of her own, and they were summoned into the lists to support contentions put forth by the Reverend Ezra Ripley, who published his anti-Lexington tract in 1827. . . .

Two results of this controversy are worth noting: the first, a development of local interest and enthusiasm in the subject, which remains unimpaired as bitterness has waned; the second, the accumulation of a mass of questionable evidence, which in exaggerated forms has gradually become accepted as history. . . . "Tradition, legend, tune, and song" all played their

105

part in the reconstruction of the Lexington story, until the schoolboy of my generation, however dull in history, knew for facts that Revere rode into Concord before dawn with news that the regulars were out, and that Major Pitcairn stirred his whiskey in the Concord Tavern, with blood-curdling threats that would have done credit to a pirate king. . . .

By way of clarifying what I have said concerning the evolution of the Lexington story, let us refer to the accompanying illustrations, four reproduced from old prints, and one from Sandham's painting, which belongs to the Lexington Historical Society and hangs in the Town Hall. The earliest print to be examined is that of Doolittle, engraved in the fall of 1775; and it is to be noted that Pendleton, Billings, and Sandham all portray the scene from the same spot, giving the same landscape that Doolittle depicted. . . .

If you will examine our faithful reproduction of the Doolittle print, you will notice that the British are

MASSACHUSETTS HISTORICAL SOCIETY

Harold Murdock

firing by platoons and that the Lexington company is dispersing in all directions. Even the magnifying glass fails to reveal any member of that company in an attitude of resistance; no suggestion of a return fire, or even of loading. One wonders why the title was not engraved, the "massacre," instead of the "battle, of Lexington." Evidently our Connecticut soldiers felt that the facts of the case, or political expediency, justified such a treatment of the subject. Then we should glance at the reduced replica of this print, which Doolittle executed in 1832 for Barber's *History of New Haven*. There could have been no political considerations to influence him at that time. Lexington was then stoutly asserting the belligerency of her minute-men; and yet, as you will see, Doolittle varied in no detail from his conception of nearly sixty years before. It is still a massacre, perpetrated upon armed but unresisting men.

The next picture to be noted, in chronological order, is Pendleton's lithograph, executed about 1830. Pendleton had evidently given heed to the current controversy and to the Lexington depositions of 1824. The British are firing, the minute-men are dispersing, as Doolittle portrayed them, but eight devoted souls are still facing their enemies, six of whom are returning the British fire while two are loading. . . .

When we come to the Billings sketch, executed a quarter of a century later, and which was used to

adorn the first edition of Hudson's *Lexington* in 1868, we find the dispersing confined to the extreme left of the line, while the firing has been extended to a round dozen or more. The Sandham painting of 1886 throws off all restraint and departs definitely from the Doolittle idea. Here at last is a battle, indeed. Where in Sandham's spirited work is there any sign of wavering, any suggestion of dispersing? The line holds firm from end to end, while, unterrified by the running blaze of British musketry and the sight of stricken comrades, the minute men stand grimly to their work, emptying their firelocks at close range into the broad and glittering target offered by the Light Infantry. Is this a true picture of what occurred on Lexington Common, or does it violate the truth beyond the limits of poetical license? I shall have occasion to refer to this picture again, but for the moment I leave this query with you, as suggesting the basis for an historic doubt. . . .

The rivalry between Concord and Lexington for the glory of shedding the first British blood was carried to even greater extremes than Mr. Murdock alleged. As the intertown feud went on, the heroics ascribed to the minutemen became so preposterous that if their bravery should not be questioned, their sanity could be doubted. The towns refused to celebrate the centennial jointly in 1875, and President Grant, the Governor of Massachusetts, and other dignitaries were whisked back and forth between Concord and Lexington throughout the day like shuttlecocks. The result of all this was such a mishmash of fact and fancy that Mr. Murdock needed no new sources to create a radically revisionist account of what really had happened on April 19, 1775. He needed only to take a calm, cold look at the existing material.

Let me say at the outset that I am in possession of no evidence regarding my subject that has not been accessible to historians for years. It is not my purpose to laud villains or to depreciate heroes; but as all the actors who played their part at Lexington were Englishmen, and professed loyalty to the British King, I shall discuss the episode as belonging as much to English as to American history. The Tory and the Redcoat will be given a fair hearing on the stand. . . .

Earl Percy, whose principles were all of the Whig persuasion, had come over well affected toward the Province; but, before he had been in Boston two months, he was writing home: "The people here are a set of sly, artful, hypocritical rascals, cruel and cowards. I must own I cannot but despise them compleately." Captain Evelyn, a less conspicuous officer, writing to his reverend father, in 1774, declares: "You who have seen mobs, generous ones compared to these, may have some idea of the wretched situation of those who were known or suspected to be friends to the King or government of Great Britain. Our arrival has in a great degree restored that liberty they have been so long deprived of, even liberty of speech and security to their persons and property, which has for years past been at the mercy of a most villainous mob." So you will see how natural it was that the army came into sufficient agreement with Mr. Samuel Adams to declare that dangers did threaten the Goddess of Liberty in the Province of Massachusetts Bay. . . .

Under the stress of local circumstances, reenforced perhaps by instructions from London, [General] Gage felt himself obliged to take some steps to assert the outraged dignity of King and Parliament. So the expedition to Concord was decided upon, and every precaution taken to ensure secrecy.

It was an arduous task, involving a practically continuous march of thirty-five miles under service conditions. The Grenadiers and Light Infantry received the necessary orders; Smith, of the 10th Regiment, was assigned to command, and Bernard, of the 23d, ordered to the Grenadiers. There were more than a score of lieutenant-colonels and majors of foot eligible for the Light Infantry; and when it was learned, on the morning of the 19th of April, that Pitcairn of the Marines had gone out as the General's choice, I fancy there was approving comment in the Boston garrison. Why was Pitcairn thus honored? It is, of course, a mere matter of speculation; but, as the fateful hour approached, it is possible that the humane General became oppressed with a fear of possible bloodshed. The people were possessed with a dangerous fanatical enthusiasm, and he knew that even among his officers there was a sense of irritation, a keen desire to "have at the damned dogs." So, while perhaps it was not customary for Light Infantry to look to the Marines for commanders in the field, Gage called for Pitcairn, an officer who was not only a rigid disciplinarian, with a long and honorable record of service, but also a man whose humanity and tact had won him the love of his command, and the respect of people of all shades of political opinion in the town. . . .

And now, as we shift the scene to Lexington, let me ask if it has ever occurred to you to question the wisdom of sixty or seventy men going out and forming on the level ground of the Common, in plain sight of an advancing force of seven hundred of their enemies? . . . Captain Parker stated, in his deposition in 1775, that he ordered the militia "to meet upon the Common to consult what to do, and concluded not to be discovered nor meddle or make with said regular troops unless they should insult or molest us." How could he expect that sixty or seventy armed men,

Doolittle and Barber's 1832 print is still faithful to the facts: Parker's men are obeying Major Pitcairn's order to disperse.

But in Pendleton's drawing of 1830, fiction had already crept in: six minutemen are firing back, while two others are reloading.

It is now 1855, eighty years after the battle, and in Hammatt Billings' drawing only a few men on the left are dispersing.

Fiction finally triumphs: Henry Sandham's 1886 painting shows a firm and defiant line of patriots making a genuine fight of it.

grouped between the meeting-house and the Buckman Tavern, should fail of discovery by troops passing along the road but a few steps away; and how could he imagine that these troops would ignore them, standing as they did with shotted arms and in a posture of war?

Captain Parker was a soldier of experience, and yet he chose a post for observation and consultation where his men would be almost brushed by the scarlet trappings of the passing enemy. Had the village been fired, had women and children stood in danger of outrage and death at the hands of a brutal soldiery, I imagine that every Lexington man would have died in defence of his home and fireside; but no outrage or insult had been reported as attending the British march; high land and thick woods, admirable spots for observation and consultation, were close at hand; and yet Parker and his men stood quietly by the wayside, inviting insult and molestation.

Has it ever occurred to you that Parker acted under orders; that the post he took was not of his choosing? Samuel Adams, the great agitator, had been a guest at Parson Clark's for days, and he was the dynamo that kept the revolutionary machinery in motion. The blood shed by Preston's men in [the Boston Massacre] had been ably used by Adams to solidify the popular cause; and now did he feel that the time had come to draw once more the British fire? It is perhaps a foolish query, but it is engendered by an historic doubt. I cannot satisfy my mind that Parker was the responsible agent in the affair. At all events, it was a group of brave men that gathered with the Lexington captain on the Green that morning, the first flush of dawn lighting their bronzed faces as they stood looking squarely into the face of death.

There was more to Mr. Murdock's wild surmise, that the decision of some 40 minutemen to make a stand before some 700 British regulars was not a military one, than he supposed. Later study of the papers of the Reverend Jonas Clark, brilliant minister of the Lexington church, at whose house Hancock and Samuel Adams had been staying for a month during the session of the Provincial Congress, reveals that Clark was the undisputed political leader of Lexington. Examination of the papers of General Thomas Gage, brought to the United States in 1930, gives further forceful circumstantial evidence to support Mr. Murdock's theory. In the Gage papers, now at the University of Michigan, are the traitorous letters of Dr. Benjamin Church, a member of the Provincial Congress, to General Gage, not only reporting details of the sessions but diagnosing with thoroughness and accuracy the moods of the members and the basic problems facing the patriots. The thrust of the Church documents is that the patriot cause was slipping, that support for it was weak, and that Sam Adams needed a new crop of martyrs—an episode like the splendidly exploited Boston Massacre.

Now, add to this the further information that Captain Parker first put the problem to his minutemen at midnight and that they "concluded not to be discovered, nor meddle or make with said regular troops." But the company did exactly the opposite three hours later—after Hancock, Adams, and probably Clark had consulted with Captain Parker. The reversal in Parker's very sound military decision was obviously a political one. And the result was exactly what the experienced strategist Samuel Adams would have anticipated: an immovable object, an irresistible force, somebody fired.

Since both parties stoutly maintained their innocence, it is a difficult matter to decide who fired the first shot on the 19th of April. . . .

Let us recall the witnesses for a hasty examination. Nearly fifty men of Parker's company subscribed to two blanket depositions. They declared, in effect, that the company which was gathering dispersed on the approach of the troops. "Whilst our backs were turned on the troops, we were fired on by them . . . not a gun was fired by any person in our company on the regulars to our knowledge, before they fired on us." This final clause, intimating that at some stage of the affair Lexington men did fire, should be especially noted, as the same hint is contained in nearly all the depositions. *Captain Parker* testified that, upon the sudden approach of the troops, he ordered his men "to disperse and not to fire. Immediately said troops made their appearance, and rushing furiously, fired upon and killed eight of our party without receiving any provocation therefor from us." *Smith*, a spectator, "saw the regular troops fire on the Lexington company," which was "then dispersing." There is no hint from the foregoing group of witnesses of any verbal preliminaries to the firing of the troops, or any suggestion as to whether this firing was spontaneous or the result of orders. *Tidd* and *Abbott* were spectators. They saw the body of troops "marching up to the Lexington company which was then dispersing; soon after, the regulars fired, first a few guns, which we took to be pistols from some of the regulars who were mounted on horses; and then the said regulars fired a volley or two." *Mead* and *Harrington* also state that pistol-shots from the officers prefaced the British volleys. *Robbins* says nothing of pistol-shots, but has a good ear for speech. They came "on a quick pace towards

us with three officers in their front on horseback, and on full gallop towards us, the foremost of which cried, '*Throw down your arms,* ye villains, ye rebels,' upon which said company dispersing, the foremost of the three officers ordered their men saying, 'Fire, by God, fire,' at which moment we received a very heavy and close fire from them." *Winship, . . .* a prisoner in the midst of the troops, observed an officer at the head of the troops, "flourishing his sword and with a loud voice giving the word Fire!" He says nothing of the command to disperse. *William Draper* avers that Captain Parker's company were turned from the troops, "making their escape by dispersing," when the regular troops made an huzza and rushed on. "After the huzza was made the commanding officer of said troops . . . gave the command to the troops, 'Fire, fire, damn you, fire.'" *Fessenden* testified that, being in a pasture near by, he viewed the whole proceeding from a distance of eighteen or twenty rods. He saw the three officers on horseback, and heard one of them cry out, "Disperse, you rebels, immediately," at the same time brandishing his sword three times over his head. The company immediately dispersed, while a second officer more to the rear fired a pistol. The regulars kept huzzaing till the leading officer finished brandishing his sword. He then pointed his sword toward the the militia and immediately the troops fired. *Elijah Sanderson* heard an officer say, " 'Damn them, we will have them,' and immediately the regulars shouted aloud, ran and fired upon the Lexington company." Finally, I quote *Willard,* who viewed the event from a window in the Harrington house, and who in some respects is the most satisfactory witness of the day: "The commanding officer said something, what I know not, but upon that the regulars ran till they came within about eight or nine rods of about an hundred of the militia of Lexington, . . . at which time the militia dispersed; then the officers made an huzza, and the private soldiers succeeded them; directly after this, an officer rode before the regulars to the other side of the body, and hollowed after the Militia, . . . and said, 'Lay down your arms, damn you, why don't you lay down your arms,' and that there was not a gun fired till the militia of Lexington were dispersed."

This, in effect, is the Lexington case so far as the evidence of participants and eye-witnesses is concerned. Upon it was based the report of the Provincial Congress. . . .

The evidence for the soldiers is of a different char-acter, and far less voluminous than that offered for the Province. None of it is given under oath, but it all tends to contradict the provincial charge that the troops were the aggressors at Lexington, averring that the British fire was given in return for shots that inflicted wounds upon British soldiers. . . . The most important witness in this group is Major Pitcairn. Now, what did Pitcairn say? We are fortunate in having his statement through President Stiles of Yale, as stanch a patriot as one could wish, with no disposition to whitewash the British case. "Major Pitcairn," says Stiles, "who was a good Man in a bad Cause, insisted upon it to the day of his Death, that the Colonists fired first; and that he commanded not to fire, and endeavored to stay and stop the firing after it began: But then he told this with such Circumstances as convince me that he was deceived tho' on the spot. *He does not say that he saw the Colonists fire first.* Had he said it, I would have believed him, being a man of Integrity and Honor. *He expressly says he did not see who fired first;* and yet believed the Peasants began. His account is this—that riding up to them he ordered them to disperse; which they not doing instantly, he turned about to order his Troops so to draw out as to surround and disarm them. As he turned he *saw* a Gun in a Peasant's hand from behind a Wall, *flash in the pan without going off:* and instantly or very soon 2 or 3 Guns went off by which *he found his Horse wounded* and also a man *near him wounded. These Guns he did not see,* but believing they could not come from his own people, *doubted not* and so asserted that they came from our people; and that thus they began the Attack. The Impetuosity of the King's Troops were such that a promiscuous, uncommanded, but general Fire took place, which Pitcairn could not prevent; tho' he struck his staff or Sword downwards with all Earnestness as a signal to forbear or cease firing."

Now this testimony of Pitcairn's troubled Stiles, who declared that it was a very great justification of Gage's claims; but I agree with him that it has an honest ring and meets the probabilities of the case. What would any conscientious officer have done on finding the Lexington company drawn up under arms by the roadside, at an hour when most good subjects of the King were supposed to be in bed? In the first place he might have ripped out an oath, and we have evidence to the effect that this was what Pitcairn did. Here was a pretty kettle of fish for an officer bound upon a secret mission, and who was due in Concord within the next two hours. That group of armed men created a situation that called for treatment. Bloodshed was not to be thought of, prisoners could not be

Americans harry the British as they retreat from their "ill plan'd and ill executed" march on to Lexington and Concord.

handled on a rapid march, and I imagine that the Major was not long in deciding that these foolhardy fellows must be surrounded, disarmed, and then sent about their proper business. They had been ordered to disperse, with appropriate epithets; and, according to Captain Parker, they were dispersing when the command was given. You remember that Willard testified that "the commanding officer said something, what I know not, but upon that the regulars ran till they came within 8 or 9 rods of the militia." I fancy that the "something" which Willard did not hear was Pitcairn's order to surround and disarm the company. Then followed a second order, but from another officer as Willard heard it—*"Lay down your arms, damn you, why don't you lay down your arms."* That was the crux of the whole situation. Sixty desperate men were getting away with their arms, and the regulars were behind in the race. This may have been when Sanderson heard an officer say "Damn them we will have them," referring, of course, to the arms.

The situation here becomes hopelessly involved in the confusion of pistol-shots and huzzas. Three Lexington men testify that they heard the command to fire. . . . The Provincial, with his hatred of the powers that would enslave him, and the soldier burning with long-suppressed resentment, were in close contact, and firing soon began. Perhaps a firelock in the hands of some stern fanatic first flashed in the pan; perhaps some hot-headed subaltern in scarlet did hiss out the words, "Fire, by God, fire." At all events, the volleys were British volleys, and Pitcairn came riding in, striking right and left among the levelled muskets and cursing the day that had brought the Light Infantry within the scope of his activities. . . .

Had Pitcairn known that generations of unborn Americans were to condemn him as a bloody butcher, I do not think he could have been any more chagrined or miserable than he was that day. The disgrace of it

all, his men out of hand and raging like a mob, the success of the march imperilled, perhaps war begun—this was a pretty situation for an honest Major of Marines. . . .

After the publication of Mr. Murdock's then very bold essay, some historians—including David S. Murrey (who was born in Lexington) in the American Historical Association's journal—accused him of erring on the side of too much sympathy for the position of the British. But later documentary evidences showed Mr. Murdock to be right. The complete war diary of Lieutenant Frederick Mackenzie of the Royal Welch Fusiliers, who was easily the most responsible of the junior officers of the day, came to light in the late 1920's. An extremely valuable letter from Lieutenant Colonel Smith to Major R. Donkin was found in the Gage Papers. Another letter from Lieutenant Sutherland, this one to Gage's secretary, was discovered by Allen French to have significant supplementary information. Most importantly, Major Pitcairn's field report to Gage was found and established Mr. Murdock to have been astonishingly accurate in his analysis of the character, the role, and the feelings of Major Pitcairn—except that Pitcairn was specific in reporting that the firing started when a minuteman's musket flashed in the pan, and shots followed from other minutemen not on the Common. Another British account of the episode, also discovered after Mr. Murdock's essay, was that of Ensign Jeremy Lister of the Tenth Regiment. He agrees with Pitcairn that the Americans fired first. Who fired first still remains a mystery, but the view of the affair held by the British military men as reconstructed by Mr. Murdock has been solidly confirmed by these later evidences.

That the Lexington company, as a company, did not fire upon the Light Infantry on the Common is, I believe, as clearly proved as any historical fact need be; that certain individuals belonging to the company, or numbered among the spectators, did, before or after the British attack, discharge their pieces, is also clear. The British were subject to the political temptation of magnifying their losses at this point, but all they claim is that a private soldier was wounded, and that Major Pitcairn's horse was struck in two places. Now it is clear that this wounded soldier tramped on with his company to Concord, while Pitcairn's horse not only carried him through the morning, but, somewhere about one o'clock, he was still so antic that he unseated his portly rider and ran snorting into the enemy's lines, with that brace of pistols which are now among the most cherished possessions of the Lexington Historical Society. From these facts, I conclude that the injuries sustained by the British on the Common were of the order known as flesh wounds—either glancing scratches, or contusions inflicted by spent balls fired from distances almost out of range. No Lexington historian has ever contended that Parker's men were deficient in the knowledge and handling of firearms, or that they were bad shots. Had they disobeyed the order to disperse, and conducted themselves as they are represented in Sandham's painting, it is certain that Pitcairn's advance companies would have been torn to shreds, and the hands that signed the depositions of 1775 would all have been clenched in death.

The present version of the Lexington story has been hallowed by long usage, and so it is a matter for some regret that Phinney in 1825 should have been induced to strive against such odds, to prove that this man or that let fly "the guts of his gun," and that British blood shed by Parker's marksmen did in the early April dawn anoint the sacred soil of Lexington. It is the more regrettable because unnecessary, the glory and fair fame of Lexington resting securely upon a sound and impressive basis of achievement. . . .

It is a singular fact that the imagination of no great artist has been stirred to portray the glory of Lexington's great day in any fashion that does not involve those few moments of tragic confusion on the Common. . . . Why could not Sandham, in choosing his subject, have turned the hands of the clock back one short half-hour? I can see a picture in the gray of the early morning, the first tinge of dawn flushing the cloudless east, the flicker of guttering tapers, or the dull glow of the taproom fire shining dimly through windows in the Buckman Tavern. The thin line is forming, and dusky groups are moving across the Green, to take their accustomed places. All is silence. The rolling drum has ceased its warning, the last echo of the belfry's brazen voice has died away; and then through the stillness we seem to hear the rhythmic footfall of marching feet. The King's troops are at hand; and as we look into the depths of the gray picture, and mark that devoted band standing steadfast by the church, we feel that here is a faithful portrayal of a strangely impressive historic fact. . . .

"Historic Doubts on Lexington" marked the end of the romantic, insipid view of the origin of hostilities in the war of the American Revolution. To most historians and to other commentators, it was a welcome relief, coming as it did during the almost irresponsible nationalism of the 1920's. In The Saturday Review of Literature, *the Murdock essay was "prayerfully recommended to over-zealous patriotic societies and the begetters of 'pure history' laws." Charles A. Beard, then at the height of his own powers as a revisionist historian, writing in* The New Republic, *proclaimed that the essay marked, after a century and a half, the end of Anglo-American hostilities.*

Harold Murdock became the leading American authority on Hugh, Earl Percy, who commanded the brigade that Gage sent out to rescue the British companies resisted by the minutemen. He wrote two delightful antiquarian reconstructions of Lord Percy as a man. Continuing his searching probes into the local military origins of the Revolution in Massachusetts, he published, in 1927, some invaluable notes and queries on the Battle of Bunker Hill. In 1934, this banker son of a Boston clergyman died at the age of 73, having written probably the most forceful single revision of a major episode in American history.

Arthur Bernon Tourtellot has written several books, including The Charles (Rivers of America Series) *and* An Anatomy of American Politics. *He has edited the public papers of Woodrow Wilson and is the author of a study of the beginnings of the war of the American Revolution,* William Diamond's Drum, *published last year.*

MR. DOOLEY LOOKS AT HISTORY

I know histhry isn't thrue, Hinnissy, because it aint like what I see ivry day in Halsted Sthreet. If any wan comes along with a histhry iv Greece or Rome that'll show me the people fightin', gettin' dhrunk, makin' love, gettin' married, owin' the groceryman an' bein' without hard coal, I'll believe they was a Greece or Rome, but not befure. Historyans is like doctors. They are always lookin' f'r symptoms. Those av thim that writes about their own times examines th' tongue an' feels th' pulse an' makes a wrong diagnosis. Th' other kind iv histhry is a post-mortem examination. It tells ye what a counthry died iv. But I'd like to know what it lived iv.

—*Finley Peter Dunne's "Mr. Dooley"*

SKETCH BY CHARLES DANA GIBSON

AN

NARRATIVE of EVENTS,

AS THEY OCCURRED FROM TIME TO TIME,

IN THE

Revolutionary War;

WITH AN ACCOUNT OF THE BATTLES,

OF TRENTON, TRENTON-BRIDGE,

AND PRINCETON.

By J. WHITE, who was an Orderly Sergeant, in the Regt. of Artillery.

Published at the earnest request of many Young Men.

Sold at No. 206, Main-Street, Charlestown.

Joseph White was born in Weymouth, Massachusetts, and was living in Charlestown when, at 18, he enlisted in General Washington's army. Like Allen Heyn, the survivor of the Juneau *whose story appears elsewhere in this issue, he was an ordinary man thrust into the great business of war. Although cast in an earlier idiom, his "Narrative" is equally the record of highly personal adventures. Looking across the chasm of time, veterans of the last war will recognize Sergeant White, patriotic, occasionally brave, but an inveterate trader, a G.I. who could maneuver through red tape to his own advantage, no man to protest too loudly when a "featherbed" assignment proffered itself.*

For the privilege of presenting White's "Narrative" in its original form, uncorrected, AMERICAN HERITAGE *is indebted to the National Archives in Washington, which displays the original pamphlet in the New Jersey case of the Formation of the Union Exhibit. Karl L. Trever, Chief of the Exhibits and Publications Section, has tracked down the information about White and his work which appears here and in the postscript. The spelling, punctuation, and syntax are all Sergeant White's, for he printed the pamphlet himself, on his own rude press.*

The Good Soldier White

Modern G. I.'s will recognize a fellow spirit in the sergeant

who wrote this account of life in General Washington's army

I enlisted in the regiment of artillery commanded by Col. Richard Gridley, the beginning of May 1775, for 8 months, as a bombardier, in Capt. Samuel Gridley's company; but had not been very long in that capacity, before the Adjutant came to me and said, I understand that you are a good speller, I told him I could spell most any word. Why cannot you come and be my Assistant said he. . . . He said he paid five shillings per week, besides his rations, and mine would be the same, which he would pay. . . .

I consented and bought a uniform coat, of an officer, he had when he belonged to capt. Paddock's company of artillery in Boston, but not the uniform of our regiment; the button holes and hat were trimmed with gold lace.

On the evening of the 16th of June 1775, our whole army were drawn up in a circle, to attend prayers. After which, they marched off towards Bunker Hill. I had a lame hand, and they would not let me go.

I then commenced acting the adjutant. I now sat off to take general orders, to the deputy adjutant general, which I followed every morning at 10 o'clock, with all the adjutants of the army. This deputy adjutant general was a sour, crabbed old fellow; he says to me, what do you want? I told him I wanted the general orders.—What are you? said he, I am an assistant adjutant of the regiment of artillery. An assistant adjutant, said he, I never heard of such an officer. Well, set down and take them. . . .

One day the Col. sent for the adjutant, or assistant, I went to him, he told me to go to Gen. Washington's quarters, and tell him what I want; you must see him yourself. After a great deal of ceremony, I was admitted into the house. One of his aid-de-camps stood at the bottom of the stairs, (the Gen. being up chamber) he said tell me, and I will go up and tell him. I told him my orders was to see him myself. The Gen. hearing that, came to the head of the stairs, and said, "tell the young man to walk up." I did, and told my business. "Pray sir, what officer are you"? I said I was Assistant Adjutant of the regiment of artillery. "Indeed,

said he, you are very young to do that duty." I told him I was young, but was growing older every day.— He turned his face to his wife, and both smiled. He gave me my orders, and I retired.

About the middle of summer, Henry Knox, Esq. took command of the regiment, and Col. Gridley retired. I did that duty until the last of December; the time I enlisted for expired. I was a feather bed soldier all this time, and slept with the Commissary-General of military stores.

I then went to Capt. Perkins, and with him I engaged to do the duty of an orderly sergeant, for the year 1776.

In March the enemy left Boston, and we were ordered to New-York. We marched to Providence, then to New-London, and there embarked for New-York.

About the middle of June, the British arrived, with about twenty thousand troops, and landed on Staten-Island, but a few miles distant. Soon afterwards, there was a conspiracy against Gen. Washington, to take his life. Many were implicated in it, but three condemned, and but one hung—one of his own guard, his name was Thomas Hickey, an Irishman. . . .

The English landed on Long-Island and defeated our troops, and kept possession of it. then Gen. Washington made all haste, to evacuate New-York. I was just recovering from a dangerous sickness, went on board a row galley * and sailed up the north river, 20 miles. Sailing up, I saw heaps of peaches, of the best kind, lying under the trees; I got the capt. to send a boat ashore and get some, which he did; I eat so many, was bad as ever, and went into a barn for the hospital. The owner of which was a quaker; after some time, went into his house to buy some milk. The quaker said, we can't sell thee any. Then I told them I would

* There was an old sea captain, whose name was Cook, enlisted in our company to do duty as a private; I told our captain, that I did not like to see such an old man stand sentry; I intend to get the men to do his duty. and they consented. I told him of it, and he was thankful. He happened to command the very galley that I went on board of, He treated me well.

milk the cows; the woman consented to let me have a pint every morning, by paying her three coppers. My health gained fast.

One morning I sat off for camp. but was so weak, had to set down every few rods, and by sunset reached Fort Washington, after travalling about 10 miles.

I now got to my old company, capt. Perkins told me, that I looked so weak, was not able to fight; that they expected to be attacked every moment. I

At Trenton: "I being weary, laid down and took a knap."

had better go to Fort Lee, to capt. Allen, so I went.

We encamped at Fort Lee a long time, and saw Fort Washington taken. The General seemed in an agony when he saw the fort surrended.

One night about 12 o'clock, I heard some body inquiring after me, I lay still, in hopes they would not find me, thinking some of the guard had deserted, that I had to go and get a new countersign. It poved to be Richard Frothingham, Esq. waggon-master of the army, Gen. Knox's right hand man. He called once or twice, I answered him: Come turn out, here is an appointment for you, said he. You are appointed commissary of military stores, of General Wayne's brigade. Here are the orders and 8 waggons load of ammunition. The orders were, that I must not deliver a single cartridge without Gen. Wayne signs the return—that I might mess with any of the officers, or by my self, and have a waiter—to draw two rations.

About a day or two after a lieutenant came for a number of cartridges, I told him he must go to Gen. Wayne, and get him to sign the return, he disputed a long time. I told him that I could not, nor would not, let him have any, unless he did. Off he sat, & not long after, the Col. came, what is the reason you did not let my lieut. have some cartridges? I told him that I could not let him, nor any body else have any, without having it signed by Gen. Wayne. I had so much trouble for two or three weeks, I resigned it.

About two or three weeks after, early one morning an express arrived, screaming "turn out! turn out! we are all surrounded, leave every thing but your blankets —you must fight your way through, or be prisoners." We were on the march in about 10 minutes, they let us march by them, leaving all the camp equipage.

As soon as we marched by them they followed us through the Jersey, to the river Delaware; here we crossed—after 2 or 3 weeks march.—The privations and

sufferings we endured, is beyond description—no tent to cover us at night—exposed to cold and rains day and night—no food of any kind but a little raw flour.

After crossing the river, we were put into the back part of a tavern; the tavern-keeper refused to take rebel money, as he called it. I went to Gen. Putnam and told him that he had every thing we wanted, but he will not take paper money, he calls it rebel money. You go and tell him, from me, that if he refuses to take our money, take what you want, without any pay —I went and told the man what the General said. Your yankee Gen. dare not give such orders, said he. I placed two men at the cellar door, as centries; let nobody whatever go down, I said. I called for a light, and two men to go down cellar with me.—We found it full of good things, a large pile of cheeses, hams of bacon, a large tub of honey, barrels of cider, and 1 do. marked cider-royal, which was very strong; also, all kinds of spirit. The owner went to the Gen. to complain. The sergeant told me, said the Gen. that you refused to take paper money. So I did, said he, I do not like your rebel money. The Gen. flew round like a top, he called for a file of men; a corporal and four men came—take this tory rascal to the main guard house.

I sent a ham of bacon, one large cheese, and a bucket full of cider-royal, to general Putnam. He asked who sent them, he told him the sergeant that he gave leave to take them. Tell him I thank him, said he.

On the afternoon of the 25th of December 1776, our whole army after marching several miles up the river Delaware, in a violent snow storm, crossed it, in order to attack a body of Hessians, posted at Trenton, under the command of Col. Rhol, who was killed in the battle. At day light, their out guard, posted about three or four miles off from their main body, turned out and gave us a fire. Our advanced guard opened from right to left, we gave them four or five cannisters of shot,

At Princeton: "I never saw men looked so furious."

following them to their main body, and displayed our columns.

The 3d shot we fired broke the axle-tree of the piece, —we stood there some time idle, they firing upon us. Col. Knox rode up and said, My brave lads, go up and take those two held pieces sword in hand.—There is a party going, you must go & join them. Capt. A. said Sergeant W. you heard what the Col. said,—you must take the whole of those that belonged to that piece, and join them. This party was commanded by Capt. Washington and Lieut. Munroe, our late President of the U. States, both of which were wounded. The party inclined to the right. I hallowed as loud as I could scream, to the men to run for their lives right up to the pieces. I was the first that reach them. They had all left it, except one man tending vent—run you dog, cried I, holding my sword over his head, he looked up and saw it, then run. We put in a cannister of shot, (they had put in the cartridge before they left it,) and fired. The battle ceased.

I took a walk over the field of battle, and my blood chill'd to see such horror and distress, blood mingling together—the dying groans, and "garments rolled in blood." The sight was too much to bear; I left it soon, and in returning I saw a field officer laying dead on the ground and his sword by him, I took it up and pulling the sheathe out of the belt, I carried it off. It was an elegant sword, and I wore it all the time I staid in the army, and part of the way home. At Hartford I met with a young officer, I sold to him for 8 dollars

Col. Knox told us to leave that piece with the broken axle-tree. This field piece was called the best in the regiment. I was determined to get it off. I hired 4 of our men and one of them had been a mate of a vessel; he contrived it and off we moved. The rear guard came on with a whole regiment. The Col. came to me and said, you had better leave that cannon, I will not take charge of it, said he. I told him I rather ran the resque of being taken, than to leave now, we had got so far. They marched on and left us. We kept marching on; here comes the enemy's light horse, said they. I looked told them they were nothing but a party of old quakers; they had handkerchiefs tyed over their hats, for there had been a snow storm all the day.

Col. Knox rode up to me, and said, Sergeant what piece is that? I told him the piece that he ordered to be left, I wanted the victory complete. You are a good fellow, said he, I will remember you, and they happened to be all the Generals, and they rode on.

After getting back to the place where we crossed, I being weary, laid down upon the snow and took a knap; the heat of my body melted the snow, and I sunk down to the ground. . . .

This victory [at Trenton] raised the drooping spirits of the American army, and string anew every nerve for our Liberty and Independence.

After staying in Pennsylvania from 26th of December 1776, to January 2d, 1777, our whole army crossed over to Trenton again, with about one half the number less than we had when we retreated over the river Delaware. . . .

The night before, a large body of malitia joined our army, and they were sent out to meet the enemy, and fight upon their retreat. As soon as they had got over the bridge, we had all our cannon placed before it, consisting of 18 or 19 pieces. The enemy came on in solid columns; we let them come on some ways, then by a signal given, we all fired together. The enemy retreated off the bridge and formed again, and we were ready for them. Our whole artillery was again discharged at them.—They retreated again and formed; they came on the third time. We loaded with cannister shot, and let them come nearer. We fired altogether again, and such destruction it made, you cannot conceive.—The bridge looked red as blood, with their killed and wounded, and their red coats. The enemy beat a retreat, and it began to grow dark.

We were dismissed for an hour or two, to pull down all the fences we could find, to build fires with them—and get some refreshment. The fires were made to deceive the enemy; to make them suppose that we were there encamped.

About 9 or 10 o'clock, orders came by whispering, (not a loud word must be spoken), to form the line and march. We took such a circuitous rout, we were all night marching from Trenton to Princeton.

Capt, Benjamin Frothingham, came to me and said, you and I must march together; we marched some ways, I being exceeding sleepy, I pitched forward several times, and recovered myself. Said he, you are the first person I ever see, sleep while marching. Do you know that you are to command that left piece to-morrow morning? I expect we shall have some hard fighting; we are going to attack Princeton, the enemy's head-quarters. I told him I could not;—I want to know where all the commissioned officers were? Whose orders is it? It is Col. Knox's, said he. I do not think that I am capable—the responsibility is too great for me;—I cannot think why he should pitch upon me; why, he remembers what you did at Trenton, said he. I began to feel my pride arising, and I said no more.

A little before we got in sight of the enemy, our whole army halted.

The captain sent me a sergeant with a bucket full of powder and rum, every man must drink a half gill. He came to me to know if I had drank any, I told him no; drink some, said he, I have, so I took a little.

We marched on a short distance, we see them all formed in a line, and ready to receive us.

We marched forward so did they. I ordered the limbers off, and to man the drag ropes—They were to the north of us, the sun shone upon them, and their arms glistened very bright, it seemed to strike an awe upon us.

The Capt: said to me, are we not nigh enough to give them a shot? I replied yes, I think so. You fire, and I will follow suit, I told the sergeant to get a strong man to take the spung. I took aim and said fire! then he did the same. Then the enemy began;—both armies advancing towards each other, firing as fast as possible,—We then loaded with cannister shot, they made a terrible squeaking noise. Both armies kept on marching towards one another, until the infantry come to use the bayonets. Our company being on the extreme left, had to face the enemy's right; consising of granadiers, highlanders, &c. their best troops.

Our left line gave way—but before I moved, saw the second come up, and Gen. Merser, who was killed, leading them. I never saw men looked so furious as they did, when running by us with their bayonets charged. The British lines were broken, and our troops followed them so close, that they could not form again. A party of them ran into the colleges, which is built of stone. After firing some cannon, they surrendered.

After the battle was over, I went into a room in the college, and locked myself in; I saw a plate of toat, a tea pot, and every thing handy for breakfast. I sat down and helped myself well.—I was very hungry, marching all night, and fighting in the morning, I felt highly refreshed; after I was done, I looked round the room, and saw an officer's coat—I went to it, and found it a new one; the paper never taken off the buttons, was plated or solid silver, I could not determine which, lined with white satin; there was a silk skirt, an elegeant one. and a pair of silk shoes, and small a gilt bible; all of which, I took.

Orders came for all the men to throw away their dirty old blankets, and take new ones.—The barrels of flour were great indeed, after filling all the waggons, they knocked the heads out of the remainder and strewed it about the ground. The women came and looked at it, but seemed afraid to meddle with it. I being nigh, told them to scoupe it up by aprons full, before the enemy come.

I had rolled a barrel to the ammunition waggon, and told the captain that I was only going to that house, pointing to it, should be back in a few minutes. I engaged a woman to bake me some cakes.

I asked the woman if she had any daughters? what do you want to know that for? said she. I told her that I was steady as a pious old deacon. How many have you? she replied two. I have got presents for both, said I, when I come again, will bring them.

I went to see how the cakes come on, and carried my presents, here mother, said I, are the presents, call your daughters. She went to the stairs and called Sally, come down, but she come part way and stopt; I went to the bottom of the stairs and said, Sally come down, here is a present for you. She came, here try this peticoat on, and if it fits you keep it. Tell your sister to come, I have got something for her. She came, I told her to take the shoes and try them on, if they fitted her, to keep them.

I went to the company and stayed some time, orders came to get ready to form the line and march in half an hour. I ran to see if the caks were done. The woman said the oven was heating, I could have some in an hours time.

The coat I sold to an officer of an rifle regiment. (The uniform answered to his all but the buttons. It belonged to the 40th regiment faced with white,) for 18$. That regiment all the commissioned officers wore red coats, faced with white.—

An express arrived and informed us, that the enemy were marching quich time after us. They supposed we were incamped up to Trenton bridge, where they saw our fires the night before; but hearing our cannon in their rear, it supprized them.—They thought it very strange that we could get by them unperceived.

They did not come to Princeton, but turned off to the right, and went to Elizabethtown, opposite their shipping.

We concluded that they got frightened, and their main body embarked and went over to Staten Island. A little while after, we received orders to march down to Elizabethtown. They had a party stationed there; as we entered one part of the town, they left the other. The Jersey was entirely free from any public enemy; but only privates ones. We had too many of them in every state. We left this town in about ten days. The British took possession of it, with a large body of troops. We left it, our main body went to a place called Bon Brook, and were stationed there all winter. Our company was stationed at a place called Chatham, four miles nearer the enemy, to watch their motions.

We had a bad time of it, for they tried to surround us every little while; if their body were large, we fired three cannon for an alarm to the main army. Some times we would be alarmed two or three times in a night. I got entirely wore out—I wanted to know of the captain, why we were not relieved. I told him I was willing to do my share of the duty, but not all. I suppose they think us the best fellows, said he.

The term of my enlistment being out, General Knox addressed the artillery in a pathetic manner to stay two months longer. Most of our regiment did.—The Capt. said to me, do perswade the men to stay two months, until the new recruits learn how to handle the cannon. Have you put down your name? said he. I said I had not made up my mind. However, I put my name down to stay until the first of March, 1777. If I had left it when my time was out, I should have escaped many dangers and sufferings I experinced that winter.

When we were at Chatham, was put into a small school house for barracks, as many as forty men; not room enough for all to lay down. I told the captain that place would not do for us. He said that we were going further back; we did about a mile. We had room plenty, being the back part of an large house. Here I staid the rest of my time.

My time I engaged for had expired, I told the captain the last day of February, that I should set out for home the next morning. I wanted him to give me a discharge, and a month's pay. Step here, said he, and take your pay. You are crazy to leave us now. Col. Knox is made Brigadier Gen. and two regiments more are to be raised, and every sergeant will have a commission. Your name is the third on the list for one. You will be at least, a captain lieutenant, and I think, a full captain, said he. I told him that I should go home; did not care about a commission.

All our officers met that evening, and gave me very flattering discharge.

I left the army and in about two weeks time marched home safe and sound.

The above was written merely to keep in memory, the great Struggle we had with Great Britain, in obtaining our Independence and Liberty!—May the Almighty continue them to us, "Till the sun grows dim with age, and nature sink in years."

Charlestown, October, 1833.

A Postscript

With his departure in 1777, Sergeant White disappears from history's sight until 1818. Then, only two weeks after President Monroe signed a pension act for Revolutionary veterans, White materializes in the pension records. On March 31, he appeared before a Massachusetts judge to file a declaration of eligibility. By May of the following year (then as now, government did not move at reckless speed), he had been certified a legitimate veteran. And he had established, as the act required, that he was in sufficiently "reduced circumstances" to deserve the $8 per month enlisted man's pension. (Officers got $20.)

The schedule he submitted of his personal property, excluding only his clothes and necessaries, is a picture of indigence. There was an old printing press, worth $20; type worth another $10; and a cutting press valued at $1—the tools of the trade at which, apparently, he was a failure. "Books and ballads" came to $5; "toys, &c." to $3; four spoons to $2. The whole pathetic total is $61.55. He was owed $18, but his debts were $11.50. The judge who forwarded this document to the War Department added his comment that "A decrepit soldier 63 years old can not do much at any labor." White got the pension.

General Washington at Cambridge; from an old woodcut.

To early Americans

the Old Testament and its scenes,

even its speech and names,

were as familiar as their own backyard

The Garden of Eden and

Noah's Ark (1846) is a primitive masterpiece in the vast field of American Biblical art. The artist, farmer-evangelist Edward Hicks, thought painting "unworthy."

George Whitefield Preaching *shows the Great Awakening's leader as painted by John Wollaston in 1742. Founder of Calvinist Methodism, this former Anglican divine seven times toured the Colonies evangelizing, died here in 1770. "I love those," he said, "that thunder out the word."*

he Deacon's Meadow By PERRY MILLER

"Polly certainly missed her vocation when she was trained for a servant," says Miss Mehitable in Harriet Beecher Stowe's *Oldtown Folks*. "She is a born professor of theology. She is so circumstantial about all that took place at the time the angels fell, and when the covenant was made with Adam in the Garden of Eden, that I sometimes question whether she really might not have been there personally."

Mrs. Stowe published this delicious piece of cultural history in 1869, purporting to describe a New England of about 1790; actually, she was pushing back into an Eighteenth-Century setting everything she remembered (and she remembered everything) about the world of her childhood, in Litchfield, Connecticut, around 1820. In New England, but also in every intensely Protestant community within the United States which is to say, as of that date, virtually all American communities—there were innumerable Pollys. Mary Ann Willson was one, but they did not all have to be females or servants, as both Edward Hicks and Erastus Salisbury Field here make evident to us. They could all be as circumstantial about the Garden of Eden or the pit into which Joseph was thrust as about Deacon Badger's meadow probably more circumstantial. Field's painting of the Garden was hardly a work of the creative imagination: thousands of his contemporaries could recognize it as readily as we do a photograph of the Eiffel Tower.

The remarkable aspect about this sort of painting, and of such daily conversation as we find reliably recorded, is that the Biblical vision out of which these particular examples come was so predominantly, almost exclusively, confined to the Old Testament. There are hundreds of Edens, Josephs, Elijahs for every rare Crucifixion or still more rare re-creation of the Manger, while Madonnas are, of course, nonexistent. Scenes and themes from Hebrew history are so pervasive in the literature—from Captain Ahab down to Mrs. Lydia Sigourney's *Aaron on Mount Hor* —that one can only stand today in speechless amazement at what a large intimacy with the Old Testament writers could assume as a matter of course among their readers:

> *But then, as Moses raised*
> *The mystic breastplate, and that dying eye*
> *Caught the last radiance of those precious stones,*
> *By whose oracular and fearful light*
> *Jehovah had so oft his will reveal'd*
> *Unto the chosen tribes, whom Aaron loved,*
> *In all their wanderings—but whose promised land*
> *He might not look upon—he sadly laid*
> *His head upon the mountain's turfy breast,*
> *And with one prayer, half wrapp'd in stifled groans,*
> *Gave up the ghost.*

One might well suppose that Lydia Sigourney also had been there personally! Her myriad admirers had no difficulty accepting on her say-so the botanical fact that Mount Hor was "turfy."

The Old Testament is truly so omnipresent in the American culture of 1800 or 1820 that historians have as much difficulty taking cognizance of it as of the air the people breathed. But as soon as you pause to ask the reason for this preoccupation with the Old Testa-

119

ment by a people intensely concerned about securing for themselves the salvation promised in the New, you find yourself in the realm of those intangibles which are the warp and woof of history, upon which politics and even economics are comparatively surface embellishments. But the deeper irony of the situation is the fact that in these very decades which produced in folk art and in popular literature the greatest efflorescence of the Hebraic imagination, Protestant piety was turning steadily away from the Old Testament toward an ecstatic rediscovery of the New. Such poems as Mrs. Sigourney's or such panels as Mary Ann Willson's *Prodigal Son* are not harbingers of the Nineteenth Century: they are the last lingering rays from a sun that set with the Eighteenth Century. If these creations are to be properly characterized, they should be called not "primitives" but the end products of a sophisticated culture that was receding before the onslaught of a new primitivism, that of the camp meeting.

It was this revolution in Protestant piety, with its communal shouting to the Lord for a mass salvation, that gradually shifted attention away from the Old Testament. However, in a curious way, the political Revolution of 1776 delayed the change. The Great Awakening of 1740, that which George Whitefield ignited, pointed the way to a surging emotionalism that might have washed out the traditional churchly standards of doctrine and practice, but as it subsided the "Old Lights" regained so much ground that their Biblicism was still vivid enough to provide symbolic parallels to the cause of the patriots. Though we think of the Revolution as led by rationalists like Jefferson or Franklin, who based the cause on scientific nature and common sense rather than on the example of Israel, still among the masses the Hebraic analogy was at least as powerful an incentive as the declaration of inalienable rights. "My dear countrymen," begins a typical communication in the Boston *Gazette* for May 6, 1782, "my sincere wish and prayer to God is, that our Israel may be saved from the rapacious jaws of a tyrant." After the victory, in 1785, Timothy Dwight published what he conceived to be a native American epic, *The Conquest of Canaan*. This is as full of gore and battle and savage exultation as the most inveterate student of the Old Testament could desire; the hero, the "Leader," is Joshua, but the book is dedicated to "George Washington, Esquire," thus tactfully but emphatically making the point that a colossal retelling of the Jewish conquest of Canaan was in fact a narrative of Washington's conquest of America.

The fixation of colonial Protestantism upon the Old Testament—a phenomenon to be noted in every settlement—has one obvious explanation: bands of European immigrants seemed, to themselves at least, the modern equivalents of a chosen people taking possession of the promised land. It was natural, indeed inevitable, for William Bradford, looking back to the landing at Plymouth in the harsh December of 1620 and reviewing the desperate predicament, to cry out, even in his old age, "What could now sustain them but the Spirit of God and His Grace?" and then to answer his rhetorical question by quotations not from the Sermon on the Mount but by quotations from Deuteronomy and the Psalms. In 1648 Thomas Shepard had to defend the Bay Colony against the charge then being made in England by the Puritans who had stayed home and fought the Cavaliers, that the New Englanders had fled from the post of danger. Shepard went immediately to Hebrew precedent: "What shall we say of the singular providence of God bringing so many shiploads of His people, through so many dangers, as upon eagles' wings, with so much safety from year to year?" Thereupon he bolstered his thesis with attestations from Exodus and Micah.

Furthermore, the Calvinist elements among the settlers—this applies to Presbyterians in the middle colonies and even to the original pioneers of Virginia as well as to the Puritans of New England—had still a further reason to think of themselves as Israel: even before they reached these shores, their theology had been considerably recast into the terminology of the covenant. To secure a perspective on themselves and their place in universal history, they had elaborated the "federal" doctrine that the covenant made with Abraham was that Covenant of Grace which replaced the Covenant of Works that God made with Adam—that first covenant on which Miss Mehitable's Polly was so circumstantial. The covenant of Abraham had, according to this theology, extended unbroken from the children of Abraham to the present church, and was most binding on those churches that were then reforming the abuses of Antichrist. The effect was to give the migrants a deep sense of their being directly connected with the histories of Jacob, Noah and Moses.

"Thus stands the cause between God and us," Governor John Winthrop preached to the Great Migration in 1630, even before it reached the coast of Massachusetts. "We are entered into a covenant with Him for this work, we have taken out a commission; the Lord hath given us leave to draw our own articles, we have professed to enterprise these actions upon these and these ends." To make clear his meaning, the Governor invoked three passages from the Old Testament—Leviticus, I. Samuel, and Micah—and only one from Ephesians. The great crime of Roger Williams, in the eyes of the orthodox, was not so much that he advocated religious liberty but that he came to this heresy out of a previous and more shocking heresy; he denied that the covenant made with Abraham had continued unbroken down to the covenant of God with the Commonwealth of Massachusetts Bay. He repudiated the hold of the Old Testament upon the churches of Christ, with the result that the orthodox the more vigorously reaffirmed their allegiance to it. Thus from Rhode Island in 1676 could come the jibe of Benjamin Franklin's grandfather, Peter Folger:

New England they are like the Jews,
as like as like can be.

The dreadful experience of English Calvinism with the "sectaries" of the English civil wars has always to be kept in mind as the factor which sealed its Hebraism, a state of mind that would persist for another century and a half. Long after the Levellers and Anabaptists had gone, long after Roger Williams' "typology" was forgotten, the churches shuddered at the memory of these radicals. Far from London, on the frontier outpost of Concord in Massachusetts, Peter Bulkeley preached upon *The Gospel-Covenant,* his manuscript being sent home for publication in 1651, so that Englishmen could heed this American warning:

And yet now some are risen up, renewing again that vile doctrine in these days of grace, teaching us to cast aside the scriptures of the Old Testament, as if they were like a bond cancelled and out of date. O Lord, whither will our deluded hearts carry us, if thou, Lord, keepest us not in the way of thy truth!

By keeping resolutely in the way of the Lord's truth as set forth in both Testaments, but by reading the New always in the light of the more dramatic Old, American Protestants grew to regard themselves as so like the Jews that every anecdote in the tribal history seemed a part of their own recollection. They proclaimed, says Harriet Beecher Stowe, a religion of asceticism, but they would never have achieved the tremendous success of pushing the frontier steadily back or of sailing and trafficking in the seven seas had they not added to this asceticism "the spirit of the Old Testament, in which material prosperity is always spoken of as the lawful reward of piety, in which marriage is an honor, and a numerous posterity a thing to be desired." By its isolation and its homogeneity New England seemed most close to the pattern of Israel, but the archetype was almost as present to the imagination of Kentucky pioneers. Describing the migration in 1780 of his parents, James B. Finley could remark: "Like ancient Israel, who, while rebuilding the temple in troublous times, had to bear about them the weapons of war, so the ministers of the Gospel at that day were obliged to carry carnal as well as spiritual weapons."

Thus they felt a kinship with Joshua and Hiram, closer than any relationship to their cousins in Europe, and accordingly named their numerous posterity Samuel, Benjamin and Eli, Mehitable and Judith, Abraham, and even Peleg.

Consequently, by the time of the Revolution a mentality had long been sustained and perfected that made easy an identification of the new nation with the children of Abraham. This secularizing of the covenant, as it might be called, was so natural and so unconscious a maneuver that it was enacted without anyone's being particularly aware that it had happened, let alone appreciating its implications. It became, as is obvious, one of the sources, perhaps the principal one, for American exceptionalism. For a long time, well into the Nineteenth Century, the image could be constantly invoked by nationalistic writers. Thus Herman Melville, arguing in 1850 that this nation should give up the barbarous custom of flogging in its navy whether or not Britain retained it, exhorted: "Escaped from the house of bondage, Israel of old did not follow after the ways of the Egyptians." Exulting in all the proverbial intoxication of the metaphor, Melville could shamelessly assert: "We Americans are the peculiar, chosen people—the Israel of our time; we bear the ark of the liberties of the world."

Yet all during these decades from 1800 to 1850 the continuous, self-renewing revival that historians call the Second Great Awakening—the one that commenced at Cain Ridge in Kentucky, that burned over and over the farms of upstate New York and rolled over the plains of Illinois, and finally was carried by evangelists like Charles Grandison Finney and Lyman Beecher into the burgeoning cities, there to blaze fitfully as fanned by Dwight Moody and Billy Sunday—this Awakening was exciting a new sort of piety which put aside the legalistic covenant and focused the Christian life entirely on the orgy of conversion. The orthodoxy of the Seventeenth and Eighteenth Centuries was theological, logical, metaphysical; therefore it could devise and elaborate such a complex conception as the covenant. The new revival was everywhere anti-intellectual. Whether they were Methodists or Baptists or Campbellites, the motto of all these exhorters was in effect Wesley's "I know, because I feel." As one convert said of Parson John Ingersoll, "He made salvation seem so plain, so easy, I wanted to take it to my heart without delays." Few may have gone to quite such extremes as Alexander Campbell, but he was representative in so stressing the New Testament that the remaining adherents of the older Protestantism could accuse him of "throwing away the Old Testament." To generalize—not too sweepingly—one may say that by the end of the century the most popular presentations of Protestantism in this country dwelt comparatively little on the stories of Noah or the Prodigal Son, while lithographs of the Resurrection or the Supper at Emmaus drove from the walls of ordinary families and into their attics the embarrassing paintings they may have inherited from their colonial forebears.

Therefore the survival into the early Nineteenth Century of such a recalcitrant Hebraism as these "primitives" exhibit is to be found mainly in older settlements where pastoral conditions still reinforced the analogy with Israel, or where the more complex (and conservative) theology of pristine Calvinism resisted the emotionalism of the frontier and the city. Mrs. Stowe was herself one who moved with the century further and further from the intellectuality of her heritage.

Uncle Tom's Cabin was an effective book because it spoke the language of revived pietism, and Uncle Tom was made a sentimentalized Christ-figure, not an Israelite in bondage. *Oldtown Folks* is in part a bitter attack upon what she called the "tragedy" of New England life: this, she says, consisted of a "constant wrestling of thought with infinite problems which could not be avoided, and which saddened the days of almost every one who grew up under it." Yet at the same time she looked back with an irresistible nostalgia to a grandeur that had, with the softening of doctrine, been lost. And the heart of this magnificence, she explicitly realized, had been that people then lived in constant face-to-face intimacy with Hebrew literature. The dramas of the Old Testament were their own dramas, the ordeals were theirs and the triumphs.

Just as a child brought up under the shadow of a cathedral, Mrs. Stowe mused, would have his mind stocked with legends of saints and angels which he could not understand, "so this wonderful old cathedral book insensibly wrought a sort of mystical poetry into the otherwise hard and sterile life of New England." She was undoubtedly speaking out of her own experience when she had her hero remark that, "although in details relating to human crime and vice, the Old Bible is the most plain-spoken book conceivable, it never violated the chastity of a child's mind, or stimulated an improper curiosity." To her dismay, she says through her alias, she was in later years astonished to learn the real meaning of passages she had formerly

listened to "with innocent gravity." (Innocent gravity may well stand as expressing the essential charm of the illustrations for this article.) Harriet thus reveals, as no social historian can, why the colonial acceptance of the Old Testament gave way, however reluctantly, to the pragmatic pietism of the revival: she and her generation could no longer stand up to the violence in the Old Testament which their grandparents had taken in stride, not as pertaining to the record of a distant and exotic people in Palestine, but as the axiomatic premise of their own existence.

Indeed, as Harriet continues, she casts more and more light onto the world out of which these paintings came, a civilization that was steadily being transformed during her lifetime and that she could describe in 1869 as utterly vanished. The hero remarks that his grandfather's prayers were completely Hebraistic: "They spoke of Zion and Jerusalem, of the God of Israel, the God of Jacob, as much as if my grandfather had been a veritable Jew; and except for the closing phrase, 'for the sake of thy Son, our Saviour,' might all have been uttered in Palestine by a well-trained Jew in the time of David."

Henry Adams, searching at the beginning of *The Education* to indicate how remote the time in which he wrote was from the world into which, in 1838, he had been born, instinctively compared his status as an Adams to that of one "born in Jerusalem under the shadow of the Temple and circumcised in the Synagogue by his uncle the high priest, under the name of Israel Cohen." Just that real, just that tangible, just that comprehensible had the Old Testament been to the primitive American mind. Though the mood of the culture has undergone many changes since then, and no doubt will move even further from the original, still the stamp of this long period of Hebraistic imagination will always be impressed upon it. This is part of our submerged memory; from day to day we ignore it, until suddenly we are confronted with such crude but eloquent tableaux as are here reproduced, and before them, to our astonishment, we recognize our own forgotten selves.

Professor Perry Miller teaches American literature at Harvard. He is the author of Orthodoxy in Massachusetts; The Puritans *(with T. H. Johnson);* The New England Mind; Jonathan Edwards; *and* Errand into the Wilderness.

General Clinton's Dumbbell Code

Late in July, 1777, the British general John Burgoyne found himself trapped by a colonial army in the upper reaches of the Hudson; he was about to lose the Battle of Saratoga. In desperation he wrote to Sir Henry Clinton in New York, asking for reinforcements. But the only available troops, under Sir William Howe, were off in Maryland. Clinton's discouraging answer was a letter which had no apparent meaning until Burgoyne's staff fitted a prearranged dumbbell-shaped mask over it. A replica of that letter and the superimposed mask (treated as if it were semitransparent) are shown below; they appear in John Bakeless' *Turncoats, Traitors and Heroes*, published earlier this year by the J. B. Lippincott Company.

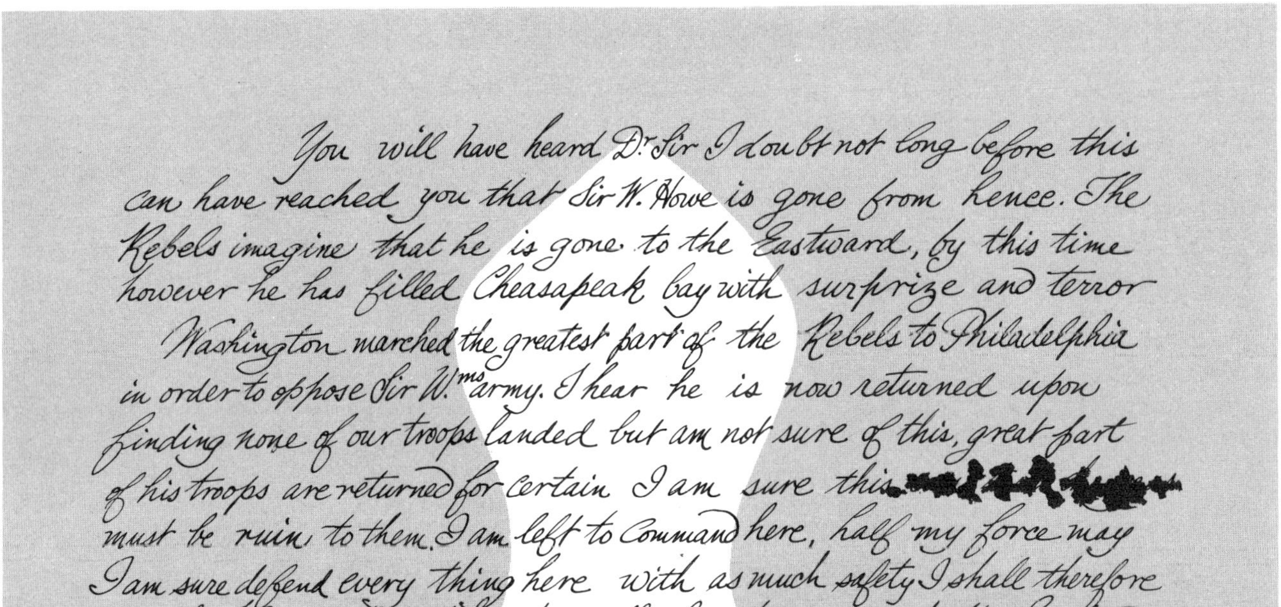

You will have heard Dr Sir I doubt not long before this can have reached you that Sir W. Howe is gone from hence. The Rebels imagine that he is gone to the Eastward, by this time however he has filled Cheasapeak bay with surprize and terror Washington marched the greatest part of the Rebels to Philadelphia in order to oppose Sir W.ms army. I hear he is now returned upon finding none of our troops landed but am not sure of this, great part of his troops are returned for certain I am sure this ▓▓▓▓▓ must be ruin to them. I am left to Command here, half my force may I am sure defend every thing here with as much safety I shall therefore send Sir W. 4 or 5 Batn. I have too small a force to invade the New England provinces, they are too weak to make any effectual efforts against me and you do not want any diversion in your favor I can therefore very well spare him 1500 men I shall try some thing certainly towards the close of the year not till then at any rate. It may be of use to inform you that report says all yields to you. I own to you I think the business will quickly be over now. Sr W.s move just at this time has been Capital Washingtons have been the worst he could take in every respect I sincerely give you much joy on your success and am with great Sincerity your hbl obt st

H C

THE ADAMS PAPERS

"Whatever you write preserve"

All that the Adamses saw they were schooled to put down and save. The

result is a collection of historical records beyond price and without peer

By L. H. BUTTERFIELD

In Philadelphia, just five days before the Virginia delegates to the Continental Congress moved a momentous resolution of independence, John Adams sat writing a letter to Mrs. Adams in Braintree, Massachusetts. The day before, he told her, it being the first day of June, he had dined with a friend. "We had Cherries, Strawberries, and green Peas in Plenty. I believe the Fruits are three Weeks earlier here than with you—indeed they are a fortnight earlier on the East, than on the West side of Delaware River. . . . The Reason is the Soil of New Jersey is a warm sand, that of Pensylvania a cold Clay. So much for Peas and Berries."

Now [he went on] for Something of more Importance. In all the Correspondencies I have maintained, during a Course of Twenty Years, at least that I have been A Writer of Letters, I never kept a Single Copy. This Negligence and Inaccuracy, has been a great Misfortune to me on many Occasions. I have now purchased a Folio Book, in the first Page of which, excepting one blank Leaff I am writing this Letter, and intend to write all my Letters to you in it from

this Time forward. This will be an Advantage to me in several Respects. In the first Place, I shall write more deliberately—in the second Place, I shall at all times be able to review what I have written. 3. I shall know how often I write. 4. I shall find out by this Means, whether any of my Letters to you miscarry.

It was really wonderful to think how many birds he could kill with this one stone! For that matter, so could Abigail. John Adams' pen scratched on:

If it were possible for me to find a Conveyance, I would send you such another blank Book as a Present, that you might begin the Practice at the same Time, for I really think that your Letters are much better worth preserving than mine. Your Daughter and Sons will very soon write so good Hands that they will copy the Letters for you from your Book, which will improve them, at the same Time that it relieves you.

John Adams' purchase of this book was, I believe, the first conscious act toward the making and preserving of a matchless family archive. Adams was aware that he, like his country, was on the threshold of great events. They had better be recorded as fully and accurately as possible. Acting on this conviction, he made, later this same month, the earliest copy of Jefferson's draft of the Declaration of Independence and sent it home soon afterward, thus providing scholars of the present century with invaluable evidence on the early stages of the composition of that celebrated document. Upon his arrival in Paris in the

Following his diplomatic mission to England during the Civil War, Charles Francis Adams built the Stone Library at Quincy as a fireproof repository for the family records. Here they remained from 1870 to 1905, when they were moved to the Massachusetts Historical Society in Boston. The library and its portrait of President John Adams, along with the Old House at Quincy, were given to the government in 1946.

spring of 1778, Adams was horrified by the offhand way in which his fellow commissioner Franklin had been conducting public business. "There never was before I came," he wrote, "a minute Book, a Letter Book, or an Account Book; or, if there had been Mr. Deane and Dr. Franklin had concealed them from Mr. Lee, and they were no where to be found. It was utterly impossible to acquire any clear Idea of our Affairs. I was now determined to procure some blank books, and to apply myself with Diligence to Business." The product of this diligence is an assemblage of records relating to the financing of the war and the negotiating of peace, still preserved in the Adams Papers, second in importance only to the official records of the Continental Congress, now in the National Archives.

We take you now, as the broadcasters say, to Ghent, some three decades later. Another Adams is now representing his country in another peace negotiation every bit as delicate and difficult as that of the 1780's, for in this case the enemy, instead of having been brought to her knees, is winning victory after victory over France, and the very city in which the American and British commissioners are meeting is garrisoned with Wellington's red-coated veterans. In no hurry to take care of so minor a matter as the war with the United States, the British government is letting the American commissioners cool their heels. This may be all very well for his colleagues, but John Quincy Adams, as usual, is busy.

"They sit after dinner, and drink bad wine, and smoke Cigarrs," he complains for only his diary to hear, "which neither suits my habits nor my health, and absorbs time which I cannot spare. I find it impossible even with the most rigorous economy of time, to do half the writing that I ought."

It was the most natural thing in the world to assign to a man of this temperament the bulk of the commission's paper work, and though his colleagues frequently objected to both the substance and form of his drafts, Adams had at least the compensation of being able to complain of their ingratitude. He was also able to take custody of the records of the mission. Beyond the strictly official records turned over by Adams to the Department of State, there is a mass of material on the Treaty of Ghent still in his files, awaiting full exploitation.

But of course the classic example of the family's record-keeping habits is John Quincy Adams' personal journal, a dinosaur among diaries and probably the most extensive and faithful record of its kind ever compiled. The earliest childish entries were made in 1779, when he was twelve; the last in 1848, a few weeks before the old warrior died. This is a span of seventy years, and during sixty of those years there are virtually no breaks whatever in the daily entries.

Adams complained bitterly about this self-imposed burden, saying that his effort to keep the diary up to date was "like the race of a man with a wooden leg after a horse," and the net result "a multiplication of books to no end and without end." Time and again he reproached himself for spending so much time on it, observing that he might have accomplished something really worthwhile in science or in literature if he had not devoted so much of his life to journalizing. Just the opposite of ordinary diarists, he would resolve that he would *not* write so fully and faithfully hereafter—and then would go on and write longer entries than ever.

One of the most graphic passages in the whole record occurs in August, 1817, when Adams was in New York with his family on the way from Washington to Quincy. Up at dawn to write his stint on the events of the day before, he totally forgot himself until, a few minutes before 7 o'clock, the boys knocked on his door to tell him if he did not hurry they would all miss the steamboat for New Haven. They missed it. In the spring of 1840, when Adams was approaching 73, he tripped on some matting newly laid on the floor of the House chamber, fell heavily, and dislocated his right shoulder. The first attempt to reset it was unsuccessful; he was then taken out of the House and physicians were summoned to reset the bone. Next day he reported that he had had "rather an uneasy night" and that his arm was in a sling. "I write against the kindest remonstrances of my family, and attended the morning sitting of the House against those of both my doctors." The point was that there was business afoot that needed his attention. Someone might slip something over on him, and on the country, if he were not at his post of duty.

Charles Francis Adams did not quite maintain the pace his father had set. One reason is that the son was drawn slowly and reluctantly into public life rather than early and eagerly. And so, though he began to keep a journal while in his teens, for a long time he had less to record in it than his father had had during the corresponding period in his life. Still, Charles Francis Adams became a highly conscientious maker and keeper of records. He was tidier about it, too, because he seems to have been born with a talent and taste for archival housekeeping. During intervals in his public service he spent, all told, a good many years in this kind of work. Toward the close of his life he wondered whether the effort had been worthwhile. In 1876, almost a hundred years after John Adams had made the first entries in his new letterbook, his grandson recorded in his diary a day's work in his library, gathering up materials for binding and so on, and then added gloomily:

Yet it often occurs to me whether all my labor will prove of any use. The continuation of families is so uncertain, and the changes of habitation so much depend on the growth of the neighborhood that it is idle to expect permanency. This is the only large house left from the early part of the last century, excepting that occupied by Mr. Butler, and this has only been occupied by our family less than ninety years.

At the Old House in Quincy (occupied by Adamses for a mere ninety years or so), the process of accumulation was now nearly complete. But a whole generation of tireless scribblers was just coming on the stage. Three of the four sons of Charles Francis were active publicists, reviewers, and lecturers; Henry only for a time, but his brothers Charles Francis II and Brooks throughout their lives. Being Adamses, they had to instruct the public how to think and act on a great variety of topics. Ultimately much of what they wrote was added to the collection of family manuscripts and swelled it by some thousands of letters and other papers. Henry came to think that everybody in the family had written far too much. "Thanks entirely to the family habit of writing," he remarked in a letter to Brooks in 1900, "we exist in the public mind only as a typical expression of disagreeable qualities. Our dogmatism is certainly odious, but it was not extravagant until we made it a record."

The creation of this great family archive had resulted from a unique combination of opportunity, talent, and training. From that August day in 1774, when John Adams rode off from Braintree to attend the first Continental Congress, the Adamses displayed a kind of genius for being in interesting places at interesting moments. Their collective memory embraced the Bunker Hill battle, the voting of independence, the making of two major peace treaties, two residences in the White House (including the very first), *Te Deums* in St. Petersburg for Russian victories over Napoleon, glimpses of Napoleon himself during the Hundred Days, the framing of the Monroe Doctrine, the glorious fight that defeated the southern "gag rule" and preserved the right of popular petition in the thirties and forties, the excitements of the Free Soil campaign and the fugitive slave cases, the great "secession winter," London during the blockade and intervention crises in the 1860's, Antietam, Gettysburg, the fall of Richmond (with the second Charles Francis Adams leading a colored regiment into the burning city), and the successful negotiation of the *Alabama* claims at Geneva. They had known Washington, Franklin, and Lafayette, Jefferson, Madison and Monroe, Jackson and Calhoun, Clay and Webster, Lincoln, Seward and Grant, Schurz and Tilden, and pretty nearly every major European chancellor and diplomat from the Comte de Vergennes to Lord Bryce, many of them on intimate terms.

All that the Adamses saw they were schooled from childhood to put down. To two young grandsons who were about to sail from Boston to join their parents in England in 1815, John Adams wrote:

I wish you to have each a Pencil Book, always in your Pockett, by which you minute on the Spot any remarkable thing you may see or hear. A pocket Inkhorn, any cheap Thing of the kind, and a sheet or two of paper, ought always to be about you. A Journal, a Diary is indispensible. "Studium Sine Calamo, Somnium." Without a minute Diary, your Travels, will be no better than the flights of Birds, through the Air. They will leave no trace behind them. Whatever you write preserve. I have burned Bushells of my Silly notes, in fits of Impatience and humiliation, which I would now give anything to recover. "These fair Creatures are thyself." And would be more useful and influential in Self Examination than all the Sermons of the Clergy.

And so it went from one generation to another, the very children themselves in their various points of vantage in the capitals of Europe addressing one another and their elders, sometimes in numbered series of dispatches that remain in the family files with careful endorsements indicating the dates of receipt and reply. It was obviously a heavy literary responsibility to be born into this family, but very few of the children shirked it.

An equally important responsibility was how to care for the mounting accumulation of papers. Before John and Abigail Adams returned from Europe in 1788 they had purchased a handsome country seat on the road between Milton and Braintree. Disappointed to find it was less commodious than they had remembered, they had to improvise library and muniment rooms in a tenant house that stood close behind the residence. Several times enlarged and revamped, and variously referred to as "the farm building" or "the office," this wooden structure continued to house most of the family's books and papers until after the Civil War. It is a wonder they survived, for there were fires or threats of fire again and again during those seventy years.

In his old age John Adams used the great airy room on the second floor of the Old House, now known as the Presidents' Study, as a combined bedroom and literary workroom. On the day he signed his will, September 27, 1819, John Adams prepared and signed a separate deed of gift by which he turned over to his son John Quincy Adams "all my Manuscript Letters, and Account Books, Letters, Journals, and Manuscript papers," contained in several trunks, a bureau, and an escritoire, each carefully described.

The old President died while his son was President in *his* turn. Not until after John Quincy Adams came back to the Old House in the summer of 1829 was he able to consider what should be done with his parents' papers and his own. During the first few months of what he then supposed would be permanent retirement, he thought seriously of building a new house with good library facilities, or at the very least a separate fireproof office. His means were not sufficient for either scheme. He made long lists of the papers, set some of the neighbors' boys to copying the fragile early diaries of John Adams, and projected a memoir of his father. He started, characteristically, by plunging into the chronicles of early New England, to provide a setting for the arrival of the first Adamses in these parts, about 1640.

He got very little further with his memoir. It was not long before a committee waited on him to ask if he would serve his district in Congress. Adams tried without much success to conceal his eagerness to accept. To the distress of his son Charles, who had distinct ideas on how ex-Presidents should comport themselves, the elder Adams showed no liking for literary and philosophical retirement, was filled with weariness at the thought of "raking over" the stale excitements of John Adams' political career, and took as much interest in current controversies, Charles noted with surprise and annoyance, "as if he was a young man." He plunged back into public service and remained there until the day of his death, for as he had once predicted, life would retire from him before he would retire from life.

Meanwhile great masses of additional correspondence and other papers accumulated in his files. He did not have time to sort the worthless from the valuable, and so he would throw away none of them, though as he ruefully remarked in December, 1842, "I have not chests and boxes and bureaus and drawers sufficient in numbers and capacity to contain them." His only hope lay in the archival and historical inclinations of his single living son. By the sixteenth article in his will, the phrasing of which he had very carefully thought out, John Quincy Adams bequeathed to his son Charles Francis "my library of books, my manuscript books and papers and those of my father, . . . and I recommend to my said son . . . , as soon as he shall find it suit his own convenience, to cause a building to be erected, made fire-proof, in which to keep the said library, books, documents and manuscripts safe." He added a hope that "as long as may be practicable" the books and manuscripts would be kept together as a single collection and in the possession of the family.

Charles Francis Adams moved immediately to carry out his father's wishes. He loved history more than he did politics and diplomacy, but they kept interrupting him—and, of course, adding to the bulk of the papers he had to care for. Not until after his seven-year mission in England could he go ahead with his long delayed plans for a fireproof library to replace the old wooden farm or office building. He engaged Edward Clarke Cabot (best known for having designed the Boston Athenaeum) as architect, and in April, 1869, they selected a site just west of the mansion and on the edge of the garden. By the fall of 1870 the new building of Quincy granite, with its tile floor, lofty tiers of bookshelves, and mezzanine gallery, was complete. Its owner had scarcely arranged his books and papers ready for use before being obliged to take off for Europe once more to represent the United States in the Geneva arbitration proceedings of 1871-72.

The provision for the family books and records in Charles Francis Adams' will extended his father's and grandfather's wishes regarding them. Charles Francis left his "papers, manuscripts and printed books . . . to such of my four sons as may survive me, and the survivors and survivor of them, in trust," to be kept together in the Stone Library as long as "any of my male descendants bearing the family name shall continue to reside upon the said mansion house estate."

The custodial responsibility now devolved on four brothers, all of them gifted but all strikingly different in temperament. The handling of the extensive family real estate and other assets, also left undivided, was a relatively easy task, for there were solid Bostonian precedents for this sort of thing, and good financial advice could be had for the hiring. But what precedents were there for administering a private collection of papers including those of two Presidents and three ministers to the Court of St. James's? More by accident than by inclination, perhaps, it was Henry, the professional historian in the family, who first gave attention to the problem. During the summers from 1887 to 1889 he was writing and proofreading his *History of the United States* in the Stone Library at Quincy, not because he enjoyed life there, but because he had a job to finish and because his widowed and ailing mother had to be cared for. As an assistant on both the *History* and the family papers, Adams retained Theodore F. Dwight, who had been librarian of the State Department and who later went on to the Boston Public Library. Surrounded by the assemblage of his forebears' diaries, Henry reread and committed to the flames his own, kept since college days, leaving, so far as I know, only the single gathering of sheets that recorded this systematic destruction. After his mother's death, in June, 1889, he wrote his friend Mrs. Cameron:

I am left here with Dwight for a solitary summer. . . . As I expect it to be the last, and am absorbed in publishing, the punishment is not severe. . . .

Apparently I am to be the last of the family to occupy this house which has been our retreat in all times of trouble for just one hundred years. I suppose if two Presidents could come back here to eat out their hearts in disappointment and disgust, one of their unknown descendants can bore himself for a single season to close up the family den. None of us want it, or will take it.

Soon afterward, Henry's brother Brooks nevertheless decided to take the Old House; Dwight left; and the family archives slumbered.

It was not that the brothers were unaware of their responsibility as custodians of a unique treasury of historical records. They were very well aware of it, but they did not know what to do about it. Henry's brothers Charles and Brooks were both historical writers, but they approached history from different directions and for very different purposes. Neither of them was likely to agree to a publishing program planned or carried out by the other.

The solution they finally hit upon was primarily a delaying action, and hardly more than that. But under the circumstances this was exactly what was needed. The establishment of the Adams Manuscript Trust in December, 1905, simply deferred the ultimate disposition of the family archives for a full generation or more. It thereby prevented any division of them among the joint owners, and the almost inevitable consequences of such a division—pilfering, weeding, and loss at worst; sale and wide dispersion at best. By consent of all the heirs of full age to the undivided estate of Charles Francis Adams, a formidable legal instrument vested in four trustees (the three surviving brothers and C. F. Adams III, son of the deceased eldest brother) the ownership and care of the historic Adams houses in Quincy, the Stone Library, and the furnishings and the literary contents. Eventually the Adams birthplaces at Penn's Hill were given to the city of Quincy, and the mansion house was given to the United States, so that after 1946 the only property remaining in the hands of the trustees was the family archives, long since removed for safekeeping to the Adams Room in the Massachusetts Historical Society.

The earliest use of the Adams manuscripts was by John Adams in preparing the rather fragmentary sketches that are collectively known as his autobiography. Written at different times between 1802 and 1807, the autobiography was an attempt to supply gaps in and amplify Adams' contemporary diary record. For this purpose it is useful, but it is also disappointing because it does not go beyond his diplomatic career into his vice-presidency and Presidency, for which, unfortunately, there are virtually no diary entries either.

John Quincy Adams thought he was going to supply this major gap by writing a substantial memoir of his father and editing a selection of his papers. The memoir got only as far as 1770 and was then dropped. The publication of the papers did not get beyond some copying work. Charles Francis Adams before long abandoned hope that his father would perform these filial tasks, but Mrs. John Quincy Adams was more persistent. And she did not mince words in pointing out to her husband the clear path of duty.

Three years ago [she wrote him in 1839] I laid before you a Letter written by you to [your] affectionate Mother, in answer to one of hers on the subject of your Fathers Papers, in which you in your strong language, promise if God spares your life, to perform this sacred duty; and will you let this Letter go down to your posterity, to show the nothingness of such promises; while you are frittering away your precious time in oft repeated observations, beneficial to no one; and wearisome to yourself?

On the back of this letter her husband meekly wrote: "Good advice." But he did not follow it.

Thus the work fell into the hands of *his* son, who fortunately found it wholly congenial. To be engaged in literary labors gave one social prestige in the Boston of that era, and young Charles Francis Adams, who was well-to-do and cared little for the drudgery of legal practice, was not averse to such prestige. His work on the family papers proceeded in several distinct stages. There was the first or exploratory period, in the 1830's, culminating in publication of the two pleasant little collections of his grandmother's and his grandfather's letters. The *Letters of Mrs. Adams*

John Adams, second President of the U.S., was born at Quincy, Massachusetts, in the frame farmhouse at right; his son John Quincy, sixth President, in the "salt-box" at left. Quincy now maintains both houses as historic monuments.

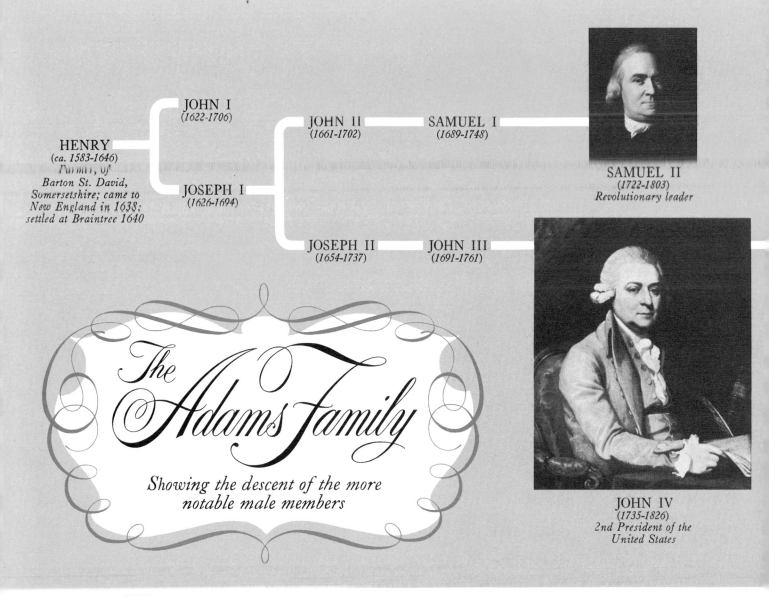

The Adams Family

Showing the descent of the more notable male members

HENRY
(ca. 1583-1646)
Farmer, of Barton St. David, Somersetshire; came to New England in 1638; settled at Braintree 1640

JOHN I
(1622-1706)

JOSEPH I
(1626-1694)

JOHN II
(1661-1702)

JOSEPH II
(1654-1737)

SAMUEL I
(1689-1748)

JOHN III
(1691-1761)

SAMUEL II
(1722-1803)
Revolutionary leader

JOHN IV
(1735-1826)
2nd President of the United States

(1840) met with a phenomenal and unexpected success. To us there can be no cause for surprise in this, since it has long been recognized that Abigail Adams was one of the most charming and spirited commentators on the life around her who ever put pen to paper.

The family editor shrewdly capitalized upon this success by promptly bringing out a matching collection of *Letters of John Adams, Addressed to His Wife* (1841)—a wish having been expressed, as the preface genteelly put it, "that the mode and degree in which the affection and sensibility of the lady were returned should be shown." In other words, the editor was now enabled to present to the public for the first time that amiable side of old John Adams that only his family and intimates had known. But the editor was also breaking new ground in a general as well as in a particular way. His preface contains a statement of editorial principles so far in advance of those current in an age when myths were forming round the leading names of the American Revolution, and it remains so basically sound even today, that it should be much more widely known.

Very early in the period of the Editor's labor [Adams wrote] a grave question sprung up for his decision, how far he had a right to use his judgment in altering or omitting such portions of these papers as might for various reasons appear to him to be unsuitable for publication. . . . There were some passages which, although well enough when considered as written in the careless way of confidential correspondence, yet looked too trifling for a grave character when publication was in question. Others presented him as holding opinions upon various subjects which clash with the fashionable sentiments of the present day and with the prevailing political dogmas of the sovereign majority in the United States. And still others contain reflections upon individuals which might by possibility . . . offend the feelings of sensitive descendants or friends. . . . Yet, however strong these arguments appeared, obstacles of a very serious nature presented themselves to the performance of the duty which

ABIGAIL (SMITH)
(1765-1813)

THOMAS BOYLSTON
(1772-1832)

CHARLES
(1770-1800)

JOHN QUINCY I
(1767-1848)
6th President of the
United States

GEORGE
WASHINGTON
(1801-1829)

JOHN V
(1803-1834)

CHARLES FRANCIS I
(1807-1886)
U.S. Minister at London,
1861-1868

ARTHUR
(1841-1846)

LOUISA CATHERINE
(KUHN)
(1831-1870)

MARY (QUINCY)
(1845-1928)

HENRY
(1838-1918)
Writer and historian

BROOKS
(1848-1927)
Writer and historian

CHARLES FRANCIS II
(1835-1915)
Railroad executive and historian

JOHN QUINCY II
(1833-1894)
Political leader and
gentleman farmer

CHARLES FRANCIS III
(1866-1954)
Banker, yachtsman,
Secretary of the Navy,
1929-1933

they recommended. In the first place it is a matter of doubt to the Editor how far any person, by virtue of a self-constituted office, has a right to alter and modify the language of another so as to make him appear before the public as saying more or less than he really thought. Secondly, admitting such a right to exist in its full extent, the exercise of it, to any great degree, appears to be of questionable expediency. For however it may effect the introduction of a tolerable degree of uniformity in literature this benefit can be gained only at the expense of all its vitality. The evils attending it appear to be of two kinds. The first, that it inevitably makes the character and opinions of an Editor the standard for judging those of the writer, and thus confounds all ability to discriminate between them. The second, that it tempts him to too great subserviency to the popular doctrines of the existing generation at the hazard of sacrificing of what may after all be the truth. If there is one recommendation of a literary work more than any other to be prized, it is that it should present the mind of the writer in as distinct a shape and as free from all extrinsic modeling as possible.

On September 20, 1824, John Quincy Adams wandered among the tombstones of the family burial plot at Quincy musing on the past and future of his line. "Four generations, of whom very little more is known," he wrote in his Diary, *"than is recorded upon these stones. There are three succeeding generations of us now living. Pass another century, and we shall all be mouldering in the same dust, or resolved into the same elements. Who then of our posterity shall visit this yard? And what shall he read engraved upon the stones? This is known only to the Creator of all. The record may be longer. May it be of blameless lives!"*

—James Truslow Adams, *The Adams Family,* Little, Brown & Company.

Samuel Adams II, portrait by Copley, City of Boston, photograph courtesy Museum of Fine Arts; John Adams IV, portrait by Mather Brown, Boston Athenaeum, courtesy Time; John Quincy Adams I, portrait by Thomas Sully, National Gallery of Art, courtesy Time; Charles Francis Adams I, Fogg Museum of Art; Henry Adams, Massachusetts Historical Society; John Quincy Adams II, collection of his daughter, Mrs. Robert Homans; Charles Francis Adams II and Brooks Adams, Brown Brothers.

Running deliberately counter to the prevailing mode of making the founding fathers as immaculate and heroic as possible by discreet textual omissions and "improvements," Charles Francis Adams declared for fidelity to the record as written. His distinction as an editor is that he not only declared for this principle, but adhered to it with far greater consistency than other historical editors did until a much later time. Having said this, however, it is necessary to say that the second stage of his editorial labors, expended on *The Works of John Adams* (Boston, 1850–56), was much less successful than one might have hoped.

That formidable set of books, bound in black, as Zoltán Haraszti has remarked, "as if for mourning," is useful only because no substitute for it has yet been provided. It is exceedingly cluttered and confusing in plan, so that one never knows where one will find anything in it. Indeed the chances are good that the inquirer will *not* find what he is looking for, because the work is devoted so very largely to the public and official writings of John Adams, which are usually lengthy and dull, to the exclusion of his much more spirited and informative personal writings.

When Charles Francis Adams had finished with his grandfather's papers, there remained, he noted in the preface, "yet larger stores" of material in reserve for another work, "to elucidate the history of the generation immediately succeeding." But fifteen crowded years were to pass before he could get at this other great task. As finally issued from 1874 to 1877, the *Memoirs of John Quincy Adams* ran to twelve large octavo volumes. "At last, on a certain day in August, 1877," the editor's son later wrote, Charles Francis Adams "found the final volume lying on his table. The labor imposed on himself nearly forty years before in connection with his grandmother, his grandfather, and his father was completed; and, laying down the volume, he wrote: 'I am now perfectly willing to go myself. My mission is ended, and I may rest.'"

The great merit of the *Memoirs* as a monument of editing is their textual trustworthiness, so far as the text goes. The available evidence shows that Adams stuck firmly to his assertion that "Whatever does appear . . . remains just as the author wrote it." What appears, however, is very largely that which relates to the writer's role in public affairs. His private life is illustrated only by occasional passages, and these are not wholly representative, since all references to at least one tragic but extremely important event in his domestic history—the suicide of his eldest son in 1829, just when his father had suffered his grievous political defeat—are suppressed. Yet for all that, the student who must often ply the pages of nineteenth-century editions of statesmen's writings will find his respect for the editorial standards and skill of Charles Francis Adams constantly growing.

Upon Charles Francis' death, the ever-recurrent question in this family arose once more. How could father's career best be memorialized? Should there be a biography, an edition of his papers, or both? Who should write the biography, and who should edit the papers? There was an abundance of talent in the family for these tasks if only a plan could be agreed on among the brothers. The best qualified brother, Henry, shied off. He had used the family papers for a couple of projects that had briefly interested him, but though he wrote and edited important biographical and historical works on national subjects, he made surprisingly little use of these papers in any of them.

His older brother, Charles, a man of versatile talents and incredible energy, grew more deeply interested in family history as Henry grew less. During the 1890's, while managing his far-flung business enterprises and writing and speaking on an amazing variety of public issues, he studied his father's diary and other papers and projected a biography and an edition of his writings, both of them on an ambitious scale. All that he ever published was a very abridged version of the biography, as a volume in the American Statesmen series (1900). His plans exceeded even his capacity: he died in 1915 with the greater work unfinished.

But long before this, both Charles Francis II and his brother Brooks had given some attention to those papers of their grandfather that had not been used in the great edition of his *Memoirs*. Charles contributed a valuable early section of John Quincy Adams' diary, hitherto unpublished, covering his years as a law student in Newburyport, to the Massachusetts Historical Society's *Proceedings,* and it was promptly reprinted by a trade publisher. Brooks worked for some years on a biography of his grandfather, documenting it heavily with the correspondence of several generations of the family. Brother Henry's strictures on the manuscript discouraged the author from publication, and no doubt fortunately, for the biography delineated John Quincy rather too obviously, as a philosophical precursor of Brooks Adams.

The formation of the trust in 1905, and the deposit of the Adams papers in the new building of the Massachusetts Historical Society in Boston, presented a new opportunity for scholarly use of the collection—always, of course, under family oversight. Charles Francis Adams II, then president of the society, wanted to see this kind of use made of the papers, and it was he who induced Worthington C. Ford in 1909 to leave the Library of Congress and come to Boston to serve as editor of the society and consultant to the trust. Ford at once proposed to edit a large-scale collection of John Quincy Adams' writings. All three brothers promptly approved; this lifted a responsibility from their shoulders. But Henry sounded a warning:

I doubt a little [he wrote to Brooks] whether Ford quite appreciates the magnitude of the job he has planned or the difficulty of fixing a limit at Speeches and Letters. . . . The old man did nothing but write, during seventy years without stopping.

In the face of the difficulties Ford did admirably. He planned an edition in twelve volumes and produced seven, covering very selectively the years 1779 to 1823, before his work was broken off, without explanation, in 1917.

The most puzzling thing in Ford's edition is the editor's acknowledgment to the Adams brothers, not for what it says but for what it does not say. He announced his deep indebtedness to them but did not mention their connection, as trustees, with the ownership of the papers he printed. In fact, the reader never learns who owned the collection or where it was. Apparently the name of the trust, like the name of the deity in some primitive religions, was something that could not be mentioned aloud.

From the standpoint of scholarship, this was not a healthy situation. Manuscripts do not exist in a vacuum, and the printed text of a letter often raises questions in the mind of a student that can be answered only by seeing the original or the other letters and papers around it. As an expert historical investigator himself, Ford surely knew this but probably could do nothing about it. Following the death of Charles Francis Adams II in 1915, Ford's freedom of action was further curtailed; and after Brooks Adams' death, in 1927, the collection seems, in effect, to have been sealed off from him.

So it remained for many years under the trusteeship of two members of the fourth generation since President John Adams: Charles Francis Adams III (1866–1954) and Henry Adams II (1875–1951), the first of whom had been one of the original trustees and the second of whom succeeded his uncle, Brooks Adams, in 1927. Their policy of custodianship rested on an assumption that, by and large, whatever *ought to be* published from the collection *had been* published. Since it is the business of historians to make discoveries, and the trustees thought it their duty to keep discoveries from being made, intercourse between inquiring scholars and the official custodians was seldom easy.

To be sure, there were exceptions. Even before the trust was established, the use of letters written *to* members of the family by their eminent contempo-

raries had from time to time been permitted, and after its establishment this policy was continued with more or less liberality. By far the most important instance occurred near the end of the trust's fifty-year existence. In Professor Samuel F. Bemis of Yale the family at last found, and fortunately realized that it had found, the answer to its century-old question of who should write the life of John Quincy Adams. Mr. Bemis' book was an overwhelming demonstration of the riches available in the Adams family papers.

While Mr. Bemis was completing his biography, important events were occurring in the trust itself. Henry Adams II died in 1951, and two young trustees bearing the historic names of Thomas Boylston Adams and John Quincy Adams were appointed by the surviving trustee to serve with him. Not being historians themselves, but having no predisposition to distrust members of that profession, they promptly called on a group of historical scholars to advise them concerning what should be done with the family archives.

As one of the scholars called upon, I have a confession to make. I came to the Old House in Quincy on that lovely summer day in 1952 prepared to argue a case. We sat around the baize-covered table in the Stone Library where Charles Francis Adams had edited his father's *Memoirs* and Henry Adams had finished his *History of the United States*. The scent of roses, some of them growing on bushes planted by Abigail Adams on her return from London in 1788, drifted in from the garden. When the senior trustee present rose to tell us why we were there, it was at once apparent to my colleagues and me that all we were doing was breaking in an open door. The trustees had already made up their minds. They had reached a decision as historic in its way as any that their statesmen-forebears had made.

What followed is familiar from public announcements: the launching of a microfilming program, under the sponsorship of the Massachusetts Historical Society (in co-operation with the Microreproduction Service of the Massachusetts Institute of Technology libraries), to make available the entire corpus of the Adams Papers in major research libraries; the proposal by the Harvard University Press to undertake a comprehensive letter-press edition of the papers over its Belknap Press imprint; the offer of Time, Incorporated, to furnish editorial funds in return for the right to serialize selections from the edited copy in *Life;* and the setting up of the editorial office at the society late in 1954. Two years later the family trust was liquidated and the papers were deeded outright to the society.

Of its kind, the collection now known as the Adams Papers is beyond price and without peer. No such assemblage of historical records touching so many aspects of American life over so long a period—just short of three centuries (1640–1920)—has ever been created and kept together by any other family in this country. The history of practically every other collection of early statesmen's papers important enough to bear comparison makes a tragic contrast with that of the Adams Papers. Benjamin Franklin's papers were divided between two continents, largely lost, then partly recovered from a stable in Pennsylvania, a tailor's shop in London, and elsewhere. George Washington's carefully preserved official and personal archives were plundered by autograph hunters and carted about the country before they were, so far as possible, reassembled in Washington by an act of Congress that purchased them from the heirs.

As conscientious a record-keeper as any man who ever served his country, Thomas Jefferson left his incomparably complete files of papers to his family, who contrived to keep them for some time, even though they lost the rest of his estate. In 1848 Congress moved to purchase them for the nation, but in its wisdom supposed that only the "official" papers of the Virginia statesman could have historic value. The result was that a bungling sorting process went on for many years, and Jefferson's papers are now divided in two unequal shares between the Library of Congress and the Massachusetts Historical Society, with uncounted other pieces, largely due to an incredibly careless editor, scattered among half a dozen other repositories.

Nothing is more instructive than to read the debates in Congress on the proposed purchases of historical manuscripts during the middle decades of the nineteenth century, when the American people were first growing conscious of their heritage. In 1848 the papers of both Jefferson and his great colleague and antagonist Hamilton became available, and in view of sectional jealousies then prevailing, it seemed best to present the two collections together for congressional action. This strategy proved successful, but by a narrow margin, and not until after a great deal of wind had risen on Capitol Hill.

Members of the House rose to point out that the Constitution said nothing about the purchase of statesmen's papers. It was none of the federal government's business to see that such papers were safeguarded and published. If they were worth publishing, let other agencies undertake the work, but let us keep our chaste Constitution inviolate. One southern representative said he would "vote for the purchase of these papers [those of Jefferson and Hamilton] as soon as for those of anybody; but if this course was to be pursued, it would not be many years before the hundred volumes of Mr. J. Q. Adams' journal and writings and perhaps

the papers of ex-president Tyler would be purchased." (John Quincy Adams, who had been laid in an honored grave only a few months before, would have shuddered at this conjunction of his name with that of "His Accidency" John Tyler.) Adams' good friend John G. Palfrey, a member from Massachusetts and the historian of New England, immediately rose to deny "with some warmth . . . that the House would ever be asked to purchase the papers of Mr. Adams."

And so it has proved. Thanks, however, to the collective vigilance, pride, financial solvency, and wisdom of the Adams family, their representatives have been enabled to turn over to the public, and have now turned over, intact, a uniquely extensive and significant body of historical records. After the manner of Adamses, down through the republic's history, they have discharged their trust well.

Of one thing those of us who have worked with the papers are especially confident: they will unfold a great human story. In the preface to his recent biography of Gladstone, Philip Magnus mentions that Gladstone's son said of Morley's monumental life of Gladstone, published in 1903, that "luminous and interesting as are Lord Morley's pages, they do not preserve for those who did not know Mr. Gladstone, a true and complete view." The burden of his complaint was that Morley had followed the dictates of nineteenth-century taste, which forbade lifting the curtain on a great man's private life—however significant such details might be—unless to show him in a conventional pose amongst his family.

Yet today it is beyond dispute that we cannot fully comprehend a man's public conduct, to say nothing of the man himself, if we see only his public face. The job of the historian is to scrutinize all the sources available to him, including both official documents and personal records in the form of diaries and correspondence, and to sift from them every scrap of evidence bearing on the subject in hand. The Adams Papers are almost inexhaustibly rich in both these kinds of records. And by an act of unparalleled generosity they are now placed before those whose task it is to interpret the past to the present and the future.

L. H. Butterfield, editor-in-chief of the Adams Papers, read a longer form of this article to the Massachusetts Historical Society in May, 1956. The multi-volume edition of the Adams Papers now under way is a joint enterprise of the society and of the Harvard University Press, over whose Belknap Press imprint the volumes will appear. Editorial funds have been furnished to the society by Time, Inc., on behalf of Life, which will publish in serial form materials from the Adams diaries, correspondence, and other writings as they are edited.

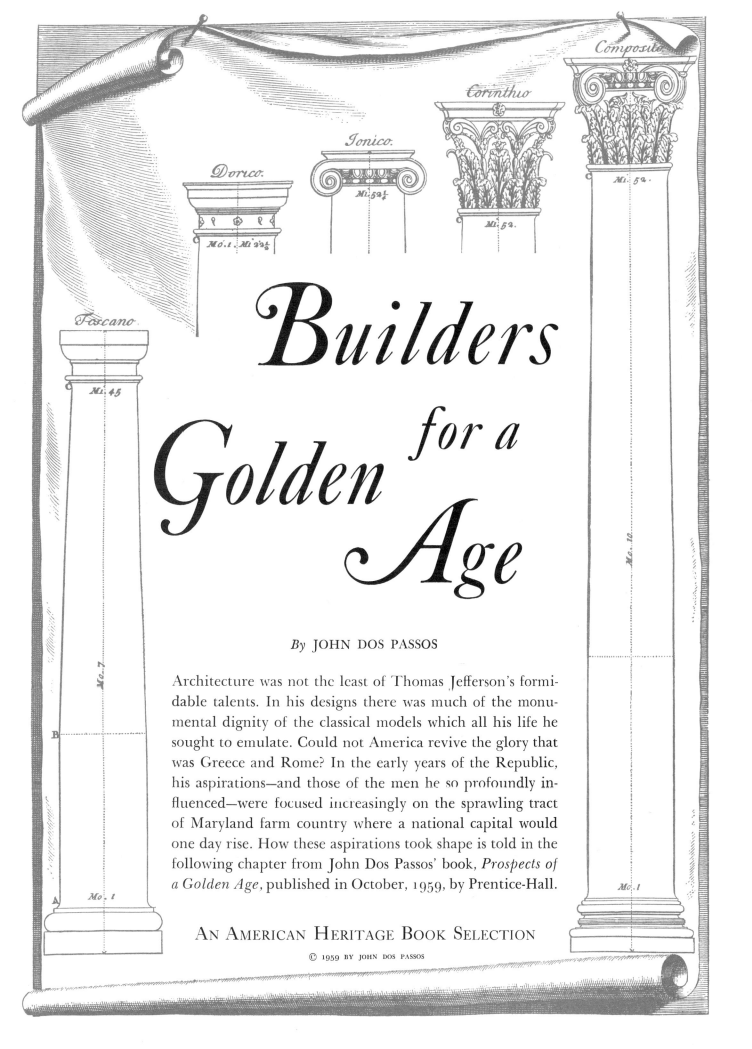

Builders for a Golden Age

By JOHN DOS PASSOS

Architecture was not the least of Thomas Jefferson's formidable talents. In his designs there was much of the monumental dignity of the classical models which all his life he sought to emulate. Could not America revive the glory that was Greece and Rome? In the early years of the Republic, his aspirations—and those of the men he so profoundly influenced—were focused increasingly on the sprawling tract of Maryland farm country where a national capital would one day rise. How these aspirations took shape is told in the following chapter from John Dos Passos' book, *Prospects of a Golden Age*, published in October, 1959, by Prentice-Hall.

AN AMERICAN HERITAGE BOOK SELECTION

Thomas Jefferson used to say that he considered architecture the most important of the arts "because it showed so much." Jefferson was responsible, more than any other single man, for the introduction into America of the Greek Revival style. As the state-builders searched the histories of the Greek and Roman republics for models for their institutions, the architects studied the classical forms so lately rediscovered by Johann Joachim Winckelmann and his school of Roman archaeologists. They wanted to put up dwelling houses and public buildings that would express the ambitions for human dignity and social order which so many of them felt. For them the style of the Greek Revival stood for those "prospects of a golden age" on which they had set their hopes for mankind.

Jefferson became one of the leading architects of his day. His influence did a great deal to form the architectural ideas of men like William Thornton and Benjamin Henry Latrobe and Robert Mills. In all his designs, from his forgotten work at Williamsburg to the final establishment of a distinctive style in the University of Virginia, he sought always proportions that would enhance the human figure.

His mind was already full of plans for building when, in 1766, during the summer of the repeal of the Stamp Act, he took time off from his law studies with George Wythe in Williamsburg to drive to Philadelphia in a two-wheel chair. The pretext was to get himself inoculated against smallpox. An eager, curious young man, he wanted to see the world. In his pocket he carried a letter from his friend Dr. George Gilmer to Dr. John Morgan, a Philadelphia physician freshly arrived from Europe.

Dr. Morgan was just the man Jefferson needed to put him in touch with everything and everybody. The young physician, already among Philadelphia's best-known, had traveled to England armed with that indispensable letter from Dr. Franklin. After some study under Dr. Fothergill in London, he had moved on to Edinburgh. There he had followed the lectures of James Watt's scientific patron, Joseph Black, on physics, and won his degree with a thesis on the nature and formation of pus, which remains one of the few medical works of the time not to be later discredited.

"Laureated" by the town fathers of Edinburgh, Dr. Morgan crossed to the Continent for the grand tour. In Rome he visited the museums and antiquities and made careful notes, which survive with a fragment of his journal to this day. He met the painter Angelica Kauffmann, and all the *cognoscenti* of Winckelmann's group. Dr. Morgan treated "Miss Angel" for some ailment, and in return she not only presented him with her portrait but painted his.

As full of enthusiasm for painting and architecture as for medicine, he collected paintings as he traveled, bought copies of Titians and Veroneses and drawings attributed to the great masters, and jotted down what he was told about the architectural proportions of the colonnades and the rules of fenestration. On his way north from Padua he went to Vicenza, visited palaces built by the great Renaissance architect, Andrea Palladio, marveled at his triumphal arch and at his magnificent reproduction in wood of a Roman theater. He procured, so he noted, "a pretty exact plate" of Palladio's theater.

Dr. Morgan arrived home bursting with the beauty of classical ruins. He settled in a fine house and unpacked his collection of paintings and, what must have been particularly interesting to Jefferson, his architectural drawings, which included a temple façade by Mansart and a plan of a country house.

As he visited Dr. Morgan's collections, undoubtedly Jefferson's soul was struck and his ideas expanded by this glimpse into the European world of fashion and science and elegance and evolving thought. Morgan's talk of the marvels of the antique background must have stirred up all Jefferson's longings to travel abroad. With the family at his Albemarle County birthplace, Shadwell, dependent on his management of the estates now that his father was dead, and his way to make as a lawyer, that was now out of the question. The notion may have started sprouting in his mind that here in America, on the shaggy hills of his own Virginia, a civilization could be built, new, separate, and superior. This was the aim to which, more ex-

FROM LEONI's *The Architecture of A. Palladio* (ca. 1715)

plicitly than any other man of his generation, he was to dedicate his life.

A civilization meant a setting. Man's setting was architecture. Jefferson was already familiar with some of the builders' manuals so much in use at the time. As early as the summer of 1763 his thoughts had turned to building himself a house of his own in Williamsburg. "No castle, though, I assure you," he wrote his college friend John Page; "only a small house which shall contain a room for myself and another for you."

Not long after Jefferson returned home from his trip up the coast, he started to build himself a house. He was already steeped in Palladio when he designed the first version of Monticello. It was typical of his radical and personal approach to everything he handled that he immediately worked his way through the superficially fashionable elements of English Palladianism and came to grips with the basic problem.

He wanted a manor house that would afford airy rooms and plenty of windows through which to look out on the big Virginia hills and the blue plain that moved him as much as music. He wanted a manor house which would combine under one roof the barns, storehouses, harness rooms, butteries, pantries, kitchens, tool sheds, stables, and carriage houses that were essential to the functioning of a plantation.

Palladio's villas were a combination of dwelling house and barn.

There must be proper covers made for everything belonging to the *Villa* in proportion to the product of the Ground and the number of Cattle and contiguous to the main house [wrote the sixteenth-century Italian (this is Leoni's translation)] that the Master may easily go everywhere sheltered, without being hindered from minding his business by either Snow or Rain or the scorching heat of the Sun. This will serve also to shelter the Wood and other numberless country provisions, which too much moisture of the Air, or the heat will spoil: besides that such Piazzas will make the Building look much greater.

When the style was adapted for the British noblemen (of whom Jefferson's schoolmaster James Maury had written that their vast annual revenue ranked them with, "nay set them above many, who, in other countries, claim the royal Style and Title"), the practical features that attracted the frugal Italians were forgotten.

Jefferson's design for Monticello went back to Palladio's practical villa, which was essentially a farmhouse flanked by sheds; and by skillful use of his hilltop managed to go Palladio one better by establishing the working part of the building in the wings built into the hill and lighted by loggias—roofed open galleries—which could be used to shelter his equipment. Their roof he used as a terrace from which to enjoy his unobstructed view.

Thus Monticello embodied in its structure the basic plan of his life, and of the lives he wanted for his friends and neighbors: a combination of practical American management of plantations large or small with the freedom enjoyed by the British noble, which warranted (to quote again from Maury's letter)

his indulging himself in the Enjoyment of that calm Retreat from the Bustle of the World, of that studious Leisure & philosophical Repose which furnish him with the happiest of Opportunities, not barely of making transient visits to, but even of fixing his Residence, within those sacred Recesses, sequestered Seats & classic Grounds which are the Muses' favorite Haunts.

Jefferson threw into the building of Monticello all his capacity for original planning and for meticulously detailed work. Whether or not he had already designed the porches at Shirley and the Randolph-Semple house at Williamsburg, as Thomas Waterman suggests in his *Mansions of Virginia,* by the time he tackled the plan

No architect influenced Jefferson more than the sixteenth-century Italian Andrea Palladio. Like Palladio, Jefferson believed that the proportions of good building were derived from the laws of nature. His own home, Monticello (right), was based on plans of practical Palladian villas, one of which is pictured at the left.

for the first version of Monticello late in the 1760's, he was enough of an architect to make innovations in his own right.

The war, public service, his beloved wife's death, the difficulties of a widower trying to raise a brood of small girls—everything took Jefferson's mind off architecture during the stormy decade that followed. It wasn't until 1785, when he was established in Paris as American minister, that he found the leisure to study the art that "showed so much."

Outside of the diplomatic grind, he had been entrusted with two commissions that gave him real pleasure to execute. One was to find a sculptor worthy of carving a statue of Washington, and the other was to furnish Virginia with plans for a new capitol.

For the sculptor he immediately picked Jean Antoine Houdon, whose seated figure of Voltaire was already famous. Houdon at 44 was undoubtedly the best sculptor in Europe. He had won the grand prize at the Beaux Arts at eighteen and hurried off to Rome and Winckelmann. After ten years of studying fragments of Roman copies of Greek fragments, through which artists were beginning to re-imagine the cool purity of the Attic style, Houdon carved a Diana so thinly draped that she caused great scandal when she was exhibited at a *salon* in the Louvre. Catherine of Russia, who was the patron of the avant-garde arts of the time, carried the naked lady off to St. Petersburg. As a result Houdon found himself with orders from all the "enlightened" European courts.

When Jefferson went to see him, he consented to leave the statues of kings unfinished and to make the hazardous voyage to America to do a head of the greatest man of the age. They agreed it was absurd to try to work from a portrait when the original was at hand at Mount Vernon.

A certain amount of republicanism already went along with a taste for the Hellenic. Attracted by George Washington's glory, Houdon agreed to do a bust for considerably less than he charged royalty, but insisted that his life must be insured at ten thousand livres for the benefit of his family in case he perished on the Atlantic. For Houdon the professional attraction of the trip was that beyond the bust he hoped to win the commission for an equestrian statue of Washington which Congress had voted. He was taken ill when the time came for him to sail, but Jefferson finally managed to pack him and a couple of his workmen off on the same ship with Dr. Franklin, who, finally released from his embassy, was being conveyed to Havre, amid the blessings and *bon voyages* of all France, in a royal litter.

In the execution of his second commission, a capitol for Virginia, Jefferson found himself embarked on the full current of the same classical revival that had helped clear Houdon's style of baroque angularities during the years he studied in Rome. Ever since Jefferson had drawn up the first bill for the removal of the Virginia capital from Williamsburg to Richmond he had been exercised about what sort of buildings would be constructed there. He had slipped into his bill the clause which he hoped he could turn into something new and fine: "said houses shall be built in a handsome manner with walls of Brick or stone, and Porticos, where the same may be convenient or ornamental."

At some early date he had already been experimenting with a tentative sketch of a plan to transform the governor's palace in Williamsburg into a temple-form building with columns in front and back. From the moment he first opened a copy of Leoni's *Palladio* he must have been taken with Palladio's drawings and measurements of the "Maison Quarrée" (he always followed Palladio's spelling of Carrée) at Nîmes.

As Jefferson pondered an architecture that would

Jefferson much admired the Maison Carrée, the Roman temple at Nîmes. Viewing it for the first time in 1787, he wrote, "Here I am . . . gazing whole hours at the Maison Quarrée [sic] like a lover at his mistress."

express the essence of the young republic, his mind settled more and more on the Maison Carrée. Now in Paris he discovered a man who had recently published a set of drawings of the Augustan temple even more carefully measured than Palladio's had been.

Charles-Louis Clérisseau was dean of the academy of painting and sculpture which had its seat in a set of apartments in the Louvre. He had returned from Rome after years of study. Under Winckelmann's influence he had measured the ruins at Nîmes, and crossed the Adriatic to Spalato on the Dalmatian coast to sketch Diocletian's gigantic palace there.

The capitol at Richmond was to plant this classical revival in the New World. Both in England and America, and in Russia too, the style in its various forms stemmed directly from Clérisseau's album of archaeological drawings.

When Jefferson went around to Clérisseau's studio, soon after arriving in Paris, the elegance and balanced strength of the Greek temple form burst on him anew. Immediately he bought Clérisseau's book on Nîmes, and engravings of Baalbek and Palmyra and of the mighty temples at Paestum which architects were barely beginning to look upon with favor.

At Clérisseau's for the first time, Jefferson found himself with the resources of a proper architect's drafting room. Modelers and draftsmen were ready to put his amateur's improvised sketches into a form usable by a contractor. He learned to work with a hard pencil. Henceforth his architectural drawings had a professional air. He bought enough co-ordinated paper in Paris to last him most of his life. In Clérisseau's portfolios he could thumb through pictures of about what had been so far unearthed of the Greek and Roman heritage. He kept coming back to the Maison Carrée. He was choosing Roman architecture at the moment when it was nearest to Greek. "We took for our model," he wrote Madison of Montpelier,

what is called the Maison Quarrée of Nîmes, one of the most beautiful if not the most beautiful & precious morsel of architecture left to us by antiquity. It was built by Caius & Lucius Caesar, & repaired by Louis XIV & has the suffrage of all the judges of architecture who have seen it, as yielding to no one of the beautiful monuments of Greece, Rome, Palmyra, & Balbec, which late travellers have communicated to us. It is very simple, but it is noble beyond expression, & would have done honor to our country, as presenting to travellers a specimen of taste in our infancy, promising much for our maturer age.

"Would have," he wrote, in the past tense, because he had received the news that the contractors appointed by the Assembly were already laying the foundations for a capitol, and was afraid that they would go ahead with the building without waiting for his plans, which Clérisseau's draftsmen were at that moment drawing up.

Clérisseau seems to have been surprised and delighted to find in this tall, angular envoy from the Virginia mountains *un vrai amateur de l'antiquité*. He furnished the archaeological information, but the plan was essentially Jefferson's. For simplicity, or perhaps because he despaired of getting Corinthian capitals properly executed in America, he changed the order of the porch to Ionic and thereby helped give the whole school of architecture that was to follow in the United States its distinctively Ionic flavor. He designed the interior chambers for the House and Senate and the conference room between, which the constitution called for. The arrangement of the windows was Jefferson's, and it was he who insisted against the Frenchman's advice on following exactly the proportions indicated by Clérisseau's own measurements of the actual temple at Nîmes.

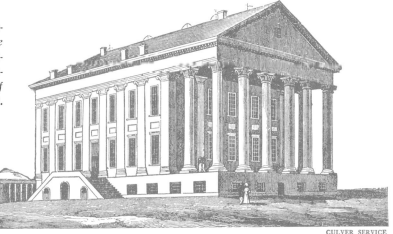

The Virginia state capitol at Richmond was a modified version of the Maison Carrée. It was not unintentional that Jefferson chose the temple form to house the machinery of American democratic government.

It is likely that Clérisseau sketched a good deal of the decorative detail. His draftsmen polished up Jefferson's drawings, and to make sure the contractors in Virginia wouldn't go wrong they made a scale model in plaster, which is still preserved in the now very much transformed state capitol in Richmond.

The drawings and the model were finally shipped off to James Monroe in Virginia, who was urged to make sure they were executed even if it meant tearing down some of the work already done. "Do my dear friend exert yourself to get the plan begun on set aside," Jefferson wrote Madison, "& that adopted which was drawn here. It was taken from a model which has been the admiration of sixteen centuries; which has been the object of as many pilgrimages as the tomb of Mahomet; which will give unrivalled honor to our State, & furnish a model whereon to form the taste of our young men."

Jefferson never quite admitted that he was the author of this first adaptation of the classical temple form to modern uses. He tried to give the impression that he had merely made suggestions to an established European architect who had drawn up the plan. Patrick Henry was governor of Virginia, and although their correspondence was polite, rightly or wrongly Jefferson suspected that the "great whale" and his friends would oppose any project of his just because it was his.

He had reason to be uneasy because he was far in advance of the taste of his time. His design anticipated by 22 years Napoleon's rebuilding of the Church of the Madeleine in imitation of a Roman temple. Although there had been small models of temples on the great English estates, as in the gardens at Stowe, the temple form was not put to practical use in England until well along in the nineteenth century. In America, the capitol at Richmond became the prototype from which developed the style of the early republic.

In spite of the efforts of Madison and Monroe, Jefferson's original plan was changed by the commissioners in charge of construction. The pitch of the roof was altered, a bastard type of Ionic capital was used on the porch, the fluting was left off the columns, and three ugly windows were put in the pediment to give light to the attic. Even so, in its essence the transformed temple remains to this day as Jefferson planned it. From Latrobe's water color of Richmond in 1796 you can get an inkling of how elegantly the capitol with its high white porch stood guard on its hill over the clapboard houses and the log huts and the shanties and the rattletrap fences of the raw little town at the falls of the James. Monsieur Clérisseau could never have guessed how admirably, translated into wood in the years to come, the Ionic style would express the civic dignity of the republican frontier.

When Jefferson returned from Europe in 1789 his plan was, after settling his daughters with their cousins and aunts, to sail back to France to see what he was looking forward to as the glorious accomplishment of a moderate revolution. Before that he hoped

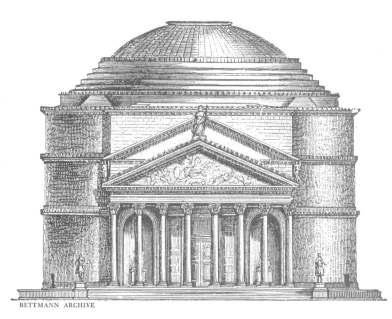

The Pantheon in Rome (left) was another classical building that inspired Jefferson. Although he had never seen that huge and well-preserved structure, with its great dome, he had studied carefully the drawings made of it by Palladio. The result was the Rotunda (right) at the University of Virginia, a building that was, if anything, more graceful than the original.

to steal a little time for rebuilding Monticello somewhat on the plan of the Hôtel de Salm he had so admired in Paris.

From his brother-in-law's home at Eppington he wrote his former private secretary William Short, whom he had left as chargé d'affaires in Paris, to describe the new buildings at Richmond. Way's new bridge across the James, carried on pontoons and boats, was 2,200 feet long; the locks on the Westham canal were completed. "Our new capitol, when the corrections are made, of which it is susceptible, will be an edifice of first rate dignity, whenever it shall be finished with the proper ornaments belonging to it (which will not be in this age) will be worthy of being exhibited alongside the most celebrated remains of antiquity, it's extreme convenience has acquired it universal approbation," he added with understandable pride. It was stirring to see that the building he had worked so hard on had already taken form in stone and mortar.

When instead of returning to Paris Jefferson accepted the post of Secretary of State, he found Congress sitting in New York in L'Enfant's remodeling of the old statehouse. The adventurous Frenchman's adaptation of the Louis Seize styles of his native Versailles to the American scene for Federal Hall, as it was called, was to be the forerunner of one trend in American building, as Jefferson's Richmond capitol was the forerunner of another. In Washington City both styles were to fuse.

Though Jefferson's political differences with George Washington multiplied as the years went on, the two men found it easy to agree on one subject. That was in the establishment of a capital city below the falls of the Potomac.

As early as his term in the Continental Congress just before he went to France, Jefferson had argued in favor of a federal capital on one of the waterways flowing into the Chesapeake. As soon as he joined Washington's administration he went to work with the same end in view. On June 20, 1790, he was writing Monroe:

It is proposed to pass an act fixing the temporary residence of 12 or 15 years at Philadelphia, and that at the end of that time it shall stand *ipso facto* & without further declaration transferred to Georgetown. In this way, there will be something to displease & something to soothe every part of the Union, but New York, which must be contented with what she has had.

Once the residence bill had passed, Jefferson felt there was no time to lose. He and the President needed no bargains to make them work together for Washington City. They were both Virginians. Always happiest when they looked to the West, they both believed the Potomac valley was the natural route to the Mississippi. Washington, as a dealer in western lands, an accomplished merchant of town lots, and an able promoter, was deeply involved in the Potomac and Ohio canal. Jefferson's vocation as an architect, his local patriotism, and his conviction that if the eastern and western states were to remain united, a cheap and easy passage through the Appalachians must be opened at once, combined to involve all the great enthusiasms of his life in the project.

When Congress adjourned in August to meet in Philadelphia in the fall, Jefferson and Madison, who was still a bachelor, traveled home together. These jaunts in Jefferson's phaeton were getting to be increasingly important to both men as their intimacy increased. They could talk as they drove. They studied the flora and fauna. They examined the buildings. They stopped at the best inns. The care with which they chose their meals did not escape the eyes of their political enemies, who would soon be accusing them of scorning their "native victuals."

They pushed on to Georgetown, where Congressman Daniel Carroll took them riding, with a cavalcade of the local landowners, over the tract of farmland and meadow that lay between Rock Creek and muddy little Goose Creek, which Jefferson already was glorifying by the name of Tiber. After dinner they rowed in a boat up to the Little Falls and admired the romantic beauty of the river. It's quite possible that, looking back from the water at the richly wooded lands of the

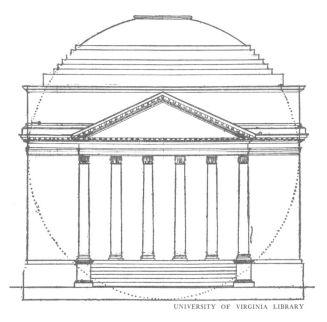

UNIVERSITY OF VIRGINIA LIBRARY

saucer-shaped depression which his imagination was already filling with the white-columned porches and the noble domes of the federal city-to-be, Jefferson was able, against the blue highlands of Washington County that hemmed it about, to count seven hills.

When they drove down to Mount Vernon, they were well primed with the lay of the land. The plan of the city was the chief subject of their conversation with Washington. The three of them seem to have agreed that the best site on the Maryland shore was somewhere between the wharves of Georgetown, at the head of navigation of the tidal estuary of the Potomac, and the Eastern Branch, for which Jefferson soon dug up the old Indian name of Anacostia. Jefferson wanted the city laid out in squares (on the plan of Babylon, he said), like Philadelphia, though he wondered whether that city's ordinance placing the houses at a certain distance from the street didn't tend to produce "a disgusting monotony." It is likely that for this conversation with Washington he sketched out the little plat that has come down to us of a gridiron of streets fronting on the creek.

Jefferson was in favor of a certain conformity of height and of a harmony of style. He had shipped home from France—now somewhere among the immense number of crates that were headed for Philadelphia—a collection of engravings of the best modern dwellings he had seen in Europe, where he felt builders and architects would be able to find hints for the style of private houses. The public buildings should be modeled on the antique, either in the spherical forms that stemmed from the domed buildings of the Romans, or the cubical that originated in the colonnaded and cunningly proportioned temples of the Greeks. The water front along the shallow Tiber should be preserved for public walks and the houses for government officials.

Washington, as he had shown in his rebuilding of Mount Vernon, had a taste for architecture himself and gloried in the spacious laying-out of grounds. The following month he himself rode round the edges of the marshes and up under the great trees on the hills between Rock Creek and the Eastern Branch to establish definitely where the limits of the city should be. He chose for the federal district a region ten miles square straddling the Potomac. The southern point of the square would include Alexandria and its wharves as far south as Hunting Creek. He hoped to find a way of taking in Bladensburg to the east. As the reporter for the *Times and Patowmack Packet* of Georgetown put it, the President "with the principal citizens of this town . . . set out to view the country adjacent to the river Patowmack in order to fix on a proper selection for the Grand Columbian Federal City."

Next day he rode over the hills toward the northern right angle of the square in the direction of Elizabeth Town (now Hagerstown), where he was received by enthusiastic citizens on horseback and saluted by a company of militia presenting arms amid the ringing of church bells. Bonfires blazed and the windows were illuminated. At a supper served to him at the tavern, the President presented the toast, "The River Potowmac. May the residence law be perpetuated and Potowmac view the Federal City."

To the Virginians it must have seemed too good to be true. Washington, never sanguine that his dearest hopes would be fulfilled, wrote of his gloomy apprehensions. Jefferson agreed with him that there was a danger that Congress might change its mind. There was no time to be lost.

As soon as he was back in his office on High Street in Philadelphia, Jefferson drew up for the President's attention a highly characteristic document that stretched Congress' vague enact-

MARYLAND HISTORICAL SOCIETY

The crudely drawn statues in Philip Hart's competitive design for a national capitol added a lively, primitive quality to a conventionally Georgian building.

ment to the point where it could be put to practical use.

Speaking of his conversations with local landowners he wrote:

. . . they were properly impressed with the idea that if the present occasion of securing the Federal seat on the Patowmack should be lost, it could never more be regained . . . & that therefore measures should be adopted to carry the residence bill into execution . . . and that the requisites were: 1st land enough to place the public buildings on; & 2ndly money enough to build them, and to erect moreover about 20 good dwelling houses . . . about as many good lodging houses, and half a dozen taverns.

He went on to suggest various methods which could be used to pay the owners for the land turned to public use without needless expenditure of public funds. He was for playing on their hopes of rising values once the city was a going concern.

Meanwhile the President was appointing a board of commissioners to superintend the work, and a surveyor was being found to lay out the boundaries of the district. As early as February 2 of the following year Jefferson wrote Andrew Ellicott, one of the ablest surveyors of the time, instructing him in professional language how to make his preliminary rough survey along the lines President Washington had decided on. A few days later, in spite of the wintry weather, Ellicott was writing back that he would soon submit a plan "which will I believe embrace every object of advantage which can be included within the ten miles square."

Ellicott had hardly started to carry his lines across the wooded hills overlooking the Potomac when Washington and Jefferson, in a fever to get sod turned for the foundations, sent frothy Major L'Enfant after him to draw a plan for the "Grand Columbian Federal City."

Pierre Charles L'Enfant arrived in America at his own expense as a volunteer to fight the British. The son of a court painter, some of whose vast seascapes and battle pieces still hang in the gray light of the royal palaces, he was brought up at Versailles. The father drew designs for the Gobelin tapestry works. The son was trained as a painter.

In America L'Enfant served with credit in the artillery, was wounded in the assault on Savannah under Colonel John Laurens, and discharged with the rank of major. Washington thought highly of him. He was thick with the leaders of the Society of the Cincinnati, who, after the war, sent him back to France to have manufactured for them from his own design the gold eagles which were their emblem.

He was a man of grandiloquent notions with a sense of scale that appealed to Washington. In the Federal Hall in New York he made the first essay toward a distinctive American style. In decoration he was a brilliant innovator, but he doesn't seem to have had the necessary training as an architect to execute his grand ideas.

As soon as he arrived he wrote Jefferson that he'd reached Georgetown in spite of the sleet and the mud, "after having travelled part of the way on foot and part on horseback leaving the broken stage behind . . . As far as I was able to judge through a thick fog I passed on many spots which appeared to me rarely beautiful and which seem to dispute with each other who [to] command." He went on in his tumultuous English:

In the most extensive prospect of the water the gradual rising of the ground from Carrollborough toward the Ferry Road, the level and extensive ground from there to the bank of the Potomack as far as Goose Creek present a situation most advantageous to run streets and prolong them on grand and far distant point of view; the water running

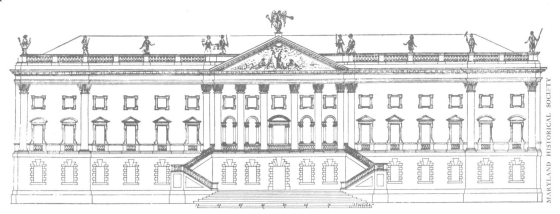

A much more sophisticated design for a capitol was submitted to the competition of 1792 by Samuel McIntire, the famous master builder of Salem, Massachusetts.

MARYLAND HISTORICAL SOCIETY

from spring to some distance into the creeks, appeared also to me possible to be conducted without much labor so as to form pounds [*sic*] for watering every part of that spot.

L'Enfant had with him Jefferson's modest sketch with its suggestion of an open mall between the President's house at one end and the house for Congress at the other. As soon as he saw Jenkins' Hill far to the east, he seized on that as a site for the Capitol, and placed the President's house about on the spot Jefferson had indicated. He immediately tripled the scale of Jefferson's sketch. Jefferson had furnished him with maps of a number of European cities, but freshest in L'Enfant's mind was the plan of Versailles. It was in Versailles that he had spent his youth. So he took Jefferson's gridiron and imposed on it the arrangement of broad avenues branching out from round points, like the claws in a goose's foot, which the royal city planners of France most likely copied from the goose-foot of streets branching out from the Piazza del Popolo in Renaissance Rome.

L'Enfant was so impressed by the grandeur of the work and with his own importance as the founder of the city that he quite lost his head. He wouldn't co-operate with the commissioners. He wouldn't explain his plans. He suddenly and without warning ordered his men to tear down a house one of the Carrolls had started to build in what L'Enfant decided was the middle of one of his favorite avenues. Before long, to the horror of Jefferson and Washington, who wanted to have the city an accomplished fact before there was too much talk about it, he had managed to flush every local vested interest so that the Georgetown people and the speculators who had laid out lots at Hamburgh on the Eastern Branch and the great tribe of Carrolls were all at sixes and sevens. There appeared a L'Enfant faction and an anti-L'Enfant faction.

He became so embroiled that although Jefferson had sent him Clérisseau's drawings for the Richmond capitol from which to study details, he never found time to prepare plans for the federal buildings. He had them in his head, he told Jefferson. "I rest satisfied the President will consider," he wrote,

that erecting houses for the accommodation of Government is not the only object, nay, not so important a one, as the encouragement to prepare buildings at those principal points, on the speedy settlement of which depends the rapid increase of the city . . . to change a wilderness into a city, to erect beautiful buildings etc. to that degree of perfection necessary to receive the seat of Government of a vast empire in the short period of time that remains to effect these objects is an undertaking vast as it is novel.

Houses for the accommodation of government Jefferson and Washington were determined to have. The foundations must be laid before some faction reared up in Congress and squelched the whole grandiose scheme. After some further urging that L'Enfant present the plans he kept talking about but never divulged, they decided to hold a competition. In March, 1792, Jefferson drew up an announcement that the commissioners would offer $500 for a suitable plan for the President's house.

When few architects appeared to take part in the competition, Jefferson submitted a drawing of his own, in which he set a skylighted dome, similar to the dome that had so intrigued him on the Paris grain market, on a version of his favorite Villa Rotonda. He signed it with the initials A.Z. and kept the secret of his authorship so close that for years the sketch, which remained among the papers of his friend Latrobe, was attributed to an Alexandria builder, Abraham Faws.

The prize was awarded to James Hoban, a young Irish immigrant who had won a fine arts medal in Dublin and been induced to come out to Charleston

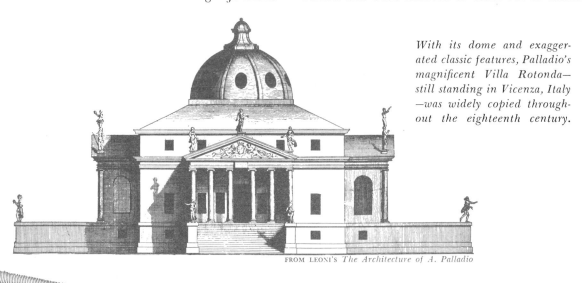

With its dome and exaggerated classic features, Palladio's magnificent Villa Rotonda— still standing in Vicenza, Italy —was widely copied throughout the eighteenth century.

FROM LEONI'S *The Architecture of A. Palladio*

to design the first South Carolina statehouse. The drawing he presented was eminently practical and had a pleasing modesty which immediately attracted Washington, and Jefferson too. Jefferson was not the man to push his own project. It was part of his gentleman's code, already quaintly archaic in his lifetime, that a gentleman didn't claim authorship of designs for a building any more than he used his own name when he wrote in the newspapers or published books. But neither was Jefferson a man to neglect making his influence felt. Much of the architectural character of the White House as it stands today depends on those later additions such as the terraces and the curved south portico which Jefferson either designed or had built under his direction.

When the time came to open the competition for the Capitol, Jefferson wrote the commissioners, as usual putting his own ideas in another man's mouth, that the President felt that instead of facing the buildings with stone of different colors as had been suggested, he would prefer them faced with brick, possibly above a stone water-table, and using stone for ornament and trim.

"The remains of antiquity in Europe," he added, "prove brick more durable than stone." He gave the exact dimensions of the flat Roman bricks. He had measured them himself. "The grain is as fine as our best earthenware." The prospectus he drafted called for a brick building, gave dimensions for a Senate chamber and a House chamber, and left about everything else to the ingenuity of the architect.

By this time news of the competition had spread through the states. The projects submitted for the Capitol showed an unexpectedly high order of invention. A great period in American building was about to begin. In all the seaport towns, merchants and ship-owners and successful sea captains were rummaging in

their strongboxes for funds to pay for mansions and public buildings of frame and brick which would express the new dignity of Americans as citizens of an independent republic.

Samuel Dobie, who had helped in the building of Jefferson's Virginia statehouse and may have known that Jefferson had a fancy for this work of Palladio's, sent in a monumental Villa Rotonda.

Samuel McIntire, already busy ornamenting sea captains' houses at Salem and Newburyport with his New England version of the style of the Adelphi, worked out a highly accomplished design in the full tradition of the late eighteenth century in England, which some architects still consider his most interesting project.

A man named Diamond, probably a practical contractor with a feeling for brick construction, presented a square building set about a court that harked back even further in English taste, but struck an up-to-date note by indicating locations for water closets. There were some enlarged versions of the Annapolis statehouse. There were some intriguing experiments with oval rooms. A recently arrived Frenchman whose name was Americanized as Hallet drafted a dome over a pediment supported by Ionic columns, which presented a compromise between the ornate dome of the Invalides and the beautifully simple dome of the Ecole Mazarine in Paris. He had been talking to Jefferson, who wanted a domed building and who had made a vigorous little sketch of his recollections of the Panthéon, the great domed church on the hill above the students' quarter on the left bank of the Seine.

When the drawings were shown to Washington, the President found only one which satisfied his sense of pomp and his desire for great scale. This was a drawing submitted by a Dr. Thornton, who boasted of being a rank amateur. Jeffer-

Submitted under the anonymous initials A.Z., Jefferson's design for a President's house had a skylighted dome; in all other respects, it practically duplicated the Villa Rotonda.

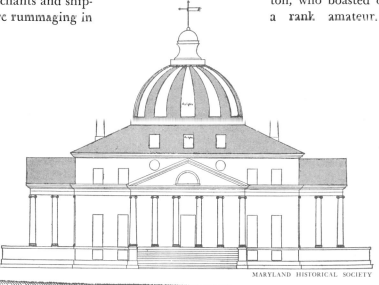

son immediately concurred. Thornton had put the antique forms to modern use. The center of Thornton's plan was a bold Roman pantheon set up on a sturdy set of rusticated arches. It had the New World flavor.

Born of a family of rich Lancashire Quakers on the tiny island of Jost Van Dyke off Tortola in the Virgin Islands, William Thornton had been educated for medicine in Scotland, and being a young man of some wealth had set out on the customary grand tour. He had been captivated by the classical revival and had spent a season in Paris subject to the fascinations of the *salon* of Josephine de Beauharnais, whom the clinging new tunics in Hellenic style became so exquisitely. He had turned up in Philadelphia in time to dine with Dr. Franklin before he died, had married a Pennsylvania girl, and had become a naturalized citizen of Delaware. William Dunlap, the historian of the arts of the early republic, speaks of him as "a scholar and a gentleman—full of talent and eccentricity—a quaker by profession, a painter, a poet and a horse racer, well acquainted with the mechanic arts."

Thornton claimed that he had never thought of architecture till he saw an advertisement in a Philadelphia newspaper of a competition for a library. He bought himself some books, fudged a set of plans, and carried off the prize. Now President Washington could think of nothing but his elevation of the façade for the national capitol.

Jefferson agreed. Yet he and the commissioners had already virtually engaged Stephen Hallet and approved his project. It was a case that demanded more than a normal amount of healing oil to keep everybody happy. On February 1, 1793, Jefferson wrote Daniel Carroll, now retired from Congress and a commissioner:

Doctor Thornton's plan of a capitol has been produced and has so captivated the eyes and judgement of all as to leave no doubt you will prefer it . . . It is simple, noble, beautiful, excellently distributed, and moderate in size . . . The Doctor will go with it to your meeting in the beginning of March. In the meantime, the interval of *apparent* doubt may be improved for settling the mind of poor Hallet, whose merit and distresses interest everyone for his tranquility and pecuniary relief.

The prize had no sooner been awarded to Dr. Thornton than it became apparent that it would be impossible to erect the building as planned. The columns of the portico were too far apart, there was no way indicated to support the floor of the central peristyle, there was no headroom on the stairways, and important parts of the interior totally lacked light and air. It was up to Jefferson to get the plan into shape.

Hallet had been awarded second prize. Jefferson, who recognized the Frenchman as a competent technician, promptly engaged him to work on Thornton's drawings. He called in Dr. Thornton, Stephen Hallet, Hoban, and a practical contractor named Carstairs to a conference on ways and means. Dr. Thornton brought along a certain Colonel Williams, who claimed all difficulties could be handled by the use of "secret arches of brick" for support.

Jefferson abhorred the notion, but he kept his feelings to himself. He managed to keep all these gentlemen pulling together to the extent that, by August 15 of the same year, he had a set of workable drawings ready to send on to Washington City. Somehow, in spite of all the burnings and reconstructions and the thousandfold modifications of the original plan, the Capitol, as it stands at present, has, in the relationship of the dome to the general mass and balance of the wings, more affinity to Jefferson's tiny sketch than it has to Thornton's original plan.

Meanwhile a miasma of contention arose from the

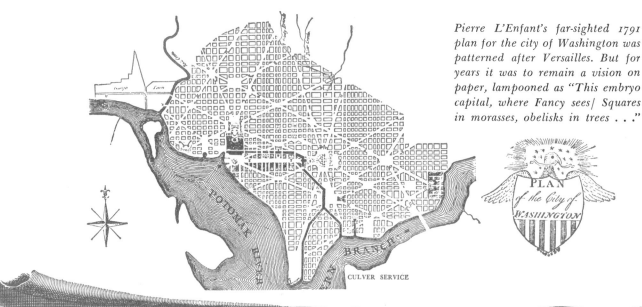

Pierre L'Enfant's far-sighted 1791 plan for the city of Washington was patterned after Versailles. But for years it was to remain a vision on paper, lampooned as "This embryo capital, where Fancy sees/ Squares in morasses, obelisks in trees . . ."

muddy flats of the Potomac. Though many loved him and all admired his talent, nobody could work with L'Enfant. His disregard for money was epic. He was too grand to study ways and means. For him it always had to be rule or ruin. Jefferson wrote tactful letters. Washington sent one of his personal secretaries with soothing explanations to try to induce the Major to co-operate with the commissioners. The secretary was rebuffed. Washington took the rebuff as a personal slight, closed his lips over his uncomfortable dentures, set his jaw, and retired into his implacable dignity.

For years L'Enfant, with his mighty imaginings unrealized, haunted the unfinished city, the first of a long train of injured men waiting for redress. When Ellicott resigned in a huff as surveyor, Jefferson wrote begging him to keep his complaints out of the newspapers. In the end Thornton, too, in spite of the sudden establishment of his reputation as America's leading architect, joined the ranks of the disappointed. The federal city seemed to devour men of talent.

As Jefferson's collaboration with Washington's administration became more and more uneasy, his personal influence diminished at the federal city. The project was beset by every difficulty conceivable. Flocks of speculators rode in, bought lots on borrowed money, took fright in the panic that followed the inflation of the stock in Hamilton's Bank of the United States, sold at a loss, and were ruined. The streets were a morass. At high tide the creeks backed up into the low-lying lots. Clumps of unfinished buildings moldered in the scrubby undergrowth. There was never enough money to pay the workmen. There were never enough workmen to do the work. When workmen arrived they found no houses to live in.

Washington and Jefferson were both stubborn men.

Each in his own way pushed the work on the government buildings on through inconceivable disappointments. It was not till the triumph at the polls in 1800 of the western settlers and the farmers, planters, mechanics, and tradesmen who made up the Republican party that Washington's survival was assured.

Jefferson as President in the fresh air of the new century was able to take full charge of the work in progress..He appointed Benjamin Latrobe as surveyor of the public buildings. Latrobe was a really great architect, a man of true originality who was able to reconcile Jefferson's meticulous taste with the grandiose plans inherited from L'Enfant and Thornton. His artistic education had been steeped in the classical revival. In Charles Cockerell's office in London he had learned to prefer an Attic plainness to the spindling elegances of the Adam style. He was a competent engineer versed in the mechanical inventions which were transforming European society. Jefferson found Latrobe's inventive mind stimulating and congenial; together they were able, pulling down the bad workmanship and shoring up the good, to complete the White House and the Capitol's two wings and to set the print of their fresh republican style on the government buildings so that Washington City became the center of this first great period in American architecture.

After his own retirement Jefferson was to write Latrobe, when at last he too resigned, like the others, disappointed, underpaid, and resentful after having devoted years of his life to the Capitol: "I shall live in the hope that the day will come when an opportunity will be given you of finishing the middle building in a style worthy of the two wings, and worthy of the first temple dedicated to the sovereignty of the people, embellishing with Athenian taste the course of a nation looking far beyond the range of Athenian destinies."

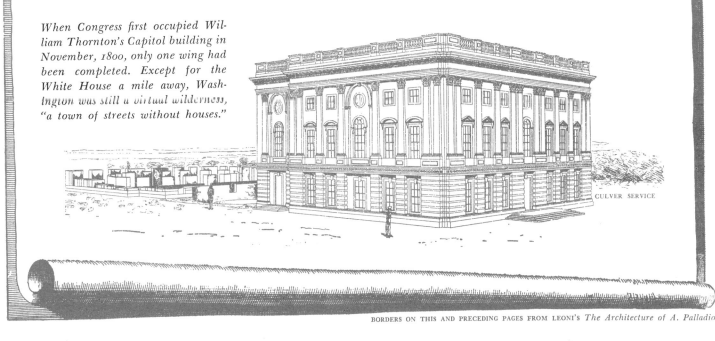

When Congress first occupied William Thornton's Capitol building in November, 1800, only one wing had been completed. Except for the White House a mile away, Washington was still a virtual wilderness, "a town of streets without houses."

CULVER SERVICE

For the young ex-slave a Vermont schoolteacher opened the door to civilization

THE WASHED WINDOW

By DOROTHY CANFIELD FISHER

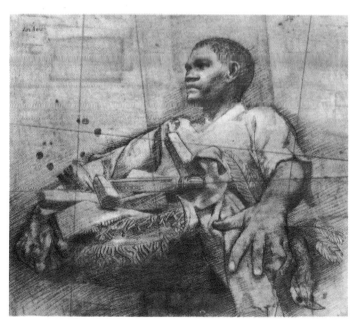

"I don't know that I ever in my life afterwards cared about doing anything right as much as getting that little old woodshed clean."

Older people in Arlington, Vermont, have a special interest in the last house you pass as you leave our village to drive to Cambridge. It was built and lived in for many years by our first, local skilled cabinetmaker. In the early days nearly every house had one or a few good pieces of professionally made furniture, brought up from Connecticut on horseback or in an oxcart. These were highly treasured. But the furniture made here was, for the first generation after 1764, put together by men who just wanted chairs, beds, and a table for the family meals—and those as fast as they could be slammed into shape.

For many years Silas Knapp lived in that last house practicing his remarkable skill. Nearly every house of our town acquired in those years one or two pieces of his workmanship. They are now highly prized as "early Nineteenth-Century locally made antiques."

He not only made many a fine chest of drawers and bedside stand there; he also brought up a fine family of children. You may never have noticed this house as you drove by, but once, some twenty or thirty years ago, a great American leader, who chanced to pass through Vermont, asked to be shown the old Knapp home. He had been delivering an important address to a large audience in Rutland. When he stood in front of the low old house he took off his hat and bowed his gray head in silence. Then he explained to the person who had driven him down to Arlington, "For me it is a shrine."

This is the story behind that visit and of why it was to him a shrine. It goes back to the exciting, heart-shaking years of the Civil War. When that terrible passage in our history ended, it left in the South thousands and thousands of newly emancipated Negroes, free, but dishearteningly ignorant—ignorant not only of their letters but of the simplest ways of civilized life. In prewar days in the South, it had been a grave legal offense, punishable with heavy social and legal penalties, to help a Negro to literacy. Naturally, the white people of the South could not at once shift gears into the opposite attitude. Many of the first schools were taught by northern girls, keyed up to the crusader tensity of purpose by the four years of war.

Among these was young Viola Knapp, the schoolteacher daughter of the cabinetmaker who lived in that small house which we Arlington people pass every time we go to see a "down-the-river" friend. To the accompaniment of great anxiety, and great pride

ILLUSTRATED FOR AMERICAN HERITAGE BY ARTHUR LIDOV

in her courage from her Arlington family and neighbors, she made the difficult trip from Arlington down South to one of the newly established schools for illiterate Negroes—they were all illiterate.

When she arrived at the rough, improvised little school, not nearly as well built or well equipped as the little district schools on our back roads, Viola Knapp found that she was regarded as a social outcast by all the white people in town. No one spoke to her, no one even looked at her. She had great difficulty in finding a place to live, and finally moved herself into a tumble-down, two-room, abandoned poor-white frame house close to the new school.

The ostracism was as complete as human imagination could make it. Her existence was ignored with great ingenuity. If she walked down one side of the street, any white person who happened to be on that side silently and instantly crossed over and walked on the other side. If she went into a shop to buy something, every white person present turned at once and went out, leaving her alone with the clerk, who served her without speaking or looking at her.

One would have thought that a blooming young woman in her twenties away from a good home for the first time would have suffered a good deal from this. So she might, except that she was from Vermont, and wasn't too much cast down, even by disapproval from others, if she herself felt sure she was doing the right thing. I won't say that she did not also find considerable satisfaction (she was human) in undergoing some martyrdom for a cause she considered good.

But evidently, from what followed, what most helped her ignore the disagreeable parts of her experience was her liking for another northern white person who was being ignored and ostracised in the same way. This was young Lieutenant Ruffner of the U.S. Army, stationed there to care for the military cemetery where Federal soldiers, killed in a battle near the town, were buried.

It did not take the two lively young outcasts long to make each other's acquaintance, and the acquaintance soon became an engagement. After a while, a suitable while, they were married. It turned out a very happy, lifelong mating. As time went on, the young lieutenant rose in the Army, became a major, became a general. The Ruffners lived in many cities, towns and army posts, bringing up a fine crop of children who also turned out well.

Our Vermont Viola had a much more colorful and wide-horizoned life than she would have had if she had not gone a-crusading. Many years later, after his wife's death, Major Ruffner (I never understood why we always called him Major) used to come every once

in a while to Arlington to see the people who had known his wife in her girlhood. He was quite an old man then, and glad to talk about his past to any younger generationer who would listen. I've heard him, many's the time, tell the story I'm setting down here.

But I have also heard it from the lips of the distinguished American educator who, as a boy, had been a student of Viola Knapp Ruffner. He became one of my father's valued friends in later years. This is about as he used to tell it to us, with many more details than I ever saw it given in print.

"I never knew exactly how old I was when I first saw Mrs. Ruffner, for in the days of slavery, family records—that is, black family records—were seldom kept. But from what I have been able to learn, I was born, a slave, on a Virginia plantation, about 1858. My home had been a log cabin with a dirt floor about fourteen by sixteen feet square. We slept on frowsy piles of filthy rags, laid on the dirt floor. Until I was quite a big youth I wore only one garment, a shirt made out of agonizingly rough refuse flax.

"We slaves ate corn bread and pork, because that could be grown on the plantation without cash expense. I had never seen anything except the slave quarters on the plantation where I was born, with a few glimpses of the 'big house' where our white owners lived. I cannot remember ever, during my childhood and youth, not one single time, when our family sat down together at a table to eat a meal as human families do. We ate as animals do, whenever and wherever an edible morsel was found. We usually took our food up in our fingers, sometimes from the skillet, sometimes from a tin plate held on our knees, and as we chewed on it held it as best we could in our hands.

"Life outside our cabin was as slovenly and disordered as inside. The white owners made no effort to keep things up. They really could not. Slaves worked; hence any form of work was too low for white people to do. Since white folks did no work, they did not know how work should be done. The untaught slaves, wholly ignorant of better standards, seldom got around to mending the fences, or putting back a lost hinge on a sagging gate or door. Weeds grew wild everywhere, even in the yard. Inside the big house, when a piece of plastering fell from a wall or ceiling, it was a long time before anybody could stir himself to get it replastered.

"After the end of the Civil War, when we were no longer slaves, my family moved to a settlement near a salt mine, where, although I was still only a child, I was employed—often beginning my day's work at four in the morning. We lived in even more dreadful squalor there, for our poor rickety cabin was in a crowded slum, foul with unspeakable dirt—literal and moral. As soon as I grew a little older and stronger, I was shifted from working in the salt mine to a coal mine. Both mines were then owned by General Lewis Ruffner.

"By that time I had learned my letters and could after a fashion read. Mostly I taught myself but with some irregular hours spent in a Negro night school, after an exhausting day's work in the mines. There were no public schools for ex-slaves; the poor, totally unequipped, bare room where colored people young and old crowded in to learn their letters was paid for by tiny contributions from the Negroes themselves.

"About that time I heard two pieces of news which were like very distant, very faint glimmers in the blackness of the coal mine in which nearly all my working hours were spent. One was about a school for colored students—Hampton Institute it was—where they could learn more than their letters. The other was that the wife of General Ruffner was from Vermont, that before her marriage she had been a teacher in one of the first schools for Negroes, and that she took an interest in the education of the colored people who worked for her.

"I also heard that she was so 'strict' that nobody could suit her, and that the colored boys who entered her service were so afraid of her and found her so impossible to please that they never stayed long. But the pay was five dollars a month, and keep. That was better than the coal mine—and then there was that chance that she might be willing to have me go on learning. I got up my courage to try. What could be worse than the way I was living and the hopelessness of anything better in the future?

"But I can just tell you that—great, lumbering, muscle-bound coal-mining boy that I was—I was trembling when I went to ask for that work. The Ruffners had just moved into an old house that had been empty for some time and they were not yet established, their furniture not unpacked, the outbuildings not repaired. When I first saw her Mrs. Ruffner was writing on an improvised desk which was a plank laid across two kegs.

"I falteringly told her I had come to ask for work. She turned in her chair and looked at me silently. Nobody had ever looked at me like that, not at my rags and dirt but as if she wanted to see what kind of person I was. She had clear, steady gray eyes, I remember. Then she said, 'You can try.' After reflection she went on, 'You might as well start in by cleaning the woodshed. It looks as though it hadn't been touched for years.'

"She laid down her pen and took me through a narrow side passage out into the woodshed. It was dark and cluttered with all kinds of dirty, dusty things. A sour, mouldy smell came up from them. Great cobwebs hung down from the rough rafters of the low, sloping roof. Stepping back for a moment, she brought out a dustpan and a broom. A shovel leaned against the woodshed wall. She put that in my hand and said, 'Now go ahead. Put the trash you clean out on that pile in the yard and we'll burn it up later. Anything that won't burn, like broken glass, put into that barrel.' Then she turned away and left me.

"You must remember that I never had done any work except perfectly rough, unskilled heavy labor. I had never cleaned a room in my life, I had never seen a clean room in my life. But I was used to doing as I was told and dead set on managing to go ahead with learning more than I would in that poor beginners' schoolroom. So I began taking out things which anybody could see were trash, like mildewed rags, which fell apart into damp shreds the minute I touched them. There were, also, I remember, some mouldy heaps of I don't know what, garbage maybe, that had dried into shapeless chunks of bad-smelling filth. Glass was everywhere, broken empty whiskey bottles, bits of crockery ware. These I swept with the broom and picking up my sweepings in my hands (I had no idea what a dustpan was for) carried them outside.

"The shed looked to me so much better that I went in to find Mrs. Ruffner. She was still writing. I told her, 'I cleaned it.' Pushing back her chair she went out to the woodshed with me.

"She made no comment when she first opened the door and looked around her with clear gray eyes. Then she remarked quietly, 'There's still some things to attend to. Those pieces of wood over there you might pile up against the wall in the corner. They would do to burn. Be sure to clean the floor well before you start piling the wood on it. And here's another pile of rotten rags, you see. And that tangle behind the door. You'd better pull it all apart and see what's there. Throw away the trash that's mixed with it.' She turned to go back, saying, 'Just keep on till you've got it finished and then come and tell me.'

"She didn't speak kindly. She didn't speak unkindly. I looked at the woodshed with new eyes and saw that, sure enough, I'd only made a beginning. I began to pull at the odds and ends in that dusty mess behind the door. And to my astonishment I saw I was perspiring.

"The work wasn't hard for me, you understand. It was like little boy's play compared to the back-breaking labor I had always done. And it wasn't that I minded carrying around in my bare hands things slimy with rot nor having liquid filth drip on my ragged pants. I was used to dirt, and my hands were as calloused as my feet. I couldn't feel much with them. What made me sweat was the work I had to do with my mind.

"Always before, when somebody had given me a piece of work to do, he had stood right there to do all the thinking. 'Pull that piece of sacking out. That stick, put it on top of the woodpile. Those dried chicken bones, scrape them up from the dirt and throw them in the trash pile.' All I had to do was to plod along, doing what I was told.

"I was determined to do it right this time. Now that I was really thinking about what I was doing, I was amazed to see how little I had done, how much more there was to do than I had seen.

"I stooped to pull apart the grimy, mud-colored tangle heaped up back of the door. As I stirred it, a snake crawled out from under it and wriggled towards the door. A big fellow. I wasn't surprised. I was used to snakes. I dropped a stone on his head.

"Now I had come to a corner where chickens had evidently roosted. Everything was covered with their droppings, like smearings of white paint. I thought nothing of handling them, and taking up the body of one I found lying stiff and dead in the midst of the rubbish. More rotted rags, a stained, torn pair of pants, too far gone even for me to wear, still smelling foul. Some pieces of wood, not rotten, fit for fuel. Everything I came to, had first to be pulled loose from the things it was mixed up with, and enough of the dirt shaken off to let me make out what it was. And thus I had to think what to do with it. No wonder that the sweat ran down my face so that, to see, I had to wipe my eyes with the back of my hands.

"Finally, the last of the refuse was taken apart and cleared away and the litter and filth which had dropped from it to the floor as I worked was swept together and carried out to the trash pile. I kept looking over my shoulder for somebody to make the decisions, to tell me what to do. 'Throw that away. Save that. Put it with the firewood. Toss that into the barrel with the broken glass.' But there was nobody there to give me orders. I went in to get Mrs. Ruffner. 'I got it done,' I told her.

"Laying down her pen, she came again to see. I felt nervous as, silent and attentive, she ran those clear eyes of hers over what I had been doing. But I wasn't at all prepared to have her say again, 'That's better, but there's a great deal still to do. You haven't touched the cobwebs, I see.'

"I looked up at them, my lower jaw dropped in astonishment. Sure enough, there they hung in long, black festoons. I had not once lifted my head to see them. 'And how about washing the window? Here, step in here and get a pail of water for that. Here are some clean rags. You'll have to go over it several times.'

"She went back into the house and I stood shaken by more new ideas than I could tell you. I hadn't even noticed there was a window, it was so thick with dust and cobwebs. I had never had anything to do with a glass window. In the dark cabins I had lived in, the windows were just holes cut in the walls.

"I set to work once more, the sweat running down my face. Suppose she wouldn't even let me try to do her work. I never could get into Hampton. What if I just never could get the hang of her ways? Stricken, scared, I began again to clean that woodshed! I went over and over every corner of it. Once in a while I stopped stock-still to *look* at it, as I had never looked at anything before, trying really to see it. I don't know that I ever in my life afterwards cared about doing anything right as much as getting that little old woodshed clean.

"When I came to what I thought was the end, I stopped to get my breath. I looked up at the slanting roof. The rafters were not only cleared of cobwebs but bare of dust; the floor was swept clean, not a chip, not a thread, not a glint of broken glass on it. Piles of firewood against the walls. And the window! *I* had washed that window! Five times I had washed it. How it sparkled. How the strong sunshine poured through it. The woodshed was no rubbish pile. It was a room. To me it looked like a parlor. I was proud of it. I had never been proud of anything I had done until then.

"Then for the third time I went to call Mrs. Ruffner to inspect. Big boy as I was, twice her size, my hands were shaking, my lips twitching. I felt sick. Had I done it right this time? Could I ever do anything right?

"I watched her face as she passed my work in review, looking carefully up, down, and around. Then she turned to me and, looking straight into my eyes, she nodded and said, 'Now it's clean. Nobody could have done it any better.'

"She had opened the door through which I took my first step towards civilized standards of living."

. . .

His name was Booker Washington.

The late Dorothy Canfield Fisher, scholar and author, was born in Lawrence, Kansas, and lived out her productive late years in Arlington, Vermont. Her work includes not only many famous short stories but books on English rhetoric (1906) and on the Montessori educational method (1913), a translation of Papini's Christ *(1921), and novels like* The Deepening Stream *and, recently,* The Vermont Tradition.

Written and illustrated by ERIC SLOANE

The MILLS of EARLY AMERICA

An artist recalls the picturesque

devices that helped a young nation get ready

for the age of machinery

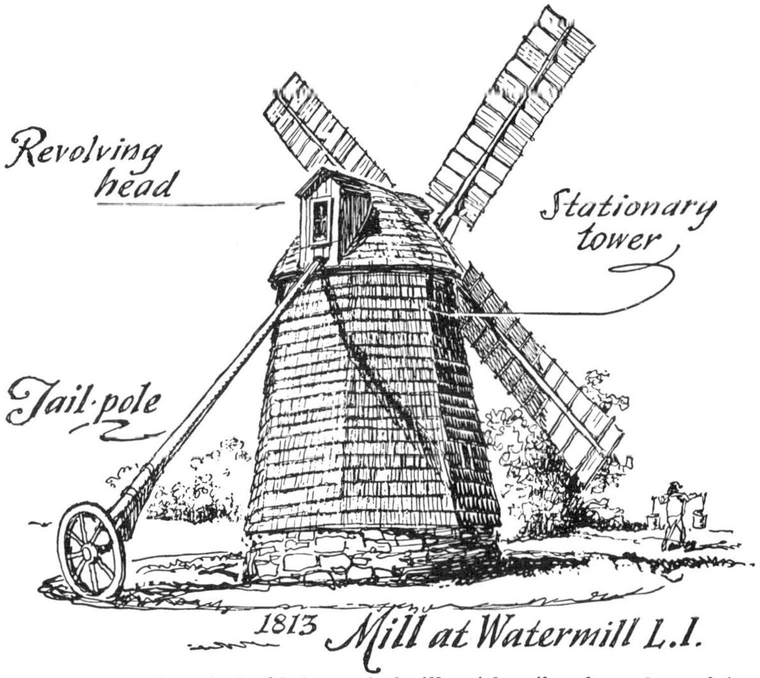

Revolving head

Stationary tower

Tail-pole

1813 *Mill at Watermill L.I.*

A typical old-time windmill, with tail pole and revolving head by which the miller could adjust it to varying winds.

While the antiquarian still coos over many a useless relic of the past, the American miller and his mill have often been forgotten. Like the farmer and the barn builder, his name is seldom recorded; but his place in the fabric of our history is distinct.

The miller was America's first industrial inventor. He was builder, banker, businessman and host to the countryside. When highways were no wider than today's bridle paths, the first good roads were built to the mills. Where there was a mill site, there was a nucleus for a town. America had so many Millvilles, Milltowns, Milfords and other towns named after original mills, that the Post Office Department sponsored the changing of many such names to stop the confusion.

There are still abandoned millponds, forgotten mill roads and millstreams that wind through the "old sections" of cities. But the structure with its machinery, once the hub of the village, is usually lost in the oblivion of a vanished landscape.

Over a hundred years ago, roads were used for travel, but almost never for commercial transportation. Even to transport a simple wagonload of wood could cost more than the value of the load; to move salt from Long Island to Danbury, Connecticut, by horse, cost eight times its worth. In Philadelphia, coal shipped from Newcastle, England, cost less than coal hauled over the road from nearby Richmond, Virginia. Every small village had to depend upon itself for almost

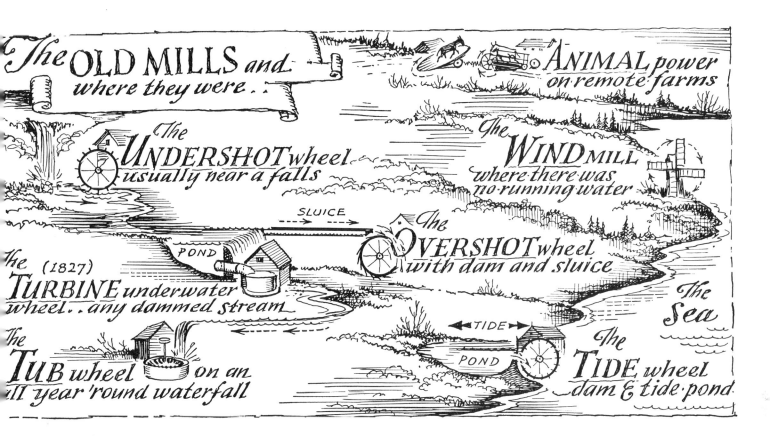

The OLD MILLS and where they were...

The UNDERSHOT wheel usually near a falls

SLUICE

POND

The (1827) TURBINE underwater wheel...any dammed stream

The TUB wheel on an all year 'round waterfall

ANIMAL power on remote farms

The WIND MILL where there was no running water

The OVERSHOT wheel with dam and sluice

TIDE

POND

The Sea

The TIDE wheel dam & tide pond

every necessity, and the mills were the answer. It would have a sawmill and a gristmill: there would also be mills for making cider, salt, flax, plaster, linseed oil, tobacco, barrel staves, axes, bone meal, mustard, and on down to smaller mills that turned out simple necessities of everyday life. In the hamlet of New Preston, Connecticut, there is still a water-powered sawmill. Its saws are actuated by a new turbine which operates underwater and therefore does not ice up the way its original water wheels did. The small stretch of waterway that feeds its turbine is no longer than you can walk in a minute or two, yet there were once about thirty mills on it, almost as many mills as there were residences.

People of today might think of the old-time miller as just another merchant. But if they could step inside an early water-wheeled mill and watch it at work, the miller might be added to their list of American greats. The ponderous wheels and massive gears spring to life with a surge of power that makes the mill house shudder, and which explains why early mills had hand-hewn beams of such tremendous proportions.

"Killed in his mill" was a frequent epitaph of two hundred years ago. The careless miller's life was a short one, and whether he was lifted aloft and thrown from a windmill, whacked in the head by a spar or caught by his hand or clothing in the gigantic gears and ground up, his everyday work had to be as exacting and careful as that of an airplane pilot.

Millstones have a lore and language of their own. The *runner* stone turned above the fixed *nether* stone, and according to the *dress* of the *run* (pair), different consistencies of meal were ground. Because of the resemblance to plowed land, the millstone dresses, or pattern of cut grooves, were called the *furrows*, while the uncut area was called the *land*. The interesting patterns of millstone dresses are becoming lost records, yet many a Pennsylvania barn's hex sign and farm wife's patchwork quilt has been inspired by some favorite millstone design.

The first mills were hand-turned mortar and pestle arrangements. The first water-powered mill had no wheel; it consisted of a pounding mortar that was lifted upward by the weight of water running into a box on one end of a beam. When the box filled, it lowered and tipped itself, actuating the beam up and down ceaselessly and pounding a stone pestle into a hollowed tree mortar. Travelers could tell when they were nearing a village by the steady beat of these "plumping mills."

We think of the windmill as being entirely Dutch, yet travelers from Holland were impressed by the windmills of New York. "As we sailed into the harbor," wrote one Hollander, "the horizon was pierced by scores of windmills, taller than any we have seen elsewhere." Sailing ships set their sails according to the position of windmills and Long Island ferries advertised "daily services except when the windmills on

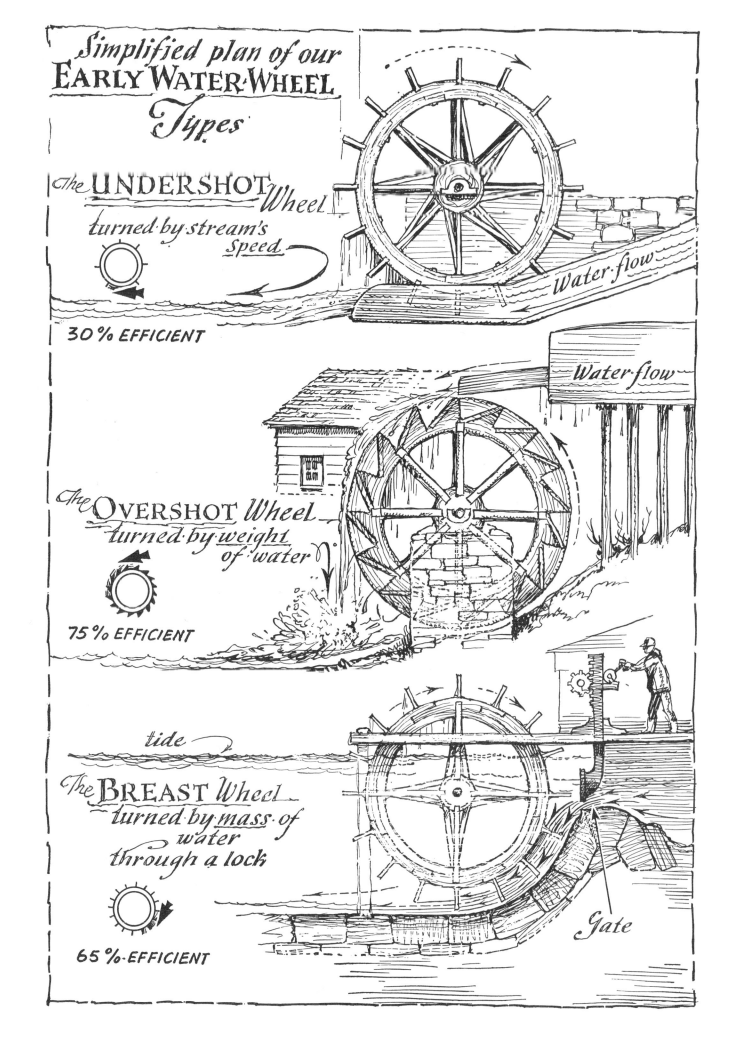

Simplified plan of our
EARLY WATER-WHEEL
Types

The UNDERSHOT Wheel
turned by stream's speed

30% EFFICIENT

Water-flow

Water-flow

The OVERSHOT Wheel
turned by weight of water

75% EFFICIENT

tide

The BREAST Wheel
turned by mass of water
through a lock

65% EFFICIENT

Gate

the opposite shore have taken in their sails."

The Dutch erected windmills in Manhattan in 1640 and the idea spread to Long Island, where the mills pumped sea water into large vats for the manufacture of salt. Although wind-powered mills were designed for riverless areas, they had an advantage over water-wheeled mills in that they did not freeze. During the great cold winters of early New England days, the water wheels were often frozen solid for months.

Except for a few restored or ornamental examples, time has run out on the American windmill. But the water-wheeled mill still turns in many a hidden glen throughout the country, grinding meal and doing other chores, just as if progress had never come through the land. City folks drive long distances to see these mills and to pay fancy prices for stone-ground corn meal, but few realize they are purchasing more than quaintness. The country people know that the best corn bread only comes from a water-powered burrstone mill, where the meal has absorbed the dampness of the mill site and has not been scorched by fast-moving machinery. When the meal is fresh from the slow-turning stones, "as warm as from the underside of a settin' hen," it makes bread the country way.

Nearly all the early water wheels were variations of three basic designs: the overshot wheel, the undershot wheel and the breast wheel. The overshot wheel was fed from above, and the weight of falling water gave it the most efficiency. The undershot wheel was moved by the velocity and mass of a moving stream; the breast wheel was fed from the middle section, often by tidewater. There were bucket wheels and tub wheels and countless inventions of the American mind, but these three designs, hewn from native timber, have become Americana despite earlier overseas models. From their pattern has evolved the industrial machinery that electricity now actuates and even in the jet airplane engine you may find early mill theories put to use.

When steam power took over, the mill had reached its Rube Goldberg age, and even the smallest farm owned treadmill machines where oxen and horses and even dogs churned butter, sawed logs and ground out linseed oil for barn paint. Even the spit in the fireplace was turned by a dog or a tame squirrel in a treadmill cage. Wherever animals, wind or water could make chores simpler, the American mind enjoyed the spectacle.

Eric Sloane is an artist living in a Brookfield, Connecticut, farmhouse built in 1782. He has written and illustrated many books, including the recent American Barns and Covered Bridges *and* Our Vanishing Landscape, *from which these sketches are taken.*

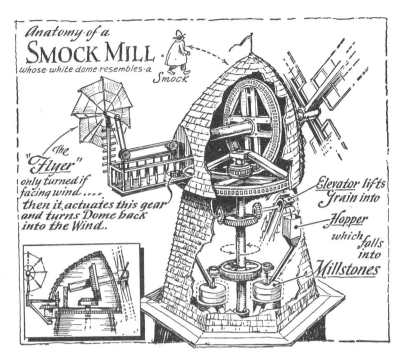

A windmill could be complicated. This cut-away diagram shows some of the intricate machinery by which the wind's power was put to work. The sketches below show various stages in the development and use of the earliest mills.

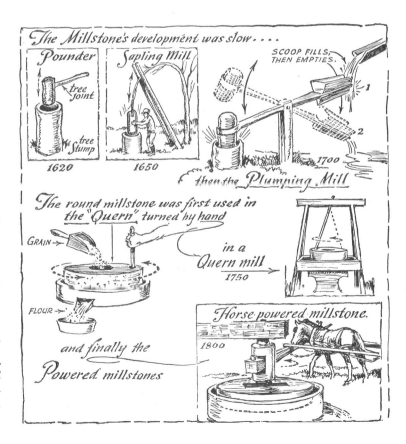

The
WILD FREEDOM
of the
MOUNTAIN MEN

The imagined liberty of Rousseau's primitive individual was actually attained by the free trappers who helped America gain a continent

By WILLIAM BRANDON

Jim Baker, a typical trapper; from a painting by Waldo Love.

Freedom is a word that has had many meanings. In all its disguises it has been relentlessly pursued, but perhaps it has been longest hunted under its most artless aspect—the simple notion of individual liberty and unrestraint. Jean Jacques Rousseau reduced this ancient and naive dream of individual freedom to concise statement in 1750, mistakenly choosing primitive man, the noble savage dancing in the forest primeval, as his example; but a half century later a phenomenon began to emerge in western America that in many respects brought the dream remarkably to life. This was the free trapper, the Rocky Mountain man.

The mountain man first appeared with the Lewis and Clark report of beaver swarming in the streams of the western mountains. He lived a brief uproarious generation and vanished in the early 1840's when the market for beaver dwindled and vanished, and the bea-

The mountain men "floated on the rolling rivers . . . and were repaid in freedom, a freedom they could accept." The spirit of those fabulous days is caught in this expressive painting by George Caleb Bingham called "The Trappers' Return."

ver nearly disappeared with it, almost trapped out.

Due to the remoteness of his hunting grounds, the Shining Mountains of the Far West, the mountain man was the first inhabitant of America to find himself at ease with the familiar concept of great land distances that Europeans still remark as one of our national attributes. He was seldom a pioneer consciously clearing a way for others to follow—he was only hunting beaver. He was seldom an integrated unit of an organized company, with a big business character branded on his pack, as in the case of the hired pork-eaters of the North West Company. He was not a family man in a covered wagon, a settler. He was, at his best, defiantly independent and individual, and he forthrightly referred to himself as free—a free trapper.

He lived on his own in a neolithic world far removed from the Steel Age civilization that had bred him. He brought along only a few of its tools: traps, rifle, knife, awl, powder and lead. He traveled with small, loosely organized groups of his own kind, a handful of men swallowed in an infinity of dark forests and strange winds. His joy was the sensual animal pleasure of life lived for its moments, one by one. He hunted with glowing eyes and spilled blood on pine needles unstirred for centuries.

He owned a mule or horse or two and an Indian girl. He dressed in skins she worked up for him, and she had warm water ready for his feet when he came in to his camp from wading the icy beaver streams. In the summer, when trading caravans came from St. Louis, he packed the spoils of his year's plunder to the great trappers' rendezvous in the mountains, bartered it for

157

a whoop and a holler and a howling hangover, and set out on the next long hunt.

He floated on the rolling rivers in boats of skin or bark or rafts of logs. He probed out trails that are railroads and highways today, and learned the way from the plains of Kansas to California and from the deserts of New Mexico and Utah to the fern grown rain forests of Oregon.

Probably the mountain men surpassed the Indians in at least a number of the necessary skills of reading sign, hunting, living off a wild and ominous land, fighting and hiding and running like agile beasts, lying concealed in brush and rocks throughout a thirsty day if necessary, starving, stealing horses, going dirty, enduring sun and cold and cracking alkali. In some of these things they must have surpassed the Indians to survive, for the Indians were living at home, cushioned by the web of their established society, and the mountain men were interlopers with no support to back them up other than what they carried in their hands, so far in time and space from the established society from which they had sprung that they had all but forgotten its existence.

They were a variegated, highly individualistic bunch, much more so than any vocational group in the confines of civilization. Their lonely, self-sufficient lives developed separatist tendencies, and they were apt at any moment to be subjected to unique experiences for which the group had provided no adjustment, thus inducing bizarre modifications in individuals—which is to say each man lived in his own hide, hair side out and plenty of it.

There were men from what are called good homes among them and scrapings from the muddy waterfronts of the big rivers from New Orleans to the Yellowstone; intelligent men and mental defectives from backwoods slums, heroes and victims and villains and clowns and all the shades between in sunburst colors, heightened and brightened to the wearer's pleasure.

They had in common only a constant insecurity and a boundless freedom, both of such dimensions as to be appalling to those sheltered by a civilized world. In their brief time, and it is noteworthy that it was without intention on their part—they were only hunting beaver—the mountain men created a vector of force that was an important factor in extending the sovereignty of the United States over the whole enormous western half of the continent. And coincidentally in their brief time they approached, in a very literal sense, the status of exalted freedom which Rousseau's fantasy portrayed.

Freedom apparently entails challenge and is achieved, not bestowed. The achievement of the mountain men was to go where others had not been, in the face of a constant challenge from an awesome and unbroken wilderness. They were repaid in freedom, a freedom they could accept, not being fettered by the fixed taboos and rigid life patterns of their contemporaries, the Indians. They were the freedom fantasy made flesh, even to an uncanny identity with the incidental details of Rousseau's picture: preoccupation with savagery, violence, sensation, and megalomania. Beaver was only a reason for beginning; unconscious contempt for the tangible rewards of their achievement was demonstrated by many of them over and over again at rendezvous, when a year's catch went for a few days of Old Sledge, *aguardiente,* and bells and beads for the woman in the lodge, and it was back to the mountains empty-handed. The mountain men were rewarded by their way of life.

To some, the lack of restraint and the challenge resulted in the realization of lives of monumental stature, lives which stamped their mark on the changing world, and afforded to an extraordinary degree that

The mountain man lasted while the beaver lasted. Here is Alfred Jacob Miller's painting, "Setting Traps for Beaver."

inner recognition of a reason for living, the feeling that here and for this one had been born, the sense of recognition and fulfillment, the intimation of immortality, for which all life strives.

Such were Jedediah Strong Smith, the triumvirate of Jim Bridger, Kit Carson and Thomas Fitzpatrick, and a number of others.

Jed Smith was a rather mystical, probably inspired young man, the greatest explorer among all the far-ranging mountain men. It seems that as a youth he dreamed of going forth and cracking the vast shell of the unknown new world of the West, and when he grew up he went and did it. It is difficult for us today to settle on a comfortable evaluation of those mightiest names of that wild, free time.

Kit Carson is still a dime novel hero, as he was during his lifetime, but his own biographer disclaims any notion that Kit may have been an orthodox great man. A great man may be a famous general or politician but scarcely someone dressed in buckskins and dirt who says "thar" and "mought be" and grunts with satisfac-

tion over the strenuous business of ripping off an enemy's scalp. Achilles could slit dead Hector's ankles and lace through thongs and drag him to his chariot, while the women of Troy screamed in anguish from the walls, but that is different. Kit Carson had a profound influence on shaping the world around him, the new West, and he had, according to most contemporary accounts, an exceptional integrity and greatness of soul, being apparently equally remarkable for modesty and bravery, kindliness and honesty.

Maybe all this makes him a great man, maybe not. What is more interesting, or at least more worthy of speculation, is the thought that Kit Carson and others like him may well have attained, during their development, a high point of freedom in the career of humankind. And the spectacular results of that development, in the case of the Carsons and Jed Smiths, the outer accomplishment and inner nobility grown from small beginnings and made to flourish in the hostile environment of the farthest wilderness, give rise to the suspicion that perhaps freedom, as a French poet said of happiness, is indeed the natural and intended condition of the human character.

But the human character is an individual thing, and in the hour of the mountaineers' leathery blue-blazing reality there were many for whom the lack of restraint led only to lives that were orgies of unrestraint, and the room they had to strive in was never recognized. They were accustomed to coming upon dismembered bodies of their companions—the head put up on a stake (with the hat on) and shot full of arrows—so they might go among wounded Indians after a battle and butcher them in grotesque fashion also. Or they might indulge the vacuum of restraint by simply yelling.

They yelled when they fought Indians and they yelled when they fought grizzlies and they yelled when they dashed to meet strangers; they sang and shouted around a nightly feast, just to fill up the infinite starry space with noise. They yelled when they stampeded and stole horses and when they chased and stole women. They killed anything that moved on the slightest provocation, including each other, and sometimes for no reason at all, as when Jim Higgins of Ewing Young's company felt an urge while in his cups to shoot and kill Big Jim Lawrence, and did so.

A much quoted passage of Ruxton, the British author and traveler who knew the mountain men, runs: "Not a hole or corner in the vast wilderness of the 'Far West' but has been ransacked by these hardy men . . . the beaver hunter has set his traps in every creek and stream." But this is preceded by a passage that has not been so much quoted: "Constantly exposed to perils of all kinds, they become callous to any feeling of

159

danger, and destroy human as well as animal life with as little scruple and as freely as they expose their own. Of laws, human or divine, they neither know nor care to know. . . . They may have good qualities, but they are those of the animal; and people fond of giving hard names call them revengeful, bloodthirsty, drunkards [when the wherewithal is to be had], gamblers, regardless of the laws of *meum* and *tuum*. . . . However, there are exceptions, and I *have* met honest mountain men."

The free trapper who owned to the most unrestrained reputation in the mountains and was proud of it, and was therefore in certain literal respects at least the freest of them all, was one William Sherley Williams, known as Old Bill. He lived more than forty years withdrawn from civilization. The last 23 or 24 were spent in the Rocky Mountains. As a young man he had been for a time a preacher in backwoods Missouri; in his old age he was famous even among the mountain men for his rugged individualism.

Old Bill carried free self-determination a step farther than most of his colleagues. Generally, the trappers liked to move and camp together in small parties. This meant added protection against Indians, help in case of injury or accident, more hunters to bring in meat, and the human satisfaction of companionship. But Old Bill went much alone, especially as he grew older, so much so that one of his many titles came to be Old Solitaire. He frequently spent the winters living with Indians, most often with the Utes, in the heart of the Rocky Mountains, but through the long hunting seasons he walked by himself. Companies of other trappers occasionally came across him in deserts or mountains, far from a base, and wholly alone.

He was secretive about his trapping grounds. If Bill Williams was the envy of the shaggy, independent mountain men because among them he was the most independent, the shaggiest, the dirtiest, and could go on the biggest sprees, he was also envied for the rich loads of furs he brought to rendezvous or Bent's Fort. But only he knew where he had trapped them, and so an air of mystery was added. Stories were told of his mountain knowledge and trail wisdom, his witchery at trapping, his supernatural skill in hunting, at which he outrivaled the predatory beasts of the forests; his uncanny instinct for danger, his boldness and ferocity in a fight, and the scalps he had taken, and the wounds he had received; his pranks and his hell-

The beaver, prize game of the trapper.

roaring Taos drunks; and his solitudes, and it was this last that impressed the mountain men more solemnly than all the rest.

Stories were told of his unbelievable strength and endurance. Stories were told that pictured him as rabid and treacherous, or as compassionate, generous, warmhearted and true.

Ruxton made of Old Bill a character typed so strikingly that he has lived ever since in western fiction—the old man of the mountains, the past master frontiersman who has seen more things with his faded eyes than can be dreamed of in tenderfoot philosophies, the eccentric old-timer, full of hard liquor and ancient reputation, who saves the wagon train in between comical jets of tobacco juice.

"Do'ee hyar now," Ruxton has him say, as a constant expression. "Do'ee hyar now, boys, thar's sign about? this hos feels like câching." And "Do'ee hyar now, boys? thar's *Injuns* knocking round, and Blackfoot at that; but thar's plenty of beaver too, and this child means trapping anyhow." And the trappers, scattered at work on the streams, are attacked, and one of the boys staggers into camp, dripping blood, with a Blackfoot arrow in his back. Old Bill, graining a skin, looks up to say, "Do'ee feel bad, now, boy? Whar away you see them darned Blackfoot?" The wounded trapper not unreasonably tells him first to pull the arrow out of his back and then he'll feel like talking, and Old Bill, going on with his work, says, "Do'ee hyar now!" And Old Bill, all alone in the mountains, makes himself known to a startled trapping party by rising out of the brush six feet away and saying, "Do'ee hyar now? I was nigh upon gut shootin' some of e'e—I was now; thought e'e was darned Rapahos, I did . . ."

But Old Bill Williams was more enigmatic than comic, and toiling, godless, worn Ishmaelite, he was essentially more pathetic than either.

When he was 61 years old he betrayed his friends, the Utes, while on an extended Taos binge, and led a detachment of soldiers against them. In the ensuing fight his arm was shattered by a bullet "most horribly." (He kept on fighting until the battle was over.) A few months later he joined John Charles Frémont's fourth expedition as guide. The expedition ended in disaster in a Rocky Mountain winter, nearly a third of the men died of cold or starvation, and Old Bill, after desperate efforts to save the expedition, was brought into Taos unable to walk, nearly sightless, frozen, according to one report, as high as his hips, and so emaci-

A year's earnings were bartered "for a whoop and a holler and a howling hangover" at the annual rendezvous. Alfred Jacob Miller painted this one in the Wind River Mountains.

ated as to be unrecognizable. And accused, incidentally, of cannibalism. Only a few weeks later he returned to the mountains after the expedition's baggage. He and his companion, another survivor of the expedition, disappeared and were never heard of again. It is presumed they were killed by Indians.

Schopenhauer parabled the social structure in his story of the porcupines, who huddled together for warmth, in spite of being pricked and tormented by each other's sharp quills: it was better to suffer the annoyances of the crowd than to be cold and alone. They fell into a pattern, these porcupines, a tight little knot of the coldest and most dependent in the center, surrounded by somewhat more independent porcupines not quite so close together, and on the outermost fringes those few individuals, proud and strong, who could stand the cold best of all. These might represent the mountain men. And the one far-

thest apart from all the rest was Old Bill Williams.

Curious parallels can be found between the compulsive, unmuzzled life of such a man as Old Bill Williams and the riotous lives of some of the men of the early Renaissance. Perhaps a line could be drawn from Renaissance humanism to the American idea—the idea of revolutionary America, supporting human dignity by placing authority on the side of individual liberty and the pursuit of happiness—and the line continued to the mountain men.

It is eminently suitable that they were instrumental (all unknowing, while they hunted beaver) in accomplishing a continental America before they vanished.

Writer of books, short stories, and magazine articles, William Brandon has spent much time in the West. This article has been adapted from his book The Men and the Mountain *(William Morrow & Co.).*

AFTER ALONZO CHAPPEL

Stephen Decatur

THE GREAT SEA WAR

Fine printmakers celebrated the heroes and heroics of 1812

By ROBERT M. LUNNY,
Curator, Delaware State Museum

The illustrations in this portfolio are reproduced through the courtesy of Irving S. Olds, former chairman of the board of the U.S. Steel Corporation and outstanding collector of naval prints, and with the assistance of Harry Shaw Newman.

For all its diplomatic blunders and often disastrous land campaigns, the War of 1812 is best remembered in this country as a great drama of the sea. The popular imagination never forgets the wooden ships clashing close aboard in single combat, and it calls up quite easily the ringing names of William Bainbridge, Stephen Decatur, David Porter, Jacob Jones, Isaac Hull, Thomas Macdonough, and Oliver Hazard Perry—the captains who fought the ships and coined the famous slogans. This strange war had a David and Goliath quality, even if the former was unprepared and the latter deeply preoccupied in a much vaster struggle against Napoleon. A U.S. Navy of fifteen-odd ships had nothing with which to meet the British ships of the line, and but nine frigates to match over one hundred flying the white ensign. Thus there could be no classic actions like Trafalgar, but only privateering, blockade running, and duels between single ships, demanding every ounce of skill and seamanship.

It was a war of broadsides fired at pistol range, of maneuvering to cross the enemy's bows and rake his decks until the tall spars toppled. There was boarding, hand-to-hand fighting with the cutlass, sharpshooting in the maintop—a far cry from modern naval warfare, fought with mechanical devices above the clouds, beneath the surface, and beyond the horizon. Naturally such a war stirred the burgeoning patriotism of the young republic. Artists seized on the theme and printmakers on both sides of the Atlantic copied their oils and water colors to exploit an eager market. In the eyes of many collectors, nothing quite equals in skill and charm the copper engravings, aquatints, and lithographs which record this romantic age.

The most popular of all 1812 subjects was (top) *the victory of the* Constitution, *Captain Hull, over the* Guerrière, *fought off Halifax on August 19, 1812. Then the country went wild when Decatur in the frigate* United States (bottom) *made a prize of the British* Macedonian *on October 25, 1812, and brought her into New York*

162

The great frigate

The most memorable American man-of-war, the frigate *Constitution*, was launched in 1797 at Boston, where she lies moored today. Rated at 44 guns (actually she carried more), built of live oak and red cedar with bolts from Paul Revere's shop, she shipped about 450 men and some of the most famous commanders in U.S. history. Under Hull, she made the famous escape (*below*) and then took the *Guerrière*. Just as the same year, 1812, was drawing to a close, she scored another brilliant victory, by sinking the frigate *Java,* 46 guns, off Brazil. This action, commencing in the afternoon of December 29, was described in the journal of the *Constitution*'s new commander, Commodore Bainbridge: "Considerable maneuvers were made by both vessels to rake and avoid being raked." The first three aquatints at right show the progressive destruction of the British ship. Totally dismasted and helpless, the Englishman "most prudently struck his flag." After survivors were removed the ship was blown up (*bottom right*). These pictures were drawn and etched by Nicholas Pocock, an English shipmaster turned marine painter, from sketches on the spot by a Lieutenant Buchanan, and published in London in 1814. One cannot imagine enemy successes being so impartially celebrated in the bitter atmosphere of war in modern times.

I

II

One morning at daybreak, the Constitution *found herself becalmed amidst a British squadron; only the ingenuity of Hull saved her. By towing with small boats and warping from an anchor dropped ahead—for sixty hours—Hull found a light breeze which sprung him from the trap.*

ENGRAVING IN *The Naval Monument,* 1816

III

IV

Overleaf: The Chesapeake, *Captain Lawrence, sailed from Boston on June 1, 1813, to engage the British frigate* Shannon, *Captain Broke. Bostonians, lining the shore to glimpse the spectacle, were disappointed as the engagement began at too great a distance. The fight was a sharp one. In fifteen minutes it was over; the* Chesapeake *was a British prize, her commander a mortally wounded man. As he was carried below during the battle, Lawrence uttered those words which ever since that day have inspired the Navy: "Don't give up the ship!" This handsome lithograph and that on page 19 were made from a series of paintings by J. C. Schetky, "under the inspection of Captain R. H. King R.N.," published in London in 1830.*

This diagram, based on an undated lithograph published in the U.S. Military Magazine *in 1840, shows the positions at various times of the* Constitution *and the* Java *during the famous battle shown above. From the beginning of the battle at 2:10 P.M., until the crippled British frigate surrendered at 5:25, Bainbridge steadily outmaneuvered him, crossing his bow perhaps eight times. Since the times are not indicated for each vessel separately, definite conclusions are difficult.*

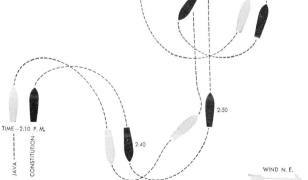

James Lawrence was no armchair officer but had served with distinction as
one of "Preble's boys" against the Tri-
politans in 1804. Early in 1813, when
commanding the sloop of war Hornet,
he captured the sloop Peacock. This
late print was published in 1862.

David Porter commanded the Essex on
her epic cruise in the South Pacific in
1813. There he broke up the British
whaling fleet by capturing twelve whalers around the Galapagos Islands and,
among other adventures, became involved in a native war. (Porter's writings are the finest from the War of
1812.) This engraving is from The
Analectic Magazine of September, 1814.

Defeats that won glory

After the battle shown on the preceding two pages, the captured *Chesapeake*
was led into the harbor of Halifax by her captors (*right*), the white ensign
symbolically flying over the flag of the United States. This was one of several
notable American defeats, which nevertheless had certain aspects in which the
new nation would take pride.

The *Chesapeake* had been in port less than two months since her last cruise
and most of her personnel, officers and men, were new to the ship. Her orders
were to cruise on the British line of communications to Canada, a most important assignment because of impending land operations. What was needed most
was a period of intensive training to develop the competence necessary to sail
the ship and man the guns and to carry out all orders with precision in the stress
of battle. All chance of such a period of preparation was lost when the *Shannon*
was discovered to be cruising within sight. It was folly to seek a fight under the
circumstances, and naval experts still criticize Lawrence for not evading the
Shannon in darkness or fog. But many a lost battle, even such ill-advised ones
as this, or the ones at Balaklava or the Little Big Horn, enshrines the dead
loser in history.

Another remarkable defeat was that of the *Essex* by the frigate *Phoebe* and
the sloop of war *Cherub* (*below*) off Valparaiso on March 28, 1814. When word
was received of Porter's successes—he captured twelve British whalers, drove the
balance to seek shelter in neutral ports, and cleared the area for American
whalers, having previously taken a prize carrying £11,000—a squadron was sent
to catch him. For six weeks he was blockaded and eventually, when his vessel
had been severely damaged in a squall, was forced to fight both ships. The battle
lasted nearly two and one-half hours, resulting in the capture of the *Essex*. The
great disparity of forces and the length of the engagement caused tremendous
American losses which would undoubtedly have been less had Porter surrendered
earlier. Out of 255 men, only 75 were effective when the colors were struck.
Even in her defeat, the *Essex* was the most successful of all the frigates.

WOODCUT IN *The Naval Monument*, 1816

Decisive battles on the lakes

At Lake Erie, on September 10, 1813 (top), Perry, in the Niagara, *at center, pushed through the British line. At Lake Champlain (below), on September 11, 1814, Commodore Macdonough and General Macomb's army repulsed the British pushing down from Canada.*

The most colorful and decisive sea battles of the war were fought far from salt water; in each of the two an American fleet was called suddenly into being, and in each a youthful American commander defeated a whole British squadron.

A series of American disasters had greeted all attempts to invade Canada, and 1813 found the British in control of Lake Erie. But in Erie, Pennsylvania, an American fleet was created, literally from green timbers, and in its flagship, the brig *Lawrence,* flying a flag reading "Don't Give Up The Ship," 28-year-old Commodore Oliver Hazard Perry set out, with eight other ships, to meet the British. When concentrated British fire put the *Lawrence* out of action, Perry seized his flag and transferred it to the *Niagara.* In her he sailed through the enemy line, raking at close range until, after a fifteen-minute cannonade, the British surrendered and Perry could send his famous message to General William Henry Harrison: "We have met the enemy and they are ours."

The victory of Thomas Macdonough, thirty, over a superior British fleet on Lake Champlain a year later, accompanied by an American victory on the land, was probably the most important naval action of the war. It thwarted an invasion from the north.

Under heavy fire, Perry transfers his flag to the undamaged Niagara, *his twelve-year-old brother, a midshipman, beside him in the sternsheets. Perry's success made it possible for him later to transport Harrison's army to victory in Canada, and re-establish American control in the Northwest.*

Over 350 years a mighty pageant of history has moved through the myth-haunted

The beauties of the river are evident even in dramatic exaggeration. This painting, The Hudson, *is by an unknown primi*

valley of the "Great River of the Mountains"

THE LORDLY HUDSON

By CARL CARMER

ist who flourished in the early nineteenth century.

Orientals were first upon the river. They came by land, and their journey eastward across the continent from its northwest coast to the banks where, their soothsayers had said, they might rest beside a water-that-flows-two-ways, had lasted many generations. There is no knowing who first saw the ocean-bound current turn about and run toward the mountains whence it came, but the realization of a prophecy fulfilled must have come upon him with a stunning impact.

The salty tides of the estuary encounter spring-borne floods that join among the high old rocks to the north, conquer them for measured periods, and then give way, leaving messages for men. Among the slant-eyed, red-brown tribes that gathered by the river were poets whose sensitivity to natural phenomena inspired legends. By the fireplaces within their rounded twig-and-clay houses they heard the rush of wind, the roll of thunder, the tattoo of rain, and a goddess who controlled all these and lived in highlands of the sky beyond the river mountains. From her perch above the wide valley she ordered her votaries cursed by lightning or blessed by sun. When the once slim moon hung fat, she lifted it from its hidden hook, cut it into stars, and sowed them like yellow seed into the night's black furrows. She had plucked and scattered countless full-blown golden blossoms from the sky before European explorers saw from under white sails the river landscape and its habitants, and speculated on its future. Verrazano, the Florentine, de-

HOLLAND'S

HEYDAY

ON

THE HUDSON

Dutch rule came to the river in 1609 with Henry Hudson. For most of its half-century of life the colony of New Neth erland was governed by a succession of director-generals appointed by the West India Company. No likeness survives of the first, Peter Minuit, but peg-legged Peter Stuyvesant (above) was painted, as well as another plain Dutchman, Cornelis Steenwyck (left), who served as burgomaster under the English in 1668-69. The able, efficient Minuit bought Manhattan Island from the Indians in 1626 for about $24, built Fort Amsterdam upon it, and made it his capital. Fort Orange—now Albany—had been founded as a trading post in 1617, and these two towns anchored and controlled the colony. The pioneers were rough fur traders. But by 1646, when Stuyvesant came, New Netherland was a thriving col ony of tidy farmers and solid burghers. "I shall be," Stuyve sant told them at the outset, "as a father over his children." But "Peter the Headstrong," as Washington Irving called him, soon alienated popular support, and this, combined with the continued refusal of the West India Company or the States-General to reinforce the colony against the New England settlements—grown hostile after a war broke out between England and Holland in 1652— boded ill for the Dutch foothold in New Netherland.

NIEUW AMSTERDAM OFTE NUE NIEUW IORX OPT TEYLANT MAN

New Amsterdam (above), with its windmill and gabled roofs, was pure Dutch in 1653. The Trumpeter (below), *by Susan Rivington Stuyvesant, illustrates a humorous passage in Irving's* Knickerbocker History, *showing the scapegrace trumpeter Van Corlear with an angry Stuyvesant. The Swedes had just captured Fort Casimir, a Dutch outpost on the Delaware.*

PROUD PATROONS

AND THEIR LADIES

Soon after the Dutch put down their first tentative roots along the Hudson, a shrewd Amsterdam jeweler named Kiliaen Van Rensselaer (below, left) gave some sound advice to the West India Company. "Open up the country with agriculture," he said; "that must be our first step." Accordingly, beginning in 1629, the Company offered the title of Patroon of New Netherland to anyone who would settle a group of fifty adults on grants of land across the sea. Over his grant the patroon (the word means patron) was to have complete control: he administered justice (fairly, in most cases); his tenants, indentured to him, had to pay rents up to $200 a year, render him many services, and give him one-tenth of everything the manor produced. Though he never set foot on it himself, Van Rensselaer, through agents, established in Rensselaerswyck a large and thriving settlement. But his agents found themselves ground between two stones: recalcitrant tenants who felt themselves exploited, and especially in Peter Stuyvesant director-generals jealous of their authority. Eventually the attempt to transplant this feudal system to the New World failed. Most patroons, like Adriaen Van der Donck (below, center), whose grant lay just north of Manhattan Island around Yonkers, never fully complied with the terms of their charters, and allowed title to revert to the Company. Then, in 1664, a seaborne English invasion force brought Dutch rule to an end (except for a few brief months again in 1673-4). New Netherland became New York, but the patroons who still had holdings along the river were allowed to retain them, and these Dutchmen, together with subsequent English grantees like the great Robert Livingston (below, right), laid the foundations of a powerful aristocracy that retained control over the Hudson Valley for generations to come.

The Land Grants of the Hudson

1. Staten Is.~Cornelis Melyn
2. Pelham~Thomas Pell
3. Lloyd's Neck~James Lloyd
4. Fordham~John Archer
5. Morrisania~Lewis Morris
6. Scarsdale~Caleb Heathcote

MAP FOR AMERICAN HERITAGE BY JOHN TEPPICH

Ariaantje Schuyler Van Rensselaer   *Ariaantje Coeymans*   *Mrs. Petrus Vas*

Captain Johannes Schuyler and his wife, attributed to John Watson about 1730. Schuyler fought against the French and helped keep the Iroquois loyal to England, but the Revolution divided his descendants.

JUGULAR

VEIN

OF REVOLUTION

When the Revolution came, control of the Hudson became a keystone of British strategy, for if the river could be won, New England could be divided from the Middle Colonies and the rebellion strangled. Late in 1776 the English seized the river's lower hinge by boldly forcing a passage north between Forts Washington (above, right) and Lee, then attacking and capturing them. But subsequent attempts to secure the Hudson's upper reaches—first by arms (below), and then by stealth (opposite page, top)—failed. The colonies' jugular vein was safe.

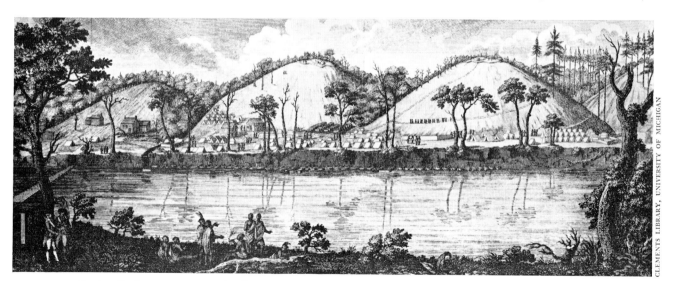

England's first attempt to win the upper Hudson, in 1777, was blocked at Saratoga. In this view of the enemy camp the funeral procession of the British General Simon Fraser winds up the hill.

HUDSONS RIVER

CONSTITUTION ISLAND

PLAN
OF
WEST POINT.

Copied from the Original Map of
Major VILLEFRANCHE (Engineer)

Scale of a Mile

The British tried again in 1780, when Benedict Arnold—ironically, one of Burgoyne's conquerors —offered to surrender West Point. But the capture of Arnold's British contact, Major John André —seen here in a self-portrait sketched before his execution—foiled the plot. In his boot heel were plans of the fort at West Point like the one above, showing the iron chain blocking the channel.

Seizing the lower Hudson in 1776, Cornwallis' men scale the Palisades to take Fort Lee. The loss of this post and Fort Washington to the east precipitated the costly American retreat across New Jersey.

BUSY RIVER LIFE

In this 1836 oil by George Harvey, a lumber raft drifts lazily down toward the Palisades. As the side-wheeler (rear) indicates, the steamboat's great day was at hand.

This view of Newburgh, as well as that of Troy at right, was painted in the 1820's by Irish-born W. G. Wall. Newburgh, originally settled by Palatine Germans in 1709, began to fade as the Erie Canal diverted its commerce. But in the 1830's and 1840's it took new life from an unlikely source: it became a thriving whaling center.

The Hudson at Bear Mountain, with a family picnicking on the bank at left, was painted about 1850 by George Loring Brown. The funnel-stacked locomotive being flagged at right was a herald of change: railroads snaked up both riverbanks, bringing wealth to the river towns. Today railroad service is contracting back to just one bank.

Wall painted the city of Troy from nearby Mount Ida. The site, at the head of navigation on the river, was visited by Hudson in 1609 and was originally part of Rensselaerswyck, the patroonship of Kiliaen Van Rensselaer. When this water color was painted, Troy was a center for Irish immigrants building new railroads and canals.

In the decades before and after the Civil War wealthy New Yorkers began dotting the lower Hudson Valley with immense piles of stone and masonry which, though far from humble, were nonetheless home. In 1855, one observer noted that suburban mansions were "starting up like mushrooms on spots which five years ago were part of the dense and tangled forest . . ." Some, like the still-standing Jehiel Read house in Hastings (top left) and ex-President Martin Van Buren's Lindenwald at Kinderhook (bottom left), were frank imitations of Italian villas; others, like John J. Herrick's crenelated country seat at Tarrytown (below), resembled castles on the Rhine. Octagon House (left), in Irvington, now the home of the author, Carl Carmer, combines the architectural ideas of Orson Squire Fowler, a prominent phrenologist responsible for the wide adoption of the eight-sided type, and a Chinese decorative influence contributed by the builder, an importer of Chinese teas. And on Pollopel Island arms dealer Francis Bannerman built a baronial castle (above), complete with arsenal. Thus, with the valley's old Dutch and English aristocracy a new strain mingled, and the Hudson's Victorian period became, as the paintings opposite show, a time of leisure and opulence.

Villas on the Hudson

These two scenes offer glimpses into the lives of the Hudson River gentry. Outing on the Hudson (above) was painted by an unknown primitive artist about 1876. Below is Thomas P. Rossiter's A Picnic on the Hudson *(1863). Seated at extreme right is Gouverneur Kemble, whose West Point Foundry was turning out the Civil War Parrott gun invented by Robert Parker Parrott, here standing behind Kemble. The white-bearded man at center is George Pope Morris, editor of the New York* Mirror *and author of* Woodman, Spare That Tree. *The artist himself stands at farthest left.*

Washington Irving and His Literary Friends, *by Christian Schussele. From left: H.T. Tuckerman, O.W. Holmes, William G. Simms, Fitz-Greene Halleck, Nathaniel Hawthorne, Henry W. Longfellow, Nathaniel P. Willis, William H. Prescott, Irving, James K. Paulding, Ralph W. Emerson, W. C. Bryant, J.P. Kennedy, James Fenimore Cooper, George Bancroft.*

THE HUDSON IN ART AND LEGEND

Millions of Americans who have never walked the green and hilly banks of the Hudson know the river well—through the stories of Washington Irving, who peopled its valley with comic Dutchmen, headless horsemen, and bowling gnomes, and through the peaceful, realistic canvases of the Hudson River school. The connection between the two is real, for in addition to his wide literary acquaintanceship (above), Irving knew and encouraged many of the Hudson River painters and recommended their work to wealthy art collectors. One of the best of their pictures is Asher B. Durand's Kindred Spirits *(left), in which the school's founder, Thomas Cole, shows William Cullen Bryant the glories of the valley. Henry Inman's* Picnic in the Catskills *(right) recalls an 1840 letter from Irving to his sister: "We have picnic parties, sometimes in some inland valley or piece of wood, sometimes on . . . some woodland point jutting into the Tappan Sea, with gay groups on the grass under the trees . . ."*

he revealed the potency of Daniel Webster in the modern world more precisely than any factual historian has revealed it.

The potency does not rest upon the statutes Webster drew, the contracts he negotiated, nor the politics he played. It is based upon his success as the establisher of moods, and that kind of success is never attested by documents. On the contrary, the documentary evidence frequently seems to contradict it, which is so much the worse for the documentary evidence. It is just this failure of the letter to capture the spirit that is the ruin of biographers and historians and the opportunity of poets. Talking of Daniel Webster conveys little that is of importance today; it was when Benét began to sing that the still surviving power and glory appeared.

The industrious pedestrians have uncovered the facts down to astonishingly small details. A New Hampshire farmer, wise beyond most of his generation, spared one of his many children the hard labor of the fields because the boy was physically sickly, although mentally precocious. Instead, the boy was sent to the best teachers available and eventually to Dartmouth College. He justified this indulgence twice, first by helping one of his brothers through college, and later by abandoning a promising professional career to care for his parents in their declining years. But the lofty intelligence, like the Scriptural city set upon a hill, could not be hid; at 31 the man was in the House of Representatives from New Hampshire. This was in 1813, just before the final wreck of the Federalist party in the Hartford Convention at the beginning of 1815. With his party shot from under him, the young man repaired to Boston in 1816 and in ten years had pushed his income from legal practice to $15,000 a year—in purchasing power the equivalent of $50,000 to $75,000 today. He went to the Senate in 1827, became secretary of state in 1841, returned to the Senate in 1845, became secretary of state again in 1850, and died in 1852.

Like every first-rate American who goes into politics, he wished to be President of the United States, and like most first-rate men he suffered the mortification of seeing second-raters chosen in his stead. During his time in Washington, Webster saw ten individuals occupying the White House and knew in his heart that he was superior to eight of them. No doubt he thought he was superior to the other two, Madison and Jackson, but history disallows that claim.

The second most brilliant period of American politics was beginning when Webster entered Congress, and he was, in popular estimation, one third of it. That was, of course, the same kind of exaggeration that gives the most brilliant period one half to Jefferson and the other half to Hamilton, although they were merely the two brightest stars in a galaxy. In the second period, Webster, Clay, and Calhoun outshone all other members of Congress, but not by much. Benton, Hayne, John Quincy Adams, Van Buren, Marcy, and John Randolph were no dim lights, and outside of Congress stood the gigantic figures of Andrew Jackson and John Marshall.

Of the illustrious trio, Webster was the latest arrival and, on technicalities, the least successful. All of them made Cabinet rank, but Calhoun was Vice President for seven years and Clay was three times a candidate for President, twice as the nominee of a major party. Thus it may fairly be said that both came closer to the White House than Webster did, although none reached it.

Without doubt Webster was refused even a nomination because his affiliations made him politically unavailable. He was the recognized spokesman of Big Business, and even at that early date party leaders were sure that nomination of such a candidate would be party suicide. It was not regarded as scandalous for a member of Congress to continue to serve his rich clients even—indeed especially—before government agencies, but it was regarded as a political handicap, and Webster's party was never strong enough to assume that handicap. Curiously enough, this favorite advocate of astute businessmen had so little "money sense" that in spite of an income that was, for the time, a huge one, he was perpetually in debt and therefore never able to break away from subservience to wealth.

But there is another aspect of this man that is even more curious. The spokesman of Big Business, the great corporation lawyer, is a familiar figure. There is always at least one in Congress, frequently half a dozen in the Administration, and they are conspicuous, often dominant, figures, so we know the type or think we do; and the common opinion is that the agent of Big Business, whatever his merits, is decidedly a cold fish, emphatically not the kind of material out of which popular heroes are made. Is it imaginable that a poet could have woven a folk tale around Thomas C. Platt or Nelson W. Aldrich or Elihu Root or Andrew Mellon? But Webster was legendary even before his death, and since that event the legend has grown until it overshadows that of Henry Clay, much the more popular figure while he lived.

The inescapable inference is that there was a link between the ordinary American and this extraordinary individual, some quality that enables the common man to feel a kinship with Webster that he never feels with any cold fish. The easy assumption is that his faults endeared him to the sinful majority, and no doubt they did to some extent.

Dan Webster stoked his boilers with brown jugs of apple cider,
And when he made a speech he yanked the spigot open wider.
Sing ho! those spirited debates, bereft of all restrictions,
When statesmen carried on their hip the strength of their convictions,

is evidence that his fondness for the bottle passed into the legend, and his amorous adventures, probably apocryphal, have been the theme of innumerable smoking-room stories. But these things the people regard with indulgence, not with approval; and somewhere in the American mind there is a deep and powerful approval of Daniel Webster, and a proprietary pride.

Yet when one examines any of his specific activities it seems far away and long ago, frequently without much logical significance even at the time. The celebrated Reply to Hayne, for example, was not a reply to Hayne at all. It was the evocation of a mood, not the refutation of an argument, a histrionic, not a logical triumph. "Liberty *and* Union, now and forever, one and inseparable!" had nothing whatever to do with the points that Hayne had raised, but it stirred up a tremendous emotional reaction against the idea of disunion. Logic frequently eludes the grasp of the masses, but they understand feeling instantly; and they understood Webster. His heart was in the right place.

At least four of his exploits have affected and still affect the destinies of every man and woman in the United States, and each of them was of the same order —the establishment of a mood rather than the defense of a thesis. These were the Dartmouth College case, the case of *McCulloch v. Maryland*, the negotiation of the Webster-Ashburton Treaty, and the Compromise of 1850.

Examined in the cold light of reason all of these are without significance as of the year 1957; but in the warm glow of emotion it is apparent that each of them grips us today with an unbreakable hold. None was the work of Daniel Webster alone, but he was an operative force in all four, and he remains an operative force to this day.

The Dartmouth College case established the sanctity of contract. The case revolved around an effort by the state of New Hampshire to move in and take control of a college that it had chartered, perpetually, as a private institution; which, Webster argued, was an effort by the state to repudiate its own contract, which not even a sovereign has a right to do. The court presumably was moved by the logic of the argument, but Webster's passing remark, "She is small, but there are those who love her," hit the country with an impact that no kind of logical exposition could achieve. The fact that this case came dangerously close to repealing the Statutes of Mortmain and delivering the future into economic bondage was something for jurisconsults to worry over; the people saw in it only the rescue of cherished and threatened institutions, and that mood has persisted through all the discomforts that immortality of corporations has brought upon us.

The case of *McCulloch v. Maryland* successfully asserted the right of judicial review of legislation. Logically, it is untenable, but practically it has worked, and that is enough for the common man. Possibly the hard core of that decision was John Marshall's determination to bow his arrogant head to no man, even at the behest of the Aristotelian syllogism. That is as it may be. But deep in the heart of the common man is a conviction that logic is an invention of schoolmasters that bears precious little relation to life as he lives it; so if the advocate in this case departed from the accepted rules he did not thereby offend the typical American. Rather, he aroused a fraternal understanding among men more intent upon devising a workable method than upon making their reasoning conform to BARBARA or FRESISON. So even in this legalistic matter they have felt close to Daniel Webster; and the mood then established, the feeling that the Constitution must be made to work, even if it has to be bent into the shape of a pretzel, has persisted from that day to this.

The Webster-Ashburton Treaty is one of the most remarkable in the history of diplomacy, not for what is contained so much as for the manner in which it was nego-

tiated. Alexander Baring, Lord Ashburton, was sent over in 1842 as a special envoy to take up with Webster, then secretary of state, a number of issues in dispute between the United States and Great Britain, the most important of which was the boundary line between Maine and Canada. That line had never been properly surveyed, but simply marked out on maps which were supposed to be attached to the treaty, but which had somehow become detached. The matter then hinged on discovery of the right map, and both parties ransacked the archives.

Through the agency of Jared Sparks, in Paris, Webster was supplied with a map said to have been marked by Benjamin Franklin and given to the French ministry—and it knocked the bottom out of the American claim. About the same time someone discovered in the British archives a map supposed to have been marked for the information of King George III—and it knocked the bottom out of the British claim. But neither negotiator suspected the existence of the other map; all either knew was that his own position was exceedingly precarious.

Thus each went into the discussions warily and with the most scrupulous regard for punctilio. When the citizens of Maine threatened to become obstreperous, Webster privately showed their leaders the Jared Sparks map, and they instantly subsided. So, since neither principal could risk being adamant, the dickering and dealing proceeded smoothly to a conclusion reasonably satisfactory to both sides.

But much more was accomplished than the boundary settlement, much that does not appear in the written records and, indeed, was never formally admitted by either side. This accomplishment was a marked softening of our diplomatic contacts with Great Britain. His lordship discovered that the American, far from being a raucous and semiliterate backwoodsman, was an urbane and gentlemanly fellow. The American, on his part, discovered that a noble lord is not necessarily arrogant and supercilious, but may be a reasonable, fair-minded character with whom it is a pleasure to do business. The discovery that each was carefully polite because he distrusted his own case came long afterward and did not destroy the mood created in 1842.

Of course this mood was reinforced by many other factors, but without doubt it was helped along by the Webster-Ashburton negotiations; and 115 years later it still persists. Before that date our contacts with the British were, as a rule, unpleasantly rough, but since then they have been the smoothest of all. Even the Anglophobes among us feel the effect and hold that while to swindle the English may be permissible and even praiseworthy, it must always be done with a certain suavity amid expressions of the utmost good will. Daniel Webster had much to do with establishing that mood and therein he touches your life and mine.

But it was on March 7, 1850, that Daniel Webster probably saved the Union and ruined himself by rising to greatness. The aftermath of the Mexican War had had the usual effect of war's aftermath—it had driven the more emotional elements of the population into raving insanity. It is at such times that formerly gentle souls turn into vipers, and formerly shrewd fellows take to a braying that drowns the voice of reason. As far as the United States is concerned certainly, and perhaps as regards other nations as well, the loss of blood and treasure that attends the actual conflict has never been as permanently injurious to the nation as the loss of common sense and common decency that follows the cessation of hostilities.

The Mexican affair had ended in 1848, and by 1850 mass hysteria had reached its height. In Congress John C. Calhoun, for the South, and William H. Seward, for the North, were no longer arguing, they were merely screeching; and each was attended by a rabble of noise-makers whose din all but obliterated calm counsel. It was plain, all too appallingly plain, that any small spark might set off an explosion that would destroy the Union.

Then old Henry Clay, already mortally ill, summoned the last of his strength to devise the nine measures known as the Compromise of 1850 and, dying on his feet, prevented the death of his country. His success was not immediate. Since it was a genuine compromise, it was furiously attacked by both Calhoun and Seward, and its fate wavered in the balance week after week and month after month. So evenly matched were the contestants that eventually it became plain that all depended upon Webster, who had so far said nothing.

On March 7 at last he rose to speak, ". . . not as a Massachusetts man, nor as a Northern man, but as an American . . . I speak today for the preservation of the Union. 'Hear me for my cause.'" They heard. They heeded. The squabbling continued for months, but eventually the compromise was adopted and the Civil War was postponed for ten years.

But Webster's reward was such denunciation from his own people as few American statesmen have had to endure. John Greenleaf Whittier, that singularly bloodthirsty Quaker, promptly consigned him to the tomb without waiting for a physician's certificate:

from those great eyes
The soul has fled:
When faith is lost, when honor dies,
The man is dead!

196

and less melodious calumniators poured cruder vituperation on him wherever two or three lunatics were gathered together.

Yet every measurement known to statistics shows clearly that from 1820 on the South had been steadily losing and the North steadily gaining in relative strength. Nevertheless, when war did break in 1861, it took every ounce of Northern strength to win through four years of the bloodiest fighting in modern times. Few Americans stop to realize that, in proportion to the numbers engaged, the American Civil War was several times as deadly as either World War I or World War II. If it had come ten years earlier the border states would almost certainly have gone with the South, and the outcome can hardly be doubted.

Henry Clay's Compromise of 1850 saved this Union; and Daniel Webster saved the compromise.

But it was not by logic that he did it. Logically, he was a Massachusetts man, a Northern man, but emotionally he was an American; and the emotional appeal, not the logic, carried the compromise. More than that, it carried Daniel Webster into the hearts of an emotional people, and there he abides. We do not believe, we cannot believe, that knowledge, logic, might, or the Devil himself can prevail against a man who loves anything strongly enough to invite ruin in its defense.

This characteristic of human nature is the great weakness of democracy, as has been vociferously proclaimed by every logician from Plato down. Alcibiades played upon it; so did Huey Long and Joe McCarthy and all the demagogues between. But under favorable circumstances it is also the great strength of democracy, as Webster, Lincoln, and the second Roosevelt instinctively recognized. It is the factor that transforms government from a science into an art, maddening the scientists, including—perhaps one should say especially—the social scientists; and inspiring poets and other irresponsible characters.

The obvious fact that democracy is—apparently incurably—emotional rather than logical is the despair of men who have subjected their minds to rigorous intellectual discipline, and who are therefore convinced that intellectual discipline is the only conceivable approach to truth. Thus when they perceive that the great heroes of democracy seem to bear more family likeness to Roscius, the actor, than to Aristotle, the philosopher, they tend to despair of democracy. Webster is a case in point. He was certainly a great constitutional lawyer, which is to say, a logician; but he became immortal only when he abandoned his logic and appealed to the emotions as frankly as Cleon of Athens ever did. The legal precedents he set— as, for example, his arguments for the bank, for and then against free trade, and on municipal and international law—have been largely superseded or abandoned, but the moods he established have endured for more than a hundred years. Superficially, this suggests that demagoguery casts its works in bronze, while statecraft carves in butter, which is a patent absurdity.

What the rigid logicians tend to overlook is that emotionalism as a political instrument is not monolithic. It is divided into separate and antipodal branches, one of which relies on love, the other on hate as its chief agency. Hope is subsidiary to love as fear is to hate. The artists, as distinguished from the scientists, in government can be classified accordingly. If one relies on the emotions of hate and fear of the enemy, it is safe to classify him with Alcibiades; but if he relies on love of country and hope for the future, there you have Pericles.

There is not the slightest doubt on which side of the line Daniel Webster's appeal to emotions lay. He spoke as an American. He spoke for the future. He was extravagant, yes; he was turgid and bombastic, if you will. But his worst extravagance and bombast were never designed to foment hatred and fear, but always to stimulate love and pride. Therefore the people, greatly needing both, have looked with an indulgent eye on his faults and frailties and, because he spurred them in the direction of greatness, deemed him, and still deem him, a great man.

True, the eye with which they have regarded him is not only indulgent, but a little sardonic. When his last words were reported, folklore quickly invented an explanation of the utterance. People said that the physician remarked to an attendant when the end was obviously at hand, "If he is still living in an hour, give him brandy," whereupon Daniel Webster with his dying breath murmured, "I still live."

Never mind. Whom the American people love, they laugh at. It has always been so, and it will be so until the character of the nation is changed. If his spirit could return to observe what has come of the nation that he saved, it is easy to believe that it would be less impressed by the miraculous changes that have taken place than by the lack of any change in the common people's love of and pride in their country. And seeing this lack of change the disembodied spirit could repeat, "I still live."

Gerald W. Johnson, formerly associated with the Baltimore Sun *and now a contributing editor of* The New Republic, *has written more than a score of books on the American social, political, and historical scenes, among them* The Lunatic Fringe *and, more recently,* America Is Born.

The pride of early locomotive builders is evidenced in their fine lithographs. This one shows a classic "American" type

FAREWELL TO STEAM

The iron horses that built America are nearly all gathered on the other side of Jordan

By OLIVER JENSEN

ner, built in 1856 by the Amoskeag Manufacturing Company of Manchester, N.H. Behind are the great Amoskeag textile mills.

It was the way they worked the cord and changed the steam pressure that made the whistle almost seem to talk. Of course, there was a regular language of signals—two long blasts for starting up; one long tremolo for approaching a station; and, at grade crossings, the familiar *whoooo, whoooo, hoo, whooooooooo!* mournful and infinitely expressive—but within these supposed rigidities there was plenty of room for individuality. An engineer was a man of importance, admired by young and old, and the whistle was his signature. It was the notes of a whippoorwill, they say, that signified to the Mississippi field

199

law is at work which has no regard for romance: the diesel is cheaper to operate. And, apparently in a desire to underscore the point, every nerve and sinew has been bent toward making the diesel as ugly as possible.

The surviving engines in operation today are the country cousins—motive power of branches, short lines, logging and quarry roads. ("Thank God for sand and gravel pits!" cried the editor of a railroad fanciers' magazine.) These survivors are generally little fellows of quaint and ancient cut, better adapted than the giants to short trains, light rails, fragile trestles, and uneven roadbeds. Often they are graying at the temples, to say the least. With a little renewing here and there and some deft cannibalizing of sister locomotives, however, a steam engine practically never wears out. *Smoky Mary*, brought over from England to a Louisiana line in 1832, operated satisfactorily for 100 years, and *John Bull*, built in 1831 by Robert Stephenson & Company at Newcastle-upon-Tyne, is still in working condition, although admittedly it spends most of its time these days just resting in the Smithsonian. In its own museum, the Baltimore & Ohio keeps a number of pre-Civil War engines like the *William Mason* ready to be steamed up and run out on the line whenever the movie-makers call.

The South, and particularly Georgia, has been a holdout in the era of the diesel, a kind of home to aging steam locomotives, but even here the new prosperity is falling on steam like a blight. The wood-burner lingered long in this area of cheap timber, but most of them too have vanished. Ironically, operable small engines of this type have grown so rare that their curio, or antique, value to museums and hobbyists has risen *ten times* in the 1956 to 1960 period.

Steam engines, it should be explained, are classified for most purposes by their wheel arrangement. Thus the so-called "American" type of locomotive, of which many specimens are illustrated in these pages, is called a 4-4-0—signifying that there are four wheels under the front truck, four driving wheels, and no trailing wheels under the cab. Wheels under the tender, of course, are ignored. It tends to be the famous older (and smaller) types that survive—Consolidations (2-8-0); freight-hauling Moguls (2-6-0); ten wheelers (4-6-0); Mikados (2-8-2); and Pacifics (4-6-2). Big as they are in relation to the little engines of the Civil War era, they are dwarfed by the great articulated Mallets, with their two sets of driving wheels, each rigged to its own set of cylinders, running in series as complex as 2-10-10-2.

The disappearance of a steam engine is rarely a publicized or even public event; it is a thing done privately in an undistinguished setting. One night old 567 rolls a way freight into the yard, uncouples, backs off on a rusty spur, and has her fires raked out and boilers drained for the last time. There she rusts a few weeks or months, depending on the market for scrap iron. Generally someone in authority comes by to chalk her boiler with a notice of disposition (or perhaps some more personal message like the "Goodbye, old Pal" one traveler observed in a Philadelphia yard) and eventually she goes to the torch. The public is on the highways, and there is no audience to see the corpse borne off, like Hamlet's by the soldiers, with a dead march, drums, and peals of ordnance. But the drama is there, for this is the end of something entirely heroic, of a century and a quarter in which one great invention transformed a scattering of towns and settlements into a united nation.

The story of America and the steam locomotive can be told in many ways. There is, for example, a tale of inventors frustrated and prophets ignored. Consider a strange genius named Oliver Evans, who was chattering about steam carriages as early as 1786. He built

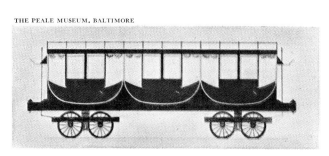

The first cars were basically coach bodies. The Winchester *(about 1832) was three Imlay coaches run together, built by Ross Winans, a horse trader who became a great engine and car builder. He patented the pivoted four-wheel trucks.*

Peter Cooper's Tom Thumb, *first American-built locomo on a regular railroad, ran its famous race with a horse*

202

a strange, crawling, amphibious monster which he called the *Orukter Amphibolos;* it moved on land to the Schuylkill River, waddled in and kept right on going. Naturally no one listened to a man like this when he suggested a wooden railway, with steam-drawn carriages to move between New York and Philadelphia at fifteen miles an hour. After him there was John Stevens of Hoboken, who operated the world's first steam ferry and, at the age of 76, designed and built with his own hands a toy engine which he operated on a circular track in his yard. This was 1825, the same year Stephenson's *Locomotion* appeared in England. After 1825, railroad projects sprang up everywhere, and railroading now became a story of inventors not only listened to but acclaimed. And the world had a new toy, viewed with horror by some and astonishment by others. Listen to an elegant gentleman of New York, George Templeton Strong, writing in 1839:

It's a great sight to see a large train get under way . . . As to the engine, the most pithy and expressive epithet I ever heard applied to it is "Hell-in-Harness." Just imagine such a concern rushing unexpectedly by a stranger to the invention on a dark night, whizzing and rattling and panting, with its fiery furnace gleaming in front, its chimney vomiting fiery smoke above, and its long train of cars rushing along behind like the body and tail of a gigantic dragon—or like the d——l himself—and all darting forward at the rate of twenty miles an hour. Whew!

When the rails came to Amherst, Emily Dickinson characteristically crouched in the woods to see the train move off and then rushed home to dash off a poem (*I like to hear it lap the miles, and lick the valleys up . . .*) Over in another wood lot, in Concord, Henry David Thoreau was opposed in principle but could not conceal a certain admiration:

. . . when I hear the iron horse make the hills echo with

his snort like thunder, shaking the earth with his feet, and breathing fire and smoke from his nostrils . . . it seems as if the earth had got a race now worthy to inhabit it. If all were as it seems, and men made the elements their servants for noble ends!

There is a story of great feats of engineering too—of speed and danger, of wilderness tamed, rivers bridged, tunnels drilled, mountains surmounted. Here, for example, is Henry Flagler, 82 years old, achieving his dream at last, making the first ride across the railroad he built out to sea to reach Key West—twenty miles on embankments, seventeen on bridges. Here between Batavia and Buffalo is the famous speed trial of old 999, making 112.5 miles an hour, back in 1893. Out at Promontory, Utah, is the greatest denouement of all, as the Golden Spike goes down in 1869, in a burst of booze and oratory. Bret Harte writes a poem:

> *What was it the Engines said,*
> *Pilots touching, head to head*
> *Facing on a single track,*
> *Half a world behind each back?*

(They might have said: Achievements pass. For the rails bypass Promontory on a shorter route today, Mr. Flagler's railroad has been blown away, and old 999 has become a state fair exhibit. Where she passed, the trains today move no faster than eighty or less.)

Then, for a time, the railroad story becomes an extravagant tale of wild speculation, swindled bondholders, great systems devouring little ones, Wall Street coups, freight-rate scandals, rival financial titans. The harsh word is robber baron, and two notable quotations come down to us from that era. There is the long argued-over retort of Vanderbilt, "The public be damned!" And there is the more characteristic remark, half aloud, half to himself, of another rail-

History of the First Locomotives in America, BY W. H. BROWN, 1871

B&O in 1830, losing only when a belt slipped steam pressure sank. It was the horse's last victory.

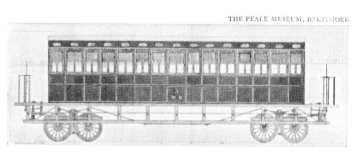

Winans' later design, the Washington, *had a center aisle instead of the coach compartments; this set the custom for America although the British, respecting privacy, retained the older arrangement. This car joined the B&O in 1835.*

203

TWENTYFIVE TON PASSENGER ENGINE.
LAWRENCE MACHINE SHOP
LAWRENCE MASS.

Great builders and gaudy eight-wheelers

ENGINES OF THIS PLAN WEIGHING FROM 37000 TO 64000 LBS.
M. W. BALDWIN & CO, LOCOMOTIVE BUILDERS,
PHILADELPHIA.

Peter Cooper's experimental four-wheeled engine weighed barely a ton, used old musket barrels as boiler tubes, and applied power to only one axle. More power was needed and a number of great locomotive builders before long responded with the engine type that was pre-eminent throughout the nineteenth century, the sturdy "American" eight-wheeler. The forward truck was pivoted to help hold the sharp, bumpy curves; connecting rods added tractive power by turning all four main wheels into drivers. Bells, whistles, tight and efficient cylinders, covered cabs, oil head lamps, and other devices appeared; proud owners saw no need for somber colors. The Lawrence (upper left) was constructed in 1853, the gaudy Wyoming (above) shopped out by Richard Norris & Son of Philadelphia in 1857. The eight-wheeler below, the Highland Light, built in 1867 for the Cape Cod Central Railroad, typifies the work of the greatest artist in engine design, William Mason of Taunton, Massachusetts, who once observed that locomotives should "look somewhat better than cookstoves on wheels." The Tiger, all scroll and panel work (below left), was turned out in 1856 by Matthias Baldwin of Philadelphia, a jeweler who got into vastly successful locomotive building after making a miniature locomotive which operated on a small track in the Philadelphia museum of his friend Franklin Peale. One of Baldwin's durable engines, the Pioneer, built in 1836, with a few repairs was able to give reliable service under its own power during the Chicago Railroad Fair in 1949.

The Lackawanna Valley *foreshadows as early as 1854 the new industrial look of America, and with it introduces an early specimen of the train watcher, or fan. The canvas was commissioned by George D. Phelps, first president of the Delaware, Lackawanna & Western Railroad, a penny-pinching patron of the arts who wished to immortalize his new round-house in Scranton, offering $75 for the job to a struggling young painter named George Inness. Mrs. Inness pressed her reluctant husband to accept and he, not trusting the steam cars, went to Scranton by stage coach, to be greeted by a demanding employer. For example, Phelps desired all the line's three engines in the picture, each lettered with the company's interminable name. For $75, said Inness, he could have only one, uninscribed. A single track then led into the roundhouse, but the president persuaded Inness to include others on the grounds that the line planned eventually to build them. Later the painting disappeared for many years, until Inness himself found it in Mexico City in 1892; he bought it back for a few dollars.*

Steam reshapes the landscape

Held Up, *by N. H. Trotter, well expresses the confrontation between the locomotive and the Wild West it came to civilize. The buffalo herds, once estimated to number some fifteen millions, vanished after the continent-binding spike was driven in 1869, yet the tracks followed their paths. The bison always took the easiest grades.*

The marriage of the railroads and the cities brought its problems, not the least of which were murderous grade-crossings. Politicians, reformers, even novelists like Winston Churchill fought them bitterly. Here on a temporary trestle, in 1875, the New York Central crosses the Harlem wastes, bound for Grand Central Terminal.

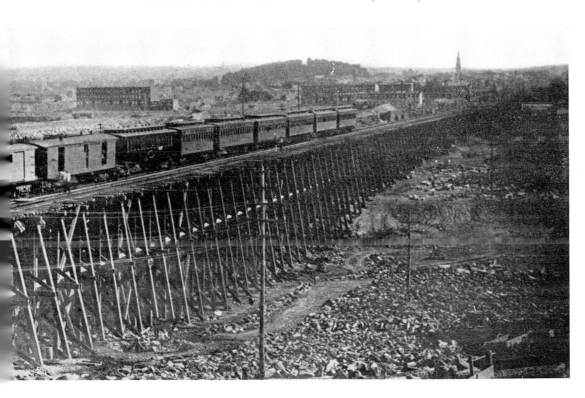

The 9:45 a.m. Accommodation, Stratford, Connecticut, *painted by E. L. Henry in 18* *recalls the day when the depot was the center of town, the engineer a great man,*

road Avenue a select address. Even the solitary Thoreau thought the depot atmos-
e "electrifying" and called steam-car movements "the epochs in the village day."

In 1836 a combined highway and railroad bridge brought the Baltimore & Ohio into Harpers Ferry, crossing the Potomac and the Chesapeake & Ohio Canal (foreground). When this picture was made, in 1857, the B&O, via connecting lines, had just reached the Mississippi at St. Louis, Missouri. Beyond the river lay fresh perils, as shown in the highly imaginative 1870 scene below on the Little Rock & Fort Smith Railroad. The handsome engine McKay might scatter the red men, but it would never make that curve.

COLLECTION OF HOWARD STEBBINS, LITTLE ROCK

Though since overshadowed by the Moffat, Cascade, and other tunnels, the 4.73-mile Hoosac Tunnel in Massachusetts, on the line of the Fitchburg Railroad, was the wonder of the age when, after 21 years and 105 deaths, it was completed in 1876. This is one of its early advertising posters, when it served several railroads. Cutting through this east-west barrier in the Berkshires, the contractors, first to employ compressed air and nitroglycerine, encountered everything, even soluble rock which, when exposed to air, ran like quicksand. As one laborer said, it was "like trying to shovel live eels."

In the days of the Comstock Lode, the Afternoon Express on the Virginia & Truckee, the legendary mining railroad of Nevada, brought the gaudy new gentry of San Francisco up steep grades to the fleshpots of Virginia City. This painting by Howard Fogg depicts the late 1870's, and a string of Pullmans double-headed behind No. 12, the Genoa, and No. 11, the Reno. Genoa, built by Baldwin in 1872 and retired but not scrapped in 1912, is a fine example of the eight-wheeler in its prime. The V&T ran ancient engines and brightly painted wooden cars right down to the bitter end in 1950. Then the rolling stock went to Hollywood, but the rails, alas, joined the sorrowful roster of picturesque but vanished American short lines.

Double-headed behind little diamond-stacked engines, the Denver & Rio Grande Western three-foot gauge threads its precipitous way through the canyon of the Lost Souls from Durango to Silverton, Colorado. The date is 1885, but much the same sort of train still operates this route today, its ten period cars packed with enthusiasts well aware that they are riding the sole surviving narrow-gauge passenger route in America. Yet once upon a time, America boasted some 750 such lines.

Competition was real and advertising vigorous. Commodore Vanderbilt's New York Central gloried in its four new tracks.

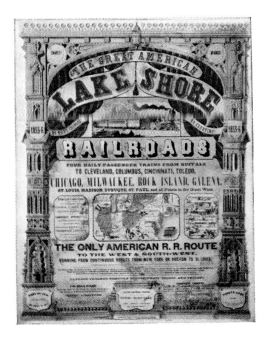

The rival Erie had a six-foot gauge, Currier & Ives posters, and three rascals (Drew, Gould, and Fisk) running it. Before the great systems gobbled up the smaller ones, outlying routes like the Lake Shore (left) were independent. In 1856, when this poster came out, the Erie had just reached the lake whose name it bears. Its broad-gauge cars could go no farther. These were times when railroad managements vaunted their steam engines and actually cared, as someone has remarked, about the passenger element.

Back in 1909, when this highly symbolic chromolithograph was printed for the adornment of depot and schoolroom walls, steam ruled the world of transportation, undaunted by flimsy aircraft or newfangled automobiles. Earth satellites were provided strictly by the Almighty.

road king, on learning of a little railroad that no one had yet gobbled up: "Great Scott! Is there anything like that still left outdoors?" This was a time when, as Philip Guedalla noted, the names of railroad presidents were apt to be a good deal more significant than those of the occupants of the White House.

There was a railroad of song and folklore, where Jesse James stopped the mail car every night, where the cars just barely cleared the burning trestle, where the brave engineer kept his hand on the throttle, where Dinah blew her horn all the day. But the most significant story is found in a series of railroad maps, by decades. Here at the start are only a few little wiggly lines around Charleston, Baltimore, New York, and Boston. Expanding steadily, as in an animated movie, they eventually envelop America in a giant

spider web. They carry the emigrants west. They bring the crops east to be traded for the products of industry. They build cities, and woe betide those they pass by. They make the desert, as the orator said, bloom like a garden. They create wealth and opportunity. In 1848, old Number One of the Galena & Chicago Union smokes her way into Chicago, first steam locomotive to reach what would become the railroad capital of the country. The same story is told over and over again, of all the western cities, until the big balloon stacks appear under the southern California sky to touch off a boom that is not over yet. No wonder the railroad and the steam behemoth that moved along it were the symbols of America.

Steam could not last forever, any more than the stage coach, after the invention of a more efficient device. The perilous state of most railroad finances —beset by subsidized highway, air, and water competition, regulated as though a nineteenth-century monopoly still existed—required some drastic economies, and this the diesel provided. The public, deserting the railroad passenger services in droves, saw less and less of the changeover.

But steam is dying hard, nevertheless, and it retains an ever-growing army of admirers. They turn out by the thousands for one "last" ride after another; they swap endless pictures, spikes, tickets, old timetables, even recordings of railroad noises; and they jabber away happily in professional jargon. They organize a great many clubs and societies; they have authors and prophets like Lucius Beebe and Stewart Holbrook and Archie Robertson; they sustain several magazines of substantial circulation. They organize excursions, a sizable business, and even buy and maintain old engines. They attract rich members like Vincent Astor and the late William Gillette, the actor, who built little lines on their own land. Enthusiasm is their hallmark. Here is an item from one fan publication, offering pictures of the Western Pacific Railroad:

The Take Off! Wide open (running late), drivers spinning, hogger reefs her to the pin, down in the corner! . . . One of the most dynamic starts in steam I've ever lensed. Sand! L.I. L 3/4 complete, heavy train with desert background —clouds.

The steam lover appeared early on the scene. He insisted on a special preview ride, before regular service began, on the very first train in America. He went on camera excursions to Harpers Ferry before the Civil War. He reappeared in sizable numbers, in the middle twenties of this century, camera in hand and eager to be allowed, please, in the locomotive cab. Just as resolutely, at first, management ignored this unexpected offer of good will. Then, at last, it offered to show the fan around, but it failed abysmally to understand him. Come over here, said management, and see the streamliner. See our new diesel! But the fan wanted to ride a local and climb over a rusting steamer out behind the roundhouse. Management might as well have offered a date with a chorus girl to a man standing by the deathbed of his childhood sweetheart.

Perhaps the most outstanding example of what this organized enthusiasm can do is the story of the narrow-gauge Silverton passenger service of the Denver & Rio Grande Western Railroad, last survivor of a network of narrow-gauge lines hacked out of the Colorado mountains many decades ago—last, indeed, of all narrow-gauge passenger lines in America. A few years ago, it had dwindled to a twice-weekly mixed train, with a single passenger car, and application was made for its abandonment. Then the steam admirers took notice and moved in, until now, throughout the summer tourist months, the astonished railroad runs a train every day, with all its ten surviving cars packed solid. Not the least of the lures is that the power at the head end is honest old-fashioned steam. As in a horse opera, the rescue came in the nick of time, for the company had been gradually getting rid of its steamers by destroying them in head-on collisions staged for the movies.

From the steam fancier's standpoint, there is one more heartening piece of news, the situation at Lionel Lines, one of the healthiest corporations in the railroad business. Lionel, which manufactures model trains, has paid steady dividends since 1937 and the future looks only optimistic. As its president explains, he considers that his market comprises some 60 per cent of American males, young and old, and that demand for his product simply goes along with the birth rate. He has nowhere to go but up, and he plans to keep right on making steam engines.

worthy of the scene and the consequences of their action. James Buchanan faced three main groups holding three divergent views of the sectional problem.

The proslavery group (that is, Robert Toombs, Alexander H. Stephens, Jefferson Davis, John Slidell, David Atchison, and many more) demanded that slavery be allowed to expand freely within the territories; soon they were asking also that such expansion be given federal protection against any hostile local action. This stand involved the principle that slavery was morally right, and socially and economically a positive good. Reverdy Johnson of Maryland, in the Dred Scott case, had vehemently argued the beneficence of slavery.

The popular sovereignty group, led by Douglas and particularly strong among northwestern Democrats, maintained that in any territory the issue of slavery or free soil should be determined *at all times* by the settlers therein. Douglas modified the Dred Scott doctrine: local police legislation and action, he said, could exclude slavery even before state-making took place. He sternly rejected the demand for federal protection against such action. His popular sovereignty view implied indifference to or rejection of any moral test of slavery. Whether the institution was socially and economically good or bad depended mainly on climate and soil, and moral ideas were irrelevant. He did not care whether slavery was voted up or voted down; the right to a fair vote was the all-important matter.

The free-soil group, led by Seward and Chase, but soon to find its best voice in Lincoln, held that slavery should be excluded from all territories present or future. They insisted that slavery was morally wrong, had been condemned as such by the Fathers, and was increasingly outlawed by the march of world civilization. It might be argued that the free-soil contention was superfluous, in that climate and aridity forbade a further extension of slavery anyhow. But in Lincoln's eyes this did not touch the heart of the matter. It might or might not be expansible. (Already it existed in Delaware and Missouri, and Cuba and Mexico might be conquered for it.) What was important was for America to accept the fact that, being morally wrong and socially an anachronism, it *ought* not to expand; it *ought* to be put in the way of ultimate eradication. Lincoln was a planner. Once the country accepted nonexpansion, it would thereby accept the idea of ultimate extinction. This crisis met and passed, it could sit down and decide when and how, in God's good time and with suitable compensation to slaveholders, it might be ended.

The Buchanan who faced these three warring groups was victim of the mistaken belief among American politicians (like Pierce, Benjamin Harrison, and Warren G. Harding, for example) that it is better to be a poor President than to stick to honorable but lesser posts. He would have made a respectable diplomat or decent Cabinet officer under a really strong President. Sixty-six in 1857, the obese bachelor felt all his years. He had wound his devious way up through a succession of offices without once showing a flash of inspiration or an ounce of grim courage. James K. Polk had accurately characterized him as an old woman—"It is one of his weaknesses that he takes on and magnifies small matters into great and undeserved

The Battle of Hickory Point typifies the warfare that swept "Bleeding Kansas." S. J. Reader sketched free staters, newly equipped with Sharps rifles ("Beecher's Bibles"), firing on a proslavery settlement near Leavenworth in 1856.

218

importance." His principal characteristic was irresolution. "Even among close friends," remarked a southern senator, "he very rarely expressed his opinions at all upon disputed questions, except in language especially marked with a cautious circumspection almost amounting to timidity."

He was industrious, capable, and tactful, a well-read Christian gentleman; he had acquired from forty years of public life a rich fund of experience. But he was pedestrian, humorless, calculating, and pliable. He never made a witty remark, never wrote a memorable sentence, and never showed a touch of distinction. Above all (and this was the source of his irresolution) he had no strong convictions. Associating all his life with southern leaders in Washington, this Pennsylvanian leaned toward their views, but he never disclosed a deep adherence to any principle. Like other weak men, he could be stubborn; still oftener, he could show a petulant irascibility when events pushed him into a corner. And like other timid men, he would sometimes flare out in a sudden burst of anger, directed not against enemies who could hurt him but against friends or neutrals who would not. As the sectional crisis deepened, it became his dominant hope to stumble through it, somehow, and anyhow, so as to leave office with the Union yet intact. His successor could bear the storm.

This was the President who had to deal, in Kansas and Washington, with men of fierce conviction, stern courage and, all too often, ruthless methods.

In Kansas the proslavery leaders were determined to strike boldly and unscrupulously for a slave state. They maintained close communications with such southern chieftains in Washington as Senator Slidell,

The governor's "mansion" at frontier-town Lecompton, limned by Harper's Weekly *in 1857, was a political hot seat.*

Speaker James L. Orr, and Howell Cobb and Jacob Thompson, Buchanan's secretaries of the Treasury and the Interior. Having gained control of the territorial legislature, they meant to keep and use this mastery. Just before Buchanan became President they passed a bill for a constitutional convention—and a more unfair measure was never put on paper. Nearly all county officers, selected not by popular vote but by the dishonestly chosen legislature, were proslavery men. The bill provided that the sheriffs and their deputies should in March, 1857, register the white residents; that the probate judges should then take from the sheriffs complete lists of qualified voters; and that the county commissioners should finally choose election judges.

Everyone knew that a heavy majority of the Kansas settlers were antislavery. Many, even of the southerners, who had migrated thither opposed the "peculiar institution" as retrogressive and crippling in character. Everybody also knew that Kansas, with hardly thirty thousand people, burdened with debts, and unsupplied with fit roads, schools, or courthouses, was not yet ready for statehood; it still needed the federal government's care. Most Kansans refused to recognize the "bogus" legislature. Yet this legislature was forcing a premature convention, and taking steps to see that the election of delegates was controlled by sheriffs, judges, and county commissioners who were mainly proslavery Democrats. Governor John W. Geary, himself a Democrat appointed by Pierce, indignantly vetoed the bill. But the legislature immediately repassed it over Geary's veto; and when threats against his life increased until citizens laid bets that he would be assassinated within forty days, he resigned in alarm and posted east to apprise the country of imminent perils.

Along the way to Washington, Geary paused to warn the press that a packed convention was about to drag fettered Kansas before Congress with a slavery constitution. This convention would have a free hand, for the bill just passed made no provision for a popular vote on the instrument. Indeed, one legislator admitted that the plan was to avoid popular submission, for he proposed inserting a clause to guard against the possibility that Congress might return the constitution for a referendum. Thus, commented the *Missouri Democrat,* "the felon legislature has provided as effectually for getting the desired result as Louis Napoleon did for getting himself elected Emperor." All this was an ironic commentary on Douglas' maxim: "Let the voice of the people rule."

And Douglas, watching the reckless course of the Kansas legislators with alarm, saw that his principles

The hatreds engendered by the long struggle in Kansas gave a specially vengeful character to incidents after war began. In retaliation for the 1863 sacking of Lawrence by Quantrill's Confederate raiders, Union General Thomas Ewing forcibly evacuated pro-Confederate communities on the Kansas-Missouri border. A famous eyewitness, George Caleb Bingham, though a Union sympathizer, was so outraged by it that he portrayed the brutal incident in this painting, Order No. 11.

and his political future were at stake. When his Kansas-Nebraska Act was passed, he had given the North his solemn promise that a free, full, and fair election would decide the future of the two territories. No fraud, no sharp practice, no browbeating would be sanctioned; every male white citizen should have use of the ballot box. He had notified the South that Kansas was almost certain to be free soil. Now he professed confidence that President Buchanan would never permit a breach of fair procedure. He joined Buchanan in persuading one of the nation's ablest men, former Secretary of the Treasury Robert J. Walker, to go out to Kansas in Geary's place as governor. Douglas knew that if he consented to a betrayal of popular sovereignty he would be ruined

forever politically in his own state of Illinois.

For a brief space in the spring of 1857 Buchanan seemed to stand firm. In his instructions to Governor Walker he engaged that the new constitution would be laid before the people; and "they must be protected in the exercise of their right of voting for or against that instrument, and the fair expression of the popular will must not be interrupted by fraud or violence."

It is not strange that the rash proslavery gamesters in Kansas prosecuted their designs despite all Buchanan's fair words and Walker's desperate efforts to stay them. They knew that with four fifths of the people already against them, and the odds growing greater every year, only brazen trickery could effect their end. They were aware that the South, which believed that a fair division would give Kansas to slavery and Nebraska to freedom, expected them to stand firm.

They were egged on by the two reckless southern Cabinet members, Howell Cobb and Thompson, who sent an agent, H. L. Martin of Mississippi, out to the Kansas convention. This gathering in Lecompton, with 48 of the 60 members hailing from slave states, was the shabbiest conclave of its kind ever held on American soil. One of Buchanan's Kansas correspondents wrote that he had not supposed such a wild set could be found. The *Kansas News* termed them a body of "broken-down political hacks, demagogues, fire-eaters, perjurers, ruffians, ballot-box stuffers, and loafers." But before it broke up with the shout, "Now, boys, let's come and take a drink!" it had written a constitution.

This constitution, the work of a totally unrepresentative body, was a devious repudiation of all the principles Buchanan and Douglas had laid down. Although it contained numerous controversial provisions, such as a limitation of banking to one institution and a bar against free Negroes, the main document was not to be submitted to general vote at all. A nominal reference of the great cardinal question was indeed provided. Voters might cast their ballots for the "constitution with slavery" or the "constitution without slavery."

But when closely examined this was seen to be actually a piece of chicanery. Whichever form was adopted, the 200 slaves in Kansas would remain, with a constitutional guarantee against interference. Whenever the proslavery party in Kansas could get control of the legislature, they might open the door wide for more slaves. The rigged convention had put its handiwork before the people with a rigged choice: "Heads I win, tails you lose."

Would Buchanan lay this impudent contrivance before Congress, and ask it to vote the admission of Kansas as a state? Or would he contemptuously spurn it? An intrepid man would not have hesitated an instant to take the honest course; he would not have needed the indignant outcry of the northern press, the outraged roar of Douglas, to inspirit him. But Buchanan quailed before the storm of passion into which the proslavery extremists had worked themselves.

The hot blood of the South was now up. That section, grossly misinformed upon events in Kansas, believed that *it* was being cheated. The northern free-soilers had vowed that no new slave state (save by a partition of Texas) should ever be admitted. South-erners thought that in pursuance of this resolve, the Yankees had made unscrupulous use of their wealth and numbers to lay hands on Kansas. Did the North think itself entitled to every piece on the board—to take Kansas as well as California, Minnesota, Iowa, Nebraska, Oregon—to give southerners nothing? The Lecompton delegates, from this point of view, were dauntless champions of a wronged section. What if they did use sharp tactics? That was but a necessary response to northern arrogance. Jefferson Davis declared that his section trembled under a sense of insecurity. "You have made it a political war. We are on the defensive. How far are you to push us?" Sharp threats of secession and battle mingled with the southern denunciations. "Sir," Senator Alfred Iverson of Georgia was soon to assert, "I believe that the time will come when the slave States will be compelled, in vindication of their rights, interests, and honor, to separate from the free States, and erect an independent confederacy; and I am not sure, sir, that the time is not at hand."

Three southern members of the Cabinet, Cobb, Thompson, and John B. Floyd, had taken the measure of Buchanan's pusillanimity. They, with one northern sympathizer, Jeremiah Black, and several White House habitués like John Slidell of Louisiana, constituted a virtual Directory exercising control over the tremulous President. They played on Buchanan's fierce partisan hatred of Republicans, and his jealous dislike of Douglas. They played also on his legalistic cast of mind; after all, the Lecompton Constitution was a legal instrument by a legal convention—outwardly. Above all, they played on his fears, his morbid sensitiveness, and his responsiveness to immediate pressures. They could do this the more easily because the threats of disruption and violence were real. Henry S. Foote, a former senator from Mississippi and an enemy of Jefferson Davis, who saw Lecompton in its true light and hurried to Washington to advise the President, writes:

"It was unfortunately of no avail that these efforts to reassure Mr. Buchanan were at that time essayed by myself and others; he had already become thoroughly *panic-stricken*; the howlings of the bulldog of secession had fairly frightened him out of his wits, and he ingloriously resolved to yield without further resistance to the decrial and vilification to which he had been so acrimoniously subjected."

And the well-informed Washington correspondent of the New Orleans *Picayune* a little later told just how aggressively the Chief Executive was bludgeoned into submission:

"The President was informed in November, 1857,

that the States of Alabama, Mississippi, and South Carolina, and perhaps others, would hold conventions and secede from the Union if the Lecompton Constitution, which established slavery, should not be accepted by Congress. The reason was that these States, supposing that the South had been cheated out of Kansas, were whether right or wrong, determined to revolt. The President believed this. Senator Hunter, of Virginia, to my knowledge, believed it. Many other eminent men did, and perhaps not without reason."

Buchanan, without imagination as without nerve, began to yield to this southern storm in midsummer, and by November, 1857, he was surrendering completely. When Congress met in December his message upheld the Lecompton Constitution with a tissue of false and evasive statements. Seldom in American history has a chief magistrate made a greater error, or missed a larger opportunity. The astute secretary of his predecessor, Franklin Pierce, wrote: "I had considerable hopes of Mr. Buchanan—I really thought he was a statesman—but I have now come to the settled conclusion that he is just the damndest old fool that has ever occupied the presidential chair. He has deliberately walked overboard with his eyes open—let him drown, for he must."

As Buchanan shrank from the lists, Douglas entered them with that *gaudium certaminis* which was one of his greatest qualities. The finest chapters of his life, his last great contests for the Union, were opening. Obviously he would have had to act under political necessity even if deaf to principle, for had he let popular sovereignty be torn to pieces, Illinois would not have sent him back to the Senate the following year; but he was not the man to turn his back on principle. His struggle against Lecompton was an exhibition of iron determination. The drama of that battle has given it an almost unique place in the record of our party controversies.

"By God, sir!" he exclaimed, "I made James Buchanan, and by God, sir, I will unmake him!" Friends told him that the southern Democrats meant to ruin him. "I have taken a through ticket," rejoined Douglas, "and checked my baggage." He lost no time in facing Buchanan in the White House and denouncing the Lecompton policy. When the President reminded him how Jackson had crushed two party rebels, he was ready with a stinging retort. Douglas was not to be overawed by a man he despised as a weakling. "Mr. President," he snorted, "I wish you to remember that General Jackson is dead."

As for the southern leaders, Douglas' scorn for the extremists who had coerced Buchanan was unbounded. He told the Washington correspondent of the Chicago *Journal* that he had begun his fight as a

Fraudulent voting was no rarity in Kansas; here the line goes from the polls to the free whisky, probably back to the polls.

contest against a single bad measure. But his blow at Lecompton was a blow against slavery extension, and he at once had the whole "slave power" down on him like a pack of wolves. He added: "In making the fight against this power, I was enabled to stand off and view the men with whom I had been acting; I was ashamed I had ever been caught in such company; they are a set of unprincipled demagogues, bent upon perpetuating slavery, and by the exercise of that unequal and unfair power, to control the government or break up the Union; and I intend to prevent their doing either."

After a long, close, and acrid contest, on April 1, 1858, Lecompton was defeated. A coalition of Republicans, Douglasite Democrats, and Know-Nothings struck down the fraudulent constitution in the House, 120 to 112. When the vote was announced, a wild cheer rolled through the galleries. Old Francis P. Blair, Jackson's friend, carried the news to the dying Thomas Hart Benton, who had been intensely aroused by the crisis. Benton could barely speak, but his exultation was unbounded. "In energetic whispers," records Blair, "he told his visitor that the same men who had sought to destroy the republic in 1850 were at the bottom of this accursed Lecompton business. Among the greatest of his consolations in dying was the consciousness that the House of Representatives had baffled these treasonable schemes and put the heels of the people on the neck of the traitors."

The Administration covered its retreat by a hastily concocted measure, the English Bill, under which Kansas was kept waiting on the doorstep—sure in the end to enter a free state. The Kansas plotters, the Cobb-Thompson-Floyd clique in the Cabinet, and Buchanan had all been worsted. But the damage had been done. Southern secessionists had gained fresh strength and greater boldness from their success in coercing the Administration.

The Lecompton struggle left a varied and interesting set of aftereffects. It lifted Stephen A. Douglas to a new plane; he had been a fighting Democratic strategist, but now he became a true national leader, thinking far less of party and more of country. It sharpened the issues which that summer and fall were to form the staple of the memorable Lincoln-Douglas debates in Illinois. At the same time, it deepened the schism which had been growing for some years between southern Democrats and northwestern Democrats, and helped pave the way to that disruption of the party which preceded and facilitated the disruption of the nation. It planted new seeds of dissension in Kansas—seeds which resulted in fresh conflicts between Kansas free-soilers or jayhawkers on one side and Missouri invaders or border ruffians on the other, and in a spirit of border lawlessness which was to give the Civil War some of its darkest pages. The Lecompton battle discredited Buchanan in the eyes of most decent northerners, strengthened southern conviction of his weakness, and left the Administration materially and morally weaker in dealing with the problems of the next two and a half critical years.

For the full measure of Buchanan's failure, however, we must go deeper. Had he shown the courage that to an Adams, a Jackson, a Polk, or a Cleveland would have been second nature, the courage that springs from a deep integrity, he might have done the republic an immeasurable service by grappling with disunion when it was yet weak and unprepared. Ex-Senator Foote wrote that he knew well that a scheme for destroying the Union "had long been on foot in the South." He knew that its leaders "were only waiting for the enfeebling of the Democratic Party in the North, and the general triumph of Free-soilism as a consequence thereof, to alarm the whole South into acquiescence in their policy." Buchanan's support of the unwise and corrupt Lecompton Constitution thus played into the plotters' hands.

The same view was taken yet more emphatically by Douglas. He had inside information in 1857, he later told the Senate, that four states were threatening Buchanan with secession. Had that threat been met in the right Jacksonian spirit, had the bluff been called—for the four states were unprepared for secession and war—the leaders of the movement would have been utterly discredited. Their conspiracy would have collapsed, and they would have been so routed and humiliated in 1857 that the Democratic party schism in 1860 might never have taken place, and if it had, secession in 1861 would have been impossible.

The roots of the Civil War of course go deep; they go back beyond Douglas' impetuous Kansas-Nebraska Bill, back beyond the Mexican War, back beyond the Missouri Compromise. But the last good chance of averting secession and civil strife was perhaps lost in 1857. Even Zachary Taylor in 1850 had made it plain before his sudden death that he would use force, if necessary, to crush the secessionist tendencies which that year became so dangerous. A similar display of principle and resolution seven years later might well have left the disunionist chieftains of the Deep South so weakened in prestige that Yancey and his fellow plotters would have been helpless. The lessons of this failure in statesmanship, so plain to Douglas, ought not to be forgotten. The greatest mistake a nation can make is to put at its helm a man so pliable and unprincipled that he will palter with a clean-cut and momentous issue.

Allan Nevins, the eminent and prolific historian who heads the Society of American Historians as well as the Advisory Board of this magazine, has twice won the Pulitzer Prize for biography. His latest work is The War for the Union.

and, whatever the result may be, I shall carry to my grave the consciousness that I at least meant well for my country.

James Buchanan

In a message to Congress on January 8, 1861, when his policies had brought the nation to the brink of disaster, Buchanan made this tragic protestation of good intentions.

223

GETTYSBURG NATIONAL MILITARY PARK, PHOTOGRAPH WALTER LANE; COURTESY *Time*

"We were there, waiting–"

The repulse of Pickett's charge, described in a little-known

account written shortly after the battle by a Union officer

Frank Aretas Haskell   *An introduction by* BRUCE CATTON

One of the genuine but little-known classics of Civil War literature is a book called *The Battle of Gettysburg*, written by a Northern soldier named Frank Aretas Haskell. Haskell fought in the battle, and less than two weeks after the fighting ceased he wrote a detailed account of what he had seen and experienced and sent the manuscript to his brother, back in Wisconsin.

Haskell had seen and experienced a good deal, for he was an aide on the staff of Brigadier General John Gibbon, commander of the 2nd Division of the Army of the Potomac's Second Army Corps; and it was this division which held the ground against which the most famous assault in American military history was directed—the charge of 15,000 Confederates led by Major General George Pickett, on the afternoon of the third day of the fight. Haskell was at storm center throughout the action, and when he wrote his manuscript the heat of battle was still on him; the town of Gettysburg was still full of wounded men, and the fearful debris of battle still littered its fields.

The book had a curious history. Haskell's brother offered the manuscript to the editor of a small-town paper, who found it far too long for his pages. Some fifteen years later the brother had it printed in pamphlet form, for private distribution. In 1898 an abbreviated version was published as part of the history of

On the facing page is a depiction of the climactic struggle at "the angle," taken from Paul Philippoteaux's epic painting. Pickett's men have broken through the Union line and overrun Cushing's guns, with Unionists rallying at left.

the class of 1854, Dartmouth College—Haskell's own class. This version was reprinted in 1908 by the Commandery of Massachusetts, Military Order of the Loyal Legion of the United States; and the full, unabridged version was printed shortly thereafter under the auspices of the Wisconsin History Commission, in an edition of 2,500 copies. It quickly became a standard reference work for students of the battle, but the general reader rarely saw it.

Now, ninety-seven years after it was written, *The Battle of Gettysburg* is available to everyone, in an unabridged edition published not long ago by the Houghton Mifflin Company of Boston. By special arrangement with this publisher, AMERICAN HERITAGE is presenting herewith an excerpt from that part of the book which deals specifically with the repulse of Pickett's charge. (The book as a whole covers the entire battle, which lasted three days, from July 1 through July 3, 1863.)

Haskell himself never saw his narrative in print, for he did not survive the war. Born in Vermont in 1828, he had gone to Madison, Wisconsin, immediately after his graduation from college and had entered the practice of law. When the Civil War broke out he promptly enlisted, and on June 20, 1861, he was commissioned first lieutenant in Company I of the 6th Wisconsin Infantry. This regiment was sent east that summer, and in the spring of 1862, along with the 2nd and 7th Wisconsin and the 19th Indiana regiments (to which, a bit later, was added the 24th Michigan), it became a unit in what was to be one of

225

the most distinguished combat outfits in the Army of the Potomac, the celebrated "Iron Brigade."

This brigade was commanded by Brigadier General John Gibbon, a tough West Pointer in his mid-thirties, who promptly made Lieutenant Haskell an aide on his staff. The two served with the brigade in the battles of Gainesville, Second Bull Run, South Mountain, and Antietam, and in the fall of 1862, when Gibbon was raised to divisional command, he saw to it that Haskell remained on his staff. Haskell stayed with him through Fredericksburg, Chancellorsville, and Gettysburg and won both Gibbon's professional admiration and personal affection. In his report on Gettysburg, Gibbon wrote that Haskell had distinguished himself in every battle "by his conspicuous coolness and bravery," and added: "It has always been a source of regret to me that our military system offers no plan for rewarding his merit and services as they deserve."

The reward came shortly after this. Gibbon was wounded at Gettysburg, and after serving for some months on the staff of the general who replaced him, Haskell was sent to Wisconsin and made colonel of the newly organized 36th Wisconsin Infantry. In the spring of 1864 this regiment was assigned to the Army of the Potomac—Gibbon, by now restored to duty, arranged to get it in his division and in the battle of Cold Harbor, on June 3, 1864, Haskell was killed leading his regiment in a hopeless assault on the Confederate entrenchments. Informed of his death, Gibbon remarked that he had lost his best friend and that the Army of the Potomac had lost one of its best soldiers.

The reader of Haskell's narrative needs to remember that it was written without benefit of the backward glance and without those inevitable revisions that grow out of long reflection and fuller knowledge. Haskell expresses all of the prejudices which an ardent officer in a hot combat unit might be expected to have, both toward other units in his own army and toward the enemy against whom he was fighting. He had, for example, nothing but contempt for the luckless Eleventh Army Corps in the Army of the Potomac; it was badly mauled at Gettysburg, just as had been the case at Chancellorsville two months earlier, and Haskell wrote it off as a half-hearted group. He also had scant use for such Union officers as Major General Daniel Sickles and Major General Abner Doubleday, and when he wrote about the battle he saw no reason to disguise his feelings.

In addition, Haskell was (naturally enough) red-hot for the Union, and the Confederates were in his eyes no better than outright traitors. The word "Rebel," as he used it, was meant as a word of bitter criticism, and although he was ready to admit that the Southern-

ers were very valiant soldiers—no veteran in the Army of the Potomac was in any doubt on that point—he was not disposed to give them credit for anything else.

In his book, Haskell covers the entire battle of Gettysburg, even though he himself missed the action of the first day.

The great three-day fight began shortly after dawn on July 1, on the ridges west of the town, when advancing Confederate infantry in Lieutenant General A. P. Hill's Third Corps collided with Union cavalry. Major General George Gordon Meade, who had just taken command of the Army of the Potomac, had his army spread out over a considerable area, trying to find Lee's army and bring it to battle, and his First Corps, led by Major General John F. Reynolds, was nearing Gettysburg when the firing started. Reynolds brought his troops into town fast, got to the western ridges, and the battle began. Reynolds was killed, but his troops held their ground—Gibbon's old Iron Brigade was in the thick of the action and suffered fearful casualties—and toward midday reinforcements arrived in the shape of Major General Oliver Otis Howard and the Eleventh Corps, which promptly took position north of town.

The fortunes of war were with the Confederates that day. Lee's Second Corps, under Lieutenant General Richard Ewell—Stonewall Jackson's old troops, these—came into town from the north and northeast, and since Confederate army corps were a great deal larger than Union corps (although there were fewer of them) Lee had a powerful numerical advantage. The Union First and Eleventh Corps were driven from their positions with heavy losses, and as the day ended they took position on Cemetery and Culp's hills, south of Gettysburg, and awaited developments.

On July 2 Lee had most of his army on hand, while a good part of Meade's was still on the road. Lee attacked Culp's Hill with Ewell's corps, and struck the extreme left of Meade's line, at the Round Top hills, with Lieutenant General James B. Longstreet's corps, winning a good deal of ground and knocking the Federal Third Corps completely out of action, but failing to drive the Unionists from Cemetery Ridge, the rounded stretch of high ground that goes south from dominant Cemetery Hill. Both armies remained in position overnight, and when July 3 came it was clear to everyone that the climactic assault of the battle was in the making. At a conference late on the evening of July 2, Meade had remarked that if Lee attacked on the third he would strike Gibbon's front.

That part of Haskell's story which is printed here picks up the situation at dawn on July 3, with Gibbon's division waiting on the crest of Cemetery Ridge for the action which everybody was sure would come.

THE THIRD DAY
AT GETTYSBURG

By FRANK ARETAS HASKELL

First lieutenant on Brigadier General John Gibbon's staff, at Gettysburg;

later colonel of the 36th Wisconsin; killed at Cold Harbor.

As the sun arose to-day, the clouds became broken, and we had once more glimpses of sky, and fits of sunshine—a rarity, to cheer us. From the crest, save to the right of the Second Corps, no enemy, not even his outposts could be discovered, along all the position where he so thronged upon the Third Corps yesterday. The men were roused early, in order that the morning meal might be out of the way in time for whatever should occur. Then ensued the hum of an army, not in ranks, chatting in low tones, and running about and jostling among each other, rolling and packing their blankets and tents.

They looked like an army of rag-gatherers, while shaking these very useful articles of the soldier's outfit, for you must know that rain and mud in conjunction have not had the effect to make them clean, and the wear and tear of service have not left them entirely whole. But one could not have told by the appearance of the men, that they were in battle yesterday, and were likely to be again to-day. They packed their knapsacks, boiled their coffee and munched their hard bread, just as usual—just like old soldiers who know what campaigning is; and their talk is far more con-

cerning their present employment—some joke or drollery—than concerning what they saw or did yesterday.

The dispositions to-day upon the left are as follows: The Second and Third Divisions of the Second Corps are in the position of yesterday; then on the left come Doubleday's—the Third Division and Col. Stannard's brigade of the First Corps; then the First Division of the Second Corps; then the Third Corps, temporarily under the command of Hancock, since Sickles' wound. Note well the position of the Second and Third Divisions of the Second Corps—it will become important. There are nearly six thousand men and officers in these two Divisions here upon the field, who occupy a line of about a thousand yards. The most of the way along this line upon the crest was a stone fence, constructed of small, rough stones, a good deal of the way badly pulled down, but the men had improved it and patched it with rails from the neighboring fences, and with earth, so as to render it in many places a very passable breastwork against musketry and flying fragments of shells.

These works are so low as to compel the men to kneel or lie down generally to obtain cover. Near the right of the Second Division, and just by a little group of trees, this stone fence made a right angle, and extended thence to the front, about twenty or thirty yards, where with another less than a right angle it followed along the crest again.

[*The "little group of trees" mentioned by Haskell was, and remains, one of the landmarks of the battlefield. Situated near the center of the Second Corps line, it was the guide for the men in Pickett's charge; they aimed at it, they got to it, and a good many of them died near it. The trees, or their descendants, are still there, enclosed by a little iron fence, and today's visitor can see them; and in front of them there is the old stone wall, making an angle which, to the men who fought at Gettysburg, was "the" angle. A great many young men lost their lives in and about the trees and the angle, and a visitor to the spot somehow can feel their presence there.*]

The lines were conformed to these breastworks and to the nature of the ground upon the crest, so as to occupy the most favorable places, to be covered, and still be able to deliver effective fire upon the enemy should he come there. In some places a second line was so posted as to be able to deliver its fire over the heads of the first line behind the works; but such formation was not practicable all of the way. But all the force of these two divisions was in line, in position, without reserves, and in such a manner that every man of them could have fired his piece at the same instant.

I could not help wishing all the morning that this line of the two divisions of the Second Corps was stronger; it was, so far as numbers constitute strength, the weakest part of our whole line of battle. What if, I thought, the enemy should make an assault here today, with two or three heavy lines—a great overwhelming mass; would he not sweep through that thin six thousand?

But I was not General Meade, who alone had power to send other troops there; and he was satisfied with that part of the line as it was. He was early on horseback this morning, and rode along the whole line, looking to it himself and with glass in hand sweeping the woods and fields in the direction of the enemy, to see if aught of him could be discovered. His manner was calm and serious, but earnest. There was no arrogance of hope, or timidity of fear discernible in his face; but you would have supposed he would do his duty conscientiously and well and would be willing to abide the result. You would have seen this in his face.

The enemy, so far as we could see, was very quiet all the morning. Occasionally the outposts would fire

a little, and then cease. Movements would be discovered which would indicate the attempt on the part of the enemy to post a battery. Our Parrotts would send a few shells to the spot, then silence would follow.

[*The Parrotts mentioned by Haskell were rifled field pieces with heavy iron bands shrunk over the breach. For field artillery they came in 10-pound and 20-pound sizes—meaning that they fired shell of that weight, with a caliber of approximately three inches. The Napoleons mentioned in the following paragraph were brass smooth-bores of about 4.5 inches caliber; their range was much less than that of the Parrotts, but for close action they were extremely effective. Firing canister—which meant that they were loaded with tin cans full of round lead pellets—they were like sawed-off shotguns of stupendous size, and against closely-ranked infantry at ranges of 250 yards or less they were simply murderous.*]

Eleven o'clock came. Not a sound of a gun or musket can be heard on all the field; the sky is bright, with only the white fleecy clouds floating over from the West. The July sun streams down its fire upon the bright iron of the muskets in stacks upon the crest, and the dazzling brass of the Napoleons. The army lolls and longs for the shade, of which some get a hand's breadth, from a shelter tent stuck upon a ramrod. The silence and sultriness of a July noon are supreme.

Now it so happened that just about this time of day a very original and interesting thought occurred to Gen. Gibbon and several of his staff; that it would be a very good thing, and a very good time, to have something to eat. Of the absolute quality of what we had to eat, I could not pretend to judge, but I think an unprejudiced person would have said of the bread that it was good; so of the potatoes before they were boiled. Of the chickens he would have questioned their age, but they were large and in good *running* order. The toast was good, and the butter. General Hancock is of course invited to partake, and without delay we commence operations. We were just well at it when General Meade rode down to us from the line, accompanied by one of his staff, and by General Gibbon's invitation, they dismounted and joined us. Fortunate to relate, there was enough cooked for us all, and from General Meade to the youngest second lieutenant we all had a most hearty and well relished dinner. Of the "past" we were "secure." The Generals ate, and after, lighted cigars, and under the flickering shade of a very small tree, discoursed of the incidents of yesterday's battle and of the probabilities of today.

And so the time passed on, each General now and then dispatching some order or message by an officer or orderly, until about half-past twelve, when all the Generals, one by one, first General Meade, rode off their several ways, and General Gibbon and his staff alone remained.

We dozed in the heat, and lolled upon the ground, with half-open eyes. Time was heavy and for want of something better to do, I yawned, and looked at my watch. It was five minutes before one o'clock. I returned my watch to its pocket, and thought possibly that I might go to sleep, and stretched myself upon the ground accordingly. My attitude and purpose were those of the General and the rest of the staff.

What sound was that? There was no mistaking it. The distinct sharp sound of one of the enemy's guns, square over to the front, caused us to open our eyes and turn them in that direction, when we saw directly above the crest the smoke of the bursting shell, and heard its noise. In an instant, before a word was spoken, as if that was the signal gun for general work, loud, startling, booming, the report of gun after gun in rapid succession smote our ears and their shells plunged down and exploded all around us.

We sprang to our feet. In briefest time the whole Rebel line to the West was pouring out its thunder and its iron upon our devoted crest. The wildest confusion for a few moments obtained sway among us. The shells came bursting all about. The servants ran terror-stricken for dear life and disappeared. The horses, hitched to the trees or held by the slack hands of orderlies, neighed out in fright, and broke away and plunged riderless through the fields.

The General at the first had snatched his sword, and started on foot for the front. I called for my horse; nobody responded. I found him tied to a tree, near by, eating oats, with an air of the greatest composure, which under the circumstances, even then struck me as exceedingly ridiculous. He alone, of all beasts or men near was cool. I am not sure but that I learned a lesson then from a horse. General Gibbon's groom has just mounted his horse and is starting to take the General's horse to him, when the flying iron meets him and tears open his breast. He drops dead and the horses gallop away. No more than a minute since the first shot was fired, and I am mounted and riding after the General. The mighty din that now rises to heaven and shakes the earth is not all of it the voice of the rebellion; for our guns, the guardian lions of the crest, quick to awake when danger comes, have opened their fiery jaws and begun to roar.

I overtake the General half way up to the line. Before we reach the crest his horse is brought by an orderly. Leaving our horses just behind a sharp declivity of the ridge, on foot we go up among the batteries. How the long streams of fire spout from the guns, how the rifled shells hiss, how the smoke deepens and rolls. The men of the infantry have seized their arms, and behind their works, behind every rock, in every ditch, wherever there is any shelter, they hug the ground, silent, quiet, unterrified, little harmed.

[*General Lee had a long rank of guns in line, and all of these opened fire in an attempt to soften the Union line for Pickett's charge. The Union guns instantly replied, and for an hour or thereabouts the greatest artillery duel yet seen on the American continent was waged. The fire was so intense and the racket was so terrific that Union gunners confessed afterward that they could hardly hear the noise their own guns made. The Union line might have been obliterated by the bombardment except for the fact that the Confederate gunners for some reason were firing just a little too high. Most of their shell exploded on the reverse slope of Cemetery Ridge.*]

The enemy's guns now in action are in position at their front of the woods. A hundred and twenty-five rebel guns, we estimate, are now active, firing twenty-four pound, twenty, twelve and ten-pound projectiles, solid shot and shells, spherical, conical, spiral. The enemy's fire is chiefly concentrated upon the position

Major General George Gordon Meade, U.S.A.

of the Second Corps. From the Cemetery to Round Top, with over a hundred guns, and to all parts of the enemy's line, our batteries reply.

Who can describe such a conflict as is raging around us? To say that it was like a summer storm, with the crash of thunder, the glare of lightning, the shrieking of the wind, and the clatter of hailstones, would be weak. The thunder and lightning of these two hundred and fifty guns and their shells, whose smoke darkens the sky, are incessant, all pervading, in the air above our heads, on the ground at our feet, remote, near, deafening, ear-piercing, astounding; and these hailstones are massy iron, charged with exploding fire. And there is little of human interest in a storm; it is an absorbing element of this. You may see flame and smoke, and hurrying men, and human passion at a great conflagration; but they are all earthly and nothing more. These guns are great infuriate demons, not of the earth, whose mouths blaze with smoky tongues of living fire, and whose murky breath, sulphur-laden, rolls around them and along the ground, the smoke of Hades. These grimy men, rushing, shouting, their souls in frenzy, plying the dusky globes and the igniting spark, are in their league, and but their willing ministers.

We thought that at the second Bull Run, at the Antietam and at Fredericksburg on the 13th of December, we had heard heavy cannonading; they were but holiday salutes compared with this. Besides the great ceaseless roar of the guns, which was but the background of the others, a million various minor sounds engaged the ear. The projectiles shriek long and sharp. They hiss, they scream, they growl, they sputter; all sounds of life and rage; and each has its different note, and all are discordant. We see the solid shot strike axle, or pole, or wheel, and the

Lieutenant General James Longstreet, C.S.A.

tough iron and heart of oak snap and fly like straws. And these shot and shells have no respect for men. We see the poor fellows hobbling back from the crest, or, unable to do so, pale and weak, lying on the ground with the mangled stump of an arm or leg, dripping their lifeblood away; or with a cheek torn open or a shoulder mashed. And many, alas! hear not the roar as they stretch upon the ground with upturned faces and open eyes, though a shell should burst at their very ears. Their ears and their bodies this instant are only mud.

We watched the shells bursting in the air, as they came hissing in all directions. Their flash was a bright gleam of lightning radiating from a point, giving place in the thousandth part of a second to a small, white, puffy cloud, like a fleece of the lightest, whitest wool. These clouds were very numerous. We could not often see the shell before it burst; but sometimes, as we faced towards the enemy, and looked above our heads, the approach would be heralded by a prolonged hiss, which always seemed to me to be a line of something tangible, terminating in a black globe, distinct to the eye, as the sound had been to the ear. The shell would seem to stop, and hang suspended in the air an instant, and then vanish in fire and smoke and noise.

We saw the missiles tear and plow the ground. All in rear of the crest for a thousand yards, as well as among the batteries, was the field of their blind fury. Ambulances, passing down the Taneytown road with wounded men, were struck. The hospitals near this road were riddled. The house which was General Meade's headquarters was shot through several times, and a great many horses of officers and orderlies were lying dead around it. The percussion shells would strike, and thunder, and scatter the earth and their whistling fragments; the Whitworth bolts would pound and ricochet, and bowl far away sputtering, with the sound of a mass of hot iron plunged in water; and the great solid shot would smite the unresisting ground with a sounding "thud," as the strong boxer crashes his iron fist into the jaws of his unguarded adversary.

[*The Whitworth bolts referred to by Haskell came from a few artillery pieces imported from England: Whitworth guns, breech-loaders, with a range of four or five miles, which fired hexagonal shells out of barrels which were hexagonal in cross section, twisted to give the missiles the effect of rifling. The shells made a horrendous noise in flight, and although they were no more effective than those of the other field pieces—Civil War artillerists had not yet learned the trick of indirect fire, and the Whitworths had more range than could profitably be used—troops on the receiving end*

230

of such fire had come to detest the weapons, and hugged the ground intently when Whitworth projectiles came over. Technically, a bolt from a field piece was a solid shot, but Whitworth missiles were uniformly given that name even though they usually carried a charge of high explosive.]

Such were some of the sights and sounds of this great iron battle of missiles. An hour has droned its flight since first the war began. There is no sign of weariness or abatement on either side. So long, it seemed, that the din and crashing around began to appear the normal condition of nature there, and fighting man's element.

The General proposed to go among the men and over to the front of the batteries, so at about two o'clock he and I started. We went down in front of the line some two hundred yards, and as the smoke had a tendency to settle upon a higher plain than where we were, we could see near the ground distinctly all over the fields. No infantry was in sight, save the skirmishers, and they stood silent and motionless—a row of gray posts through the field on one side confronted by another of blue. Under the grateful shade of some elm trees, where we could see much of the field, we made seats of the ground and sat down.

On either crest we could see the great flaky streams of fire, and they seemed numberless, of the opposing guns, and their white banks of swift, convolving smoke; but the sound of the discharges was drowned in the universal ocean of sound. Over all the valley the smoke, a sulphury arch, stretched its lurid span; and through it always, shrieking on their unseen courses, thickly flew a myriad iron death. With our grim horizon on all sides round toothed thick with battery flame, under that dissonant canopy of warring shells, we sat and heard in silence. What other expression had we that was not mean, for such an awful universe of battle?

Half-past two o'clock, an hour and a half since the commencement, and still the cannonade did not in the least abate; but soon thereafter some signs of weariness and a little slacking of fire began to be apparent on both sides. The General and I started to return, passing towards the left of the division, and crossing the ground where the guns had stood. Our infantry was still unshaken, and in all the cannonade suffered very little. The batteries had been handled much more severely. Guns had been dismounted. A great many caissons, limbers and carriages had been destroyed, and usually from ten to twenty-five men to each battery had been struck, at least along our part of the crest. Altogether the fire of the enemy

had injured us much; the scenes that met our eyes on all hands among the batteries were fearful.

All things must end, and the great cannonade was no exception. In the number of guns active at one time, and in the duration and rapidity of their fire, this artillery engagement, up to this time, must stand alone and pre-eminent in this war. It has not been often, or many times, surpassed in the battles of the world. Two hundred and fifty guns, at least, rapidly fired for two mortal hours. Cipher out the number of tons of gunpowder and iron that made these two hours hideous.

General Robert Edward Lee, C.S.A.

At three o'clock almost precisely the last shot hummed, and bounded and fell, and the cannonade was over. Men began to breathe more freely, and to ask, What next, I wonder? There was a pause between acts, with the curtain down, soon to rise upon the great final act, and catastrophe of Gettysburg.

We have passed by the left of the Second Division, coming from the First; when we crossed the crest the enemy was not in sight, and all was still—we walked slowly along in the rear of the troops, by the ridge cut off now from a view of the enemy in his position, and were returning to the spot where we had left our horses. We were near our horses when we noticed Brigadier General [Henry J.] Hunt, Chief of Artillery of the Army, swiftly moving about on horseback, and apparently in a rapid manner giving some orders about the guns. Thought we, what could this mean? In a moment afterwards we met Captain Wessels and the orderlies who had our horses; they were on foot leading the horses. Captain Wessels was pale, and he said, excited: "General, they say the enemy's infantry is advancing." We sprang into our saddles, a score of bounds brought us upon the all-seeing crest.

None on that crest now need be told that *the*

Major General Winfield Scott Hancock, U.S.A.

231

enemy is advancing. Every eye could see his legions, an overwhelming resistless tide of an ocean of armed men sweeping upon us! Regiment after regiment and brigade after brigade move from the woods and rapidly take their places in the lines forming the assault. More than half a mile their front extends; more than a thousand yards the dull gray masses deploy, man touching man, rank pressing rank, and line supporting line. The red flags wave, their horsemen gallop up and down; the arms of eighteen thousand men, barrel and bayonet, gleam in the sun, a sloping forest of flashing steel.

[*Haskell exaggerates slightly; Pickett had approximately 15,000 men with him when he made his charge.*]

Right on they move, as with one soul, in perfect order, over ridge and slope, through orchard and meadow, and cornfield, magnificent, grim, irresistible.

All was orderly and still upon our crest; no noise and no confusion. General Gibbon rode down the lines, cool and calm, and in an unimpassioned voice he said to the men, "Do not hurry, men, and fire too fast, let them come up close before you fire, and then aim low and steadily." The coolness of their General was reflected in the faces of his men.

Five minutes have elapsed since first the enemy have emerged from the woods. Should these advancing men pierce our line and become the entering wedge, driven home, that would sever our army asunder, what hope would there be afterwards, and where the blood-earned fruits of yesterday? None of these considerations either depressed or elevated us. They might have done the former, had we been timid; the latter had we been confident and vain. But, we were there waiting, and ready to do our duty—that done, results could not dishonor us.

Our skirmishers open a spattering fire along the front, and, fighting, retire upon the main line—the first drops, the heralds of the storm, sounding on our windows. All our available guns are now active, and from the fire of shells, as the range grows shorter and shorter, they change to shrapnel, and from shrapnel to canister; but in spite of shells, and shrapnel and canister, without wavering or halt, the hardy lines of the enemy continue to move on. The Rebel guns make no reply to ours, and no charging shout rings out to-day, as is the Rebel wont; but the courage of these silent men amid our shots seems not to need the stimulus of other noise.

And so across all that broad open ground they have come, nearer and nearer, nearly half the way, with our guns bellowing in their faces, until now a hundred yards, no more, divide our ready left from their advancing right. The eager men there are impatient to begin.

Let them. First, Harrow's breastworks flame; then Hall's; then Webb's. As if our bullets were the fire coals that touched off their muskets, the enemy in front halts, and his countless level barrels blaze back upon us. The Second Division is struggling in battle. The rattling storm soon spreads to the right. All along each hostile front, a thousand yards, with narrowest space between, the volleys blaze and roll; as thick the sound as when a summer hail-storm pelts the city roofs; as thick the fire as when the incessant lightning fringes a summer cloud.

[*The three officers mentioned by Haskell here were the brigade commanders in Gibbon's 2nd Division— Brigadier General William Harrow, Brigadier General Alexander S. Webb, and Colonel Norman J. Hall.*]

When the Rebel infantry had opened fire our batteries soon became silent. The conflict

is left to the infantry alone. It was tremendous, but I had seen no wavering in all our line.

Wondering how long the Rebel ranks, deep though they were, could stand our sheltered volleys, I had come near my destination, when—great heaven! were my senses mad? The larger portion of Webb's brigade, by the group of trees and the angles of the wall, was breaking from the cover of their works, and was falling back, a fear-stricken flock of confusion! The fate of Gettysburg hung upon a spider's single thread!

A great magnificent passion came on me at the instant. My sword, that had always hung idle by my side, the sign of rank only in every battle, I drew, bright and gleaming, the symbol of command. All rules and proprieties were forgotten; all considerations of person and danger and safety despised; for, as I met the tide of these rabbits, the red flags of the rebellion began to thicken and flaunt along the wall. I ordered these men to "halt," and "face about" and "fire," and they heard my voice and gathered my meaning, and obeyed my commands. On some unpatriotic backs of those not quick of comprehension, the flat of my sabre fell not lightly, and at its touch their love of country returned, and, with a look at me as if I were the destroying angel, as I might have become theirs, they again faced the enemy.

[*Haskell's paragraphs about the supposed rout of Webb's brigade drew down on him, early in the twentieth century, the distilled wrath of the organized survivors of that brigade. Reading his narrative after it had been reprinted by the Wisconsin History Commission, the survivors assembled and passed a series of resolutions upholding the valor of their own brigade and denouncing Haskell as a vainglorious person who had denigrated the bravery of a combat unit in order to magnify*

his own role as staff officer. The fact seems to be that Webb's brigade was driven away from the stone wall but that nothing like a genuine rout took place. The Confederates did break the Union line at this point, but the break was not large enough for them to exploit properly.]

The men that had fallen back, facing the enemy, soon regained confidence in themselves, and became steady. This portion of the wall was lost to us, and the enemy had gained the cover of the reverse side, where he now stormed with fire. But our men, with their bodies in part protected by the abruptness of the crest, now sent back in the enemies faces as fierce a storm. Little could be seen of the enemy, by reason of his cover and the smoke, except the flash of his muskets and his waving flags. These red flags were accumulating at the wall every moment, and they maddened us as the same color does the bull.

Webb's men are falling fast, and he is among them to direct and to encourage; but, however well they may now do, with that walled enemy in front, with more than a dozen flags to Webb's three, it soon becomes apparent that in not many minutes they will be overpowered, or that there will be none alive for the enemy to overpower. Webb has but three regiments, all small, the 69th, the 71st and 72d Pennsylvania—the 106th Pennsylvania, except two companies, is not here to-day—and he must have speedy assistance, or this crest will be lost.

Oh, where is Gibbon? where is Hancock?—some general—anybody with the power and the will to support that wasting, melting line? No general came, and no succor! I thought of Hayes upon the right, but from the smoke and war along his front, it was evident that he had enough upon his hands, if he stayed the inrolling tide of the Rebels there. Doubleday upon the

R. Houlday

left was too far off and too slow, and on another occasion I had begged him to send his idle regiments to support another line battling with thrice its numbers, and this "Old Sumpter Hero" had declined. As a last resort I resolved to see if Hall and Harrow could not send some of their commands to reinforce Webb. I galloped to the left in the execution of my purpose, and as I attained the rear of Hall's line, from the nature of the ground and the position of the enemy it was easy to discover the reason and the manner of this gathering of Rebel flags in front of Webb.

[Haskell obviously had a low opinion of Major General Abner Doubleday, who had been a member of the original garrison at Fort Sumter (which Haskell, like many others in that day, consistently misspelled "Sumpter"). His assertion that Doubleday on an earlier occasion had refused to send help may refer to the battle of Antietam, in which Gibbon's brigade was very heavily engaged, with severe losses. In that fight Doubleday had succeeded to the command of the division in which Gibbon's brigade belonged, and Haskell seems to have blamed him for Gibbon's inability to get reinforcements. It might be noted that at Gettysburg, when Reynolds was killed, Doubleday took over command of the First Corps by right of seniority, but that Meade refused to let him retain the command; while the battle was still being fought, Meade detached Major General John Newton from command of a division in the Sixth Corps and sent him over to replace Doubleday at the head of the First Corps. The "Hayes" Haskell mentions was Brigadier General Alexander Hays, commander of the 3rd Division of the Second Corps.]

The enemy, emboldened by his success in gaining our line by the group of trees and the angle of the wall, was concentrating all his right against and was further pressing that point. There was the stress of his assault; there would he drive his fiery wedge to split our line. In front of Harrow's and Hall's Brigades he had been able to advance no nearer than when he first halted to deliver fire, and these commands had not yielded an inch. To effect the concentration before Webb, the enemy would march the regiment on his extreme right of each of his lines by the left flank to the rear of the troops, still halted and facing to the front, and so continuing to draw in his right, when they were all massed in the position desired, he would again face them to the front, and advance to the storming. This was the way he made the wall before Webb's line blaze red with his battle flags, and such was the purpose there of his thick-crowding battalions.

Not a moment must be lost. Colonel Hall I found just in rear of his line, sword in hand, cool, vigilant, noting all that passed and directing the battle of his brigade. "How is it going?" Colonel Hall asked me, as I rode up. "Well, but Webb is hotly pressed and must have support, or he will be overpowered. Can you assist him?" "Yes." "You cannot be too quick."

He gave the order, and in briefest time I saw five friendly colors hurrying to the aid of the imperilled three. The regiments marched by the right flank. Col. Hall superintended the movement in person. The movement was difficult; but in reasonable time, Hall's men are fighting gallantly side by side with Webb's before the all important point. I did not stop to see all this movement of Hall's, but from him I went at once further to the left, to the 1st brigade. Gen'l Harrow I did not see, but his fighting men would answer my purpose as well. All men that I could find I took over to the right at the double quick.

As we were moving to, and near the other brigade of the division, from my position on horseback I could see that the enemy's right, under Hall's fire, was beginning to stagger and to break. "See," I said to the men, "see the chivalry! See the gray-backs run!" The men saw, and as they swept to their places by the side of Hall and opened fire, they cheered, and this in a manner that said more plainly than words—for the deaf could have seen it in their faces, and the blind could have heard it in their voices—the crest is safe!

[Pickett's men advanced over a very wide front, but wheeled together as they neared the crest in order to mass numbers in front of the chosen objective—the ground in and around the little group of trees and the angle in the stone wall. A certain part of the Confederate maneuvers here were not so much due to the punishing effect of Union rifle fire as to the tactical necessity for massing men at the decisive point.]

Before the 2nd Division the enemy is massed, the main bulk of his force covered by the ground that slopes to his rear, with his front at the stone wall. Formation of companies and regiments in our ranks is lost; but commands, companies, regiments and brigades are blended and intermixed—an irregular extended mass—men enough, if in order, to form a line of four or five ranks along the whole front of the division. The twelve flags of the regiments wave defiantly at intervals along the front; at the stone wall,

The map on the facing page shows general positions of the two armies on the afternoon of July 3, when Pickett made his famous charge. The previous afternoon's fighting had causd many changes in Federal troop dispositions, and many of the elements of different corps were intermixed. The charge was received by two divisions of the Second Corps.

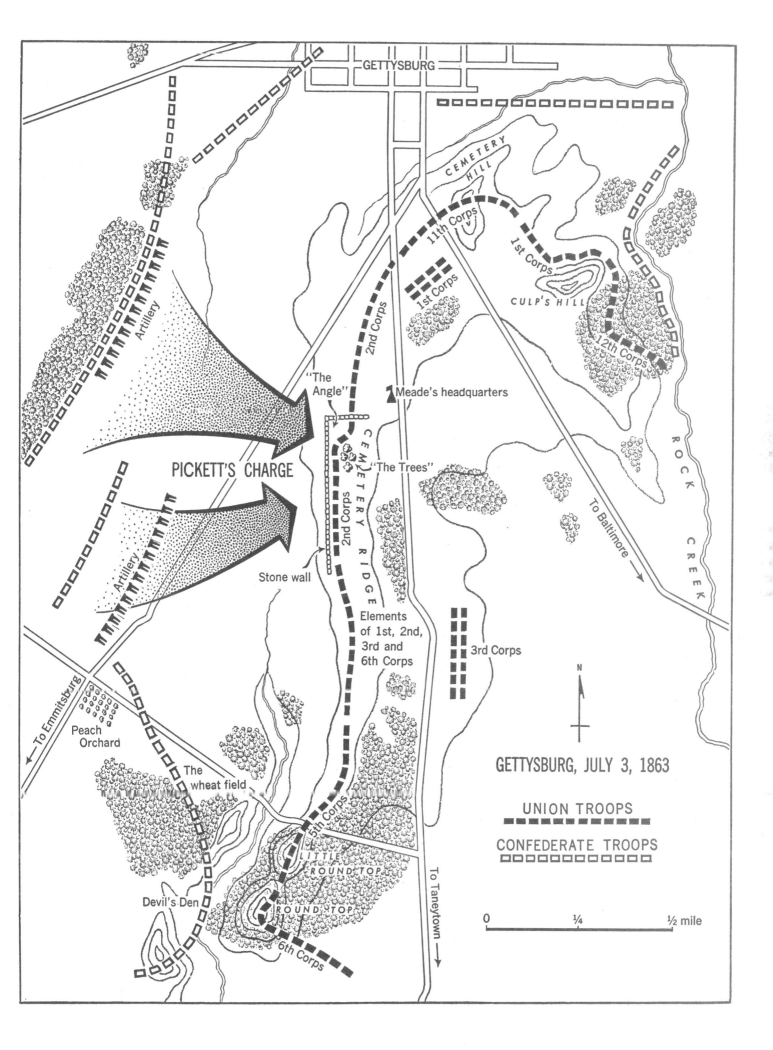

GETTYSBURG

CEMETERY
HILL

11th Corps

1st Corps

1st Corps

CULP'S HILL

12th Corps

Artillery

"The
Angle"

Meade's headquarters

2nd Corps

ROCK CREEK

PICKETT'S CHARGE

CEMETERY RIDGE

"The Trees"

To Baltimore

Artillery

2nd Corps

Stone wall

Elements
of 1st, 2nd,
3rd and
6th Corps

3rd Corps

N

To Emmitsburg

Peach
Orchard

The
wheat field

GETTYSBURG, JULY 3, 1863

UNION TROOPS

CONFEDERATE TROOPS

5th Corps

LITTLE
ROUND TOP

ROUND TOP

To Taneytown

Devil's Den

0   ¼   ½ mile

6th Corps

at unequal distances from ours of forty, fifty or sixty yards, stream nearly double this number of the battle flags of the enemy. Now it was as if a new battle, deadlier, stormier than before, had sprung from the body of the old.

The jostling, swaying lines on either side boil and roar and dash their flamy spray, two hostile billows of a fiery ocean. Thick flashes stream from the wall, thick volleys answer from the crest. All depths of passion are stirred, and all combatives fire, down to their deep foundations. Individuality is drowned in a sea of clamor, and timid men, breathing the breath of the multitude, are brave. The men do not cheer or shout; they growl, and over that uneasy sea, heard with the roar of musketry, sweeps the muttered thunder of a storm of growls.

Now the loyal wave rolls up as if it would overleap its barrier, the crest. These men of Pennsylvania, on the soil of their own homesteads, the first and only to flee the wall, must be the first to storm it.

"Major—, *lead* your men over the crest, they will follow." "By the tactics I understand my place is in rear of the men." "Your pardon, sir; I see *your* place is in rear of the men. I thought you were fit to lead." "Sergeant, forward with your color. Let the Rebels see it close to their eyes once before they die."

The color sergeant of the 72d Pennsylvania, grasping the stump of the severed lance in both his hands, waved the flag above his head and rushed towards the wall. One man only starts to follow. Almost half way to the wall, down go color bearer and color to the ground—the gallant sergeant is dead. The line springs —the crest of the solid ground, with a great roar, heaves forward its maddened load, men, arms, smoke, fire, a fighting mass. It rolls to the wall—flash meets flash, the wall is crossed—a moment ensues of thrusts, yells, blows, shots, and undistinguishable conflict, followed by a shout universal that makes the welkin ring again, and the last and bloodiest fight of the great battle of Gettysburg is ended and won.

[*It needs to be borne in mind in this portion of the narrative that the Union line was approximately 100 yards in front of the actual crest of Cemetery Ridge. When Pickett's men broke through, the Union defenders retired to the crest of the ridge and held their ground there, keeping up a sharp fire; eventually they swept down the slope and drove the gallant survivors of Pickett's spearhead out of the ground that had been seized. It should be pointed out that although the Confederates brought up the slope many more men than the Second Union Corps had for defense, their troops were actually outnumbered at the actual point of penetration. Once the Unionists were rallied for a counterattack, Pickett's case was hopeless.*]

Many things cannot be described by pen or pencil —such a fight is one. Some hints and incidents may be given, but a description or picture never. From what

is told the imagination may for itself construct the scene; otherwise he who never saw can have no adequate idea of what such a battle is.

When the vortex of battle passion had subsided, hopes, fears, rage, joy, of which the maddest and the noisiest was the last, and we were calm enough to look about us, we saw that, as with us, the fight with the Third Division was ended, and that in that division was a repetition of the scenes immediately about us. In that moment the judgment almost refused to credit the senses. Are these abject wretches about us, whom our men are now disarming and driving together in flocks, the jaunty men of Pickett's Division, whose steady lines and flashing arms but a few moment's since came sweeping up the slope to destroy us? Are these red cloths that our men toss about in derision the "fiery Southern crosses," thrice ardent, the battle flags of the rebellion that waved defiance at the wall? We know, but so sudden has been the transition, we yet can scarce believe.

Just as the fight was over, and the first outburst of victory had a little subsided, when all in front of the crest was noise and confusion—prisoners being collected, small parties in pursuit of them far down into the fields, flags waving, officers giving quick, sharp commands to their men—I stood apart for a few moments upon the crest, by that group of trees which ought to be historic forever, a spectator of the thrilling scene around. Some few musket shots were still heard in the Third Division; and the enemy's guns, almost silent since the advance of his infantry until the moment of his defeat, were dropping a few sullen shells among friend and foe upon the crest.

It is not an hour since these legions were sweeping along so grandly; now sixteen hundred of that fiery mass are strewn among the trampled grass, dead as the clods. More than seven thousand, probably eight thousand, are wounded, among them Generals Pettigrew, Garnett, Kemper and Armistead, the last three mortally, and the last one in our hands. "Tell General Hancock," he said to Lieutenant Mitchell, Hancock's aide-de-camp, to whom he handed his watch,

"that I know I did my country a great wrong when I took up arms against her, for which I am sorry, but for which I cannot live to atone."

[Brigadier General Lewis A. Armistead, commanding a brigade in Pickett's division, had been a close friend of Hancock before the war, and the two had exchanged emotional good-byes at a farewell party in an army post in California in the spring of 1861, when Armistead and other Southern officers resigned their commissions in order to come east and serve with the Confederacy. Armistead died among Cushing's guns at the point where Pickett's men briefly broke the Union line, and his last thought apparently was of Hancock.]

Four thousand, not wounded, are prisoners of war. Our men are still "gathering them in." Some hold up their hands or a handkerchief in sign of submission; some have hugged the ground to escape our bullets and so are taken; few made resistance after the first moment of our crossing the wall; some yield submissively with good grace, some with grim, dogged aspect, showing that but for the other alternative they could not submit to this.

Such was really the closing scene of the grand drama of Gettysburg. After repeated assaults upon the right and the left, where, and in all of which repulse had been his only success, this persistent and presuming enemy forms his chosen troops, the flower of his army, for a grand assault upon our center. The manner and result of such assault have been told—a loss to the enemy of from twelve thousand to fourteen thousand, killed, wounded and prisoners, and of over thirty battle-flags. This was accomplished by not over six thousand men, with a loss on our part of not over two thousand five hundred killed and wounded.

[Haskell substantially overstates the total of Confederate losses in this fight.

The three Confederate divisions involved in the attack had total casualties of approximately 7,600 men at Gettysburg. Two of these divisions had incurred a good part of these losses in the fighting on the first day; and the over-all losses in the charge on July 3 were undoubtedly much nearer 5,000 than the 12,000 to 14,000 mentioned by Haskell. Pickett's own division, of course—numbering about one-third of the total in the assaulting column—was practically wrecked by its losses.]

Would to Heaven General Hancock and Gibbon could have stood there where I did, and have looked upon that field! It would have done two men, to whom the country owes much, good to have been with their men in that moment of victory. But they are both severely wounded and have been carried from the field. One person did come then that I was glad to see there, and that was no less than Major General Meade, whom the Army of the Potomac was fortunate enough to have at that time to command it.

To appreciate the incident I give, it should be borne in mind that one coming up from the rear of the line, as did General Meade, could have seen very little of our own men. One who did not know results, so coming, would have been quite as likely to have supposed that our line there had been carried and captured by the enemy—so many gray Rebels were on the crest—as to have discovered the real truth.

General Meade rode up, accompanied alone by his son, who is his aide-de-camp. The principal horseman was no bedizened hero of some holiday review, but he was a plain man, dressed in a serviceable summer suit of dark blue cloth, without badge or ornament, save the shoulder-straps of his grade, and a light, straight sword of a General or General staff officer. He wore heavy, high-top boots and buff gauntlets, and his soft black felt hat was slouched down over his eyes. His face was very white, not pale, and the lines were marked and earnest and full of care.

As he arrived near me, coming up the hill, he asked, in a sharp, eager voice: "How is it going here?"

"I believe, General, the enemy's attack is repulsed," I answered.

Still approaching, and a new light began to come in his face, of gratified surprise, with a touch of incredulity, of which his voice was also the medium, he further asked: *"What! Is the assault already repulsed?"* his voice quicker and more eager than before. "It is, sir," I replied.

By this time he was on the crest, and when his eye had for an instant swept over the field, taking in just a glance of the whole, he said, impressively, and his face lighted: "Thank God." And then his right hand moved as if it would have caught off his hat and waved it; but this gesture he suppressed, and instead he waved his hand, and said "Hurrah!" The son, with more youth in his blood and less rank upon his shoulders, snatched off his cap, and roared out his three "hurrahs" right heartily. The General then surveyed the field, some minutes, in silence. He at length asked who was in command—he had heard that Hancock and Gibbon were wounded—and I told him that General Caldwell was the senior officer of the Corps and General Harrow of the Division.

He asked where they were, but before I had time to answer that I did not know, he resumed: "No matter, I will give my orders to you and you will see them executed." He then gave direction that the troops should be reformed as soon as practicable, and kept in their places, as the enemy might be mad enough to attack again. He also gave directions concerning the posting of some reinforcements which he said should soon be there, adding: "If the enemy does attack, charge him in the flank and sweep him from the field; do you understand." The General then, a gratified man, galloped in the direction of his headquarters.

[*Haskell's description of his meeting with Meade drew the sarcasm of the survivors of Webb's brigade when they read his story in 1909. In a pamphlet which they published the survivors referred scornfully to Haskell as "this Wellington of Lee's Waterloo," and suggested that Meade would hardly have left all arrangements for a counterattack in the hands of a mere first lieutenant. Since Meade's army made no gesture toward such an attack the point hardly seems to be of great importance.*]

Then the work of the field went on. First, the prisoners were collected and sent to the rear. "There go the men," the Rebels were heard to say, by some of our surgeons who were in Gettysburg, at the time Pickett's Division marched out to take position—"There go the men that will go through your d——d Yankee lines, for you." A good many of them did "go through our lines for us," but in a very different way from the one they intended—not impetuous victors, sweeping away our thin lines with ball and bayonet, but crestfallen captives, without arms, with the cheers of their conquerors ringing in their ears. There was a grim truth after all in this Rebel remark.

In view of the results of that day—the successes of the arms of the country—would not the people of the whole country, standing there upon the crest with General Meade, have said, with him: "Thank God?"

I have no knowledge and little notion of how long a time elapsed from the moment the fire of the infantry commenced, until the enemy was entirely re-

pulsed, in this his grand assault. I judge, from the amount of fighting and the changes of position that occurred, that probably the fight was of nearly an hour's duration, but I cannot tell, and I have seen none who knew. The time seemed but a very few minutes, when the battle was over.

When the prisoners were cleared away and order was again established upon our crest, where the conflict

Brigadier General Lewis Addison Armistead, C.S.A.

had impaired it, until between five and six o'clock, I remained upon the field, directing some troops to their position, in conformity to the orders of General Meade. Of the pursuit of the enemy and the movements of the army subsequent to the battle, until the crossing of the Potomac by Lee and the closing of the campaign, it is not my purpose to write. Suffice it that on the night of the 3d of July the enemy withdrew his left from our front, and on the morning of the 4th we again occupied the village of Gettysburg, and on that national day victory was proclaimed to the country; that floods of rain on that day prevented army movements of any considerable magnitude, the day being passed by our army in position upon the field, in burying our dead, and some of those of the enemy, and in making the movements already indicated; that on the 5th the pursuit of the enemy was commenced—his dead were buried by us—and the corps of our army, upon various roads, moved from the battlefield.

With a statement of some of the results of the battle, as to losses and captures, and of what I saw in riding over the field, when the enemy was gone, my account is done.

The magnitude of the armies engaged, the number of the casualties, the object sought by the Rebel, the result will all contribute to give Gettysburg a place among the great historic battles of the world. That General Meade's concentration was rapid—over thirty miles a day was marched by some of the Corps—that his position

Major General George Edward Pickett, C.S.A.

was skillfully selected and his dispositions good; that he fought the battle hard and well; that his victory was brilliant and complete, I think all should admit. I cannot but regard it as highly fortunate to us and commendable in General Meade, that the enemy was allowed the initiative, the offensive, in the main battle; that it was much better to allow the Rebel, for his own destruction, to come up and smash his lines and columns upon the defensive solidity of our position, than it would have been to hunt him, for the same purpose, in the woods, or to unearth him from his rifle-pits. In this manner our losses were lighter, and his heavier, than if the case had been reversed. And whatever the books may say of troops fighting the better who make the attack, I am satisfied that in this war, Americans, the Rebels as well as ourselves, are best on the defensive.

[*Haskell's remark that both Federals and Confederates "are best on the defensive" simply highlights the fact that Civil War weapons had been improved much more than infantry tactics. The rifled infantry musket, muzzle-loader though it was, had vastly increased defensive fire power. The old smooth-bore, on which infantry tactics were still based, was very inaccurate, and was so limited in range that it was ineffective at any distance greater than about 150 yards. The rifle used by Civil War troops could begin to kill at half a mile or more, and the advance in the massed formation—still standard, by the old tactics—was simply out of date. A straight frontal assault against good troops in a properly chosen defensive position had very little chance to succeed, by the 1860's: a lesson that was impressed on the Unionists at Fredericksburg, on Lee at Gettysburg, and on U. S. Grant at the battle of Cold Harbor.*]

But men there are who think that nothing was gained or done well in this battle, because some other general did not have the command, or because any portion of the army of the enemy was permitted to escape capture or destruction. It should be enough, perhaps, to say that men who have knowledge enough of military affairs to entitle them to express an opinion on such matters will be most likely to vindicate the Pennsylvania campaign of Gen. Meade, and to see that he accomplished all that could have been reasonably expected of any general of any army. Complaint has been, and is, made specially against Meade, that he did not attack Lee before he had time to withdraw across the river. These were the facts concerning this matter:

The 13th of July was the earliest day when such an attack, if practicable at all, could have been made. The time before this, since the battle, had been spent in moving the army from the vicinity of the field, finding something of the enemy and concentrating before him. On that day the army was concentrated and in order of battle near the turnpike that leads from Sharpesburg to Hagerstown, Md. The mean distance to the Potomac was some six miles, and the enemy was between Meade and the river.

The Potomac, swelled by the recent rain, was boiling and swift and deep, a magnificent place to have drowned all the Rebel crew. I have not the least doubt but that Gen. Meade would have liked to drown them all, if he could, but they were unwilling to be drowned, and would fight first. To drive them into the river then, they must be routed. Gen. Meade, I believe, favored an attack upon the enemy at that time, but at daylight on the morning of the 14th, strong reconnaissances showed that between the enemy, except a thousand or fifteen hundred of his rear guard, who fell into our hands, and the Army of the Potomac, rolled the rapid unbridged river. The enemy had constructed bridges, had crossed during all the preceding night, but so close were our cavalry and infantry upon him in the morning, that the bridges were destroyed before his rear guard had all crossed.

Among the considerations against the propriety of attack at that time were the following: The army was wearied and worn down by four weeks of constant forced marching or battle. What such weariness means few save soldiers know. Since the battle the army had been constantly diminished by sickness or prostration and by more straggling than I ever saw before. The men were near the point when further efficient physical exertion was quite impossible.

The enemy was in position in a ridgy, wooded country, abounding in strong defensive positions, his main bodies concealed, protected by rifle-pits and epaulements, acting strictly on the defensive. To have had a battle there then, Gen. Meade would have had

to attack a cunning enemy in the dark, where surprises, undiscovered rifle-pits and batteries, and unseen bodies of men might have met his forces at every point.

I felt the probability of defeat strongly at the time. I believe the Army of the Potomac is always willing, often eager, to fight the enemy, whenever, as it thinks, there is a fair chance for victory; that it always will fight, let come victory or defeat whenever it is ordered so to do. Of course the army, both officers and men, had very great disappointment and very great sorrow that the Rebels *escaped*—so it was called—across the river; the disappointment was genuine, at least to the extent that disappointment is like surprise; but the sorrow to judge by looks, tones and actions, rather than by words, was not of that deep, sable character for which there is no balm.

[*Abraham Lincoln was one who felt that Meade should not have permitted Lee to get his army back across the Potomac into Virginia, and he expressed himself in a rather bitter letter which he wrote, in the White House—and then decided not to send. It may be worth noting that in the summer of 1957 President Dwight D. Eisenhower and Field Marshal Viscount Montgomery, sauntering about the field at Gettysburg, came to much the same conclusion Lincoln had reached: that Lee should not have been allowed to get his beaten army back to safety. At the same time it should be remembered that Lincoln did not actually send Meade his letter of criticism, and that he retained Meade in command of the Army of the Potomac to the end of the war.*]

On the 6th of July, while my bullet bruise was yet too inflamed and sensitive for me to be good for much in the way of duty—the division was then halted for the day some four miles from the field on the Baltimore turnpike—I could not repress the desire or omit the opportunity to see again where the battle had been. With the right stirrup strap shortened in a manner to favor the bruised leg, I could ride my horse at a walk without serious discomfort. It seemed very strange upon approaching the horse-shoe crest again, not to see it covered with the thousands of troops and horses and guns, but they were all gone—the armies, to my seeming, had vanished.

The recent rains had washed out many an unsightly spot, and smoothed many a harrowed trace of the conflict; but one still needed no guide save the eyes, to follow the track of that storm, which the storms of heaven were powerless soon to entirely efface. The spade and shovel, so far as a little earth for the human bodies would render their task done, had completed their work. The scattered small arms and the accoutrements had been collected and carried away, almost all that were of any value; but great numbers of bent and splintered muskets, rent knapsacks and haversacks, bruised canteens, shreds of caps, coats, trowsers, of blue or gray cloth, worthless belts and cartridge of harness, of all that men or horses wear or use in battle, were scattered broadcast over miles of the field.

I stood solitary upon the crest by *"the trees"* where, less than three days ago, I had stood before; but now how changed is all the eye beholds. Do these thick mounds cover the fiery hearts that in the battle rage swept the crest and stormed the wall? I read their names—them, alas, I do not know—but I see the regiments marked on their frail monuments—"20th Mass. Vols.," "69 P. V.," "1st Minn. Vols.," and the rest—they are all represented, and as they fought commingled here. So I am not alone. These, my brethren of the fight, are with me. Sleep, noble brave! The foe shall not desecrate your sleep. Yonder thick trenches will hold them. As long as patriotism is a virtue, your deeds have made this crest, your resting place, hallowed ground!

Hayfoot,

By BRUCE CATTON

This youthful warrior, a bit bewildered in his oversized coat and boots, is poignantly typical of the citizen-soldiers of the Civil War. Winslow Homer's oil sketch was painted about 1862.

The volunteer soldier in the American Civil War used a clumsy muzzle-loading rifle, lived chiefly on salt pork and hardtack, and retained to the very end a loose-jointed, informal attitude toward the army with which he had cast his lot. But despite all of the surface differences, he was at bottom blood brother to the G.I. Joe of modern days.

Which is to say that he was basically, and incurably, a civilian in arms. A volunteer, he was still a soldier because he had to be one, and he lived for the day when he could leave the army forever. His attitude toward discipline, toward his officers, and toward the whole spit-and-polish concept of military existence was essentially one of careless tolerance. He refused to hate his enemies—indeed, he often got along with them much better than with some of his own comrades —and his indoctrination was often so imperfect that what was sometimes despairingly said of the American soldier in World War II would apply equally to him: he seemed to be fighting chiefly so that he could some day get back to Mom's cooking.

What really set the Civil War soldier apart was the fact that he came from a less sophisticated society. He was no starry-eyed innocent, to be sure—or, if he was, the army quickly took care of that—but the America of the 1860's was less highly developed than modern America. It lacked the ineffable advantages of radio, television, and moving pictures. It was still essentially a rural nation; it had growing cities, but they were smaller and somehow less urban than today's cities; a much greater percentage of the population lived on farms or in country towns and villages than is the case now, and there was more of a backwoods, hay-seed-in-the-hair flavor to the people who came from them.

For example: every war finds some ardent youngsters who want to enlist despite the fact that they are under the military age limit of eighteen. Such a lad today simply goes to the recruiting station, swears that he is eighteen, and signs up. The lad of the 1860's saw it a little differently. He could not swear that he was eighteen when he was only sixteen; in his innocent way, he felt that to lie to his own government was just plain wrong. But he worked out a little dodge that got him into the army anyway. He would take a bit of paper, scribble the number *18* on it, and put it in the sole of his shoe. Then, when the recruiting officer asked him how old he was, he could truthfully say: "I am *over* eighteen." That was a common happening, early in the Civil War; one cannot possibly imagine it being tried today.

242

Strawfoot!

The Civil War soldier marched to his own individualist cadence, but he was much like today's G. I.

Similarly, the drill sergeants repeatedly found that among the raw recruits there were men so abysmally untaught that they did not know left from right, and hence could not step off on the left foot as all soldiers should. To teach these lads how to march, the sergeants would tie a wisp of hay to the left foot and a wisp of straw to the right; then, setting the men to march, they would chant, "Hay-foot, straw-foot, hay-foot, straw-foot"—and so on, until everybody had caught on. A common name for a green recruit in those days was "strawfoot."

On the drill field, when a squad was getting basic training, the men were as likely as not to intone a little rhythmic chant as they tramped across the sod—thus:

March! March! March old soldier march!
Hayfoot, strawfoot,
Belly-full of bean soup—
March old soldier march!

Because of his unsophistication, the ordinary soldier in the Civil War, North and South alike, usually joined up with very romantic ideas about soldiering. Army life rubbed the romance off just as rapidly then as it does now, but at the start every volunteer went into the army thinking that he was heading off to high adventure. Under everything else, he enlisted because he thought army life was going to be fun, and usually it took quite a few weeks in camp to disabuse him of this strange notion. Right at the start, soldiering had an almost idyllic quality; if this quality faded rapidly, the memory of it remained through all the rest of life.

Early days in camp simply cemented the idea. An Illinois recruit, writing home from training camp, confessed: "It is fun to lie around, face unwashed, hair uncombed, shirt unbuttoned and everything un-everythinged. It sure beats clerking." Another Illinois boy confessed: "I don't see why people will stay at home when they can get to soldiering. A year of it is worth getting shot for to any man." And a Massachusetts boy, recalling the early days of army life, wrote that "Our drill, as I remember it, consisted largely of running around the Old Westbury town hall, yelling like Devils and firing at an imaginary foe." One of the commonest discoveries that comes from a reading of Civil War diaries is that the chief worry, in training camp, was a fear that the war would be over before the ardent young recruits could get into it. It is only fair to say that most of the diarists looked back on this innocent worry, a year or so afterward, with rueful amusement.

There was a regiment recruited in northern Pennsylvania in 1861—13th Pennsylvania Reserves officially, known to the rest of the Union Army as the Bucktails because the rookies decorated their caps with strips of fur from the carcass of a deer that was hanging in front of a butcher shop near their camp—and in mid-spring these youthful soldiers were ordered to rendezvous at Harrisburg. So they marched cross-country (along a road known today as the Bucktail Trail) to the north branch of the Susquehanna, where they built rafts. One raft, for the colonel, was made oversized with a stable; the colonel's horse had to ride, too. Then the Bucktails floated down the river, singing and firing their muskets and having a gay old time, camping out along the bank at night, and finally they got to Harrisburg; and they served through the worst of the war, getting badly shot up and losing most of their men to Confederate bullets, but they never forgot the picnic air of those first days of army life, when they drifted down a river through the forests, with a song in the air and the bright light of adventure shining just ahead. Men do not go to war that way nowadays.

Discipline in those early regiments was pretty sketchy. The big catch was that most regiments were recruited locally—in one town, or one county, or in one part of a city—and everybody more or less knew everybody else. Particularly, the privates knew their officers—most of whom were elected to their jobs by the enlisted men—and they never saw any sense in being formal with them. Within reasonable limits,

243

the Civil War private was willing to do what his company commander told him to do, but he saw little point in carrying it to extremes.

So an Indiana soldier wrote: "We had enlisted to put down the Rebellion, and had no patience with the red-tape tomfoolery of the regular service. The boys recognized no superiors, except in the line of legitimate duty. Shoulder straps waived, a private was ready at the drop of a hat to thrash his commander—a thing that occurred more than once." A New York regiment, drilling on a hot parade ground, heard a private address his company commander thus: "Say, Tom, let's quit this darn foolin' around and go over to the sutler's and get a drink." There was very little of the "Captain, sir" business in those armies. If a company or regimental officer got anything especial in the way of obedience, he got it because the enlisted men recognized him as a natural leader and superior and not just because he had a commission signed by Abraham Lincoln.

Odd rivalries developed between regiments. (It should be noted that the Civil War soldier's first loyalty went usually to his regiment, just as a navy man's loyalty goes to his ship; he liked to believe that his regiment was better than all others, and he would fight for it, any time and anywhere.) The army legends of those days tell of a Manhattan regiment, camped near Washington, whose nearest neighbor was a regiment from Brooklyn, with which the Manhattanites nursed a deep rivalry. Neither regiment had a chaplain; and there came to the Manhattan colonel one day a minister, who volunteered to hold religious services for the men in the ranks.

The colonel doubted that this would be a good idea. His men, he said, were rather irreligious, not to say godless, and he feared they would not give the reverend gentleman a respectful hearing. But the minister said he would take his chances; after all, he had just held services with the Brooklyn regiment, and the men there had been very quiet and devout. That was enough for the colonel. What the Brooklyn regiment could do, his regiment could do. He ordered the men paraded for divine worship, announcing that any man who talked, laughed, or even coughed would be summarily court-martialed.

So the clergyman held services, and everyone was attentive. At the end of the sermon, the minister asked if any of his hearers would care to step forward and make public profession of faith; in the Brooklyn regiment, he said, fourteen men had done this. Instantly the New York colonel was on his feet.

"Adjutant!" he bellowed. "We're not going to let that damn Brooklyn regiment beat us at anything. Detail twenty men and have them baptized at once!"

Each regiment seemed to have its own mythology, tales which may have been false but which, by their mere existence, reflected faithfully certain aspects of army life. The 48th New York, for instance, was said to have an unusually large number of ministers in its ranks, serving not as chaplains but as combat soldiers. The 48th, fairly early in the war, found itself posted in a swamp along the South Carolina coast, toiling mightily in semitropical heat, amid clouds of mosquitoes, to build fortifications, and it was noted that all hands became excessively profane, including the one-time clergymen. A visiting general, watching the regiment at work one day, recalled the legend and asked the regiment's lieutenant colonel if he himself was a minister in private life.

"Well, no, General," said the officer apologetically. "I can't say that I was a regularly ordained minister. I was just one of these —— —— local preachers."

Another story was hung on this same 48th New York. A Confederate ironclad gunboat was supposed to be ready to steam through channels in the swamp and attack the 48th's outposts, and elaborate plans were made to trap it with obstructions in the channel, a tangle of ropes to snarl the propellors, and so on. But it occurred to the colonel that even if the gunboat was trapped the soldiers could not get into it; it was sheathed in iron, all its ports would be closed, and men with axes could never chop their way into it. Then the colonel had an inspiration. Remembering that many of his men had been recruited from the less savory districts of New York City, he paraded the regiment and (according to legend) announced:

"Now men, you've been in this cursed swamp for two weeks—up to your ears in mud, no fun, no glory and blessed poor pay. Here's a chance. Let every man who has had experience as a cracksman or a safeblower step to the front." To the last man, the regiment marched forward four paces and came expectantly to attention.

Not unlike this was the reputation of the 6th New York, which contained so many Bowery toughs that the rest of the army said a man had to be able to show that he had done time in prison in order to get into the regiment. It was about to leave for the South, and the colonel gave his men an inspirational talk. They were going, he said, to a land of wealthy plantation owners, where each Southerner had riches of which he could be despoiled; and he took out his own gold watch and held it up for all to see, remarking that any deserving soldier could easily get one like it, once they got down to plantation-land. Half an hour later, wishing to see what time it was, he felt for his watch . . . and it was gone.

If the Civil War army spun queer tales about itself,

it had to face a reality which, in all of its aspects, was singularly unpleasant. One of the worst aspects had to do with food.

From first to last, the Civil War armies enlisted no men as cooks, and there were no cooks' and bakers' schools to help matters. Often enough, when in camp, a company would simply be issued a quantity of provisions—flour, pork, beans, potatoes, and so on—and invited to prepare the stuff as best it could. Half a dozen men would form a mess, members would take turns with the cooking, and everybody had to eat what these amateurs prepared or go hungry. Later in the war, each company commander would usually detail two men to act as cooks for the company, and if either of the two happened to know anything about cooking the company was in luck. One army legend held that company officers usually detailed the least valuable soldiers to this job, on the theory that they would do less harm in the cook shack than anywhere else. One soldier, writing after the war, asserted flatly: "A company cook is a most peculiar being; he generally knows less about cooking than any other man in the company. Not being able to learn the drill, and too dirty to appear on inspection, he is sent to the cook house to get him out of the ranks."

When an army was on the march, the ration issue usually consisted of salt pork, hardtack, and coffee. (In the Confederate Army the coffee was often missing, and the hardtack was frequently replaced by corn bread; often enough the meal was not sifted, and stray bits of cob would appear in it.) The hardtack was good enough, if fresh, which was not always the case; with age it usually got infested with weevils, and veterans remarked that it was better to eat it in the dark.

In the Union Army, most of the time, the soldier could supplement his rations (if he had money) by buying extras from the sutler—the latter being a civilian merchant licensed to accompany the army, functioning somewhat as the regular post exchange functions nowadays. The sutler charged high prices and specialized in indigestibles like pies, canned lobster salad, and so on; and it was noted that men who patronized him regularly came down with stomach upsets. The Confederate Army had few sutlers, which helps to explain why the hungry Confederates were so delighted when they could capture a Yankee camp: to seize a sutler's tent meant high living for the captors, and the men in Lee's army were furious when, in the 1864 campaign, they learned that General Grant had ordered the Union Army to move without sutlers. Johnny Reb felt that Grant was really taking an unfair advantage by cutting off this possible source of supply.

If Civil War cooking arrangements were impromptu and imperfect, the same applied to its hospital system. The surgeons, usually, were good men by the standards of that day—which were low since no one on earth knew anything about germs or about how wounds became infected, and antisepsis in the operating room was a concept that had not yet come into existence; it is common to read of a surgeon whetting his scalpel on the sole of his shoe just before operating. But the hospital attendants, stretcher-bearers, and the like were chosen just as the company cooks were chosen; that is, they were detailed from the ranks, and the average officer selected the most worthless men he had simply because he wanted to get rid of men who could not be counted on in combat. As a result, sick or wounded men often got atrocious care.

A result of all of this—coupled with the fact that many men enlisted without being given any medical examinations—was that every Civil War regiment suffered a constant wastage from sickness. On paper, a regiment was supposed to have a strength ranging between 960 and 1,040 men; actually, no regiment ever got to the battlefield with anything like that strength, and since there was no established system for sending in replacements a veteran regiment that could muster 350 enlisted men present for duty was considered pretty solid. From first to last, approximately twice as many Civil War soldiers died of disease—typhoid, dysentery, and pneumonia were the great killers—as died in action; and in addition to those who died a great many more got medical discharges.

In its wisdom, the Northern government set up a number of base hospitals in Northern states, far from the battle fronts, on the theory that a man recovering from wounds or sickness would recuperate better back home. Unfortunately, the hospitals thus established were under local control, and the men in them were no longer under the orders of their own regiments or armies. As a result, thousands of men who were sent north for convalescence never returned to the army. Many were detailed for light work at the hospitals, and in these details they stayed because nobody had the authority to extract them and send them back to duty. Others, recovering their health, simply went home and stayed there. They were answerable to the hospital authorities, not to the army command, and the hospital authorities rarely cared very much whether they returned to duty or not. The whole system was ideally designed to make desertion easy.

This merely reflected the loose discipline that prevailed in Civil War armies, which in turn reflected the underlying civilian-mindedness that pervaded the rank and file. The behavior of Northern armies on the march in Southern territory reflected the same thing—

and, in the end, had a profound effect on the institution of chattel slavery.

Armies of occupation always tend to bear down hard on civilian property in enemy territory. Union armies in the Civil War, being imperfectly disciplined to begin with—and suffering, furthermore, from a highly defective rationing system—bore down with especial fervor. Chickens, hams, cornfields, anything edible that might be found on a Southern plantation, looked like fair game, and the loose fringe of stragglers that always trailed around the edges of a moving Union army looted with a fine disregard for civilian property rights.

This was made all the more pointed by the fact that the average Northern soldier, poorly indoctrinated though he was, had strong feelings about the evils of secession. To his mind, the Southerners who sought to set up a nation of their own were in rebellion against the best government mankind had ever known. Being rebels, they had forfeited their rights; if evil things happened to them, that (as the average Northern soldier saw it) was no more than just retribution. This meant that even when the army command tried earnestly to prevent looting and individual foraging, the officers at company and regimental levels seldom tried very hard to carry out the high command's orders.

William Tecumseh Sherman has come down in history as the very archetype of the Northern soldier who believed in pillage and looting; yet during the first years of the war Sherman resorted to all manner of ferocious punishments to keep his men from despoiling Southern property. He had looters tied up by the thumbs, ordered courts-martial, issued any number of stern orders—and all to very little effect. Long before he adopted the practice of commandeering or destroying Southern property as a war measure, his soldiers were practicing it against his will, partly because discipline was poor and partly because they saw nothing wrong with it.

It was common for a Union colonel, as his regiment made camp in a Southern state, to address his men, pointing to a nearby farm, and say: "Now, boys, that barn is full of nice fat pigs and chickens. I don't want to see any of you take any of them"—whereupon he would fold his arms and look sternly in the opposite direction. It was also common for a regimental commander to read, on parade, some ukase from higher authority forbidding foraging, and then to wink solemnly—a clear hint that he did not expect anyone to take the order seriously. One colonel, punishing some men who had robbed a chicken house, said angrily: "Boys, I want you to understand that I am not punishing you for stealing but for getting caught at it."

It is nearly a century since that war was fought, and things look a little different now than they looked at the time. At this distance, it may be possible to look indulgently on the wholesale foraging in which Union armies indulged; to the Southern farmers who bore the brunt of it, the business looked very ugly indeed. Many a Southern family saw the foodstuffs needed for the winter swept away in an hour by grinning hoodlums who did not need and could not use a quarter of what they took. Among the foragers there were many lawless characters who took watches, jewels, and any other valuables they could find; it is recorded that a squad would now and then carry a piano out to the lawn, take it apart, and use the wires to hang pots and pans over the campfire. . . . The Civil War was really romantic only at a considerable distance.

Underneath his feeling that it was good to add chickens and hams to the army ration, and his belief that civilians in a state of secession could expect no better fate, the Union soldier also came to believe that to destroy Southern property was to help win the war. Under orders, he tore up railroads and burned warehouses; it was not long before he realized that anything that damaged the Confederate economy weakened the Confederate war effort, so he rationalized his looting and foraging by arguing that it was a step in breaking the Southern will to resist. It is at this point that the institution of human slavery enters the picture.

Most Northern soldiers had very little feeling against

To city-bred soldiers on the foraging detail, the land of milk and honey seemed to contain only balky cows and angry bees.

slavery as such, and very little sympathy for the Negro himself. They thought they were fighting to save the Union, not to end slavery, and except for New England troops most Union regiments contained very little abolition sentiment. Nevertheless, the soldiers moved energetically and effectively to destroy slavery, not because they especially intended to but simply because they were out to do all the damage they could do. They were operating against Southern property—and the most obvious, important, and easily removable property of all was the slave. To help the slaves get away from the plantation was, clearly, to weaken Southern productive capacity, which in turn weakened Confederate armies. Hence the Union soldier, wherever he went, took the peculiar institution apart, chattel by chattel.

As a result, slavery had been fatally weakened long before the war itself came to an end. The mere act of fighting the war killed it. Of all institutions on earth, the institution of human slavery was the one least adapted to survive a war. It could not survive the presence of loose-jointed, heavy-handed armies of occupation. It may hardly be too much to say that the mere act of taking up arms in slavery's defense doomed slavery.

Above and beyond everything else, of course, the business of the Civil War soldier was to fight. He fought with weapons that look very crude to modern eyes, and he moved by an outmoded system of tactics, but the price he paid when he got into action was just as high as the price modern soldiers pay despite the almost infinite development of firepower since the 1860's.

Standard infantry weapon in the Civil War was the rifled Springfield—a muzzle-loader firing a conical lead bullet, usually of .54 caliber.

To load was rather laborious, and it took a good man to get off more than two shots a minute. The weapon had a range of nearly a mile, and its "effective range"—that is, the range at which it would hit often enough to make infantry fire truly effective—was figured at about 250 yards. Compared with a modern Garand, the old muzzle-loader is no better than a museum piece; but compared with all previous weapons—the weapons on which infantry tactics in the 1860's were still based—it was a fearfully destructive and efficient piece.

For the infantry of that day still moved and fought in formations dictated in the old days of smoothbore muskets, whose effective range was no more than 100 yards and which were wildly inaccurate at any distance. Armies using those weapons attacked in solid mass formations, the men standing, literally, elbow to

elbow. They could get from effective range to hand-to-hand fighting in a very short time, and if they had a proper numerical advantage over the defensive line they could come to grips without losing too many men along the way. But in the Civil War the conditions had changed radically; men would be hit while the rival lines were still half a mile apart, and to advance in mass was simply to invite wholesale destruction. Tactics had not yet been adjusted to the new rifles; as a result, Civil War attacks could be fearfully costly, and when the defenders dug entrenchments and got some protection—as the men learned to do, very quickly—a direct frontal assault could be little better than a form of mass suicide.

It took the high command a long time to revise tactics to meet this changed situation, and Civil War battles ran up dreadful casualty lists. For an army to lose 25 per cent of its numbers in a major battle was by no means uncommon, and in some fights—the Confederate army at Gettysburg is an outstanding example—the percentage of loss ran close to one-third of the total number engaged. Individual units were sometimes nearly wiped out. Some of the Union and Confederate regiments that fought at Gettysburg lost up to 80 per cent of their numbers; a regiment with such losses was usually wrecked, as an effective fighting force, for the rest of the war.

The point of all of which is that the discipline which took the Civil War soldier into action, while it may have been very sketchy by modern standards, was nevertheless highly effective on the field of battle. Any armies that could go through such battles as Antietam, Stone's River, Franklin or Chickamauga and come back for more had very little to learn about the business of fighting.

Perhaps the Confederate General D. H. Hill said it, once and for all. The battle of Malvern Hill, fought on the Virginia peninsula early in the summer of 1862, finished the famous Seven Days campaign, in which George B. McClellan's Army of the Potomac was driven back from in front of Richmond by Robert E. Lee's Army of Northern Virginia. At Malvern Hill, McClellan's men fought a rear-guard action—a bitter, confused fight which came at the end of a solid week of wearing, costly battles and forced marches. Federal artillery wrecked the Confederate assault columns, and at the end of the day Hill looked out over the battlefield, strewn with dead and wounded boys. Shaking his head, and reflecting on the valor in attack and in defense which the two armies had displayed, Hill never forgot about this. Looking back on it, long after the war was over, he declared, in substance:

"Give me Confederate infantry and Yankee artillery and I'll whip the world!"

247

On Saturday morning, October 25, 1851, Horace Greeley's New York *Tribune*, entrenched after a decade of existence as America's leading Whig daily, appeared with twelve pages rather than its usual eight. The occasion was too noteworthy to be passed over without comment by the paper itself. So a special editorial was written—probably by Greeley's young managing editor, the brisk, golden-whiskered Charles A. Dana—to point it out.

Besides a "press of advertisements," the editorial ran, this morning's enlarged paper contained "articles from some foreign contributors that are especially worthy of attention." Among these were "a letter from Madame Belgioioso, upon the daily and domestic life of the Turks, and another upon Germany by one of the clearest and most vigorous writers that country has produced—no matter what may be the judgment of the critical upon his public opinions in the sphere of political and social philosophy."

Turning the pages to see who this most clear and vigorous German might be, readers glanced past such items as a "Grand Temperance Rally in the 13th Ward"; a Philadelphia story headlined "Cruelty of a Landlord—Brutality of a Husband"; a Boston campaign telegram announcing a Whig demonstration "in favor of Daniel Webster for President." Then they reached a long article entitled "Revolution and Counter-Revolution," over the by-line, Karl Marx.

"The first act of the revolutionary drama on the Continent of Europe has closed," it began upon a somber organ tone; "The 'powers that were' before the hurricane of 1848, are again the 'powers that be.'" But, contributor Marx went on, swelling to his theme, the second act of the movement was soon to come, and the interval before the storm was a good time to study the "general social state . . . of the convulsed nations" that led inevitably to such upheavals.

He went on to speak of "bourgeoisie" and "proletariat"—strange new words to a readership absorbed at the moment with the Whig state convention, the late gale off Nova Scotia and with editor Greeley's strictures against Tammany and Locofocoism. "The man goes deep—very deep for me," remarked one of Greeley's closest friends, editor Beman Brockway of upstate Watertown, New York. "Who is he?"

Karl Marx, a native of the Rhineland, had been for a short time the editor of a leftist agitational newspaper in Cologne until the Prussian police closed it down and drove him out. At thirty, exiled in Paris, he had composed as his own extremist contribution to the uprisings of 1848 an obscure tract called the *Communist Manifesto*. At least at this moment it was still obscure, having been overtaken by events and forgotten in the general tide of reaction that followed the surge of 1848 abroad. Thrown out of France in turn as a subversive character, he had settled in London, tried unsuccessfully to launch another left-wing journal there, spent the last of his small savings, and now was on his uppers with his wife and small children in a two-room hovel in Soho, desperately in need of work.

PHOTOGRAPH OF KARL MARX FROM BETTMANN ARCHIVE

WHEN KARL MARX WORKED

The following week Karl Marx was in the *Tribune* again, continuing his study of the making of revolutions. And again the week after that. "It may perhaps give you pleasure to know," managing editor Dana wrote him as his series of pieces on the late events in Germany went on, "that they are read with satisfaction by a considerable number of persons and are widely reproduced." Whatever his views might be, evidently the man could write. Next he branched out and wrote for Greeley and Dana on current political developments in England, France, Spain, the Middle East, the Orient—the whole world, in fact, as seen from his Soho garret. News reports, foreign press summaries, polemics, and prophecies poured from his desk in a continuous, intermixed flow, sometimes weekly, often twice-weekly, to catch the next fast packet to New York and so to earn from Greeley five dollars per installment.

This singular collaboration continued for over ten years. During this period Europe's extremest radical, proscribed by the Prussian police and watched over by its agents abroad as a potential assassin of kings, sent in well over 500 separate contributions to the great New York family newspaper dedicated to the support of Henry Clay, Daniel Webster, temperance, dietary reform, Going West, and, ultimately, Abraham Lincoln. Even at his low rate of pay—so low that his revolutionary friend and patron, Friedrich Engels, agreed with him that it was "the lousiest petty-bourgeois cheating"—what Marx earned from the *Tribune* during that decade constituted his chief means of support, apart from handouts from Engels. The organ of respectable American Whigs and of their successors, the new Republican party, sustained Karl Marx over the years when he was mapping out his crowning tract of overthrow, *Das Kapital*.

In fact, much of the material he gathered for Greeley, particularly on the impoverishment of the English working classes during the depression of the late 1850's, went bodily into *Das Kapital*. So did portions of a particularly virulent satire he wrote for the *Tribune* on the Duchess of Sutherland, a lady who had taken the visit of Harriet Beecher Stowe to London as the occasion to stage a women's meeting that dispatched a lofty message of sympathy to their "American sisters" in their cause of abolishing Negro slavery. Marx scornfully asked what business the Duchess of Sutherland had stepping forth as a champion of freedom in America, when at home she herself was living off vast Scottish estates from which not so long ago her own family had driven off 3,000 tenant families and burned their villages in order to turn the land back to pasture lands and ducal hunting preserves.

The *Tribune* was not only Marx's meal ticket but his experimental outlet for agitation and ideas during the most creative period of his life. Had there been no *Tribune* sustaining him, there might possibly—who knows?—have been no *Das Kapital*. And had there been no *Das Kapital*, would there have been a Lenin and a Stalin as the master's disciples? And without a

OR HORACE GREELEY

By WILLIAM HARLAN HALE

Charles A. Dana met Marx in Europe and got Greeley to hire him as London correspondent.

Marxist Lenin and Stalin, in turn, would there have been . . . ? We had best leave the question there. History sometimes moves in mysterious ways.

Few episodes in journalism seem more singular and unlikely than this association of the frowning ideologist of Soho on one hand and, on the other the moon-faced, owlish New Hampshire Yankee who was known to legions of readers in North and West as "Uncle Horace" as he traipsed around the country on the steamcars with his squeaky rural voice, his drooping spectacles, his carpetbag, and his broad-brimmed white hat. It is startling enough today that their careers should ever have become intertwined. What is even more odd in retrospect is the degree to which they did. Although Marx filed well over 500 pieces to the *Tribune,* just how many there were nobody knows, since many were "spiked," killed and forgotten, while others were cut up and cannibalized, and still others were taken over bodily and printed without his by-line as leaders in the special precincts of Greeley's own editorial page. Precisely which of Marx's pieces were so used only a process of deduction and guesswork can tell, since no copies were kept. Today, scanning the *Tribune*'s files, one cannot be sure whether the voice one encounters thundering on its most famous page is that of the great Greeley himself or that of his rabid man in London, Herr Doktor Marx.

And the puzzle goes one step further. Even on those occasions when a *Tribune* contribution is clearly labeled as by Karl Marx, one cannot be sure that it really was written by Marx at all. Managing editor Dana, who conducted the office's day-to-day dealings with its London correspondent, evidently believed that whatever Marx sold the *Tribune* as his own really was his own. But today we know better. From Marx's immense correspondence with his acolyte, financial angel, and amanuensis, Friedrich Engels (still published for the most part only in the original German) we can discover something his American employers at the time never suspected, namely that much of what they bought as by "Karl Marx" was actually ghostwritten by the ever-helpful Engels.

Not one word of the opening article which the *Tribune* heralded as being by this "clearest and most vigorous" of German writers, Karl Marx, was penned by Marx at all. Nor was anything he sent to the paper under his own name for the next six months or so. Even after that, what was really Marx's and what was Engels' is a question that remains to be explored by Ph.D.'s in search of occupation. But all that matters is that much of what the *Tribune*'s subscribers in the 1850's took to be the work of Greeley was the work of Marx, and what they took to be the work of Marx was often that of an unknown assistant in Manchester, England, named Engels.

If readers were astonished at their Uncle Horace for bringing so alien a person as this Marx into their fold, they had only to remember that he had surprised them often before. In the ten years of its existence, his paper had espoused more varied causes and assembled around itself a more unconventional array of talents than any major daily had ever done before (and, one may safely add, than any has done since). It had come out for free homesteading and labor unions at a time when these were drastic new ideas. It had also backed socialist community experiments, the graham bread cult, pacifism, vegetarianism, and Mrs. Bloomer's clothing reform. The utopian Albert Brisbane had preached in its pages the virtues of his North American Phalanx, a communal colony set up according to the principles of the Frenchman Charles Fourier. The formidable, rhapsodic Margaret Fuller, whom Nathaniel Hawthorne had once called "the Transcendental heifer," had preached feminism in it—and then moved right into Greeley's own married home. The paper's star performers ranged from Bayard Taylor, the romantic poet and world traveler whose profile made him look the part of an American Lord Byron, to George Ripley, the exuberant Unitarian minister who had broken away to found the cooperative retreat at Brook Farm where intellectuals carried on Socratic discourse and took in each other's washing.

Greeley himself was always inquiring and imaginative, and with the priceless possession of an independ-

Marx set the "line," but his patron Friedrich Engels actually wrote many Tribune *articles.*

ent popular newspaper at his command he stood at the center of the turbulence as a barometer, a bellwether, a broker of new notions and ideas. Nothing was quite alien to him in the assorted stirrings of that era—not even the Fox sisters of Rochester, who had attracted much attention with their clairvoyant "spirit-rappings," and whom he invited to his house for a séance along with the famed Swedish soprano, Jenny Lind, newly brought to this country as the protégée of his somewhat gamy yet still moralistic crony, Phineas T. Barnum.

For such a man as Greeley, then, not even Karl Marx was quite beyond the pale. What was meant by this new gospel of socialism, after all? Did it really involve total overthrow? One of the *Tribune*'s intellectual friends, Henry James senior, speaking at a time when his more famous sons, William and Henry junior, were still playing with building blocks, had put the case for socialism on a religious basis. Our present society, he had said, "affords no succor to the divine life in man." Yet every creature of God was entitled to ample physical as well as social subsistence—that is, the respect and brotherly affection of every other creature of God. Greeley, deeply devotional himself, had been moved by the force of the argument. At the same time he balked at the idea of an all-knowing new system that would paternally take care of everyone. The ancient conflict between freedom and order burned in his mind. Better go on listening to both sides, then, he thought.

Up to a point, the apostles of change had a good

case, he said in the *Tribune*. "We . . . who stand for a comprehensive Reform in the social relations of mankind impeach the present Order as defective and radically vicious in the following particulars. . . . It does not secure opportunity to labor, nor to acquire industrial skill and efficiency to those who need it most. . . . It dooms the most indigent class to pay for whatever of comforts and necessaries they may enjoy . . . at a higher rate than is exacted of the more affluent classes . . . [and] for the physical evils it inflicts, Society has barely two palliatives—Private Alms-giving and the Poorhouse. . . ." Yet he did not want a class revolution, he insisted. He wanted to see co-operation and harmony. He looked forward to a reorganization of life amid the threatening weight of the factory system that would give each worker a share of the proceeds of the enterprise or else an opportunity to strike out on his own on free land from our national domain, where he could build his own enterprise.

Such ideas, far from seeming subversive, pulsed like wine through the veins of a young generation. One of those who had been swept up was a well-bred Harvard junior named Charles A. Dana. Young Dana, handsome, well-spoken, and idealistic, joined Ripley's colony when it was set up at Brook Farm and lived there for five years, milking the cows, teaching other intellectuals' children German and Greek, and waiting on tables to such distinguished visitors as Hawthorne, William Ellery Channing, Miss Fuller, and Greeley himself.

When Brook Farm burned down both Ripley and his young helper found berths on Greeley's ever-hospitable *Tribune*. The year 1848 broke—a time of real revolution abroad as against the pastoral make-believe of Brook Farm at home. Young Dana, fired by the reports the first packet steamers were bringing in, managed to get a leave of absence from the fourteen-dollar-a-week job he then held as Greeley's city editor to go to Europe and see the drama. He was in Paris at the height of the insurrection that overthrew the July Monarchy. Paris went to the barricades, and reporter Dana climbed them too. He saw blood flow in the rue de Rivoli.

From this scene Dana sped on to Germany for more hopeful signs. There, in Cologne, he called on editor Karl Marx, then functioning during a brief lifting of the police ban as editor of the grubby *Neue Rheinische Zeitung*.

Just what young Dana of the *Tribune* and Marx of the *Communist Manifesto* said to each other that midsummer day in Cologne is not of record. In later years, when he had graduated to become editor of the New York *Sun* in his own right and thereby a pillar of

251

American society, Dana seems to have expunged all memory of that meeting from his mind. But it was there that the contact was made which led to Marx's ten-year connection with the *Tribune*. And if Dana remained reticent, another caller on Marx that same summer has left a vivid impression of what the Cologne radical was then like. This other visitor was Carl Schurz, then himself a fledgling fellow-revolutionist of the Rhineland, and destined—like Dana himself—to a distinguished public career in the United States. Marx that summer, Carl Schurz recalled, "was a somewhat thickset man, with his broad forehead, his very black hair and beard and his dark sparkling eyes. I have never seen a man whose bearing was so provoking and intolerable. To no opinion which differed from his, he accorded the honor of even a condescending consideration. Everyone who contradicted him he treated with abject contempt. . . . I remember most distinctly the cutting disdain with which he pronounced the word 'bourgeois.'"

Dana returned to the home office, aroused and enlarged by all he had seen abroad. Greeley, who had never been abroad himself, encouraged his bright young acquisition and made him managing editor. In this role, in 1851, he extended the *Tribune's* invitation to Marx, then living in penury and exile at 28 Dean Street, Soho. Would he begin with a series on the late revolution in Germany? Marx jumped at it as a lifesaver. No English newspaper had wanted him as a contributor. For one thing, although he spoke a thickly accented English, he could not write the language. Yet this could be overcome by his getting in his friend and fellow exile, Friedrich Engels, to translate for him. Engels, the highly cultivated scion of a prosperous German textile family, was busy managing his father's branch factory in Manchester and was always eager to assist.

Then Marx had a further thought. Why not have Engels write the whole series for him and thus leave him free to go on undisturbed with his studies for *Das Kapital*? So he wrote Engels imperiously, "You must, at this moment when I am entirely absorbed in political economy, come to my aid. Write a series of articles on Germany since 1848. Spirited and outspoken. These gentlemen [the *Tribune* editors] are very free and easy when it comes to foreign affairs." Soon acolyte Engels obliged, sending in his draft for Marx's signature. "Mes remerciements pour ton article," Marx acknowledged it, in that mixture of tongues he resorted to as a kind of exiled lingua franca; "Er . . . ist unverändert nach New York

Fragments of a Marx dispatch in the Tribune *for February 9, 1853, show how he combined news, research, and polemic.*

gesegelt. Du hast ganz den Ton für die *Tribune* getroffen." *

So, while Marx from his garret gave Engels the political line for his articles, saying he was too busy to do more than that, his faithful partner sat down after work at the factory to write what was required and then hurried downtown through Manchester's midnight fogs to put his copy on the late express to London, where Marx would see it and pass it on across the sea. It was a demanding life for Engels, as he sometimes pointed out. Once he minuted to Marx, "Busy the whole day at the office; supper from seven to eight; then right to work, and sending all I could get done off now at 11:30." Or "In spite of my greatest efforts, since I got your letter only this morning and it's now eleven P.M., I haven't yet finished the piece for Dana." Marx, for his part, cashed the monthly payment drafts coming in from the *Tribune.*

Still Marx's own life at that time was not one of ease. It resembled a nightmare. He was living and trying to do his thinking in a squalid two-room flat which he shared with his wife and as many as six children. Three died there while he went out begging from friends for food and medicine, and, in the case of one little girl whom the Marxes lost, the price of a coffin in which to bury her. When he finally did commence writing himself for Greeley in German in order to reduce the pressure on his friend, he sometimes found it impossible to go on. "My wife is sick," he complained to Engels one day, "little Jenny is sick, Lenchen [the family's factotum, also quartered in the same two rooms] has a sort of nerve fever. I couldn't and can't call the doctor, because I have no money for medicine. For eight to ten days I've fed the family on bread and potatoes, and it's doubtful whether I'll be able to chase up any today. . . . I haven't written anything for Dana because I didn't have a penny to go out and get newspapers to read."

Under such circumstances, the relationship to the *Tribune* of a man who was haughty and irascible to begin with, and stone-broke, bitter, and fearful of his family's very survival besides, promised to be stormy. Marx constantly importuned his New York employers for more linage, better treatment of his copy, and, above all, more pay. When this was not forthcoming, he vented his spleen in scribblings to Engels in which he variously described the *Tribune* as *Löschpapier* (that blotter) or *Das Lauseblatt* (that lousy rag), its editors as *Kerle* and *Burschen* (those guys, those bums), Dana as *Der Esel* (that ass) and Greeley him-

self as "*Dieser alte Esel* with the face angelic." The two German intellectuals consoled themselves by looking down their noses at the the mass-circulation Yankee daily for which they found themselves having to work. "One really needn't put one's self out for this rag," said Engels to Marx; "Barnum struts about life-size in its columns, and its English is appalling." And Marx in turn muttered to Engels, "It's disgusting to be condemned to regard it as good fortune to be taken into the company of such a rag. To pound and grind bones and cook up soup out of them like paupers in the workhouse—that's what the political work comes down to which we're condemned to do there."

Moreover, Marx disagreed with many of the *Tribune*'s policies—although he avoided an open break, fearful of losing his meal ticket. One particular anathema to him was the idea of a protective tariff. Yet Greeley, whose dallyings with socialism had never interfered with his enthusiasm for American business enterprise, felt that protectionism was just the thing. When he heard this, Marx erupted darkly to Engels, "Das alles ist very ominous."

Managing editor Dana had a difficult time with the impetuous pair in London. Most of the letters in which he answered Marx's multilingual torrent of demands and protests have been lost. But Dana was a born diplomat, shrewd, worldly, a trifle sardonic, and his responses were always smooth. He addressed Marx gracefully "in the name of our friendship," but avoided paying him the triple rate Marx had asked for, and eventually also cut down his space. Marx stormed but went on writing for the *Tribune,* which at least let him say what he wanted to say. "Mr. Marx has indeed opinions of his own, with some of which we are far from agreeing," an editorial note in the paper remarked; "but those who do not read his letters neglect one of the most instructive sources of information on the great questions of European politics."

For, in spite of all their letting off steam to one another about the "lousiness" of the *Yankeeblatt* the partners Marx and Engels finally settled down together to do an extraordinary journalistic job for it. In a day before the coming of the transatlantic cable, and when Europe's own overland telegraph lines were still too sparse and costly to carry more than fragmentary press reports, England was the world's great communications center by reason of its unrivaled sea traffic in every direction. Marx and Engels were keenly aware of this and set themselves up as a sort of central agency amassing world news and intelligence for their American client—with their own slant, of course. With Teutonic diligence they dredged up from diplomatic dispatches, statistical abstracts, government files, the British Museum, gossip, and newspapers in half a

* "My thanks for your article. It . . . sailed off unchanged to New York. You have hit the tone for the *Tribune* precisely."

dozen languages gathered from Copenhagen to Calcutta, a mass of information on going topics such as had never reached the readers of an American newspaper before.

In 1853 the eyes of Europe turned apprehensively toward the growing crisis between the Western powers and Russia over the control of weak but strategic Turkey—a contest that soon led to the Crimean War. Marx and Engels provided their American readers with a background series that discussed the ethnic make-up of the area, reviewed its diplomatic history as far back as the treaty of 1393 between the Sublime Porte and Walachia, characterized all its chief personalities, and estimated down to battalion strengths the military forces and capabilities of the contenders. Some of this made for dry reading, but Marx had a way of breaking through into language of a vigor any American could understand. He poured vitriol on the Western rulers who were trying to maintain decadent Turkey as their tool:

"Now, when the shortsightedness of the ruling pygmies prides itself on having successfully freed Europe from the dangers of anarchy and revolution, up starts again the everlasting topic, 'What shall we do with Turkey?' Turkey is the living sore of European legitimacy. The impotency of legitimate, monarchial governments ever since the first French Revolution has resumed itself in the axiom, Keep up the *status quo*. . . . The *status quo* in Turkey! Why, you might as well try to keep up the present degree of putridity into which the carcass of a dead horse has passed at a given time, before the putridity is complete."

Equally, he turned on czarist Russia, in whose "good will" toward Turkey the *Times* of London was at the moment voicing hopeful confidence. "The good will of Russia toward Turkey!" he snorted. "Peter I proposed to raise himself on the ruins of Turkey. . . . Czar Nicholas, more moderate, only demands the exclusive Protectorate of Turkey. Mankind will not forget that Russia was the *protector* of Poland, the *protector* of the Crimea, the *protector* of Courland, Georgia, Mingrelia, the Circassian and Caucasian tribes. And now Russia, the protector of Turkey!"

On this score there was trouble again between Marx and Greeley. Greeley, a perennial twister of the British lion's tail, was inclined to take sides with Russia's aspirations. Marx was violently against *all* imperial ambitions in Europe. "The devil take the *Tribune*!" he exploded to comrade Engels. "It has simply got to come out against Pan-slavism. If not, we may have to break with the little sheet." But he added quickly, "Yet that would be fatal."

When Marx turned around again and let fly at the British government and social system, he spoke a language more pleasing to Greeley and his American constituents. The foreign secretary, Lord Palmerston, was "that brilliant boggler and loquacious humbug." Lord John Russell was "that diminutive earth-man." Gladstone was "a phrase-mongering charlatan." And as for Queen Victoria's consort, Prince Albert, "He has devoted his time partly to fattening pigs, to inventing ridiculous hats for the army, to planning model lodging-houses of a peculiarly transparent and uncomfortable kind, to the Hyde Park exhibition, and to amateur soldiery. He has been considered amiable and harmless, in point of intellect below the general average of human beings, a prolific father, and an obsequious husband." By the time he wrote this, Karl Marx had clearly mastered English on his own, and very well indeed; from then on, he needed little further help from Engels.

But from under this coruscating surface there always emerged before the end of the article the same Marxian refrain. It was that of the inevitable approach of new and sweeping revolution. Marx saw it coming everywhere. One of his most scathing pieces, written with the atmosphere of a columnist's exclusive, was a detailed forecast of the cynical maneuvers which he said the five Great Powers were about to stage over the Middle East. "But," he wound up, "we must not forget that there is a sixth power in Europe, which at any given moment asserts its supremacy over the whole of the five so-called Great Powers, and makes them tremble, every one of them. That power is the Revolution. Long silent and retired, it is now again called to action. . . . From Manchester to Rome, from Paris to Warsaw to Perth, it is omnipresent, lifting up its head. . . ."

And so on. Eventually the *Tribune* began to weary of Marx's obiter dicta. For the next revolution in Europe showed no signs of coming. Instead of making for Marx's barricades, the masses seemed intent simply on pursuing their own business. In 1855 editor Greeley traveled to Europe, a somewhat incongruous figure in his Yankee whiskers and duster. But he refrained from calling upon his chief correspondent and revolutionary expert in London, Karl Marx. So the two men, moving like tall ships on contrary courses in the narrow seas of Europe, never met.

Perhaps Marx had laid on too thickly. Perhaps, while marshaling his massive batteries of facts and handing down his imperious conclusions, he had presumed too much on the hospitality of his readership. Or perhaps America, open-minded yet realistic and absorbed in the practicalities of its own fast-changing existence, had outgrown him. In any case he was not talking about unleashing the "divine life" in man, as the idealists around Greeley had done not so many years before. (Once a *Tribune* editor appended to a homily of Marx's that was run as an editorial a wind-up sentence beginning, "God grant that——" which at once aroused Marx's ire. He wasn't asking God to grant anything.) Marx was calling for revolutionary wars and barricades. A war did come— but not the one Marx had projected. It was our own.

In 1857, a year when American minds were intent on our imminent crisis over the extension of slavery, Dana wrote Marx circumspectly on Greeley's behalf to say that because of the current economic depression the *Tribune* found itself forced to reduce drastically all its foreign correspondence. "Diese Yankees sind doch verdammt lausige Kerle" (damned lousy bums), Marx burst out to Engels in his original German, charging that they now wanted to toss him aside like a squeezed lemon. But Dana, knowing Marx's financial situation, came through with an offer of outside help. He himself was editing on the side a compilation to be called the *New American Cyclopaedia.* Wouldn't Marx like to do a number of short sketches on historic personalities for it, at two dollars per printed page? Marx had no alternative but to accept. So the twin revolutionists sat down, grumbling as ever, to deliver hack-work biographies beginning under letter *B* with Barclay, Bernadotte, Berthier, Blücher, Bourrienne . . . an extraordinary potpourri.

A trickle of further letters from Marx and Engels to the *Tribune* did continue, and Greeley and Dana used them when they found inclination or space. But the spacious enthusiasm of the days that had prompted the first of them had died away. It had been smothered partly by the rush of American events and partly by the realization that Marx, for all his efforts to stake a claim in the *Tribune,* did not, after all, speak our language. Dana, ever the diplomat, and appreciative of what Marx (alias Engels) had contributed over the years, notified him when the war between North and South broke out that while all other foreign correspondence had been suspended because of the emergency, he himself could continue contributing—although on a still more reduced basis. Marx, increasingly dubious of his American outlet, wrote for a while longer, only to learn that Dana himself, after what was reported to have been a falling-out with Greeley, had left the staff of the *Tribune* to become assistant secretary of war. Not long afterward, Marx's own arrangement was canceled, too.

Now the frustrated team in London, who had so often reviled Dana as their immediate taskmaster, came around to the view that he, no less than they themselves, had been just the exploited wage slave of Greeley. "It's that old ass himself who is really responsible for everything," said Engels, as the curtain of their life with the *Tribune* rang down.

Marx was never again a correspondent for another newspaper. He had by now finished a great part of *Das Kapital,* for one thing, and henceforth went on to lead in organizing the Communist First International. Greeley, for his part, never once mentioned in his own memoirs the name of the most famous and controversial man who had ever worked for him on the *Tribune.*

Today all that remains of their episode together is a bundle of faded letters, a rash of multilingual expletives, and a file of published articles of whose authorship one can only rarely be quite sure. For Marx the collaboration was something less than a total success, for he never made Marxists of the subscribers to the New York *Tribune.* Did Greeley's *Tribune,* in turn, with its hospitality and willingness to give free run to new ideas, have any effect upon Marx?

Perhaps it was too much to expect that any outside influence (particularly when money was involved) would have any effect on that somber man, pursued by his own demon of the absolute. Still, although Marx and Greeley found they had little in common save sheer journalistic energy and a gift for rhetoric, there were occasions when what either one of them said could well be put into the mouth of the other. Such an instance occurred on the last day of 1853, when many of the readers of the *Tribune* were as absorbed with the issues of East and West, of freedom and organization, as their descendants are today:

"Western Europe is feeble . . . because her governments feel they are outgrown and no longer believed by their people. The nations are beyond their rulers. . . . But there is new wine working in the old bottles. With a worthier and more equal social state, with the abolition of caste and privilege, with free political constitutions, unfettered industry, and emancipated thought, the people of the West will rise again to power and unity of purpose, while the Russian Colossus itself will be shattered by the progress of the masses and the explosive force of ideas."

That passage was written by Karl Marx, not by Horace Greeley. You will not find it, though, in the official collected works of the father of Soviet communism.

William Harlan Hale, a former editor of The New Republic *and of* The Reporter, *served with the Office of War Information and the Foreign Service in London and Vienna. Currently managing editor of* Horizon, *he has written several books, among them* Horace Greeley, Voice of the People. *He is now at work on a book about notable Americans abroad.*

CITIES
OF THE
MIDDLE BORDER

Some became great, others stayed as they were—

and their story tells of the rise of the Midwest

By PAUL M. ANGLE

One hundred and fifty years ago the story of America was a story of the open country—of rural people, living for the most part in villages or on farms. A great part of the country had not even been explored, and huge sections of it did not belong to the United States. By 1830, although the number of Americans living west of the Alleghenies was fast approaching the number east of them, many intelligent men seriously believed that it would take anywhere from 500 to 2,000 years to settle and develop the country.

Today, in contrast, the story of America has become very largely a story of the city. Of all the changes that have come to America, one of the most striking has been the country's amazing urbanization. A few generations ago the average American was a farmer; today he is a city dweller.

At the beginning of the nineteenth century, Boston, New York, Philadelphia, and Baltimore were the only cities in the United States with white populations of more than 10,000. When the 1950 census was taken, 484 cities had passed the 25,000 mark, and within their limits lived 41 per cent of the entire population.

Nowhere has the change been more dramatic than along what used to be called the Middle Border—the great Middle West, an open land of frontier communities and small towns only a century ago, today a thickly settled, highly industrialized area of thriving cities that have burgeoned far beyond anything imaginable in 1860.

The enormous difference can be seen, visually, in such exhibits as the set of contrasting lithographs and photographs from the Chicago Historical Society on the next four pages. But while the visual disparity is evident, what is not so clear is the reason behind the cities' changing faces.

What happened, out on the Middle Border, to make some of these cities double, treble, or quadruple their populations in so short a time? Why should one city grow so much faster than another? Why should St. Paul, Minnesota, have a population of 300,000 today while Davenport, Iowa, has 75,000—when both were approximately the same size a hundred years ago?

We start with Galena, Illinois, not because the town is typical, but because it is not. Almost alone among middle western cities, Galena has lost population over the last hundred years. A century ago it had 10,000 inhabitants; today it has fewer than 5,000.

256

GALENA, ILLINOIS

This center of lead mining in 1856 was all bright promise, but growth stagnated and the town today is smaller than it was.

DAVENPORT, IOWA

This is the thriving young river town in 1856. It prospered, yet St. Paul, tiny at that time, has long since outstripped it.

St. Louis, Missouri

This view in the 1850's looks down from the bluffs at Lucas Place. Across the Mississippi is Illinoistown (now East St. Louis). In the white-domed building at right, Dred Scott lost his first legal battle for freedom; here an unsuccessful ex-army captain named U. S. Grant was selling real estate. Busy, attractive St. Louis lived up to its early promise.

other industries. In the 1880's, nearby limestone quarries were opened and the manufacture of cement was begun. Plants for fabricating iron and steel were founded about the same time. Davenport became, and remains today, a city of diversified industry, at least keeping pace with the country as a whole in growth.

Industry, transportation, and a location that brings trade—these seem to be the factors that make cities. Certainly these are the factors that made St. Louis. When Pierre Laclède Liguest picked its site in December, 1763, he announced that he was establishing a settlement "which might hereafter become one of the finest cities in America." Each passing decade has proved that the prediction was not idle talk. Before the Revolutionary War St. Louis had become the center of the western fur trade. The acquisition of Louisiana Territory made it the crossroads of western expansion. Year after year caravans of settlers bound for the West crossed the Mississippi at St. Louis and bought their outfits for the long trip across the plains.

But it was the traffic on the river that made a city. By 1840, after 77 years, St. Louis had a population of 16,400. In 1850 the census takers counted 78,000; in 1860, 160,000. These were the years when the stacks and masts of the river steamers tied up at St. Louis looked like the denuded trunks in a burned-over forest. The rivermen sinned boisterously in the dives along the wharves and brawled in the streets, but in spite of their picturesque ways, the city impressed visitors by its substance and maturity.

Chicagoans, a boastful breed, like to recall that in forty years their own upstart city passed long-established St. Louis, and subsequently left it far behind. The implication is that when the railroads supplanted the river steamers, St. Louis withered and Chicago bloomed. But St. Louis didn't wither. Railroads could be built to and from the city on the Mississippi as well as anywhere, and they quickly replaced the commerce that the river had carried. Industry, moreover, was firmly established as early as 1850.

Optimistic St. Louisans predicted in 1850 that by 1900 the city would have a population of a million. The actual 1900 figure turned out to be 575,000, but that represented a steady, decade-by-decade gain which has continued in the twentieth century. In 1950, with 850,000 inhabitants, St. Louis ranked eighth among the cities of the country.

St. Louis, in fact, outran a rival that had taken what appeared to be, in the first thirty or forty years of the nineteenth century, a lead that would hold up forever. During most of these years Cincinnati deserved to be called the Queen City. Even the acidulous Frances Trollope, who lived there from 1828 to

1831, admitted that in spite of all shortcomings it was "a city of extraordinary size and importance." Later English visitors were less restrained. In 1859 the English reformer Richard Cobden recorded in his diary:

"The City has a substantial and prosperous appearance.—Like Philadelphia it depends very much on its manufactures, besides being the centre of a very rich agricultural region, its pork market being the most famous in America.—Lying along the right bank of the Ohio river, with its wooded banks on both sides and its graceful reaches as it winds its course below the City, it is one of the most beautiful sites for a town I have ever seen.—The population is about 200,-000 [actually it was 160,000] of which nearly one half are Germans & Irish. . . . At dinner at the hotel heard a discussion as to the number of people in Cincinnati who are worth $500,000, when it seemed to be the opinion that there were 20 to 25 persons owning that amount of property.—It was thought there were hundreds possessing $100,000."

Mrs. Trollope confessed that upon her arrival she thought "the many tree-covered hills around, very beautiful," but went on to say that she tired of the view so quickly that long before she left she would have welcomed the sight of Salisbury Plain. But to Isabella Bird, in 1855, the view from any of the hills which ringed the city was magnificent. "I saw it first bathed in the mellow light of a declining sun," she wrote, ". . . hill beyond hill, clothed with the rich verdure of an almost tropical clime, slopes of vineyards just ready for the wine-press, magnolias . . . and everywhere foliage so luxuriant that it looked as if autumn and decay could never come."

But Cincinnati had more to be proud of than pleasing vistas. In mid-century, no other city in the interior United States could offer more convincing evidence of industry and prosperity. Mrs. Bird catalogued the signs of well-being: "heavily laden drays rumbling along the streets—quays at which steamboats of fairy architecture are ever lying—massive warehouses and rich stores—the side walks a perfect throng of foot-passengers—the roadways crowded with light carriages, horsemen with palmetto hats and high-peaked saddles, galloping about on the magnificent horses of Kentucky —an air of life, wealth, bustle, and progress."

Yet Cincinnati had reached its zenith, at least comparatively. The city had profited from the westward movement of the American people; but the flood tide had passed. After 1850 Cincinnati would grow so slowly that at the end of a century seventeen cities would rank ahead of it. Even in Ohio, it would slip to second place, outstripped by what was a mere village when Cincinnati was the queen of the old Northwest.

In 1850 Cleveland had a population of 17,034. But

Cleveland also had a fine harbor, canal connections, and ten miles of railroad. By 1860 the population had jumped to 43,417, and the ten miles of railroad had become hundreds, connecting the city with the eastern seaboard and with Chicago, Cincinnati, and St. Louis. And by 1860 Cleveland was an iron ore port with a red avalanche spilling on its docks to be distributed for smelting to the coal-rich neighboring area. To this day, the flow continues.

Oil soon paired with ore to push Cleveland ahead. For ten years after Edwin L. Drake brought in the nation's first great oil field in northwestern Pennsylvania, Pittsburgh, the nearest large city to the wells, held first place as a refining center. Then Cleveland's superior transportation facilities—a water route and two competing railroad connections with the East against Pittsburgh's one—made the city on the lake the oil capital of the country.

The two great industries attracted manufacturers of other products. New railroads were soon built to transport raw materials and finished products. Thousands of foreigners flocked in to fill the ever-increasing number of jobs. Cleveland grew—to 160,000 in 1880, to 380,000 in 1900. In the twentieth century Cleveland spurted to fifth place among American cities, but by 1950 a newcomer, Los Angeles, and an old stalwart in the East, Baltimore, had forced it back to seventh place. Yet with almost a million inhabitants, fine transportation facilities that have become even better with the completion of the St. Lawrence Seaway, and a solid base of diversified industry, Cleveland should hold its high relative position indefinitely.

Cleveland had natural advantages, but it also had, to a remarkable degree, another asset often ignored when attempts are made to appraise the forces that raise one city above another. Cleveland had bold, imaginative, and highly successful enterprisers. Samuel L. Mather and Stephen V. Harkness in iron and steel; Daniel P. Rhodes and his son-in-law, Mark Hanna, in coal, ore, and lake shipping; John D. Rockefeller and Henry M. Flagler in oil—to these men, one could contend, Cleveland owes as much as it owes to all the other factors in its expansion.

The same case can be made for the last of our seven cities, St. Paul. When St. Paul became the capital of the newly created Minnesota Territory in 1849, it was a frontier village with fewer than a thousand inhabitants, many of whom were French Canadians and half-breeds. After ten years St. Paul counted 10,000 inhabitants, most of them brought up the Mississippi by wood-burning side-wheelers which returned downriver loaded with furs and buffalo robes from the Indian country to the north and west.

By this time, the city had given up its early name, Pig's Eye—the change is understandable—and was beginning to ship its grain to the East.

Among the immigrants, Swedes and Germans and Irishmen, who poured in to make St. Paul large and powerful, one would not have particularly noticed James Jerome Hill. All that marked this little fellow of eighteen was a blind eye, put out by an arrow in his native Ontario, and a yen to continue west, to the Pacific, with the next brigade of trappers. Because no brigade left soon after his arrival, Jim Hill had to wait. Meanwhile he got a job labeling flour bags, and St. Paul gained a maker of cities who transformed the little settlement into a great trading center. Here was a railroad builder not ashamed to doff his fine coat and spell the workmen digging his own railroad, a man of choler who would, according to his whim, put a town on the railroad or not, in the manner of the Lord giving or taking away. Acquiring control of the St. Paul and Pacific Railroad in the 1870's, Hill expanded it into the Great Northern, extended its lines, and induced many thousands of ambitious men from Europe and the older states of the East to settle in the territory it served. The Northwest prospered, the Great Northern prospered, St. Paul prospered. By 1900 the village of 1850 had become a city of 163,000; fifty years later it had almost doubled in size. To credit this result to James J. Hill alone would be the grossest kind of oversimplification, yet one can easily imagine slower growth, and a smaller city today, had chance led the well-named Empire Builder to some other place of residence.

One certain deduction can be made from this cursory survey of what has happened to seven cities of the interior United States in the last hundred years. Of all the factors which contribute to growth, the greatest is industry. But industry has brought blight as well as wealth. Look at the attractive, almost bucolic aspect of the cities shown in the old lithographs. Discount the pictures, if you please, on the score that they were made to sell, and that the buyers wanted realism no more than the subject of a portrait photograph desires it. The old prints still represent pleasanter surroundings than we live in today. But not, perhaps, pleasanter surroundings than we might enjoy if we only wanted them badly enough to zone our cities properly and keep them as clean and attractive as they once dreamt of being, in the fresh youth of the Middle Border.

Paul Angle is director of the Chicago Historical Society and is the author of a number of books on Lincoln and American historical subjects.

BLONDIN

THE

HERO OF NIAGARA

Entered according to act of Congress AD 1861 by Blodgett & Bradford in the Clerks' Office in the Dist Court of the North. Dist of N York.

By day and by night, frontward and back, his feet in baskets, his

head in a sack, he crossed the torrent on a cable—190 feet up

By LLOYD GRAHAM

On Thursday, June 30, 1859, the atmosphere at Niagara Falls was charged with excitement. A slightly built Frenchman, dressed in tights and carrying a long balancing pole, was planning to attempt the impossible—he was going to walk across the terrible gorge of the Niagara River about a mile below the Falls on a slender rope cable, 190 feet above the swift and boiling flood. As they watched in fascination, shading their eyes with their parasols, ladies in crinolines nearly swooned. Strong men in top hats and stocks were tense, for many had wagered large sums on the outcome. Little girls clung to the skirts of their nurses and small boys skylarked. Three hundred thousand people —or was it ten thousand?—held their breath as Jean François Gravelet, better known as Blondin, edged out onto the sloping cable.

For people of fashion, wealth, beauty, and culture, northerners and southerners alike, the Falls were already a great attraction a century ago. Whole families with their servants visited Niagara in the new steam cars. Here they spent entire summers in the gentle, stimulating coolness which still is characteristic of the area in the hot months. They registered at luxurious hotels like the Clifton House or the Cataract House, with its huge ballroom and superb crystal chandeliers. They listened to the soft music and danced through the mellow evenings. They sat on the long verandas facing the river gorge and rocked away the long afternoons, listening to the rumble of the Falls and watching the ever-shifting clouds of mist roll up and make rainbows as the waters crashed on the rocks below.

There were plenty of livery stables with carriages of all kinds drawn by shining-coated horses, for it was customary to drive out daily and view the Falls from various vantage points. There were no parks in those days, but the areas on both sides of the Niagara were cluttered with free-enterprising activities. There were restaurants and drinking places and Punch-and-Judy shows and two-headed calves and bearded ladies. It was a place made to order for Blondin.

Physically, Blondin was a small man, distinguished

Blondin, the Hero of Niagara, a march whose colorful cover enhanced the acrobat's features, enjoyed a vogue in 1861.

by blue eyes and the blond hair that had given him his nickname. He stood only five feet five and weighed a mere 140 pounds. Nimble and wiry, he had developed superb co-ordination on the tightwire during years of experience in theaters and circuses. He possessed imagination and courage and tremendous self-assurance— even enough courage and assurance to perform without a single slip the fantastic acts that were the fruit of his imagination. He began experimenting on the tight-rope when he was five years old. When he first appeared at Niagara early in June, 1859, it was with the intention of picking up a few dollars during the summer while waiting to begin an engagement in late August with Franconi's Equestrian Troop. He was then 35 years old and had come to the United States eight years earlier.

As he prepared for the great event, Blondin displayed his genius for publicity and his understanding of the morbid curiosity of the multitude. He had arranged for the use of a rope cable two inches in diameter and 1,300 feet long. Stringing this cable across the roaring gorge and securely anchoring it on both sides presented a considerable problem. A light rope, seven-eighths of an inch in diameter, was attached to one end of the cable and used to convey it across the river. On the American side it was wound around a huge oak tree in White's Pleasure Grounds. When it had been drawn to within about 200 feet of the Canadian side, some of Blondin's helpers expressed the fear that the light rope would not be sufficiently strong to bear the weight of the heavy cable as it was drawn up from the Niagara gorge for anchorage in Canada.

Blondin knew just what to do. While onlookers stared, he attached another rope to his body, went down the 200 feet on the small rope, attached the second rope also to the end of the cable, and then calmly climbed back to Canadian ground. With the two lines supporting it, the cable was pulled ashore and secured to a rock.

Actually, there was about 1,200 feet of cable over the gorge. Some fifty feet were taken up by the inevitable sag in the center, and a few feet at each end were needed to provide for tautness and secure anchorage. It was stretched midway between the Suspension

275

Some of Blondin's Imitators

Signor Farini followed Blondin in 1860.

In 1873 Signor Balleni survived a 160-foot leap into the river with a rope around him.

Maria Spelterini performed in 1876. Some years later Daring Dixon (below) twirled a hoop around his ankles.

Bridge and the Clifton House. To keep it from swaying, guy ropes ran from it at about twenty-foot intervals to anchorage posts on both banks. But there was a considerable portion in the center, perhaps as much as fifty feet, where it was impractical to fasten guy ropes. At the points where the cable came ashore, the ground was about 240 feet above the level of Niagara water. This meant that, allowing for the sag, the center was actually about 190 feet above the tumbling waters of the gorge.

On Thursday, June 30, the day scheduled for Blondin's first crossing, Niagara had a carnival air. On the American side were special grandstands—to which admission was charged. Early in the day, Blondin performed preliminary feats on a tightrope in White's Pleasure Grounds while bands played "God Save the Queen," "Hail, Columbia," and other popular airs. At both ends of the cable Harry Colcord, Blondin's manager, had provided small enclosures with "every facility" for reporters. It was, said the Buffalo *Morning Express,* "just the day for this sort of thing."

All at once the noise subsided to an expectant murmur as Blondin appeared at the American end of the cable. What the spectators saw was reported next morning in the *Express:*

Mons. Blondin has just successfully accomplished the feat of walking across the Niagara River on a tight rope in the presence of a crowd variously estimated at from five to ten thousand persons. He first crossed from the American side, stopping midway to refresh himself with water raised in a bottle with a rope from the deck of the steamer *Maid of the Mist.* The time occupied in the first crossing was seventeen and a half minutes.

When Blondin arrived at the Canadian side, he greeted the reporters, joined in a toast drunk to his health, and announced that he would return over the cable to the American side in half an hour. A collection was taken up for him, and he was conveyed in a carriage drawn by four flag-decorated bays to the Clifton House for a short rest. When he came back to the cable for the return crossing, the reporter wrote that he partook of some "refreshments furnished by Mr. Kavanagh of the Great Western Hotel." The return trip—made quickly and without incident—was almost an anticlimax. "He certainly stands at the head of tight rope walkers and the possession of so much coolness and utter lack of fear must be a luxury," said an *Express* editorial. *"Vive Blondin."*

Blondin's plans for the future, especially for a crossing on the Fourth of July, were widely publicized. The river scene, when that holiday arrived, must have been a strange one. Every vantage point—every tree, every rock, as well as every seat in the grandstands—was occu-

FERNAND BOURGES, COURTESY *Life*

pied by a huge crowd, morbidly confident that Blondin would lose his balance and plunge into the Niagara gorge. They never took their eyes off him lest they miss the awful moment. Betting on the outcome was said to have been huge.

At the appointed hour, Blondin appeared at the American end of the cable without his 38-foot balancing pole. Halfway across, he lay down full length on the cable, putting one foot above the other. He walked backward swiftly, balanced on one foot, extended the other and also his body over the "boiling flood," whirled himself around as if he had been "on a pivot stool," repeated this in the center of the cable, took a flask from his pocket and drank, then completed his journey.

After resting about an hour, he appeared at the Canadian end of the cable, waving a sack. When it was put over his head, spectators saw that it reached to his knees, depriving him of his sight and the use of his arms and hands. With this handicap, he repeated on his return trip the evolutions of the earlier crossing. "In fact," wrote the ecstatic *Express* reporter, "one can scarcely believe the feat was indeed real, and stands gazing upon the slender cord and the awful gulf in a state of utter bewilderment. . . . I look back upon it as upon a dream."

On July 15 the *Express* reported what was billed as Blondin's "farewell" performance. He was reported to have made his first crossing walking backward from the American to the Canadian side. On the return trip he pushed a wheelbarrow, "pausing in the center to do several stunts." On this day he had the greatest crowd so far assembled.

But there was more to come. Blondin had no intention of making his farewell while the crowds continued to grow. On Wednesday, August 3, no doubt "by popular request," he advertised a fourth crossing. The communities on both sides of Niagara Falls were jammed with visitors, surpassing the crowds of all previous exhibitions. Multitudes arrived, not only from Buffalo and Toronto but also from Rochester and many other cities. Railroads and steamship lines ran excursions.

Blondin appeared about four thirty in the afternoon and quickly crossed from the American to the Canadian side at what a reporter described as a "tripping pace." He rested for about fifteen minutes in Canada and began his return. About halfway to the center, he stopped and sat down, and then stretched out full length. After this, he proceeded to do "a number of

This contemporary print, curious in its distortion of perspective, shows Blondin crossing in 1859, his first season at Niagara. The Maid of the Mist *is pictured in the river below.*

get my dying words. This country holds your father's body. Never sell the bones of your father and your mother."

The crisis came soon after Old Joseph's death. Settlers from Oregon's Grande Ronde found a route into the Wallowa and moved in, claiming the Indians' land. Young Joseph protested to the Indian agent on the Nez Percé reservation in Idaho, and an investigation by the Bureau of Indian Affairs resulted in a decision that the Wallowa still belonged legally to the Indians. On June 16, 1873, President Grant formally set aside the Wallowa "as a reservation for the roaming Nez Percé Indians" and ordered the whites to withdraw.

Recognition of their rights brought joy to the Indians. But it was short-lived. The settlers, refusing to move, threatened to exterminate Joseph's people if they didn't leave the valley. In defiance of the presidential order, more whites rolled in by the wagonload. As friction increased Oregon's governor, La Fayette Grover, attacked Washington officials for having abandoned the government's position of 1863 and forced the Administration to reverse itself. In 1875 a new and confusing presidential edict reopened the Wallowa to white homesteaders.

The Nez Percés were dismayed. Young Joseph, whom they called Heinmot Tooyalakekt, meaning "Thunder Traveling to Loftier Mountain Heights," counseled patience. He moved the Indian camps from the neighborhood of the settlers and again appealed to the federal authorities. The assistant adjutant general of the Military Department of the Columbia, Major H. Clay Wood, was assigned to make a survey of the conflicting claims, and in his report, forwarded to Washington by his commanding officer, O. O. Howard, the one-armed "Christian" general of the Civil War, stated: "In my opinion, the non-treaty Nez Percés cannot in law be regarded as bound by the treaty of 1863, and insofar as it attempts to deprive them of a right to occupancy of any land, its provisions are null and void. The extinguishment of their title of occupancy contemplated by this treaty is imperfect and incomplete."

At first the government took no action, but as harassment of the Indians continued and the threat that they might retaliate with violence increased, a commission of five members was appointed to meet with the Nez Percés in November, 1876, with authority to make a final settlement of the matter for "the welfare of both whites and Indians."

The commissioners, Howard, Wood, and three eastern civilians, found Joseph a disquieting figure. Only 36 years old, tall and powerfully built, he seemed

At the Cow Island crossing Nez Percé warriors stand guard until their women and children are safely away. Then, in

strangely amicable and gentle; yet he bore himself with the quiet strength and dignity of one who stood in awe of no man. And when he spoke, it was with an eloquent logic that nettled the whites, who found themselves resenting their inability to dominate him.

Why, they asked him, did he refuse to give up the Wallowa? He answered by referring to the land as the Mother of the Indians, something that could not be sold or given away. "We love the land," he said. "It is our home."

But, they persisted, Lawyer had signed it away in 1863.

Joseph had a ready reply that embarrassed them. "I believe the old treaty has never been correctly reported," he said. "If we ever owned the land we own it still, for we never sold it. In the treaty councils the commissioners have claimed that our country has been sold to the government. Suppose a white man should come to me and say, 'Joseph, I like your horses, and I want to buy them.' I say to him, 'No, my horses suit me, I will not sell them.' Then he goes to my neighbor,

nidating—but not harming—the Army guards, they plun-
red the stores to replenish supplies for the flight ahead.

and says to him, 'Joseph has some good horses. I want to buy them but he refuses to sell.' My neighbor answers, 'Pay me the money, and I will sell you Joseph's horses.' The white man returns to me and says, 'Joseph, I have bought your horses and you must let me have them.' If we sold our lands to the government, this is the way they were bought."

To all their arguments, Joseph replied with an uncompromising "No" and when the council ended, the exasperated commissioners had made no progress with him. But events were moving against the Indians. The situation in the Wallowa had grown perilous, and the commission was under political pressure. Two excited white men had killed an Indian youth after mistakenly accusing him of stealing their horses. Joseph had had all he could do to keep his people calm, and the settlers, fearing an uprising, were arming and calling for military protection.

To the commissioners, despite the fact that it was unjust and there was no legal basis for it, there could be only one decision, and before they left the reserva-

tion headquarters at Lapwai, they rendered it: Unless, within a reasonable time, all the non-treaty Nez Percés (the other bands that had not signed in 1863, as well as Joseph's people in the Wallowa) voluntarily came onto the reservation, *they should be placed there by force.* General Howard, symbolizing the force that would be used, signed the report along with the three easterners. Only Major Wood's name was absent, and it is believed that he submitted a minority report, though it has never been found.

Immediately after the decision, the Indian Bureau defined the "reasonable time" and ordered the Indians to come onto the reservation by April 1, 1877. Unable to move their herds and villages across the rugged canyons in the dead of winter, the Nez Percés appealed for another conference, and, as April 1 came and went, General Howard agreed to one last meeting with all the non-treaty chiefs at Lapwai. It did no good. The die had been cast, and Howard adamantly refused to discuss the commission's decision. As the Indians pleaded in proud but pitiable terms to be allowed to remain in the lands where their fathers were buried, the General finally lost patience and threw one of the most respected old chiefs, a deeply religious war leader and tribal orator named Toohoolhoolzote, into the guardhouse. It broke the spirit of the others. To gain Toohoolhoolzote's release, they capitulated with bitterness and agreed to have their bands on the reservation in thirty days.

All of Joseph's skill as a diplomat had to be called into play when he returned to his people. He had abandoned his father's counsel and trust, and there were cries to ignore him and go to war rather than to move to the reservation. When Joseph argued that the white man's power was too great for them to resist and that it was "better to live at peace than to begin a war and lie dead," they called him a coward. But he received strong assistance from his younger brother, Ollokot, a daring and courageous buffalo hunter and warrior who had won many tribal honors and held the respect of the more belligerent younger element. Eventually the two brothers won agreement to the capitulation from the band's council. With heavy hearts, the Indians prepared to round up their stock and move.

A half year's work was crowded into less than thirty days as the people combed the mountains and forests for their animals and drove them down the steep draws to the Snake. The river was in flood, and hundreds of head of stock were swept away and drowned during the tumultuous crossing. Other portions of the herds, left behind on the bluffs and plateau, were driven away by whites who attacked the guards and harassed the withdrawing Indians. By June 2, with

The rumors this time were true. With Howard's troops floundering in the wilds, the non-treaties had managed to cross again to the north side of the Salmon. Howard tried to follow them, couldn't get his men and equipment across the river, and had to go back over the entire dreadful mountain trail to the place of his original crossing, where he had left his boats. Meanwhile Whipple, forgetting Looking Glass in the face of the full Nez Percé force, sent out a reconnoitering party of ten men under Lieutenant S. M. Rains and dug in for an expected attack. The Indians wiped out Rains's party to a man, cut up another group of scouts and several hastily formed bodies of civilian volunteers, and finally, bypassing Whipple and the terrified settlers barricaded in Cottonwood and Grangeville, moved to another hiding place on the South Fork of the Clearwater River. Here they were joined by Looking Glass's infuriated band. It gave the Indians another forty fighting men but also raised the number of women and children, who would have to be carried along and protected from the soldiers, to a peak figure of 450.

From the beginning it had been assumed by the whites that Joseph, spokesman for the non-treaties in peacetime, had also been leading them in war. Howard had credited him with skillfully contriving the ambush of Perry at White Bird. Now Joseph was being given grudging praise for the masterful way in which the Indians had evaded Howard in the wilderness and doubled back to get between him and Whipple. In addition, the Nez Percés had been conducting themselves in an unusual manner for Indians "on the warpath," refraining from scalping or mutilating bodies, treating white women and noncombatants with humanity and even friendliness, and otherwise adhering to what was considered the white man's code of war. This too was credited to Joseph, whose dignity and decency at prewar councils were recalled by Howard and the Indian agents.

The truth was that Nez Percé successes were resulting from a combination of overconfidence and mistakes on the part of the whites, the rugged terrain that made pursuit difficult, and, to a very great extent, the Indians' intense courage and patriotic determination to fight for their rights and protect their people. Indian strategy and tactics had also played a role, but at each step of the way these were agreed upon in coun-

A colorfully beaded Nez Percé breastplate, worn for decoration.

cils of all the chiefs and were carried out on the field by the younger war leaders and their warriors. Joseph sat in the councils, but since he had never been a war chief his advice carried less weight than that of men like Five Wounds, Toohoolhoolzote, and Rainbow. On the march and in battle Joseph took charge of the old men, women, and children, an assignment of vital importance and sacred trust, while Ollokot and the experienced war chiefs led the young men on guard duty or in combat. The whites had no way of knowing this, and, as events continued to unfold, the legend that Nez Percé strategy was planned and executed by one man, Joseph, was spread far and wide by the hapless army officers opposing him and accepted without question by correspondents and the U.S. public.

On July 11, with a reinforced army of 400 soldiers and 180 scouts, packers, and teamsters, Howard was back in pursuit of the Nez Percés. Suddenly he sighted their camp lying below him on the opposite side of the Clearwater River, opened fire with a four-inch howitzer and two Gatling guns, and prepared to launch an attack. The Nez Percés were taken by surprise, but old Toohoolhoolzote and 24 warriors raced across the river, scaled a bluff to the level of the soldiers, and, taking shelter behind boulders, engaged the troopers with a fierce and accurate fire that held them up until more Indians could come across and get into the fight. The firing was sharp on both sides, but as increasing numbers of mounted Nez Percés began appearing over the top of the bluff to circle the troops' rear and flanks, Howard hastened his men into a square and ordered them to dig in on the open, rocky ground with their trowel bayonets.

The fighting raged all day and continued in the same spot the next morning, an almost unprecedented length of time for Indians to maintain battle in one location. The Nez Percés, outnumbered almost six to one and occasionally under artillery fire, kept the troopers pinned down and on the defensive with marksmanship that Howard's adjutant, Major C. E. S. Wood, described as "terribly accurate and very fatal." Several times small groups of Indians darted forward to engage the soldiers in hand-to-hand fights, and once they almost captured Howard's supply train. In addition, the Nez Percés held the only spring in the area and controlled access to the river; under the blazing July sun the soldiers suffered unmercifully from thirst.

By noon of the second day the chiefs had decided that there had been enough fighting without decision. Many of the warriors had become restless and tired and wanted to leave. Holding the line long enough for Joseph to get the families packed and safely away with the herds, the Indians, one by one, ceased fighting and withdrew down the bluff. Howard's troops followed the last of them across the river and through the abandoned camp. It was an anticlimactic and hollow finish to a battle that had cost the army thirteen killed and twenty-seven wounded, two of them fatally. Howard could count four Indians killed and six wounded, but the hostiles had escaped from him again.

The Nez Percés crossed the Clearwater north of the troops and paused at an old meeting ground on the Weippe Prairie to decide what to do next. They had had enough of Howard and thought that if they left Idaho and went somewhere else, the General would be satisfied and would leave them alone. Looking Glass, who many times had hunted buffalo and fought with the Crows in Montana, urged that they cross the mountains and join that tribe. They could then hunt on the plains in peace, he told them, and the war would be over. It was a harsh proposal, for it meant the final abandonment of their homeland, but with the people's safety weighing heavily on them, Joseph and the other chiefs reluctantly agreed to the exodus. On July 16, having named Looking Glass as supreme chief for the trek to the Crows, the bands set off on the arduous Lolo Trail across the wild and precipitous heights of the Bitterroot Mountains.

Smarting under increasing criticism from Washington, as well as from the press and public, Howard once more took after the Indians, doggedly following their trail up through the thick and tangled forest growth of mountain slopes to the high, ridge-top route that led from Idaho to Montana. It was a painful and grueling trip for both pursuers and pursued. The Indian families, stumbling along over steep and rocky trails, guarded by the warriors and driving some 2,000 horses with them, managed to keep well ahead of the troops, who, with their guns and camp equipment, found the going even rougher. In the meantime, word of the Indian flight had been telegraphed ahead to Montana, and from Missoula Captain Charles C. Rawn, with 35 men of the 7th Infantry and 200 citizen volunteers from the Bitterroot Valley, hastened to the eastern end of the Lolo Trail and threw up a log fort from which to block the hostiles' passage until Howard could catch up to them from the rear.

On July 25, after nine days in the mountains, the Nez Percés appeared above Rawn's fort, and Joseph, Looking Glass, and an elderly chief named White Bird came down for a parley. Explaining that they were on their way to the Crows, the Indians promised to move peacefully through the Bitterroot Valley, respecting the settlements and paying for any supplies they needed. This satisfied the volunteers, who, having no stomach for an Indian fight, deserted Rawn and stole back to their homes. As a federal officer, Rawn was obliged to continue his posture of resistance, but fortunately for his depleted garrison the Indians shrewdly bypassed his fort and, making a noisy feint in front of him, quietly filed around him on another mountain trail that led them into the Bitterroot Valley. The embarrassed Captain withdrew to Missoula, and his log bastion was promptly dubbed Fort Fizzle by the many wags who were beginning to root for Joseph and the apparently unconquerable Nez Percés in their fight-and-run battle with the military.

Moving through the heavily settled valley, the Indians scrupulously maintained their promise to commit no hostile act. At Stevensville they paused to buy coffee, flour, sugar, and tobacco and paid the merchants with gold dust and currency. The friendly treatment they received from the Montana citizens made the Indians believe that, now that they were out of Idaho, the war was over and they were safe. They leisurely moved south to the Big Hole Valley and, on an open meadow beside the willow-lined Big Hole River, pitched camp to rest.

General Howard was still far back in the Bitterroot Mountains, temporarily out of the picture. But, unknown to the Nez Percés, a new force of 163 army regulars and 35 volunteers under Colonel John Gibbon was hurrying across country from Fort Shaw, on the Sun River, by forced marches to attack them. On the night of August 8 Gibbon gained a wooded hill above the unsuspecting Nez Percé camp and, the next morning at dawn, launched a surprise attack. Firing volleys into the sleeping village, the soldiers charged down the hill in a long line, forded the shallow river, and swept into the camp, shooting and clubbing men, women, and children. Some of the Nez Percés were able to seize their weapons and ammunition belts and escape to the shelter of the willows. There they were rallied by the aged White Bird, who cried at them, "Why are we retreating? Since the world was made, brave men have fought for their women and children! Fight! Shoot them down! We can shoot as well as any of these soldiers!"

Gibbon's commanding officer on the left had been killed during the opening charge and, without a leader, that part of the line faltered as Indians stood their ground and fought back desperately from the tepees. The troopers were forced toward the right,

287

Walking slowly toward General Howard and Colonel Miles, Joseph raises his arm in salute and accepts the honorable terms given him. Over the protests of Howard and Miles, the government promptly violated the agreement. This painting and those on pages 281 and 282–83 are part of a series of miniature historical oils executed by Olaf C. Seltzer, Danish-born painter of the American West.

allowing the Nez Percés in that sector to erect a firing line against them. This brought confusion to the main part of the camp, where Gibbon's men, in complete control, were unsuccessfully trying to set the leather tepees afire. With his milling troops being pushed together and soldiers being struck both by the Indians on the left and by White Bird's snipers on the right, Gibbon, who had been wounded in the leg, ordered a withdrawal across the river to the protection of the wooded knoll from which the attack had been launched. To his chagrin the Nez Percés swarmed after him, and in a few moments he found himself on the defensive, fighting fiercely, his position encircled by well-concealed Indian sharpshooters.

As the soldiers pulled out of the village, the old men, women, and children, directed by Joseph, hur-ried back in, picked up their dead and wounded, struck the tepees, and, driving their pack strings and pony herds ahead of them, moved off toward the south. The warriors remained behind, continuing the siege on the hill throughout the day and into the night, pinning down Gibbon's men in shallow holes and behind fallen trees, and picking off anyone who showed himself. Cut off and without prospect of relief, the soldiers' position rapidly became desperate. The men ran out of water, and cries from the unattended wounded filled the air. Gibbon's howitzer, ordered to come up after the initial attack, arrived on the scene and was immediately captured by a group of wild-charging Nez Percés, who rolled it over a steep bluff. Another body of Indians seized a packload of 2,000 rounds of Gibbon's ammunition. By eleven that night,

288

with their camp safely away, the warriors mercifully decided to break off the engagement and spare the surviving troopers. Backing off slowly to guard against pursuit, they took the trail after Joseph.

Gibbon's men, cut up and dazed, were in no condition to follow. Thirty-three soldiers were dead and thirty-eight wounded. Fourteen of the seventeen officers were casualties. Howard's men, coming up hurriedly the next day, found the troops still in a state of shock, burying the dead and trying to care for the groaning wounded.

The Indians' losses at the Big Hole had also been high. Between sixty and ninety Nez Percés had lost their lives, including Rainbow, Five Wounds, and some of the tribe's most able warriors. Many of the casualties had been women and children, slain during the initial attack on the tepees. Joseph's wife had been among the seriously wounded, and Joseph had been seen fighting his way through the early part of the battle sheltering his new baby in his arms.

The Nez Percés now quickened their retreat across southwestern Montana. Gone were illusions that the whites would let them be. In their desperation to escape, only one haven seemed left to them. Like Sitting Bull, they would go to Canada and seek refuge among the tribes in the country of Queen Victoria. Canada was hundreds of miles away, but they would get there somehow. Looking Glass, blamed for the false sense of security that had led to so many deaths at the Big Hole, was relieved of command, and a tough fighter named Lean Elk, whom the whites had known as Poker Joe, was elevated to supreme chief. The column headed eastward toward Targhee Pass, which would lead the refugees over the Continental Divide to the Yellowstone, where they could turn north to Canada. West of the pass, rear-guard scouts brought word that Howard was catching up and pressing close behind them again. In a bold night attack, 28 warriors led by Ollokot and three other chiefs stole back to Howard's camp and ran off the General's entire pack string. Howard came to a dead halt, forced to scour the settlements for more animals, and the Indians hurried on, unhampered, across the Divide and into the area which five years before had become Yellowstone National Park.

A sight-seeing party, of which General William Tecumseh Sherman was a member, had just left the area, but the Nez Percés swooped up two other groups of campers and took them along. The chiefs insisted on humane treatment for the frightened tourists, who included a number of women. In time, as the Indians continued across the park, past geysers and bubbling mudpots, the sight-seers were allowed to escape. On the eastern side of the park, the Indians found themselves harassed by new bodies of troops, coming at them from posts on the Montana plains. One force of the 7th Cavalry under Colonel Samuel Sturgis tried to set a trap for the Indians in the upper Yellowstone Valley, but the Nez Percés fought their way skillfully through a mountain wilderness where the whites thought passage would be impossible and emerged on the Clark's Fork River in Sturgis' rear. Realizing he had been tricked, Sturgis gave chase with 300 men, following the Indians across the Yellowstone River and down its northern bank past present-day Billings, Montana.

On and on the Indians hurried. Near Canyon Creek they passed a stage station and captured a stagecoach. Letting its occupants escape into some nearby willows, the warriors had a day of great fun, driving the incongruous-looking coach along in the rear of the column. The sport ended abruptly. At Canyon Creek the bands turned north, and here, on September 13, Sturgis' hard-riding cavalry overtook them. There was a furious fight. A rear guard of Indians, hiding behind rocks and in gullies, held off the troopers while the Nez Percé women and children drove the pack strings and herds to the protection of a narrow canyon that cut north through rimrock country. Sturgis ordered his men to dismount, an error that allowed the Indians to escape into the canyon. Later the cavalry tried to follow the Nez Percés in a running fight up the canyon, but the Indians succeeded in making pursuit difficult by blocking the canyon floor behind them with boulders and brush. At darkness, weary and running out of ammunition and rations, Sturgis gave up the chase. Three of his men had been killed and eleven wounded. The Indians counted three wounded, but the long pursuit was beginning to tell heavily on them. They too were becoming tired and dispirited, and they were losing horses. Many of the animals were going lame from the difficult trek and had to be abandoned. Others were being lost in the hurry to keep moving.

Beyond Canyon Creek their old allies, the Crows, now in service as scouts for the army, began to attack them. The Nez Percés fought them off in running engagements and continued across the Musselshell to the Missouri River, helping themselves to army stores at a military depot on Cow Island while a frightened sergeant and twelve men looked on helplessly from behind an earthwork. Just across the Missouri, the Indians fought off a half-hearted attack by a small force from Fort Benton and hastened on across badlands and open, rolling plains to the Bear Paw Mountains. About thirty miles short of the Canadian line, exhausted by the long flight, they paused to rest, confident that they had outdistanced all pursuers.

Once more they were wrong, outflanked again by

the telegraph, and this time the pause would end in their last stand. From Fort Keogh in the east, Colonel Nelson A. Miles, with nearly 600 men that included the 2nd and 7th Cavalry, the mounted 5th Infantry, and a body of Cheyenne warriors, was hastening obliquely across Montana, hoping to intercept the hostiles before they crossed the border. On the cold, blustery morning of September 30, Miles's Cheyenne scouts sighted the Nez Percé tepees in a deep hollow on the plains close to Snake Creek on the northern edge of the Bear Paw Mountains. Miles ordered an immediate attack, and the Cheyennes and 7th Cavalry, supported by the 5th Infantry, charged across the open ground toward the village.

The assault caught the Nez Percés in three groups. Some, including women and children, were on the distant side of the camp and were able to mount and flee to the north, where they scattered on the broken plains, to die from hunger and exposure or to eventually reach Canada in small, pitiful groups. Others, including Joseph, were trapped with the horses at some distance from the camp. A third group, at the village, found protection behind a low-lying ridge. These warriors, hidden behind rocks, opened a deadly fire on the attackers, inflicting heavy casualties and sending the troopers reeling back short of the camp. Two officers and twenty-two soldiers were killed in the assault and four officers and thirty-eight enlisted men wounded.

The 2nd Cavalry, meanwhile, had been sent around the camp to capture the Nez Percé pony herd and try to cut off escape. This unit had better luck. The troopers crashed into the herd, stampeding the horses and splitting the Indians into small groups that fought back hand-to-hand or sought cover in gullies or behind rocks. A few of the Indians got away on ponies and disappeared to the north. Others, among them Joseph, crawled or fought their way back to the main body of Nez Percés, reaching the camp under cover of darkness. The troopers drove off at least a third of the horses, however, and most of the Nez Percés' remaining war leaders, including the brave Ollokot and Toohoolhoolzote, were killed in the fighting.

The heavy casualties Miles had sustained deterred him from ordering another charge, and he decided to lay siege to the village. He made one attempt to cut off the Indians from their water supply by establishing a line between the camp and the river, but the troops detailed to the task were driven back by fierce Indian resistance. As the siege settled down, both sides dug in, continuing a desultory sharpshooting fire between the lines. The weather turned bitterly cold, and the next morning five inches of snow covered the unretrieved bodies of the dead. The Indians, wounded, hungry, and cold, suffered intensely. Using hooks, knives, and

pans, the people tried to dig crude shelters in the sides of the hollows. One dugout was caved in by a hit from Miles's howitzer that had been tilted back for use as a mortar, and a woman and child were buried alive.

As the siege continued, Miles grew concerned. There were rumors that Sitting Bull, with a band of Sioux, was coming to the Nez Percés' rescue from Canada. And, even if they didn't show up, Howard was getting closer, and Miles wanted the glory of Joseph's end for himself. Hoping to hurry the surrender, he hoisted a white flag over his trenches and, after negotiations with a Nez Percé who could speak English, lured Joseph across the lines. The two men parlayed amicably for a few moments, but when Joseph began to detail terms for an honorable surrender, Miles had him seized and made prisoner. The same day, however, the Nez Percés captured one of Miles's officers. The next morning an exchange was agreed to, and Joseph was returned to his camp.

The siege went on amid cold and snow flurries, and on October 4 Howard reached the battlefield with a small advance party that included two treaty Nez Percés. The appearance of their old enemy, heralding the arrival of reinforcements for Miles, took the final heart out of the suffering Nez Percés. The next morning the two treaty Nez Percés crossed the lines and told the chiefs that if they surrendered, they would be honorably treated and sent back to Lapwai. The chiefs held a final council. White Bird and Looking Glass still opposed surrender. Joseph pointed to the starving women and children in the shelter pits and to the babies that were crying around them. "For myself I do not care," he said. "It is for them I am going to surrender."

As the council broke up, Looking Glass was suddenly struck in the forehead by a stray bullet and killed. As the surviving warriors gathered around the slain chief, Joseph mounted a horse and, followed by several men on foot, rode slowly up the hill from the camp and across to the army lines where Howard and Miles awaited him. As he reached the officers, he dismounted and handed Miles his rifle. Then, stepping back, he adjusted his blanket to leave his right arm free and, addressing Miles, began one of the most touching and beautiful speeches of surrender ever made:

"Tell General Howard I know his heart. What he told me before I have in my heart. I am tired of fighting. Our chiefs are killed. Looking Glass is dead. Toohoolhoolzote is dead. The old men are all dead. It is the young men who say yes or no. He who led the young men is dead. It is cold and we have no blankets. The little children are freezing to death. My people,

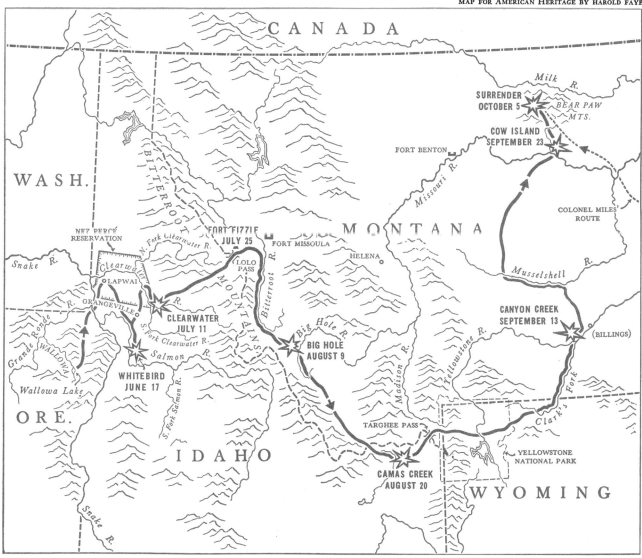

The Nez Percé retreat covered 1,300 miles in about four months. Miles cut them off just short of Canada and safety.

some of them, have run away to the hills, and have no blankets, no food; no one knows where they are—perhaps freezing to death. I want to have time to look for my children and see how many I can find. Maybe I shall find them among the dead. Hear me, my chiefs. I am tired; my heart is sick and sad. From where the sun now stands, I will fight no more forever."

The fact that neither Joseph nor any other individual chief had been responsible for the outstanding strategy and masterful successes of the campaign is irrelevant. The surrender speech, taken down by Howard's adjutant and published soon afterwards, confirmed Joseph in the public's mind as the symbol of the Nez Percés' heroic, fighting retreat. Although the government failed to honor Miles's promise to send the Indians back to Lapwai, sympathy was aroused throughout the nation for Joseph's people. At first the

Indians were shipped by flatboats and boxcars to unfamiliar, hot country in the Indian Territory, where many of them sickened and died. But friendly whites and sympathetic societies in the East continued to work for them, and public sentiment finally forced approval of their return to the Northwest. In 1885 Joseph and most of his band were sent to the Colville Reservation in Washington. Joseph made many attempts to be allowed to resettle in the Wallowa but each time was rebuffed. In 1904 he died, broken-hearted, an exile from the beautiful valley he still considered home.

Alvin M. Josephy, Jr., formerly an associate editor of Time, *recently became managing editor of American Heritage Books. He wrote "Was America Discovered Before Columbus?" for the April, 1955, issue and "First 'Dude Ranch' Trip to the Untamed West," in the February, 1956, issue.*

291

HOW THEY KILLED

In the mid-Nineteenth Century, enormous herds

*Family portrait of the American bison, or buffalo, shows a bull, weighing
about 2,000 pounds, and a cow, weighing about 1,200, with her spring calf.*

THE BUFFALO

roamed the western plains. In a few years only scattered remnants of these survived.

By WAYNE GARD

Stories of the vast size of the buffalo herds that once roamed the Great Plains of the West sound like the imaginings of a Paul Bunyan. They would hardly be credited today except that they were attested by many reliable travelers and by early settlers.

Often the herds of shaggy beasts darkened the whole horizon. In 1832, after skirting the north fork of the Platte River, Captain Benjamin Bonneville climbed a high bluff that gave him a wide view of the surrounding plains. "As far as the eye could see," he reported, "the country seemed absolutely blackened by innumerable herds." John K. Townsend, while crossing the Platte Valley, stopped on the rise of a hill to view a similar scene. The whole region, he wrote, "was covered by one enormous mass of buffaloes. Our vision, at the least computation, would certainly extend ten miles; and in the whole of this vast space, including about eight miles in width from the bluffs to the river bank, there apparently was no vista in the incalculable multitude."

These accounts were matched by others that came from the high plains of northwest Texas. One pioneer there described a herd which he said covered fifty square miles. Another reported that he saw between two and three million buffaloes at one time. A third told of herds that he estimated held four million head. Many frontiersmen, like the Indians, thought there were enough buffaloes to last forever.

Sometimes the herds were so solid that they impeded travel. On the upper Missouri River in the summer of 1867, the steamer *Stockdale*, in charge of Captain Grant Marsh, was held up while a herd of snorting and bellowing shaggies crossed the stream. The buffaloes became so thick that the boat could not move, and the captain had to stop its engines. Many of the animals became entangled with the wheel, while others beat against the sides and stern, blowing and pawing. It was hours before the whole herd had crossed and the boat could continue its voyage.

Two years later, buffaloes were so thick in western Kansas that an immense herd held up a Kansas Pacific train for nine hours while it crossed the track. As late as the early 1870's, Texas drovers taking longhorn cattle up the Chisholm Trail had to stop in the Indian Territory to let buffalo herds cross their path. The cowmen feared that the buffaloes would cause the cattle to stampede and that some of the longhorns would join the shaggies.

Many of those who saw the enormous buffalo herds in the West and assumed that they always would be there lived to see the plains cleared of them. Except for a remnant in the north, the whole slaughter was completed in little more than a decade. The near extermination of the buffalo came because his hide was worth a dollar or so to hardy hunters willing to take chances on being scalped by Indians.

For as long as they could remember, the Indians had been hunting buffaloes. The tribes living on the Great Plains were especially dependent on them for their meat, for robes for winter warmth, and for hides used in making tepees. When the early Spanish explorers first saw the buffaloes on the plains, they called them Indian cattle.

Yet the Indians, although sometimes they hunted for pleasure, as a rule killed the buffaloes only when they needed meat or hides. Until the Spaniards brought horses from Europe, the Indians hunted afoot with bows and arrows or with lances, sometimes disguising themselves under wolf skins. After they began to steal horses from the Spaniards and to capture and tame those that had gone wild, they became expert riders and used their mounts in hunting.

"The Indian is a great epicure," said Colonel Richard Irving Dodge. "He knows the choicest tidbits of every animal and how to cook them to his taste. The great fall hunt yields him the fullest enjoyment of his appetite." Most of the red men, though, were less patient. The warrior who killed a buffalo likely would cut it open and eat at once the raw liver and some of the other meat.

293

The Grand Duke Alexis of Russia (right) hunted buffalo in royal style in 1872, with George A. Custer (left) as guide.

Some of the early travelers in the West hunted buffaloes for sport as well as for meat. One such was Washington Irving, who, with several companions, went on a buffalo hunt in the Indian Territory in October, 1832. Irving, after several misses, downed an enormous bull with his pistol. He took the tongue on his saddle and carried it back to camp.

A number of European visitors traveled to the West to try their marksmanship on the shaggies. Among them was Sir William Drummond Stewart, who came from Scotland in 1843 to shoot buffaloes. In the Platte Valley he and his party found all they could want—a herd estimated at a million head. On some days when they finished shooting the prairie was strewn for miles with dead animals. [See "First 'Dude Ranch' Trip to the West," AMERICAN HERITAGE, February, 1956.]

The most publicized hunt of this type was that of the Grand Duke Alexis, a son of Czar Alexander II of Russia. Early in 1872 the Grand Duke went by rail to the Kansas frontier town of Hays, where General Philip Sheridan arranged a hunting party. Chief Spotted Tail of the Sioux staged a war dance for the entertainment of the royal visitor, and William F. Cody, better known

as Buffalo Bill, coached him on shooting. Soon after Alexis had downed a buffalo and the other hunters had drunk his health in champagne, he was ready to return to his private car.

At the time of the Grand Duke's hunt, the decade of the slaughter of the buffaloes for their hides was about to begin. In that span the vast herds—estimated to have held 75,000,000 head before the Indians acquired horses—were reduced to a fragmentary herd in the north and a few stragglers elsewhere. Already the mounted Indians had begun to trim the size of the herds, especially after they could sell choice robes to white fur traders and mountain trappers.

In the 1840's the American Fur Company sent large cargoes of robes down the Missouri River to St. Louis. The count included 76,000 robes in 1840 and 110,000 robes and 25,000 tongues in 1848. The skins of the cows only were used for robes, since those of the bulls were too heavy. Meanwhile butchering by the whites was increasing. Pioneer farmers in Kansas and Nebraska killed thousands of buffaloes for their meat. On January 9, 1873, the Wichita *Eagle* reported, "Choice humps and rounds of buffalo are selling at three cents a pound on our streets." As early as 1844, Josiah Gregg had viewed with alarm the excessive killing of the buffaloes, and other warnings followed. Yet to most eyes the herds seemed as large as ever.

The start of the great buffalo hunt is linked with the name of J. Wright Mooar, who became the mightiest of the hide men. Mooar, of Scotch ancestry, was born in Vermont in 1851. He traveled west in 1869 and, after working as a horsecar conductor in Chicago and as a carpenter at Rochelle, Illinois, went on to Hays, Kansas, in the fall of 1870. There he chopped cordwood for a government contractor on Walnut Creek, thirty miles south of the fort.

As this was buffalo country, Mooar soon joined in the more lucrative occupation of hunting. With five associates he equipped a small outfit, with two horse teams and one ox team. At that time the market for hides was limited largely to their use in making lap robes. Mooar and his fellows killed for meat. Mooar shipped the hind quarters to Quincy, Illinois, and to Kansas City, leaving the rest of each carcass, including the hide, to rot on the prairie.

In the winter of 1871-72, Mooar learned from another hunter, Charlie Rath, that the Leavenworth firm of W. C. Lobenstein had an order for 500 buffalo hides. A firm in England wanted them for experimental use in making leather. After Mooar had provided a quota of this order, he had 57 hides left. He shipped the surplus hides to his brother, John Wesley Mooar, who was a clerk in a jewelry store in New York, asking him to see if he could interest tanners in them.

The tanners were so interested that Wright Mooar soon had orders for all the hides he could deliver, and his New York brother went to Kansas to handle the business end of the enterprise. As more tanners discovered that buffalo hides made leather good for many uses, the demand became so great that a whole army of hunters surged into the buffalo ranges.

With Dodge City as the principal outfitting and shipping point, most of the hunters worked in small groups, going out with wagons for hauling back the hides. They used heavy rifles, some of them Sharps made especially for killing buffaloes. In some cases, two hunters worked together, sharing both the shooting and the skinning. In a bigger outfit, two or three expert marksmen might hire a larger number of less skilled men for the more menial work of skinning and drying.

The buffaloes, although suspicious of strange smells, had poor eyesight and were less alert than most game animals. If the hunter approached against the wind, usually he could come close to the herd without being noticed. Often he could kill many of the animals before the others sought safety in flight. Some hunters fired from the saddle, but more preferred to work afoot and thus have steadier aim and take more hides with less ammunition. The hunter tried to shoot the buffalo just behind the shoulder blade and to penetrate the heart. A wounded bull could be dangerous, but usually the rifleman could dodge long enough to place the mortal shot.

One of the Kansas hunters, who hired fifteen skinners, claimed to have killed 1,500 buffaloes in a week, 250 of them in a single day. Billy Tilghman took 3,300 hides in one season. With a long-range Sharps rifle, even an ordinary marksman could average fifty hides a day. At one place on the prairie a surveying party found 6,500 carcasses from which the hides had been stripped. The untouched meat had been left to rot or to be devoured by wolves. A Santa Fe railway conductor, J. H. Helton, said he could have walked for a hundred miles along the right of way without stepping off the carcasses. So great was the slaughter that in 1872 and 1873 the railroads hauled 1,250,000 hides out of Kansas and nearby territory.

This hide hunting, plus the killing of an estimated 350,000 head by Indians in that period, thinned the Kansas herds enough to make further shooting less profitable there. In search of new herds, J. Wright Mooar and John Webb saddled their horses and took a trip through the Texas Panhandle. For five days they rode through a sea of grazing buffaloes.

Their report excited the other hunters, but there was some hesitation because the Medicine Lodge treaties of 1867—by implication and interpretation—had reserved for the Indians all hunting grounds south of the Arkansas River. However, Texas, which owned the land now in question, had not been a party to the treaty. Mooar asked advice from the Third Infantry commander at Fort Dodge, Richard Irving Dodge.

"Boys," replied the officer, "If I were hunting buffalo I would go where the buffalo are."

That was enough for the hunters. Willing to risk the danger of Indian scalpers, they quickly formed parties and set out to the south. They were followed in the spring of 1874 by dealers in hunting supplies and hides. The first of these, Charlie Myers, drove south with about forty hunters and teamsters, taking eight wagons and six-yoke teams of oxen. On the Canadian River in the Texas Panhandle he cut cottonwood logs and built a branch of his Dodge City store. This site was a mile and a half east

A SWELL SPORT ON A BUFFALO HUNT.
Aw-I say! Don't see any Buffalo!

In the early American West the English dude was always good for a laugh. Actually the buffalo had neither the eyesight nor the disposition to charge.

of the ruins of the Adobe Walls trading post that a party sent out by William Bent had established about 1843. Around the Myers store the men built a corral and a stockade.

Soon afterward another Dodge merchant, Charlie Rath, also arrived to set up a Texas branch. He opened for business in a sod house near the Myers cabin. Next, James Hanrahan, also from Dodge City, came in with a supply of whisky and built a sod-house saloon between the two stores and near the Myers stockade. Then Tom O'Keefe set up a picket house for a blacksmith shop between the saloon and the Rath store. All were ready for business by the first of May, and the newcomers called their village Adobe Walls.

Business flourished with the success of the hide hunters, but danger from Indians was never far away. Hostile warriors, who had killed and scalped several of the hunters in isolated camps, made a concentrated attack on Adobe Walls at dawn on the morning of June 27, 1874. The 700 attackers were mainly from the Cheyenne, Comanche, and Kiowa tribes and were led by Quanah Parker and Lone Wolf. Mooar and others had gone north with hides, but the outpost had 28 men and one woman. The defenders successfully fought off the Indians but lost four men.

Other temporary headquarters of the Texas buffalo hunters in the next few years included Tepee City, on Tepee Creek, and Rath City, near the Double Mountain Fork of the Brazos River. The latter outpost, established by Charlie Rath in January, 1877, lasted until May of the following year. In addition to offering supplies and a market for hides, it had a wagon yard, a Chinese laundry, and a combination saloon and dance hall.

In the middle and late 1870's the principal Texas headquarters for the hunters was Fort Griffin, on the Clear Fork of the Brazos. From this outpost long wagon trains hauled the hides to Dallas and Denison. One of the trains might include as many as forty wagons, each drawn by six or eight mules. As the hides made light freight, they were piled high and were held in place with poles and ropes. After Fort Worth obtained its first railroad, on July 4, 1876, it became the chief Texas shipping point for hides.

In the winter of 1876-77 an estimated 1,500 hunters were shooting buffaloes on the Texas plains, and by early spring Fort Griffin had about four acres filled with piles of hides waiting for the wagon trains to haul them to Fort Worth. In the latter town, one morning in May, 1877, a reporter noted a caravan of ten wagons coming in. "In front were eleven yoke of oxen driven by one man and dragging after them four large wagons, heavily laden. Two other teams, with seven yoke each, drawing three wagons, followed. There probably were 2,500 to 3,000 hides in the train."

In the same spring another Fort Worth observer was impressed with one lot of 60,000 hides piled high on a platform near the Texas and Pacific Railroad. During the season, Fort Griffin sent in about 200,000 hides, which brought the hunters about a dollar each. But the peak of the slaughter had passed, and the end was in sight. The hunters had broken up the great southern herd, leaving only scattered remnants.

In the winter of 1877-78 the skinners took more than 100,000 hides in Texas. This virtually wiped out the southern herd. The only noteworthy commercial hunting left was that in the northern plains in the early 1880's. Like many of his fellows, J. Wright Mooar put away his buffalo guns and turned to cattle ranching in Texas. His careful aim had downed 20,000 of the shaggies in eight years.

The widespread and wasteful slaughter had aroused shocked opposition, especially in the East. Several western states passed laws to curb the killing, but these

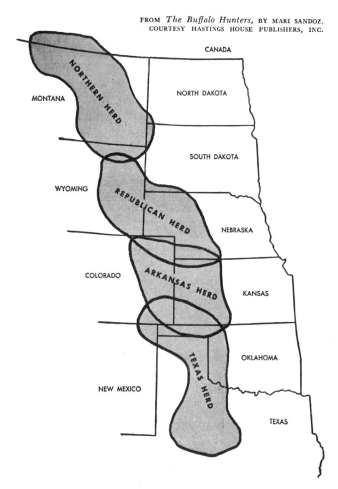

FROM *The Buffalo Hunters*, BY MARI SANDOZ, COURTESY HASTINGS HOUSE PUBLISHERS, INC.

Four great buffalo herds roamed the American prairie. Their ranges overlap because the herds moved with the seasons.

296

A buffalo stampede was a terror of the covered wagon trains. This one, caused by Indian hunters, was painted by William H. Jackson and is reprinted with permission of the publishers from The Old West Speaks *by Howard Driggs, copyright 1956, by Prentice-Hall Inc.*

measures came too late and were not strictly enforced. Realists in the West knew that the buffaloes would have to go before the hostile Indians of the Great Plains could be subdued and the ranges opened for cattle ranching.

Representative James A. Garfield expressed this view in 1874 when, in a debate in Congress, he reported that the secretary of the interior would rejoice, as far as the Indian question was concerned, when the last buffalo was killed. Early in the following year General Phil Sheridan put it even more clearly when he addressed a joint session of the Texas legislature, which was considering a bill to protect buffaloes.

The hunters, said the General, ". . . will do more in the next year, to settle the vexed Indian question than the entire regular army has done in the last thirty years. They are destroying the Indians' commissary. . . . Send them powder and lead . . . let them kill, skin and sell until the buffaloes are exterminated. Then your prairies can be covered with speckled cattle and the festive cowboy, who follows the hunter as

a second forerunner of an advanced civilization."

When the hunters had completed their slaughter, only the white bones remained strewn over the plains. Many a pioneer farmer and ranchman eked out his meager income in a drought year by gathering these bones and hauling them in his wagon to the nearest railroad town, where they were shipped off to be made into carbon or fertilizer.

In isolated valleys enough buffaloes were left to let the breed survive and to supply circuses and zoos and those ranchmen who liked to keep a few for sentimental reasons. Today the federal game preserves are so well supplied that every year or two the government has to sell a few hundred head to keep the ranges from being overgrazed. Yet the vast herds have vanished; they roam only in song and story and in the minds of a few old men with long memories.

Wayne Gard is an editorial writer for the Dallas Morning News *and contributes to various magazines. He is the author of several books; the most recent is* The Great Buffalo Hunt.

This view of the serpent's appearance in Glou-cester in 1817 is allegedly "taken from life," yet observers reported neither scales nor teeth.

When New England Saw the Serpent

By EVARTS ERICKSON

Recently I went down to Cape Ann and stood on the Stage Rocks overlooking Gloucester Bay. There were a few sailboats in sight and occasionally a fishing trawler would round the Dog Bar Breakwater. A strong odor of fish hangs over the town as it has for several centuries, but the air over the Stage Rocks was clean and the visibility was excellent. I stayed there for some time, trying to visualize the bay as it must have appeared in August, 1817, when something occurred that put this spot in all the newspapers of the world.

One day that month the skipper of a coasting vessel, forced into Gloucester by bad weather, came into Lipple's auction room with a curious story. At the entrance to the bay, he said gravely, he and his crew had seen a terrible creature that looked like a sea serpent—sixty feet long! He was laughed out of the room, but in two weeks all Gloucester was in an uproar. Everyone seems to have seen it—or, by local usage, him. He was colored like an eel. He made the bay his home. Sometimes he lay extended on the surface; sometimes he played like a porpoise, but mostly he preyed on the herring, caught in record numbers that year. When he swam with his head raised above the surface, his head and long neck moved slowly from side to side, while his body proper

seemed to move with the vertical motion of a cater-pillar. Most witnesses agreed that they saw neither horns, gills, teeth, or scales on the snub-headed animal, though some women claimed that his eyes were "as large as pewter plates."

He was the strangest, biggest fish that New England had ever seen, and the professional cod catchers and sailors of Gloucester determined to kill him, skin him, and place him on exhibition. They baited shark hooks and attached them to buoys anchored in the bay; they set out nets. The revenue cutter had a brush with him and took on extra four-pounders; Nantucket whale-men came with their harpoons to try for an announced reward of $5,000.

For a month the serpent basked in the public eye. "He was seen by two hundred, at one time, sporting the whole afternoon, under Wind-Mill Point," wrote David Humphreys, a former aide-de-camp of Washing-ton, who had received Cornwallis' colors at Yorktown.

If the "Great American Sea Serpent" (as European naturalists jocularly called him) was a mass hallucina-tion, he at least provided some exciting moments. On August 14 a local marksman named Mathew Gaffney fired a one-ounce ball at him from a distance of, he

claimed, thirty feet. Someone else in another boat said it was closer to thirty yards. It didn't really matter much, because the creature sounded, reappeared in the distance, and sped away from his pursuers. On August 20, we are told, an unwarned ship from the banks arrived off the bay, saw him, and fled in horror. There were a few later reports of sightings from Long Island Sound, off Connecticut, and then—silence.

One would expect a diminution of excitement. On the contrary, the situation now took a chilling turn for the worse. Soon after, a Cape Ann farmer pitchforked in his seagirt pasture a three-and-one-half-foot snake with humps like the monster's. Boston's Linnaean Society, to whom the snake had been brought, decided it was the serpent's progeny. They dissected it, made an engraving of its innards, and named it *Scoliophis atlanticus*. This piece of news from the Hub sent small fry along the coast in a frenzied hunt for sea serpent eggs until a French naturalist pointed out that the reptile in question was actually a common black snake in a diseased condition. It was a bitter blow for the Linnaean Society (which really included some very eminent people) but then, in July and early August, 1819, another vintage sea serpent year, an event occurred which provoked even more of a sensation than the serpent's original visit. In the dog days of that year he showed up off Nahant, then a resort of Boston's wealthier families. Hundreds of people watched him disport off Long Beach; certain Cabots wrote detailed reports of him for the Boston newspapers.

And on August 26, almost two years to the day since the monster had last been seen in Gloucester Bay, he was spotted there by a naval surveying vessel, permitting the Reverend Cheever Felch, who taught navigation to the midshipmen on board and prided himself on making measurements, to add a further detail. The length of the monster from his head down to the last hump on his back, he estimated, was at least one hundred feet—not counting the tail.

Such was the Leviathan's last stand on the New England coast. Backed now by science, naval authority, and the Cabots, one Boston newspaper decided it would print no further news of him. After all, as the editor told his readers, "the existence of this fabulous animal is now proven beyond all chance of doubt."

Evarts Erickson is a free-lance writer who lives in Boston and denies that he has ever seen a sea serpent.

Sophia Peabody in 1830, at age 21, by Chester Harding.

The Hau in Para

Nathaniel was poor and sunk in his

invalid, but a late-flowering love

By MALCOLM

There are only a few great love stories in American fiction, and there are fewer still in the lives of famous American writers. Nathaniel Hawthorne wrote one of the greatest, *The Scarlet Letter*. He also lived a story that deserves to be retold—with all the new knowledge we can bring to bear on it—as long as there are lovers in New England; it was his courtship and conquest of Sophia Peabody. Unlike his first novel, the lived story was neither sinful nor tragic. Everything in the foreground was as softly glowing as a June morning in Salem, but there were shadows in the background and obstacles to be surmounted; among them were poverty, seemingly hopeless invalidism, conniving sisters, political intrigues, a silken temptress, a duel that might have been fought to the death, and inner problems more threatening than any of these. It was as if Hawthorne had needed to cut his way

through a forest of thorns—some planted by himself—in order to reach the castle of Sleeping Beauty and waken her with a kiss, while, in the same moment, he wakened himself from a daylong nightmare.

When he first met Sophia, Hawthorne was thirty-three years old, and he had spent twelve of those years in a dreamlike seclusion. Day after day he sat alone in his room, writing or reading or merely watching a sunbeam as it bored through the blind and slowly traveled across the opposite wall. "For months together," he said long afterward, in a letter to the poet R. H. Stoddard, "I scarcely held human intercourse outside of my own family; seldom going out except at twilight, or only to take the nearest way to the most convenient solitude." He doubted whether twenty people in Salem even knew of his existence.

In remembering those years, Hawthorne sometimes

solitude; Sophia seemed a hopeless

gave them at last "a perfect Eden"

COWLEY

Nathaniel Hawthorne in 1840, aged 36, by Charles Osgood.

pictured his solitude as being more nearly absolute than it had been. There were social moments even then. Every summer he took a long trip on his Manning uncles' stagecoach lines and "enjoyed as much of life," he said, "as other people do in the whole year's round." In Salem he made some whist-playing acquaintances and learned a little about the intricacies of Democratic party politics. He had a college friend, Horatio Bridge, of Augusta, Maine, to whom he wrote intimate letters, and Bridge was closely connected with two rising political figures, also Democrats and college friends of Hawthorne's, Congressman Jonathan Cilley of Maine, and Franklin Pierce, the junior senator from New Hampshire. All three were trying to advance Hawthorne's career, and Bridge had rescued him from complete obscurity by guaranteeing a publisher against loss and thereby inducing him to

issue the first book with Hawthorne's name on it, *Twice-Told Tales.*

After the book appeared in the early spring of 1837, its author made some mild efforts to emerge into Salem society, where the young ladies admired him for his courtesy, his deep-set eyes—so blue they were almost black—and his air of having a secret life. He thought of marriage and even fancied himself in love that spring, as Romeo did before meeting Juliet, but his courtship of a still-unidentified woman was soon broken off. Hawthorne was beginning to fear that he would never be able to rejoin the world of living creatures. His true solitude was inward, not outward, and he had formed the habit of holding long conversations with himself, like a lonely child. His daylong nightmare was of falling into a morbid state of self-absorption that would make everything unreal in his

301

The eldest of the three Peabody sisters was the formidable Elizabeth, later famous as a writer, founder of kindergartens, and a bustling figure in the New England literary ferment. She sought out Hawthorne, only to see his attention fasten not on her but on quiet, pretty Sophia.

eyes, even himself. "None have understood it," says one of his heroes, Gervayse Hastings of "The Christmas Banquet," who might be speaking for the author, "—not even those who experience the like. It is a chilliness—a want of earnestness—a feeling as if what should be my heart were a thing of vapor—a haunting perception of unreality! . . . All things, all persons . . . have been like shadows flickering on the wall." Then putting his hand on his heart, he says, "Mine—mine is the wretchedness! This cold heart . . ."

Sophia Amelia Peabody, five years younger than Hawthorne, never suffered from self-absorption or an icy heart, but she had a serious trouble of her own. A pretty rather than a beautiful woman, with innocent gray eyes set wide apart, a tiptilted nose, and a mischievous smile, she had beaux attending her whenever she appeared in society; the trouble was that she could seldom appear. When Sophia was fifteen, she had begun to suffer from violent headaches. Her possessive mother explained to her that suffering was woman's peculiar lot, having something to do with the sin of Eve. Her ineffectual father had her treated by half the doctors in Boston, who prescribed, among other remedies, laudanum, mercury, arsenic, hyoscyamus, homeopathy, and hypnotism, but still the headaches continued. Once as a desperate expedient

she was sent to Cuba, where she spent two happy years on a plantation while her quiet sister Mary tutored the planter's children. Now, back in Salem with the family—where her headaches were always worse—she was spending half of each day in bed. Like all the Peabody women, she had a New England conscience and a firm belief in the True, the Beautiful, and the Transcendental. She also had a limited but genuine talent for painting. When she was strong enough, she worked hard at copying pictures—and the copies sold—or at painting romantic landscapes of her own.

Sophia had been cast by her family in a role from which it seemed unlikely that she would ever escape. Just as Elizabeth Peabody was the intellectual sister, already famous as an educational reformer, and Mary was the quiet sister who did most of the household chores, Sophia was the invalid sister, petted like a child and kept in an upstairs room. There were also three brothers, one of them married, but the Peabodys were a matriarchy and a sorority; nobody paid much attention to the Peabody men. It was written that when the mother died, Sophia would become the invalid aunt of her brother's children; she would support herself by painting lampshades and firescreens, while enduring her headaches with a brave smile. As for Hawthorne, his fate was written too; he would become the cranky New England bachelor, living in solitude and writing more and more nebulous stories about other lonely souls. But they saved each other, those two unhappy children. Each was the other's refuge, and they groped their way into each other's arms, where both found strength to face the world.

2

It was Elizabeth, the intellectual sister, who first brought them together, unthinkingly, in a moment of triumph for herself. She had long admired a group of stories, obviously by one author, that had been appearing anonymously in the annual editions of a gift book, *The Token,* and in the *New England Magazine.* Now she learned that the author was a Salem neighbor. Always eager to inspire a new genius, she made patient efforts to inveigle him into the Peabody house on Charter Street, with its square windows looking over an old burying ground where Peabodys and Hathornes—as the name used to be spelled—were sleeping almost side by side. She even took the bold step of paying several visits to the Hawthorne house on Herbert Street, known as "Castle Dismal," where nobody outside the family had dared to come for years.

Usually she was received by Hawthorne's younger sister, Louisa, who, Miss Peabody said disappointedly, was "quite like everybody else." The older sister, Elizabeth—usually called Ebe—was known with good reason as "the hermitess," but she finally consented to take a walk with her enterprising neighbor. Madam Hawthorne, the mother, stayed in her room as always, and Nathaniel was nowhere to be seen. He did, however, send Miss Peabody a presentation copy of his book, and she replied by suggesting some journalistic work that he had no intention of doing. Then, on the evening of November 11, 1837, came her moment of triumph. Elizabeth was sitting in the parlor, looking at a five-volume set of Flaxman's classical engravings that she had just been given by Professor Felton of Harvard, when she heard a great ring at the front door.

"There stood your father," she said half a century later in a letter to her nephew Julian Hawthorne, "in all the splendor of his young beauty, and a hooded figure hanging on each arm." The figures were Louisa and Ebe. Miss Peabody bustled them into the parlor and set them to looking at Flaxman's illustrations for *The Iliad*. Then she ran upstairs to the invalid's room and said, "Oh, Sophia, Mr. Hawthorne and his sisters have come, and you never saw anything so splendid— he is handsomer than Lord Byron! You must get up and dress and come down. We have Flaxman too."

Sophia laughed and said, "I think it would be rather ridiculous to get up. If he has come once he will come again."

A few days later he came again, this time in the afternoon. "I summoned your mother," Miss Peabody said in the same letter,

and she came down in her simple white wrapper, and glided in at the back door and sat down on the sofa. As I said, "My sister, Sophia—Mr. Hawthorne," he rose and looked at her—he did not realize how intently, and afterwards, as we went on talking, she would interpose frequently a remark in her low sweet voice. Every time she did so, he looked at her with the same intentness of interest. I was struck with it, and painfully. I thought, what if he should fall in love with her. . . .

Miss Peabody explained why that was a painful thought; it was because "I had heard her so often say, nothing would ever tempt her to marry, and inflict upon a husband the care of such a sufferer." But there was an unspoken reason too, for it is clear from other letters that Elizabeth Peabody wanted Nathaniel Hawthorne for herself. Whether she hoped to marry him we cannot be sure, but there is no question that she planned to become his spiritual guide, his literary counselor, his muse and Egeria.

Sophia had no such clear intentions. She told her children long afterward that Hawthorne's presence exerted a magnetic attraction on her from the beginning, and that she instinctively drew back in self-defense. The power she felt in him alarmed her; she did not understand what it meant. By degrees her resistance was overcome, and she came to realize that they had loved each other at first sight. . . . That was Sophia's story, and Hawthorne did not contradict her. There is some doubt, however, whether he told her about everything that happened during the early months of their acquaintance.

3

What followed their first meeting was a comedy of misunderstandings with undertones of tragedy. Hawthorne was supposed to be courting Elizabeth— Miss Peabody, as she was called outside the household; *the* Miss Peabody, as if she had no sisters. There was a correspondence between them. In one of her missives—and that is the proper word for them—she warned Hawthorne that her invalid sister would never marry. His answer has been lost, but Miss Peabody quoted him as saying, "Sophia is a rose to be worn in no man's bosom." Satisfied on this point, she advised him to study German, write books for children, and have no truck with Democratic politicians. She liked to think of him as an other-worldly genius who might save the soul of America, if only he would read the German philosophers in the original. Hawthorne obediently studied German, but he did not take kindly to advice about his personal affairs, and Miss Peabody went off to West Newton to live with her married brother. While she was there, Sophia wrote her a series of letters. Most of them mentioned Mr. Hawthorne, more and more warmly, but Sophia maintained the pretense that her interest in him was intellectual, or at most sisterly, and that he was still Elizabeth's suitor. Meanwhile Hawthorne himself was secretly involved with a Salem heiress.

The story of his involvement, and of the duel to which it nearly led, was told in some detail by Julian Hawthorne in his biography of his parents. Unfortunately Julian did not give names (except "Mary" and "Louis") or offer supporting evidence. Poor Julian, who was sometimes irresponsible, has never been trusted by scholars, and the result is that later biographers of Hawthorne either questioned the story or flatly rejected it. Quite recently Norman Holmes Pearson of Yale, who is preparing the definitive edition of Hawthorne's letters, discovered an interesting document in the Morgan Library. He wrote an article about it for the *Essex Institute*'s quarterly, one for which other scholars stand in his debt. The article was a memorandum by Julian on a conversation with Miss Peabody, one in which she described the whole affair, giving names and circumstances and supporting Julian's story at almost every point. She even explained by implication why the principal figures in the story had to be anonymous. Two of them were still living in 1884, when Julian's book was published, and one of them was the widow of a president of Harvard.

Her name when Hawthorne knew her was Mary Crowninshield Silsbee, and she was the daughter of former United States Senator Nathaniel Silsbee, a great man in New England banking and shipping. Julian says that she was completely unscrupulous, but admits that she had "a certain kind of glancing beauty, slender, piquant, ophidian, Armida-like." Armida—in Tasso's *Jerusalem Delivered*—was a heathen sorceress, daughter of the king of Damascus, who lured the boldest of the Crusaders into her enchanted garden. Mary Silsbee exercised her lures on the brilliant young men she met in her travels between Salem and Washington. One of them was John Louis O'Sullivan of Washington, who was laying ambitious plans for a new magazine to be called the *Democratic Review*.

The young editor was a friend of Hawthorne's classmate Jonathan Cilley, the rising congressman from Maine. Cilley had given him a copy of *Twice-Told Tales* as soon as the book appeared. O'Sullivan was impressed by it and wrote to the author soliciting contributions at the generous rate, for the time, of five dollars a page. He also told Miss Silsbee about Hawthorne. Fascinated by O'Sullivan's picture of a mysterious Salem genius, Armida at once determined, Julian says, "to add him to her museum of victims."

Her method of operation was to cast herself on Hawthorne's mercy by revealing what she told him were the secrets of her inmost soul. She read him long and extremely private passages from her diary—"all of which," Julian says, "were either entirely fictitious, or such bounteous embroideries on the bare basis of reality, as to give what was mean and sordid an appearance of beauty and a winning charm." Hawthorne, who had never considered the possibility that a Salem young lady might be a gratuitous liar, began to regard himself as Miss Silsbee's protector and champion. But he disappointed her by offering none of his own confidences in return.

She tried a new stratagem. Early in February, 1838, she summoned Hawthorne to a private and mysterious interview. With a great deal of calculated reluctance she told him that his friend O'Sullivan, "presuming upon her innocence and guilelessness"—as Julian tells the story—"had been guilty of an attempt to practise the basest treachery upon her; and she passionately adjured Hawthorne, as her only confidential and trusted friend and protector, to champion her cause." Hawthorne promptly wrote a letter to O'Sullivan, then in Washington, and challenged him to a duel. The letter has disappeared, but there is another to Horatio Bridge written on February 8—possibly the same day—in which he speaks darkly of a rash step he has just taken.

O'Sullivan must have discussed the challenge with their friend Jonathan Cilley; then he wrote a candid and friendly letter to Hawthorne refusing the challenge. But he did more than that; he made a hurried trip to Salem and completely established his innocence of the charge against him. Although Hawthorne could scarcely bring himself to believe that Miss Silsbee had made an utter fool of him, he had to accept the evidence. In Miss Peabody's words, he called on Armida and "crushed her."

To this point the story had been a comedy, or even a farce, but it soon had a tragic sequel on the national scene. In 1838 the House of Representatives was equally divided between conservatives and radicals, not to mention the other division between southerners and northern antislavery men. Jonathan Cilley was a rising leader among the radical free-soil Democrats, and there are some indications that his political enemies had decided to get rid of him. On a flimsy pretext, he was challenged to a duel by a fire-eating southern congressman, William J. Graves of Kentucky. He was still hesitating whether to accept the challenge when somebody said to him—according to Julian's story—"If Hawthorne was so ready to fight a duel without stopping to ask questions, you certainly need not hesitate." Horatio Bridge denied this part of the story, but there is no doubt that Hawthorne considered himself partly responsible for what followed. The duel, fought with rifles at ninety yards, took place on the afternoon of February 24. After the first exchange of shots, and again after the second, Cilley's

Nathaniel brought his bride to the Old Manse in Concord in 1842, and here they passed their three truly idyllic years.

second tried to effect a reconciliation, but Graves and his second both declined. Cilley said, "They thirst for my blood." On the third exchange, he was hit in the body and fell dying.

Hawthorne brooded over the duel for a long time. His memorial of Cilley, which was among the first of his many contributions to the *Democratic Review,* reads as if he were making atonement to the shade of his friend. In a somewhat later story, "The Christmas Banquet," from which I have quoted already, he describes a collection of the world's most miserable persons. One of them is

a man of nice conscience, who bore a blood stain in his heart—the death of a fellow-creature—which, for his more exquisite torture, had chanced with such a peculiarity of circumstances, that he could not absolutely determine whether his will had entered into the deed or not. Therefore, his whole life was spent in the agony of an inward trial for murder.

Julian's story would lead us to believe that Hawthorne, once again, was thinking of himself.

4

There were other causes for worry in those early months of 1838, when Hawthorne was still supposed to be courting Sophia's intellectual sister. One of the chief causes was Mary Silsbee, who refused to let him go. Miss Peabody's memorandum says that Mary somehow "managed to renew relations with him," and that she then offered to marry him as soon as he was earning $3,000 a year, a large income for the time. Hawthorne answered that he never expected to have so much. When his sister Ebe heard the story, she remarked—according to Miss Peabody—"that he would never marry at all, and that he would never *do* anything; that he was an ideal person." But Hawthorne did something to end the affair; he disappeared from Salem.

Before leaving town on July 23, he paid what was known as a take-leave call on Sophia. "He said he was not going to tell any one where he should be for the next three months," she told Elizabeth in a letter; "that he thought he should change his name, so that if he died no one would be able to find his gravestone. . . . I feel as if he were a born brother. I never, hardly, knew a person for whom I had such a full and at the same time perfectly quiet admiration." Then, suspecting that she had gone too far, she added, "I do not care about seeing him often; but I delight to remember that *he is.*" It was as near as she could come to telling Elizabeth that she was already in love.

At the end of September when Hawthorne came back to Salem—from North Adams, his mysterious hiding place—Miss Silsbee had disappeared from his life. She had renewed her acquaintance with another suitor, now a widower of 49 with an income well beyond her minimum requirement; he was Jared Sparks, the editor of George Washington's papers, who would become president of Harvard. Hawthorne now had more time to spend at the house on Charter Street. He was entertained by whichever sister happened to be present, or by all three together, but it began to be noticed that his visits were longer if he found Sophia alone. One day she showed him an illustration she had drawn, in the Flaxman manner, for his story "The Gentle Boy." It showed the boy asleep under the tree on which his Quaker father had been hanged.

"I want to know if this looks like your Ilbrahim," she said.

Hawthorne said, meaning every word, "He will never look otherwise to me."

Under the Peabody influence, he was becoming almost a social creature. There was a sort of literary club that met every week in one of the finest houses on Chestnut Street, where the Salem merchants lived. The house belonged to Miss Susan Burley, a wealthy spinster who liked to patronize the arts. Hawthorne was persuaded to attend some of Miss Burley's Saturday evenings—usually as an escort for Mary or Elizabeth, since the invalid sister was seldom allowed to venture into the night air. There was one particularly cold evening when Sophia insisted that she was going to Miss Burley's whether or not she was wanted. Hawthorne laughed and said she was not wanted; the cold would make her ill. "Meanwhile," Sophia reported in a letter, "I put on an incalculable quantity of clothes. Father kept remonstrating, but not violently, and I gently imploring. When I was ready, Mr. Hawthorne said he was glad I was going. . . . We walked quite fast, for I seemed stepping on air."

The evening at Miss Burley's marked a change in their relations. From that time Sophia began taking long walks with Mr. Hawthorne in spite of the winter gales. Elizabeth was busy with her affairs in Boston, and Mary, the quiet sister, looked on benevolently. Sophia never felt tired so long as she could hold Mr. Hawthorne's arm. It was during one of their walks, on a snowy day just before or after New Year's, 1839, that they confessed their love for each other. Clinging together like children frightened of being so happy, they exchanged promises that neither of them would break. They were married now "in the sight of God," as old-fashioned people used to say, and as Hawthorne soon told Sophia in slightly different words, but that was a secret they would keep to themselves for a long time to come.

5

In the middle of January Hawthorne went to work as a weigher and gauger for the Boston Custom House. It was a political appointment made by the collector of the port, who was George Bancroft, the historian. Hawthorne had been recommended to him by several influential persons, including Miss Peabody, who may have hoped to get him out of Salem. Bancroft justified the appointment to Washington by writing that Hawthorne was "the biographer of Cilley," and thus a deserving Democrat. Cilley again. . . . It was as if the college friend for whose death Hawthorne felt responsible had reached out of the grave to help him. Many other deserving Democrats had sought for the post, but it was not a sinecure, and he worked as hard as Jacob did for Rachel, while saving half his salary of $1,500 a year. Every other Saturday he took the cars to Salem and spent an evening with Sophia. On the Saturdays in Boston he sent long letters, sometimes written in daily installments.

"What a year the last has been!" he wrote on January 1, 1840. ". . . It has been the year of years—the year in which the flower of our life has bloomed

out—the flower of our life and of our love, which we are to wear in our bosoms forever." Three days later he added,

Dearest, I hope you have not found it impracticable to walk, though the atmosphere be so wintry. Did we walk together in any such weather, last winter? I believe we did. How strange, that such a flower as our affection should have blossomed amid snow and wintry winds—accompaniments which no poet or novelist, that I know of, has ever introduced into a love-tale. Nothing like our story was ever written—or ever will be—for we shall not feel inclined to make the public our confidant; but if it could be told, methinks it would be such as the angels might delight to hear.

As a matter of fact, Hawthorne wrote the story from day to day, in that series of heartfelt letters to Sophia, and the New England angels would delight to read them. It is true that the tone of them is sometimes too reverent for the worldly taste of our century. "I always feel," Hawthorne says in July, 1839, "as if your letters were too sacred to be read in the midst of people, and (you will smile) I never read them without first washing my hands." We also smile, but in a different spirit

from Sophia's. We feel a little uncomfortable on hearing the pet names with which he addresses her, almost all superlatives: "Dearissima," "mine ownest love," "Blessedest," "ownest Dove," "best, beautifullest, belovedest, blessingest of wives." It is confusing to find that he calls her "mine own wife," and himself "your husband" or "thy husband," for three years before the actual marriage. His use of "thee" and "thou" in all the letters written after March, 1840, though it reveals his need for deeper intimacy of expression, still gives an archaic look to the writing. But the feelings expressed are not in the least archaic; they are those of a restrained but passionate man, truly in love for the first and last time, and gifted with an extraordinary talent for self-awareness.

Long afterward Sophia, then a widow, tried to delete the passion before she permitted the letters to be read by others. She scissored out some of the dangerous passages, and these are gone forever. Others she inked out carefully, and most of these have been restored by the efforts of Randall Stewart—the most trustworthy biographer of Hawthorne—and the staff of the Huntington Library. They show that Hawthorne was less of an other-worldly creature than Miss Peabody pictured him as being. "Mine own wife," he says in one of the inked-out passages (November, 1839), "what a cold night this is going to be! How I am to keep warm, unless you nestle close, close into my bosom, I do not by any means understand—not but what I have clothes enough on my mattress—but a husband cannot be comfortably warm without his wife." There is so much talk of beds and bosoms that some have inferred, after reading the restored text, that Hawthorne and Sophia were lovers for a long time before their marriage—and most of these readers thought no worse of them. But the records show that this romantic notion has to be dismissed. Much as Hawthorne wanted Sophia, he also wanted to observe the scriptural laws of love. "Mr. Hawthorne's passions were under his feet," Miss Peabody quoted Sophia as saying. If he had made Sophia his mistress, he would have revered her less, and despised himself.

"I have an awe of you," he wrote her, "that I never felt for anybody else. Awe is not the word, either, because it might imply something stern in you; whereas—but you must make it out for yourself. . . . I suppose I should have pretty much the same feeling if an angel were to come from Heaven and be my dearest friend. . . . And then it is singular, too," he added with his Salem obduracy, "that this awe (or whatever it is) does not prevent me from feeling that it is I who have charge of you, and that my Dove is to follow my guidance and do my bidding." He had no intention of submitting to the Peabody matriarchs. "And will not you rebel?" he asked. "Oh, no; because I possess the power to guide you only so far as I love you. My love gives me the right, and your love consents to it."

Sophia did not rebel, but the Peabodys were confirmed idealists where Hawthorne was a realist, and sometimes she tried gently to bring him round to their higher way of feeling. Once she refused to kiss him good night because she had smelled a cigar on his breath. Another time she made the mistake of urging him to hear the famous Father Taylor, who preached to the sailors. "Dearest," he said,

I feel somewhat afraid to hear this divine Father Taylor, lest my sympathy with thy admiration of him should be colder and feebler than thou lookest for. Belovedest wife, our souls are in happiest unison; but we must not disquiet ourselves if every tone be not re-echoed from one to the other—if every slightest shade be not reflected in the alternate mirror. . . . I forewarn thee, sweetest Dove, that thy husband is a most unmalleable man; thou art not to suppose, because his spirit answers to every touch of thine, that therefore every breeze, or even every whirlwind, can upturn him from his depths.

But this conflict of wills is a minor note of comedy in the letters. In time Sophia learned to yield almost joyfully, not so much to Hawthorne's unmalleable nature as to his love. It is love that is the central theme of the letters—unquestioning love, and beneath it the sense of almost delirious gratitude that both of them felt for having been rescued from death-in-life. Sophia refused to worry about her health. "If God intends us to marry," she said to Hawthorne, "He will let me be cured; if not, it will be a sign that it is not best." She depended on love as her physician, and imperceptibly, year by year, the headaches faded away. As for Hawthorne, he felt an even deeper gratitude for having been rescued from the unreal world of self-absorption in which he had feared to be imprisoned forever. "Indeed, we are but shadows," he wrote to Sophia, "—we are not endowed with real life, and all that seems most real about us is but the thinnest substance of a dream—till the heart is touched. That touch creates us—then we begin to be. . . ." In the same letter he said:

Thou only hast taught me that I have a heart—thou only hast thrown a deep light downward, and upward, into my soul. Thou only hast revealed me to myself; for without thy aid, my best knowledge of myself would have been merely to know my own shadow—to watch it flickering on the wall, and mistake its fantasies for my own real actions. . . . Now, dearest, dost thou comprehend what thou hast done for me?

His four novels, beginning with *The Scarlet Letter,* were written after his marriage and written because

Sophia was there to read them. Not only Nathaniel Hawthorne but the world at large owes the gentle Sophia more than can be expressed.

6

When Miss Peabody was told of the engagement, after more than a year, she took the news bravely. Her consolation was that having Hawthorne as a brother-in-law might be almost as rewarding as having him for a husband; she could still be his Egeria. Not yet knowing how unmalleable he was, she still thought of forging him into the shape of her dream. Meanwhile she offered to serve as a secret courier and forward his letters to Salem. With Sophia's health improving, it was Hawthorne's inability to support a wife —especially a delicate wife who needed a servant in the household—that now seemed to be the chief remaining obstacle to the marriage.

The post in the Boston Custom House did not solve the problem. It left him with little time alone or energy for writing, and he could not be sure of keeping it after the next election. Hawthorne resigned at the end of 1840, a few months before he would have been dismissed—as were almost all his colleagues—by the victorious Whigs. After some hesitation he took a rash step, partly at the urging of Miss Peabody. He invested his Custom House savings in George Ripley's new community for intellectual farmers: Brook Farm. It was the last time he would accept her high-minded advice.

The dream was that Hawthorne would support himself by working in the fields only a few hours each day, and only in the summer; then he could spend the winter writing stories. He and Sophia would live in a cottage to be built on some secluded spot. Having bought two shares of stock in the community at $500 each— later he would lend Ripley $400 more—he arrived at Brook Farm in an April snowstorm. Sophia paid him a visit at the end of May. "My life—how beautiful is Brook Farm!" she wrote him on her return. ". . . I do not desire to conceive of a greater felicity than living in a cottage, built on one of those lovely sites, with thee." But Hawthorne, after working for six weeks on the manure pile—or gold mine, as the Brook Farmers called it—was already disillusioned. "It is my opinion, dearest," he wrote on almost the same day, "that a man's soul may be buried and perish under a dung-heap or in a furrow of the field, just as well as under a pile of money." By the middle of August he had decided to leave Brook Farm. "Thou and I must form other plans for ourselves," he told Sophia; "for I can see few or no signs that Providence purposes to give us a home here. I am weary, weary, thrice weary of waiting so many ages. Yet what can be done? Whatever may be thy husband's gifts, he has not hitherto shown a single one that may avail to gather gold."

"Thy husband" and "mine own wife" were drawing closer to marriage, simply because they had exhausted their vast New England patience. "Words cannot tell," Sophia had written, "how immensely my spirit demands thee. Sometimes I almost lose my breath in a vast heaving toward thy heart." Hawthorne, now vegetating in Salem—while the Peabodys were in Boston, where Elizabeth had opened a bookshop—was looking desperately for any sort of literary work. In March, 1842, he went to Albany to see John Louis O'Sullivan, who was again editing the *Democratic Review.* On the strength of the promises that O'Sullivan was always ready to make, Hawthorne decided to wait no longer; he would try to support a wife on what he could earn as a writer. It was a bold decision for an age when American writers were miserably paid and when Poe, his principal rival, had never earned as much as $1,000 in one year.

The wedding was set for the last day of June. During a visit to the Emersons, Miss Peabody found a home for the young couple; it was the Ripley house in Concord, where the parson used to live. Hawthorne could no longer defer telling his family about the engagement, after keeping it secret for three years. Now at last it became evident that there was and had always been another obstacle to his marriage.

The final obstacle was his older sister, Ebe the hermitess. She adored her handsome brother and clung to him as her only link with the world. The stratagem she found for keeping him was to insist that their mother would die of shock if she learned that he was marrying an invalid. Hawthorne loved his mother, though he had never been able to confide in her. This time he finally took the risk. "What you tell me is not a surprise to me," Madam Hawthorne said, ". . . and Sophia Peabody is the wife of all others whom I would have chosen for you." When Ebe had recovered from

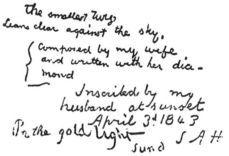

The Hawthorne inscriptions still may be seen on a window of the Old Manse.

her fury at hearing the news, she wrote Sophia a frigid letter of congratulation.

Your approaching union with my brother [she said] makes it incumbent upon me to offer you the assurances of my sincere desire for your mutual happiness. With regard to my sister and myself, I hope nothing will ever occur to render your future intercourse with us other than agreeable, particularly as it need not be so frequent or so close as to require more than reciprocal good will.

There would be, in fact, no intercourse with Ebe. She retired to a farmhouse in Beverly, where she spent the rest of her long life reading in her room and walking on the shore.

Three weeks before the date set for the wedding, Sophia terrified everyone by taking to her bed. There was talk of an indefinite postponement. Fortunately a new doctor explained that it was nothing unusual for a bride to run a fever, and so another date was chosen: Saturday morning, July 9. It was a few days after Hawthorne's thirty-eighth birthday, while Sophia was almost thirty-three. At the wedding in the parlor behind Miss Peabody's bookshop, there were only two guests outside the immediate family. It started to rain as the bride came down the stairs, but then the sun broke through the clouds and shone directly into the parlor. Hawthorne and Sophia stepped into a carriage and were driven across the Charles River, along the old road through Cambridge and Lexington, into the Land of Eden.

7

And so they lived happily ever after? They lived happily for a time, but as always it came to an end, and the lovers too. For Hawthorne after twenty years of marriage, the end was near when he went feebly pacing up and down the path his feet had worn along the hillside behind his Concord house, while he tried to plan a novel that refused to be written. For Sophia the end was a desolate widowhood without the man who, she never ceased to feel, "is my world and all the business of it." But the marriage was happy to the end, and at the beginning of it, during their stay at the Old Manse, they enjoyed something far beyond the capacity of most lovers to experience: three years of almost unalloyed delight.

On the morning after their first night in the Old Manse, Hawthorne wrote to his younger sister, Louisa, the one who was quite like everybody else. "Dear Louse," he said affectionately, "The execution took place yesterday. We made a christian end, and came straight to Paradise, where we abide at the present writing." Sophia had the same message for her mother, although she expressed it more ecstatically. "It is a perfect Eden round us," she said. "Everything is as fresh as in first June. We are Adam and Eve and see no persons round! The birds saluted us this morning with such gushes of rapture, that I thought they must know us and our happiness." The Hawthornes at 38 and 33 were like children again—like children exploring a desert island that every day revealed new marvels. Their only fear was that a ship might come to rescue them. Once the great Margaret Fuller wrote them and suggested that another newly married couple, her sister Ellen and Ellery Channing, might board with them at the Manse. Hawthorne sent her a tactful letter of refusal. "Had it been proposed to Adam and Eve," he said, "to receive two angels into their Paradise, *as boarders,* I doubt whether they would have been altogether pleased to consent." The Hawthornes were left happily alone with Sarah the maid and Pigwiggin the kitten.

They were exercising a talent that most New Englanders never acquire, that of living not in the past or in dreams of the future, but in the moment itself, as if they were already in heaven. Sophia wrote letters each morning or painted in her studio, while Hawthorne worked meditatively in the garden that Henry Thoreau had planted for them. In the afternoon they explored the countryside together or rowed on the quiet river, picking waterlilies. Hawthorne wrote in his journal,

My life, at this time, is more like that of a boy, externally, than it has been since I was really a boy. It is usually supposed that the cares of life come with matrimony; but I seem to have cast off all care, and live with as much easy trust in Providence, as Adam could possibly have felt, before he had learned that there was a world beyond his Paradise.

Sometimes they ran footraces down the lane, which Sophia grandly called "the avenue." Sometimes in the evening she wound the music box and, forgetting her Puritan training, danced wildly for her lover. "You deserve John the Baptist's head," he teased her. In the records of that time—there are many of them, and all

a delight to read—there is only one hint of anything like a quarrel. It arose when one of their walks led them to an unmown hayfield. Hawthorne, who had learned about haying at Brook Farm, told Sophia not to cross it and trample the grass. "This I did not like very well and I climbed the hill alone," Sophia wrote in the journal they were keeping together.

We penetrated the pleasant gloom and sat down upon a carpet of dried pine leaves. Then I clasped him in my arms in the lovely shade, and we laid down a few moments on the bosom of dear Mother Earth. Oh, how sweet it was! And I told him I would not be so naughty again, and there was a very slight diamond shower without any thunder or lightning and we were happiest.

There was some thunder and lightning even during those three sunny years at the Old Manse. Sophia's mother and her sister Elizabeth had insisted that she must never bear children, but she longed for them ardently. One day in the first February she fell on the ice—where she had been sliding while Hawthorne skated round her in flashing circles—and suffered a miscarriage. When her first baby was born in March, 1844, it lingered, as Hawthorne said, "ten dreadful hours on the threshold of life." It lived and the parents rejoiced, but now they had financial worries: O'Sullivan took years to pay for the stories he printed, and Ripley hadn't returned the money advanced to Brook Farm. There were weeks when Hawthorne was afraid to walk into Concord for the mail, lest he meet too many of his creditors. Sophia's love did not waver, then or for the rest of her life, nor did her trust in the wisdom and mercy of Providence. It had snatched her from invalidism and spinsterhood and transported her to Paradise. It had made her "as strong as a lion," she wrote to her sister Mary, "as elastic as India rubber, light as a bird, as happy as a queen might be," and it had given her a husband whose ardent love was as unwavering as her own. She was expressing in five words all her faith in Providence, and indeed all her experience of life, when she stood at the window in Hawthorne's study one April evening at sunset and wrote with her diamond ring on one of the tiny panes —for him to see, for the world to remember:

Man's accidents are God's purposes.

Sophia A. Hawthorne 1843

Pennsylvania-born Malcolm Cowley has edited the works of many leading American writers, including Hawthorne, Whitman, Fitzgerald, Hemingway, and Faulkner. Mr. Cowley's own works include The Dry Season, Exile's Return, *and* The Literary Situation. *Since 1936 he has lived in Sherman, Connecticut, where he is currently writing a series of studies in American literature.*

INDEPENDENT GREENBACK PARTY.

Headquarters, Union Square (cor. 14th Street and 4th Ave.,) New York.

HON. PETER COOPER, of New York, Candidate for the Presidency.

HON. SAMUEL F. CARY, of Ohio, Candidate for the Vice-Presidency.

PETER COOPER THE CARRIAGE MAKER

PETER COOPER AT THE TURNING-LATHE

NATIONAL PROSPERITY CANNOT BE RESTORED BY ENFORCING IDLENESS ON A LARGE PORTION OF THE PEOPLE — PETER COOPER

EXORBITANT RENT (COMMONLY CALLED INTEREST) SILENTLY BUT SURELY DEVOURS THE SUBSTANCE OF THE PEOPLE — PETER COOPER

COOPER UNION READING ROOM
EXIT TICKET
PLEASE RETURN AT THE DOOR
(OVER)

THE FIRST LOCOMOTIVE IN AMERICA. BUILT BY PETER COOPER.

COOPER UNION. TO SCIENCE AND ART.

I am convinced that when a true American System of Finance is adopted which shall put all that circulates as Money entirely and exclusively under the Control of the Government, MAKING IT RECEIVABLE FOR ALL DUTIES AND DEBTS, Employment for all the Working Classes, and Prosperity for the whole Country will be the natural and permanent result.—PETER COOPER.

The American People and Government cannot too constantly remember that it is utterly impossible for us as a Nation to buy anything cheap from foreign countries *that must be bought at the expense of leaving our own good Raw Materials unused, and our own Labor unemployed.*—PETER COOPER.

[ENGRAVED EXPRESSLY FOR THE "IRISH WORLD."—RE-PRINTED BY THE NEW YORK MERCANTILE JOURNAL CO., 350 PEARL STREET, NEW YORK.]

In a day of rampant money-making, gentle Peter Cooper was not only a reformer but successful, widely loved, and rich

The HONEST MAN

By PETER LYON

Around 1875, at the feverish height of the Gilded Age, when conventional citizens were in greedy pursuit of the dollar, when the executive branch was vying with the legislative and the judicial as to which would prove the most venal, when monstrous fortunes lay ripe for the hook or the crook, an elderly gentleman of benign aspect commenced to make some distressing remarks, right out loud and in public.

"The dealers in money," said he, "have always, since the days of Moses, been the dangerous class." And again:

"There is fast forming in this country an aristocracy of wealth, the worst form of aristocracy that can curse the prosperity of any country." And again:

"There may at some future day be a whirlwind precipitated upon the moneyed men of this country."

What manner of man was this, who launched such jeremiads against the rich and respectable? Was he socialist? Senile? Simple?

As it happens, he was a shrewd and exceedingly rich Republican; a leading citizen of New York and, indeed, of the whole country; inventor, industrialist, and ironmaster; troubled social thinker whose ideas came at least a half-century too soon. Above all, he was the conscience of his times.

This was Peter Cooper. During the last decade of his life, when the seven deadly sins—and especially Pride, Envy, Covetousness, Gluttony, and Lust—were in riotous command of the social scene, Peter Cooper, almost alone among the wealthy, insisted that worldly goods created a grave responsibility. "The production of wealth," he declared, "is not the work of any one man, and the acquisition of great fortunes is not possible without the co-operation of multitudes of men; and . . . therefore the individuals to whose lot these fortunes fall . . . should never lose sight of the fact that as they hold them by the will of society expressed in statute law, so they should administer them as trustees for the benefit of society as inculcated by moral law."

A singular sentiment, and one that surely appalled his contemporaries. Consider some of those contemporaries: William Marcy Tweed, whose political gang plundered New York City of at least $100,000,000; Cornelius Vanderbilt, who growled, "Law? What do I care about the law? Hain't I got the power?"; Collis P. Huntington, the railroad titan, who bought entire Congresses for up to $500,000 a session; Jim Fisk and Jay Gould, who almost succeeded in beggaring the country by cornering all the gold in circulation; and sanctimonious old Uncle Dan Drew, who clawed his way to the top of the heap in Wall Street, swindling and gutting as he climbed, and who murmured, "It's the still hog that eats the most." All these were men who were out for number one. Money was what they wanted: money to get power to get more money, no matter how ruthless or cynical or swinish the means. And yet here was Peter Cooper saying, in his stubborn, disconcerting way, "Money is so unlike every other

Left: This Greenback handbill from the 1876 campaign stressed Candidate Peter Cooper's working background.

"The Judge to the Millionaires: GO THOU AND DO LIKEWISE"

article that I believe a man has neither a legal or a moral right to take all that he can get."

Such talk was sufficiently embarrassing, but Cooper went further. He deliberately gave his money away in great gobs. Not for business reasons, for he couldn't expect his gifts to profit him. There was no income tax at the time, and death duties were very modest: he could have left his entire fortune to his family. No, Cooper simply chose to march out of step. Where custom decreed he should become a robber baron, instead he became this country's first large-hearted philanthropist; it was his precept and example that later nudged Andrew Carnegie, George Peabody, Matthew Vassar, Ezra Cornell, and a dozen others to the same unlikely course.

Cooper's perverse behavior warrants a closer look. To be decent and disinterested is, in any age, to invite derision; in the Gilded Age it was positively ludicrous. Rascality, unfortunately, is ever so much more colorful, and so Cooper's solid virtues have been elbowed into obscurity by the sins of his gaudy contemporaries. He deserves better.

Peter Cooper lived a long life. He was born in 1791, during George Washington's first presidential term; when he died, in 1883, Chester Arthur was President. In his last years, Cooper liked to say that his life had fallen into three periods—thirty years to get started, thirty years to amass a fortune, thirty years to dispose of that fortune wisely—and the implication was that he had planned his life to fit those three tidy compartments.

The actual events of his career, moreover, lend the notion a certain plausibility. To be sure, his first thirty years were aimless; during the next thirty his fortunes did indeed rise steadily, until he was rolling in a most gratifying bed of clover; his philanthropies preoccupied him for the rest of his life. But this view was considerably assisted, and distorted, by hindsight. It failed to take any account of the customary leading role played by chance, and it failed to give due credit to Cooper's sturdy and inventive mind. It was a humorless mind, clogged by naïveté, but nonetheless tough and original.

The tonic note of Cooper's eventful and empirical career was struck when he was still in short pants. His mother required him to help with the family wash: dull work, pounding dirty clothes in a barrel of soapy water; the same dreary chore performed once a week by thousands of groaning, arm-weary boys all over the country, and by them accepted as inevitable. But young Cooper, being an original, was bound to tinker with the inevitable, to take it apart and remake it, testing whether it might not be made to work better. He actually contrived a primitive washing machine, involving a geared wheel, double lever, and ratchet, thereby cutting his labor in half and washing the clothes cleaner and quicker.

When, at seventeen, he apprenticed himself for four years to a New York carriage maker, signing on for his board and twenty-five dollars a year, his virtues throbbed monotonously. There were at the time some 3,500 oases serving strong drink in New York, or about one for every four families, nor were the brothelkeepers behindhand. But, Cooper related later, while the other apprentices were "in the habit of going out nights to indulge in sports of all kinds," he retired to a monastic chamber provided him by his grandmother, where he carved wood, pored over the Bible, and committed to memory long passages from Pope or Burns.

The truth was, he was ashamed of himself; ashamed of his lack of education, of his lack of polish and urbanity; ashamed, for he was a hayseed—born in New York, to be sure, but reared in the wilderness up the Hudson River Valley near Peekskill. He felt himself a bumpkin; with a certain low skill at mechanical contrivances, perhaps, but no fit company for his fellows at the taphouse or bagnio.

There were, however, compensations. "I was always fussing and contriving," he said later, "and was never satisfied unless I was doing something difficult—something that had never been done before, if possible." He devised a machine for mortising the hubs of carriages, a contrivance his employer was happy to buy from him. He attempted to convert the power from the tides of the East River into compressed air, and thus drive the ferries from New York to Brooklyn. After rejecting his employer's offer to set him up in trade, he invented first a lawn mower (never, however, patented), then a mechanically-rocked cradle fitted with "a musical instrument that would sing the child to sleep" and a cloth to "keep the flies off the little one." This anticipation of Rube Goldberg he called a "Pendulous & Musical Cradle," and traded his Connecticut rights in it to a peddler who offered his horse and wagon and all it contained in exchange. Since there was a hurdy-gurdy in the wagon, Cooper concluded he got the better of the trade.

There were other inventions: an endless chain, powered by water elevated in the locks, to haul canalboats along the brand-new Erie Canal; and a rotary steam engine. Both these contraptions seem to have had merit but, for one reason or another, neither was in a way of making Cooper any money. He was drifting: in ten years he had gone from carriage maker to machinist to cabinetmaker to grocer; he was in danger of becoming that familiar figure, the handy man who is all

dreams but no dollars. Any adept of the then infant science, phrenology, might by palpating his pate have diagnosed the difficulty: where he should have had a Bump of Acquisitiveness, instead there was a crater. Invent, yes; exploit, no. But all at once, in 1821, chance proffered him a gilt-edged proposition: a successful business enterprise, priced at only $2,200. Cooper snatched at it so quickly that, since he offered cash down, he was able to get it for $2,000.

He was now thirty years old, and for the next thirty-odd years this enterprise would make him a great deal of money and would, indeed, be the cornerstone of his substantial fortune. And what was this business? It was making glue.

Now there is patently nothing offensive, nor disgraceful, nor ridiculous about the manufacture of glue. Glue is a useful commodity, even necessary to a great many folk; glue, in its humble fashion, holds our society together. Having said all of this, it must be admitted that a Glue King sounds like a character out of P. G. Wodehouse. And not only today: in his own time New York's Knickerbocker society fleered at Cooper and called him "the self-made millionaire glue-boiler."

Fortunately, being armored with a powerful humorlessness, Cooper could ignore the gibes and settle down to making money. In his fragrant business, he was presently associated with some important figures of New York's financial future: Henry Astor, John Jacob's brother, was the town's biggest wholesale butcher, and from him Cooper purchased cattle hoofs and heads; the cattle yards and the cattle drovers' favorite rendezvous, the Bull's Head Tavern, up in the country at 24th Street and Third Avenue, were both owned by that unique amalgam of piety and rascality, Dan Drew.

And from the start the money rolled in. Cooper had bought at the bottom of the severe Panic of 1818-20, and the decade that followed brought the country's first sizable manufacturing boom. As the national industrial plant expanded, so did Cooper's enterprise: he made, as well as glue, neat's-foot oil, isinglass, and gelatin. Never did his products earn him less than $10,000 a year, and indeed before long his earnings were closer to $100,000 a year. Ever the empiricist, he plunged into the complexities of gluemaking and emerged with techniques that an organic chemist could hardly have bettered. His commercial methods were simplicity itself: he kept no formal books, never borrowed a cent, abjured both banks and bankers as creatures of Satan, paid off all his obligations at each year's end in gold, worked his employees hard but fairly, and trusted to the excellence of his wares to do his selling for him. Providence, in the years before the Civil War, smiled on such methods.

His profits he cannily invested in real estate, especially on Manhattan. Since the boom enriched New York more than any other city in the country, the value of his investments soared most delectably. Boom gave way to bust with painful frequency in the antebellum period, but no financial panic ever caught Cooper napping. Insulated as he was from the vagaries of contracting credit, he had only to wait for the moment when he considered a slump had scraped bottom and then rake in the best securities, drawing on his copious supply of ready gold. Indeed, so often did he repeat this maneuver that, his grandson reported later, "when his gig appeared in Wall Street during a panic, the word went all up and down the Street that the storm was now about over because Peter Cooper had bought his securities and all would now be well." In 1833 Cooper could write, in a little brown notebook of accounts, that he was worth $123,459; by 1846, this figure was up to $383,500; by 1856, to $1,106,000. What, he might have retorted to those who cracked jokes behind his back, what is so funny about glue?

More than glue was, of course, involved. There was also Cooper's thrift, pluck, industry, sobriety, enterprise, ingenuity, self-reliance, and all the others in the catalogue of his virtuous traits—to each of which, as he grew older, Cooper loved to allude in his speeches and in the growing stream of homiletic pamphlets that flowed from his pen. There was also the fact that the times could scarcely have been more propitious for a manufacturer, combining, as they did, the first fruits of the Industrial Revolution with a market apparently destined for unchecked expansion. But most important of all, there was Cooper's happy faculty of transforming adversity into prosperity—what might, in the case of anyone less virtuous, have been termed his sheer dumb luck. One or two examples of this golden touch will suffice.

In 1828 two New Yorkers approached Cooper with a gleaming proposition: the purchase of 3,000 acres of land at Lazeretto Point, within the city limits of Baltimore. How could they lose? The citizens of Baltimore, alarmed by the Erie Canal's threat to their midwestern commerce, had rammed through the state legislature a charter for a railroad, the Baltimore & Ohio. All these citizens were running high temperatures over the speculative prospects; one excited Baltimorean was so entranced by the promise of future profits as to predict that the rails could be built of silver. Cooper hesitated, but when friends urged him on, he plunked down $20,000 as his first payment for one third of the land, which was going for $105,000. He had been bilked. His *soi-disant* partners milked him of a few more hundreds, alleging there were taxes that had to be paid, but, as he later discovered, they were using his funds to pay their board.

Now clearly what can be detected here is, so far from the surly snarl of a commercial man-eater, merely the meek snuffle of an all-time chump. But Peter Cooper was no man to let his simple-mindedness stand in the way of making a quick recovery. Promptly he set to work. In no time he had found that there was iron ore in his land; he had it dug up, had kilns built, and began smelting his ore into iron. Here again his native wit almost fatally deserted him: the coal in his kiln caught fire and would not be doused; Cooper then went to the door of the kiln and peered in, at which instant the gas itself caught fire and lifted him up, out, back, and down in a fine parabola, dumping him base over apex, ten feet away, with his eyebrows and whiskers all singed away.

Even, however, before his whiskers had grown back, Cooper found his investments harassed from another direction. The directors of the B&O faced blank despair: despite labor troubles and frequent cave-ins they had managed, at hideous expense, to lay thirteen miles of track; their plans, in order to avoid the cost of deep cuts through rocky hillsides, included track that would curve around a radius of 150 feet. But it had become clear by 1829 that the most economical locomotion for railroads would be steam, and George Stephenson, the English engineer who had successfully built the first steam locomotives, flatly insisted that they could never negotiate a curve that sharp.

It was a moment ready-made for an empirical inventor like Cooper. "In the abandonment of [the B&O]," he wrote later, "I saw the defeat of my enterprise. It would have been a terrible defeat to me, for I saw that the growth of the city of Baltimore depended upon the success of that road, and I had purchased that tract with a view of taking advantage of the rapid growth of the city which was anticipated." What to do? Obviously, there was only one solution. He went to the president of the railroad and promised that he "would put a small locomotive on" that, he declared, would pull a train around those short curves. And sure enough, as he said later, "I got up a little locomotive."

This was the celebrated "Tom Thumb," the first American locomotive to run on an American railroad. It was, as Cooper himself put it, "about as temporary [a makeshift] as any you ever saw," but considered as a means of demonstrating that the railroad had a glossy future—and that in consequence, Cooper's flier in Baltimore real estate would pay off—it was a rousing success. Cooper conducted his lesson in applied mechanics at the Mount Clare Railroad Shop. Here he found some old wheels, to which he rigged a platform. He sent to New York for the rotary steam engine that he had invented some years before; it had one cylinder and generated one horsepower. He had a boiler made; it was five or six feet high, with a diameter of twenty inches; "it was difficult to imagine," said a man who examined it later, "that it had ever generated steam enough to drive a coffee mill." When it came to attaching the engine to the boiler, Cooper was stumped, but only momentarily. "I couldn't find any iron pipes," he wrote later. "The fact is that there were none for sale in this country. So I took two muskets and broke off the wood part, and used the barrels for tubing to the boiler, using one on one side and the other on the other." To keep a head of steam, he contrived a "blowing apparatus, driven by a drum attached to one of the car wheels, over which passed a cord that in its turn worked a pulley on the shaft of the blower." To save space on his platform, he stood his boiler up straight. This improvised miracle was ready for the road in July, 1830, but there ensued a series of those tragicomic mishaps that seem always to attend on an initial experiment of any significance: a wheel broke, once, twice, thrice; some miscreant made off by night with some copper chopped from the engine, necessitating a week's delay. At length, however, in August, with six men on the engine platform and another three dozen perched on a car behind, Cooper drove his locomotive the thirteen miles to Ellicott's Mills in an hour and twelve minutes and back again in fifty-seven minutes. (When they were hurtling along at their top speed of eighteen m.p.h., some of the party whipped out pencil and paper and wrote "some connected sentences to prove that even at great velocity it was possible to do so.")

Here was a sensation, but there was better to come, for Baltimore's stagecoach owners were determined to squash this new competition before it got out of hand. And so a match was arranged: the Tom Thumb vs. a powerful gray horse hitched to a car on a parallel track. The race would be run from the Relay House eight miles into town.

"Away went horse and engine," reported John H. B. Latrobe, a B&O lawyer who was an eyewitness, "the snort of the one and the puff of the other keeping time and time." At first the horse drew ahead, for the engine needed time to get up a head of steam. "The blower whistled, the steam blew off in vapory clouds, the pace increased, the passengers shouted, the engine gained on the horse, soon it lapped him—the silk was plied—the race was neck and neck, nose and nose— then the engine passed the horse, and a great hurrah hailed the victory." Alas! too soon; for Cooper's blower all at once conked out: "the horse gained on the machine, and passed it; and although the band was presently replaced, and steam again did its best, the horse

By way of contrast:

"Uncle Dan" Drew

CULVER SERVICE

Daniel Drew (1797-1879) was a short, chunky man with a face as seamed and wrinkled as a prune; he walked with a stealthy tread, like a cat; his attire was downright dowdy; he affected the bland, who-me? air of a hedgerow parson. Yet for a quarter-century this man was one of the most justly feared in the financial circles of nineteenth-century America.

He began his business career as a cattle drover. It was rough and risky work, attracting chiefly the quick-witted and unscrupulous, and from the start Drew proved himself peerless as a swindler. He conceived the ruse of feeding his steers salt on the last night before a sale; next morning each animal, crazed with thirst, swilled enough water to add fifty pounds to its weight, and presently a new phrase, "watered stock," had entered the language.

In 1834 Drew had enough capital to engage in an epic duel with Cornelius Vanderbilt over who should control the Hudson River steamboat business. By a sustained policy of rate cutting and betrayal of his own associates Drew won; and by 1844 he was off on his fearsome, singlehanded career as the Great Bear.

In the spring of 1866 Drew, who had by that time wangled his way to treasurer of the Erie Railroad, advanced the line $3,500,000, taking as security 28,000 shares of unissued stock and $3,000,000 worth of bonds convertible into stock. He then cheerfully went short in a rising market, dumped 58,000 shares on the bewildered bulls, and when the stock dove from 95 to 50, shoveled in the profits, cackling. During this venture, Drew's lieutenants were two young scoundrels on the make—Jim Fisk and Jay Gould.

When a Vanderbilt judge ordered Drew's arrest, he prudently retreated across the Hudson to Jersey City with Fisk and Gould, taking with him $6,000,000 in greenbacks. It was estimated that in the final settlement of the "Erie War" the line was milked of no less than $9,000,000; and in October, 1868, Drew, Fisk, and Gould used their loot to attack bank credit, stock prices, and the foreign exchange. Thousands of businessmen in and out of Wall Street were ruined in the process, banks were brought to the verge of suspension, and the national credit was seriously threatened.

But suddenly, in 1870, Drew's luck ran out. He was cornered in a bull market, lost $1,500,000, and in the Panic of 1873 was irrevocably ruined. On no hand was there any mercy. In March, 1876, he filed a schedule in bankruptcy. He was old and broken, hated and scorned.

He died, not particularly mourned, in September, 1879.

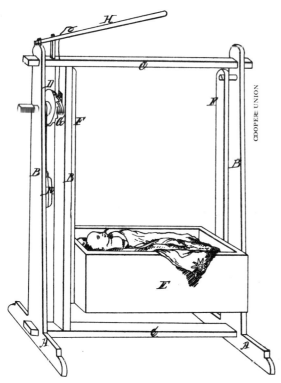

COOPER UNION

As a young father Peter Cooper designed this automatic cradle, rocked by a pendulum, for his own babies. Later he attached to it "a musical instrument that would sing a child to sleep."

was too far ahead to be overtaken, and came in the winner of the race."

The defeat provoked some merriment at Cooper's expense, but he was satisfied. For one thing, as he noted, "the bonds of the [B&O] were sold at once, and there was no longer any doubt as to the success of the line." For another, his real-estate venture panned out very well indeed: he sold the land in 1832 at a profit; some of his payment was in stock worth only $44 a share, but it obligingly rose to $235 a share before he sold the last of it. Out of what had at first seemed a most unhappy investment, Cooper got a handsome return and a full measure of fame.

Again, when a man to whom he had loaned $5,000 went bankrupt in the severe Panic of 1837, Cooper looked like a loser. All he got in compensation was his debtor's small and floundering wire factory, and what did he know about making wire? Precisely nothing. But almost at once he was fighting customers off like flies from honey. For—thanks to the new railroads, structural iron bridges, and telegraph—the national economy in the 1840's was starving for iron. It began to seem as though iron would prove even more profitable than glue. Cooper was obliged to build a rolling mill; soon he was experimenting with anthracite for puddling; naturally he invented an improved

blast furnace; and by 1847 he had organized the Trenton Iron Company, which was to become one of the biggest in the country.

A man like this wins the respect, however grudging, of his fellows. Who among them dared to to say that Cooper's most demented scheme might not turn out a winner? And indeed he did come up with some tolerably daft notions. There was, for instance, his plan for sluicing brine through the Erie Canal to Albany, where, by evaporation, the salt would be recovered for domestic use. He actually tried to patent this idea. Again, he financed an experimental ship to be powered by submerged vertical paddle wheels. At his behest, a boat was built with one vast paddle wheel even with the keel; Cooper himself rang the starting bell, the engines speeded up, and the boat at once sank like a stone, coming to rest with her decks awash. The paddle box had burst. Cooper studied the situation. "Well," he commented, "I guess that experiment is a failure."

But no matter his occasional imbecilities, he was by common consent recognized as one of New York's leading citizens, perhaps, indeed, the foremost. He had become a character. Tall, robust, big-beaked, lantern-jawed, he dressed simply, affecting a black stock at this period, and always taking care to have with him a small pneumatic rubber cushion that he placed beneath him before he sat. Whiskers encircled his chin; and his spectacles, too, were remarkable, consisting of four octagonal lenses, one pair in front of his eyes in the usual way and the other pair flanking them, at the outside. His expression, for many years stiff and forbidding, clearly indicative of his shyness and reserve, was softening now as his years mounted through middle age; there was, one saw at once, a surpassing kindliness that had come hand in hand with assurance. He had always been painfully ashamed of his lack of education and social graces, painfully aware of the fact that he could scarcely write a sentence without misspelling a word or dropping a comma. Now he had come to sense that a flaw in spelling or punctuation held no more horror than a drop of rain, so long as his thought carried true to its mark; and while his respect for education had never flagged, his skepticism of the learning that came only from books was waxing. Wherever he went he was recognized and, more and more, beloved.

There was, to be sure, a solid foundation for the public esteem. Dimly at first but with increasing clarity, his fellow citizens, and especially the humbler among them, perceived that Cooper earnestly professed, in everything he did, to serve mankind. Hence his inventions; hence even his manufacture of glue. To Cooper the fact that he made money was, if not actually irrelevant, at least not the main goal. Money was a kind of temporary reward for moral behavior, for doing good; the main goal was, as he phrased it, "to give the world an equivalent in some form of useful labor for all that I consumed in it." His inventions, his commercial enterprises, were not enough. He found time to work in other ways as well: for the Public School Society, which fought to make education compulsory; on New York City's Common Council, where he had in his charge the project of insuring the city's water supply; for the Juvenile Asylum, for New York faced then as now the problem of juvenile delinquency; for the New York Sanitary Association; for a free milk dispensary.

Whenever a committee was formed on behalf of some public need, all hands thought first of Peter Cooper when nominations for chairman were in order; and Cooper, incorrigibly naïve, accepted all nominations. He was chairman of Tammany committees formed for the purpose of whiting sepulchers, and he was also chairman of committees formed for the purpose of freeing New York forever from Tammany's grip. He was chairman of a public meeting called to raise funds for the odoriferous Erie Railroad, and almost simultaneously one of a committee of twelve appointed to raise funds for the bitterly competitive New York & Albany Railroad.

In any well-regulated society, such chairmanships are traditionally assigned to elderly gentlemen of more than average pomposity and fatuity who have retired from the struggle for money. At first glance Cooper seemed to fit these specifications admirably. In 1860 he was 69 years old; his glue business was running smoothly, and he had all but formally relinquished control; he had turned over active management of the iron mines and mills to his son Edward and to Abram Hewitt, who five years earlier had become his son-in-law ("I don't know," he had said to Hewitt, "that you can get books far enough out of your head to let even a little business in, but if you'd like to try here's a chance"), and these two were successfully expanding the business. But while Cooper was no longer actively in pursuit of money, he was far from retired. He was, indeed, just launched on what was to prove the most fruitful phase of his long life. A year earlier he had officially opened the doors of that unique institution, his pride and his joy, the Cooper Union for the Advancement of Science and Art.

Cooper's plans had been afoot for nearly twenty years. In 1830 a fellow member of the Common Council, one Dr. David Rodgers, had told him about a polytechnical school in Paris. "What made the deepest impression on my mind," Cooper said later, "was . . . that he found hundreds of young men from all parts of France living on a bare crust of bread in order to get the benefit of those lectures. I then thought how glad I should have been to have found such an institution in the city of New York when I was myself an apprentice . . . I determined to do what I could to secure to the youth of my native city and country the benefits of such an institution . . . and throw its doors open at night so that the boys and girls of this city, who had no better opportunity than I had to enjoy means of information, would be enabled to improve and better their condition, fitting them for all the various and useful purposes of life." By 1852 he had assembled his parcels of land (on Astor Place, between Third and Fourth avenues) and the cornerstone was laid the next year. In May, 1858, the Cooper Union was finished; the first students were admitted in the fall of the following year. Then (as now) they paid no tuition; then (as now) the only entrance requirement was a superior intelligence.

At first New York viewed Cooper Union with considerable mistrust. "Cooper is very well meaning but very silly for a self-made millionaire," his neighbor, George Templeton Strong, noted in his diary. "All his conceptions [for Cooper Union] are amorphous, preposterous, and impractical. . . . He will produce nothing but $500,000 worth of folly." And Allan Nevins has told the story of how Cooper, riding up the Bowery in a horsecar, overheard the talk of two men sitting ahead of him. "There's Peter Cooper's building," said one; "that man is a snake in the grass. See the stores on the ground floor? It's a commercial building, and he's trying to evade tax payments by calling it an educational institution." Cooper broke in. "Alight, gentlemen," he bid them, "and come in with me. You have maligned me. Let me show you the building and explain it." He took them through, and made such believers out of them that one of them later contributed some money to the Union.

Very rapidly all of New York came to respect the Union. Why not? Here was a night school ready to instruct all comers in chemistry, elementary physics, mathematics, music, and drawing (freehand, mechanical, and architectural); here was a school of design for women; here, perhaps most important, was a large and well-stocked reading room open to the general public from eight in the morning till ten at night, the only library of its sort in the city. Before long as many as three thousand people a week were availing themselves of its resources. As for the classes proper, Hewitt later recalled that on registration day, "There was a mob assembled so large and eager that the efforts to register students almost resulted in a riot. It was incredible"— although, clearly, not to Cooper—"that there should be

Cooper Union's first building was designed by F. A. Peterson, but Cooper himself planned its mechanical ventilating system and other innovations. Opened in 1859, the structure is still in use today as the Union marks its centennial.

such a passion for learning among the toilers. Every class was filled in one night, and from that day there was never a vacancy in the Cooper Union classes." Those first students ranged in age from sixteen to fifty-nine. And the graduates, it might be added, have since included such eminent men as the sculptor Augustus Saint-Gaudens and the inventor Michael Pupin.

But it was chiefly as a forum for new and exciting ideas that Cooper Union was noted. Almost from the first it was the center of thought in the country's largest city. In February of 1860 there was Lincoln, delivering the speech that he himself later credited with winning him the Presidency. And later there was Susan B. Anthony, Horace Greeley, Mark Twain, Ulysses S. Grant, Robert Ingersoll, Victoria Woodhull, Henry Ward Beecher, and from England, John Tyndall and Thomas Huxley. Over and over again the Union's great hall filled with the city's most influential people, to hear the most influential ideas of the day. This year, as it marks its centennial, the Union's vitality remains undiminished: over 1300 students attend its thriving art and engineering schools, while many hundreds more benefit from its extensive adult education program, its museum, and its library.

During his lifetime, its founder affably haunted its corridors. There was scarcely a day, from the time it opened in 1859 until he died in 1883, when Cooper absented himself. There were plenty of other things on his mind: he was intimately involved in Cyrus Field's efforts to span the Atlantic with a telegraph cable, and was even for a time the president of one of the companies that essayed to establish a monopoly over American telegraph lines; later, when all right-thinking citizens of New York were straining shoulder to shoulder to shove Boss Tweed out of power, Cooper could always be depended upon, if he were not too busy chairing

committees devoted to getting the Boss what he wanted, to chair a reform committee formed to oust the Boss. But none of this really touched Cooper at the core.

For forms of government let fools contest;
Whate'er is best administer'd is best.
For modes of faith let graceless zealots fight;
His can't be wrong whose life is in the right.
In Faith and Hope the world will disagree,
But all mankind's concern is Charity.

So said Cooper's favorite poet, Pope, in Cooper's favorite poem, "An Essay on Man," and Cooper heartily agreed. Called upon to put it in his own words he said, "God is love, love in action—love universal."

A man, so one might have thought, hopelessly mired in platitude and pietistic cant. And then, all at once, Cooper once again showed the sturdy and original fiber of his mind. The difficulty was that he would not slope into senility, like any other rich old man; he had to keep on educating himself, and what was worse, thinking for himself. As Allan Nevins has said, "For a rich man, he was singularly successful in avoiding the preconceptions of his own moneyed group." And so, at the age of 85, Cooper undertook to run for President of the United States on a radical, third-party ticket. The year was 1876, when, despite a popular majority for Samuel Tilden, the Presidency was "won" by Rutherford B. Hayes.

Cooper ran as the standard-bearer of the National Independent party, popularly called the Greenback party. This was a party of protest. During the Civil War the government had issued greenbacks that were not redeemable at their face value in gold; with the war's end the bankers and financiers commenced to clamor for an end to all this cheap money. By 1868 the Congress had managed to reduce the outstanding greenbacks to the amount of $356,000,000, but then the howl from southern planters and western farmers forced a halt. Their farms were mortgaged: if the greenbacks were still further reduced—that is, if the nation's available total of cash were reduced—how would they pay their debts? In the East, moreover, men were out of work; if there were less money available, how would they feed their children? Farmers and laborers, then, began to insist that the greenback issue of the Civil War be made permanent. Such was the pressure, indeed, that in the Panic of 1873 the secretary of the treasury reissued $26,000,000 worth of greenbacks previously withdrawn from circulation. But in 1874, when the Congress passed a bill increasing the volume of greenbacks to $400,000,000, Grant vetoed it. The bankers and the creditors generally applauded vigorously; the mortgaged farmers, the laborers, and the debtor classes generally as vigorously wailed. Quite naturally, since this was the Gilded Age, there followed the Resumption Act of 1875, according to which more greenbacks were to be retired and the balance of the fiat money backed by a sale of bonds. The Greenbackers saw here only a plot to enrich the eastern bankers; they girded their loins for battle and prevailed on Cooper to be their champion.

His extraordinary venture was, of course, greeted with a chorus of catcalls and horselaughs from every influential newspaper editor in the country, and the jeers persisted throughout the campaign. He could not rely even on his own family, for his son-in-law, Abram Hewitt, was Tilden's campaign manager.

Truths would you teach, or save a sinking land?
All fear, none aid you, and few understand.

Once again Cooper could reflect on how wise was his favorite poet. He was shrewd enough to realize—indeed, even to hope—that he hadn't a chance whatever of election. Why, then, did he accept the nomination?

As the old man looked about him in 1876 he saw workers grossly underpaid, farmers fettered by mortgages, rising unemployment, a Congress committed to legislate in favor of the rich, and a federal government committed to a financial policy that still further lined the pockets of the rich at the expense of the poor. Would neither the Republicans nor the Democrats undertake campaign pledges to give aid to the unemployed? To regulate the privately owned railroads? To halt the huge land grabs in the West? To control the nation's currency? Cooper appealed to the candidates of both major parties; when they did not take action, he decided it was his duty to run, if only as a gesture.

He received only one per cent of the vote. Yet time has treated his ideas most kindly. For in retrospect the impression will not down that, so far from being ludicrous, those ideas were sane, intelligent, liberal, and practical. Eighty-three years later a majority supports the notion of a government-controlled currency backed by long-term, low-interest bonds rather than by gold or silver; we are long accustomed to federal works programs for the unemployed, to federal regulation of the railroads, to civil service—in sum, to a strong Executive in Washington, using federal powers to help all segments of the population.

But in the Gilded Age Cooper was a freak. His mind looked backward with approval to the days of Jackson; if he could have looked forward to the days of Franklin Roosevelt, he would have found as much to approve.

The old man went back to his Union. In truth, he had never been away, for his campaign had scarcely been an active one. His son was elected mayor of New York; before long, although old Cooper wouldn't live to see it, his son-in-law would be elected to the same

A key part of Cooper's industrial empire was the Trenton Iron Company, which he organized in 1847. It turned out the first wrought-iron structural beams, used not only in Cooper Union (opposite page) *but in the dome of the Capitol.*

office. And there was another generation coming along; Cooper had a fine workshop built in his house just off Gramercy Park so that his grandchildren might learn to work with their hands. And two of these—Peter Cooper Hewitt and Edward Ringwood Hewitt—grew up to become distinguished inventors themselves. Cooper used to take them down to the Union with him, one or the other importantly carrying along the old man's air cushion.

He drove to his Union for the last time on March 31, 1883. He caught a cold; it grew worse, and pneumonia developed. Early on April 4 he died.

All over the city flags were lowered to half-mast. The family wanted to bury him quietly and privately, but such was the love in which he was held by the city's nameless thousands that this proved impossible. His coffin was brought to All Souls' Church on April 7, and the mourners streamed past from nine in the morning till mid-afternoon. When the coffin was lifted into the hearse, a cortege formed spontaneously and followed for miles through streets in which the shops had been closed, while from one after another of scores of churches along the way the bells slowly tolled. Seldom before or since has a citizen of New York been mourned from such a full heart.

Over his coffin, the Reverend Dr. Robert Collyer spoke the funeral address. "Here lies a man," said Collyer, "who never owned a dollar he could not take up to the Great White Throne." It was a thought to give Cooper's contemporaries pause.

Peter Lyon is a New York free-lance writer whose previous articles for AMERICAN HERITAGE *have included "The Master Showman of Coney Island" (June, 1958) and "Isaac Singer and his Wonderful Sewing Machine" (October, 1958). He is co-author of* The American Heritage Book of the Pioneer Spirit.

The undimmed appeal of

THE GIBSON GIRL

By AGNES ROGERS

In the dear, nostalgic days of the 1890's and early 1900's a vibrant, radiant young woman took the country by storm. She was the Gibson Girl, a brilliant invention, something quite new. She was lovely, animated, and unquestionably American. And today, though four change-filled decades have passed, more men are still in love with her than you might think.

Why is her appeal still so potent? She was far removed from our current notions of the ideal American woman. She was not particularly bright and not highly educated. She was not politically informed, and her social conscience, in present-day terms, was dormant. She could not cook or manage a home, nor did she resemble today's pin-up girl, whose charms are so candidly revealed in certain large-circulation magazines.

Yet even now she evokes worshipful sighs from men too young ever to have known anyone resembling her. One reason, I think, is that the Gibson Girl was forever a girl—forever young and beautiful. She was femininity incarnate without being (in today's terms) sexy. And nowadays, when sex is portrayed in such blatant detail, it is refreshing to be given the promise of future raptures rather than the play-by-play accounts of bedroom romps in current novels.

In any discussion of the Gibson Girl there is a word, now taboo, that one cannot avoid. She was a lady. In fact, John Ames Mitchell, founder of *Life* (the original one), explained that one of the reasons he accepted the first drawings of Charles Dana Gibson was that he could draw a lady. The Gibson Girl represents the rosiest aspect of Society (with a capital S) at a period in American life when Society was more clearly defined, less complex, and far more admired than it is today. Gibson himself, by virtue of his birth, his engaging personality, and his agreeable manners, had the entree to New York's

Her infinite variety

FORE!

THE AMERICAN GIRL TO ALL THE WORLD

THE AMERICAN GIRL ABROAD

HERE SHE IS, CHAPERONED BY A REAL DUCHESS, WITH TWO NOBLEMEN OF AN-
CIENT LINEAGE READY TO MARRY HER, AND YET HER HAPPINESS IS NOT COMPLETE.

WHEN DOCTORS DISAGREE

Man proposes, She disposes

MELTING

PICTURESQUE AMERICA

ANYWHERE ALONG THE COAST

THE WEAKER SEX

THE YOUNG MAN IMAGINES HIMSELF THE LATEST VICTIM OF SOME FAIR ENTOMOLOGIST.

LIFE'S VAUDEVILLE

"I'LL BE A SISTER TO YOU."

HEARTS ARE TRUMPS

HAS DIFFICULTY KEEPING HIS MIND ON THE GAME AND REPEATEDLY TRUMPS HIS PARTNER'S TRICKS.

Everything brings them together...

ALL BROKEN UP

ANOTHER COLLISION WITH SERIOUS RESULTS

TWO'S COMPANY,
THREE'S A CROWD

THE OTHER MAN SHOULD
REMEMBER THAT HE IS A CROWD.

A LITTLE INCIDENT

SHOWING THAT EVEN INANIMATE OBJECTS CAN ENTER INTO THE SPIRIT OF THE GAME.

...Or almost together

THE PARTY WALL

A CASTLE IN THE AIR

THESE YOUNG GIRLS WHO MARRY OLD MILLIONAIRES SHOULD STOP DREAMING.

ANOTHER MONOPOLY

WIRELESS TELEGRAPHY

Love conquers all

THE LAST GUEST

highest social circles and found the best it had to offer highly sympathetic. By "best" I mean a group of congenial people of established family, inherited wealth, and cultivated tastes, who employed their leisure in genuinely graceful (not "gracious") living.

Gibson hated snobbishness and the vulgarity of those newly rich who attempted to buy their way into elite circles. The Society that he did approve of, and in which he was most at home, was the old guard—scornful of public entertainers and of the attentions of the press. A lady's name appeared in newspapers just three times: when she was born, when she married, and when she died. That Society stoutly resisted the idea that wealth and position are synonymous, confident that in itself it represented all that was best and most important in American life. And many people of less exalted position agreed.

Though the Gibson Girl dwelt in high society, she was the darling of the less affluent as well. In countless houses all over the land prints of Gibson drawings were hung on the walls and Gibson's long red picture books were on parlor tables. Girls all over the country wanted to be as nearly like her as possible. They dressed like her; they wore their hair like her. Nor did the young men escape her influence. The Gibson man was usually clean-shaven (as were the artist himself and his father before him) and strong-jawed, the precursor of the Arrow Collar man. Many a luxuriant moustache was shaved off. The Gibson Girl was tall. Young men stood erect to gain inches.

Just who was the original model for the Gibson Girl? Many people have said that she was Mrs. Gibson, the lovely Irene Langhorne from Virginia, one of four sisters of legendary beauty. It is true that after their marriage—and a spectacularly happy marriage it proved to be—on November 7, 1895, Mrs. Gibson often posed for her husband, but the Gibson Girl was already in existence before then. She was a composite, not an individual. The artist's earliest models were often young society girls whom he knew and who were only too happy to come, carefully chaperoned, naturally, to the attractive young man's studio for a sitting. (The original Gibson Man, by the way, was Richard Harding Davis, Gibson's friend and author of numerous stories illustrated by the artist.)

Everybody agrees that the Gibson Girl connotes romance. Love, courtship, and marriage are the themes that engaged Gibson's liveliest interest. And he was truly romantic about his darling creation. It revolted him to think of a girl's being married off for money, especially to an old man, and this subject appears time after time. His fury was roused also by those international alliances in which American dollars were exchanged for the benefits of a foreign title.

For the most part, Gibson portrays the foreigners who fall prostrate at the feet of the Great American Girl as rather seedy specimens, but very occasionally he permits himself to show us a presentable Englishman. This may have been a gesture toward his wife's sister, Nancy Langhorne, who married Lord Astor. Or the change may have resulted from his own trips to Britain, during which he fraternized with and was feted by the foe and learned that most English lords preferred to marry English ladies.

It is often said that the American girl prior to World War I lived a pretty dull life, at least a carefully confined one, and mostly indoors. Not so the Gibson Girl. As early as the nineties we see her on the tennis court, on the golf links, on a bicycle, even driving a motor car. To be sure, when she went into the water at the seashore, she wore a decorous bathing suit (with the obligatory stockings). But she wore no bathing cap. Either she never got her head under water or Gibson couldn't bear to hide her crowning glory.

Actually, by the turn of the century, the outdoor life was an accepted thing in upper class circles, chiefly along the eastern seaboard. With the exception of bicycling (that great liberator of American women as a whole) most outdoor sports suitable for mixed company began as diversions for the well-to-do and gradually filtered downward in the social scale to become the property of the masses. Public tennis courts and golf courses were many years in the future. The automobile was a rich man's toy.

Oddly enough, when the Gay Nineties are revived today in revue skit or greeting card, the spectacle bears no resemblance to the Gibson Girl or her circle. All the men have handle-bar moustaches and the girls are made up as Sweet Rosie O'Grady or Mamie O'Rourke. In other words, they are low life. Very merry, very gay, but definitely low life. The Gibson Girl was just as definitely high life. Moreover, whereas these jovial modern revivals from the Bowery are comic valentines, the Gibson Girl defies caricature. The short-haired, short-skirted hoyden of the twenties, the flapper immortalized by John Held, was something of a caricature to begin with. It is almost impossible to exaggerate her. For quite another reason, the Gibson Girl remains as she was created, immaculate and bewitching. To burlesque her would be sacrilege.

Agnes Rogers, associate editor of the Reader's Digest Condensed Book Club, is the author of Women Are Here to Stay, From Man to Machine, *and, with her late husband, Frederick Lewis Allen, of* The American Procession *and* I Remember Distinctly.

My Mouth Hurts
PRESIDENT GROVER CLEVELAND

When the

When Charles Francis Adams called what happened to the United States in 1893 its "most deep-seated financial storm," his metaphor was weak. More than a storm, it was a major earthquake, a violent onset of national growing pains which upheaved the young country's financial crust and shook the whole continental economy along major fault lines.

The Republicans' high protective tariffs had put fat gold surpluses into the Treasury which not even Republican largess to Civil War pensioners depleted. But the tariffs and gold were no good for farmers, just then in a run of their leanest years. Despairing for cheaper money and more of it, the westerners turned to silver, of which some of the new states just admitted to the Union had mountains at bargain prices. In 1890 their senators very nearly obtained the free and unlimited coinage of silver. When the Republican-controlled

Cancer, Definitely
DR. WILLIAM H. WELCH

House blocked that, the compromise Sherman Silver Purchase Act required the Treasury to buy 4,500,000 ounces of the white metal per month (the estimated total U.S. output), at market, and to issue notes against it redeemable either in silver or in gold. Most people, of course, took gold.

This was a particularly hazardous fiscal gesture at a time when European countries, and even Russia and India, had demonetized silver. The way foreigners queued up at his Treasury windows to get something for nothing gave Uncle Sam one of his early glimpses of himself as Uncle Sucker.

By putting on their ticket little Adlai E. Stevenson of Illinois, a former assistant postmaster general and a flirt with the Populist movement, the Democrats in 1892 were able to re-elect New York's trusted Grover Cleveland as President. No friend of soft money or Treasury raids, Cleveland had stood against both in his 1884-88 term, and he still maintained his opposition. But even before he retook office,

ACADEMY OF MEDICINE

I'd Operate
DR. JOSEPH BRYANT

the earthquake was in motion and much of the havoc wrought.

More than $100 million in silver notes had been issued, redeemable in gold. The gold reserve was down from $185 million to $101 million and was soon to fall lower yet. That winter and spring of 1893, the Treasury was kept solvent only by omitting sinking fund payments and not spending appropriations voted by Congress.

The clang of closing bank doors reverberated through the land; 642 would shut this year. Savings banks required thirty days notice for withdrawals. Call money was 60 per cent in March and headed for 73 per cent. In February the solid old Reading Railroad went into receivership.

President Disappeared

'893, Grover Cleveland suffered his own secret ordeal on a yacht in Long Island Sound

By JOHN STUART MARTIN

As unemployment spread, not only did panic grip industrialists and financiers, but stark desperation and actual starvation gripped the working masses. Not for another year would Coxey's Army march on the White House, but Grover Cleveland could already hear it being recruited. His solid sense was sickened, and his honest heart.

The whole trouble, he saw, was the Silver Act, which only he might be able to get Congress to repeal. When it failed to do so before recessing in June, President Cleveland, on that month's last day, issued a call for a special session to convene on August 7, to save the nation's fiscal health and sanity.

Those two dates in black 1893—June 30 and August 7—are worth closer scrutiny. Between them lay an act of personal courage and determination un-

Keep It Secret
ADVISER
DANIEL LAMONT

paralleled in the annals of our Presidents.

For on June 30, at as dark an hour as his country had ever known, the President of the United States disappeared entirely. He did so for a dire reason which was national as well as personal. As he saw it, both he and his country were in sight of the gates of death, and only by a lonely act of his could these be avoided.

Take My Yacht
COMMODORE
ELIAS C. BENEDICT

On June 18, gruffly as was his wont, Grover Cleveland had asked Dr. Robert M. O'Reilly, the White House physician, to have a look at a "rough place" in the roof of his cigar-chewing mouth. It had, he said, been bothering him for a mat-

ter of weeks and felt worse all the time.

What O'Reilly saw was an angrily inflamed area about the size of a silver quarter, extending out to the median line from the left bicuspids and back to the soft palate. He took tissue samples and sent them anonymously to the Army Medical Museum and also to the country's top pathologist, Dr. William H. Welch at Johns Hopkins.

Cigar-chewing, whisky-drinking Ulysses Grant had lately died, slowly and painfully, of a neglected mouth cancer. Thus O'Reilly and Cleveland were shocked but not exactly surprised when the pathologists' reports concurred in one horrid word: "Malignant."

Cleveland's instant reply to this news was one other word: "Secrecy." The already shaken country must not know.

A hurried visit to Washington by his great and good friend Dr. Joseph Bryant of New York aroused no suspicions. These two were hunting and fishing cronies as well as doctor and patient. But when Joe Bryant, after confirming the diagnosis, told him, "Were it in my mouth, I would have it removed at once!" Grover Cleveland had to cogitate, to plot and plan. He did so almost instantly and with forthright resolution. Calling in Dan Lamont, his former press secretary, now his secretary of war, he concerted with Bryant for an operation on July 1, under conditions as cleverly contrived as they were critical.

Waiting at Home
YOUNG MRS. CLEVELAND

A few minutes after issuing his call to Congress for a date only six weeks beyond his private ordeal, Grover Cleveland left the White House with Dan Lamont and Dr. Bryant in the afternoon of June 30. They boarded the 4:20 northbound train. (There were no detectives, for secret service men were not assigned as regular presidential guards until after McKinley's assassination in 1901.) The press was not told that he was leaving. The story would be, if his move were discovered, that he was just slipping away to rest at Gray Gables, his summer home on Buzzard's Bay, where his young and again pregnant wife had gone already.

Unnoticed in the dusk, the President left his train at New York and with Dr. Bryant went from the station to the Battery in a common carriage. Dim in the night offshore lay Commodore Elias C. Benedict's graceful yacht *Oneida*. Her tender quietly ferried the President of the United States out to and aboard her, unseen, unsuspected.

BROWN BROTHERS

Interested Party
VICE PRESIDENT
ADLAI E. STEVENSON

The tender had already made a few other such unobtrusive trips that afternoon and evening. At casually spaced intervals it had fetched Dr. O'Reilly; Dr. Edward G. Janeway, the country's foremost physiologist; Dr. William W. Keen of Philadelphia, an oral surgeon of highest repute; Dr. Bryant's brilliant young assistant, Dr. John F. Erdmann (who was to succeed him as "top knife" of New York for a long span of years); and a Dr. Ferdinand Hasbrouck of 147 West 126th Street, Manhattan. No surgical bigwig, the latter was a young dentist, but urgently required by the others for his knowledge of the new "laughing gas," nitrous oxide, for anesthesia.

The dumpy but distinguished patient greeted all these gentlemen tersely and sat with them a while on deck, smoking one more cigar. He did not discuss his ugly ailment but did growl, "Oh, those office seekers! They haunt me even in my dreams!"

About midnight Dan Lamont and Joe Bryant went to their Manhattan homes to sleep, returning before the first sun of July had burned the mist off Manhattan's rivers. The *Oneida* sailed betimes, moving up the East River and out through Hell Gate into a glassy Long Island Sound, with Commodore Benedict and Dan Lamont plainly in evidence on deck to make it look to any curious eyes on shore like an ordinary rich man's pleasure cruise over the Fourth. Inside the

yacht's main saloon the scene was far less usual.

This space, with wide overhead transoms, had been fitted up as a floating surgery. A straight-back chair was lashed to the mast to receive the patient. Sheeted paraphernalia were ranged about, including besides Dr. Hasbrouck's gas machine a standard ether-giving rig, a manually operated generator for magneto-cautery, tables of instruments for surgeons Bryant and Keen, and a chair beside the patient's for Dr. Janeway, who would check pulse, blood pressure, and respiration throughout the hacking and scraping. The yacht's steward was put into a surgical gown so that he could function as orderly. Boiling water and cracked ice were on hand in good supply.

Several times during the morning Cleveland's mouth was washed out and disinfected. Shortly before noon he was led pajamaed from his stateroom to the chair and there strapped in, head tilted back as though for a shave.

Dr. Bryant, in charge of everything, nodded to Dr. Hasbrouck for the gassing to begin. The importance of this part was that, deep under heavy ether, oral patients might choke to death on their own blood. From the lighter gas they could more easily be aroused to cough it up. Moreover, Cleveland was precisely the overweight, hypertensive type to go into an apoplexy if he choked at all.

Cleveland went under the gas readily, and the skillful Hasbrouck, with heavy forceps, swiftly extracted two bicuspids to make room for the surgeons' work. Now came the moment for Dr. Keen's specialty. From Paris he had lately brought back an ingenious cheek retractor, which would give Joe Bryant's strong big fingers free play without a hole being cut through the face.

Into the posterior dental ridge now bared by this instrument, Joe Bryant grimly carved with his white-hot electric knife, excising with it a section of the mouth's roof out to the midline and back to an apparently affected portion of the palate. His great concern was not to invade the orbital palate, that is, eye socket.

BROWN BROTHERS

The Leak, Denied
REPORTER
E. J. EDWARDS

BROWN BROTHERS

Years Later,
The Truth
DR. WILLIAM W. KEEN

When Bryant was about half through cutting, Dr. Hasbrouck warned that the gas would soon wear off and the patient awaken. So at 1:14 Dr. O'Reilly administered ether and presently Dr. Bryant resumed his work.

When Cleveland's left antrum was fully exposed, it was seen to be filled with "a soft, gray, gelatinous mass"—the lethal sarcoma. Scooping and scraping this away, Dr. Bryant pared the excavation's limits to remove as many wild fringe cells as possible.

Bleeding was kept to a fortunate minimum—only about six ounces (one tumblerful). What with hot water, ice packs, pressure, and the cauterizing effect of the heated blade, they had to tie off only one blood vessel. Before 2 P.M. all was finished, the cavity stuffed with gauze, the patient back in bed. When he started coming to, about three o'clock, they gave him one-sixth of a grain of morphine. Pulse, blood pressure, and temperature all behaved well, the latter at no time rising above 100.8 degrees.

While the President slept, all hands took a stiff drink and a late lunch. In their vigils that night they knew what no one else in America or the world knew: that the President of the United States had, with their aid, confronted a mortal enemy and, in all likelihood, defeated it for himself and his nation in silence.

Late the next afternoon, July 2, Cleveland felt well enough to leave his bed and walk around a bit. His spirit matched his iron constitution, and through the packings in his mouth he did not complain but thanked those who came in turn to read to him.

He was not told about a difficulty that had arisen with Dr. Hasbrouck. As soon as his job was done the first day, this gentleman asked to be set ashore. The others firmly declined. To go in now might jeopardize their tremendous secret, and besides there might be complications such as hemorrhaging, with more gas needed. But by the afternoon of July 2 Hasbrouck was frantic as well as disgruntled. He was, he said, 48 hours late for another critical operation. Now the rest relented, and the tender put Dr. Hasbrouck ashore at New London.

On July 3 Cleveland was up and around all day. He belatedly signed the ship's register with a hand that was quick and firm.

On July 4 the *Oneida* ran in to Sag Harbor, where Dr. Keen was put ashore.

Late in the afternoon of the fifth, the *Oneida* moored in Buzzard's Bay and a squat, limping figure wrapped in a cloak made his way up the private dock at Gray Gables. The world was told that he had been treated for two ulcerated teeth and a recurrence of his pedal rheumatism. While he went to bed, his friends

mounted guard, Joe Bryant not far from bedside, Dan Lamont to cope with a hornets' nest.

At nearby Buzzard's Bay village, the gentlemen of the nation's press had been kicking their heels for five full days and nights with no word of any kind as to their President's whereabouts. When the *Oneida* was sighted offshore, fretfulness became fury which Lamont confronted in an old gray barn on the Cleveland estate. With a smoothness to match anything later displayed by a Steve Early or a Jim Hagerty, Dan Lamont gave them the rheumatism routine and expressed hurt dismay at all questions probing for a "malignancy," a mortal illness. He sent the reporters away silenced if not mollified, but they were back again the next day with a fresh line of attack.

Vice President Stevenson, they said, had heard the President's condition was so serious that he was entraining at once from New York to come up and investigate. Dan Lamont squelched this move by announcing that Mr. Stevenson was neither invited to nor expected at Gray Gables.

In view of Stevenson's cahooting with the Silverites and his influence in the Senate, a hard money New York columnist cracked: "The Buzzards will please keep aloof from Buzzard's Bay!"

So no "buzzard" came, but on July 7 the President's devoted friend and favorite actor, Joe Jefferson, came, cheering him vastly. And Dan Lamont and Joe Bryant stayed on, the latter taking Cleveland out, as was their custom, to fish for stripers and drumfish from a rowboat, where the salt air was as good therapy as any. An orthodontist, Dr. Kasson C. Gibson was brought

The Scene Itself, THE YACHT *Oneida*

up from New York to make impressions, and he quickly fashioned a hard-rubber plug for the gaping jaw hole.

Despite his continuing discomfort, by July 12 Cleveland was doggedly at work on his message to Congress for August 7. It went slowly. He had got little done by the seventeenth, when Joe Bryant ordained another trip to sea in the *Oneida*. This time their object was, again in utmost secrecy, to remove the rubber plug and see how the wound was healing. As they had feared, patches of evil tissue were regrowing; so they managed another gas job by themselves as Dr. Bryant, using his electric knife, scraped the hole with thorough diligence.

Back ashore, where the press had not missed him, Cleveland yielded to Dan Lamont's insistence that the attorney general be allowed to come up and help with the message to Congress. When Richard Olney arrived he was shocked to see how haggard the round face had become, how gaunt the robust body. "My God, Olney, they nearly killed me!" grunted Cleveland, and went to work on the draft speech Olney had brought with him. He retained only about one-sixth of it, cutting, substituting, rephrasing, and finally writing the rest of 2,800 words himself in his own laborious longhand.

With the advent of August, Cleveland was still feeling miserable, but he insisted on journeying back to Washington not later than the fifth. He wanted a couple of days to collar returning members of Congress and impress upon them their duty to pass the Sherman Act repealer with all speed. The Senate, Lord knew, would be trouble enough, but the House must not hesitate.

The Congress met on the seventh and duly received the President's uncompromising message. ". . . The operation of the silver purchase law now in force," he wrote, "leads in the direction of the entire substitution of silver for gold in the Government Treasury, and . . . this must be followed by the payment of all Government obligations in depreciated silver. . . .

"The people of the United States are entitled to a sound and stable currency, and to money recognized as such on every exchange and in every market of the world. Their government has no right to injure them by financial experiments opposed to the policy and practice of other civilized states."

Cleveland stayed in hot Washington four more days. Then, with the repealer measure introduced, and all his personal pressures to bear, he crept back to his commodious retreat, Gray Gables, to resume the process of getting well.

Meantime, on the very day he went to Washington, something occurred in New York City which came very near to unmasking Cleveland's entire high conspiracy.

When the disgruntled Dr. Hasbrouck left the *Oneida* at New London, it was to assist a very high-toned medico indeed named Leander P. Jones, vet to the blue bloods of Newport and Manhattan. To save skin off his own nose, Hasbrouck let Jones know just who and what it had been that had made him so late in getting to Newport.

Miffed at being treated so highhandedly, even by Dr. Joe Bryant and the President of the United States, Dr. Jones tipped off a newspaper friend of his, one E. J. Edwards, a reporter for the Philadelphia *Press*, who signed all his work rather grandly "Holland."

Holland wasted no time getting up to 147 West 126th Street. There Dr. Hasbrouck, persuaded that the story was publicly known at least in outline, and far from ashamed of his own conspicuous part in it, con-

---

DR. KEEN MAKES ANOTHER APPEARANCE

Twenty-eight years later, at the age of 84, the surgeon who helped save President Cleveland appeared again at an important medical moment in the annals of the presidency, although he could not have known it at the time. In August, 1921, while vacationing nearby, Dr. Keen was summoned to Campobello Island in New Brunswick, Canada, as a consultant in diagnosing Franklin D. Roosevelt, who had, apparently, caught cold after extensive sailing, running, and swimming in the frigid Bay of Fundy. The second day Roosevelt lost the ability to move his legs, and Keen, examining him the third day, according to a letter from Mrs. Roosevelt (*F.D.R.: His Personal Letters, Vol. II*), concluded "that a clot of blood from a sudden congestion has settled in the lower spinal cord temporarily removing the power to move though not to feel." He prescribed massage and predicted that recovery might "take some months." Mrs. Roosevelt added, "He also sent his bill for $600!" As Roosevelt's condition worsened over the next few days, Keen altered his diagnosis from a clot to a "lesion" in the spinal cord. It was some days before other doctors discovered that Roosevelt in fact had infantile paralysis, for which, of course, massage was the wrong treatment.

—Based on an article by Noah D. Fabricant, M.D., on the possible causal relationship between tonsillectomy and poliomyelitis (F.D.R.'s tonsils had been removed not long before), in Eye, Ear, Nose & Throat Monthly, *June, 1957.*

Gray Gables, the Clevelands' summer home on Buzzard's Bay, served as a salubrious haven for the President's recovery.

firmed the entire story to the eager Holland in full detail.

Thus, just four days before his fight in Congress began and in time for the grave question about his health to affect the fight perhaps fatally, Cleveland's secret was out.

And yet it wasn't out—not quite. As conscientious as he was alert, Holland sought to check his colossal scoop. Imperatively his sources must be Dr. Bryant, Dr. Keen, Dan Lamont, and, of course, the White House itself.

For his pains poor Holland was rebuffed by all these sources as a scandal-mongering scoundrel, a journalistic guttersnipe, and worse. Dr. Hasbrouck was branded a vicious prevaricator, an unknown dentist who had been called in on a routine extraction job and been fired for bungling.

The publishers of the Philadelphia *Press* withheld the story. Not for nearly four weeks did they get up enough confirmation and nerve to print it. By that time the huge white lie that it exposed had succeeded and changed places with the truth.

Congressman William Jennings Bryan orated for three hours on August 16 against the repealer (warming up for his "Cross of Gold" speech three years later) but on August 28 the House voted 239 to 108 in Cleveland's favor. When the Holland story came out next day, it had been so bruited about and discredited in advance that, though it was widely quoted, the conspirators' denials were quoted also and preponderantly believed.

Helpful also in supporting his great deception through its final stage was Cleveland's health. With more rest, fishing, and sea air, he now rebounded. By September 5 he was in shape to address a Pan-American Medical Congress in Washington, at which the most jaundiced professional eye could but agree that he never looked livelier or more robust. Keen's cheek retractor had obviated any outward scar. Gibson's refitted jaw plug filled any telltale hollow and, if anything, improved his always heavy diction. And on September 9 his wife bore the President, who was only 52 and now had begun to look it again, another girl child.

In the Senate the final victory of Gold over Silver, and the beginning of the end of the earthquake, came less through Cleveland's efforts than through the Silverites' own folly. With the little Vice President's connivance, they filibustered so long—and so absurdly—that by October 30 enough in-betweeners were fed up to make the vote 48 to 37.

So ended an arch cabal in allegiance to the nation's well-being. As to its violence to veracity, that was not mended until 1917. Then, with most of the other principals dead (Cleveland of heart trouble, and not one more trace of cancer, in 1908), aged Dr. Keen found it fit and profitable to publish a book telling the whole story.

E. J. (Holland) Edwards was long dead, too, and still dishonored. But the press which had reviled him now made such amends as it could. Failing a marble monument, it at least erected in his memory a paramount policy from which it is doubtful that any President will ever find it possible again to escape: the full and instant truth about the White House occupant's whereabouts and his health.

John Stuart Martin is a former managing editor of Time, *author of a novel,* General Manpower, *a picture history of Russia and many magazine articles. He lives at Great Meadows, New Jersey, where he operates a commercial shooting preserve.*

Eugene Ely, with crash helmet and inner tube, poses in the pilot's seat of his plane. At left, his plane takes off from U.S.S. Pennsylvania; right, the improvised flight deck on the ship, with sandbags as retarding gear.

Rickety flight deck, primitive plane —

and the Navy got its wings

By REAR ADMIRAL G. VAN DEURS, *U.S. Navy (Retired)*

U.S.S. *Pennsylvania,* a four-stacker armored cruiser with massive hitting power but only moderate speed, lay at anchor south of Goat Island in San Francisco Bay in the clear morning of January 18, 1911. Her afterdeck was disfigured by a temporary wooden platform, 119 feet in length; just forward of this, heavy canvas was draped from the searchlight platform. Most of the ship's company crowded the upper works; lifeboats floated, ready, alongside. All manner of naval and civilian craft dotted the nearby water. An act of history was about to be performed.

Coming in low over the water from dead astern was a frail-looking Curtiss biplane, piloted by a young civilian named Eugene Ely. He was about to make the first of all airplane landings on the deck of a warship. Ely and the *Pennsylvania*'s skipper—a stocky, friendly officer, Captain C. F. Pond, nicknamed "Frog"—and a few other enthusiasts believed that this might be an important achievement. Actually, a complete revolution in naval warfare was riding down the wind with the flimsy crate that was coming in for its risky landing. U.S.S. *Pennsylvania* looked odd, with its rickety flight deck, but it was at that moment the ultimate ancestor of all the mighty carrier fleets that would rule the seas in the future.

Ely was a barnstormer. Less than twelve months earlier he had bought a badly damaged Curtiss, had patched it up, and then (lacking an instructor) had taught himself to fly; it seems he kept taxiing around a field until finally he bounced into the air, and from

then on it was more or less easy. He had made money barnstorming, he held U.S. aviator's license number 17, and by now he was no stranger to the Navy. In the fall of 1910 he had tried a take-off from a platform built on the bow of U.S.S. *Birmingham,* in the Chesapeake. He got off all right, but he bounced on the water, damaged his propeller, got lost in the fog, and made an emergency landing on the first beach he saw. Today he was out to make both a landing and a take-off, and hardly anybody really thought that he could do it.

Except for a few enthusiasts, the Navy itself was rather cool to the idea. The famous Wright brothers had refused to provide either a plane or a pilot, considering the stunt too dangerous. Glenn Curtiss himself shared their feeling, and he had tried to talk Ely out of it, without success. So now Ely was coming in for his landing.

Ely sat out in front, grotesque in crash helmet, with an inflated bicycle inner tube wrapped around his chest as a safety measure. The canvas draped over the searchlight platform was meant to protect him from injury in case he could not stop in time. Along the flight deck was a primitive "retarding gear"—a series of sandbags connected by lines. On a slat between the wheels of the plane were three spring-loaded hooks. With any luck, these hooks ought to catch the lines and bring the plane to a tolerably smooth stop.

Ely had taken off from a field twelve miles to the south of the *Pennsylvania*'s anchorage. He cruised over the bay at 1,200 feet, his eight-cylinder engine purring

344

just behind him. Then he came down to 400 feet and came up to the line of warships, steadily cutting his altitude. At topmast level he rounded the *Pennsylvania*'s stern and roared up her starboard side. The air was cold and smooth as he flew back down her port side at nearly a mile a minute. A hundred yards astern he banked steeply and headed slightly to windward of the platform. Fifty feet from the ship he cut the switch—there was no room to go round again. He did not have the wave-off option of a modern carrier pilot. The propeller stopped in swishing quiet. He was almost there.

It looked perfect till the last moment; then Ely felt the settling plane suddenly jump up. The shipside updraft, well-known now, was unsuspected then, but Ely's reflexes had been sharpened by nine months of flying. They took charge. Like many a latter-day flyboy he "dove for the deck" as he floated over the third line. The spring hooks snatched the next ten and stopped him with forty feet to spare.

Before Ely's jaws relaxed men surrounded his machine. Diminutive Mabel Ely, his wife, who had been on the bridge with Captain Pond, burst through the crowd, flung herself into his arms, and kissed his cold face. "Oh, you boy," she shouted for the benefit of reporters. "I knew you could do it."

Captain Pond pumped Ely's hand, kissed Mabel's cheek and declared, "This's the most important landing of a bird since the dove flew back to the ark." They posed for photographers before the skipper maneuvered his celebrity below. At the cabin hatch he turned to the officer of the deck. "Mr. Luckel," he said, "let me know when the plane is respotted ready for take-off." Thus Frog Pond originated the order that carrier men still hear, "Respot the deck."

In the Captain's cabin, officers and guests lifted champagne glasses to toast "Ely," next "the birth of naval aviation," and "this landing which has opened a new chapter in naval history." Ely quietly passed up his favorite drink to sip ginger ale. His mind was on the job still ahead.

It was a good party, but he was glad when his machine was ready. At his wave, a mechanic jerked the toggle and for the second time a plane flew from a ship. This time it did not splash. From the end of the ramp it circled up till Ely was some 2,000 feet above his friends on deck. Then he headed straight for Selfridge Field. Thirteen minutes after take-off he rolled to a stop in front of the stands where people were gathering for the afternoon show. More champagne and more lunch were spread before him. This time he relaxed and enjoyed both. "It was easy enough," he told the battalion officers. "I think the trick could be turned nine times out of ten."

At about the same time the watch changed on the *Pennsylvania*. Midshipman Luckel signed this log entry:

> 8 A.M. to meridian:—
> Cloudy and pleasant. Calm to light airs from the East. Barometer rising. The steamer *Herald* cast off at 10:25. Eugene Ely of the Curtiss team alighted upon the aviation platform of this ship at 11:01 A.M., a feat that never before had been successfully accomplished. At 11:58 the aviator departed from the ship in his flying machine without accident and returned safely to the aviation field. Received H.M. Bogart, sea., from the U.S.S. *Lawrence* for further transfer to the U.S.S. *California*. Signals as per book.

Lt. Commander Standley, the navigator, approved the log without comment on the unique event sandwiched with the routine. Was he unimpressed then? (In 1941, as a retired admiral, the President sent him to investigate the destruction wrought by Japanese carrier planes at Pearl Harbor.)

Eugene Ely never again flew from a ship. Nine months later he died in a crash at Macon, Georgia. He always distrusted the sea, never wore a Navy uniform, and never saw any "wings-of-gold"—they had not been designed yet—but he was the first naval aviator and first carrier pilot.

Rear Admiral Van Deurs, born in Portland, Oregon, in 1901, entered the Navy in 1917, qualified as a naval aviator in 1923, and retired from active service in 1951.

THE STANLEYS AND

BROWN BROTHERS

Teetotaling twin brothers

built the most wonderful car of

their era, and its day of glory

may not be over yet

At the turn of the twentieth century, the American automobile industry was in a stage of youthful indecision. Two courses lay open to it: to follow the already well-defined path of steam propulsion, or to explore the lesser-known byway of gasoline power. Steam seemed to have the brighter future and, at this point, was heavily favored by the early auto makers. In the year 1900 more than 1,600 steam cars were produced, compared to only 900 driven by gas.

The course of an industry, however—like that of an individual or an entire nation—is sometimes influenced by isolated incidents. Such an incident occurred in 1907 at Ormond Beach, Florida, where a crowd had gathered to watch the annual automobile speed trials. After a number of gasoline cars had made their runs, none reaching the 100 m.p.h. mark, the Stanley Steamer entry appeared. It was a frail vehicle that looked like a canoe turned upside down and mounted on spindly wheels. The press of the day had dubbed it "The Flying Teapot."

As the Steamer started its run, it was silent except for a low, soft whistle. This rose to a faint whine, and a jetlike white stream flowed from the tail of the car. Soon the head of the driver could hardly be seen in the blur of speed. The car passed the 100 m.p.h. mark

THEIR STEAMER

By JOHN CARLOVA

F. E. and F. O. Stanley in a handmade 1897 Steamer. Two years later they began producing the car commercially.

and surged up to 197 m.p.h. As it was about to touch 200 m.p.h., however, the racer hit a slight bump on the beach. The light car took off like a wingless glider, soared for about 100 feet at a height of 10 feet, then crashed to the cement-hard sand in an explosion of steam and flames. The driver was flung clear, badly injured but not dead.

Out of the flaming wreckage was born another of the legends surrounding the Stanley Steamer, the best car of its era but also the most misunderstood and maligned. No man, it was said, could open the throttle and stay with the Steamer. Anyone who could even hold the throttle open for three minutes, went another

story, would be rewarded by the company with a prize of $1,000. Rumors went the rounds about men who had been blown to bits trying to win this prize.

These stories persist to this day, although all are false. The truth is that the Stanley Steamer was constructed in such a way that it was impossible for it to blow up. Early models, however, did have a tendency to let off steam in a noisy manner. One time in Boston, for example, a man drove up to a tavern, parked his Stanley Steamer at the curb, and went inside, forgetting to turn off a valve. The Stanley Steamer, in protest, gave off a thunderous blast of steam. The tavern windows rattled, glasses danced on shelves, and several startled patrons fell to the floor. The Stanley Steamer owner glanced at the prostrate patrons, remarked to the bartender, "Mighty powerful stuff you're serving here these days," and calmly walked out to his car.

This *savoir-faire* was typical of adventurous Stanley Steamer owners, who, according to a company announcement of 1916, had "the courage to buy the house they want, or the overcoat they want, or the automobile they want, even though their neighbors advise them not to." They had to have courage of another kind, too. The fuel burners of the early Stanleys used to "flood," shooting out sheets of smoke and flame. This looked a lot more dangerous than it actually was, since the front part of the car was virtually a fireproof compartment and the flames would go out of their own accord. Experienced drivers simply ignored the blaze and continued on their way, much to the consternation of all human and animal life in the vicinity. They did not always escape unscathed, however. One of them was driving a flaming Steamer through the streets one day, when a hastily summoned horse-drawn fire engine clattered around a corner, pulled alongside, and doused both vehicle and driver.

Incidents such as this—and the tales that grew out of them—eventually contributed to the death of the Stanley Steamer in 1925. This was a sad passing, for the Stanley Steamer was more than an automobile. It was the symbol of an era, an era of individuality and independence—an era that has been replaced, for better or worse, by standardization and conformity.

Appropriately, the highly individualistic Steamer was the brain child of two of the most rugged individuals in American industrial history—the Stanley twins, Francis E. and Freeland O., better known as "F. E." and "F. O." They were born in 1849 into a particularly large family in Kingfield, Maine.

F. E. and F. O. were identical twins. One was seldom seen without the other, and both were always whittling. This led them into their first enterprise, the carving and making of fine violins. Such an artistic beginning for a pair of auto makers is not as incongruous as it may seem. The Stanley Steamer, when it was produced, was as much a work of art as it was of mechanics. For instance, instead of employing patternmakers, the Stanleys themselves whittled the precise wooden forms required for casting machinery.

From violins the twins moved on to photography. They pioneered the dry photographic plate and perfected early X-ray equipment. The sale of these inventions set them up financially for the next stage of their career—the production of the Stanley Steamer. This important stage opened almost casually. In 1896 the Stanley twins went to a fair to see a widely advertised "horseless carriage." The car, imported from France, was billed as "The Marvel of the Age." Actually it was not impressive, continually snorting, jerking, and stalling.

The Stanley twins decided they could do better. Within a year, without any previous knowledge of steam engineering, they turned out the first Stanley Steamer. This was simply a small engine and boiler slung beneath a carriage, but it was an immediate success. Spectators were particularly impressed by the vehicle's brisk pace and strange silence. "It was like watching a pair of pants run down the street with nobody in them," one old-timer graphically recalls.

The Stanley twins had the New England characteristics of taciturnity and dry humor. They enjoyed a practical joke and were not above taking advantage of their car's silence. Noiselessly pulling up to a toll bridge one time, they found the keeper sound asleep. When awakened, the keeper stared at the two men in the carriage and demanded, "How did you get up here without me hearing you? Where's your horse?"

"He got away from us," said F. E. "Have you seen him?"

The keeper shook his head. "No—but you're blocking the bridge. You'll have to get that carriage out of the way."

"Of course," said F. E., and covertly touched the throttle. The carriage silently glided across the bridge, leaving the keeper staring after it with open mouth.

Horses also suffered from the silent Steamer. They apparently couldn't figure out what kind of invisible beast was drawing the carriage, and some horses wouldn't even go near a trough that had been used by a Steamer taking on water. Dogs were another story. As soon as a Stanley Steamer appeared, the entire canine population would come running, barking, and howling. It used to be a mystery how a dog, sometimes more than a mile away, would know an unobtrusive Stanley was in the neighborhood. With today's scientific knowledge, it is not hard to guess that the sharp-eared dogs were attracted by the supersonic pitch of the Steamer's burner.

To discourage dogs, some Stanley owners installed steamboat whistles on their cars. One blast and the dogs would scamper for home. More than a few humans were sent scampering, too—astonished by the sudden sound of a steamboat on Main Street.

Train whistles were used on Stanleys, too. These were fine for "whistling down" the barriers at a train crossing—*after* the Stanley was safely across the tracks and on its way. The crossing keeper would then come out and stand scratching his head, wondering what had happened to the train he had heard.

Despite their wry humor, the Stanleys were austere in their private lives. Neither of the twins drank or smoked, and both were shrewd, hardheaded businessmen. They took pleasure, however, in mystifying people with their similarity in appearance. They dressed alike and wore the same full-blown type of beard. For such a conservative pair, they also developed a strange passion for speed. This led to confusion among police all over New England.

For instance, in taking trips, the Stanleys would start out in two Steamers, F. O. a few minutes in advance of F. E. Sooner or later, F. O. would be stopped by a constable. While the lawman was lecturing F. O. on the evils of speeding, his twin would solemnly whiz past, identical in all respects. This numbed more than one rural arm of the law.

In 1899, after several years of making and selling individual Steamers, the twins bought a factory at Newton, Massachusetts, and formally launched what soon became known as the Stanley Motor Carriage Company. Two hundred cars were made that year, and the firm went down in history as the first American company to produce steam automobiles commercially.

This by no means meant that the Steamers were turned out on anything resembling a mass-production basis. On the contrary, the mechanics—all hand-picked by the Stanleys and all highly skilled if somewhat temperamental craftsmen—were encouraged to assemble the cars as they thought best. Consequently, each craftsman put into his cars something of himself as an individual, and, unlike the twins, no two Stan-

This photograph of cars and spectators at the Ormond Beach races of 1907 shows the wildly individualistic character of early auto design. This was the meet at which a Steamer became air-borne and crashed; the Stanley twins never raced again.

ley Steamers were ever exactly alike. One mechanic even insisted on putting in the engine upside down, a principle he claimed was better than the Stanleys'. This was too much for F. E., who, after fruitless argument, went to F. O. and complained about the stubborn mechanic. "Better let him have his way," F. O. advised. "He's just as cussed as we are."

And the Stanleys were "cussed" indeed. A customer simply couldn't walk in and buy a Stanley Steamer. He had to be "screened," like a candidate for an exclusive club. If the Stanleys decided he didn't have the right personality for their car, they wouldn't even take his order. Even when a customer's order was accepted, this didn't necessarily mean he would get a Steamer. If he did or said anything to displease the Stanleys between the time of placing the order and the actual production of the car, he would be refused delivery. This happened to a customer who asked for a written guarantee. The Stanleys, who figured their word was guarantee enough, showed the gentleman to the door.

This was hardly the way to build a business, let alone sell cars, and a modern automobile salesman would blanch at such treatment of a customer. It is a measure of the Stanley Steamer's worth that it continued to sell as well and as long as it did, especially since one never left the factory until it had been paid for in hard cash.

The price of a Steamer was high for its day—in 1917, about $2,500—and there weren't many people around who had that kind of cash. Sales were steady but never spectacular. The Stanley was a prestige car, and although many people would have liked one, they simply couldn't afford it. If the car had been sold on credit, and more people had gotten to own one and know its wonderful qualities, it is possible the Steamer would never have been allowed to pass away.

However, there were other matters that contributed to its death. The Stanleys didn't believe in advertising. They figured that it was a waste of money that should go into the improvement of their product. In later years, when the Stanley Steamer was suffering from all sorts of rumors, some judicious advertising might have saved the firm. Instead, the Stanleys stubbornly stuck by their policy of letting the Steamer "advertise itself."

Nor would they give in to the demands of style and mass production, which would have increased the popularity of the car and brought its price down. Except for a few streamlined racers and an early rakish model known as the Gentlemen's Speedy Roadster, the lofty, solid, individually-created Stanleys bore a resemblance to a prairie schooner. Almost always painted black, they had long, rounded hoods, which added to their funereal aspect. They looked like coffins.

Beneath that dark, gaunt exterior, however, beat a heart of mechanical ingenuity. The Stanley Steamer was—and still is—a model of engineering skill, combining comfort and economy with almost unbelievable speed and power. Yet with all this, it was surprisingly simple. The 1916 model had only 32 moving parts.

George Woodbury, a New Hampshire sawmill owner who reconstructed a 1917 Steamer, wrote a book about his experiences. The source of the car's power, Woodbury wrote in *The Story of a Stanley Steamer*, was a twenty-gallon water tank set under the floor boards. The water was pumped into a small, drumlike boiler—23 inches in diameter and 18 inches high—located under the hood. This boiler, bound with three layers of fine, high-grade steel wire, could easily take the 600 pounds of pressure considered necessary for ordinary driving. Actually it was virtually impossible to burst the boiler, as the Stanleys once proved. They dug a hole in a field, placed a boiler in it, and pumped

349

Fred Marriott at the wheel of the Stanley Rocket, virtually identical with the racer which took off and crashed in 1907.

steam pressure up to 1,500 pounds. At that point, instead of exploding, the tubes within the boiler began to leak, allowing the steam to escape.

Inside the boiler were 751 small, seamless steel tubes, looking somewhat like metallic spaghetti in a big pot. In effect, they were tiny chimneys, conveying heat through the boiler from the pressure burner beneath and turning the water to steam. The cheaply operated kerosene burner—its jets fed from a twenty-gallon tank safely situated at the extreme rear of the car—worked on the blowtorch principle. Although small, the burner could generate intense heat.

The steam drove a two-cylinder horizontal engine, geared directly to the rear axle, which almost literally had the power of a locomotive, although its horsepower rating was low. Its tremendous performance sprang mainly from the peculiar nature of steam. This is best described by John Bentley, who states in *Old-time Steam Cars:* "At best, the thermal efficiency of the internal-combustion engine may reach 35 per cent, whereas that of the steam engine tops 90 per cent.

The Stanley Steamer also benefited from its single gear. In other words, when the engine turned over once, the rear wheels also turned once. This means that in a mile the simple Stanley engine turned only 980 times, compared to the 4,000 or 5,000 times of a complicated internal-combustion engine. No wonder the Stanleys asserted that their engine could "last forever."

When the live steam had accomplished its job at the rear of the Stanley, it was piped back to a condenser in the nose. Here it was cooled to water and returned to the water tank, where it could be used again on an endless circuit. In this way, a Steamer could go for more than 200 miles before taking on a fresh supply of water. This was not so with the early Stanleys,

which had no condenser and could manage only one mile on a gallon of water, requiring so many stops at horse troughs that an outraged legislator in Vermont once demanded that "these vile, smelly, snorting steam demons be barred by law from facilities set out for the comfort and well-being of man's noble friend and helper, the horse."

The actual driving of a Stanley Steamer was simplicity itself. In fact, the Stanley anticipated modern automatic transmission by nearly half a century. A touch of the throttle—a sliding lever conveniently located just beneath the steering wheel—set the Steamer into silent motion. There was no clutch, and no gears to shift, which meant that a speed as low as 1 m.p.h. could be maintained all day without shaking, shuddering, rattling, overheating, or stalling. Another touch of the throttle would accelerate the car.

There were two foot-pedals on the floor. The right one was for the brake, the left for reverse. The Stanley, incidentally, could go as fast backward as forward—and Stanley pranksters sometimes *passed* gasoline-driven cars in that manner.

The Steamer could also be thrown into reverse even while it was going ahead at speed. Since the old-time rear-wheel brakes were none too efficient anyway, this quick reverse action was helpful in times of emergency. During one race in New York State, a Stanley whirled around a corner just as a group of spectators was straggling across the road. The driver threw the Steamer into reverse, even though it was doing better than 60 m.p.h. With a shriek the tires tore loose, and then the body, which slid along the road and came to rest a few inches from the spectators, the driver draped over the windshield. The chassis, meanwhile, was obediently going backward. It slanted off the road, bumped across a field, and disappeared into a forest; finally it encountered a solid line of trees, and only then did it grind to a halt.

On another occasion, a brick wall failed to stop a Stanley. It happened in a garage in Chicago, where a mechanic was tinkering with a Steamer. He "fired up" all right and opened the throttle, but still the car wouldn't go—for the simple reason that the emergency brake was on. After steam pressure had been building up for some time, the mechanic finally remembered the emergency brake. As soon as he released it, the Stanley rammed through the wall of the garage and emerged into the street, leaving a trail of bricks.

This trick of building up steam with the emergency brake on was used by racing drivers to get greater acceleration out of a Stanley. The Steamer, in its heyday, was limited in acceleration only by the amount of strain its old-type wheels and structure could stand. As early as 1914, however, a Stanley went from 0 to

60 m.p.h. in 11 seconds. This compares with the 11.7 seconds it takes a 1958, 310-horsepower Cadillac to go from 0 to 60 m.p.h. At a recent sports-car meet in California, this writer did 0 to 60 m.p.h. in 9 seconds in a reconstructed and improved Stanley, which put the old Steamer right up there with such modern speedsters as a British-made Triumph and a Studebaker Golden Hawk.

The accelerating action of a Steamer is different from that of a gasoline car. Instead of a grabbing, jerking, neck-snapping forward lunge, the motion is smooth and gliding, strangely rubbery, like being flung out of a slingshot. Out on the highway, at speed, it is the ground, rather than the Steamer, that seems to be moving. With the silence, one has the feeling of forever coasting down a hill—even when the car is going *up* a hill.

It was at hill climbing, in fact, that the Stanley Steamer first attracted nationwide notice. In 1899 F. O. Stanley, with his wife as a passenger, drove a Steamer to the top of 6,288-foot Mount Washington, the highest peak in New England. The rugged dirt wagontrack wound for ten miles at a twelve per cent grade, but the Stanley made it in two hours and ten minutes —a remarkable feat for its day and the first time a motor vehicle had accomplished anything like it. It was not until three years later that the first gasoline-powered car managed to struggle up Mount Washington in a little less than two hours. F. E. promptly took a new model Stanley up the mountain in only 27 *minutes.*

This showed how much the Steamer had been improved—and, incidentally, stopped any argument as to which was the best car on the road in those days. One proud Stanley owner even boasted that his Steamer could "climb a tree if it could catch ahold." There was more than a little truth in the boast, for a Stanley once literally climbed a tree—in fact, two trees. The car had been left standing at the foot of a bank of earth, which was topped by a grove of young birch trees. A boy, playing around the car, opened the throttle wide. The Steamer threw the boy aside, plunged up the bank, and slammed into two trees growing close together. The pliant trees bent back nearly to the ground, and the Steamer stopped only when it became entangled in the branches. A few minutes later the birch trees, noted for their elasticity, rose into the air again, carrying the car with them. There it was eventually found, suspended about ten feet from the ground.

This was the sort of incident that wove an almost mystic aura around the Stanley Steamer. Owners of the car were not above thickening the mystery. One of their favorite tricks was to walk down the road about a dozen yards ahead of a parked Steamer, then turn and whistle. The car, responding like an alert and well-trained dog, would roll down the road to its master.

The explanation for the trick was simple enough. The Steamer, after standing for half an hour or more, would "cool off." If the throttle was open very, very slightly, there would be a space of some seconds before the engine took hold. This would give the owner time to walk down the road and "whistle" his car to him. The effect on a group of spectators can easily be imagined.

Another trick was more nerve-racking. F. O., who once accompanied a Stanley Steamer shipped to New Orleans, assembled the car in a field near the Mississippi River. Every day a crowd gathered to watch the vehicle taking shape. When the Steamer was ready to roll, F. O. began "firing up." The crowd stared in tense apprehension. Up and up went the steam pressure—100 pounds, 200 pounds, 400 pounds, 600 pounds. Suddenly there was a terrific explosion.

F. O., not too concerned, turned to reassure the crowd. There was nobody to reassure. Everyone had scuttled out of sight. F. O. turned back to the car and examined it. There didn't seem to be anything wrong. Perplexed, F. O. finally heard a snicker in some bushes behind him. Turning, he saw a couple of kids trying to hold back their mirth. One pointed beneath the Steamer, where F. O. spotted the remains of a big firecracker.

F. O. enjoyed this joke so much he took to carrying firecrackers around himself. When a crowd gathered to watch him "fire up," he would wait till a particularly suspenseful moment, then drop a firecracker beneath the car.

These pranks—which, of course, added to the wild tales about the Stanley Steamer—also obscured many practical (although unusual) uses of the car. For instance, it made a fine peanut roaster. Before starting on a trip, a bag of peanuts could be placed on top of the boiler. By the end of the journey, the peanuts would be done to a turn.

A Stanley's steam pressure was also excellent for blowing out clogged drains. In addition, several cities used Steamers to thaw out frozen fire hydrants in winter.

On the other hand, there were a number of drawbacks to the old Stanley. It sometimes took up to half an hour to get up steam in a cold boiler. Although driving the car was easy enough, the "firing up" process was complicated and cumbersome, calling more for a plumber than a mechanic. The driver's seat, faced with a bewildering array of gauges, valves, and pump controls, looked something like a boiler room. In fact, one of the most persistent canards about the Stanley was that a driver needed a steam engineer's license, as well as a regular driver's license, to operate it competently.

There was also the matter of smell. Kerosene, although cheap, has a pungent, penetrating odor. An old saying went, "You can see a Stanley Steamer before you hear it—and you can smell its owner before you see him."

The Stanley twins and the head of their maintenance department, Fred Marriott, raced Steamers all over the country, particularly at fairs. Nothing on wheels could stand up to the Stanley, which usually beat its nearest opponent by as much as five minutes in a twenty-mile race.

In 1906, at Ormond Beach, driving a streamlined but otherwise stock-model Steamer, Fred Marriott set a world speed record of 127.66 m.p.h. and became the first human to travel two miles a minute. This record was set by a car weighing only 1,600 pounds. Actually, it was lack of weight that hurled the little "Flying Teapot" to its doom in 1907 on the same track. In that year, so fateful to the Steamer, Fred Marriott brought the racer back to Ormond Beach. Piling the pressure up to 1,300 pounds, Fred opened the throttle and sent the car speeding down the beach. Nearly fifty years later, Marriott was still around to describe what happened next:

I quickly got up to 197 miles an hour and the speed was rising fast when the car hit a slight bump. I felt it lift and then rise clear off the ground and twist a little in the air. It took off like an airplane, rose about 10 feet off the beach and traveled 100 feet before it struck. I was thrown clear and pretty badly smashed up. The machine broke in two and was bashed to kindling wood. The boiler rolled, blowing steam like a meteor, for a mile down the beach.

The cause of the crash was a simple one, although few could understand it at the time. In designing the streamlined body of the car, the Stanleys had left the underside flat. When the wind got under this at high speed, it lifted the light car and made it air-borne, creating the myth that a Steamer was just too fast to stay on the ground. It is interesting to note that the 200 m.p.h. mark touched by the 1,600-pound Stanley was not bettered by a gasoline car until 1927, and then only by a four-ton monster powered by two twelve-cylinder airplane engines.

The Stanley twins were badly shaken by the near disaster at Ormond Beach. They never built another racer and, in fact, tried to play down the speed potential of the Steamer. This, then, brings up the natural question: What about that well-known and widely believed story that the Stanleys would pay $1,000 to anyone who could hold the throttle open for three minutes? Fred Marriott had a definite answer:

I'll tell you what's in that yarn—*nothing*. We did our best to kill it, but it always kept coming back. It used to make the Stanleys sore—and kind of sad, too. I guess they could see the way things were going.

In 1918, F. E. Stanley started out on a trip in his Steamer. Coming up over the crest of a hill, he found the road blocked by two farm wagons. Rather than hit them and possibly kill the drivers and horses, he turned off the road and crashed into a ditch. He was killed instantly.

F. O., heartbroken over the tragedy, retired. (He eventually died of a heart attack in 1940.)

Early English steamer, built by James and Anderson in 1829, had two boilers and engines and traveled fifteen m.p.h. carrying fifteen passengers, including a tootling footman.

First successful U.S. steamer was Oliver Evans' "Orukter Amphibolos" (Amphibious Digger), a combined boat-carriage which was "launched" in 1805 to dredge Philadelphia docks.

The Stanley Motor Company passed into other hands. It lingered on for a few years, out of tune with the fast-changing times, lost without those "cussed" dreamers and craftsmen, the Stanley twins. In 1925, the firm went out of business. In its last full year of production it turned out only 65 cars. Ford alone was producing more than that in a single day. Mass production and the internal-combustion engine had won out over steam and individuality.

Today there are many automobile experts who cannot understand why the Steamer was allowed to pass away. They argue that with modern improvements—such as a boiler capable of a quick start—the Steamer would be a far better car than the present gasoline auto. And who can deny that our cities would be finer, pleasanter places if we all had silent Steamers, rather than the noisy, fumes-belching gasoline cars that now pollute the air?

There is also the matter of economy. During World War II, with gas rationing, many old Stanley Steamers were brought out of barns or rescued from junk yards. Aside from the low cost of operation, the gallant Stanleys brought back to many motoring enthusiasts the thrill of driving a truly outstanding and individual car. This set off a revival of interest in steam autos that is still growing. The era of the Stanley Steamer is gone, but the spirit of the time and the car has not perished.

Not long ago a petroleum engineer, who improved an old Stanley, drove from Los Angeles to New York on $4.50 worth of furnace oil. Another engineer designed and built a steam car capable of taking off from a cold start in one minute and maintaining a steady seventy or eighty m.p.h. on the open road. Some steam fans, like Charles Keen, a Wisconsin businessman,

hide their silent secret under the modern exterior of a reconverted gas car. Others, like Hollywood writer Nick Belden, take their improved Stanleys to sports-car meets and beat some of the latest models from the Detroit assembly lines.

Some observers contend that it is performances such as these that keep the steam car from coming back. They claim that powerful automobile and gasoline interests, having long ago won the battle against steam, are certainly not going to allow their old rival to be revived commercially. In at least one instance, this is not true. Not long ago, the Chrysler Corporation brought Calvin and Charles Williams to Detroit from Philadelphia to demonstrate their highly improved steam motor, which works equally well in cars, trucks, buses, or boats. It can be built for one third the price of a gasoline engine and can perform with greater efficiency and economy, operating on fuel oil costing sixteen cents a gallon.

The Chrysler Corporation is reported to be interested in producing the Williams' steam motor. It is perhaps significant that the Williams brothers are twins. Automobile history may yet repeat itself. In fact, one auto expert, Ken Purdy, writes in *Kings of the Road:* "The steam-lovers may have to wait just a bit longer—until the atomic-powered automobile is ready. Chances are that it will be a steam car, for it seems doubtful that we will find a way to use atomic energy for transport except by converting it to steam."

The greatest glory of steam cars, therefore, may lie just ahead.

A sports-car enthusiast, John Carlova has worked all over the world as a newspaperman and magazine writer, and now lives in Laguna Beach, California.

Deliveries by steam were made in this buglike wagon produced by the White Sewing Machine Company, which made steamers until 1910, then switched to gasoline automobiles.

DRAWINGS BY EVELYN CURRO

Stanley's last stand was the 1922 phaeton, continued until 1924, when the company was sold. The purchasers made Stanley cars for another year or so, but steam was about dead.

T.R.
ON THE TELEPHONE

By private wire from Oyster Bay Roosevelt angled for the 1916 Progressive and

Republican nominations, but his strategy backfired and killed the Progressive party

Edited by JOHN A. GARRATY

On June 7, 1916, the national conventions of the Progressive and Republican parties were about to open simultaneously in Chicago. Of the many presidential candidates who would be suggested at the Republican convention only two, ex-President Theodore Roosevelt and Supreme Court Justice Charles Evans Hughes, seemed to have a real chance of being nominated. Almost to a man, the Progressive delegates were determined to name Roosevelt, who had fashioned the party in righteous indignation four years earlier, when William Howard Taft had "stolen" the Republican nomination that Roosevelt believed his.

Defeat had thinned the Progressive ranks, but the survivors were zealous and loyal. Roosevelt, whatever his personal wishes, felt a sense of obligation to them. Ideally he would have liked to be nominated by both parties, which would have been a tacit admission by the Republicans that they had mistreated him in 1912. Failing that, he wanted to see some other candidate chosen whom both groups could endorse. President Wilson, fortified by his New Freedom domestic reforms and by his obviously sincere dedication to keeping the United States out of the bloody European war, would be a formidable opponent even for the combined Republican and Progressive forces; if they were split, he would be well-nigh invincible. Most sensible politicians in both the Progressive and Republican parties were eager to unite.

Each side had one mighty asset the other lacked. The Republicans had a powerful political organization, but no candidate of national stature or appeal. The Progressives were woefully lacking in experienced workers at the precinct level, but they had in Roosevelt a proved and colorful national leader. While both parties were willing to work for union, neither was willing to surrender much of its independence, and on the eve of the conventions no real progress had been made. For this reason the confusion common to all national conventions was even greater than usual, for, with the fate of both parties at stake, the politicians worked frantically and often at cross purposes. Understanding Roosevelt's key role and knowing that important decisions would have to be made on short notice, his chief representative at Chicago, the retired Morgan banker George W. Perkins, had installed a private telephone line between his own rooms at the Blackstone Hotel and Roosevelt's home in Oyster Bay, Long Island. To allay Roosevelt's fears that he would be misquoted, Perkins had his secretary, Miss Mary Kihm, monitor the conversations. First published in the December, 1957, AMERICAN HERITAGE, Miss Kihm's transcript, from which the following excerpts are taken, reveals the mounting tension of that hectic week and lights up the events that went on behind the scenes.

★ ★ ★

Monday and Tuesday, June 5 and 6
With the formal opening of the conventions two days away, Republican and Progressive leaders began to assemble in Chicago. As they canvassed the delegates, it became increasingly clear that the leading Republican candidate was Hughes. Roosevelt did not want to support him, partly because of his own ambitions and partly because he felt that Hughes was, if not actually pro-German, at least insufficiently enthusiastic for preparedness and "Americanism" in the face of the European war. Hughes had taken the position that as a judge he ought not to seek the nomination—a stand that, however sincerely held, enabled him to be discreetly silent on the issues of the day. Roosevelt, therefore, argued that he could not support Hughes until he knew where the Justice stood on these issues.

Perkins worked assiduously among the delegates before the conventions opened. Among conservative Republicans he found Senator Boies Penrose of Pennsylvania and Senator Henry Cabot Lodge of Massachusetts willing to support Roosevelt. Lodge and Roosevelt had been friends for more than 30 years; not so Penrose, but his bluff remark, "I don't want Hughes; I cannot do business with Hughes; I can do business with Roosevelt," was very encouraging to Perkins.

At 12:30 A.M. on June 6, Perkins put Penrose and Lodge on the private wire to Oyster Bay.

Penrose: This Hughes proposition has assumed proportions none of us dreamed of before we came here. . . . I do not suppose more than a quarter of [the delegates] are here yet. Mr. Perkins is making a careful canvass and so am I, to see where we are at. . . . Have you any suggestions to make?

Roosevelt: No, Senator, except that I want to say one thing. Supposing that matters come about so that I am nominated; I want to say to you what I have said to Mr. Perkins . . . that you will be the leader in the Senate at that time.

Penrose: . . . That side of it is not the question with me. . . . I really do not think the question of patronage, while a factor with a percentage of the delegates, is the controlling factor at present. . . . There is a general desire to win. . . . Lodge is here. Think it would be a good thing for you to talk with him. . . .

Lodge: Hello, Theodore.

Roosevelt: Hello, Cabot Lodge.

Lodge: It is a very mixed up situation we have here. . . .

The thing lies just this way: It looks like the nomination of Hughes [by the Republicans]. There is no enthusiasm for him at all but there is a wide-spread feeling that he can be more easily elected than any one else. Now to nominate you in that convention—I do not know if the votes are there or not. Of course if the Progressives nominate you before we act, that blows our plans all up and destroys them; you know there is a lunatic fringe to the Progressive party—I use your own words.

Roosevelt: Rightly said.

Lodge: . . . It is going to be either you or Hughes, in my judgment. . . . It is very hard to get at the convention. You know these delegates are all elected independently and are uninstructed and they cannot be handed around and delivered. . . . The question is how many votes they can show for you, and that I do not know. . . .

Roosevelt: As far as my personal interests are concerned, if they do not nominate me I shall breathe a sigh of relief. I have no ambition to go into a purely political campaign. . . . I can earnestly say I am not interested in my personal welfare at all; but in international matters and in the present situation I know I am worth two of Hughes.

Late that evening John T. King, Republican national committeeman from Connecticut, made the same point to Roosevelt.

King: . . . I am very much afraid of this Hughes situation tonight.

Roosevelt: I think myself that is the way the thing is drifting.

King: Yes, very fast, and if [Hughes's opponents] do not get a program pretty quick it is going to be almost impossible to stop it. . . . Here is the stand I am taking, Colonel: No matter whether the two conventions can get together or not as far as politics is concerned it is the duty of us fellows to stop Hughes by all means. Even though the Progressives and the Republicans cannot get together there is no sense in nominating Hughes. So let us go down on that principle.

Between them, Lodge and King had outlined the course which Roosevelt's supporters were to follow for the rest of the week: to stop Hughes and to seek to build support among the Republicans for Roosevelt or for a candidate he could support; and simultaneously to hold off the eager Progressives from immediately nominating Roosevelt, behind whom the Republicans, in their convention, were not yet ready to unite.

Roosevelt spoke again with Lodge regarding a speech Hughes had given at a girls' school. Then he brought up the question of who should place his name in nomination at the Republican convention:

Lodge: How are you, all right?

Roosevelt: Right as a trivet. Very much amused by Hughes's speech. It is exactly like a Wilson speech to the Colonial Dames. . . . Now I wish to ask whether it would

not be a good thing to have [Senator Albert] Fall of New Mexico * nominate me?

Lodge: He would do it very well.

Roosevelt: . . . Suppose you talk it over with Perkins now. I think that perhaps to have Fall nominate me would emphasize what I would like to have emphasized, that if you want the antithesis of Wilson you want to take me.

Perkins then took the phone and gave Roosevelt a rundown on the results of his own canvassing among the Republican delegates.

Perkins: . . . Curiously enough we figure up 81 or 82 votes on the first ballot. . . . Now I have purposely tried to minimize the vote on the first ballot and have given out that we expect 70 or 75. . . . On the second ballot we know we will have more than 75 and then we will be in the running. . . . A good many are after me about your not being a Republican. I have made this suggestion to [Idaho's Senator William E.] Borah, for him to think over. . . . I said, "You want the Colonel and his party. Now suppose that I could get our people [the Progressives] to authorize me to say to you, confidentially, that provided the Colonel, the right Vice President and the platform were put up, we would immediately pick up our banners, walk down to the Coliseum and surrender, body, boots and breeches." Borah said, "That is some suggestion."

Roosevelt: George, that is a master stroke. It must have made a great impression.

"I think Hughes a good deal of a skunk in the attitude he has taken."

Wednesday and Thursday, June 8 and 9 As the conventions opened the professionals of each party managed to maintain control of the convention machinery and to pave the way for compromise. Progressive William Draper Lewis met with Senator Lodge and together they drafted the party platforms, which were nearly identical. Party leaders also managed to engineer the appointment of a conference committee consisting of five Progressives and five Republicans. On Thursday evening Medill McCormick of Illinois, a pro-Roosevelt Republican, explained to the Colonel the composition of the Republican committee.

McCormick: . . . The Republican convention has just appointed a conference committee consisting of [Murray] Crane [of Massachusetts], Nicholas Murray Butler, ex-Congressman Johnson of Ohio, Borah and Reed Smoot. . . .

* *This was the same Albert Fall who, as Secretary of the Interior in the Harding Administration, became involved in the Teapot Dome oil-lease scandals and was forced to resign from the Cabinet. He was later tried and convicted in criminal court and sent to prison.*

In my delegation the tide today turned very strong for Hughes. For instance, some fellows who have been close friends of mine personally, although I have opposed them politically, have given me a private tip to get out of the way. . . .

Roosevelt: Now tell me, when do you think the nominations will come?

McCormick: The nominations will be made some time tomorrow. The Bull Moose [Progressive] crowd are now over in the auditorium, appointing their conference committee. . . .

Roosevelt: Of course I have never believed that there was a chance of my nomination and I have been very anxious that the thing should work out right for the country's best interest. Hughes has been a big disappointment thus far. I guess there is no need to tell you that I think Hughes a good deal of a skunk in the attitude he has taken.

While Roosevelt and McCormick were talking, the Progressives appointed their delegates to the conference committee. Perkins headed the group, which also consisted of Governor Hiram Johnson of California, Charles J. Bonaparte of Maryland, John M. Parker of Louisiana, and H. S. Wilkinson of New York.

Their first session with the Republicans, held at the Chicago Club, was orderly, congenial, frank—and fruitless. When the Progressives offered Roosevelt as a "compromise" candidate, Nicholas Murray Butler stated that "under no circumstances whatever would the Republican convention consent to his nomination." Perkins asked the Republicans to suggest someone else. This they refused to do, saying that they could not commit the convention to any man so early in the game. At 3:30 A.M. on Friday, June 9, the conferees adjourned, having accomplished nothing.

Friday, June 9
After learning of the failure of the meeting, the Republican convention proceeded to the nomination of candidates, a complicated, windy process which consumed most of Friday. Many Progressive delegates reacted by demanding that Roosevelt be selected at once, without regard for the Republicans. At 3:30 on Friday afternoon William Allen White of Kansas was on the private wire to Oyster Bay, asking Roosevelt's permission to go ahead with his nomination in the Progressive convention.

White: . . . We feel that we can go over a couple of ballots but that it would be a little dangerous to go further than that.

Roosevelt: I do not think we ought to nominate until they [the Republicans] have had a full chance. . . . You know I haven't committed myself in any way about running on a third ticket, but as you know I am very reluctant to do so.

White: Naturally.

Roosevelt: I can see that only damage would come from

Charles Evans Hughes

it. I think it would hurt to nominate me until they have acted. . . .

White: If the Republican convention does not show a decided tendency to come our way they [the Progressives] will nominate you pretty soon.

Roosevelt: Try to keep our convention from acting today. Keep them from acting until tomorrow. Let us see the drift of this evening and then call me up tomorrow. . . .

White: I think it can be very easily handled for tonight provided the Republicans do not go into session tonight and stampede for Hughes. Our people do not like the Hughes proposition.

Roosevelt: I do not like the Hughes proposition myself; I loathe it. I think Hughes is a man of the Wilson type; I think he is little better than Wilson. . . .

White: He must get out from under that German proposition before our people will consider him.

Yet White was a self-confessed leader of a group of "conspirators" who worked day and night to undermine Perkins' control of the convention and proceed at once to the nomination of Roosevelt. At 8 P.M. Perkins reported to Roosevelt.

Perkins: We have had an extraordinary day here. . . . I really feel hopeful tonight for the first time. . . .

Roosevelt: George, I should like to be where I could hold your hand. . . . Did White tell you what he came down to tell me? He came to tell me that he had consulted with . . . the conservative side of the Progressive party, and said that they had decided that they were willing to yield to my wishes to the extent of waiting for one ballot. They wanted to know if I wished to be nominated after the first, or whether they should wait until after the second.

Perkins: When I got back to the convention I found they had it all framed up to nominate you, and [Raymond] Robins [chairman of the convention] told me that they did not propose to listen to any more nonsense about postponing your nomination and were going to put you through.

Roosevelt: George, there is no doubt about it; the other fellows have all the crooks and we have all the cranks.

(Note from Mary Kihm: I was called away at this point and did not get back to the telephone until the following remark by Colonel Roosevelt.)

Roosevelt: However, much as I despise Hughes I would prefer him to one of the burglars [i.e., those who had "stolen" the nomination from him in 1912—Ed.]. Even the members of our lunatic fringe take that view.

Twenty minutes later Roosevelt was getting a report on the Republican convention from John W. McGrath, Roosevelt's private secretary, and Dr. Edward A. Rumely, owner of the New York Evening Mail.

McGrath: They have gone to ballot in the other convention but we haven't heard anything from it as yet.

Roosevelt: Oh, Mac, go get your gun!

Rumely: I was at the Republican convention when you were nominated. The reporters said it was the first live demonstration. . . . Hughes was cheered for twenty minutes but it was a weak, thin thing. Joe Cannon and Harding looked down from one side of the platform and then down the other to see what was doing. Here's the proposition: They are a very astute bunch of poker players. I watch the delegates. I talked with one Massachusetts delegate, Patch, who is known not to favor you. He stood up on a chair and I said, "What are you up for?" and he said, "I'm for Roosevelt but I haven't been able to say it until now." There are others like him, but here's the situation: If they come to a vote and are only guessing whether or not there is a third party in the field they are very likely to follow their leaders; but if they know there is a third party in the field they will be afraid not to endorse you. . . .

Gifford Pinchot, pioneer conservationist and one of Roosevelt's closest friends and staunchest Progressive supporters, was then put on the line.

Pinchot: Our weakness here from the start, as indicated in my letter to you, remains the same—the doubt on the part of your opponents as to what you will do in case of your nomination by the Progressives; in other words, the feeling has got around among them, from somewhere or other, that if you are nominated and they had anyone that is even approximately bearable, you would withdraw and their nomination would stand. That is what has made us weak in dealing with them. We have been playing poker with them substantially without chips in that direction. Now I realize,

of course, the difficulty of that situation; at the same time, if you could send to some one here a telegram or a message over the telephone which could be circulated and which, without directly committing you finally to make the race, would indicate that that was your intention, and that could become known to the other side, it would very much strengthen our case.

Roosevelt. . . . I do not believe that good would come from such a communication as you suggest. . . .

White and the other "radicals" were unable to get control of the Progressive convention on Friday. Over at the Coliseum, the Republicans wound up their oratory and began to vote. The first ballot was a great disappointment to the friends of Roosevelt in both conventions. Hughes had an impressive lead over the field, whereas Roosevelt was far down the list of candidates with only 65 votes. The second ballot greatly increased Hughes's lead and added only a handful of new supporters to Roosevelt's candidacy. At this point the nomination of Hughes seemed inevitable unless a deal with the Progressives could be arranged. The Republican leaders therefore adjourned the session to allow for a final effort at compromise.

The results of the first two ballots had demonstrated clearly that Roosevelt could not win the Republican nomination. For Roosevelt, this practically settled the question of his own action. So long as he had hopes of a double nomination he was willing to consider the possibility of running independently, should the Republicans make an objectionable choice; without those hopes the possibility disappeared.

Fearing just this development, some of the Progressives attempted to force Roosevelt's hand.

"I am not going to dictate to that convention as if I were a Tammany chieftain."

Pinchot: Have you heard the result of the first ballot?

Roosevelt: Yes, I got [65], did I not? The Republicans must [realize] that if they carry things too far they may make it absolutely necessary for me to run on a third ticket but I absolutely will not commit myself in advance. I wish you would look around and see who else would run; see Hiram Johnson.

Pinchot: He will not. As things stand tonight I do not see how it is possible for anything of that sort to happen, and your refusal to run would kill the Progressive party entirely. That seems to be self-evident. . . .

Roosevelt: I wish to say this—that there is a very wide difference between making a young colonel and a retired major general lead a forlorn hope. I have simply got to reserve judgment.

Pinchot: There is one thing I want to say. There is apparently throughout the convention a very strong fear that if we wait until after the Republicans have nominated, and if they nominate Hughes, an effort will be made at that time to force our convention to nominate Hughes.

Roosevelt: I do not see how. I can only say for myself: If the Republican convention now nominated Hughes I would have to say that even though the Progressives endorsed him I would not endorse him until he repudiated the German-American alliance.

Pinchot: I want you to make it evident that our people will nominate you; then you decide afterwards what to do.

Roosevelt: Now see here; that is a big order.

Pinchot: I do not want you to make a public statement but I want you to make it evident to your managers here that you do not want anyone to take steps to have our convention nominate Hughes.

Roosevelt: I'll take those steps.

Pinchot: There is a very strong fear among men whose judgment is to be respected that an effort of that kind will be made.

Roosevelt: Now I'll tell you, Gifford, I have purposely arranged that I would tell everything to Hiram Johnson and George Perkins. . . . Now you consult Hiram Johnson.

Pinchot: Now will you tell George Perkins the same thing? You cannot expect our convention to wait until Hughes makes a statement. We have got to act before that happens. You cannot keep our people here a week.

Roosevelt: Now, Gifford, take that up with Hiram Johnson and Perkins and have them make some suggestions to me.

Pinchot: All you have to do, Theodore, is to let your will be known to your managers.

Roosevelt: My will known to the managers? I am not going to dictate to that convention as if I were a Tammany chieftain. That is just what I want to avoid doing.

Pinchot: There is no question of your dictating. The convention wants to do only one thing and is afraid that plans are being put in operation to prevent it from doing so, and I want you to make it plain that those plans have not your approval, if they exist.

Roosevelt: Very good; now you mean that plans are being put in existence to secure the endorsement of Hughes if he is nominated—the endorsement of Hughes before he has made any statement. Now then, I personally will not support Hughes until I know where he stands.

Pinchot: May I quote you as to that?

Roosevelt: Yes, but you must not quote me to the newspapers.

Pinchot: Well, then, whom can I quote you to?

Roosevelt: What do you mean? Do you mean to say that you think you can quote me to the newspapers? Of course you cannot. Quote me to Hiram Johnson, to William Allen White, to Henry Allen, to George Perkins.

Pinchot: Dr. Rumely wants to speak to you for one moment.

Roosevelt: O, for the Lord's sake! All right.

Rumely: They are having difficulty in keeping the Progressive convention from nominating you. Johnson is holding the floor now. He is saying that for two days he has been part of a strategy he did not believe in; that it is only your will that has kept him from going through with the plan he thought should be put through. If you could realize the situation in Chicago you would feel you have a much stronger hand than I think you now feel you have.

Roosevelt: I have told Hiram Johnson and I have told George Perkins that they must be in consultation. Let Hiram Johnson and George Perkins get together, and if they differ then let them come to me.

At 10:30 P.M. George B. Cortelyou, Roosevelt's former secretary, was on the wire, speaking to Roosevelt about the meeting—then just getting under way at the Chicago Club—of the Progressive-Republican conference committee.

Cortelyou: . . . G. W. [Perkins] asked what I thought they should do when they went into this conference committee tonight. Neither convention can push the thing to a conclusion until the conference committee reports back that their efforts have been unavailing; any other course would be a slap in the face of the convention. They cannot go on forever. I should think that tonight there ought to be a showdown. . . . I should imagine G. W. would have to be guided somewhat by the statement made to him by the Republican conferees as to the line he will take. Of course he feels now that he has about got to the point where he cannot hold that Progressive crowd much longer. They meet at 10:30 tomorrow—a half hour before the other one—so that they will get into action right away unless they are controlled and unless this conference committee has something to say.

"Now, George, it's hard to know what is best to do. What is your judgment?"

Roosevelt: My judgment is that the conference committee cannot say anything. They will have to say that they disagreed.

Cortelyou: The next question comes up after the action of the Progressive convention tomorrow. If they nominate you at once, then comes the question of whether they should complete the ticket or hold over a while to see what effect the first nomination will have.

Roosevelt: Now, George, it's hard to know what is best to do. If they nominate me shall I take a little time to decide? Should I take two or three hours to consider it? What is your judgment?

Cortelyou: I should think so, because if they nominate at once that would be before the other convention opened. You could accept it at once, but from our point of view that would look as though you wanted to take snap judgment.

Roosevelt: But, my dear boy, I do not intend to accept.

Cortelyou: I know, but in talking with the conference

committee tonight I imagine G. W. cannot show his hand on that.

The difficulty Roosevelt now faced was this: If he were to oppose Hughes, whom could he suggest (other than himself) as an alternative? As the conference committee met again in another attempt to find a common candidate, everyone realized that this was the last chance for the "bosses" to exert the control they liked to think they possessed. If they could not agree, the separate nominations of Roosevelt and Hughes would surely follow in the morning.

But agree they could not. The Progressives still insisted they had no name to offer but Roosevelt's; the Republicans rejected him, but would suggest no one else.

Shortly before 3 A.M. the committee adjourned. But as the weary conferees were leaving the club, Perkins asked Nicholas Murray Butler if he would be willing to talk to Roosevelt on the private wire. Butler asked for time to discuss this idea with some of his friends, and after they had agreed he hurried to Perkins' room at the Blackstone. Perkins got Roosevelt on the phone at ten minutes to three.

Perkins: I must talk very quickly and then will put Nicholas Murray Butler on the telephone in a minute. All I want to be sure to do is to tell you that you must not say in any way that you are for this man, that man or the other. . . . He will try hard to see if you personally will stand for [Elihu] Root, [Charles W.] Fairbanks or some one of that sort. . . .

Roosevelt: What is the use of it?

Perkins: I don't know. This is all along the line of trading out before morning. . . .

Roosevelt: Hello; this is Colonel Roosevelt.

Butler: Hello; this is Murray Butler.

Roosevelt: How do you do, President of Columbia College?

Butler: We have been having a very interesting time out here. . . . Now the situation in the Republican party is just this: The so-called [here Miss Kihm missed a phrase—probably "favorite sons"—Ed.] cannot hold their vote from Hughes much longer. The outlook now is that Hughes will be nominated on the first or second ballot in the morning. That is to me and a great many of us a desperate calamity. The fact of the matter, whether Mr. Hughes knows it or not, is that all the pussyfooters and pro-Germans in Chicago are for him, and that of itself has excited my suspicion.

Roosevelt: And he is not going to make any statement until after his nomination?

Butler: No, and then it will be futile. . . . Now I regard it as impossible to elect him, no matter who endorses him. I regard it as assuring four more years of this awful Wilson. I am most anxious—and I have a great many of our people in condition to talk sense—to find some way, if possible, to prevent Hughes's nomination, and there is only one way to prevent it, and that is to say to them that someone has

been found who is satisfactory to the Progressives and who has your support. . . .

Butler then made three suggestions: Elihu Root, Charles W. Fairbanks, who had been Roosevelt's Vice President and a senator from Indiana, and Philander C. Knox, a veteran of the Senate and of Cabinet posts. Of these Root was clearly the largest figure both in intellect and in experience, having served in the Senate and as secretary of state and of war. But he was over 65, and he was particularly hated by the Progressives for his cynical smothering of the Roosevelt forces in the 1912 Republican convention. Both Butler and Roosevelt realized he was hopeless as a compromise candidate. The others, lesser men, received serious consideration.

 "Mexico is our Balkan Peninsula and we will have to deal with it."

Butler: There is some talk of Fairbanks, whose record I am not familiar with but whose record with you I do know about. And then there is Knox, who has been little mentioned here.

Roosevelt: Let me interrupt with a word about Knox. I am devoted to Knox personally, but unfortunately he is just as responsible for this Mexican situation as the present Administration. [Roosevelt felt that Knox, as Taft's secretary of state, had been partially responsible for what Roosevelt considered the mishandling of the Mexican Revolution.—Ed.] . . . After peace the submarine episodes will be but a memory, but Mexico is our Balkan peninsula and we will have to handle it; and we will be met at every step in our condemnation of Wilson with what our candidate himself has done. Lodge will tell you that too.

Butler: What is there to be said in a general way about Fairbanks?

Roosevelt: . . . I really have a real liking for Fairbanks personally. He is to me a very much better man than Hughes, but I am horribly afraid that he will prove impossible to do anything with. . . . I need not tell you that I am in the same position you are. I have to get the Progressive convention to agree in the same way that you must get the Republican convention in agreement. Fairbanks I personally would like. . . . Would there be any chance of taking up an entirely new man?

Butler: I think it possible, although it might surprise them very much.

Roosevelt: . . . Now would there be a chance of taking up Leonard Wood?

Butler: I don't think there would be, for this reason: There would not be any objection to him personally, but it would not meet with the approval of the western and southwestern states. . . . In view of our preparedness program they would not approve of a military man. . . .

Roosevelt: Of course he would understand very speedily that the tariff and such matters were entirely outside his realm and would get on the Army and Navy question and Americanism at once. He wouldn't have to do as Brother Hughes will have to do—improvise. Would there be any possibility of putting Lodge across?

Butler: . . . I don't know what vote-getting qualities Lodge has.

Roosevelt: I don't myself; but he has the political habit and these men would get on with him. . . .

Butler: Suppose I have a talk with Perkins along the lines we have been talking? . . . Will you just hold the wire and I'll get Perkins? Sorry to have got you out of bed at this hour.

Roosevelt: Heavens and earth, man, don't speak of it. Look what you must have been doing all these nights while I have been lolling around doing nothing.

"I know Lodge's record like a book. He is just as straight as a string."

Roosevelt then reported to Perkins the main points of his conversation with Butler. Perkins rang off to confer with Butler, to whom he proposed the following plan: The Progressive leaders (presumably in Roosevelt's name) would draft a statement refusing to support Hughes. This statement could be pushed through the Progressive convention, however, only by coupling it with the nomination of Roosevelt, which the great mass of the delegates was hot to accomplish. After that the Progressives would adjourn, sending their anti-Hughes statement to the Republicans. Then the Republicans would have no choice but to accept Roosevelt if they wanted to win the election. "I want it distinctly understood," Perkins told Butler in explaining his scheme, "that if we do that you are going to say to your friends that it was we who saved them [from Hughes] and that you are not going to hold it up against us for nominating our man first." At 3:30 Butler left to confer with the other Republicans on the compromise committee, promising to let Perkins know before dawn if this course of action seemed feasible. Perkins called Roosevelt back and outlined the new plan.

Roosevelt: That is one of the most extraordinary things I have ever heard. I want to say right here, although you may not agree with me, that I am sure I was right in speaking of Wood and Lodge.

Perkins: I am sorry you mentioned Lodge. We are in the position, as it stands now, of not submitting any choice to those people except you. That is perfectly all right because they have never submitted anyone to us. . . . Still, I don't

like our record. Somebody might say that you should have suggested someone else. . . . [Yet Lodge] is the only man familiar with the international situation and one who could be agreed on by both conventions. Is there anything you can think of in Lodge's record that would be against that proposition?

Roosevelt: I know Lodge's record like a book. There has never been anything against it at any time, except, of course, George, that he does not have as advanced views as you and I.

Perkins: I think we could take care of that.

Roosevelt: We have, first of all, to deal with preparedness and Americanism, because they are questions of internal relations. Then foreign relations. [Lodge] is chairman of the Foreign Relations Committee. He is just as straight as a string. Do you want me to talk to Hiram Johnson?

Perkins: Not on your life; not for an hour or two.

Roosevelt: Then I won't say a word. I want to add this, if you will, George. Keep Hiram Johnson in touch with me so he won't fly off the handle and think I am neglecting him.

Perkins: Of course I'll do that, but at the right moment. . . . I think it was a very grave mistake to suggest Wood. He is not acceptable to anybody. He is a military man. It puts you in a bad light.

Roosevelt: It has been rejected and I will not follow it up at all. I am glad you have come to the conclusion to suggest Lodge. Fortunately, Lodge has voted for me on the second ballot, so that we can use that with our wild-eyed Progressive friends.

Perkins: I may want to call you up in the morning and get a statement from you giving your reasons why you support Lodge.

Roosevelt: From now on I will not go to bed.

Perkins: All right, I will call you pretty often.

Saturday, June 10
Butler evidently got an unfavorable response to Perkins' suggestion from his Republican colleagues, for he makes no mention of it in his memoirs and there is no further record of it in the transcript of the telephone conversations. The Republican members of the conference committee decided finally that Hughes could not be stopped and, making the best of the situation, agreed to present his name to the joint committee as their "compromise" candidate.

In the meantime Roosevelt worked on a message to the two conventions suggesting Lodge's name, while Perkins routed the Senator from his bed and got him to agree to accept if chosen. At a quarter to nine on Saturday morning Perkins was again on the phone with Roosevelt. The Colonel offered to come to Chicago to argue on behalf of Lodge if the nominations could be postponed until Monday, but that was clearly impossible.

When the compromise committee met again, the

Republicans offered Hughes as their choice. The three Progressives (Hiram Johnson and John M. Parker had dropped out in disgust when they learned that Roosevelt wanted them to support the conservative Lodge) excused themselves to think this over. Ruefully, Perkins called Oyster Bay.

Roosevelt: Now, did you read my letter [recommending Lodge] to them?

Perkins: In view of this I do not think we should deliver that. . . .

Roosevelt: Well, George, I am awfully sorry about that. . . . Of course I am not going to accept Mr. Hughes, and I am going to ask you to put my letter before that committee.

Perkins: . . . You understand, of course, that Johnson and Parker will not stand for the counter-proposition, so we will just turn it in as the major report of our committee, submitted to you. Perhaps we might just as well put it in as coming from you and not as coming from the committee.

Roosevelt: Put it right in as from me, that's right.

Several Progressives urged Roosevelt to reconsider his decision about the Lodge letter. One of these was Walter Brown, a conservative member of the Progressive National Committee.

Brown: Mr. Perkins wanted me to ask you if you had considered the fact that that letter would probably eliminate you from any further chance in that convention.

Roosevelt: . . . I have passed that stage. I have considered everything in connection with it. I wish that letter presented at once. . . .

Perkins himself made one last effort to bend the strong Roosevelt will.

Perkins: There are five or six of us here, discussing this situation. [We] feel that . . . it would be better not to turn in the Lodge letter now.

Roosevelt: I disagree with you. I considered that whole thing when I wrote that letter. I must request you definitely and at once to put that letter before the conferees.

*Against such a positive command no one could argue. Wearily, and with profound misgivings, Perkins ar-*ranged for the statement to be read to the two conventions. While he was doing so Roosevelt talked again with some of his more radical supporters. To former Governor Robert Bass of New Hampshire he explained his position with special clearness.*

Roosevelt: I do not ask our people to accept one of the burglars. I do not ask them to accept any man who isn't of the highest character and who does not stand absolutely square on the issues of today. I think Hughes has shown himself in the most contemptible possible light, and so I am not now asking any of our people to support him; that must be determined by events; but I do feel that if the Republicans are willing to do what I have asked, the Progressives should join with them. . . .

Bass: I believe the Republicans will nominate Hughes. We cannot accept a man whose position is totally unknown to us, and the only thing we can do is to place our nomination in your hands, to be held in trust and to do with as you see fit and in accordance with the things we have stood for.

Roosevelt: Well, Bob . . . you are proposing to put a very, very heavy burden on me. . . . We have got to see what the Progressive and Republican conventions do with my communication. . . .

The conventions acted as everyone but Roosevelt had expected they would act. When Perkins addressed the Progressives, his speech was continually interrupted by hoots and catcalls, and at his presentation of the names of Hughes and Lodge, "loud agonizing No's echoed through the hall." The Republicans listened phlegmatically to the reading of Roosevelt's suggestion and then proceeded to give Hughes the nomination at once, and unanimously at that. As soon as word of this reached the Progressives, they simply swept the protesting Perkins out of the way and nominated Roosevelt by acclamation.

This nomination was completed at 12:37 on Saturday afternoon. Less than ten minutes later the leaders were talking to Roosevelt again on the private wire. Different points of view were presented to him as to what he should do about the nomination, but it was

Roosevelt himself, speaking to Perkins, who made the decision.

Roosevelt: George, we have got to have our skirts absolutely clear. . . . And here is my thought: that I should answer them [the Progressive delegates] that if they wish a definite answer now I must refuse to accept and must ask them to nominate someone else; however, if they wish, and only if they wish, I am content to act as follows: that is, to turn over to the National Committee my conditional refusal to accept the nomination and run on a third ticket until the committee has had an opportunity to find out where Hughes stands. . . . Then, if the National Committee thinks Hughes's attitude is entirely satisfactory, they can so announce and no further action on my declination will be taken.

Perkins agreed and Roosevelt rang off to prepare a statement along these lines. While various drafts of his statement were being formulated and revised, he continued to talk with important Progressive delegates throughout the afternoon. Among them was his son.

Theodore, Jr.: Hello, father.
Roosevelt: Hello, my son.
Theodore, Jr.: In the first place, in connection with that statement of yours, I think we want to be particularly careful, if we are going to support Hughes as we probably will, that we say nothing that will reflect on him in our statements here. . . . The statement reads as if you did not approve of Hughes. You don't, of course.
Roosevelt: Of course I will support him, but I will not be responsible for him.

Later Roosevelt talked with Hiram Johnson. The terrible-tempered fire-eater now seemed resigned to Roosevelt's withdrawing in favor of Hughes.

Johnson: Hello, Colonel.
Roosevelt: How is the Honorable Hiram? . . . Are you in a pliable and compromising mood?
Johnson: . . . I feel this way, Colonel. I feel that the thing is coming to the point where you have to quit the nomination. I would really prefer to perform the operation today and not have you bothered and troubled. . . .
Roosevelt: My own feeling is just as you said a year ago —that I will go fishing; you said that you anticipated that in this campaign you and I would like to go fishing. I think my fishing trip has begun. If you will remember, you said then that it was not right to ask me to run and you did not regard it as right to ask you to run.
Johnson: I felt that way then and feel that way now. I think it would be a crime to ask you to run unless there is some great national thing that demands it.

★ ★ ★

The rest of the story is anticlimactic. Hughes's statements proved satisfactory to a majority of the Progressive National Committee, and on June 26 they voted to support him. Roosevelt had already made up his own mind, and on June 28 he dined with the candidate, formally making his peace. Hughes, of course, was beaten by Wilson in a close race, featured by Hughes's loss of California because of a misunderstanding with the influential Hiram Johnson.

The chief result of the dramatic developments of the two conventions was the utter destruction of the Progressive party. Its chief undertaker was Theodore Roosevelt. Had he so willed, it would have gone on, to defeat no doubt in 1916, but to no one knows what future developments. As it was, its members either returned with Roosevelt to the Republican camp or switched to Woodrow Wilson and the Democrats.

No doubt some of Roosevelt's supporters thought him a traitor. It is true that he and men like Perkins made cynical use of the Progressive convention, treating it, as Professor George Mowry has said, "as a stalking horse and a trading horse." But Roosevelt was utterly convinced that Wilson, because of his neutralism in the European war, had to be defeated if the national honor were to be preserved. And, if Roosevelt wanted the nomination himself at the beginning of the conventions, no one can deny that at the end he made a serious and unselfish effort to find a satisfactory compromise between himself and Hughes. His judgment in pushing Lodge was faulty, but his motive was neither insincere, nor corrupt, nor selfish. Nor did he at any time try to deceive those of his supporters who wanted him to run as a Progressive.

History may judge his actions to have been misguided, foolish, even tragic, when one considers that the destruction of the Progressive party made the Republican party a stronghold of super-conservatism for at least a generation. But history has the benefit of hindsight. Things might well have worked out differently. Had Roosevelt not died in 1919 he would almost certainly have been the Republican candidate in 1920, for by supporting Hughes he had rehabilitated himself with the party regulars. He would have won in 1920, and at the very least, the nation would have been spared the sorry antics of the Harding Administration. In any case, this much is beyond argument: throughout the battle of 1916 Roosevelt did what he thought was in the best interests of the nation and of those principles in which he sincerely believed.

Professor John A. Garraty, a member of the Columbia University history department, is the author of biographies of Henry Cabot Lodge, Silas Wright, and Woodrow Wilson. He has written a number of articles for AMERICAN HERITAGE.

Sketches from the Vanishing Landscape

Drawings by ERIC SLOANE

Artist Eric Sloane lives in Connecticut and roams about America seeking to recapture the look and the feel of a countryside which is inexorably changing. On these two pages are presented some of his sketches, which depict things that seem to be symbols of a bygone age. "Such symbols," he writes, "preserved by a longing tethered to the past, whether it be a distant church spire, a gracious bend in an old road, or just a reverence for trees and the old ways of farm life, become more important as they vanish. But if some good things are destined to be only memories, we can still be thankful that though they have disappeared the memory remains."

These sketches are reproduced from Mr. Sloane's recent book, *Our Vanishing Landscape*. It is reprinted by permission of the publishers, Wilfred Funk, Inc. Copyright, 1955, by Wilfred Funk, Inc.

The Blacksmith Shop
1800

Butchering Shed

Ohio 1815
Pennsylvania

The Outdoor Oven
1820
Pa.

Wash house 1840

Spring house 1850

Barns are at their best in Winter.
The snow blankets the unheated parts, yet melts over the Stalls, from Animal Heat

.. or breaks the back of the weak barn

In Summer, the Barn becomes closer to the landscape ...

the old barns blending with the landscape as only weathering wood can

DIME NOVELS

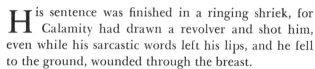

This art form dismayed the moralist, delighted small boys,

and somehow put its own stamp on the American legend

By MARY NOEL

His sentence was finished in a ringing shriek, for Calamity had drawn a revolver and shot him, even while his sarcastic words left his lips, and he fell to the ground, wounded through the breast.

" 'So much for your lyin', you miserable whelp!' the girl cried, wrought suddenly to a high pitch of anger. 'If I was dishonored once, by one such as you, no man's defiling touch has reached me since . . .'

"Now she dashed away through the narrow gulch, catching with delight long breaths of the perfume of flowers which met her nostrils at every onward leap of her horse, piercing the gloom of the night with her dark lovely eyes, searchingly, lest she should be surprised; lighting a cigar at full motion . . ."

Attracted by the glowing panatela, four desperadoes leap from ambush, Colts flashing, but this vintage cover girl simply rides them down, amid "howls of pain and rage, and curses too vile to repeat here," and gallops off unscathed, whooping like a Comanche.

Here, in capsule form, we have the prototype of the classic dime novel scene, with a fair sampling of its normal ingredients—action and sudden death, virtue preserved and ambush outwitted, rough talk

and high-flown writing. For those who appreciate the rarer spices in this vanished literary cupboard, there are finer points—the complicated syntax, delivered at a dead run by the leading character; the anticlimactical epithet ("whelp"); the new twist on the fate-worse-than-death; the totally unexplained villains; the note of pious forbearance by the author ("curses too vile to repeat here"); the difficult but admirable feat ("lighting a cigar at full motion"). That Calamity can do this while also bending both nostrils to the heady prairie flora only goes to show that the killer behind the gun is really a girl at heart. Characterization in the dime novel was terse. This, for example, is the entire description of one Silas Rodgers: ". . . a man honest and upright after the fashion of frontiersmen. He was brave, and had shot two or three in brawls, but was not regarded as quarrelsome."

The early dime novels, like the Beadle at left, dealt—however fancifully—with real folk heroes. As competition brought gaudy colored covers and slightly larger type, the authors turned to fiction. Yet a great many boys have been reared in the fond delusion that Frank Merriwell, for instance, was some sort of flesh-and-blood hero in the dim football history of Yale.

During the half century of the popularity of the dime novel, from 1860 to about 1910, millions of boys, vigorous parental opposition notwithstanding, luxuriated in this imaginative world. They took their reading straight, without benefit of "comics," and in the closest, dimmest, smallest possible print—although even this could be reduced in size if, at the end of the yarn, the cascade of words outran the space, so that the final episodes might well be visible only to those equipped with magnifying glasses. The only visual lure was the cover picture.

The problem of the age, apparently, was not why Johnny couldn't read, but how to stop him. Dime novel vocabulary was never simplified to suit a boy's "age level." An academy "derived its appellation" from a nearby lake. A man never crossed a plain—he "traversed" it. The silvery beams of the moon did not fall upon a face, but upon a "pain-distorted countenance," which was "rendered doubly repulsive by the red streaks where the mingled blood and brains had oozed from the shattered skull." Or, in another field of action: "Miss Howard patronized the elevated road to her home in the Bronx."

Dime novels, of course, were not novels at all and during most of their long vogue cost only a nickel, forced down by competition among the publishers and from the candy interests. While many of the central figures in later days were fictional, the early ones were supposedly taken from life—Daniel Boone, Pontiac, Mad Anthony Wayne, Custer, Billy the Kid—and the tales were put forward unblushingly as gospel truth, down to the last bloodstained pool of gore.

Belief, apparently, was widespread, no matter how strange the speech which emerged from the grim lips of the actors, who were capable of such interesting phrases as "Hark, pard!" Anyone under stress was ready at the drop of a hat to utter a mouthful. Consider one bride-to-be, observing a posse closing in on her groom: "Those dreadful men, of which there are so many, who I believe would murder you; they may kill you at any time!"

Or Billy the Kid, rallying his men: "Hurrah! Hurrah! my brave lads. Strike hard and strike home. Hurl back the fiends, sweep them from the face of the earth!"

Or a Texas Ranger, who has just completed the hanging of two Mexicans, whose sin seems to be a matter of mere birth: "Hang there! vile varlets! Hang, I say, and idly dangle above the mad waters, which shall soon be contaminated with thy loathsome carcasses! Hang higher than Haman, thou base, degraded sons of a semi-monthly, revolutionized, conglomerated, amalgamated, bastard republic! Hang!"

("Yer sling the dang'est, biggest words I ever knowed any one else tew let loose," remarks an admiring friend.)

If racial tolerance presented no problem to authors who classed red men, "greasers" and Latins in general with other wild game, body disposal was an acute one, constantly recurring. The writers approached it with clichés at the ready. For example, some Texas Rangers come upon "the swollen, mutilated corpse of a man, covered with blood and clotted gore. . . . Upon the dead, sun-bloated corpse . . . was his little son, seven years of age," and the lad was oozing enough blood for one thrice his years. It was "in horrible contrast to the white, delicate skin, made more livid by the loss of his life-giving fluid." A paragraph or two on the approaching buzzards, circling coyotes, buzzing flies and crawling maggots, and the boy expires, probably in despair, without ever speaking a word. How his age and relationship to the dead man are established never comes to light. The twin burial is attended, among others, by several rescued girls who avert their eyes.

Eye-averting, next to being abducted or getting confined to asylums by crooked guardians, was the favorite

"Stop! look to your own honor! I stand without a blemish!"

advertisers to support publications aimed at a pocket-money audience. The dime novel successors have been the pulp magazines, with a slightly more adult appeal. The youngsters themselves have been placated with the movies, television, and the comics.

Like the comics today, dime novels were attacked by the moralists—there was a scarcity of psychologists in those days. Anthony Comstock called the paper-backs "devil-traps for the young." As a precaution, the publishers required their writers to insert a discreet number of Sunday school platitudes that could be forked out to captious critics upon occasion. Yet the youngster who surveyed the titles could scarcely have found them repressive in spirit. Perhaps *The Doomed Dozen; or Dolores the Danite's Daughter, A Romance of Border Trails and Mormon Mysteries* appealed to his fancy; or *Cibita John, the Prickly Pear from Cactus Plains; or Red Hot Times at Ante-Bar*. In any case, he would find *Desperate Duke, the Guadaloupe 'Galoot'; or, the Angel of Alamo City* far removed from the imprisoning doors of the schoolroom and the monotonous regularity of his early bedtime hour. And

when he finished this tale he could begin *Stuttering Sam, the Whitest Sport from Santa Fe; or How the Hummer from Hummingbird Feathered His Nest.* The dime novel did not deny him the lawful right of his young manhood to a loud guffaw each and every time the worthy scout remarked, "You'll have ter excuse me a few minutes . . . gentlemen, ef ye please, for it's a scandulous fac' thet I haven't hed but six good solid snifters this hull blessed morning!"

When some of the dime novel authors were diverted from "westerns" to city detective stories, all of the moralists were up in arms. They now felt that a villain who pursued his women down rocky gorges or roasted his captive millionaire over a slow fire in the wide open air was a healthier sort than the villain whose activities were confined to windowless dance-hall chambers and dank, fetid, underground vaults. Be that as it may, the western hero had only to change his accouterments and lingo to become a detective hero, but the dime novel detective story was in no sense a predecessor of the modern "mystery." From

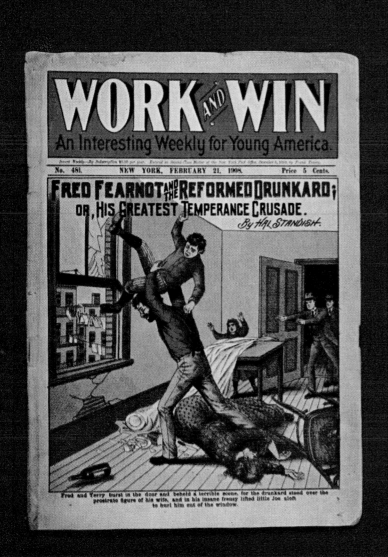

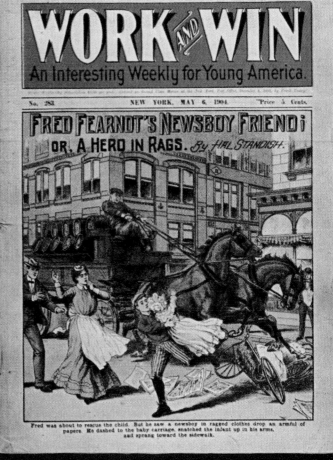

the very start it was perfectly clear to both detective and reader who had done it. The problem was simply whether the detective would catch the criminals, or would the criminals catch the detective. On the detective's side were physical strength and, in an emergency, the forces of the law. On the criminals' side were craft and imagination.

Criminals were always provided with a variety of improvised prisons—ranging from iron cells in the holds of ships to scientifically constructed torture chambers deep underground. Nevertheless, there was always a way out, especially for an inventive operative like Nick Carter. He was capable of making his escape past thirteen masked ruffians and one "radiant creature" named Elmora who carried a jeweled stiletto, through a succession of triply bolted doors separated by long passages underground, up an elevator which was guarded by a man leaning over the open hatchway with his finger on the rifle trigger, and out into the dark and vacant street. Nick then figured he had no time to go for the police, so he quickly changed his disguise and returned by himself the way he had come

out. These particular criminals were given to cowls and robes of silver and gold and blue and white, and to marching to the chant of the radiant Elmora accompanied by an automatic organ. They had a torture chamber lined with skulls through whose eyes shone ghastly red lights, and filled with skeletons bending over the intense fire of an open furnace. Over the center of the furnace hung a tackle and sling, and on one side of the room was a chair, equipped with steel fingers to sink into the skull of the occupant. To Nick this was practically a playroom.

Nick Carter was not the only dime novel hero who was heroic in so many different ways that he could be carried through hundreds of stories, year after year. Since all the central characters were stereotypes, there was really no reason for changing their names, anyway. The one essential was to change the setting. Before drawing up a contract with Gilbert Patten for the Frank Merriwell stories, his publisher specified that Frank must travel. Upon finishing school he must come into sufficient money to escape the monotony of even the most exalted of professions, and be left free

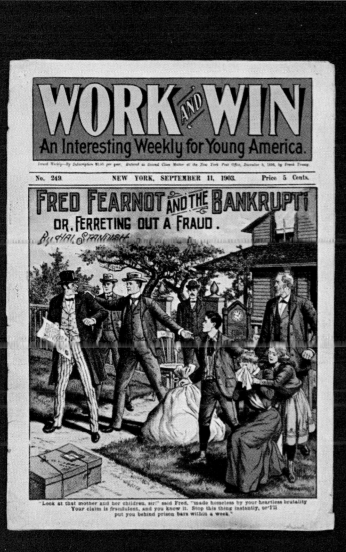

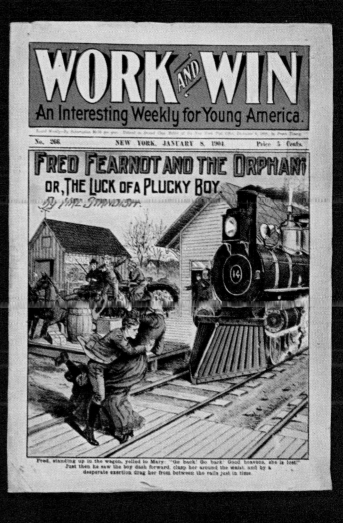

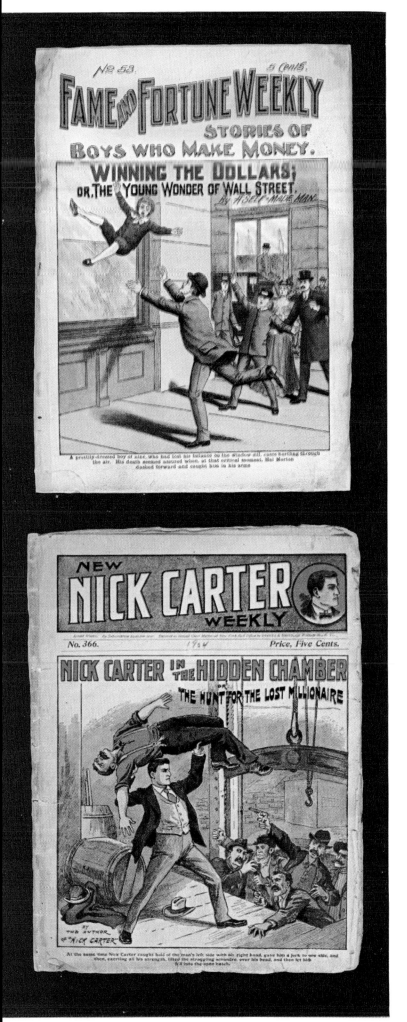

to pursue his hobby of rescuing young ladies in all parts of the world. Both he and his author lasted out some 900 of these stories.

A competing publisher produced a pale and prosaic imitation of Frank Merriwell who called himself Fred Fearnot. He was run through 1,382 issues, over 28 years. Fred was a headline hunter, pure and simple. At one time he was "Battling for the Boers"; at another, hobnobbing with the Sultan on the Island of Sulu. A little later he was, like Teddy Roosevelt, giving advice to the Kaiser in his Royal Palace. Among his more humdrum activities were playing a part in the circus he owned, running a ranch, and assisting temperance crusades. Every now and then he was forced to return to New York for a few days to look after his highly speculative stocks.

Frank Reade, Jr., a scientific type, invented his own novel means of travel in the shape of a submarine sea serpent, an amphibious device known as the Electric Boomerang—especially equipped for crossing the heart of Africa in the face of savage tribes—an electric tricycle, a steam man and a steam team, an electric snow-cutter and numerous flying machines. So equipped he could rescue one fair female from the clutches of a polar bear one day, and her twin sister from the savages of Darkest Africa the next day. Rescuing, rather than pure science, was Frank's primary business in life. He was always glad enough when his machine was accidentally wrecked at the end of the story, with all hands saved. In this way he could turn his mind to inventing and building a new and better machine.

A dime novel hero might somehow, in the midst of his rough surroundings, have about him a mysterious air of gentlemanliness. In this case the eternally surprised reader would find his hero ultimately restored to the fame and fortune which he had lost through the machinations of the villain. On the other hand, he might frankly work—or fight—his way upward from rags to riches. Even in the Nineteenth Century this Horatio Alger theme had provoked a scolding from the moralists because of its lack of realism in dealing with the problems facing youth in modern industrial society. In the latter days of the dime novel, around 1900, this particular moral defect was remedied by means of an opportunism which must have caused the Alger hero to turn over in his fictional grave. An orphan discovered by the wealthy Fred Fearnot was taught a trick he could do with a chicken. With very little urging the orphan picked up a chicken, made a tour of the local taverns, bet repeatedly on his ability to hoodoo the chicken, and cleared five hundred dollars. When a lady protested that he had been gambling, the orphan solemnly explained: "No, ma'am, I never touched a card. It was not a game of chance at all. It was betting on a fact." Thus early was it established that Our Hero was merely an enterprising Financier, not a scheming Gambler.

Getting a start in the world of dime novel finance required, almost inevitably, a rescue. The messenger boys of Wall Street, 488 of them in as many issues of *Fame and Fortune Weekly*, seemed always to be passing when a young heiress was facing death on her runaway horse, a child needed snatching from in front of a speeding horsecar, or a millionaire was going down for the third time. It was almost a matter of routine, suggesting that the rescue was only a symbol for the ability to be in the right place at the right time, an essential virtue which any businessman will recognize. As the "Young Wonder of Wall Street" himself remarked: "I'm $4,000 to the good, and it's all due to the fact that Master Jack Meredith happened to lean too far out of his papa's window and took a tumble in consequence, just as I was coming along in time to catch him. It's better to be born lucky than rich."

The Young Wonder's method of improving upon his opportunities was to eavesdrop. Whenever, in a ferry, or in a crowded train, or at the baseball stadium, he overheard two brokers discussing a tip, or two directors explaining how they were going to boom their company's stock, then unload and buy back at a low figure, the Wonder was all ears. Until such propitious moments, he cautiously kept his funds in a safe-deposit vault. But when he did invest, he staked his all—he never stultified his heroic leanings with a diversified portfolio. As his profits mounted quickly to $80,000, he continued to report regularly for his messenger boy duties. Only when he reached a quarter-million did he resign and go into business for himself, presumably employing messenger boys of his own.

The dime novel worshipped success, as it exalted danger and adventure; it instilled many of our subconscious habits of thought. It was a common thing, cheap to buy, and like most common things, rarely preserved. But those few yellowed thrillers that survive have more than a mere nostalgic interest, for they teach us a great deal about our nationalistic ways and our creed of self-reliance. To this day they reflect, however crudely, the American spirit of an earlier and perhaps more innocent age.

Mary Noel was educated at Radcliffe and Columbia University. She is the author of Villains Galore *(Macmillan, 1954), about the era of the popular story weekly, and teaches history at the Polytechnic Institute, San German, Puerto Rico.*

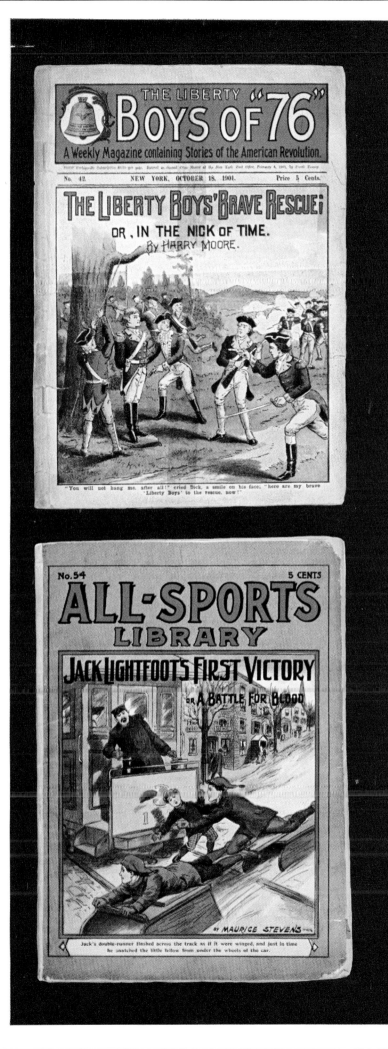

It was an innocent man's war, a simple matter for Americans, despite the millions of Europeans who lay dead already between Vilna and the Marne. We entered the tragedy at the beginning of the fifth act, like off-stage soldiers in a play; and we entered singing. Woodrow Wilson had given us our simple theme: Kaiser Bill was a villain; and we marched to make the world safe for democracy.

Our weapons were simply modifications of earlier ones. Substitute the flimsy aircraft of the day with their remarkable pilots for the balloonist-professors of the Civil War, and General Pershing could have used Lee or Grant as a corps commander after routine briefing. We had the bolt-action rifle, and a bayonet that is still unchanged. Then there were machine guns, a medley of them. There were some grenades and mortars and, for artillery, the French gave us the seventy-five, which our own crews, in true American fashion, subjected to a cadence of firing that both astonished and alarmed the French. They supplied us with tanks, too; and for a large part of our two big pushes, crewed them for us. But for his set pattern of tactics, General Pershing took to open warfare.

We had begun with some exercises in trench warfare along quiet sectors; but Pershing, in his first full-dress conference with Generalissimo Foch, announced his intention of reducing the formidable German salient at Saint-Mihiel, an engineering masterpiece that had repulsed both British and French for four years. And he would take the salient with doughboys in tin hats and rolled leggings, all moving forward in frontiersman style, whether they

Charles Meurer depicted the World War I field kit of a U.S. Army officer—complete with spurs, a lighted cigarette, and the canteen that was still standard issue a quarter century later—in a trompe l'oeil *painting called* Memories.

were farm boys from Iowa or pushcart lads from Manhattan.

It was largely, at the outset, a singing war devoted to polite songs. There were croaks about K-K-K-Katy, Beautiful Katy, who would find a man waiting beside the k-k-k-kitchen door. Then some sang that it was a long way to Berlin, "but we'll get there, Uncle Sam will find a way." There was some anticipation of the joys awaiting a man on leave: "How you Gonna Keep 'em Down on the Farm, after They've Seen Paree?" Then there was a great marching song, "Over There," which the lads overseas changed to "Underwear," with some unprintable allusions to the long drawers furnished by the quartermaster's department. But the song of songs was "Mademoiselle from Armentières," and many a platoon waited for the wit of the team to fashion new versions of that young lady's extraordinary versatility and prowess. I recall that, as a young lieutenant, my first platoon had a whole series of verses on the Mademoiselle describing the nine months of gestation in great physiological detail, terminating with the arrival in the world of a little marine. They sang these verses with great good will until one afternoon we marched to its cadences past a garden wall, unaware of the fact that our battalion commander was giving a tea party to some ladies of the *haute noblesse* behind it.

General Pershing made his declaration as to the Saint-Mihiel salient in September, 1917. He was exactly one year in preparing for the day when his men, a new army green in many divisions, would go forward with rifle and bayonet and fulfill his mission. In the winter of 1918 we had some troops manning trenches in quiet sectors while General Pershing steadfastly refused to piecemeal his troops, battalion by battalion, into British and French units. It is a tribute to his character

THE WAR TO END WAR

We went into it singing, and forty years—which included a second world war—have not dimmed its terrible gallantry

By LAURENCE STALLINGS

that he could withstand the entreaties of men like Lloyd George and Clemenceau, formidable antagonists. A casual raid or two by the Germans, catching some of us napping, meanwhile set about a wagging of heads in London and Paris, with the happiest of smiles in Berlin. Then the First Division staged its *divertissement* at Cantigny, and the real American war was on.

The Germans sustained their first true shock on the Marne around Château-Thierry, where Pershing threw in whole divisions for the first time, to bolster a shattered French line; but it was not his kind of a war. It was largely defensive, with occasional passages to the offensive, as witness the flamboyant charges of the Marine Brigade in Belleau Wood. It was the first true lesson for us, and the Germans administered it with great severity. I recall leading a digging party back from the vicinity of a town called Torcy, and watching a German sausage balloon ascending into the dawn sky. I took to the woods, hearing myself cursed by men swarming through brambles to follow. They were silent when we skirted a sunken road, for the soldiers there, grotesque in their attitudes of death, were still warm from a salvo directed by that balloon. We were new, we were ignorant, all of us; it was a matter of degree, but not of kind. And the Germans were teaching us.

No longer would the British and French ask for battalions to be brigaded into their war-weary troops. They would ask for divisions. In the July and August that followed, the requests were continuous, and battle streamers fly from many of our flags with the names of actions only the men who fought them will remember. Who recalls Foch's great counterattack at Soissons? The bloody gallantry at Blanc Mont? The Ourcq River, a little stream where a poet named Joyce Kilmer died? Pershing would lend these divisions, and by September recover enough of them to command an army of half a million men, his own men, with many of his divisions now battle-worthy.

The temper of the singing men with the wooden guns was changing. Hospitals were filling with too many their buddies would not forget—and there were no "miracle" drugs in that war. There must have been little difference between the hospital where Oliver Wendell Holmes found his son after Antietam, and a tent I recall somewhere near the vicinity of La-Ferte-Sous-Jarre. It was mainly a gangrene tent, where some of us suffered from that torment. In those days the commander of our brigade's machine-gun battalion sat bolt upright, quietly smoking away his agony. A lieutenant I had trained with would emerge from his delirium to apologize for the noise he knew he must have been making. There was no sulfa, no penicillin, to still the air. There was only morphine sulfate, and those who survived that tent had a steep cliff to climb before they could rid themselves of morphine's toxic baggage.

The first glimpse of German prisoners, those fellows Woodrow Wilson told us we were not making war against, was always a pleasant experience for green troops. Tanks stood by, hacking open tins of bully beef to see other men, trembling in *Feldgrau*, devour food scorned by the lads from Des Moines and Seattle. As the hospitals filled, as new divisions suffered from the accomplished deviltry of the veteran Germans, this attitude would change. Moreover, there was one provocation unknown in the Second World War. It was poison gas. It was everywhere. Gas had been introduced in secrecy by the Germans, but they failed to win a war by its surprise use. Time went on, and both sides possessed it. Many a platoon leader would strip down his men to find them lobster-pink at armpit and groin, eyes swollen and half-shut, breath hardcaught.

Meanwhile Saint-Mihiel's salient, a thorn in the Allied breast, was reduced by an American army with an element of surprise and a great *élan* in the attack. The first trial of true strength had been won; the great trial, the Argonne, lay ahead. Had it been left to Pershing, the name of Argonne would never have flown from a regimental staff. He had wished to push on from his victory at Saint-Mihiel, but the British protested to Foch. They had known a great day themselves on August 8 at Amiens, "the black day," Ludendorff said, "of the German army in the history of the war." The British under Haig wanted Pershing to reduce pressure on their right flank. They had begun asking for battalions, and progressed to requests for divisions, and now they wanted armies. Specifically, they wanted Pershing, who now commanded two American armies, to recapture the Argonne forest where for four years the Germans, who possess great skill in the use of fortifications, had been busy with their engineers devising tunnels and traps calculated to discourage the most aggressive opponent. Pershing, for once tractable, agreed to take the Argonne.

The saga of the Argonne is epitomized in the story of the Lost Battalion, those tough unfortunates from a New York division whose battalion commander had pushed forward into a trap. My own thoughts of it are colored by the memory of a wounded lieutenant from that outfit who was placed in a bed next to mine. He had lain for some days on the raw earth of the Argonne with multiple wounds and little care. His broken jaws were wired, front teeth extracted so he might sip nourishment through a tube. Both arms were broken and plastered across his chest as in prayer. Both legs had been fractured, and they too were in plaster. He could speak through clenched teeth, and he could wiggle the toes on his right foot. Thus accoutered, he entered the life of the hospital ward, which was teeming, after hours, with vigorous dice games and Martinique rum. He soon won a considerable sum in the dice games.

The lieutenant made his own casts of the dice, a brother officer placing the dice beneath the swollen toes for the lieutenant to wiggle, meanwhile holding a mirror so that he might "read 'em and weep." He soon found that the raw *rhum Negrito,* sucked through his glass tube, was too fiery on his jaw wounds; and so a rubber drainage tube was acquired, being inserted in his nostril toward the esophagus, well past the fractured area. Then with a fellow lieutenant holding a small funnel, he was able to drink along with the rest. To me, he was a fitting ambassador from the Argonne, representative of the million who went forward into that vast maze of caves and traps, of machine guns and cannon. My friend with the rubber tube and the swollen toes showed emotion only once, when he wept one night because he was unable to get to his feet and fight a brother officer from whom, he erroneously believed, he had suffered an insult.

The troops in the Argonne were not all of veteran caliber. Some divisions were relieved, but mainly they moved forward, halted at times by their own ineptitude, or by the sheer severity of the defense. They were humorists still. A carrier pigeon could arrive back at the pigeon wagons bearing the message: "I'm tired carrying this damned bird." The man who wrote that line was not far from the one in the Maine regiment that held the line at Gettysburg, a private who, when asked by his West Point colonel why he was chewing hardtack in the ranks, could reply: "For the juice, sir. I'm very fond of the juice."

A generation freshly memoried in the deeds of the Second World War cannot appreciate the simplicity of the first one. A brilliant defense at Château-Thierry, some fine bolstering counterattacks in the intervening two months before the reduction of Saint-Mihiel, and the great grinding sacrifices of the Argonne: that was the tale. It was told by correspondents still of the Richard Harding Davis tradition: it had no simple chroniclers such as Ernie Pyle. The result was that, when the men came home and began to write realistically of their experiences, the public was shocked at literary and dramatic works that seem, at this far-off date, rather pale by contrast with the works that followed the later war. These were true shockers;

but Pyle and his school of writing had prepared a public for them. A man will read of that first one, even in the most realistic postwar works that followed it, and have difficulty in capturing the simplicity of its mood. The gulf between the two, the abyss of sentiment, is simply unfathomable.

When the Armistice came on November 11, 1918, the victors gave their exultant cries and set out scrounging for *vin rouge*; but not so General Pershing. He had sent a regiment across the fire-raked pontoons of the Meuse the day before, for he wanted, like the boys in the song, to go to Berlin. Some years later he could say to a friend of mine, who was his officer of the guard on another occasion: "They don't know they were beaten in Berlin, and it will all have to be done all over again." The temper of his troops was such that they would have pressed forward at his word, as witness that regiment, with Armistice talk filling the air, fighting across the Meuse at Sedan.

In both wars there was, beyond the death and the mutilation, the heroism and sacrifice, an American feeling of idealism. The literature following the wake of both wars would deny this; writers try to single out the variation from the norm. The coward seems more interesting, in pedestrian literature, than the heroic figures chosen, say, by the Greeks in their great age. Even the films following the first war that were concerned with the gallantries of the aviators will show, on examination, that it is the boy who is frightened who holds the interest of the writer. It was a long while before Hemingway, in his *Farewell to Arms*, could examine a man who forsook the war, turning his back upon carnage, simply because he wanted no more of it. The play, *What Price Glory?* was attacked by many high-ranking officers; one of its authors was even subjected to the possibility of a court martial by President Coolidge; yet it could be said of its characters what Froissart said of the Plantagenets: "Whatever may have been their faults, there was not a coward among them."

One of the remarkable features of the Civil War was that, though peopled by great figures, it was followed by no great writing; only when Stephen Crane— a generation later, having never been near a battle himself—produced *The Red Badge of Courage*, were the men of its armies adequately pictured. In its way, the First World War left no great works either; some fine ones perhaps, but nothing like the work that Tolstoi, a generation after it, created from the wreck of Napoleon's dream; nothing like Stendhal's description of the field of Waterloo in *The Charterhouse of Parma*. Yet the men who returned from the first one were unhampered, uncensored; above all they were vic-

torious They could not set down, however, their deepest feelings about it, any more than could the men who shook hands at Appomattox. The best works of literature following the First World War were from the pens of men like Sinclair Lewis, who makes little mention of it, and Eugene O'Neill, who seems unaware of it. Both of them won the Nobel prize.

It may be a characteristic of the English-speaking races; for certainly the finest English work written during the period of the Napoleonic wars, when England was frequently on the ropes, is Miss Jane Austen's *Pride and Prejudice*. Written in an English garrison town, with one of its principals an officer in the army, it refers only on its last page to the war—or rather "the restoration of peace." And so it was with our war. There were no chroniclers, no painters, no writers reaching greatness because of it.

In Stendhal's account of Waterloo, in which he is actually adapting his own recollections as a French staff officer at Bautzen, where Ney failed to take an advantage and confusion followed, he restricts his field of vision to that enjoyed by a single green recruit. Actually, the men of Belleau Wood, of Saint-Mihiel, of the Argonne, saw little of their war, either. The nature of the terrain, the squirrel-hunting tactics, made it impossible to get anything like a big picture of the scene. What could a platoon leader see of it? If he was knocked down and his face bloodied by a grenade, as he scrambled forward to regain his line he might see his own platoon; a flank of the one on the right wavering temporarily because its lieutenant was knocked down and dying; and beyond the line a few of the enemy heads sighting down the barrels of light machine guns. There were isolated instances of the panorama such as must have been vouchsafed Andrew Jackson's men at New Orleans, where behind mud ramparts the fog rose above meadowland full-dressed in British redcoats, echeloned and glinting as they moved forward toward the rifles of the Kentuckians and the Tennesseans.

Thomas Mann says somewhere that nothing is so remote, so difficult to recapture, as the immediate past. It must be that way with our First World War. The men who fought it are grandfathers, their own sons recalling a far more complex affair. And no anthologist can ever bring back the full body of it; though like all wars it carries thoughts too deep for tears.

Laurence Stallings, a marine veteran of two world wars, is the co-author of one of the most popular plays of the American stage, What Price Glory? *and the editor of a picture history of the First World War.*

A WAR PORTFOLIO BY AMERICAN ARTISTS

For a World War I America, Harvey Dunn's steel-helmeted and khaki-clad machine gunner (above) was the heroic prototype of the conscript warrior; just as Kerr Eby's painting of massed infantry marching to the front in the Saint-Mihiel offensive of September, 1918, (below) symbolized a conflict that for private soldier and general alike became somber and incomprehensible.

"LAFAYETTE,
WE ARE HERE!"

America's mobilization, once under way, was rapid. In spite of the ever-present U-boat menace, fast convoys like the one shown in Burnell Poole's painting (above) ferried more than 2,000,000 men to France by November, 1918. Pushed in four years to the limits of their endurance, the Allies welcomed the Americans as their deliverers. The frenzied exchange between doughboys leaving for the front and the citizens of a Paris suburb (upper right) was a scene often repeated in the last year of the war. Gradually the Americans took their place in the trench system that stretched from the North Sea to Switzerland; like Dunn's sentry (right), with Mills bombs and potato mashers close by, the newcomers stared uneasily across no man's land, and prepared for their first taste of a brutal, molelike warfare in which the capture of a few dozen yards was reckoned as a smashing victory.

A GALLERY OF

Two Congressional Medal of Honor winners were painted by Joseph Cummings Chase. Sergeant Alvin York (far left) wiped out a battalion of 35 machine guns singlehanded; Samuel Woodfill (left), whom General Pershing called "the outstanding soldier in the A.E.F.," was cited for a similar feat in the Argonne.

A.E.F. artist Dunn sketched German prisoners and American wounded streaming back from the front lines during the Meuse-

FIGHTING MEN

Chase also painted Douglas MacArthur (right) and General John J. ("Black Jack") Pershing (far right). Decorated for his courage in action, and twice wounded, MacArthur was a division commander at thirty-eight. Pershing, as leader of the American Expeditionary Forces, refused to scatter it among the other Allied troops.

Argonne offensive of October, 1918. In these gaunt faces reflecting war's horror, it is difficult to tell victor from vanquished.

Above: Standing over the body of a fallen comrade, a dough-
boy fires at the enemy in Dunn's sketch of street combat.

A Château-Thierry street barricade (below) was painted by
W. J. Aylward. Here we won our first major engagement.

"AND WE WON'T
COME BACK
TILL IT'S OVER
OVER THERE"

From the first reckless encounters at Château-Thierry in June, 1918, through the last dreadful days of the Meuse-Argonne offensive, when the German line finally cracked, the Americans acquitted themselves brilliantly; but the 48,000 killed in battle that they left behind testified to the high price of their courage. The scene at left, painted by W. J. Aylward, was typical of many such farewells on the battlefields of France. Back home the nation waited jubilantly for the boys to return. The march of the visiting French Blue Devils down Fifth Avenue in May, 1918 (above), painted by George Luks, set the tone for the gaudy American victory parades still to come.

Homer painted this picture of himself and two friends sketching the endlessly changing light patterns made by scudding clouds over the White Mountains.

Before painting his famous seascapes,

Winslow Homer recorded a golden time which has almost

passed from the American scene

NEW ENGLAND
Summer

By RICHARD M. KETCHUM

It was the afternoon of America.

As the Nineteenth Century turned slowly into its final quarter, the life most New Englanders knew was that of the small town or the farm. In their land of long winters, the most precious time was summer when the smells, the sounds, and silences of nature were all the more acute for being crowded into so brief a span. All the world had an early-morning freshness, school was out, and ahead of every child there stretched the limitless vista of summer.

Beneath the shading elms and maples of Main Street were white houses in perverse alignment and behind them big, comfortable yards sprinkled with apple trees and honeysuckle, weathered sheds, and squeaky rope swings that lifted a child high above the vegetable patch to command, for an instant, the hills and woods beyond. Out in the meadows, insects droned their course from daisy to black-eyed Susan and boys tramped through tall grass toward still, secret pools where the big trout lay. Here and on the hilltops, where little ginghamed girls swung through forgotten clearings, looking for blueberries, only the far-off note of the dinner horn was a link with reality.

This was a world of wagons and green apples, of lemonade in tall, cool, earthenware crocks, of chicken sounds and cowbells, and dogs who wandered into church to scratch and be snickered at. There was time to laze on the warm earth, smelling the grass smell, wondering if a real agate marble was worth the trade of a jackknife with a broken blade or if the blackberry pie was for supper.

Not far from this world, but not for a moment part of it, were the resorts and hotels, the porticoed watering places of summer people. From all parts of America decorative visitors flocked to the Berkshires, the White Mountains, and to the sandy bluffs of Long Branch, New Jersey. At Newport charioteers and riders made their dignified rounds on Ocean Drive. Overdressed picnickers picked their way gingerly along the beach, and hoopskirted young ladies blessed croquet lawns with plashes of color. A few hardier souls chose the wilderness still existing in parts of New England and the Adirondacks, but most settled for places like Saratoga, where a man could tilt his chair back and sit all day on the Grand Union Hotel's endless piazza, watching the parade of parasoled elegance. Between rocker and hammock, the sensible click of knitting needles vied with fancies of Ben Hur and Marjorie Daw, then faded into thoughts of the evening Masquerade and Promenade Concert.

Just over the horizon of this good, comfortable life was a new century, a turning point; and as the time of their youth slipped by, people began to realize that what they had witnessed was irretrievably gone. Getting on in the world seemed, in America, to mean getting out of a world they had known and loved. There was no going back—but as if to prove that the memories of that other life could be relied upon, there was a man named Winslow Homer who had seen all these things and had set them down as they were.

Most of Winslow Homer's youth was spent near Boston, where he was born in 1836, and with the exception of his Civil War illustrations, his work until the early 1880's was confined almost exclusively to the New England scene, to the people and the way of life he had known and loved from childhood. Like so many of these nostalgic paintings, The Dinner Horn *captures the authenticity of an unassuming moment*

Fame first came to Homer as a Civil War artist, and after 1865 he spent winters in New York, traveling twice to Europe; yet no painting of the city came from his brush, nor did he follow a school of art. Rather, it seemed, his strength and vitality came from the long summer trips to his northeast homeland, to the White Mountains and the Adirondacks, to Gloucester or the Maine coast. Whether his subject was a pastoral Barnyard With Boy Feeding Chickens *or a boy and girl on* Gloucester Farm, *this country was the root of his art and its raw material his constant inspiration until he turned, finally, to that other powerful source— the sea—which was to occupy his energies almost continually until his death in 1910.*

The soaring joys of boyhood—the games, the love of adventure, the long, deep thoughts— were caught in mid-flight by Homer and recorded with a freshness and truth rivaled by few American artists. All the simple, exciting pleasures of a child's summer emerge from a canvas like Breezing Up, which fairly tingles with salt air and the sparkle of sunlight on the water. Time is suspended in the sketch of a ragamuffin on an idle swing or in the drowsy hour of The Nooning, where a dream is built to the soft hum of insects in the grass. In another arrested instant, the chain breaks and two youngsters tumble to the ground in a game of Snap the Whip.

THE EDITORS ACKNOWLEDGE WITH THANKS THE COOPERATION OF THE SOUTH-
ERN VERMONT ART CENTER, MANCHESTER, VERMONT, IN COLLECTING THIS
PORTFOLIO OF WINSLOW HOMER'S PAINTINGS.

Unlike other artists, Homer never idealized the American girl. His women were usually young and nearly always pretty, it is true; but never—in his croquet scenes, in his charming sketches, or in a painting like Sun-light *and* Shadow—*did he attempt to make them anything but the healthy, decorative creatures they were.*

Time and motion stop, and it is summer forever in Winslow Homer's lovely painting On The Beach.

HISTORY
AND HOW TO WRITE IT

By DIXON WECTER

In the period before the appearance of the new AMERICAN HERITAGE, *when the Society of American Historians was studying ways of establishing a sound popular magazine of history, the following article was written by the late Dixon Wecter, as a kind of charter for such a magazine. Wecter lent his buoyant personality, keen mind, and rich fund of knowledge to many worthy enterprises. This Texas-born product of Baylor, Yale, and Oxford was first of all a writer of history, as his three principal volumes,* The Saga of American Society, The Hero in America, *and* The Age of the Great Depression, *impressively attest. He was a valued university teacher and public lecturer; for a time he was director of research at the Huntington Library, and literary executor of the Mark Twain estate. As a sparkling exposition of some fundamental principles, this article will be read with interest by everyone; as a statement of Dixon Wecter's own ideals of historical writing it has a special poignancy to all who lament his untimely death as a loss to American letters.*

—Allan Nevins

THE MACMILLAN COMPANY

Dixon Wecter

A chimpanzee with a stack of empty boxes and a banana hanging out of reach soon learns by his own experience. But man alone learns from the experience of others. History makes this possible. In the broadest sense all that we know is history. More strictly, it is the road map of the past. True, the terrain never repeats itself to the last detail, any more than does the ribbon of highway sweeping past a motorist. But the contours, with all their variations, give the alert observer knowledge about safe driving and, often, clues about what lies ahead, since resemblances of a general sort occur endlessly. The past is also a fascinating story for its own sake, shedding light upon the eternal behavior of human beings, singly and in the mass, adding richly to any reader's knowledge about himself and the world he lives in.

Some think of history as the process of accumulating bundles of facts, dates, statistics, for storage in some antiquarian's bin or scholar's cupboard. But it is a great deal more, namely, a review of the success and failure of man's life on this planet. History examines the rise and fall of nations and cultures, with their heroes and political leaders, and the often ragged record of mankind's experiments in living together through war and peace, its struggles for bread and leisure and faith, its germinal ideas and collective symbols.

History was once written and taught mainly as a tale of intrigue and bloodshed. In those days arose the old French proverb that "happy is a nation which has no history." By the light of a better definition this saying seems foolish. A cultural group, and indeed the whole human race, keeps its character precisely because it cherishes some remembrance of things past. Whether this memory is an ennobling one, say, the influence of the Lincoln tradition in American life, or a corrupting one such as the effect wrought by Bismarck upon the behavior of modern Germany, is another matter. At all events, the remembered past is a present and powerful thing for good or evil. Croce spoke truly when he said that all living history is contemporaneous.

What is "the past"? One of the most elastic ideas

ever conceived by mind, it ranges from the remotest records left on earth down to the wake of the second hand as it sweeps around the dial. People who urge us to "live in the present" rarely weigh the literal meaning of their advice. "The present," that infinitesimal spark gone before we can photograph it on our brain, comes close to being an illusion. "The future" is still more impalpable since its content and impact upon us have not yet been registered. Beside these two concepts, "the past" seems curiously solid and real. It represents time and events met, realized, and built into the fabric of understood experience. Man is not only the sole creature able to learn from what happened to others, miles and centuries away, but also the only one capable of stretching the so-called present to its maximum. We do this unconsciously when talking about "the present day" or "the present generation." By just such an extension in time, all history that interests us and has something to tell us is living history.

Like other good things, history can be abused and misused. A dull narrator can make even its most meaningful chapters seem drab and unimaginative—an act of exhumation, followed by a grim inventory of the bones. Mr. Dooley once observed that "history is a post-mortem examination. It tells ye what a country died iv." Condescension toward the past is a graver mistake. For example, the darkness of what used to be termed the Dark Ages existed chiefly in the minds of the analysts.

History can also be abused by carelessness in handling the facts or a desire merely to make them sensational and shocking. Still worse, the muse called Clio can be sold down the river to become the handmaid of propaganda, brazenly perverting the truth. In a mood of cynicism Mark Twain once declared, "The very ink with which all history is written is merely fluid prejudice." To a history student forced to read between the party lines—the school children of Hitler's Reich or those under the Soviet Politburo—freedom to learn and reach one's own conclusions becomes just as impossible as to the student of sciences similarly debauched.

Yet history, along with kindred social studies like ethnology, anthropology, and sociology when honestly used helps enormously to splinter those barriers of prejudice and explode those lies which create hatred between races, sections, and national groups. Few indeed are the bigots and reactionaries found among true historians. Anybody setting out sympathetically to re-create the past can hardly help becoming less of a provincial himself, in both time and space. Among history's inescapable lessons, for example, are the folly of aggressive war, the stupidity of persecuting others because of their race or opinions, and the futility of

trying to destroy the freedom of the mind.

The American record is not flawless, as we all know. The nation whose literature and history lack vigorous self-criticism is more apt to illustrate the suppression of free speech than the attainment of alleged perfection. But on the whole, from the Founding Fathers on, the American panorama is one we need not blush to own, one in which we may often take hearty pride. This is a history good citizens need to know, to understand their world and to be able to improve it. With our faith in majority government we see the importance of clearer self-knowledge for those expected to do the thinking and voting.

This need applies not only to the nation, but to each region and state with its especial traditions and interests. Yet masses of local records, letters, diaries, private papers, business archives, and old-timers' recollections are being lost year after year, by decay, fire, and death, all through simple ignorance. A friend of mine remembers an intelligent young woman in St. Joseph, Missouri, who after hearing a talk a couple of years ago on the centennial of the Hannibal & St. Joe Railroad—in which the speaker described its background of courage and hope as it battled great odds to become an important feeder into the frontier West—came up and told him, "I didn't know that was history. I didn't know the Midwest had a history. I thought history was Plymouth Rock and Bunker Hill."

Ignorance about what happened in our town, state, region, and country, as well as to our neighbors—in this age when all nations are neighbors—is bad citizenship in any policy-making democracy. So it has always been. But today, when we find ourselves the foremost champion of democracy in times of unprecedented physical power, such ignorance is not only shameful but dangerous.

And yet a century ago the reading of history was much more popular among educated people than it seems today. The school and college student used to get at least a smattering of Xenophon, Thucydides, Caesar, Livy, Plutarch, Tacitus, and then in his adult years, for pleasure, read not only Gibbon and Macaulay and Carlyle but our home-grown historians like Washington Irving, Prescott, Parkman—best sellers all. If the decline of Latin and Greek is responsible for ground lost on the former front, the blame for our retreat on the second sector lies gravely with those now writing American history.

For all its huge, able, often highly original output, the last half century of American research has yielded almost no great books worthy to stand as literature beside the classics of our first hundred years. Industry minus art, accumulation lacking charm, data without digestion—such shortcomings explain this popular allergy against American history as written. A great many school texts are pretty repulsive, while history for the adult seems hardly more inviting. After diligently harvesting the grain of fact, too few investigators seem to have done left for threshing out the chaff or milling the flour. Their energy is exhausted long before the job is done—so that readers have to choose between the pedant's dry straw and the half-baked loaf turned out by historical romancers.

How *not* to write history is the first question. Surely it need not be penned in the grand manner once the vogue. The Duc de Sully always put on court dress before sitting down to work on his memoirs, just as French surgeons in the day of Lisfranc used to garb themselves for a major operation in white tie and tails as befitted the august encounter between life and death. Edward Gibbon, though among the greatest of historians, often wearies modern readers with his massive style. The so-called father of American history, George Bancroft, had a hankering for resonant periods like "The pusillanimous man assents from cowardice, and recovers boldness with the assurance of impunity." The stilted-heroic in writing is now as much out of fashion as the equestrian statue.

Then came the scientific approach to history, which tightened up research methods, fostered thoroughness, and pruned away some of the flowers of rhetoric. Under the guidance of many German and a few British and American scholars who gloried in the epithet "colorless," historians began to think themselves successful when their writing grew chilly and impersonal. But it is well to remember that the pioneer of that tribe, the Prussian von Ranke, called history both a science and an art.

The writing of good history is just that. As a science it can make no compromise with the slipshod and false; as an art it must seize upon the durable and significant, firmly rejecting the rest. The doting antiquary, like the untaught Mohammedan, saves every scrap of paper blown his way by the wind because it might contain the sacred name of Allah. But the scholar of broad vision cannot shirk his job of selection. Horse sense, independence, and strict integrity are vital to the good writing of good history. Neither Chesterton and Belloc, on the extreme Catholic right, nor Bukharin and Tarle, on the Marxist left, are trustworthy guides through the mazes of the past. If the historian warps his evidence to fit some prejudice or preconceived pattern, he has failed us. The late Charles Beard came more and more to advocate the deliberate cultivation of "assumptions" by the historian, but applying his own counsels of defeat Beard declined steadily from front rank into the role of propagandist and ax-grinder. Trends in whitewashing or debunking come and go, but history written with a steady hand will outlast them all.

This doesn't mean that a good historian must be drained of individuality—a research automaton for dredging up facts and offering them to the public in a mechanical scoop. Nor does it require him to lack personal stability or a core of conviction about principles, like those whom Shaw has described as having minds so open there is nothing left but a draft.

If the author's saturation in his subject is so real that he develops affections and dislikes, his writing is sure to be more warm and vigorous than if he strikes the attitude of a biologist dissecting a frog. On a basis of sound inquiry and reasoned belief he should form those value judgments from which no historian worth his salt must flinch. We simply demand that he treat the material fairly, give an accounting for the generalizations he draws, and, while playing his thesis to win, never stack the cards. He cannot fabricate evidence—whether documents, conversations, or incidents. At this fork he parts company with the romancer. What the storied and spacious past needs is not invention but insight and interpretation.

Yet the field of current literature is thickly populated with burrowing scholars too indifferent to write well and with slick fictioneers too lazy to dig for themselves. Public taste naturally favors the latter, and so the historical romance stays entrenched atop the best-seller list year after year. The quality of such books is as variable as the barometer, usually rising in direct relation to their fidelity to sources. Thus, while Kenneth Roberts and Margaret Mitchell have mixed sound history and original research with their dramatic gifts, Heaven help those whose knowledge of the past depends upon Howard Fast or Taylor Caldwell.

If the professional historians see the flag of popular following wrenched from their grasp by the romancers, as I have said, they have largely themselves to blame. A great deal of the fault lies with the bloodlessness of so much academic writing—the traditions of dull competence that have grown up about the Ph.D. dissertation and the learned monograph. Instead of "wearing all that weight of learning lightly like a flower," in Tennyson's phrase, these savants wear it not a little pridefully like a ball and chain. This is not to disparage solid scholarship or belittle necessary toil over government documents, statistics, diaries, and all manner of dusty archives. Parkman and Prescott drudged too, before achieving a distillate of crystal clarity and palatable flavor.

Some years ago, before the illustrious heyday of Winston Churchill, George M. Trevelyan grumbled that history was no longer read widely because it had ceased to be written by "persons moving at large in the world of letters or politics" like his great-uncle Macaulay. It is perhaps too much to require the average historian to sit in Parliament or Congress or Cabinet, to plunge up to the neck in the civic activities of his time, travel all over the globe, steep himself in a dozen languages and cultures, or even write poetry and fiction as aids to his craftsmanship in the manner of Carl Sandburg. Any of these experiences, however, will enrich him. Think of those lively annalists of early Virginia, for instance, like Robert Beverley, William Byrd, and Thomas Jefferson—planters and men of affairs, business, and politics, who wrote all the better for the versatility of their lives. Or of the later historian-statesmen like Theodore Roosevelt, Albert J. Beveridge, and Woodrow Wilson.

Some of our best professionals have been the least sedentary. A zest for field work adds freshness, originality, and vigor to the sinews of writing—as instanced by Francis Parkman's journey over the Oregon Trail and sojourn among the Sioux; Douglas S. Freeman's patient exploration of every crater in the battlefields of northern Virginia; Samuel Eliot Morison's sailing with the Navy in the Second World War. Before writing *Admiral of the Ocean Sea* Morison navigated the Atlantic in a sailing boat comparable to the *Santa María*—in fact doing almost everything Columbus did except discover America. The feel of an ax or a rifle butt or fishing rod in the hand, a pack at the back, wind upon the face, salt air in the nostrils, are all good disciplines for the writing of history. An apt historian learns of the past through all his senses. I once met an eccentric spinster archaeologist who claimed that she could date any Roman aqueduct by the flavor on her tongue of its crumbling masonry— she had tasted them all.

Too often the savor of drama, the sense of reliving the past, the communicable thrill of a story to tell, is buried under the accretion of data. Yet history is inevitably dramatic. The very word comes from the same root as "story"; narration is of the essence. A sense of comedy has its place at the historian's elbow no less than tragedy. The re-creation of a dominant personality, or daily life of an era, or the power generated by its ideas, calls for exact knowledge fired by historical imagination. To say also that the chronicle of great events calls for a touch of poetry is not to call down upon us showers of cadenced prose and purple passages, beloved of the swashbucklers and patrioteers. It means that powers of symmetry, proportion, aesthetic design, controlled emotion, even a knack of

EMINENT HISTORIANS

In the beginning, noble Greeks and Romans

HERODOTUS

THUCYDIDES

TACITUS

Stylists made history a high literary art

GIBBON

MACAULAY

In America a century ago, historians were best sellers

BANCROFT

MOTLEY

PRESCOTT

Some were explorers in the field... Some recluses in the study

PARKMAN

HENRY ADAMS

Some let the facts alone speak... Some relied on interpretation

VON RANKE

BEARD

CHESTERTON

Others were recruits from literature

CARLYLE

IRVING

Or themselves makers of history

CAESAR

ROOSEVELT

CHURCHILL

playfulness, and at high moments a certain unforced eloquence can be summoned into the service of truth.

The artist's structural gift—not merely the lumping together of details to be hurled at the reader like a soggy snowball—yields writing that can be read with pleasure. The structure ought to be clean and firm, yet not obtruding the bones of its skeleton. Topic sentences should marshal the squadrons of argument along without seeming to be drillmasters. Passages spongy with the deadwood of jargon or encrusted with barnacles of cliché, or ranging from the high-brow-recondite to the insultingly obvious; quotations herded in such droves as to suggest that the writer is too timid to speak for himself—these vices have no place on the pages of good history.

The best writing has been defined as the richest thoughts put into the simplest language. As applied to history, such discourse should resemble the easy, informal, but never careless talk of a well-educated man speaking to his friends. To bore, to shout, to preach, to patronize, to grow flabbily garrulous, are all bad manners in society— that is, among intelligent readers who happen to be nonspecialists. A classroom full of students cannot choose but hear, but professors should never forget that the common reader of history finds it all too easy to shut his book or chuck the magazine into the nearest wastebasket. The pretentious, the sentimental, and the flippant are prone to invite such treatment.

A good writer varies his pace to suit the mood and his reader's comfort. The crisp, clear statement is his staple. The staccato sentence belongs to the pulse of modern living, to journalism as well as the age of planes and high explosives, but it can be exaggerated just as surely as Clarendon and Hume and Montesquieu overworked the compound-complex sentence, geared to the era of Augustan Latinity, of oxcarts and sailing ships. Nevertheless, the best English and French historians of modern times give us models in writing that many an American might well imitate. These scholars overseas skillfully conceal the grubbing that laid their foundations, the scaffolding that made possible the walls—just as the bright Oxford undergraduate of my day "swotted" furiously over his books during the long vacation with no observers at hand, and returned in termtime to the unhurried career of a gentleman and sportsman. The one thing that a writer need *not* communicate is all the pain and toil that went into his finished product.

Nothing said here is meant to give aid and comfort to the elegant trifler with the Horace Walpole touch in historiography. His species has never rooted deeply in American soil. As a people we have always put such stress upon factual content, specialization, and accomplishment, as to turn the old Greek maxim "Know thyself" into the American vulgate as "Know thy stuff." Dilettantism has never been our besetting sin and needs no encouragement now.

But the historian who joins ripe learning to skill and charm in the telling commands the ear not only of the American public but also of the world—whose hunger for clarification among the welter of ideas in which we live made Spengler and H. G. Wells such phenomenal successes after the First World War, and Arnold Toynbee after the Second.

The historian who can write has a sobering responsibility. He is not only promised a wide and interested audience reading over his shoulder, but he is also assured that posterity will borrow many of its ideas from him, whether they are true or false. The reputation of Tiberius has been blackened for all time by the brilliant calumnies of Tacitus. Cromwell will always be a hero in shining armor to the devotees of Carlyle, and Warren Hastings a double-dyed villain to the thousands who still cherish their Macaulay. Two such diverse Presidents of the United States as Herbert Hoover and Franklin D. Roosevelt have been deeply concerned about the verdict of posterity—as evidenced, among other signs, by great libraries of their personal papers which they endowed supposedly to the end of time.

A readable historian of his own times will be accepted as the foremost witness par excellence, generation after generation. But by way of compensation, the historian who arrives on the scene long afterwards enjoys advantages too. Though a million details, important and unimportant, will be lost for lack of recording or proper preservation, the disclosure of diaries and secret archives, the fitting together of broken pieces from the mosaic, the settling of controversial dust and cooling of old feuds, and the broad perspective down the avenues of time, all make it possible for him to know an era in its grand design better than most men who lived through it.

To remind ourselves again of Croce's saying that all living history is contemporaneous, the recorders of that history—the writers who make it real for the largest number of people—are those who lend it the gift of immortality and the power to affect thoughts, emotions, and deeds centuries after the event.

The time when this self-confident composition was painted was a century and a half ago. It typifies the age. Defended to be sure by two still undiminished oceans, young America often felt very much alone and menaced by a world of swelling absolutisms. Yet—and perhaps it carries a lesson—the republic had faith in itself, and in the sure triumph of its institutions.

*B*eing thus arived in a good harbor and brought safe to land, they fell upon their knees and blessed the God of heaven, who had brought them over the vast and furious ocean, and delivered them from all the periles and miseries therof, againe to set their feete on the firme and stable earth, their proper elemente.

. . . If they looked behind them, ther was the mighty ocean which they had passed, and was now as a maine barr and goulfe to seperate them from all the civill parts of the world. . . . What could now sustaine them but the spirite of God and his grace? May not and ought not the children of these fathers rightly say: Our faithers were Englishmen which came over this great ocean, and were ready to perish in this willdernes; but they cried unto the Lord, and he heard their voyce, and looked on their adversitie, etc. Let them therfore praise the Lord, because he is good, and his mercies endure for ever.

William Bradford, *Of Plimoth Plantation.*

: DUE